LIBRARY
ST. MICHAEL'S PREP SCHOOL
1042 STAR RT. - ORANGE, CA. 92667

P9-EDF-094

For Reference

Not to be taken from this room

6251

American Poets, 1880-1945
First Series

Dictionary of Literary Biography

Dictionary of Literary Biography • Volume Forty-five

American Poets, 1880-1945
First Series

6251

Edited by
Peter Quartermain
University of British Columbia

A Bruccoli Clark Book

Gale Research Company • Book Tower • Detroit, Michigan 48226

Advisory Board for
DICTIONARY OF LITERARY BIOGRAPHY

Louis S. Auchincloss
D. Philip Baker
John Baker
A. Walton Litz, Jr.
Peter S. Prescott
Lola L. Szladits
William Targ

Matthew J. Bruccoli and Richard Layman, *Editorial Directors*
C. E. Frazer Clark, Jr., *Managing Editor*

Manufactured by Edwards Brothers, Inc.
Ann Arbor, Michigan
Printed in the United States of America

Copyright © 1986
GALE RESEARCH COMPANY
Foreword copyright © 1985 by Peter Quartermain

Library of Congress Cataloging-in-Publication Data
Main entry under title:

American poets, 1880-1945: first series.

(Dictionary of literary biography; v. 45)
"A Bruccoli Clark Book."
Includes index.
1. Poets, American—20th century—Biography—
Dictionaries. 2. Poets, American—19th century—Bio-
graphy—Dictionaries. I. Quartermain, Peter. II. Series.
PS129.A545 1986   811'.009 [B]   85-24601
ISBN 0-8103-1723-0

For Meredith

Contents

Plan of the Series

. . . Almost the most prodigious asset of a country, and perhaps its most precious possession, is its native literary product—when that product is fine and noble and enduring.

Mark Twain*

The advisory board, the editors, and the publisher of the *Dictionary of Literary Biography* are joined in endorsing Mark Twain's declaration. The literature of a nation provides an inexhaustible resource of permanent worth. It is our expectation that this endeavor will make literature and its creators better understood and more accessible to students and the literate public, while satisfying the standards of teachers and scholars.

To meet these requirements, *literary biography* has been construed in terms of the author's achievement. The most important thing about a writer is his writing. Accordingly, the entries in *DLB* are career biographies, tracing the development of the author's canon and the evolution of his reputation.

The publication plan for *DLB* resulted from two years of preparation. The project was proposed to Bruccoli Clark by Frederick G. Ruffner, president of the Gale Research Company, in November 1975. After specimen entries were prepared and typeset, an advisory board was formed to refine the entry format and develop the series rationale. In meetings held during 1976, the publisher, series editors, and advisory board approved the scheme for a comprehensive biographical dictionary of persons who contributed to North American literature. Editorial work on the first volume began in January 1977, and it was published in 1978.

In order to make *DLB* more than a reference tool and to compile volumes that individually have claim to status as literary history, it was decided to organize volumes by topic or period or genre. Each of these freestanding volumes provides a biographical-bibliographical guide and overview for a particular area of literature. We are convinced that this organization—as opposed to a single alphabet method—constitutes a valuable innovation in the presentation of reference material. The volume plan necessarily requires many decisions for the placement and treatment of authors who might properly be included in two or three volumes. In some instances a major figure will be included in separate volumes, but with different entries emphasizing the aspect of his career appropriate to each volume. Ernest Hemingway, for example, is represented in *American Writers in Paris, 1920-1939* by an entry focusing on his expatriate apprenticeship; he is also in *American Novelists, 1910-1945* with an entry surveying his entire career. Each volume includes a cumulative index of subject authors. The final *DLB* volume will be a comprehensive index to the entire series.

With volume ten in 1982 it was decided to enlarge the scope of *DLB* beyond the literature of the United States. By the end of 1984 fourteen volumes treating British literature had been published, and volumes for Commonwealth and Modern European literature were in progress. The series has been further augmented by the *DLB Yearbooks* (since 1981) which update published entries and add new entries to keep the *DLB* current with contemporary activity. There have also been occasional *DLB Documentary Series* volumes which provide biographical and critical background source materials for figures whose work is judged to have particular interest for students. One of these companion volumes is entirely devoted to Tennessee Williams.

The purpose of *DLB* is not only to provide reliable information in a convenient format but also to place the figures in the larger perspective of literary history and to offer appraisals of their accomplishments by qualified scholars.

We define literature as the *intellectual commerce of a nation:* not merely as belles lettres, but as that ample and complex process by which ideas are generated, shaped, and transmitted. *DLB* entries are not limited to "creative writers" but extend to other figures who in this time and in this way influenced the mind of a people. Thus the series encompasses historians, journalists, publishers, and screenwriters. By this means readers of *DLB* may be aided to perceive literature not as cult scripture in the

*From an unpublished section of Mark Twain's autobiography, copyright © by the Mark Twain Company.

keeping of cultural high priests, but as at the center of a nation's life.

DLB includes the major writers appropriate to each volume and those standing in the ranks immediately behind them. Scholarly and critical counsel has been sought in deciding which minor figures to include and how full their entries should be. Wherever possible, useful references will be made to figures who do not warrant separate entries.

Each *DLB* volume has a volume editor responsible for planning the volume, selecting the figures for inclusion, and assigning the entries. Volume editors are also responsible for preparing, where appropriate, appendices surveying the major periodicals and literary and intellectual movements for their volumes, as well as lists of further readings. Work on the series as a whole is coordinated at the Bruccoli Clark editorial center in Columbia, South Carolina, where the editorial staff is responsible for the accuracy of the published volumes.

One feature that distinguishes *DLB* is the illustration policy—its concern with the iconography of literature. Just as an author is influenced by his surroundings, so is the reader's understanding of the author enhanced by a knowledge of his environment. Therefore *DLB* volumes include not only drawings, paintings, and photographs of authors, often depicting them at various stages in their careers, but also illustrations of their families and places where they lived. Title pages are regularly reproduced in facsimile along with dust jackets for modern authors. The dust jackets are a special feature of *DLB* because they often document better than anything else the way in which an author's work was launched in its own time. Specimens of the writers' manuscripts are included when feasible.

A supplement to *DLB*—tentatively titled *A Guide, Chronology, and Glossary for American Literature*—will outline the history of literature in North America and trace the influences that shaped it. This volume will provide a framework for the study of American literature by means of chronological tables, literary affiliation charts, glossarial entries, and concise surveys of the major movements. It has been planned to stand on its own as a vade mecum, providing a ready-reference guide to the study of American literature as well as a companion to the *DLB* volumes for American literature.

Samuel Johnson rightly decreed that "The chief glory of every people arises from its authors." The purpose of the *Dictionary of Literary Biography* is to compile literary history in the surest way available to us—by accurate and comprehensive treatment of the lives and work of those who contributed to it.

The *DLB* Advisory Board

Foreword

"And what do I care if yellow and red are Spain's riches and Spain's good blood. Here yellow and red mean simply Autumn!"—William Carlos Williams (1919)

In 1835 Sir William Rowan Hamilton devised a revolutionary algebra (he called it "Quaternions") in which *ij* is not equal to *ji* but to -*ji*. In 1867 Karl Marx, in *Das Kapital*, argued that *"20 yards of linen = 1 coat"* is not necessarily the same as *"1 coat = 20 yards of linen."* The astonishing revolution of thought and art which we think of as modern, which questioned and often overthrew the commonsense assumptions of an earlier age, has its roots in the nineteenth century (and, indeed, before): Darwin proposed in 1859 that we are descended from apes; Freud proposed throughout a long career which began in 1885-1886 that the springs of behavior lie in our unconscious, that our casual or mistaken utterances are more meaningful than our deliberate ones, that dreams have meaning, that we are not, after all, reasonable or rational creatures; Jane Ellen Harrison in *Prolegomena to the Study of Greek Religion* (1903) demonstrated that ancient Greek religion and mythology originated in dark and sometimes bloody rituals, not in reasonable thought or fiction, and that Dionysus, the principle of irrationality, is as important in Greek thought and life as is Apollo, the principle of reason. Sir James G. Frazer, in his comparative study of the beliefs and institutions of mankind, *The Golden Bough* (1890-1915), helped establish the idea that folklore and myth embody ways of looking at the world and ways of thinking about it, and gave impetus on one hand to anthropological studies which gradually dispelled the notion that certain men and societies are "primitive" or "savage" and on the other to studies of language and symbolism. Meanwhile, studies of Homer and of oral poetry began to undermine orthodox grammar and conventional verbal logic by setting paratactic syntax alongside hypotaxis as a legitimate structure for the sentence. The discovery of cave paintings at Altamira in 1879 and at Pair-non-pair and La Mouthe in the last decade of the century gradually led to the recognition of archaic or paleolithic man as intelligent, artistic, and possessed of a culture, while the study of these paintings and of aboriginal art from Africa, the Americas, and Australasia con-

tributed in the early years of the twentieth century to the breakdown of perspective and verisimilitude and of the picture plane in painting. Cézanne, in any case, showed that paintings are not pictures but *paint*, and Mallarmé told Degas that "poetry is not written with ideas but with words." In the twentieth century Werner Heisenberg learned (through Willard Gibbs) how to use Hamilton's quaternions in quantum analysis: the world of quantum physics defies rationality, since light is *both* wave *and* particle, since (in the words of Niels Bohr) "an independent reality in the ordinary physical sense can neither be ascribed to the phenomena nor to the agencies of observation," since every observation of phenomena introduces uncontrollable elements, since space and time cannot be distinguished, and thus cause and effect cannot be discerned. As J. Robert Oppenheimer put it, "If we ask . . . whether the position of the electron remains the same, we must say 'No'; if we ask whether the electron's position changes with time, we must say 'No'; if we ask whether it is in motion, we must say 'No.' "

In March 1914, when T. S. Eliot was a student at Harvard Graduate School, working on the philosophy of F. H. Bradley, Bertrand Russell, who was then one of his teachers, summed it all up in a lecture on *Our Knowledge of the External World* to the Lowell Institute in Boston: "The immense extension of our knowledge of facts in recent times" he said, has—as it did in the renaissance—"made men distrustful of the truth of wide, ambitious systems: theories come and go swiftly, each serving, for a moment, to classify known facts and promote the search for new ones, but each in turn proving inadequate to deal with the new facts when they have been found. Even those who invent the theories do not, in science, regard them as anything but a temporary makeshift. The ideal of an all-embracing synthesis, such as the Middle Ages believed themselves to have attained, recedes further and further beyond the limits of what seems feasible. In such a world, as in the world of Montaigne, nothing seems worthwhile except the discovery of more and more facts, each in turn the deathblow to some cherished theory; the ordering intellect grows weary, and becomes slovenly through despair." A world, then, of uncertainty and ambiguity and contradictions; a world without unity, and unknowable; a world in which the solid security of shared (and perhaps unspoken) assumptions and traditions is no longer available; a world in which masterpieces are no longer recognizable and works of art no longer identifiable: the modern struggle is the struggle to make sense of the world by defective means, to discover how to live amid disorder. The story of modern American poetry is of those poets who do indeed have one thing in common: their perception of the world as fragmented and uncertain (and it is among them that the battlelines are drawn). It is in their attitudes toward that world, the assumptions they bring to bear, the devices and strategies that they adopt, the resources they exploit or reject, that modern American poets can be characterized, and it is in this context that their work can be read: "To be modern," Marshall Berman has observed, "is to experience personal and social life as a maelstrom, to find one's world and oneself in perpetual disintegration and renewal, trouble and anguish, ambiguity and contradiction; to be part of a universe in which all that is solid melts into air." The variety of responses among modern writers is diverse indeed, ranging from the sort of acceptance Berman's "to be part of a universe" suggests (as in the work of William Carlos Williams) through a hard-fought and uneasy compromise (as in the work of Eliot) to a complete rejection of this modern vision in favor of a more traditional perception of the universe (as in the work of William Ellery Leonard or Robert P. Tristram Coffin).

The perception of irony as a characteristic modern device or mode gave rise to a whole school of American modernist writers who, following Eliot in their poetic practice, in their theoretical work established the New Criticism, an approach and methodology that prevailed in the universities and outside them from the late 1920s through the 1940s and beyond. Viewed through the lens of the New Criticism a number of nineteenth-century writers seem strikingly modern in the ways in which they handle their disillusionment, in their adoption of irony not simply as a mask through which to view the world but as a strategy of survival. But it is not the only strategy available, nor is it the only perspective. The major issues in twentieth-century American poetry, issues which had a profound canonical effect, appear fairly early in the century, most obviously in the work of Ezra Pound, T. S. Eliot, and William Carlos Williams.

The opening poem of Pound's *Hugh Selwyn Mauberley* (first part written in 1919) has not without reason acquired a reputation for complexity

and obscurity, what with its puns, its allusions, its rhymes out of one language into another, its shifts of literary reference from one culture into another, its vocabulary, its syntax, its use of Greek. Yet what the poem is *about* is quite straightforward: bankruptcy. Bankruptcy experienced, sensed—and its accompanying frustration. The poet, aesthete perhaps, is himself bankrupt; society, indeed the whole culture, is bankrupt; there is no way at the present time in which it is possible to be a poet at all (without, at any rate, writing what the English poet Basil Bunting later called "Overdrafts"). Viewed one way, the poem is a sum of the individual life, the poet's. Viewed another, it has representative value, a summing up and a summoning up of the culture in which the poet is: its miscellaneousness, its lack of direction, its instability, its lack of focus. It is a culture too amorphous to be worked against, and the artist in any case has no idiom in that culture, nor any form in which that idiom can express itself; it is a world uncongenial to the artist, and the artist is uncongenial to the world—save in fragments, perhaps. The complexity of the poem is a complexity of surface, and what makes for the greatest difficulty is the multiplicity of the voices—just how does the poem sound? Who is the speaker? Is it Pound himself? Some clubby London literary pundit? This is the central question, and Pound deliberately leaves it not only unanswered but unanswerable—the multiplicity of voices sound *at once*, simultaneously. The reader is left in ambiguity, able to identify no voice as dominant, and unable as a result to decide what attitude to take (sympathy? hostility? approval? rejection?) toward either Mauberley or the culture in which Mauberley finds himself—and of which the reader himself is a part. Holding all judgment in abeyance then, the reader holds all the voices, the conflicts, the contradictions, the ambiguities, in mind at once; in thus accepting the multiplicity and ambiguity of the world of this opening poem, the reader discovers the complexity of his own responses to the world and of his feelings about it.

Leaving the question open in this way is what sets Pound in marked contrast to Eliot. *The Waste Land* (1922) is a very different sort of poem. Eliot himself, in the *Paris Review* interview in 1959, said he wrote it to get something off his chest, and in a lecture at Harvard he called it "the relief of a personal . . . grouse against life; it is just a piece of rhythmical grumbling." Unlike the first poem of *Hugh Selwyn Mauberley*, it is a complaint about the decline of Western culture. A cry of rage and despair, *The Waste Land* is a quest for unity in a fragmented and isolating world, using history as a means to judge the present, holding up tradition as a measure of loss; if it is at all possible to restore order—or a sense of order—it is not in the world as a whole, but only in one's personal life. The main thrust of the poem is not simply toward establishing a sense of unity (the poem has a remarkable singleness of purpose in its sequential multiplicity of voices), but toward changing the modern world, or at least shoring up the ruins. The poem is a cry against the modern world, and a resistance to it. Where Pound accepts the fragmented world and determines to build with what there is, Eliot is hungering for the world that's gone. In Canto 85 Pound notes that there are "No classics,/no American history,/no centre, no general root,/no *prezzo giusto* [that is, just price] as core," and thereby identifies *The Cantos* as an attempt to provide them. In *The Waste Land* Eliot, in saying "These fragments I have shored against my ruins," resists the modern condition.

Eliot's influence on American poetry, like Pound's, has been inescapable and far-reaching; indeed, it was Eliot, not Pound, who came to rule informed taste in America. The central issue in twentieth-century American poetics is discernible in the difference between the two poems; it is, in the long run, the difference between unity and diversity, singularity of meaning and multiplicity of meaning, monotheism and polytheism, closed form and open form. When William Carlos Williams, looking back in his *Autobiography* in 1951, called *The Waste Land* "the great catastrophe to our letters," he both enlarged and more clearly defined the terms of the disagreement among poets (and still he acknowledged "the blast of Eliot's genius which gave the poem back to the academics"): "Critically Eliot returned us to the classroom just at the moment when I felt that we were on the point of an escape to matters much closer to the essence of a new art form itself—rooted in the locality which would give it fruit." When *The Waste Land* appeared Williams was working on *Spring and All* (1922)—a book which Louis Zukofsky would carry around in his pocket until it was virtually tattered, a book which never achieved wide circulation and was extremely difficult to find until it was reprinted in *Imaginations* by New Directions in 1970 alongside the equally scarce *Kora in Hell* (1920). In 1918, Williams wrote the prologue to *Kora in Hell,* and attacked Pound and Eliot for running off to Europe. He called Pound "the best enemy U. S. verse has" for doing so (though he would always uphold the essential value of Pound's poetry), and accused

Eliot not simply of being "a subtle conformist" to European (and more specifically English) tradition, an "archbishop of procurors to a lecherous antiquity": he called his work "rehash, repetition . . . of Verlaine, Baudelaire, Maeterlinck" and imagined an international congress of poets having "parodies of the middle ages, Dante and *langue d'oc* foisted upon it as the best in United States poetry." In a 1919 essay called "Belly Music," which appeared in *Others,* he flatly asserted that "the mark of a great poet is the extent to which he is aware of his time and NOT . . . the weight of liveliness in his metres. . . . It is NOT true that we can sing the old songs. The old poetry will NOT do." Williams rejects the tradition and the learning he associates with Eliot and Pound as harmful to the American poem: all his life he insisted on two points which most clearly set out his opposition to them. These are, as he phrased them in a talk at Dartmouth College in 1936, first, that "all art begins in the local and must begin there since there only will the senses find their material"; second, that "American poetry is not written in English but American. The two languages are in many ways diametrically opposed to each other though using mostly the same words. The effect on poetry in the two is fundamental. English verse connotes a past which largely governs it. It is bound up with the English language. In America we speak a new, swiftly evolving tongue unlike English in poetic connotations. . . . Without such an understanding there can be no superlative excellence in this place so far as poetry is concerned."

It is an argument over language, culture, symbolism; it is an argument about the nature of tradition, about the materials of poetry and what a poem is. Eliot seeks to connect the world of the present and the work of the present to the work of great artists and thinkers of the past, and invokes tradition, history, and religion as powers—"the poet must develop or procure the consciousness of the past . . . and he should continue to develop this consciousness throughout his career," he said in "Tradition and the Individual Talent" (1919); Pound invokes culture and seeks in books such as *How to Read* (1929) and *Guide to Kulchur* (1938) to make the reader "dig out the vital spots" in the culture of the past, and bring them to the present; Williams invokes the power of the individual to discover and rediscover his world and lift to the imagination "those things that lie under the direct scrutiny of the senses, close to the nose." In 1942 in an essay titled "The Invisible University" he said that he envied much of what Eliot had: "I long for what I presume to be his knowledge of Greek and Latin and I pine for his reading which I never got. What, I say, should I not be able to do with them if I could only have done those things. What revolutions, what revelations! I wonder. But that is what I think. If only I had the sound and knowledge of the Greek in my head how I could put it to use today. But maybe I couldn't. I might become just as they are, helpless with it." When, four years later, he called his long poem *Paterson* (1946) "a reply to Greek and Latin with the bare hands" he meant that in that poem he was doing (he hoped) what he saw the ancient Greeks and Romans (the first poets) doing: translating the actual immediate world into the world of the poem, making it new. In insisting that poetry be made out of the local and sensible, Williams necessarily insisted that it be the spoken (American) word, not the (bookish) written one; that it be immediate in and to the world (that things be seen for what they are, not freighted with symbolic or other significance or meaning—which in the prologue to *Kora in Hell* he called "an easy lateral sliding"). He insisted, too, that the poet be inseparable from the man. Eliot, on the other hand, argued (in "Tradition and the Individual Talent" and elsewhere) that "what happens [to the poet] is a continual surrender of himself as he is at the moment to something which is more valuable. The progress of an artist is a continual self-sacrifice, a continual extinction of personality. . . . The more perfect the artist, the more completely separate in him will be the man who suffers and the mind which creates." Eliot sees the poet as creating, and what he creates is masterpieces; Williams sees the poet as perceiving, and what he writes is testimony.

The difference is crucial, for a concern for masterpiece rests on a consideration of the means by which something called "nature" becomes something called "art," and the notion of what constitutes "art" is necessarily preconditioned by a set of rules, stated or not, which exists prior to the work and to which the work must conform. The predilection for rules which the notion of masterpiece fosters separates the poem from the outside world, demands that it conform to abstract criteria. In separating the work of art from the work of nature the artist separates himself from his work, and his work from his life: the work of art is seen as immutable, and even as Absolute. A concern for testimony leads the poet to anchor the poem firmly in his life, in the process of composition, in the world of experience, in the personal. If, as Williams wrote to Harriet Monroe in 1913, "life is above all

things else at any moment subversive of life as it was the moment before—always new, irregular," then the poem must incorporate that irregularity and indeterminacy into its structure by whatever means come to hand, including, say, the poet's own errors, the mistakes in writing; it might even abandon unity (one of the classic rules): the poem must be true to its own history, the history of its own composing. The opposition between the two views has frequently been called the opposition between the classic and the romantic, but it is perhaps more accurate to view it as an opposition between singleness and multiplicity of vision. It is possible to write bad work either way, of course, just as it is possible to write good. Pound, Eliot, and Williams are all great poets.

The issue was rarely (if ever) as clear-cut as this brief description suggests, however. In "Pounding Fascism," which appeared in *Sulfur* in spring 1985, Charles Bernstein has suggested that Ezra Pound himself, who stands at the wellhead of twentieth-century American poetry, is in the form of *The Cantos* releasing the unified voice and consciousness toward a multiplex and polyphonous world and work, nomadic and fragmentary, while at the same time his desire is for a hierarchical and ordered structure. Even though Pound says (in the *New Age*, 10 January 1918) that "the monotheistic temperament has been the curse of our time," his desires and habits of thought are monotheistic: hence his fascism. The contention which is at the heart of *The Cantos* is a contention at the heart of modern American poetry, and one of the sources of its great energy in the first half of this century; few indeed are the poets whose attitudes are as clearcut as those of Eliot and Williams. Eliot and Pound enabled renaissance English or medieval Italian or modern French (or Dante, Confucius, the *Upanishads*) to enter an *American* poem; Williams, in his intense localism, posed the authenticity of American speech against their literariness, against their internationalism, and brought the colloquial and insistent rhythms of nongrammatical speech into the American poem.

Furthermore, in the late years of the nineteenth century a number of strongly individualistic writers, growing up in a nonacademic or at any rate nonliterary climate, perforce created their own poetry: Edwin Arlington Robinson (born 1869), Robert Frost (1874), and Wallace Stevens (1879), as well as William Carlos Williams (1883), Ezra Pound (1885), and T. S. Eliot (1888). The Robinson-Frost streams have not, in this century, been influential—though both poets enjoyed a wide readership and are clearly major writers. Wallace Stevens's influence has been pervasive and varied (writers as diverse as John Ashbery, Robert Creeley, and Theodore Roethke, for example, are considerably indebted to him), but historically he has not founded a tradition; there is no Stevens "school." And although Williams, Pound, and Eliot are the dominant figures in the first sixty-or-so years of the century, they were not of course working alone. What was accomplished was accomplished over a number of years, through a series of poetic generations which the organization of these three volumes of the *Dictionary of Literary Biography* seeks to reflect by grouping poets according to the years of their births. This volume covers poets born in 1885 through 1897. Later volumes will cover poets born in 1898-1916 and 1842-1884. Needless to say, the generations are not clear-cut, and inevitably there are omissions: we know virtually nothing about such writers as Alanson Hartpence, Orrick Johns, and Billy Saphier, for example, yet they are important in the history of early modernist writing in America. And there are several complicating factors. First and foremost of these is the American language itself.

Of the nearly 28 million immigrants to the continental United States in the period 1820-1910, 63.5% of them (that is, nearly 18 million) arrived during the thirty-one years 1880-1910, and 31.5% of them (more than 8.75 million) arrived in the first eleven years of the twentieth century at an average rate of more than 2,400 a day (in 1907 they came at a rate of more than 3,500 a day). Not many of them spoke English. In 1854, one of the peak immigration years, 50% of 427,833 immigrants spoke German, and 37% spoke English; in 1882, 32% of 788,922 immigrants spoke German, and 22% English; in 1907, 29% of 1,285,349 immigrants spoke German, and 8.9% spoke English. The Census Bureau reported that in 1900 more than 12 million (16.4%) of a total population of 76.3 million were foreign born, and roughly 16 million (21.4%) were native born of foreign parents; that is to say, 37.8% of the population were either foreign born or native born of foreign stock. Since the census only recorded statistics for the white population, the figures are conservative, but even if 30% of these were native speakers of English (and that estimate is surely high) then just under 20 million (26%) of the 1900 population learned English as a second language—if they learned it at all. The 1910 census reported that of the more than 32 million Americans of foreign white stock, over 22 million of them (or about 24%

of the white population) were from non-English-speaking stock. It seems reasonable to estimate that somewhere between one person in four and one person in five in the continental United States in 1910 learned English as a second language, or did not know it at all. Further, immigrants to the United States tended to cluster in New England, the Middle Atlantic states (New York, New Jersey, Pennsylvania, and Delaware), and the Midwest, and to avoid the South. In 1900 only 7.9% of the white population of the South was foreign born or native born of foreign stock (as compared to 37.8% for the continental United States), a *decline* from the figures for 1870, the earliest year in which such a count was made. In 1850, 45% of the population of the Middle Atlantic states was foreign born (655,929 of them in New York, the bulk of them presumably in New York City), while only 14% of the population of New England was foreign born (and many of them Irish). In *A Century of Population Growth From the First Census to the Twelfth 1790-1900* (1909) the Census Commissioners reported that "In both New England and the Middle States, more than half of each 1,000 of the white population in 1900 were of foreign parentage. It appears, moreover, . . . that in these two sections of the country the proportion is increasing with great rapidity." The effect of all this on the American language—and on American poetry—has been profound. Southern writing, for example, is linguistically as well as culturally distinct from that of the rest of the nation, and it is surely significant that three major innovators among twentieth-century American writers learned English as a second language: Gertrude Stein spoke German as a small child; William Carlos Williams, Spanish (though he may have learned both languages from the very beginning); and Louis Zukofsky's first language was Russian Yiddish.

Of the large number of German-speaking immigrants who entered the United States in the 1850s and the 1880s (as many as English speakers, if not more), many were both articulate and politically active. They brought with them habits of thought attendant on a language which combines and compounds words with great (and perhaps to an English ear almost pedantic) precision and concreteness (hydrogen, for instance, is *wasserstoff*); a language which reflects an almost singular taste for large abstractions for which there is in English no precise equivalent (like, say, *weltanschauung*); a language which in addition to its penchant for polysyllabic words habitually delays the verb to the end of the sentence. Such linguistic habits fed a native

American taste for rhetoric (Alexis de Tocqueville observed as early as the 1820s that Americans go to speeches where Europeans go to plays); fed into a culture which, increasingly urbanized and industrialized, increasingly needed technical terms and fairly high-order abstractions in order to cope with increasing social complexity; and fed into a literary and artistic culture which had acquired from romanticism (more specifically from Coleridge and Kant) a taste for Neoplatonic abstractions and Latinisms. The language which the immigrants learned (often, perhaps, from a grammar and/or a dictionary) had already been deracinated, and hence rendered abstract, almost from the very foundation of American colonies. The earliest settlers may have thought of themselves as Englishmen, and as far as they could they educated their children along English lines or even sent them to England for their schooling, but at the same time, willy-nilly, the fact of exile not simply from English culture but from the English landscape divorced the language from the world: William Carlos Williams observed that "they saw birds with rusty breasts and called them robins" when "what they saw were not robins. They were thrushes"; much of the language Americans used, certainly, had no visible antecedents as they walked down the street. In important respects, the American language is history-less.

It was also in important respects at the turn of the century a dead language. The history of American writing (and especially poetry) in the twentieth century can be read as the history of a language gradually acquiring native speakers, when there were none before; a dead language, reversing all customary patterns, returning to life. A dead language is a language that exists without its surrounding and supportive culture, a culture which defines the things to which the language refers. Classical Latin is a dead language because the groups of people who understood the culture that gave rise to the language are gone: as they vanished, so did the world embodied in the words set forth by them, and the history of the language, at some profound level apprehended, felt in the language by its speakers, became forgotten, and that language became a special territory reserved for special functions. Those millions of Americans who learned English as a second language through books rather than through speech rarely came to feel the kinship of words, what I. A. Richards called "the interinanimation of words." But the abstractness, the thin-ness, of the American language was not confined to immigrants. Matthew Arnold ob-

served of Emerson's poetry in 1884 that "he is not plain and concrete enough, . . . A failure of this kind goes through almost all his verse, keeps him amid symbolism and allusion and the fringes of things"; in 1901 William Butler Yeats complained of Longfellow that "no words of his borrow their beauty from those that used them before, and one can get all that there is in story and idea without seeing them as if moving before a half-faded curtain embroidered with kings and queens, their loves and battles and days out hunting, or else with holy letters and images of so great antiquity that nobody can tell the god or goddess they would commend to an unfading memory." It is almost a commonplace among twentieth-century American writers to notice, as Gertrude Stein did in her 1935 lectures on narration at the University of Chicago, that in American writing words "began to detach themselves from the solidity of anything"; elsewhere she told an audience that the American language exhibits a "lack of connection" with material daily living. Many things conspired to lay an English vocabulary over an American landscape, and Malcolm Cowley was by no means the only American of his generation to complain bitterly that in school "our studies were useless or misdirected, especially our studies in English literature: the authors we were forced to read, and Shakespeare most of all, were unpleasant to our palate; they had the taste of chlorinated water." Thus, when Williams calls *Paterson* "a reply to Greek and Latin with the bare hands" he is identifying his poem as an attempt to end the divorce between the American and his speech, between American speech and American culture and landscape, between American speech and American writing. In the context of the state of the American language, Malcolm Cowley and Slater Brown's remark in the last issue of *Broom* that "Eliot believes in tradition, form, everything dead" is both poignant and urgent.

Some other complicating factors can be fairly briefly outlined. The widespread adoption as textbooks in American colleges and universities of *Understanding Poetry* by Cleanth Brooks and Robert Penn Warren (1938, fourth edition 1976), and of anthologies such as *Modern American Poetry: An Introduction*, edited by Louis Untermeyer (1919, seventh edition 1950), had a profound effect upon the nature of American poetry, and on the shape of the canon, for they established an orthodoxy that defined both what sort of thing a poem is and (as corollary) who the worthwhile poets are. *Understanding Poetry* is perhaps the most influential textbook ever to have been published in the field; at least one generation of poets and possibly two formally studied poetry through this book (between 1938 and 1976 the book went through four editions and over fourteen printings; in 1985 it is still in print): writers as different as John Berryman and Robert Lowell learned to write—or in their schooling were encouraged to write—the kind of poetry that the book fostered. *Understanding Poetry* derived its tenets from the New Criticism as established and practiced in the United States by Brooks, Warren, John Crowe Ransom, and Allen Tate (perhaps Eliot's most astute American followers). A cardinal principle of the book is that in the long run the meaning of a poem cannot be stated at all (except by repeating the poem) but can only be perceived, understood, and appreciated; it teaches the explication of poems through the analysis of relationships between elements in the poem, but especially through the examination of irony and paradox; imagery and ambiguity are fundamental in the consideration of tone, theme, and structure, and it is through these means that the student is shown how to attempt the explication of meaning. *Understanding Poetry* discusses "intention and meaning" and works from the assumptions, first, that "the unity of a poem, like that of any work of art, is a unity of final meaning," and second, that the poet "shapes and uses" language—that the poet is, in other words, the author, the creator of the poem, and is in control. Following Eliot's lead, the book exhibits a marked preference for the work of John Donne and the English metaphysicals over that of Ben Jonson or Sir Thomas Wyatt, and sees poetry as expressive and/or communicative in its aims. As Cleanth Brooks put it in 1947 in *The Well Wrought Urn*, a poem is "a structure of meanings, evaluations, and interpretations; and the principle of unity which informs it seems to be one of balancing and harmonizing connotations, attitudes, and meanings. . . . [The unity is] an achieved harmony." Critics of the book were fond of remarking that *Understanding Poetry* taught difficulty as a virtue and lucidity as of dubious value in poetry; cynics accused the book of serving the interests of professors who, if all good poems are difficult poems, thus have something to profess. The year after the book first appeared, Basil Bunting complained in a letter that "the age of poems for commentators returns."

Understanding Poetry and its host of imitators did much to establish modern writing against the at-times-virulent conservatism of such traditionalists as A. E. Housman in England, and Stanton A. Coblentz, Max Eastman, Robert P. Tristram Coffin,

and John G. Neihardt in America. James Laughlin (later to become not only an accomplished poet himself but the most important single figure in the publishing of poetry in the United States) recorded in an interview in 1981 that when he was an undergraduate at Harvard in 1934 "You couldn't mention Pound's or Eliot's name in [Robert] Hillyer's class or you'd be sent out of the room," and there is no question at all that critics such as Brooks, Warren, Ransom, Tate, Edmund Wilson, and Yvor Winters (and Eliot himself, of course) made possible an American readership for modern British and American poets such as W. H. Auden, Hart Crane, E. E. Cummings, Robert Frost, Archibald MacLeish, Louis MacNeice, Wallace Stevens, Dylan Thomas—and, later, Richard Eberhart, Randall Jarrell, Robert Lowell, Theodore Roethke, Delmore Schwartz, Karl Shapiro, Richard Wilbur, and others. With the exception of Frost and Stevens, the diversity of this list is more apparent than real, for these writers constitute a poetic generation that, consciously influenced by Eliot's criticism, wrote in an ironic and formal mode. But in thus establishing an orthodoxy of received opinion, many British and American poets were also (to a greater or lesser degree) *excluded* from the modern canon and to all intents and purposes driven underground, becoming more or less invisible (at least to "serious critics" and trade publishers). Among these are such writers as Basil Bunting, Hilda Doolittle (H. D.), David Jones, Mina Loy, Robert McAlmon, Hugh MacDiarmid, Thomas Merton, Marianne Moore, Lorine Niedecker, Charles Reznikoff, Kenneth Rexroth, Laura Riding, Gertrude Stein, William Carlos Williams, and—later—Robert Creeley, Robert Duncan, Roy Fisher, Allen Ginsberg, Ronald Johnson, George Oppen, Charles Olson, Jeremy Prynne, Jack Spicer, John Wieners, and Jonathan Williams. Some of these writers died with their work out of print or even unpublished (H. D., Marianne Moore, Mina Loy, Lorine Niedecker), or, if it was in print, published and kept in print by James Laughlin's New Directions (Thomas Merton, Kenneth Patchen, Ezra Pound, Kenneth Rexroth, William Carlos Williams). Others first published their work outside the United States (Robert Creeley, Charles Olson, Ezra Pound, Louis Zukofsky) or privately (Lorine Niedecker, Charles Reznikoff, William Carlos Williams). H. D. at her death was remembered, if at all, for her earliest poems; it was not until twenty years later—after her long poems later published as *Hermetic Definition* had circulated in xeroxes of the manuscripts—that her *Collected Poems* were published by New Directions. The strength of the canonical tradition of modern American poetry is reflected in the reputation of Kenneth Rexroth, whom James Dickey dismissed in 1980 as "one of the worst" of American poets while Eliot Weinberger (poet, translator, and editor) only two years later would call him "America's great Christian poet" and suggest that "postwar American poetry is the 'Rexroth Era' as much as . . . the earlier decades are the 'Pound Era.' " One of the great ironies in the history of modern reputations is that William Carlos Williams, who complained that the publication of *The Waste Land* in 1922 "set me back twenty years," not only had to wait twenty-five or twenty-six years for recognition within the universities and by the general public, but achieved that recognition through the publication in 1946 of Randall Jarrell's review of *Paterson I* in *Partisan Review* and in June 1948 of Robert Lowell's review of *Paterson II* in the *Nation*. In 1948 Williams was sixty-five years old, Jarrell was thirty-four, and Lowell was thirty-one. Yet Cleanth Brooks remarked in a 1964 lecture, later printed in *A Shaping Joy*, that Williams's "The Red Wheelbarrow" remains "quite inert. I see the white chickens and the raindrops glazing red paint. But I have to take on faith the author's statement that 'so much depends' on this scene." Robert Lowell, describing the nature of his indebtedness to Williams and looking back on his education at Kenyon College in the late 1930s under John Crowe Ransom, recalled in 1961 that "My own group, that of Tate and Ransom, was all for the high discipline, for putting on the full armor of the past, for making poetry something that would take a man's full weight and that would bear his complete intelligence, passion and subtlety," that "for us Williams was part of the revolution that had renewed poetry, but he was a byline. Opinions varied on his work. It was something fresh, secondary, and minor, or it was the best that free verse could do." Yet although he is "a model and a liberator," he confessed, "the difficulties I found in Williams twenty-five years ago are still difficulties for me. Williams enters me, but I cannot enter him." The difficulty is instructive and derives in part from a predilection to read poems for the unity of their final meaning rather than for the play of possible meanings, to read them for the controlled play of ambiguity and irony rather than for the play of syntax and language per se. One view explains it as the difference between seeing life as a self-improvement course and life as an adventure.

The difference between the two camps was

never perhaps as simple as this discussion suggests, but it is nevertheless true that trade publishers tended to favor poets blessed by the university and, often, teaching in it, and that poets outside the universities had to make do with fugitive publication in little magazines, by small private presses, or overseas. The history of the politics of poetry publishing in the United States has yet to be written, but it is closely related to the fortunes of the two traditions; the central texts in the academic tradition were Eliot's two essays "Tradition and the Individual Talent" and "Hamlet and his Problems," both widely anthologized; outside the academy, they were Williams's *Kora in Hell* and *Spring and All*, both extremely difficult to find, both enjoying a substantial underground reputation and influence. The effect of the two camps on the poet, and the complexity of their interrelationship, is perhaps best shown in Robert Duncan's description of *his* education in 1935 or 1936 (he is two years younger than Robert Lowell): "Books had opened in childhood imaginations of other lives in which the idea of our own lives dwelling took on depths and heights, colors and figures, a new ground beyond self or personality in the idea of Man. But this prescribed thing was different, books became materials for examinations. English Literature with its reading lists, its established texts, its inquisitions, was to map our compulsory path in what had seemed before an open country. Work by work, author by author, the right roads were paved and marked, the important sights were emphasized, the civic improvements were pointed out where the human spirit had successfully been converted to serve the self-respect of civil men, and the doubtful, impulsively created areas were deplored. If we, in turn, could be taught to appreciate, to evaluate as we read and to cultivate our sensibilities in the ground of other men's passions, to taste and to regulate, to establish the new thing in the marketplace, we were to win some standing in the ranks of college graduates, and educated middle class, urbane and professional, as our parents had done before us." Against that orderly and ordered world Duncan sets an order of poetry "that seemed to contain a personal revelation," in which the poem is "not demanding a response but testing for an affinity," in which the reader submits to the poem as the poet is seen to submit to the language: it is writing as discovery. Such a view of the poem rejects the notion of the poet as controlling his work. It is a crucial distinction, and one that not only complicates the relations between the two traditions but confuses and blurs the boundaries: a poet like

Wallace Stevens, for example, can in poems like "A Clear Day and No Memories" write a short lyric of great beauty which works through a concentrated play of irony and paradox, and whose beauty rests in large degree upon not simply the poet's control over his materials but the reader's recognition of that control (in this he is very like Frost), but he also, in other poems, submits to the language, submits to the poem—relinquishing, one might say, conceptual as well as perceptual control—though he keeps tight hold on the *form*.

The apparently simple distinctions between the two camps, the academic and nonacademic, had by the 1960s begun to blur, and with the wisdom of hindsight it became apparent that the distinctions had probably always been blurred. Yet that blurring first became visible, probably, in 1948, with the publication not of Williams' *Paterson II* (nor of Olson's seminal book on Melville, *Call Me Ishmael*, 1947), but of Pound's *Pisan Cantos,* which won the Bollingen Prize (the fact that Allen Tate was one of the judges who awarded the prize to Pound suggests the complexity of this picture). Pound's central position in the history of modern American poetry rests in part on the fact that his early poetry (up to and through the complete *Hugh Selwyn Mauberley*) served as a model for the academic tradition, the university poets, while his *Pisan Cantos* and the early *Homage to Sextus Propertius* (1919) served as model or inspiration for such later poets as Robin Blaser, Robert Creeley, Robert Duncan, and Charles Olson, who fought that tradition vehemently and who at least were able to emerge from the underground if not come into prominence in the 1950s. With the publication in 1960 of Donald Allen's catalytic and crucial anthology *The New American Poetry 1945-1960* that underground was provided with its own college and university textbook and itself started an orthodoxy; the central critical document for the group, Charles Olson's *Projective Verse* (1950), at last achieved wide circulation. And Pound was seen to be, in his career as a whole, a seminal figure in both traditions.

It is only, then, with that complexity in mind that the following extremely oversimplified summary can be read at all: there are two traditions, or rather *camps* (for they are indeed at war); there are two ways of looking at the world, and they exist side-by-side, perhaps in the same person; they seem to have been endemic to American writing throughout its history. In his extraordinary book *All That Is Solid Melts Into Air* (1982) Marshall Berman suggests that "to be a moder*nist* is to make oneself somehow at home within the maelstrom, to

make its rhythms one's own, to move within its currents in search of the forms of reality, of beauty, of freedom, of justice, that its fervid and perilous flow allows." In that search, however, there is a difference between a man's emotions and intellections giving value to what he sees as an otherwise valueless universe and world—where the meaningfulness of experience is a construct, more or less deliberate and conscious, of the individual's; where traditional values are invoked, perhaps overtly projected onto a seemingly indifferent or impenetrable cosmos—and a man's experience of the world as the experience of a world of signs—where things and events are seen as striving to speak, where to evoke an image is to receive a sign (whose meaning may be obscure indeed), where the cosmos is experienced as potential meaning, striving to be seen and to be declared, where the act of writing is an act of translation, bringing "into human language a word or phrase in which the universe itself is written" (the phrase is Robert Duncan's). It is the difference between singleness of vision and multiplicity of vision; between the belief that the universe is knowable, and that it is essentially and perdurably ambiguous, mysterious; between making things meaningful, and working toward an awareness of meaning. Heidegger commented in *What is Called Thinking?* that "multiplicity of meanings is the element in which thought must move in order to be strict thought" precisely because the fleeting, the confused, the dim, and the uncertain are the elements of experience which best exhibit reality; in these terms, intellectual certainty is precarious if not delusory.

For the poem, the difference is telling. For in one case, form is given to or imposed on experience (the poet bringing to his experience a set of preconceptions and assumptions)—in which case the poem becomes a poetry of *content*, and the critical apparatus brought to bear upon the poem insists upon "form" and "content" as distinct aspects of the work. In the other, form is found in experience, and content is discovered in *matter* ("no ideas but in things," wrote Williams in *Paterson*). When form is given to experience, poets write poems which are closed forms; often, perhaps, asserting an absolute, or in quest of one; always, in the long run, reducible to a single unity of meaning or interpretation; monotheistic in their belief and desire, such poets write poems which have a point, have something to say. And when form is discovered in experience, poets write poems which are open forms, processes rather than products, poems of possibility and possible meanings: the poet does not know what it is he wants to say, and indeed in the course of writing discovers what it is that the poem says, for if form is discovered in experience, that experience includes the experience of language, especially the language in which the poem is written, and to which the poet is necessarily obedient. Such poems may or may not be open to a single interpretation, and, although they have (perhaps) an ending, they are not necessarily complete. Hence Williams when he died was working on book six of *Paterson* (which he originally planned in four books), and Pound, when he died, was still working on *The Cantos*, originally designed to end at Canto 100.

In the history of American writing, the dominance of one of these attitudes over the other seems to run in cycles. The early struggles of the imagists (first under Pound's aegis, then under Amy Lowell's) for recognition and dominance pushed the *Others* group (Maxwell Bodenheim, Alfred Kreymborg, Mina Loy, Marianne Moore, and others) to one side; in the 1930s the sheer prominence of Eliot (in 1932-1933 as Charles Eliot Norton Professor of Poetry at Harvard University he delivered the lectures which became *The Use of Poetry and The Use of Criticism*) pushed to one side the objectivist group (George Oppen, Carl Rakosi, Charles Reznikoff, William Carlos Williams, and Louis Zukofsky)—who have come to recognition and influence if not dominance in the 1980s—and contributed to the utter neglect of such political poets as Norman MacLeod and Lola Ridge. The essential contention between the two attitudes is the great source of energy for modern American poetry, and accounts in large part for its great diversity and power, as does the increasing confidence through the century of the American poet with a native American idiom. When the American army (in the form of six soldiers) arrived in the French village of Culoz on 1 September 1944, Gertrude

Stein was there to welcome them and, as she tells us in *Wars I Have Seen* (1946), was reminded of an earlier liberation, at the end of World War I, twenty-seven years earlier, by an American army whose soldiers spoke English, who spoke American English, but yet who were not native speakers: "[In 1944] they had a poise and completely lacked the provincialism which did characterize the last American army, they talked and they listened and they had a sureness, they were quite sure of themselves, they had no doubts or uncertainties and they had not to make any explanations. The last army was rather given to explaining, oh just anything, they were given to explaining, these did not explain, they were just conversational. . . . I think of the Americans of the last war, they had their language but they were not yet in possession of it, and the children of the depression as that generation called itself was beginning to possess its language but it was still struggling but now the job is done, the G.I. Joes have this language that is theirs, they do not have to worry about it, they dominate their language and in dominating their language which is now all theirs they have ceased to be adolescents and have become men." The story of modern American poetry to World War II is the story of successive generations of writers increasingly gaining familiarity in and security with the American idiom, increasingly gaining confidence in the possibility of being *American* poets without having to turn to Europe for models or for approval, or having to turn deliberately away from Europe. It is instructive, then, to group poets in short "generations" as these volumes of the *Dictionary of Literary Biography* do, for the complexity of the pressures on the writer, of the patterns of literary history of which he is a part, are then emphasized.

—*Peter Quartermain*

Acknowledgments

This book was produced by BC Research. Karen L. Rood, senior editor for the *Dictionary of Literary Biography* series, was the in-house editor.

Art supervisor is Patricia M. Flanagan. Copyediting supervisor is Patricia Coate. Production coordinator is Kimberly Casey. Typesetting supervisor is Laura Ingram. The production staff includes Rowena Betts, Matt Brook, Kathleen M. Flanagan, Joyce Fowler, Pamela Haynes, Judith K. Ingle, Vickie Lowers, Beatrice McClain, Judith McCray, George Stone Saussy, Joycelyn R. Smith, and Lucia Tarbox. Jean W. Ross is permissions editor. Joseph Caldwell, photography editor, and James Adam Sutton did photographic copy work for the volume.

Walter W. Ross and Jennifer Castillo did the library research with the assistance of the staff at the Thomas Cooper Library of the University of South Carolina: Lynn Barron, Daniel Boice, Connie Crider, Kathy Eckman, Michael Freeman, Gary Geer, David L. Haggard, Jens Holley, Marcia Martin, Dana Rabon, Jean Rhyne, Jan Squire, and Ellen Tillett.

Grateful acknowledgment is given to New Directions, agents for the Ezra Pound Literary Property Trust, and to Marlan Beilke, from whose book *Shining Clarity* the photograph of Robinson Jeffers on page 197 is taken.

American Poets, 1880-1945
First Series

Dictionary of Literary Biography

Conrad Aiken

Stephen Cummings
University of Western Ontario

See also the Aiken entry in *DLB 9, American Novelists, 1910-1945*.

BIRTH: Savannah, Georgia, 5 August 1889, to William Ford and Anna Potter Aiken.

EDUCATION: A.B., Harvard, 1912.

MARRIAGES: 25 August 1912 to Jessie McDonald, divorced 1929; children: John Kempton, Jane Kempton, Joan Delano. 27 February 1930 to Clarissa Lorenz, divorced 1937. 7 August 1937 to Mary Hoover.

AWARDS: Pulitzer Prize for *Selected Poems*, 1930; Shelley Memorial Award, 1930; Guggenheim Fellowship, 1934; Bryher Award, 1950; National Book Award for *Collected Poems*, 1954; Bollingen Prize in Poetry, 1956; Academy of American Poets Fellowship, 1957; National Institute of Arts and Letters Gold Medal, 1958; Huntington Hartford Foundation Award, 1960; St. Botolph Award, 1965; Brandeis University Creative Arts Medal, 1967; National Medal for Literature, 1969; Poet Laureate of Georgia, 1973.

DEATH: Savannah, Georgia, 17 August 1973.

BOOKS: *Earth Triumphant and Other Tales in Verse* (New York: Macmillan, 1914; London: Macmillan, 1914);
Turns and Movies and Other Tales in Verse (Boston & New York: Houghton Mifflin, 1916; London: Constable/Boston & New York: Houghton Mifflin, 1916);
The Jig of Forslin: A Symphony (Boston: Four Seas, 1916; London: Secker, 1922);

Courtesy of
University of Georgia Press

Nocturne of Remembered Spring and Other Poems (Boston: Four Seas, 1917; London: Secker, 1922);
The Charnel Rose, Senlin: A Biography, and Other Poems (Boston: Four Seas, 1918);

3

Scepticisms: Notes on Contemporary Poetry (New York: Knopf, 1919);

The House of Dust: A Symphony (Boston: Four Seas, 1920);

Punch: The Immortal Liar, Documents in His History (New York: Knopf, 1921; London: Secker, 1921);

Priapus and the Pool (Cambridge, Mass.: Dunster House, 1922);

The Pilgrimage of Festus (New York: Knopf, 1923; London: Secker, 1924);

Bring! Bring! (London: Secker, 1925); republished as *Bring! Bring! and Other Stories* (New York: Boni & Liveright, 1925);

Senlin: A Biography (London: Leonard & Virginia Woolf at the Hogarth Press, 1925);

Priapus and the Pool and Other Poems (New York: Boni & Liveright, 1925);

Blue Voyage (London: Howe, 1927; New York: Scribners, 1927);

Conrad Aiken, The Pamphlet Poets, edited by Louis Untermeyer (New York: Simon & Schuster, 1928);

Costumes by Eros (New York: Scribners, 1928; London: Cape, 1929);

Prelude, The Poetry Quartos (New York: Random House, 1929);

Selected Poems (New York & London: Scribners, 1929);

John Deth: A Metaphysical Legend, and Other Poems (New York: Scribners, 1930);

Gehenna (New York: Random House, 1930);

The Coming Forth by Day of Osiris Jones (New York: Scribners, 1931);

Preludes for Memnon: or, Preludes to Attitude (New York & London: Scribners, 1931);

And in the Hanging Gardens (Baltimore, Linweave Limited Editions, 1933);

Great Circle (New York: Scribners, 1933; London: Wishart, 1933);

Among the Lost People (New York: Scribners, 1934);

Landscape West of Eden (London: Dent, 1934; New York: Scribners, 1935);

King Coffin (London: Dent, 1935; New York: Scribners, 1935);

Time in the Rock: Preludes to Definition (New York: Scribners, 1936);

A Heart for the Gods of Mexico (London: Secker, 1939);

Conversation: or Pilgrims' Progress (New York: Duell, Sloan & Pearce, 1940); republished as *The Conversation: or Pilgrims' Progress* (London: Phillips & Green, 1940);

And In The Human Heart (New York: Duell, Sloan & Pearce, 1940; London: Staples, 1949);

Brownstone Eclogues and Other Poems (New York: Duell, Sloan & Pearce, 1942);

The Soldier (Norfolk, Conn.: New Directions, 1944; London: Editions Poetry, 1946);

The Kid (New York: Duell, Sloan & Pearce, 1947; London: Lehmann, 1947);

Skylight One: Fifteen Poems (New York: Oxford University Press, 1949; London: Lehmann, 1951);

The Divine Pilgrim (Athens: University of Georgia Press, 1949);

The Short Stories of Conrad Aiken (New York: Duell, Sloan & Pearce, 1950);

Ushant: An Essay (New York: Duell, Sloane & Pearce/Boston: Little, Brown, 1952; London: Allen, 1963);

Collected Poems (New York: Oxford University Press, 1953; augmented, 1970);

A Letter from Li Po and Other Poems (New York: Oxford University Press, 1955);

Mr. Arcularis: A Play (Cambridge: Harvard University Press, 1957; London: Oxford University Press, 1958);

Sheepfold Hill: Fifteen Poems (New York: Sagamore, 1958);

A Reviewer's ABC: Collected Criticism of Conrad Aiken from 1916 to the Present, edited by Rufus A. Blanshard (New York: Greenwich/Meridian, 1958; London: Allen, 1961); republished as *Collected Criticism* (London: Oxford & New York: Oxford University Press, 1968);

The Collected Short Stories of Conrad Aiken (Cleveland & New York: World, 1960; London: Heinemann, 1966);

Selected Poems (New York: Oxford University Press, 1961; London, Oxford & New York: Oxford University Press, 1969);

The Morning Song of Lord Zero: Poems Old and New (New York: Oxford University Press, 1963; London: Oxford University Press, 1963);

The Collected Novels of Conrad Aiken: Blue Voyage, Great Circle, King Coffin, A Heart for the Gods of Mexico, Conversation (New York, Chicago & San Francisco: Holt, Rinehart & Winston, 1964);

A Seizure of Limericks (New York, Chicago & San Francisco: Holt, Rinehart & Winston, 1964; London: Allen, 1965);

3 Novels: Blue Voyage/Great Circle/King Coffin (New York, Toronto & San Francisco: McGraw-Hill, 1965; London: Allen, 1965);

Cats and Bats and Things with Wings (New York: Atheneum, 1965);

Preludes: Preludes for Memnon/Time in the Rock (New York: Oxford University Press, 1966; London: Oxford University Press, 1966);

Tom, Sue and the Clock (New York: Collier/London: Collier-Macmillan, 1966);

Thee: a Poem (New York: Braziller, 1967; London: Inca, 1973);

The Clerk's Journal: Being the Diary of a Queer Man (New York: Eakins Press, 1971);

A Little Who's Zoo of Mild Animals (London: Cape, 1977; New York: Cape/Atheneum, 1977).

OTHER: Thomas Hardy: *Two Wessex Tales*, foreword by Aiken (Boston: Four Seas, 1919);

Modern American Poets, selected, with a preface, by Aiken (London: Secker, 1922); revised contents, with a new preface, by Aiken (New York: Modern Library, 1927); enlarged as *Twentieth Century American Poetry*, with an augmented preface by Aiken (New York: Modern Library, 1945; revised, 1963);

Selected Poems of Emily Dickinson, edited, with a preface, by Aiken (London: Cape, 1924);

American Poetry, 1671-1928: A Comprehensive Anthology, edited, with a preface, by Aiken (New York: Modern Library, 1929); revised and enlarged as *A Comprehensive Anthology of American Poetry* (New York: Modern Library, 1944);

An Anthology of Famous English and American Poetry, edited, with introductions, by Aiken and William Rose Benét (New York: Modern Library, 1945).

Conrad Aiken's long and productive literary career has prompted such descriptions of him as "the buried giant of twentieth-century American writing" (Malcolm Cowley), "the best known unread poet of the twentieth century" (Louis Untermeyer), and appreciations such as "When the tide of aesthetic sterility which is slowly engulfing us has withdrawn, our first great poet will be left. Perhaps he [Aiken] is the man" (William Faulkner). Hayden Carruth has suggested that Aiken's influence had significant impact "in determining, almost while no one was aware of it, the look and sound of the poetry written in our age." While no consensus has been reached, Aiken's thirty volumes of poetry, five novels, dozens of short stories, hundreds of critical articles and reviews, and his autobiography, plus collected and selected editions of poetry, short stories, novels, and criticism, constitute a major and imposing body of work. Translations have appeared in fifteen languages, and adaptations or readings of his work have been presented on radio

or television on seventy different occasions between 1936 and 1971, in the United States, Canada, England, and Germany. The argument concerning its value has extended through hundreds of journal articles and reviews of his work, and in four full-length treatments by Houston Peterson (1931), Jay Martin (1962), Frederick Hoffman (1962), Reuel Denney (1964); in two Aiken "numbers" of literary journals (*Wake, 11*, 1952; *Studies in the Literary Imagination*, 1980); in sixteen Ph.D. dissertations since 1961; and, by implication, in an edition of his letters (1978) and in a recent "confession" by his second wife (1983).

The body of work posed—and poses—a reading problem to critics, which perhaps arose from both the bulk and the nature of its content. In a bibliographical review of Aiken criticism, Catherine Harris points out that "Scholars and critics of the nineteen-seventies re-emphasized that Aiken's poetry deserved to be, indeed benefitted from being, considered as a whole," and "Many critics found Aiken's fiction to be a prose version of the poetry." This remarkable sense of integration among both poetry and prose seems to center upon Aiken's notion of the autobiographical. Freud and the apparatus of psychoanalysis are essential to his method, and his theme, as R. P. Blackmur describes it, "is the struggle of the mind which has become permanently aware of itself to rediscover and unite itself with the world in which it is lodged." The object of Aiken's autobiographical analysis is, then, not merely Aiken-the-man, but Aiken-the-consciousness, by which his work rises above the personal and becomes the record of a pilgrimage in which the reader may share. Such a pilgrimage must be, of necessity, circular in form, for the arrival at one's goal is marked only by an enlargement of consciousness in an ever-changing and at the same time alienating present. That Aiken's life reflects an astonishing symmetry attests, perhaps, to a relentless honesty and to a will to fuse the realms of art and life.

Although Conrad Potter Aiken was born in Savannah, Georgia, in 1889, lived there with his two brothers and one sister until 1901, and died there at the age of eighty-four in 1973, he was not a Southerner. Both of his parents were descendants of John Akin, a Scottish Quaker who arrived in America in 1680 and settled in New England. His mother's maiden name was Anna Aiken Potter. Thus her marriage to Dr. William Ford Aiken meant that her married name was a transposition of her maiden name: Anna Aiken Potter became Anna Potter Aiken. "It was just an accident my

Conrad Aiken, circa 1895 (courtesy of Mary Aiken)

father came to Savannah. Physician's jobs were hard to find in the North and there was a scarcity of doctors in the South," Conrad Aiken explained in an interview. His maternal grandfather, William James Potter (1829-1893), proved a lifelong influence. Potter was a radical Unitarian minister, who with Ralph Waldo Emerson and a "Colonel Higginson" (probably Thomas Wentworth Higginson), founded the Free Religious Association in 1867. Conrad Aiken later said that he always had with him a copy of his grandfather's collected sermons. He has also said that summer trips to New England were useful to him, as "Shock treatment . . . the milieu so wholly different," but simple transplantation was not to be so shocking as what happened in 1901, when he was eleven.

In his edition of Aiken's *Selected Letters* (1978), Joseph Killorin reports a conversation with Aiken: "On the morning of February 27, 1901, he awoke about seven to hear his father and mother, in their bedroom, quarreling: 'And I heard my father's voice counting: "One, two, three." And a pistol shot, and then another shot. I got out of my bed and walked through the children's bedroom, next to my parents' and where Elizabeth and Kempton and Robert were in their cribs, and opened the folding doors to my parents' room. I had to step over my father's body to go to my mother. But she was dead, her mouth wide open in the act of screaming. I came out, closed the folding doors, told the children to stay in their beds and that the nurse would come to them. I dressed myself, went downstairs and told the cook there had been an accident and to give the children breakfast downstairs, and to keep them in the dining room. Then I walked to the police station a block away and told them my father had shot my mother and himself, and they said: "Who is your father?" And I said: "Dr. Aiken." So they came with me and took command.' " The murder-suicide of his parents dramatically ended his childhood, dissolved completely his life in a family—his brothers and sister were adopted by Frederick Winslow Taylor in Philadelphia, while he was moved to Cambridge to live with his Uncle William Tillinghast where, as he says, "I more or less lost touch with them"—and opened a psychological door through which his pilgrimage in search of self began.

Aiken committed himself early on to writing, producing a handwritten and later typed magazine called the *Story Teller* at the age of thirteen, and writing for and editing the Middlesex School (Concord, Massachusetts) magazine, *Anvil*, between 1904 and his entrance to Harvard in 1907. He was part of the illustrious Harvard classes of 1910-1911, which included Heywood Broun, Stuart Chase, E. E. Cummings, Walter Lippmann, and John Reed, but perhaps his most important friendship was with T. S. Eliot, who had entered in 1906. At the end of his freshman year, Aiken was elected to the Harvard *Advocate* and began to write for it. In his junior year, he was elected its president. During his senior year he took advantage of his place on the dean's list to cut classes to translate Théophile Gautier's *La Morte Amoureuse* but was placed on probation (the translation was never published; Aiken acknowledged *La Morte Amoureuse* as the source of the vampire narrative in *The Jig of Forslin*). He felt his probation to be unfair treatment, but his resignation from Harvard was perhaps also prompted by shyness: he had been chosen class poet and would have had to perform the public duties of that office. Among the teachers who influenced his thinking were Charles T. Copeland, Dean Le Baron Russell Briggs, and George Santayana. Rob-

Aiken's parents: Dr. William Ford Aiken and Anna Potter Aiken (courtesy of Mary Aiken)

ert Wilbur has pointed out that "Santayana's ideas on poetry had a lasting importance upon Aiken. . . . Santayana's insistence that the greatest poetry was 'philosophical poetry,' said Aiken . . . 'fixed my view of what poetry would ultimately be . . . that it really had to begin by *understanding*, or trying to understand.' " After resigning from Harvard he traveled in Europe, visiting Eliot in Paris, but he returned to Harvard in autumn 1911 to complete his degree (1912).

As Aiken describes it in his autobiography, *Ushant* (1952) this interlude in Europe was formative: "He had himself a hand in the shaping of that magical spring and summer, which had, for him, the effect of finally opening doors, everywhere. It was his decision that his life must be lived *off-stage*, behind the scenes, out of view, and that only thus could he excel, . . . that had now established for the first time his freedom to maneuver as he wished to, and as he knew best he could. And this freedom, for him, must be inviolable." Aiken would, all of his life, maintain his distance from subjugating group identities, even stating this distance to be a

necessity in a *New Republic* essay (18 September 1935) titled "A Plea for Anonymity": "Our writers must learn once more in the best sense how to *stand clear*, in order that they may preserve that sort of impersonal anonymity, and that deep and pure provincialism, in which the terms approach universals, and in which alone they will find, perhaps, the freedom for the greatest work."

Upon his return to Cambridge, Aiken fell into regular meetings with Eliot (who had returned in the fall of 1911 from the Sorbonne). Much has been argued concerning the influence of the two young poets on each other; Aiken says, "the juices went both ways." The general opinion of Aiken as imitator, preferred in the 1920s and still echoed by Frederick Hoffman in 1962, has perhaps reversed. An anonymous *Times Literary Supplement* review in 1963, suggested that "the test of time had revealed Aiken as an innovator rather than a copier, a lender rather than a borrower." It was, however, Aiken who advanced Eliot when he carried typescripts of "The Love Song of J. Alfred Prufrock" and "La Figlia che Piange" to England on a trip in 1914 and showed these poems to Ezra Pound. In 1922 Aiken confirmed that their relationship was a two-way street when he wrote to Robert Linscott about Eliot's *The Waste Land* (1922): "Am I cuckoo in fancying that it cancels the debt I owed him? I seem to detect echoes or parodies of *Senlin, House, Forslin*: in the evening at the violet hour etc, Madame Sosostris etc, and in general the 'symphonic' nature, the references to music (Wagner, Strawinsky [*sic*]) and the repetition of motifs, and the 'crowd' stuff beginning 'Unreal city.' "

Aiken's earliest verse was unimpressive, at best. The lyrics published in the *Advocate*, and even the long narrative *The Clerk's Journal*—which, although written in 1910-1911, was not published until 1971—are often clumsy and labored with heavy-breathing sentiment. *The Clerk's Journal* is important, however, because it shows Aiken already at work on the problems of adapting musical structure to poetry and his use of ordinary citizens as central characters. A two-part narrative, of more than 400 lines, it relates the aspirations and general moodiness of a clerk whose love affair with a waitress has gone sour. In his preface Aiken himself described the poem as "unmistakably the work of a very young man," and noted that it was often "very funny when it didn't quite mean to be."

Three years after he completed *The Clerk's Journal*, in September 1914, Aiken's first volume of poetry was published by Macmillan. The poems in *Earth Triumphant and Other Tales in Verse* represent continuing experiment and should be viewed as products of the discipline of a poet-in-training. Many were written during a year in Europe with his wife, Jessie McDonald, whom he had married in Canada in August 1912. Others were written in Cambridge, to which they had returned in preparation for the birth of the first of their three children, John Kempton, in October 1913 (all of his three children were to publish novels, although the youngest, Joan Aiken, is best known). None of the poems in *Earth Triumphant* has been included in any subsequent selected or collected edition of his poetry, for none was considered to be, as he says in the preface to the *Collected Poems* (1953), "even remotely salvageable." The book shows no sign of experimental or original verse. Traditional and romantic in their rhythm and rhyme schemes, the poems owe much to John Masefield. The title poem, a narrative written in octosyllabics, describes a young man's disillusion with life and asserts the solid realities of earth and love over the abstractions of art and intellection.

Aiken had begun to produce, and by 1920 he would publish another five books of poetry. His next, *Turns and Movies and Other Tales in Verse* (1916), contains his first explicit experiments with musical form. "Turns and Movies," a collection of fifteen vignettes concerned with the lives of vaudeville actors, takes its title from the *Boston Transcript*, which published an entertainment column under that name. These poems are dramatic where "Earth Triumphant" was narrative and exhibit a surer hand than those of the earlier volume; as Hoffman says, "We have a sense of genuine, legitimate feeling in these statements by vaudevillians and circusmen." According to Jay Martin, Aiken produced a second series of vaudeville poems, "The Tinsel Circuit," in the fall of 1915. Although three poems from this sequence appeared in the December 1935 issue of *Esquire* and seven poems from it appeared in the Fall issue of *Carolina Quarterly*, the whole sequence, much revised from earlier appearances, was first published in *The Morning Song of Lord Zero* (1963). The full sequence reappears in the 1970 edition of his collected poems, where it is dated "1916-1961." Martin suggests that "The Tinsel Circuit" contains elements of both *Turns and Movies* and of the later symphonies and is thus transitional in nature.

Of the other four poems in *Turns and Movies*, two are love lyrics ("Discordants" and "Evensong"), one, "Disenchantment," is a narrative concerning disillusionment in a marriage, and the last, "This Dance of Life," is a second installment of the long title narrative of *Earth Triumphant*. The first section of "Discordants" became so popular with anthologists—who seemed to prefer it to more current work—that eventually Aiken refused to allow it to be reprinted. "Disenchantment: A Tone Poem" is perhaps Aiken's first explicit experiment with musical variation as a poetic method: he uses variations rather than simple repetitions of phrase, and juxtaposes cacophony and harmony, stanza by stanza and section by section. It is dedicated to Lucien Crist, an American composer Aiken met in England during his absence from Harvard.

Nocturne of Remembered Spring (1917) contains ten poems, largely concerned with themes which had become familiar to Aiken's small group of readers: disillusionment, guilt, nostalgia, anxiety, and melancholy. They may still be considered experimental, and at least half are attempts at adapting ideas of musical structure to poetry (an analogy Aiken was developing on a larger scale in his symphonies, which include *The Jig of Forslin*, published in 1916). Aiken called "Episode in Grey," to be included in his *Collected Poems*, "a sufficient example

First page of the manuscript for The Clerk's Journal *(by permission of Mary Aiken, courtesy of Eakins Press)*

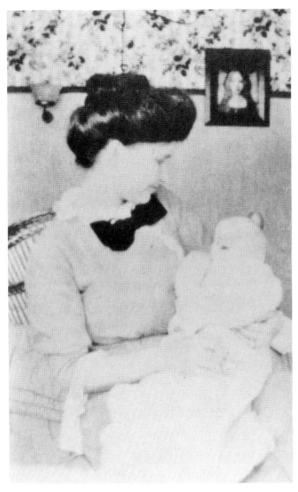

Aiken's first wife, Jessie McDonald Aiken, and their son, John, in 1913

of the lengths to which an obsession with the 'musical' analogies of poetry could be carried." The book also contains the third and final installment of "Earth Triumphant." In an anonymous review of his own work, published in the *Chicago News* (January 1917), Aiken disinflated himself: "In *Turns and Movies* he willfully sacrificed his ability to write in smoothly involute curves for a dubious gain in matter-of-fact forcefulness. In *The Jig of Forslin* he recanted, and, with occasional sops to downright and rigid realism, abandoned himself to a luxuriation of romantic virtuosity. And now, in *Nocturne of Remembered Spring*, he is more clearly than ever a schizophrenic."

Among other reviewers of his early work, the names of William Faulkner (*Mississippian*, February 1921), John Gould Fletcher (*Poetry Journal*, July 1916), H. L. Mencken (*Smart Set*, February 1917), William Dean Howells (*Harper's Monthly Magazine*,

September 1915), and Harriet Monroe (*Poetry*, November 1918) indicate an awareness of Aiken's poetry in some of the most widely read writers of the time. In general, critics both well known and little known commented upon the influence of John Masefield on the poems of *Earth Triumphant* but noted Aiken's originality; poems in *Turns and Movies* and *The Jig of Forslin* were variously praised for their vivid imagery but faulted for psychological or sensational themes; those of *Nocturne of Remembered Spring* revealed to several critics a growing mastery of technique but were called too intellectually slight. Critical reaction was, if mixed, at least constant.

By 1917 Aiken had begun to establish himself as a critic. Of the 238 articles and reviews listed in Rufus Blanshard's "Checklist of Conrad Aiken's Critical Writings," in *A Reviewer's ABC* (1958), some sixty-two appeared between 1915 and 1919 (the publication date of Aiken's first collection of criticism, *Scepticisms.*) He had distinguished himself by attacks on imagism—or "Amygism," with reference to Amy Lowell—in the *New Republic* and *Poetry Journal* and had addressed himself to recent poetry of many of his contemporaries in newspapers, the *Dial*, and *Poetry* (Chicago). That Aiken's acute, candid, and occasionally cutting observations were sometimes directed toward poets who would later review his work has been suggested as one source of the generally unfavorable reviews his work received, as book-by-book it emerged. Whatever the political wisdom of his reviewing, Marianne Moore was later to say of him, in *Wake 11* (1952) that "he was the perfect reviewer, Diogenes' one honest man, fearing only to displease himself. . . ." General reaction to the collected criticism in *A Reviewer's ABC* was very favorable. And Blanshard, in his introduction to the volume, suggests that Aiken's criticism was "everywhere informed with that natural but unassertive authority of the dedicated and engaged writer to whom the extra reputation he might win as critic is not so important as the self-rewards of the critical experience."

During this period, Aiken launched what was to be the major work of his early career, the six "symphonies." He and Jessie Aiken continued to live in Boston, where their second child, Jane Kempton, was born in December 1917. His encounter with army conscription in 1917 brought about a change in the law: he successfully argued that his profession as a writer was an "essential profession" and became the first American poet to be deferred because he was a poet. They lived on a small income, supplemented by earnings from reviewing. But neither the necessities of daily life nor the relative contentment of his domestic environment distracted him from a feverish production of poetry.

In a letter to Houston Peterson in 1928, Aiken traces the source of the symphonies back to 1912-1914 and a "passing passion for Richard Strauss," and provides this account of their writing: "In 1915, then, I began the first out-and-out symphony, on the theme of nympholepsy: *The Charnel Rose*. And it was as I was bringing this to a close, in November of that year, that I first thought of a series of symphonies which might project a kind of rough and ready 'general view.' I think Santayana's preface to *Three Philosophical Poets*, and the book itself, were deeply influencing me at this time. . . . Anyway, I began *The Jig of Forslin* on the same day that I finished *The Charnel Rose*, and had it done early in 1916. And here again the new poem led on to the next one: I saw the *House of Dust* as I was finishing *Forslin*, saw it as a corollary." After writing *The House of Dust* in winter 1916-1917, Aiken wrote the first half of his long narrative poem, *Punch: The Immortal Liar* (1921), but he put it aside in early 1918 to write another symphony, *Senlin*. Returning to and finishing *Punch* later in 1918, Aiken began

Conrad Aiken, 1914

The Pilgrimage of Festus, in fall 1919 and took "(with intermissions) two years" to complete it.

The symphonies were published in a slightly different order: *The Jig of Forslin* (1916), *The Charnel Rose; Senlin* (1918) in a single volume, *The House of Dust* (1920), *The Pilgrimage of Festus* (1923). When they were gathered in *The Divine Pilgrim* (1949), they were arranged in their order of composition and a sixth poem, *Changing Mind* (written in 1924-1925), was added as a coda to the whole series.

In the symphonies Aiken's interest in the long poem, pursued since the early experiment *The Clerk's Journal*, comes to fruition on a grand scale. Musical analogy in Aiken's "symphonic form" refers to patterns of narrative repetition and variation: words and in some cases whole lines are repeated (as in the opening and closing sections of *The House of Dust*); situations are varied (as in the morning, noon, and evening songs of *Senlin*); and words and phrases are repeated or echoed in repeated or varied situations (as in the opening passages of parts one and two of *The House of Dust*, and in such lines as "Beautiful darkener of hearts, weaver of silence," "Beautiful pale-lipped visionary," and "Beautiful woman! golden woman whose heart is silence!" in part two, section one of *The Pilgrimage of Festus*). In abandoning smooth, chronological narrative structure which might be likened to the classical symphonies of Mozart, Beethoven, and Haydn, Aiken is working in a more contemporary tradition of the symphony, derived from such composers as Anton Bruckner, Gustav Mahler, Arnold Schoenberg, Anton von Webern, and Igor Stravinsky. The juxtapositions, abrupt transitions, repetitions, and variations of his narrative structures are also analogous to the work of such artists as Cézanne, Picasso, and, for occasional cacophony, Duchamp.

The Charnel Rose is the least effective of the symphonies, as Aiken himself said in a review of his own work, published in *Poetry* in 1919 at the invitation of Harriet Monroe. Concerned with the pursuit of, possession by, and disillusionment in, love, it contains dreamlike visions of lamias and death—for which, as Steven Olson says, "Aiken has often been regarded as a latter-day decadent with Freudian proclivities." In his prefaces and in the 1919 review Aiken established for each symphony a precise though lengthy statement of theme, but Steven Olson suggests that these statements have led critics to read them "as over-structured works hopelessly burdened with musical analogies and intellectual themes verging on the didactic. Aiken so lucidly described his technique and 'themes' that he led critics down a garden-path of false scents to an architecturally impressive but ultimately empty gazebo."

The Jig of Forslin presents a sort of Everyman in reverie:

That he was oldish, and that his name was Forslin,
And that he sat in a small bare gaslit room.

In the mute evening, as the music sounded,
Each voice of it, weaving gold or silver,
Seemed to open a separate door for him. . . .

But this Everyman's fantastic inventions are peopled with prostitutes, vampires, and demons and include murders and a religious debauch, in manner not unlike Berlioz' *Symphonie Fantastique*: Aiken views the modern world as confused, rapacious, and selfish, alienating, and hostile. In some of its details it is a vision not unlike the cities of Rimbaud and Baudelaire or the hallucinations of Flaubert's *The Temptation of Saint Antony.*

The very long and complex *The House of Dust* explores an analogy between the city and the human body, playing individual against crowd and poet against collective mind. In a letter to John Freeman, Aiken said there is "a roughly orderly progression from the crowd to the individual, and again from the individual superficially seen (as a mere atom in the crowd) to the individual seen intimately, subjectively, at a moment when his consciousness is sharply focussed by an emotional crisis." Parts one and two are chronological and present events of the city and activities of individuals between sundown one day to the following night. Parts three and four are comprised mainly of vignettes of individuals, in part fulfilling the Poet's quest: "I will ask them all, I will ask them all their dreams,/I will hold my light above and seek their faces./I will hear them whisper, invisible in their veins. . . ." The quest is for quintessential identity, and the poem explores the dimensions of identity on the levels of the crowd, the individual as extension of the crowd, and the solitary individual. *The House of Dust* is a virtuoso performance, in which technique and theme seem perfectly matched. Aiken's control of variation, repetition, and tonal modulation seem more finely tuned than in the preceding symphonies.

Senlin: A Biography is generally considered to be the most successful of the symphonies. Senlin represents a fluid consciousness, seeking its own form. He incorporates the particulars of his own world—in such physical manifestations as a forest,

a desert, a city, and a house—and at the same time he exists self-consciously independent of them. Senlin is whatever he imagines himself to be; and he is also the expression of very human imperatives. The poet's quest is to identify the city with the consciousness of it:

It is morning, Senlin says, and in the morning
When the light drips through the shutters like the
　　dew,
I arise, I face the sunrise,
And do the things my fathers learned to do.

Stars in the purple dusk above the rooftops
Pale in a saffron mist and seem to die,
And I myself on a swiftly tilting planet
Stand before a glass and tie my tie.

Who and what am I, the poem asks; how can I move in my own way, with my own balance, when the planet moves on its? How be firm and upright and independent, while "on a star unstable?" The theme runs through much of Aiken's poetry.

The Pilgrimage of Festus returns to a more concrete conception of personality. Festus, searching for truth and knowledge, observes and reports his own fantasies. Nightmarish scenes such as the vivisection of the princess are counterbalanced by specific and alternate points of view, encountered in imaginary conversations with the Buddha, Confucius, Jesus, and Mephistopheles. Festus searches for wisdom, but Mephistopheles suggests that self-exploration pleases.

In *Changing Mind* (1925), added to the sequence when Aiken reorganized the symphonies as *The Divine Pilgrim* (1949), the artist directly confronts the problems of identity and reality in a shifting and indeterminate world; the self seeking its identity is the "I" of the artist looking at Forslin, Festus, Senlin, and himself; the self looks not only at the shifting external universe but also—through the offices of Doctor Wundt—at the shifting indeterminacies of the internal world of the psyche:

"Laugh if you like," she said, whose golden hair
Fell round me fine as water-sifted sunlight.
"Whistle derision from Rome to Jericho;
Sell him to Doctor Wundt the psycho-analyst
Whose sex-ray eyes will separate him out
Into a handful of blank syllables,—
Like a grammarian, whose beak can parse
A sentence till its gaudy words mean nothing."

The five symphonies up to and including *Festus* deal with humanity's experience; the "I" is generic, not specific. *Changing Mind* is the pilgrimage of the artist at a particular moment of his history and hence experience: Jay Martin suggests that in this coda to *The Divine Pilgrim* Aiken is "recreating, in order to understand, the whole process of his development." The protagonist of *Changing Mind* confronts and attempts to understand his "constituent particles" (Aiken's phrase), the elements that created him. Between the completion of *The Pilgrimage of Festus* and *Changing Mind*, Aiken had turned to the writing of short stories. He incorporates prose in *Changing Mind*, an experiment which would recur in *The Coming Forth by Day of Osiris Jones* (1931).

The 261 pages devoted to the symphonies in Aiken's *Collected Poems* contain a major achievement. Critics were quick to dismiss them as they appeared. John Middleton Murry (*Athenaeum*, September 1919) said, "We are far from saying that Mr. Aiken's poetry is merely a chemical compound of the 'nineties, Freud, and introspective Imperialism; but we do think it is liable to resolve at the most inopportune moments into those elements, and that such moments occur with distressing frequency." Allen Tate (*Nation*, January 1926) notes that repetition and diffuseness result in failures in such long poems as *Senlin*. Hoffman, too, has dismissed them as both transitional and representing "an almost wasteful brilliance." The symphonies do represent an advance in technique, from misty conception to sure execution—which is itself a statement of enlarging consciousness. Aiken would write other long poems, but in the symphonies he had completed his most literal attempts to adapt musical structure to poetry.

Punch: The Immortal Liar, Documents in His History (1921) and *Senlin*, both composed in 1917-1918, were perhaps Aiken's best-received works of this period, and it is interesting to note that, whereas *Senlin* is the most lyrical of the symphonies, *Punch* is almost purely narrative. Reviews of *Senlin* were qualified by regret that the poems were overly dependent upon psychological ideas, but they generally conclude that *"Senlin . . . is the profoundest and most unified of his allegories in this kind"* (unsigned review, *Times Literary Supplement*, August 1925). *Punch* fared better with the critics, Maxwell Anderson (*Measure*, May 1921) called the second part of *Punch* "one of the most poignant lyrics ever written." Amy Lowell (*New Republic*, September 1921) said that *Punch* was "one of the most significant books of the poetry renaissance." Aiken's Punch, the archetypal figure of the Punch and Judy puppet shows, has later literary predecessors in the

Pierrots of Jules Laforgue, Aubrey Beardsley, and Picasso; in the Harlequins of Cézanne; in Richard Strauss's Tyl Ulenspiegel; in Stravinsky's *Petrouchka* (1911) and *Pulcinella* (1920); in Schoenberg's *Pierrot Lunaire* (1912); and Ferruccio Busoni's *Arlecchino* (1917). In Aiken's version, which is devoid of authorial comment, Punch is presented from several points of view: the testimony by two old men, Punch's own story (as "the immortal liar") and its refutation by Polly Prim; an account of Punch's death. In the second part, Punch is seen from Mountebank's point of view as a misshapen hunchback trapped in a marriage to Judy but driven by lust toward Polly, who will not have him. In an epilogue Mountebank, who both carved the puppet and determined his fate, muses on Punch's story and says, "I too am a puppet." Punch's story presents life as mysterious, luxurious; Polly's presents it ironically; the Mountebank sees it mechanistically. The poem is dominated by Punch's fertile imagination—yet he is a puppet. Essentially, the poem is a balancing act between a view of man as limitless potential and resourceful imagination and of man as limited, deterministically controlled. The language of Punch is, on the whole, analytical where that of the symphonies had been emotive, evocative. *Punch* is narrative; *Senlin* is lyrical. Insofar as the symphonies other than *Senlin* had attempted a fusion of the lyrical and the narrative, they had failed to produce the new poetic form Aiken had sought and had not, in Aiken's view, adequately expressed or increased man's consciousness.

Following a scouting trip to London in 1920, Aiken decided to move his family to England in the fall of 1921. When Amy Lowell wrote to him in August of 1921, offering to review *Punch*, he replied, "I should, in any case, value your praise very highly, but I value it all the more in *this* case, first because we have so often, professionally, been at swords' points, and second because my own judgment of *Punch* has been, as it happens, and still is, singularly uncertain and wavering." Lowell's review in *New Republic* (September 1921) is an indication that Aiken was, if not well-received, then clearly established as an American poet. The move to England, however, presaged another frustration: another climb from obscurity. A few months later, in December 1921, he would write to Robert Linscott that the English edition of *Punch* "is sharing the ostracism of his author. It's been out over a month, with no sale and no reviews, save a tiny 'note' in the *Times* which appeared day before yesterday."

Aiken lived for a year in London, renewing his friendship with John Gould Fletcher (whom he had lived near in Boston). In October 1919 he had begun a series of commentaries and reviews of contemporary poetry, "Letters from America," for the London *Athenaeum*; just before his move to England in the autumn of 1921, he began contributing similar material under the same title to the London *Mercury* and continued to do so in England. He moved from London to a cottage in Winchelsea, Sussex, and then to Rye. Between 1920 and 1927—when he began his great work, the Preludes—he produced only two volumes of poetry and a relatively few shorter poems. Instead, he turned to writing short stories and a novel, *Blue Voyage* (1927). In 1922 he edited the first of several anthologies, most notable of which are the *Selected Poems of Emily Dickinson* (1924) and *An Anthology of Famous English and American Poetry* (1945), the product of what he called a "shotgun alliance" with William Rose Benét (during which he quarreled with Bennet Cerf and Saxe Commins of Random House over their exclusion of Ezra Pound, whom Commins had called a "fascist and traitor").

Priapus and the Pool (1922), which later appeared in *Priapus and the Pool and Other Poems* (1925), is in Martin's opinion Aiken's first successful use of the serial form, a musical form that is neither wholly lyrical nor wholly narrative but which permits an exploration of theme by increment and variation. The mythical Priapus, god of fertility, gardens, and herds, is here used as a grotesque and deformed phallic symbol; as Douglas Robillard points out, the fifteen poems of the series have a double theme, Priapus and Narcissus: "Priapic love is intensely phallic, entirely sexual," and the pool is the one in which Narcissus looked and fell in love with his own image. The poems play up "the themes of intense feeling and of meditation, of action and thought, transience and permanence, desire and memory." The prefatory poem (a dialogue) asks what the ego can remember. Is it merely a reflective surface like a pool, or has it its own (priapic?) identity and autonomy? The succeeding fourteen poems answer these questions and, although (as Robillard noted) not a sonnet sequence, *Priapus and the Pool* "follows the typical sonnet plot of love and loss, and the sublimation of feeling into art."

John Deth: a Metaphysical Legend (1930) was completed in 1924, shortly after Aiken moved to Rye, in England. The felicitous names of his characters—John Deth, Millicent Piggistaile, and Juliana Goatibed—were the names of the first three

Jeake's House, Rye, the seventeenth-century house where Aiken completed John Deth: A Metaphysical Legend *in 1924*

landowners of Winchelsea, near Rye: the materials of the poem have both historical and personal bases. "Here was the dance of death, localized," Aiken wrote Houston Peterson in October 1928, "and my Deth would have two complementary figures, one of whom would symbolize . . . consciousness, while the other would symbolize the unconscious or the merely physical." The narrative derives from the Dance of Death allegory and may have been prompted by Aiken's seeing, in Lucerne in 1911, Hans Holbein's series of paintings *Dance of Death*. It is a difficult and at times obscure poem (Aiken confessed to Peterson that "my meaning was, and has largely remained, obscure to me") but if the poem (following Aiken's own lead) is read as "possibly a direct reproduction of racial consciousness," it is remarkably strong. Yet it has frequently been neglected.

Part one is a fairly straightforward account of how De[a]th dances his victims away from life, willing or not; part two (which Robillard correctly calls the most difficult of the poem) joins in marriage the negative and the positive: weary, sterile Deth; sexual, carnal, fertile, and above all, lively Millicent Piggistaile—and from their union comes Juliana

Goatibed, "joint consciousness." This section of the poem is remarkable for the grotesqueness of its dream world: "Aiken has a penchant for the weird," says Robillard, "but in strangeness and eeriness this part of *John Deth* far outdoes all the vampires, lamias, dissections and Witches' Sabbaths of the symphonies."

The poem is a discussion/exploration of the Freudian notion (as expressed, perhaps, in Freud's *Civilization and Its Discontents*) that the allegorical Everyman figures Deth, Piggistaile, and Goatibed are, in Aiken's words, "doomed to an infinite and wearisome repetition of their ritual." Robillard calls part three of the poem "another *Parlement of Foules*": the birds seek in their discussion "the principle behind beauty, mortality, pain and life," and learn (from the bat) that the principle is Venus, the goddess of love. To break the endless cycle of Death-birth-love, Venus must be killed. Part four (the weakest in the poem) asserts that the love principle cannot be killed even by Death, and in part five the poem ends inconclusively: Juliana Goatibed buries John Deth and Millicent Piggistaile, but he is sleeping, not dead, and the process will go on. That the poem received lukewarm reception is perhaps a result—despite Aiken's own misgivings of its persuasiveness—more of habit among his critics than of a careful reading of the poem. Critics such as Babette Deutsch (*New York Herald Tribune Books*, 25 January 1931) and Louise Bogan (*New Yorker*, March 1931) echoed the qualified praise Aiken had so often received before. Percy Hutchinson (*New York Times Book Review*, October 1930) said, "So gifted is [Aiken] with poetic accomplishments and power that his work can never be less than distinguished, however unsatisfactory it may be in point of content."

Aiken began work on his first novel, *Blue Voyage* (1927), in 1922, but turned away to short stories in order to refine his craft and—he hoped—to increase his income. (His third child, Joan Delano, was born in 1924.) His first volume of short stories, *Bring! Bring! and Other Stories*, appeared in 1925, but his fiction did not produce the financial security for which he hoped; this led to a period of intense suffering, resulting first in divorce in 1929 and then in a suicide attempt in 1932. Yet his emotional decline did not reduce his output significantly. Aiken returned to Boston several times; there, in 1926, he met Clarissa Lorenz, whom he married in 1930 at William Carlos Williams's house in Rutherford, New Jersey. In September of 1927, he was appointed tutor at Harvard, but after graduates complained that "the author of *Blue Voyage* was not

Clarissa Lorenz and Conrad Aiken in Cambridge, Massachusetts, circa 1927 (courtesy of University of Georgia Press)

a fit teacher of the young" (though the book is innocuous enough), he was fired for "moral turpitude." One of Aiken's pupils at the time was Nathan Pusey, who later served as president of Harvard from 1953 to 1971, and it was likely with some satisfaction that Aiken refused, in 1961, the offer of an honorary degree from Harvard. In 1929 he began his long and often complex relationship with Malcolm Lowry, during which he became Lowry's guardian for a time. In 1930 his fortunes seemed to turn for he received both the Pulitzer Prize for his *Selected Poems* and the Shelley Memorial Award, and in that same year he returned to Rye with Clarissa Aiken and Lowry. Although 1931 saw the publication of two new books of poetry, *Preludes for Memnon* and *The Coming Forth by Day of Osiris Jones*, and Houston Peterson's full-

Malcolm Lowry in Cambridge, Massachusetts, July 1929
(courtesy of University of Georgia Press)

length study of his work, *The Melody of Chaos*, Aiken's frustrations mounted. In September 1932 he attempted suicide. Ironically, the next month he set in motion a series of events which led to the release of John Gould Fletcher from Bethlehem Hospital, to which Fletcher's wife secretly committed him following Fletcher's own suicide attempt. It was during this period that Aiken began, in 1927, the work for which he has since become best known as a poet, the Preludes.

The Coming Forth by Day of Osiris Jones is perhaps more poetic in attempt than in execution,

though Jay Martin (and indeed Aiken himself) views it as central to his career. A funerary book, it is a report, a document, a letter, a parable, even a myth. It is rich in resource, incorporating several voices in colloquy, choral response, dialogue. Aiken's note to the poem quotes E. A. Wallis Budge to the effect that in Egyptian funerary books the deceased (whose life is recorded there) is called Osiris (the ruler and judge of the underworld), "true of voice." The deceased must fully report the facts of his life so that he may be judged true of voice—and thereby step from darkness into light: the judgment is based on the completeness of the account, not on the deeds of the life itself. The aim at completeness, then, accounts for the resourcefulness (and difficulty) of the writing—parts of the poem are simply verbatim quotations from *The Book of the Dead* arranged as verse. As a funerary book it is a fitting complement to *John Deth*; in it the *things* of life, both physical and psychical, have their say. Their speech is often fragmentary and prosaic, as Marianne Moore commented (in *Wake 11*), "as on a late dynastic roll . . . there were sometimes illustrations, there arise here—not consecutively—favorite thoughts or might one say vignettes, and certain sensations prominent to the consciousness of Osiris Jones." As Jay Martin comments in his excellent analysis of the poem, "Jones is wholly understood as he wholly understands, completely accepted as he completely accepts."

In a preface to his 1961 *Selected Poems*, Aiken says that *The Coming Forth by Day of Osiris Jones* "was actually written after *Preludes for Memnon*, and before *Time in the Rock;* but I have now placed it ahead of those poems, and for two reasons. For one thing, it helps, I think, to explain those two sequences; and for another, it enables me to put them together, as they were meant to be—to all intents, they are one poem." The fragmentary, quasi-narrative *The Coming Forth by Day of Osiris Jones* is, in fact, a prologue to the 159 meditations of the two books of Preludes. Jay Martin calls the three books, and *Landscape West of Eden* (1934), "the central poem in Aiken's career," toward which all the earlier poems build, and from which the later poems derive. (It is curious, in light of Aiken's careful shaping and reshaping of all his poems and works, that the four poems have never—except in the *Selected Poems*—appeared together: in the Second Edition of the *Collected Poems* (1970), Aiken preserved the arrangement of the 1953 collection.)

Preludes for Memnon: or, Preludes to Attitude (1931) are "for" the colossal statue of Memnon at Luxor which, split, sang at dawn, as the rising sun

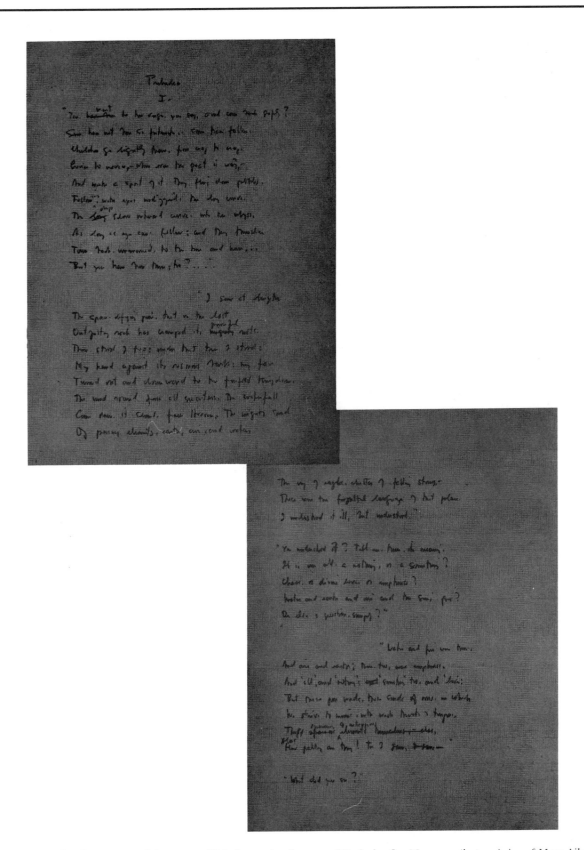

Draft for the first four stanzas of the poem published as section fourteen of Preludes for Memnon *(by permission of Mary Aiken; courtesy of the Houghton Library, Harvard University, gift of Alfred Claghorn Potter, 1936, H 1889)*

struck it, and reminded the Greeks of the Memnon who was killed at Troy, waiting for his mother Aurora (Dawn), who fought the dark. The title reasserts, then, a focus on the concerns of *The Coming Forth by Day of Osiris Jones*. The poems are preludes because they record moments of consciousness, of awareness; preserve memories against oblivion; consciousness transcends vicissitude and flux. They address the problems encountered in a search for a meaningful or consistent view of a fluid consciousness ranging between knowledge and desire, memory and sensation, matter and transcendence. There is, therefore, both a consciousness-in-flux and a consciousness-which-views the consciousness-in-flux: the epistemological mirror which is the essence of Aiken's autobiographical method. Despair and love are polar conditions of the consciousness-which-views; despair arises from the inability of the consciousness-which-views to affect or control the consciousness-in-flux, and love arises from a simple acceptance of the gulf which separates the two consciousnesses. Hope, if there is to be hope, lies in self-knowledge, in the greatest possible scope for the consciousness-which-views. The serial form of the Preludes allows Aiken to come at his theme again and again, often with great lyrical power, as in the central lines of "Prelude XXIX":

> There is no doubt that we shall do, as always,
> Just what the crocus does. There is no doubt
> Your Helen of Troy is all that she has seen,—
> All filth, all beauty, all honor and deceit.
> The spider's web will hang in her bright mind,—
> The dead fly die there doubly; and the rat
> Find sewers to his liking. She will walk
> In such a world as this alone could give—
> This of the moment, this mad world of mirrors
> And of corrosive memory. She will know
> The lecheries of the cockroach and the worm,
> The chemistry of the sunset, the foul seeds
> Laid by the intellect in the simple heart . . .
> And knowing all these things, she will be she.

In *Time in the Rock: Preludes to Definition*, Aiken explores the paradox of innocence—that those who recognize innocence in others are not themselves innocent—as a possible bridge between knowing and being. His conclusion is that innocence is transient, as transient as youth, and is lost as a mode of being to that old world-weary consciousness-which-views. Nevertheless, that same old consciousness is free to choose its attitude toward innocence, whether to despair its own loss of innocence or to celebrate the presence of innocence in others or in memory with joy. Even the "posing mind"—the

mind which pretends to be other than it is, that poses "like an acrobat" and "like an actor" in "Prelude IX" of *Time in the Rock*, that *performs* rather than *is*—is capable of the bright moment, "the bright the brief the brave, the seeming certain,"

> upon the stage of his own making
> there in the dirty wings on dirty sawdust
> against the trumpets of a vivid world.

What redeems the moment, bright or dark, from futility and pathos, is love, a transcendent angel, as in these lines from "Prelude LXXV," where, viewing unfaithful love and "a change of heart," caught in bravado and self-congratulation, knowing one's own failure to be ashamed at one's own dereliction and betrayal of others, brazening it out, grinning "at your own grin":

> Yes, and you have noted
> how the chemistry of the soul at midnight
> secretes particular virtue from such poisons:
> you have been pleased: rubbed metaphoric hands
> saying to yourself that the suffering, the shame,
> the pity, and the self-pity, and the horror,
> that all these things refine love's angel,
> filth in flame made perfect.

The higher awareness of the consciousness-which-views is neither limited to, nor does it exclude, the ironic or the pathetic. It is inclusive, luminous, and capable of liberation. One breaks out of the darkness by accepting it: knowledge is transcendence. In the words of "Prelude LXXV," "you [hold] the candle nearer that you might see/the essential horror." *Thence*, bright moments.

In *Landscape West of Eden* (1934) Aiken pursues these ideas in an allegorical geography, in which not an omnipotent God, not a fixity, but a god in the process of development proceeds west from Eden, followed by Adam, and learns that knowledge is a complex state of mind, compounded by aging and dying. With these four poems, Aiken arrives at his final philosophical position and concludes his experiments with musical form (although his poems will speak of music again, they cease to be based upon musical analogies). The clear narrative line of *Landscape West of Eden* also points to a decision as to how best he may explore the implications of his philosophical position: narrative is the means to revelatory autobiography, and lyrics are the means to record songs along the way. "Prelude XLV," of *Preludes for Memnon*, supplies the titles of two subsequent books, *Time in the Rock* (1936) and *And In The Human Heart* (1940), as well as the narrative theme of *Landscape West of Eden:*

> I have read
> Time in the rock and in the human heart,
> ....
> He moved the universe from east to west,
> Slowly, disastrously,—but with such splendor
> As god, the supreme poet of delight, might envy,—
> To the magnificent sepulchre of sleep.

Landscape West of Eden, perhaps Aiken's most complex poem, weighs the alternatives: move west, toward risk, with Adam (and develop), or resist that, seek fixity, with Eve (and stagnate).

And In The Human Heart is a sequence of forty-three sonnets, twenty-two of which were contained in letters written to his third wife, Mary Hoover, whom he married in 1937 after his divorce from Clarissa Lorenz. The book was conceived as a more formal continuance of the serial structure of the Preludes, but here the poems celebrate love more

Conrad Aiken, 1937; portrait by his third wife, Mary Hoover Aiken (courtesy of Mary Aiken)

optimistically: the sequence ends with the line, "Rejoice, my love, our histories begin!"

The complex relationships among Aiken's works of this period reveal that the "central poem" is located, in fact, in a net of many works of this period, and may or may not be limited to the four titles which Jay Martin identified. This complexity drew from R. P. Blackmur the comment that "more than any other American poet, Mr. Aiken has exhibited organic growth, has matured in sensibility, and has developed a form capable of expressing or enacting his material at the most significant level appropriate to his peculiar, and profound, talent" (*New Republic*, 13 January 1937). The "organic growth" between 1925 and 1940 most resembles an explosion, for during these fifteen years he published eight books of poetry, three collections of short stories, all five of his novels, one hundred and fifteen articles and reviews, and edited two anthologies of poetry—all of this roughly equal to half his total production, excluding selected, collected, or revised work—and in his personal life he concluded his first marriage, entered into and concluded a second, and entered into his third. During these years, in which he reached the emotional depths of attempted suicide and the heights of new love, he also conducted a summer school for artists and writers in Rye and maintained often difficult relationships with artists and writers such as Edward Burra and Malcolm Lowry. In 1934-1936 he was also London correspondent for the *New Yorker*, under the pseudonym Samuel Jeake, Jr. (His house in Rye had been built in 1689 by Samuel Jeake.)

In 1939 Aiken returned to his cottage at Cape Cod and the next year bought an old farmhouse in Brewster, Massachusetts, which he called 41 Doors. Aiken's many trips across the Atlantic by boat provided him with an image central to his work, the voyage (especially in *Blue Voyage, Great Circle,* and *Ushant*), but his return to New England signalled a change of focus, away from the voyage of self-discovery set in the immediate past and present and toward ancestral roots. His reputation among critics continued to be a source of considerable frustration. He wrote to Malcolm Cowley in 1941, "It makes me a little sad that after all this time I still can't be given to a critic who is both intelligent and not wholly unsympathetic," noting that Vincent McHugh's description of *King Coffin* as "a little masterpiece" had been cut from McHugh's review when it was published in the *New Republic*. He went on to say that "of the reviews all the way from *John Deth* and *Blue Voyage* through *Osiris Jones, Preludes for Memnon, Landscape West of*

Eden, Great Circle, and the book of short stories to *Conversation,* not one but was tepid and pejorative, not one that admitted or suggested that my work as a whole was of any importance, or added up to anything. Frankly, this has been a poisoned thorn in my side. . . ." Such reviews he concluded were in direct contrast to "the views of Graham Greene, for example, who thought *Great Circle* and *King Coffin* amongst the best novels of their decade, with a kind of Elizabethan power, or Freud, who said *Great Circle* was a masterpiece, or the *Times Literary Supplement,* which two years ago devoted half a leading article to *Festus, Senlin* and *Punch,* under the title 'Virtues of Abundance.' "

In one sense the four volumes of poetry published during the 1940s concern the American— or more often, the New England—experience within a larger historical framework. *Brownstone Eclogues* (1942)—a series of thirty-eight lyrics, in various stanzaic, rhythmic, and rhyme patterns— addresses the problems of life in the city, but without a controlling, central metaphor such as he had used in *The House of Dust.* The book also contains two longer elegies, "Blues for Ruby Matrix," in jazzy cadence with occasional playful syncopation, and the elegant "The Poet in Granada," for García Lorca. *The Soldier* (1944) can be compared to *The Coming Forth by Day of Osiris Jones* for its use of several voices in colloquy, choral response, and dialogue. War is conceived not only in terms of its simple brutalities, but as a necessary societal phase which brings forth culture as well as death. *The Kid* (1947) brings together a number of historical personages, most notably William Blackstone, John James Audubon, Kit Carson, Billy the Kid, Paul Revere, Willard Gibbs, Henry Adams, Walt Whitman, Herman Melville, and Emily Dickinson, to create a composite American figure who explores the immense regions of American geography and spirit. *Skylight One* (1949) is a mixed collection of poems containing a four-poem sequence on the seasons, an elegy for Franklin D. Roosevelt ("Crepe Myrtle"), a poem in celebration of Quaker and Puritan backgrounds ("Mayflower"), and an attack on the commercialization of Hallowe'en in which the dead retaliate.

Aiken's literary fortunes began a slow turn for the better in 1947 with his election as a Fellow in American Letters of the Library of Congress. In 1950 he became Poetry Consultant at the Library of Congress, holding the position for two years. During his tenure there, he completed work begun some twenty years earlier on his important autobiography, *Ushant* (1952). Also in 1952 *Wake 11*

Mary and Conrad Aiken, 1941 (courtesy of Mary Aiken)

devoted a special number to Aiken, and its contributors included Malcolm Cowley, Allen Tate, Marianne Moore, Mark Schorer, Malcolm Lowry, and Julian Symons, among others. Aiken's completion of *Ushant,* at the age of sixty-three, closes a cycle of productivity. *The Kid* was his last long poem and *Ushant,* his last prose narrative. He continued, however, to write articles and to comment on literary matters in letters to editors; his last appeared in the *Times Literary Supplement* in April 1971. Between 1950 and his death in 1973, he received nine major literary awards, including a National Book Award, the Bollingen Prize in Poetry, and the National Institute of Arts and Letters Gold Medal, and became the fifth winner of the National Medal for Literature.

Aiken's poetry of the 1950s and 1960s appeared in four volumes, *A Letter from Li Po and Other Poems* (1955), *Sheepfold Hill: Fifteen Poems* (1958), *The Morning Song of Lord Zero: Poems Old and New* (1963), and *Thee* (1967). In the best of these poems, such as "A Letter from Li Po," "Overture to Today," and "The Cicada," Aiken's craft is sure, sustained, and graceful. While many of the poems are serial in form, they are generally medium length rather than book length. They pursue the themes of "world and life as word." The language of art, says Aiken, is capable of surviving the ravages of time, transforming the world into "immortal text," as in "A Letter from Li Po":

> Chang Hsu, calligrapher of great renown,
> needed to put but his three cupfuls down
> to tip his brush with lightning. On the scroll,
> wreaths of cloud rolled left and right, the sky
> opened upon Forever. Which is which?
> The poem? Or the peachtree in the ditch?
> Or is all one? Yes, all is text, the immortal text,
> Sheepfold Hill the poem, the poem Sheepfold Hill,
> and we, Li Po, the man who sings, sings as he climbs,
> transposing rhymes to rocks and rocks to rhymes.

One senses here an affirmation and a reconciliation with the world which is not present in Aiken's early work. Perhaps it was this changed perspective which provided the groundwork for the extraordinary closing chapter in Aiken's life.

According to Joseph Killorin, Aiken had "revisited Savannah twice since 'the day of the long drive behind the two black-plumed hearses' and found that 'everything had waited for him.' " In 1960 Hy Sobiloff, a businessman, poet, and friend of Aiken's, visited Savannah and bought the house next door to Aiken's old home. After restoring it, Sobiloff gave Aiken the right to live in it for the rest of his life. The Aikens moved into the house in February 1962, at first living there only during the winter months. Later in his life, Aiken's illness made it impossible to return to Brewster during the summer. *A Seizure of Limericks* (1964), *Cats and Bats and Things with Wings:* (1965; a book of children's verse), and *Thee* (1967)—a sort of hymn, dedicated to his wife Mary—were among the last things Aiken wrote.

A recent revival of interest in Aiken, measured in numbers of doctoral dissertations and the publication of such scholarly tools as Catherine Harris's *Conrad Aiken: Critical Recognition, 1914-1981* (1983) and the Bonnells' *Conrad Aiken: A Bibliography (1902-1978)* (1982), suggests that Aiken is no longer the neglected or buried giant of American letters; yet the absence of Aiken's work from recent popular anthologies and textbooks also suggests that he remains unread except by specialists. The power and grace of his craftsmanship, the daring of his experiments with poetic form, the complex interrelationships of his total output, and the intelligence of his literary mind remain a rich resource to students of American literature in particular and of the human spirit in general.

Conrad Aiken, 1968 (courtesy of Mary Aiken)

A reading of Aiken would be incomplete without a sense of the man in his last years. By the time he qualified as a "senior citizen," the emotional turbulence of his youth and middle years, so painfully explored in his writing, had dropped from his life. Late interviews with Aiken record a memorable smile and his laughter. In a statement to the President's Council on Aging in 1965, at the age of seventy-five, he wrote, "It's extraordinary how little I can now remember of Cicero's famous essay on Old Age, which I had to read in Latin at school— but perhaps natural, for what does the boy want to know of old age, or what can he feel about it? All he does know is that grandfather and grandmother are old, and that this is a preliminary to death, that other mystery. He is still himself completely enthralled in what Santayana called animal faith, and of course is not in the least aware that the very act of being born is to be embarked on a process that leads to death: we live our lives, but in a sense we die them too. I find it profoundly reassuring to consider this inexplicable wonder, as I myself grow older: it has the perfection of a work of art. . . . Ignore the changed face that looks at you from the mirror, it is really the boy who still looks at you there, *he* has not changed; or if he has, it is only in the fact that he has all his life been gathering an inestimable treasure of memory: his own great poem to the universe. Encourage him to go on with it, and every morning, for this is *you*, the one and only never-to-be-replaced *you*, with its own private, but also cosmic, view of the world. Go along with him, and on crutches, if you have to, but let him enjoy it. And he will."

Letters:

Joseph Killorin, ed., *Selected Letters of Conrad Aiken* (New Haven: Yale University Press, 1978).

Interviews:

Andrew Sparks, "An Hour with Conrad Aiken," *Atlanta Journal and Constitution Magazine*, 5 May 1963, pp. 8, 46-47;

Ashley Brown, "An Interview with Conrad Aiken," *Shenandoah*, 15 (Autumn 1963): 477-488;

Patricia R. Willis, "Conrad Aiken: An Interview," *Rebel*, 8 (Winter 1965): 3-12;

Robert Hunter Wilbur, "The Art of Poetry IX: Conrad Aiken, an Interview," *Paris Review*, 11 (Winter-Spring 1968): 97-124.

Bibliographies:

R. W. Stallman, "Annotated Checklist on Conrad Aiken: A Critical Study," *Wake*, 11 (1952): 114-121;

F. W. Bonnell and F. C. Bonnell, *Conrad Aiken: A Bibliography (1902-1978)* (San Marino, Cal.: Huntington Library, 1982);

Catherine Harris, *Conrad Aiken: Critical Recognition, 1914-1981. A Bibliographic Guide* (New York & London: Garland, 1983).

Biography:

Clarissa Lorenz, *Lorelei Two: My Life with Conrad Aiken* (Athens: University of Georgia Press, 1983).

References:

Reuel Denney, *Conrad Aiken*, University of Minnesota Pamphlets on American Writers, No. 38 (Minneapolis: University of Minnesota Press, 1964);

Frederick J. Hoffman, *Conrad Aiken* (New York: Twayne, 1962);

Jay Martin, *Conrad Aiken: A Life of His Art* (Princeton: Princeton University Press, 1962);

Steven Eric Olsen, "The Vascular Mind: Conrad Aiken's Early Poetry, 1910-1918," Ph.D. dissertation, Stanford University, 1981;

Houston Peterson, *The Melody of Chaos* (New York: Longmans, Green, 1931);

Douglas Robillard, "The Poetry of Conrad Aiken: A Critical Study," Ph.D. dissertation, Wayne State University, 1965;

Studies in the Literary Imagination, special Aiken issue, 13 (Fall 1980);

Wake 11, special Aiken issue, edited by Seymour Lawrence (1952);

Robert Hunter Wilbur, "George Santayana and Three Modern Philosophical Poets: T. S. Eliot, Conrad Aiken, and Wallace Stevens," Ph.D. dissertation, Columbia University, 1965.

Papers:

The major collections of Aiken's papers are located at the Huntington Library in San Marino, California, and the Houghton Library, at Harvard University.

Hervey Allen
(8 December 1889-28 December 1949)

Paula L. Hart
University of British Columbia

See also the Allen entry in *DLB 9, American Novelists, 1910-1945.*

BOOKS: *Ballads of the Border* (El Paso, Tex.: Privately printed, 1916);

Wampum and Old Gold (New Haven: Yale University Press, 1921);

The Bride of Huitzil: An Aztec Legend (New York: James F. Drake, 1922);

Carolina Chansons: Legends of the Low Country, by Allen and DuBose Heyward (New York: Macmillan, 1922);

Earth Moods and Other Poems (New York & London: Harper, 1925);

Israfel: The Life and Times of Edgar Allan Poe (New York: Doran, 1926; London: Brentano's, 1927);

Toward the Flame (New York: Doran, 1926; London: Gollancz, 1934;

DuBose Heyward: A Critical and Biographical Sketch (New York: Doran, 1927);

New Legends (New York: Farrar & Rinehart, 1929);

Sarah Simon, Character Atlantean (Garden City: Doubleday, Doran, 1929);

Songs for Annette (New York: W. E. Rudge, 1929);

The Syllabus of a Novel to Be Called Anthony Adverse (New York: Farrar & Rinehart, 1932);

Anthony Adverse (New York: Farrar & Rinehart, 1933; London: Gollancz, 1934);

Action at Aquila (New York: Farrar & Rinehart, 1938; London: Gollancz, 1938);

It Was Like This: Two Stories of the Great War (New York & Toronto: Farrar & Rinehart, 1940);

The Forest and the Fort (New York & Toronto: Farrar & Rinehart, 1943);

Bedford Village (New York & Toronto: Farrar & Rinehart, 1944);

Toward the Morning (New York: Rinehart, 1948; London: Heinemann, 1949);

The City in the Dawn, edited by Julie Eidesheim (New York: Rinehart, 1950).

OTHER: *Year Book of the Poetry Society of South Carolina,* foreword by Allen and DuBose Hey-

Hervey Allen

ward (Charleston: Poetry Society of South Carolina, 1921);

Year Book of the Poetry Society of South Carolina, foreword by Allen and Heyward (Charleston: Poetry Society of South Carolina, 1922).

PERIODICAL PUBLICATIONS: "Poetry South," by Allen and DuBose Heyward, *Poetry,* 20 (April 1922): 35-48;

"Poe in South Carolina," *Poetry,* 20 (April 1922): 48-49.

Although Hervey Allen made his reputation as a writer with popular historical fiction, most notably *Anthony Adverse* (1933), his early writing career was devoted to poetry, most of which was published during the 1920s. This traditional verse, much of it concerned with local color and dominated by philosophical themes, no doubt provided solid apprentice work for the romantic fiction he later wrote.

William Hervey Allen, Jr., was born in Pittsburgh, Pennsylvania, to William Hervey and Helen Eby Myers Allen. He entered the U.S. Naval Academy in 1909 but withdrew two years later after suffering a leg injury in sports. After completing his bachelor of science degree at the University of Pittsburgh in 1915, he enlisted in an infantry unit of the Pennsylvania National Guard. Active service in 1916 at the Mexican border led to *Ballads of the Border*, his first published poems. Called to active duty again when the United States entered World War I, he was wounded and gassed in action. This war experience inspired his earliest poem of note, "The Blindman: a Ballad of Nogent l'Artaud," which was published in *Wampum and Old Gold* (1921). The poem's title also became the name of the poetry prize awarded annually by the Poetry Society of South Carolina, a group founded in 1920 by Allen and DuBose Heyward to promote a new interest in poetry in the South.

After a brief period of graduate study at Harvard Allen taught English at Porter Military Academy in Charleston, South Carolina, and in the public high school from 1920 to 1924. During this period two collections of his verse appeared. *Wampum and Old Gold*, published in the Yale Series of Younger Poets in 1921, contains a group of poems on experiences at the front in France and another of poems written after 1918. Reviewers of this early volume found promise in his work, a striving for an individual voice in its sincerity, strong feeling, and vivid imagery, but the reviewer for the *Springfield Republican* found it lacking in fresh ideas. His delight in the local color and rich history of South Carolina and his friendship with Heyward led to their joint authorship of *Carolina Chansons: Legends of the Low Country* (1922).

Shortly before the publication of *Carolina Chansons*, Allen and Heyward shared editorship of a Southern number of *Poetry* magazine (April 1922). Their views of the direction Southern poetry should take, expressed in their "Poetry South" editorial, may well be taken as Allen's own poetic theory, practiced not only in this collection but also in those which followed. Allen and Heyward explained that the South "will accept with modern spirit the new forms in verse, but accept them as being valuable for their loosening effect upon the old rather than as being all satisfactory in themselves; and it brings to American poetry a little known but tropically rich store of material, an unurbanized beauty, the possibility of legend, folk song, romance, historical narrative, glorious landscape, and an untired mood; in short, a content which will save it from that sure sign of literary inadequacy, a too nice preoccupation with form."

The topics mentioned in this editorial remained Allen's favorite poetic subjects, and his fondness for traditional form constantly disappointed his critics, who found his employment of it undistinguished. Allen's contribution to the *Carolina Chansons* included historical pieces on subjects such as LaFayette's landing; recreations of romantic legend, such as a story of blockade running; and depictions of a way of life infused with history, as in these lines from one of "The Sea-Islands" poems:

Sea-island winds sweep through Palmetto Town
Bringing with piny tang the old romance
Of pirates and of smuggling gentlemen.

Carolina Chansons was warmly received by contemporary critics, who saw the book as a valuable contribution of the Southern renaissance, a unique capturing of local color in poetic form. Amy Lowell, writing to an acquaintance in 1923, called Allen "the only man who has a broader vision; I have a belief in his promise, but it is too early yet to say whether my belief is justified or not." Modern critics have not been as kind. Louis Rubin, Jr., has contrasted the achievement of the South Carolinians with the innovative Fugitive poets, such as John Crowe Ransom and Allen Tate. The South Carolina poets, he says, were popularizers who dealt with concrete subjects in language "filled with abstraction."

Allen returned to the North in 1924 to take up residence for the next few years, first teaching English at Columbia University (1925-1926) and then at Vassar College (1926-1927). Annette Hyde Andrews, a student at Vassar, became his wife on 30 June 1927, and in the autumn of that year they went to live in Bermuda, on a plantation they named Felicity Hall.

During his New York days he became well known for his beer and chicken breakfasts, a festivity he delighted in throughout his life. "These breakfasts," wrote Emily Clark in the *Saturday Review of Literature* (9 December 1933), "were copious like Allen's size, conversation, and books." Although she was referring to his later prose, the 6'4" Allen also had a fondness for long narrative poems.

His 1925 collection, *Earth Moods and Other Poems,* was partially composed of long narrative poems dealing with the large themes of evolution and the importance of environment and partially of shorter lyrics dealing often with the mystical and grotesque. One of the narrative poems from this collection, "The Saga of Leif the Lucky," demonstrates his fondness for heroic figures and, in this case, historical speculation:

> Leif Erikson came rowing up the Charles
> In the sea-battered dragon ships,
> Stroked by the strong blond carls,
> The rattle of whose oars
> Had wakened sea lions on the glacial shores
> Of Greenland, where the white Christ newly ruled.

These poems, too, received positive critical attention. John Farrar of the *Bookman* was impressed by his suggestion of "the swift flow of life through the ages," and B. E. Stevenson of the *International Book Review* praised the power of his "small, colorful picture." Reviewing the book for the *New York Tribune* (21 June 1925), Babette Deutsch, while likening him to Amy Lowell, wrote, "he catches dynasties in a phrase, covers epochs in less than a stanza. But his terseness defeats itself, and the grandeur of his theme is blurred by a factual style, blunted by prose cadences." Almost ten years after Allen's first collection of poems, William Rose Benét still referred to him as a poet of promise whose work was too didactic and characterized by a "prosaic heaviness" (*Outlook,* 15 July 1925).

Louis Untermeyer included two of the *Earth Moods* poems, "Gargantuana" and "Whim Alley," in the 1930 edition of his anthology *Modern Amer-*

Hervey Allen and Bernard DeVoto in Coral Gables, Florida

ican Poetry. Calling these poems "particularly effective examples of Allen's ability to make decorations which do not suffer from picturesque affectations," he considered the collection itself an indication that Allen was more than a regional poet. Like Deutsch he felt that Allen's themes were larger than he could handle, but he found a "definiteness of execution" in "The Saga of Leif the Lucky" and the highly regarded "Funeral at High Tide."

It was four years before another collection of Allen's poetry appeared: *New Legends* (1929) is the result of his five years of plantation life in Bermuda, where he also wrote his best-selling novel *Anthony Adverse*. He loved this way of life, with its closeness to nature and tradition, and he subsequently followed it at Bonfield Manor on the Maryland shore, which he bought with the royalties from *Anthony Adverse*, and finally in Florida, on the Glades Estate in Coconut Grove, near Miami. *New Legends*, a collection of seven long narrative poems and some shorter lyrical works, includes previously published material as well as new poems. "Sarah Simon," Allen's personal favorite of the narratives, shows his fondness for colorful legend. Also published separately, with the added "Character Atlantean," "Sarah Simon" is the poetic story of the contact between a tropical native and white people. After losing her first husband, she rescues a sailor, lives with him, and bears him three children. She is eventually deserted by this man and robbed by her grown children, left to live alone until the age of ninety.

Some critics, such as Granville Hicks in the *New York World*, considered the collection a pleasant treatment of its themes; others, including L. W. Dodd (*Yale Review*), bemoaned the fact that Allen had still not found an individual poetic voice. J. T. Farrell of the *New York Evening Post* dismissed the collection cryptically, writing that Allen's own term "sweet kickshaws" defined the work. After the publication of *New Legends*, Louis Untermeyer commented in the 1930 edition of his anthology *Modern American Poetry*, "At present Allen stands at the crossroads: he has the possibilities of being either a lyricist or a writer of ambitious epics." Allen chose to write epics, but in prose rather than poetry, initiating a new trend in the lengthy historical novel.

Allen's last separately published poems appeared in *Songs for Annette* (1929), a twenty-three-page pamphlet printed in a limited edition of 100 copies. In 1933 Allen achieved recognition as a writer of popular fiction with *Anthony Adverse*. Louis Rubin has found it unsurprising "that many of the Charleston poets turned increasingly to popular fiction in the later 1920's and afterward. They were from the start *popular* writers who directed their work at a wide audience."

In the long historical novel Allen had at last found his voice. While none of his later novels was as successful as his first, the genre proved the best vehicle for his broad themes, colorful settings, and heroic action. It must be noted, too, that the sharp eye for visual detail, the appreciation for the heroic dimension in human life, and the tremendous historical knowledge that Allen first displayed in his poetry accounted for a large part of the success of both his 1926 biography of Edgar Allan Poe, *Israfel*, and his fiction. Allen was working on the fourth book in a projected five-volume series of novels set in colonial America, when he died of a heart attack in 1949. He is buried in Arlington National Cemetery.

References:

William Rose Benét, Review of *Earth Moods and Other Poems*, *Outlook*, 140 (15 July 1925): 403;

Emily Clark, "Hervey Allen," *Saturday Review of Literature*, 10 (9 December 1933): 323;

S. Foster Damon, *Amy Lowell: A Chronicle* (Boston: Houghton Mifflin, 1935), p. 636;

Babette Deutsch, Review of *Earth Moods and Other Poems*, *New York Tribune*, 21 June 1925, p. 3;

Louis Rubin, Jr., *The Curious Death of the Novel: Essays in American Literature* (Baton Rouge: Louisiana State University Press, 1967), pp. 207-221;

Louis Untermeyer, Note on Allen, in his *Modern American Poetry: A Critical Anthology*, fourth edition, revised (New York: Harcourt, Brace, 1930), pp. 614-617.

Papers:

The Hillman Library at the University of Pittsburgh has a collection of Allen's papers.

Djuna Barnes

(12 June 1892-18 June 1982)

Richard S. Donnell
Miami University

See also the Barnes entries in *DLB 4, American Writers in Paris, 1920-1939,* and *DLB 9, American Novelists, 1910-1945.*

BOOKS: *The Book of Repulsive Women: 8 Rhythms and 5 Drawings* (New York: Bruno Chap Books, 1915);
A Book (New York: Boni & Liveright, 1923);
Ladies Almanack (Paris: Privately printed, 1928; New York: Harper & Row, 1972);
Ryder (New York: Liveright, 1928);
A Night Among the Horses (New York: Liveright, 1929);
Nightwood (London: Faber & Faber, 1936; New York: Harcourt, Brace, 1937);
The Antiphon (London: Faber & Faber, 1958; New York: Farrar, Straus & Cudahy, 1958);
Selected Works of Djuna Barnes: Spillway/The Antiphon/Nightwood (New York: Farrar, Straus & Cudahy, 1962);
Spillway (London: Faber & Faber, 1962; New York: Harper & Row, 1972);
Creatures in an Alphabet (New York: Dial Press, 1982);
Smoke and Other Early Stories, edited by Douglas Messerli (College Park, Md.: Sun & Moon Press, 1982);
Interviews, edited by Alyce Barry (College Park, Md.: Sun & Moon Press, 1985).

Djuna Barnes (photograph © Berenice Abbott)

In Paris in 1924 Ernest Hemingway noted: "Djuna Barnes who, according to her publishers is that legendary personality that has dominated the intellectual night-life of Europe for a century is in town. I have never met her, nor read her books, but she looks very nice." Written long before her best-known production—the novel *Nightwood* (1936), this comment, ambiguous in tone, still sums up Barnes's literary standing. She has often seemed more a slightly pretentious legend than an author read and respected for her genuine achievements—her sophisticated literary skill and her tragic vision.

Since Barnes's present reputation is for fiction, it may seem strange—despite Faulkner's references to her as "a fine one"—to approach her as poet. Yet her writing career began in 1911 with two poems in *Harper's Weekly;* her last sizable creation, *The Antiphon* (1958), is a verse play; and her later writing—largely unpublished—is poetry. In fact, except for *Nightwood,* all her books contain some poetry, and about *Nightwood,* T. S. Eliot insisted that "only sensibilities trained on poetry can wholly appreciate it."

Born near Cornwall-on-Hudson north of New York City, Barnes grew up there and on a Long Island farm. Her father, Wald Barnes, was a nonconformist and a failed artist who had married Elizabeth Chappell, an acquiescent and longsuffering English wife. Because he disliked his father and objected to being called Henry Budington after him, he renamed himself, taking his mother's maiden name as surname. Upon his family he imposed his views, his sexual and educational theories, and his mistresses. Especially by, it seems, supervising his only daughter's sexual initiation, he earned her lasting hatred. Educated at home in literature, painting, and music, Djuna Barnes apparently learned less from her father than from her grandmother, a feminist and writer of articles, poems, and stories. Barnes's muddled family life, her English ties, her molestation, and her hatred of her father shape *Ryder* (1928) and *The Antiphon*. In fact, Andrew Field asserts that her "family history . . . would supply the basis of her art."

Diversely talented, Barnes emerged in the 1910s as poet, journalist, artist, fiction writer, dramatist, and emancipated woman. Her only formal study went on at Pratt Institute in Brooklyn around 1911-1912 and at the Art Students League in Manhattan in 1915. Employed first in 1913 to write and draw for the *Brooklyn Daily Eagle*, she quickly moved on in 1914 to write for New York papers—the *Press,* the *World,* and the *Morning Telegraph,* a theater and racing sheet. For them she wrote about such topics as the playwright David Belasco, Coney Island, the boxer Jess Willard, her own force-feeding, the evangelist Billy Sunday, and her hug from a baby gorilla. Her first poems and stories appeared in these newspapers and in popular magazines, such as *All-Story Weekly*.

Settling in Greenwich Village in 1915, where she became a widely known and striking figure in her black cape, opened new possibilities. The somewhat disreputable Guido Bruno published her first book, a collection of poems and drawings, *The Book of Repulsive Women: 8 Rhythms and 5 Drawings* (1915). He became a model for Felix Volkbein and his son in *Nightwood*. Soon she made more prestigious connections—with the Stieglitz gallery, the *Others* group, the *Little Review,* and the Provincetown Players. There were numerous affairs with men, including Putzi Hanfstaengel, who became Hitler's jester, and a marriage from roughly 1917 to 1919 to Courtenay Lemon, an intellectual. Her friendships with women included a possibly lesbian attachment to Mary Pyne, a Greenwich Village poet and actress, who died of influenza in 1915 despite Barnes's nursing. She also befriended the counterfeit Baroness Elsa von Freytag-Loringhoven, noted for such exploits as shaving and shellacking her head, but still a poet and writer. The attachment to Pyne appears in one or more of the poems in *A Book* (1923), the first collection of Barnes's writing.

Djuna Barnes, self portrait, 1917 (courtesy of G. P. Putnam's Sons)

The Baroness contributed to the portrait of Robin Vote in *Nightwood*.

Barnes's connection with the Provincetown Players, who put on three of her short plays in their 1919-1920 season, clearly announced her dramatic aspirations. Already indicated by her dialogue sketches for newspapers, these one-act dramas point forward to *The Antiphon*. Through the players she came to know Edna St. Vincent Millay, who wrote verse dramas; more important, Barnes's writing was admired by Eugene O'Neill. The first presented of her plays, *Three from the Earth,* the only one of the three that she included in *A Book*, draws on her family situation: three rustic youths come to get back their dead father's letters from a mistress. The other two short pieces are lighter: *Kurzy of the Sea* deals with a fisherman and a mermaid who turns out to be a barmaid; in *An Irish Triangle,* related to Barnes's admiration for John Millington Synge, a poor wife learns refinement through her husband's affair with a lady. Barnes wrote other dramas in the 1920s: two other one-act plays are included in *A Book* and two longer plays exist in manuscript. None of this early dramatic writing, however, is in verse.

Despite her many activities, Barnes published from 1911 to 1923 more than fifty poems. Like her most recently published poetry, these are generally traditional in meter, rhyme, stanza, and topics (sadness, nature, love, death, and time). They occasionally suggest the influence of decadent and impressionist poetry, but except in the subject of *The Book of Repulsive Women* neither they nor her later poems show a marked response to modernist developments, such as imagism and free verse. The distinctive and modern qualities of her poetry as it develops are indirection, paradoxical expression, and difficult syntax and language.

Of the poems published by 1923, about one-third had appeared before *The Book of Repulsive Women* in 1915. Usually less expert than the poems of 1916-1923, this initial group introduces Barnes's characteristic themes and methods, but it is more varied in subject and tone than the poems written after 1915. Representative of her initial verse is her first published effort, "The Dreamer." It combines personal feeling, impressionist detail, and metrical competence: "And drips the rain with seeming sad, insistent beat,/Shivering across the pane, drooping tear-wise,/And softly patters by, like little fearing feet." The topics of this group of poems include war ("Just Lately Drummer Boy"), religion ("The Personal God"), and sordid reality (" 'Six Carried Her Away,' " a ballad apparently about a prostitute).

Connected to the more adventurous poems of this initial group is Barnes's major early attempt in verse—*The Book of Repulsive Women: 8 Rhythms and 5 Drawings*. Indicative of a concern with women's experience, including lesbianism, that runs through her work, the collection presents her view of the current state of women—chiefly through portraits of women damaged or destroyed by the modern world. Although the series conveys strong sympathy, the fragmentary but suggestive portraits display repulsive grotesques, and the tone of the usually iambic, six-line stanzas is harsh to control sentimentality. The five verse portraits offer a survey of city women: a much desired Fifth Avenue figure makes "Short sharp modern/Babylonic cries"; a shabby Third Avenue woman "grins . . . vacant into space."

The remaining short poems in the book generalize: women are driven to suicide because society values them for something other than their true selves. Although Barnes offers a pessimistic outlook by such words as "repulsive/As the truth" and "Time comes to kill," she recalls better possibilities—"youth," "fancy," "wise words," "good or bad," "conscience," "soul," "Christ"—the loss of which makes her women pitiful. Despite occasionally strained writing, *The Book of Repulsive Women* is a memorable criticism of contemporary life and Barnes's most ambitious verse interpretation of experience until *The Antiphon*.

Yet if the other early poems—those of 1916-1923—usually attempt less, they manage their subjects with increased craft and greater insight. Several eventually appeared in such literary magazines as the *Little Review* and the *Dial,* and Barnes later interspersed eleven in her collection *A Book.* Usually in iambic, four- or five-line stanzas, they are developed with more grace and more reliance on, skill with, and control of diction, imagery, tone, and persona than the verse of 1911-1915. Some of the best avoid all author comment: "Antique" offers only a cameo image of a lady and "To a Dead Favorite of Liu Ch'e" is an elegy spoken by a lover.

While the poems of 1916-1923 take up fewer topics, they develop them more perceptively and persuasively. They again deal with death, love (now with possible echoes of Millay), nature, and life in general, and though some contain a positive outlook, most continue to present a depressing world. "In Conclusion" ends with the encouragement that we who "were not above/Great human pity and inhuman love,/Will not be found ignoble when we fall." Despite this assurance, the poem ends with the word *fall* and deals primarily with loss and death. In the poems in *A Book,* the dominant effect is bleakness. In the first of these, "Pastoral," any beauty in nature is balanced by disproportion: "Each is before, and each behind its time." Such ambivalence marks the poems about love in the collection. These have been read as a series about Barnes's lesbian love for Mary Pyne, to whose memory she dedicated one of the poems, "Six Songs of Khaladine." Yet series or not, the love poems, though they touch on bliss, resurrection through nature, and love's persistence after death, deal largely with betrayal, unhappiness, and dying. Certainly "Six Songs" offers an unprepossessing definition of love: "It is not gentleness but mad despair/ That sets us kissing mouths."

Having established herself as a writer in the 1910s, Barnes spent most of the 1920s and 1930s in Paris and elsewhere abroad, living and writing among expatriate artists. Especially in the 1920s she supported herself by journalism, much anon-

Illustration by Barnes for her novel Ryder, *in which she portrayed her father as the profligate Wendell Ryder, depicted here with one of his many children*

ymous, and by contributions to such magazines as *Vanity Fair, Charm, McCall's,* and the *New Yorker.* During the 1920s, too, Liveright put out Barnes's first substantial volumes: *A Book,* a collection of stories, short plays, poems, and drawings; *Ryder,* a comic novel that gained some notoriety; and *A Night Among the Horses* (1929), a new edition of *A Book* which includes three added stories. The jeu d'esprit *Ladies Almanack* (1928) was published anonymously in Paris.

As in New York, her acquaintances and friends in Paris were numerous, and a few left a definite mark on her work. Some of these she met she had already known in Greenwich Village; others, such as Robert McAlmon and Natalie Barney, she met for the first time. Especially important, she came to know major figures: Ezra Pound, Gertrude Stein, and James Joyce, whose writing, including *Work in Progress,* influenced hers. In 1921 she encountered T. S. Eliot, who would edit both *Nightwood* and *The Antiphon.* The substance of her work, however, drew on personal friendships, especially that with Thelma Wood, a sculptor and silver-point

artist, whom she lived with for eight years. Of their relationship she said, "I'm not a lesbian. I just loved Thelma." Her experience with Wood provided her with the characters and relations of Nora Flood and Robin Vote in *Nightwood.* Her friend Dan Mahoney, an untrained, homosexual doctor, abortionist, and great talker, became Dr. Matthew O'Connor, one of the most memorable figures in *Ryder* and *Nightwood.*

Barnes's involvement with the salon and lesbian circle of Natalie Barney is reflected in *Ladies Almanack.* Barney, an Ohio heiress, ran the chief expatriate salon in Paris and received such writers as André Gide, Paul Valéry, and Colette. But she was equally known for her lesbian circle, which Barnes's small, illustrated book spoofs. In this light piece about friends and acquaintances, Natalie Barney is Evangeline Musset, feigned rescuer of young women. Her major love, Romaine Brooks, an English painter, appears in coachman's dress as Cynic Sal. Radclyffe Hall, the English author of the lesbian novel *The Well of Loneliness,* becomes Lady Tilly Tweed-in-the-Blood, who believes in female marriage. Other Americans in the book include her old friend Mina Loy as Patience Scalpel, a skeptical observer, and the *New Yorker's* Gênet (Janet Flanner) and her companion, Solita Solano, a poet and novelist, as the sprightly page-figures Nip and Tuck.

Though Paris was Barnes's base in the 1920s and 1930s, she did go elsewhere. In 1921 there was a trip to Vienna, Budapest, and Berlin, where she spent the end of the year with other expatriates. She also returned for several months to New York on publishing matters in the fall and winter of 1922-1923 and 1926-1927. To be with Thelma Wood, she lived in Greenwich Village from 1929-1931, serving as a columnist for *Theatre Guild Magazine.*

Although Barnes's volumes published in the 1920s indicate a turn toward fiction that lasted from 1923 until she began work on a verse drama in 1936, Barnes never deserted poetry; instead, her development as writer and poet took place within her fiction. Both *Ladies Almanack* and *Ryder* include verse in their loosely fictional structures. These poems show Barnes discovering forms, such as couplet narrative and blank verse, that are more open than stanzas. They also use traditional devices and language to establish a perspective, witty or satirical, on contemporary material. In *Ladies Almanack* Barnes exhibits Dame Musset and her lesbian circle and lightly satirizes examples of excess by means of eighteenth-century couplets. "Portents, Signs

courtesy of George Wickes

courtesy of Mrs. Herbert Bayer
and Mrs. Frederic Benedict

Nice circa 1928-1930. Djuna Barnes with two of the models for characters in Ladies Almanack: *Natalie Barney (Dame Evangeline Musset) and Mina Loy (Patience Scalpel). The photograph of Barnes and Loy was taken by Barney.*

and Omens" makes fun of lesbian prudery about men, while "Lists and Likelihoods" ironically glorifies possible conquests: "The Vixen in the Coat of red,/The Hussy with the Honey Head."

Ryder, often described as the celebration of a lusty natural man in the New York countryside, seems better defined as "a satire on masculinity" and "a tragedy of women," who suffer from Wendell Ryder's exploits. For Ryder is based on her father, and the events of the novel draw on the humiliations of her childhood, here overcome by treating them as comedy but still very bitterly remembered, as *The Antiphon* would show. Containing several types of verse, the novel includes two Chaucerian couplet poems, "The Occupations of Wendell" and "Yet for the Vindication of Wendell," that mock the title figure. "Midwives' Lament" is a blank verse elegy for a girl dying in childbirth, who "Pricked herself upon her son and passed/Like any Roman bleeding on the blade—." The blank verse

in *Ryder* looks forward to the use of this form as the vehicle for *The Antiphon*.

With several books behind her, Barnes after 1931 devoted herself almost exclusively to her own writing. After leaving Thelma Wood, she returned to Paris in the fall of 1931 and traveled to Vienna, Budapest, and Munich with Charles Henri Ford, a young writer twenty years her junior. Thereafter, she settled down to her task of the decade, the creation of her major work of fiction, *Nightwood*, which she initially entitled "Bow Down." Much of her writing on this novel was done among the artists and writers gathered on an English estate rented by the heiress Peggy Guggenheim, whom she had known since arriving in Paris and who asked her to her manor in Devon during the summers from 1932 to 1934. She did other work on the novel in Tangier in 1933 with Charles Henri Ford, who typed up what she wrote. After a futile trip to publishers in New York with her completed manuscript in the fall and winter of 1933-1934, her novelist friend Emily Coleman succeeded in placing the novel with T. S. Eliot at Faber and Faber in London. Barnes revised the book extensively before it was published in 1936, and Eliot wrote an introduction for the first American edition. Attracted now to England, Barnes lived most of 1937-1939 in London.

Nightwood, which established her reputation and remains its basis, is typically described as "a vision of life among sexual perverts in Paris, written in a highly poetic prose." Such a description leaves out much: some of the scenes occur in Vienna, Berlin, and upstate New York, and the action takes place in the 1920s and early 1930s. The central characters—the Jewish businessman Felix Volkbein, Nora Flood and Robin Vote whom she loves, Jenny Petherbridge who steals Robin, and Doctor Matthew O'Connor who comments on the events— cannot be summarized by the term "sexual perverts." And the novel's demimonde of expatriates, lesbians, and homosexuals, most of them American, represents less an expedition into an alien and abnormal world than a study of the misery of selfish love. Some of the complexity of Barnes's treatment of her material appears in her working title, the imperative "Bow Down." Andrew Field says the phrase means "man's descent back into the kingdom of the animal, which is something both preferable to his human captivity and yet obscene." It may also suggest a recognition and acceptance of the animal in man, these being part of a continuing piety toward life despite its apparent descents into animality.

Although *Nightwood* contains no excursions into verse, it has been consistently termed "poetic." Kimon Friar and John Malcolm Brinnin even included passages from it in their anthology *Modern Poetry: American and British* (1951). It is this poetic quality in the speeches, descriptions, and narrative that justifies touching on the novel in a discussion of Barnes as poet. The quality is an eloquence that depends on the writer's use of many techniques of modern poetry: heavily freighted language, heightened rhythms, abundant, repeated images and motifs, symbol and myth, and unexpected juxtapositions. The novel, more specifically, employs symbolic settings, the myth of the Wandering Jew, and recurrent references to night, animals, the heart, and bowing down. The texture of the prose can be suggested by some often-quoted lines defining the central figure, Robin: "as insupportable a joy as would be the vision of an eland coming down an aisle of trees, chapleted with orange blossoms

and bridal veil, a hoof raised in the economy of fear." But Friar and Brinnin prefer the monologues of another major character, Dr. Matthew O'Connor: "We are but skin about a wind, with muscles clenched against mortality. We sleep in a long reproachful dust against ourselves. We are full to the gorge with our names for misery."

The 1930s ended for Djuna Barnes with her permanent return to the United States. Before coming back she had gone to Paris in 1939 and may have been there when the German occupation began. Both the bombing of England and the fall of France appear in *The Antiphon.* After her return she had very little to live on and remained for the rest of her life in straitened circumstances, even after Peggy Guggenheim gave her an allowance. In the fall of 1940 she found an inexpensive apartment in Patchin Place in Greenwich Village and took up a reclusive life there, "entertaining poetry," she said, until her death in 1982. There, helped by correspondence with T. S. Eliot and Edwin Muir, she labored over *The Antiphon,* chiefly from 1947 to 1954. Translated into Swedish by Dag Hammarskjöld and Karl Gierow, the verse play was first produced in Stockholm in 1962. In her later years Barnes wrote much other poetry, but only a handful of poems and the tiny volume *Creatures in an Alphabet* (1982), finished before her death, have yet been published. Barnes described her last years as her "Trappist" period, but they were not unproductive.

The chief of these later works was *The Antiphon,* which despite its Swedish production seems nearer to a closet drama than a play, as she intended, for the stage. It is based on the same family material that Barnes gave comic treatment in *Ryder,* but here she fashions this material into a harsh satirical tragedy. Influenced by and possibly answering Eliot's *Family Reunion* (1939), it deals not with victimized men but with victimized women and ends not with hope of expiation but deaths without reconciliation. Although shaped in action and poetry by Elizabethan and Jacobean drama, it also employs symbolic, surreal, and absurdist effects. Yet despite such modern elements, Barnes's archaic diction, crabbed syntax, and clotted figures of speech often make the verse, and hence the play, difficult to follow.

Yet the events can be sorted out and interpreted. The drama presents a family and setting symbolic of man's discordant and destructive history. At the start of World War II, the Hobbses, a divided American family, come together in a bombdamaged ancestral mansion in England. The title

Djuna Barnes in her Patchin Place apartment, 1971 (photograph by Jack Manning, New York Times)

of the play, which refers to responsive singing, points to the possibility of reconciliation—a harmony between human beings and between them and their past. In a setting suggestive of civilization and its present ruin, the family faces its past—essentially the disordered world of Wald Barnes, here named Titus Hobbs, and of the molestation. But the family cannot rise above its hostilities. To be independent of the past and its ties, the two businessmen-brothers, Dudley and Elisha, are ready to kill their mother Augusta and their sister Miranda. An actress representative of art, awareness of tradition, and responsiveness, Miranda also fails to transcend the past. Despite or perhaps because of their close ties, she and Augusta cannot agree, and their physical conflict concludes the play with both dead upon the stage. Although values exist, the play appears to say, human beings are usually incapable of rising to them.

Despite its melodramatic qualities, the play is complex and rich in its development and writing. Many of its rewards, besides those from character,

setting, and content, are in the poetry. Intended to remind us of our ancestors' powers of expression, now lost, the controlled but varied blank verse allows speeches that range from the coarse talk of the vicious brothers to eloquent statement of the themes. Miranda's speech on forgotten harmonies illustrates Barnes's most successful moments: "Where the martyr'd wild fowl fly the portal/High in the honey of cathedral walls,/There is the purchase, governance and mercy./ . . ./As the high plucked banks/Of the viola rend out the unplucked strings below—/There is the antiphon."

With the exception of *Creatures in the Alphabet*, which appears simple, the other poems of Barnes published after *Nightwood* contain verse as dense as that of *The Antiphon*. Less traditional than the early poems, they are still for the most part iambic, rhymed, and stanzaic. Serious but not always solemn, they include both pessimism and self-assertion. "Transfiguration" (1938) and "Fall-out Over Heaven" (1958) depict apocalypses, while "Galerie Religieuse" (1962) describes Christ's love as "spent,/

Dwindling." Yet in "Quarry" (1969) and "Walking-Mort" (1971), the speaker recognizes the impotence of age but protests she will "stand" and slap her soul's "face/That it fetch breath."

Creatures in an Alphabet, the tiny collection of nursery rhymes for adults that Barnes readied for publication in her final months, combines similar elements. In twenty-five octosyllabic four-line stanzas written with coolness and wit, Barnes creates a "black alphabet" portraying or satirizing, with possibly one exception, an unattractive human menagerie engaged in pointless life. Of the search for meaning she writes, "It ends the same—/An old man's titter, a young man's game." Yet she treats the yak, her final animal, with respect: "With all his craggy services,/His lowly life Himalayan is."

The long poem or poems, contemplative or satirical, on which Barnes was working in her later years remain in manuscript. Without a collection of the poems she labored on so long, Barnes's place in literature will rest on *Nightwood* and perhaps also on her stories and *The Antiphon.* Yet whether or not her poetry is widely known, she began and continued a poet, and she was recognized as a poet by such writers as Faulkner, Eliot, and Dylan Thomas. Even if *Nightwood* alone keeps its reputation, her poetry will have helped her novel demonstrate what Friar and Brinnin call "the similarity between poetry and imaginative prose of the first order."

Bibliography:

Douglas Messerli, *Djuna Barnes: A Bibliography* (Rhinebeck, N.Y.: David Lewis, 1975).

Biography:

Andrew Field, *Djuna: The Life and Times of Djuna Barnes* (New York: Putnam's, 1983).

References:

Kenneth Burke, "Version, Con-, Per-, and In-(Thoughts on Djuna Barnes' Novel *Nightwood*)," in his *Language as Symbolic Action: Essays on Life, Literature, and Method* (Berkeley: University of California Press, 1968), pp. 240-253;

Lynda C. Curry, "The Second Metamorphosis: A Study of the Development of *The Antiphon* by Djuna Barnes," Ph.D. dissertation, Miami University, 1978;

Joseph Frank, "Spatial Form in Modern Literature," in his *The Widening Gyre: Crisis and Mastery in Modern Literature* (New Brunswick: Rutgers University Press, 1963), pp. 3-62;

Louis F. Kannenstine, *The Art of Djuna Barnes: Duality and Damnation* (New York: New York University Press, 1977);

Howard Nemerov, "A Response to The Antiphon," in his *Reflections on Poetry & Poetics* (New Brunswick: Rutgers University Press, 1972), pp. 66-70;

James B. Scott, *Djuna Barnes* (Boston: Twayne, 1976);

Sharon Spencer, *Space, Time and Structure in the Modern Novel* (New York: New York University Press, 1971), pp. 39-43.

Papers:

Djuna Barnes's papers are in the McKeldin Library, University of Maryland.

William Rose Benét

(2 February 1886-4 May 1950)

John Griffith
University of Washington

BOOKS: *Merchants from Cathay* (New York: Century, 1913; London: Oxford University Press, 1915);

The Falconer of God and Other Poems (New Haven: Yale University Press, 1914; London: Oxford University Press, 1914);

The Great White Wall: A Poem (New Haven: Yale University Press, 1916);

The Burglar of the Zodiac and Other Poems (New Haven: Yale University Press, 1918);

Perpetual Light (New Haven: Yale University Press, 1919);

Moons of Grandeur (New York: Doran, 1920);

Saturday Papers: Essays on Literature from the Literary Review, by Benét, Henry Seidel Canby, and Amy Loveman (New York: Macmillan, 1921);

The First Person Singular (New York: Doran, 1922);

The Flying King of Kurio: A Story for Children (New York: Doran, 1926);

Wild Goslings (New York: Doran, 1927);

Man Possessed: Being the Selected Poems of William Rose Benét (New York: Doran, 1927);

Rip Tide (New York: Duffield & Green, 1932);

Starry Harness (New York: Duffield & Green, 1933);

The Prose and Poetry of Elinor Wylie (Norton, Mass.: Wheaton College Press, 1934);

Golden Fleece: A Collection of Poems and Ballads Old and New (New York: Dodd, Mead, 1935);

Harlem and Other Poems (London: Methuen, 1935);

With Wings as Eagles: Poems and Ballads of the Air (New York: Dodd, Mead, 1940);

The Dust which is God (New York: Dodd, Mead, 1941);

Adolphus: Or, The Adopted Dolphin & The Pirate's Daughter, by Benét and Marjorie Flack (Boston: Houghton Mifflin, 1941);

Stephen Vincent Benét: My Brother Steve, by Benét, with *For the Record,* by John Farrar (New York: Saturday Review/Farrar & Rinehart, 1943);

Day of Deliverance: A Book of Poems in Wartime (New York: Knopf, 1944);

The Stairway of Surprise (New York: Knopf, 1947);

Timothy's Angels (New York: Crowell, 1947);

Poetry Package, by Benét and Christopher Morley

William Rose Benét, etching by Henry Hoyt (courtesy of the Clifton Waller Barrett Library, University of Virginia)

(New York: Greenfield, 1949);

The Spirit of the Scene (New York: Knopf, 1951).

OTHER: *Twentieth Century Poetry,* edited by Benét, John Drinkwater, and Henry Seidel Canby (Boston: Houghton Mifflin, 1929);

The Collected Poems of Elinor Wylie, edited by Benét (New York: Knopf, 1932);

Fifty Poets, an American Auto-anthology, edited by Benét (New York: Duffield & Green, 1933);

The Oxford Anthology of American Literature, edited by Benét and Norman Holmes Pearson (New York: Oxford University Press, 1938);

An Anthology of Famous English and American Poetry, edited, with introductions, by Benét and Conrad Aiken (New York: Modern Library, 1945);

The Reader's Encyclopedia, edited by Benét (New York: Crowell, 1948).

Even at the height of William Rose Benét's prominence as a man of letters in the 1930s and 1940s, no one claimed that he was a major poet or would ever be considered one. Praise for Benét tended to emphasize his goodness: the high-minded values of love, spirituality, and patriotism which he espoused in his writing; his generosity as an adviser and critic; his unfailing patience and thoughtfulness as a friend and family man. There was respect, but not great admiration, for his poetry and great fondness for Benét himself among his intimates, his many professional associates, and his extensive reading public.

Benét was born at Fort Hamilton, New York, the son of James Walker Benét, a career army officer whose specialty was ordnance and whose avocation was poetry. "He knew more about English poetry than most poets and all professors," said family friend and poet Leonard Bacon, "and had the Elizabethan poets by heart." All three children of Colonel Benét and his wife, Frances Neill Rose

Benét, were to become poets—William, his older sister, Laura, and his younger brother, Stephen Vincent.

Benét showed some inclination to follow his father's footsteps into the military. He attended Albany Academy, a military school, graduating in 1904, and was awaiting appointment to West Point when he finally decided to enroll in the Scheffield Scientific School at Yale. He graduated from Yale in 1907, having served as chairman of the *Yale Courant* and editor of the *Yale Record*. He made a number of literary friends at Yale, among them Henry Seidel Canby and Sinclair Lewis.

After graduation, Benét went to sea briefly as a ship's clerk; then he returned to live with his family in California. In 1911 he took a job with *Century Magazine*, beginning as an office boy and working his way up to assistant editor, a position he held from 1914 to 1918. During this period he published the first of his many volumes of poetry.

In 1918 Benét volunteered for service in World War I and was accepted in the aviation section of the U.S. Signal Corps despite his bad eyesight, received flight instruction, and was commissioned a second lieutenant, although ultimately he saw only ground service in Florida and Texas. After the war he occupied himself briefly with writing advertising copy in New York City and working for the *Nation's Business*, a chamber of commerce journal in Washington, D.C. In 1920 he set out, with three collaborators, Canby, Amy Loveman, and Christopher Morley, to found the *Literary Review*, a supplement to the *New York Evening Post*. Four years later the same group moved on to launch the *Saturday Review of Literature*, with which Benét remained connected as an editor until his death twenty-six years later.

Benét was married four times: on 3 September 1912 to Teresa Frances Thompson, by whom he had three children and who died in a flu epidemic in 1919; on 5 October 1923 to the poet Elinor Wylie, who died of a stroke in 1928; on 15 March 1932 to Lora Baxter, from whom he was divorced in 1937; and on 21 June 1941 to Marjorie Flack, author of children's books, who survived him as his widow.

His first book of poetry, *Merchants from Cathay* (1913), was favorably received. Joyce Kilmer, writing in the *New York Times* (30 November 1913), said, "For the whole book we may well be grateful; it is a book of real poetry, magical, imaginative, vigorous." The reviewer for the *North American Review* (December 1913) said Benét "shows a quaint originality and a definiteness of point of view that win

Laura, Stephen Vincent, and William Rose Benét, 1900

Stephen Vincent and William Rose Benét on the Yale campus,
autumn 1915

respect and give pleasure." The title poem has the particular mixture of exotic fantasy and bumptious word music that were permanent features of Benét's poetry. The poem is generally in the line of Samuel Taylor Coleridge's "Kubla Khan" and William Butler Yeats's "Byzantium" in its evocation of a visionary *otherwhere*, radically unlike the workaday world. Benét's prosody, though, has more in common with that of Rudyard Kipling or Vachel Lindsay (Lindsay, in fact, took "Merchants from Cathay" to his heart, for a time proclaiming it his favorite American ballad and reciting it with full histrionic treatment). The poem tells, through the eyes of a startled, awestruck Everyman, the story of two "mad, antic merchants" who bound uproariously into town with silks and spices and "weird fruits" to sell, and a song to sing—"a catch and a carol to the great grand Chan," the "King of all the Kings across the sea," to whose kingdom and back, they say they have fought their way. Just as their song ends, a fiery gulf opens in the ground beneath them and they are "plunged to Pits Abysmal with their wealth untold," ostensibly destroyed for trying to share the secrets of the Chan "with silly, common folk." The fable is loosely and expansively symbolic, suggesting thoughts about the conflict between mortals and immortals, the mundane and the celestial, the prosaic and the poetic. More important

to its success, though, are the sheer theatrical effects of rhythm, exotic imagery, and portentous event that Benét achieved.

His second collection, *The Falconer of God and Other Poems* (1914), tones down somewhat the exuberant, playful fantasy, but Benét's romantic love of broad, theatrical gestures and big ideas is still evident. The title poem is a controlled, evenhanded allegory expressing an old paradox of the romantic quest: that the soul's best times are those spent in the pursuit of noble purposes rather than in the achievement of them, for one destroys the precious quarry in seizing it. In the poem a youth's soul—represented by a hunting falcon—strikes and kills a "strange white heron" which stands for "The secret of the stars, of the world's heart-strings/ The answer to their woe." The poem's conclusion has a Longfellowish stoicism about it, proclaiming that, despite the discovery that the predatory soul ultimately destroys what it desires,

> Yet I fling my soul on high with new endeavor,
> And I ride the world below with a joyful mind.
> ....
> The pledge is still the same—for all disastrous
>   pledges,
>   All hopes resigned!
> My soul still flies above me for the quarry it shall find.

The quest is worthwhile, even if the end is destruction.

The collection is varied in its subjects, verse forms, and moods, but it clearly shows Benét's allegiance to romantic and Victorian poetic traditions. Benét writes sometimes in rustic dialects and sometimes in the stateliest of high poetic diction; he conjures up the streets of modern New York and visionary dreamlands where the poets of the ages sit in conclave; he meditates on fame, religion, the imagination, beauty; he professes his love for his brother Stephen. Through it all, however, Benét's devotion to nineteenth-century conventions of thought, language, and aesthetics is consistently expressed.

In Benét's next volume, *The Burglar of the Zodiac and Other Poems* (1918), some of the poems—such as "The Quick-Lunch Counter," "The Push-Cart," "Films," "The Suffrage Procession"—demonstrate an intention to make his poetry tougher and more modern. In a letter to his friend Louis Untermeyer, though, Benét admitted that these poems were still trying "to put the splendors of anciantry into the grim of modernity."

The best-known poem in this collection—and

probably the most widely reprinted of all Benét's poems—is "The Horse Thief," a hybrid of Greek mythology and wild West cowboy yarn. Its narrative line has a fugitive outlaw, on the run from a posse, roping and riding the winged horse Pegasus in a careering flight through poetical heavens—

> The musical box of the heavens all round us rolled to a tune
> That tinkled and chimed and trilled with silver sounds that struck you dumb,
> As if some archangel were grinding out the music of the moon.

The flight ends when "the Centaur of the Stars," Sagittarius, chases the flying horse thief, causing Pegasus to buck him off. He regains his senses as the posse takes him:

> So you know—and now you may string me up. Such was the way you caught me.
> Thank you for letting me tell it straight, though you never could greatly care.
> For I took a horse that wasn't mine! . . . But there's one the heavens brought me,
> And I'll hang right happy, because I know he is waiting for me up there.

William Rose Benét

For Benét the boundaries of a homely American folk type (a horse thief pursued by vigilantes) overlap the cosmic drama that made Greek myth.

"Jesse James," published in *Golden Fleece* (1935), is another of Benét's popular variations on this idea, a Lindsay-esque yarning ballad in which Benét celebrates the famous Missouri badman with a crescendo of increasingly mythic terms:

> Jesse James rode hell for leather;
> He was a hawse an' a man together;
> In a cave in a mountain high up in air
> He lived with a rattlesnake, a wolf, an' a bear.
> . . . .
> Jesse James was a Hercules
> When he went through the woods he tore up the trees.
> When he went on the plains he smoked the groun'
> An' the hull lan' shuddered for miles aroun'.
> . . . .
> An' when you see a sunset bust into flames
> (*Lightnin' like the Missouri!*)
> Or a thunderstorm blaze—that's Jesse James!
> (*Hear the Missouri roll!*)

In such poems as this, Benét attempted to create a sense of grandeur and magic through the use of homely American dialect and the simple stanzas of hymns and ballads. His efforts perhaps echo the earlier verse of James Whitcomb Riley and James Russell Lowell's *The Biglow Papers* (1848, second series 1862).

In 1919 he published *Perpetual Light*, a memorial to his first wife, consisting of several love poems he had written to her earlier. This volume was followed by *Moons of Grandeur* (1920), a collection primarily on historical subjects—"Gaspara Stampa," "Niccolo in Exile," "Michelangelo in the Fish-Market," "The Ballad of Taillefer." In 1927 he published *Wild Goslings*, a collection of fifty-odd short prose pieces written for magazines, and he selected what he considered the best of his poems and published them in *Man Possessed*.

A new departure for Benét was his verse novel *Rip Tide* (1932), a romantic tale about a young woman who falls in love with a handsome stranger she meets at a house party. The two become engaged to marry, but, after the girl's father returns home and learns of the engagement, he realizes that the young stranger is his own son, born of a brief liaison with a woman who had since died. The father confronts the son with the facts of his birth, in a scene which Harriet Monroe praised for its emotional power (*Saturday Review of Literature*, 29 October 1932). Soon after, the boy drowns in the ocean during a storm, after saving his sweetheart/ half sister from the same fate. Garetta Busey of the *New York Herald Tribune* found the depth of Greek tragedy in Benét's story. Yet, the melodramatic resolution of its plot, with its strikingly convenient hurricane and heroic self-sacrifice of the star-crossed hero, is a serious weakness.

With *Starry Harness* (1933), Benét returned to his old practice of collecting a large number of short lyric poems in a potpourri. Some of them are light verse and some love poems, but this volume shows a new emphasis on philosophical lyrics with an increasingly mystical air. Notably absent were any story poems of the sort that had won Benét some of his most admiring readers.

The book which must stand, ultimately, as Benét's magnum opus is in a different vein: his fictionalized autobiography in verse, *The Dust which is God* (1941), which won the Pulitzer Prize for poetry in 1942. The poem describes the life of Raymond Fernandez, a persona for Benét, moving from his childhood memories around 1900, through his schooldays, his time at Yale, his experiences in World War I, and his first three marriages. Around these personal recollections Benét develops wide-ranging meditations on social history, especially the emergence of fascism from European democracy, and its impact on the hero and his friends. John Gould Fletcher (*Poetry*, January 1942) recognized in the book a fundamental American patriotism, comparing it with Sandburg's *The People, Yes* (1936) and Stephen Vincent Benét's *John Brown's Body* (1928) as a large-scale, popular celebration of the American spirit.

Benét's patriotism and his moral outrage at Germany, Italy, and Japan are most overtly the subject of his next volume, *Day of Deliverance* (1944), fifty-five poems, most of them designed to rouse martial ardor in Benét's American and English readers and to denounce the horrors of World War II. There is little that is especially original in the rhetoric or the emotions of this volume, and Benét does not hold back from clichés: Nazis "tramping with booted heel," "destruction plummeting from the sky," "Freedom striding with the sword that she can swing." The moral vision is stark and simplistic:

good against evil. But few readers seemed to find this grounds to criticize the book in its own time. It reads, as Benét intended, like strong, committed oratory.

Benét published one more volume of poetry before his death, *The Stairway of Surprise* (1947), another medley of lyrics in several forms and on several subjects that interested him: love, the imagination, people he knew, historical episodes. The title is from Emerson's poem "Merlin"—"But mount to paradise/By the stairway of surprise"— and the collection has a kind of latter-day Emersonian optimism about it, as in these lines from "Birth Funeral":

> The end in the beginning!
> And I believe, my friend,
> That wisdom worth the winning,
> Thus won, outshines the end.

His final book, *The Spirit of the Scene* (1951), published soon after his death from a heart attack, continues the mood and spirit of the previous collection.

In addition to writing poetry, Benét was a prolific editor, critic, anthologist, translator, children's storyteller, and writer of textbooks. In all, he wrote, edited, or collaborated on some thirty-six books. He was secretary of the National Institute of Arts and Letters at the time of his death. To the general reading public, he was perhaps best known for his column "The Phoenix Nest" in the *Saturday Review of Literature* (1924-1950).

References:

Fred B. Millett, *Contemporary American Authors: A Critical Survey and 219 Bio-Bibliographies* (New York: Harcourt, Brace, 1944), pp. 249-250;

Stanley Olson, *Elinor Wylie: A Life Apart* (New York: Dial, 1979);

Louis Untermeyer, *From Another World* (New York: Harcourt, Brace, 1939), pp. 229-253.

Papers:

Benét's papers are in the Beinecke Library at Yale University.

John Peale Bishop
(21 May 1892-4 April 1944)

Thomas C. Tulloss
University of Maryland, European Division

and

George F. Hayhoe

See also the Bishop entries in *DLB 4, American Writers in Paris, 1920-1939*, and *DLB 9, American Novelists, 1910-1945*.

BOOKS: *Green Fruit* (Boston: Sherman, French, 1917);
The Undertaker's Garland, by Bishop and Edmund Wilson (New York: Knopf, 1922);
Many Thousands Gone (New York: Scribners, 1931);
Now With His Love (New York & London: Scribners, 1933);
Minute Particulars (New York: Alcestis Press, 1935);
Act of Darkness (New York: Scribners, 1935; London: Cape, 1935);
Selected Poems (New York: Scribners, 1941);
The Collected Poems of John Peale Bishop, edited by Allen Tate (New York & London: Scribners, 1948);
The Collected Essays of John Peale Bishop, edited by Edmund Wilson (New York & London: Scribners, 1948);
Selected Poems of John Peale Bishop, edited by Tate (London: Chatto & Windus, 1960).

PERIODICAL PUBLICATION: "Some Unpublished Poems of John Peale Bishop," edited, with an introduction, by Robert Lee White, *Sewanee Review,* 71 (Autumn 1963): 527-537.

John Peale Bishop, circa 1922

John Peale Bishop is usually remembered for his associations with the Princeton circle of F. Scott Fitzgerald and Edmund Wilson, the expatriate group in Paris that centered around Ezra Pound and Ernest Hemingway, and the Nashville Agrarians who produced the literary magazine the *Fugitive* (1922-1925) and *I'll Take My Stand* (1930). Best known during his lifetime for his poetry, Bishop has in recent years been the subject of scholarly and critical attention focused more on his prose—fiction, essays, and letters—than on his sparse but high quality verse.

John Peale Bishop was born on 21 May 1892 in Charles Town (now Charleston), West Virginia, a quiet county seat in the eastern panhandle of the state. Founded by, and named after, a brother of George Washington, it preserves to this day a good deal of its original architecture from the late-eigh-

continued his boyhood habit of declaiming his verses the morning after their creation, a custom which either amused or amazed whomever happened to be about when he was shaving. For a brief period, both Bishop and Wilson courted Edna St. Vincent Millay, neither with any reasonable hope of success. They also collaborated on a little volume called *The Undertaker's Garland* (1922), a book that celebrated death in sardonic prose and verse. It concludes with "Resurrection."

His first New York period came to an end when Bishop married Margaret Grosvenor Hutchins of Columbus, Ohio on 17 June 1922; they departed for a two-year honeymoon in Europe, spent mostly in Paris and Sorrento. On the Continent, he would again meet Fitzgerald, renew other old acquaintances, and begin his lifelong friendship with Archibald MacLeish.

The fierce competition of individual literary careers in the so-called lost generation caught him up, and in 1924 the Bishops returned to New York, where he went to work in the offices of Paramount Pictures and began a novel called "The Huntsmen Are Up in America," which he worked on throughout 1924 and 1925. At first, Fitzgerald praised it and passed it on to his editor at Scribners, who was also initially encouraging. Unfortunately, all three parties lost interest, with Bishop the last to realize this fact. He completed a final typescript version and kept it among his papers, but a period of coolness set in between Fitzgerald and himself. Bishop was an odd man out in the New York of the mid-1920s, for as Edmund Wilson said, he had little talent for advancing himself. Thus, it is not surprising that in 1926 the Bishops again pulled up stakes for France, where they purchased an old hunting lodge that had belonged to Henry of Navarre, the Chateau de Tressancourt in the village of Orgéval, northwest of Paris.

As usual, Bishop seems to have felt most at home among the shades of history in some rustic pile of architecture where he could live in splendid isolation. For the first few years at Orgéval, Bishop wrote little and published less. For a time, he apparently considered writing for the Broadway stage, the careers of his friends Fitzgerald and Hemingway having convinced him that it was necessary to have a popular success. With the onset of the Depression, however, he was suddenly visited with a burst of creative energy that allowed him to publish four books in as many years.

Although, as Fitzgerald pointed out, 1930 was the last "season" for American expatriates on the Continent, the Bishops stayed on well into 1933,

their isolation now virtually complete. Three sons were born during these years, so the mounting financial pressures may well have added to the urge to write and, more important, to publish. In 1931 Bishop brought out a book of interrelated stories—*Many Thousands Gone*—set in nineteenth-century Charles Town (called Mordington in the tales). The book's title piece won the prestigious and lucrative Scribner's Prize. Before finally leaving for the States in 1933, Bishop saw into print his second volume of poems, *Now With His Love*, many of which reveal his idyllic conception of his wife and are surprisingly erotic for their day.

Bishop returned to live for a time in his father's native state of Connecticut, and then spent a year in New Orleans before moving his family to Cape Cod at South Chatham. There his old Princeton friend architect William Bowman built a house for the Bishops called Sea Change, where they could live in the splendor of eighteenth-century symmetries and indulge, thanks to the surrounding salt marshes, the Southerner's overriding passion for bird-watching. Before moving in, Bishop published *Minute Particulars*, another volume of verse, and his semi-autobiographical novel *Act of Darkness*, both in 1935. Afterward, however, the life of high style in the secluded chateau seems once again to have set in, and Bishop produced nothing more except his *Selected Poems* (1941), that would be published in his lifetime.

He was the chief poetry reviewer for the *Nation* during 1940, a year during which he became increasingly alarmed at the potential consequences of France's fall to the Nazis. Archibald MacLeish, at the Library of Congress and the State Department, was twice able to offer Bishop posts during World War II, but his rapidly failing health forced him to return to Cape Cod each time. With Allen Tate, he coedited an anthology of American verse for Latin American readers and worked to set up a proposed *Pan-American Review*. All this work was his contribution to the war effort as Director of Publications of the Bureau of Cultural Relations of the Council of National Defense, a post he held for about a year in 1941 and 1942. The job as Resident Fellow in Comparative Literature at the Library of Congress in 1943 lasted only two weeks before a heart attack forced him to go home. Although his friends, especially Wilson, were shocked by the violence of his reaction to the fall of France, this fact, plus Fitzgerald's sudden death in Hollywood late in 1940, seems to have stirred Bishop's interest in writing, especially poetry, one last time. "The

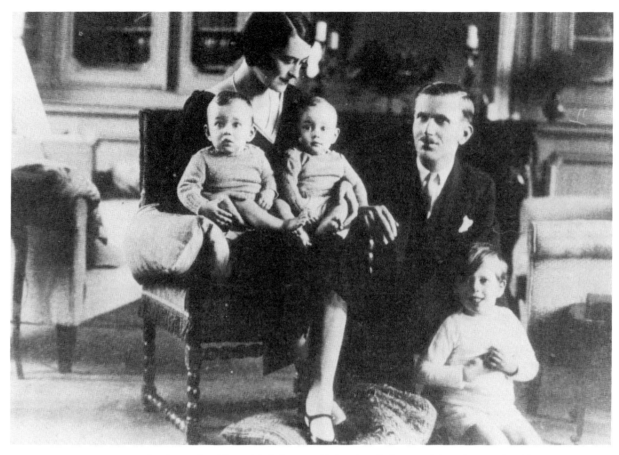

Margaret and John Peale Bishop with their sons, Christopher, Robert, and Jonathan, early 1930s
(courtesy of West Virginia University Press)

Hours," an elegy to his old friend, reflects Bishop's mournful frame of mind.

His last poems, collected by Tate after his death, were viewed by Wilson and his other old friends as despairing. They saw him as giving up on life, just as he foresaw the destruction of civilization when the Germans entered Paris. His health seems to have rallied briefly, and he wrote poems until two weeks before his death, when he could no longer recognize anyone. Bishop died in a coma at the Hyannis hospital on 4 April 1944 of coronary disease.

Bishop was given a fair-sized obituary in the *New York Times*, and in 1948 Scribners brought out his *Collected Poems* and *Collected Essays*, edited by Tate and Wilson, respectively.

Both during his lifetime and since his death, Bishop's reputation has always been that of a minor author, overshadowed by poets and fiction writers of the first rank—many of them his friends. The highly favorable opinion of Bishop held by acquaintances such as Allen Tate, Edmund Wilson,

and Archibald MacLeish has been noted by literary historians but largely ignored, despite their persistence. Indeed, Tate was so enthusiastic a champion that he sometimes recited his favorite selections from Bishop's poetry at the beginning of public readings of his own work. Nevertheless, especially during the first two decades after his death, most critics acknowledged Bishop's mastery of form but considered his work flawed, though not usually agreeing on what the flaws were.

Marxist-leaning critics such as Horace Gregory and Marya Zaturenska assailed Bishop for avoiding social issues during the Great Depression and attributed what reputation he did achieve to "fortunate" friendships. R. P. Blackmur, Howard Mumford Jones, and—to a lesser extent—Robert Penn Warren viewed Bishop as a "talented amateur" but not a major poet. R. W. Stallman praised Bishop's verse for fifteen years until he discovered a vulgar acrostic hidden in "A Recollection," in 1961. Shocked by what he considered obscenity, Stallman concluded that Bishop was mocking his own style and dismissed his work. Actually, the explanation for the coarse phrase lies in the poem's origin. Bishop salvaged this exquisite sonnet from his aborted first novel, "The Huntsmen Are Up In America," where the sheltered protagonist scrawls it on a fence after first seeing the nude portrait of a Venetian courtesan and simultaneously discovering sex.

During the last twenty-five years, Bishop's reputation has fared somewhat better, and critics such as Jesse Bier, Leslie Fiedler, Joseph Frank, Robert Lee White, and Simone Vauthier have praised his work. They acknowledge that his verse is imitative, but point to the excellence of the imitation and the wide range of styles he attempted, from Keats and Shelley to Swinburne, Yeats, Eliot, Pound, and Williams. They point to the profound moral sense which pervades his poetry and fiction and which is revealed in such ways as his drawing on archetypes, mythology, literary tradition, and psychology. They have explored his fascination with the techniques of various media seen in his reviews, essays, and poems such as "Perspectives Are Precipices" (which imitates surrealistic painting), "Ballet," "Speaking of Poetry," and "A Frieze." While still not making extravagant claims for his work, these scholars find Bishop a fruitful subject for study because he and his writings—verse, fiction, and criticism—are so typical of their time and place. His connection with the major literary figures of the period also continues to command notice.

Though only *Act of Darkness* is currently in print (a few poems also appear in anthologies), Bishop has received steadily increasing attention from critics in the past decade. Several articles have treated the whole range of his work, especially the heretofore neglected fiction; a biography has appeared; and his correspondence with Tate has been published. A full-scale edition of Bishop's letters is also in preparation. The critical pendulum may be moving to a more balanced perception of Bishop as a minor but decidedly interesting writer.

Letters:

The Republic of Letters in America: The Correspondence of John Peale Bishop and Allen Tate, edited by Thomas Daniel Young and John J. Hindle (Lexington: University Press of Kentucky, 1981).

Bibliography:

J. Max Patrick and Robert W. Stallman, "John Peale Bishop: A Checklist," *Princeton University Library Chronicle,* 7 (February 1946): 62-79.

Biographies:

Jesse Bier, "A Critical Biography of John Peale Bishop," Ph.D. dissertation, Princeton University, 1956;

Elizabeth Carroll Spindler, *John Peale Bishop: A Biography*(Morgantown: West Virginia University Library, 1980).

References:

B. Asterlund, "John Peale Bishop," *Wilson Library Bulletin,* 18 (1944): 424;

Joseph Frank, "The Achievement of John Peale Bishop," *Minnesota Review,* 2 (1962): 325-344;

Christian Gauss, "Edmund Wilson, The Campus, and The 'Lit,'" *Princeton University Library Chronicle,* 5 (1944): 41-50;

Horace Gregory and Marya Zaturenska, "The Lost Generation of John Peale Bishop," in their *A History of American Poetry 1900-1940* (New York: Harcourt, Brace, 1946): 458;

George F. Hayhoe, "John Peale Bishop's Theory of Poetry," *Markham Review,* 4 (February 1974): 34-38;

Stanley Edgar Hyman, "Notes on the Organic Unity of John Peale Bishop," *Accent,* 9 (1949): 102-113;

Stephen C. Moore, "Variations on a Theme: The Poetry and Criticism of John Peale Bishop," Ph.D. dissertation, University of Michigan, 1963;

R. W. Stallman, "The Poetry of John Peale Bishop," in *Southern Renascence,* edited by Louis D. Rubin and Robert D. Jacobs (Baltimore: Johns Hopkins University Press, 1953): 368-391;

Allen Tate, "John Peale Bishop," in his *Essays of Four Decades* (Chicago: Swallow Press, 1968): 348-357;

Robert Lee White, *John Peale Bishop* (New York: Twayne, 1966).

Papers:

Virtually all of Bishop's manuscripts are deposited at the Princeton University Library; for a brief description of this collection see Jesse Bier, "A Critical Biography of John Peale Bishop," p. 529.

Maxwell Bodenheim

(26 May 1892-7 February 1954)

Russell Murphy
University of Arkansas at Little Rock

BOOKS: *Minna and Myself* (New York: Pagan Publishing, 1918);
Advice (New York: Knopf, 1920);
Introducing Irony (New York: Boni & Liveright, 1922);
Blackguard (Chicago: Covici-McGee, 1923);
Against This Age (New York: Boni & Liveright, 1923);
The Sardonic Arm (Chicago: Covici-McGee, 1923);
Cutie, A Warm Mama, by Bodenheim and Ben Hecht (Chicago: Hechtshaw, 1924);
Crazy Man (New York: Harcourt, Brace, 1924);
Replenishing Jessica (New York: Boni & Liveright, 1925);
Ninth Avenue (New York: Boni & Liveright, 1926);
Returning to Emotion (New York: Boni & Liveright, 1927);
The King of Spain (New York: Boni & Liveright, 1928);
Georgie May (New York: Boni & Liveright, 1928);
Sixty Seconds (New York: Liveright, 1929);
Bringing Jazz! (New York: Liveright, 1930);
A Virtuous Girl (New York: Liveright, 1930);
Naked on Roller Skates (New York: Liveright, 1931);
Duke Herring (New York: Liveright, 1931);
6 A.M. (New York: Liveright, 1932);
Run, Sheep, Run (New York: Liveright, 1932);
New York Madness (New York: Macaulay, 1933);
Slow Vision (New York: Macaulay, 1933);
Lights in the Valley (New York: Harbinger, 1942);
Selected Poems, 1914-1944 (New York: Beechhurst Press/Bernard Ackerman, 1946);
My Life and Loves in Greenwich Village, attributed to Bodenheim (New York: Bridgehead Books, 1954).

OTHER: Thomas Yoseloff, ed., *Seven Poets in Search of an Answer,* symposium with Bodenheim and others (New York: Bernard Ackerman, 1944);
Hugh Ford, ed., *The Left Bank Revisited,* includes articles by Bodenheim (University Park: Pennsylvania State University Press, 1972).

Maxwell Bodenheim selling his poems in Washington Square, 1948 (Wide World Photo)

From his 1916 arrival in New York's Greenwich Village at the Bank Street apartment rented for him by Alfred Kreymborg, then editor of *Others,* to his tragic death in 1954 when he and his third wife, Ruth Fagan, were murdered in a slum rooming house near the Bowery by a former mental patient who was convinced that they were Communists, the poet and novelist Maxwell Bodenheim lived in the dissolute style of a bohemian literatus with such flair and self-destructive energy that his lifelong production of some ten volumes of poetry and fourteen novels from 1918 to 1946 must remain remarkable solely by virtue of the fact that he found the time to write them. Considered a misanthrope and freeloader by friends and enemies alike, this "queerest among the queer" and "yellow-haired child of melancholia," as Kreymborg later remembered him from their first meeting, became something of a bon vivant and redoubtable ladies' man during Greenwich Village's Jazz Age heyday in the 1920s, so much so that Kreymborg, writing toward the end of that same decade, could observe that the Bodenheim legend had grown "to such proportions that I have actually been asked whether such a person as Bodenheim exists."

The object of such queries was, surprisingly, born in Hermanville, Mississippi, a small town near Natchez, on 26 May 1892. The son of Solomon W. and Caroline Herman Bodenheimer, Bodenheim was born into a Jewish, middle-class, mercantile family. Although there is a sizeable Jewish population in Southern urban areas, Jews are decidedly a minority in the homogeneous and often fundamentalist Christian rural South. The Bodenheimers moved to Chicago when young Max was nine, but he would consider himself a Southerner for the rest of his life. In Chicago he received little formal schooling, but he did form a boyhood alliance with Ben Hecht, an individual who would become a literary collaborator, then a rival, and finally his eulogizer.

After dropping out of school, serving in the army, and traveling in the Southwest, Bodenheim returned in 1912 to Chicago (by about 1908 he had dropped the final two letters of his name); in Chicago his reputation as a sardonic wit and literary go-getter was quickly established in the circle at *Poetry* magazine, which included, along with its founder and editor Harriet Monroe, Carl Sandburg, Edgar Lee Masters, and Sherwood Anderson. Bodenheim remained there for four years with the older, more established *Poetry* crowd, having his poems published in both *Poetry* and the *Little Review*, before settling in Greenwich Village, for good, in 1916. He had traveled east after a correspondence with Kreymborg with whom he found "genuine elements of friendship." By then he had let it be known that he was at odds with the people at *Poetry*. Yet Kreymborg hailed him not as a renegade from the Chicago literary scene, where *Poetry* and the *Little Review* were stealing New York's thunder, but as the "Mississippi Hamlet"; and, as late as the time of his death in 1954, *Time* magazine would report that Bodenheim had "managed a certain courtly Southern dignity" right up to the end. the rural South, then, and not brawling Chicago had the most profound influence on Bodenheim's approach to the life of letters. He was essentially a

Mississippian, and New York remained for Bodenheim as exotic as Paris and New Orleans were to Faulkner, and Greenwich Village was his Hollywood.

By 1917 Hart Crane was writing from the Village to his mother that he had met Bodenheim, who "is at the top of American poetry today." It is true that Crane was only eighteen and impressionable. Nevertheless, although Bodenheim was himself not quite twenty-five and was still a year away from his first book-length publication, his poetry, according to Kreymborg, was "mature to the last degree" and "frankly admired" by the *Others* group, which included, in addition to Kreymborg, William Carlos Williams, Marianne Moore, and Alanson Hartpence. By 1918 Williams was writing in his prologue to *Kora in Hell* (1920) that nothing he could say "touching poetry would be complete without Maxwell Bodenheim in it."

It was as the aesthete, a turner of fine imagist verse, that Bodenheim arrived in New York all ready to let his light shine among those hard-boiled Easterners. What he found instead was a young poet from the Midwest like himself, Hart Crane, a chess genius, Alfred Kreymborg, and a pediatrician, William Carlos Williams. Easterners, he discovered, were neither urban wise guys nor effete snobs, and New York City was ripe for the picking by a street-wise Southern boy and born outsider like Bodenheim. He freely admitted to Crane at their 1917 meeting that he, Bodenheim, succeeded "in getting publication only through the adverse channels of flattery, friendships, and 'pull.'" Though he had been in the city only a year, Bodenheim already knew the editor at the *Seven Arts* well enough to offer to take several of Crane's pieces there, and he would be an editor for the next issue of the influential little magazine *Others*, its first after a considerable hiatus. By the time Guido Bruno's Pagan Publishing released Bodenheim's first volume, *Minna and Myself*, in 1918 when the poet was twenty-five, Bodenheim's poetry had been published in such excellent magazines of the period as the *Little Review*, *Poetry*, the *New Republic*, the *Seven Arts*, the *Pagan*, and the *Egoist*.

Minna and Myself, with its Parnassian posturings, imagist cryptograms, symbolist decorations, and Freudian dilemmas, is a masterful blending of what Kreymborg and others were calling the "new verse" with elements of American romanticism, especially echoes of Poe, another transplanted Southerner. The first twenty-seven poems are numbered and are written to the poet's first wife, Minna Schein (they were married in November 1918, and in 1920 their only son, Solbert, was born). In number eighteen, a dialogue between a maiden and youth, is this fine imagist emblem: "When your heart leaves mine it will be an old woman/With two of my shrunken flowers for her breasts." Number twenty-one contains another equally pointed image: "Your body is a closed fan." Yet number twenty-five includes lines that seem more like a dose of Keats via Poe:

> Upon an arched sarcophagus of pain
> Are figures painted in arrested embraces
> With outlines so light that we must bend close to see.

Meanwhile, a regionalism, "Pain is a country cousin of yours," begins number five, and an effete turn, "Your mind is a little, clandestine pastel," introduces number twenty-seven. Gradually it becomes apparent that the poet is trying out a variety of voices and styles, limiting himself to no one school.

It is in the poems of the subsequent section "Myself" that the singular, clearer voice—characterized by wit edged with a committed sorrow—of the more mature Bodenheim first begins to emerge. In "Poet to His Love" he compares his love to "an old silver church in a forest," while a "Hill-Side Tree" is "a drowsy, rain-browned saint" and in "Chorus Girl" her heart is "an old minstrel/Sleepily pawing at his little mandolin." There is still an element of posturing for the posture's sake, but the tougher voice that will triumph in later volumes is already prevailing; Bodenheim did not remain an aesthete manqué for long. Even at this point in his career, while his imagist's inclinations still occasionally obscure the poet's social sense, the book includes a poem on "Rear Porches of an Apartment Building" and another on a "Factory Girl." In "Soldiers" the faces of their dead "form a gravely mocking sentence" in "their sprawling crescent." Finally, there is a note of personal truthfulness that was perhaps too confessionally accurate for the impersonal, poem-over-poet aesthetic temperament of the times. In "To an Enemy," the poet admits that "I despise my friends more than you." Though few would later deny that Bodenheim was a good hater and very likely meant what he said, Kreymborg would come to think that poem's tone was too strident.

Bodenheim the bohemian begins to emerge with his next volume, *Advice*, published by Alfred A. Knopf in 1920. His vision has enlarged to encompass the complex vistas of experience in a city where one daily meets famous people whose "insolence drops to its knees/Before the half-won grandeur of past years" ("To a Friend"), but it is also a city where "an old Jew munches an apple/With conquering immersion" ("East-Side: New York"). In "Foundry-Workers" he captures the hellishness of the industrial behemoth spreading its way from Chicago to New York and points east, where the workers' "brown faces" are "twisted back/Into an ecstasy of tight resistance" while "eyes . . . are huge sweat-drops/Unheeded by the struggle underneath them." In a longer poem, "Steel Mills: South Chicago," the effects of that vast industrial machine on the human element once more attract the poet's attention. The steelworkers' faces "hold a swarthy stupor/Loosened by little fingers of morning light/Until it droops into reluctant life" while a young prostitute stands inside a doorway, "uttering muffled innuendos/To the drained men of her race." Bodenheim balances these bitter observations in the series of poems from which the volume takes its title, by offering lyrical advice to objects for the most part as removed from that industrial inferno and urban wasteland as a bluebird ("You alone can lose yourself/Within a sky and rob it of its blue"), a buttercup ("To the red ant eyeing you/You are giant stillness"), and even a forest ("The little men who bit into your hearts/Will stray off in a patter of rabbits' feet"). Although there is also a poem of advice to a street pavement—"Keep your passive indolence/At the dwarfs who scorn you with their feet"—by now the strategy is clear: To match waste there is wit, and to match man there is nature, impassively colorful.

The anger in Bodenheim's voice is evident, but it is as self-deprecating as it is staunch; and the logical turn for one as engagé as Bodenheim is a turn to irony. *Introducing Irony* (1922), his subsequent volume, announces the decision. The poems are ironic in the sense that life is ironic. From "Jack Rose," a poem about a heroin peddler who admires his trade's "blundering destructiveness, like a monk/Viewing a play that made him mildly drunk," to "Turmoil in a Morgue," in which a "Negro,/Chinaman,/White servant-girl,/Russian woman,/Are learning how to be dead," the poems present misery, suffering, and bitterness with sardonic wit. Death is a "grandiosely hackneyed subject" ("Meditations in a Cemetery"), while fame is "harlots' wine" ("Imaginary People"), and the poet predicts that he will die in 1962 "with a grin at the fact/That literature and art in America/Were still presenting a mildewed, decorous mien" ("Simple Account of a Poet's Life"). Fellow poets arouse much of Bodenheim's ire. "Impulsive Dialog" is between a poet and an undertaker; and in "Manners," "poets drink much wine/And tug a little at their garments/Weighing the advantages of disrobing":

(It is necessary to call them "poets"
Since, according to custom,
Titles are generously given to the attempt.)

Finally, however, man is the target of Bodenheim's choler, so much so that in "Seaweed from Mars" he introduces Torban, "a young man from Mars," as an alter ego:

We do not love and hate in Mars.
These earthly cries are flashing bars
Of sound from which our minds are free.

Torban reappears in a future volume, apparently having given Bodenheim a proper guise and perspective from which to launch his critiques of the human comedy with its bedrock of misery and pretensions.

By 1921 Hart Crane was calling Bodenheim's poetry "dull nonsense," and Ezra Pound was accusing him of an "anemia of education"; but by the end of the 1920s, he had produced eight volumes of well-received poetry and two best-selling novels. Bodenheim's development continued as his reputation increased. He was a regular contributor to the *Dial, Harper's Bazaar,* the *Nation, Broom,* and the *Bookman.*

As the titles of Bodenheim's two 1923 volumes, *Against This Age* and *The Sardonic Arm,* openly indicate, both books carry on the lyrical excoriations of modern society which had replaced the imagist delicacies of Bodenheim's writing in the 1910s. *Against This Age* includes poems such as "Nightmare and Something Delicate," in which he tells "anecdotes of microscopical towns," where the night is "Blake in combat/With an extraordinary wolf " and "transcending the rattle of this car/And every other gibberish/Uttered by civilization,/The poet plans his story." The poet's story includes a postman who carries forty years that "have massed/Exhausted lies within him" ("Regarding an American Village") and a policeman who is a "marionette-fanatic" ("Poem to a Policeman") in a world where money ("Rhymed Conversation with Money") and rats ("Highly Deliberate Poem") have all the power, and death stalks the child and the poet alike.

The Sardonic Arm, published in a limited edition of 525 copies, opens with a "Reluctant Foreword," in which Bodenheim castigates "the poetic

situation in America," where poetry has become a "verbose and blustering invitation to boredom and a slight, reviling headache" and "words conceal the essential helplessness" embodied in "the American spectacle." The poetry continues the assault. "Concerning America" portrays the nation as an "agitated child,/Listening to the words of clown,/Charlatan, blackguard, clergyman," and in "Dear Minna" the poet begs his wife to "read the newspapers/And gloat with me over death's industry." For the individual, "pain is but/A circus barker whose loud cries/Seek to reward a trivial show" ("Concerning Emotions") in cities where desperate "men with faces quicker/And more furtive than time/Stand motionless in doorways" ("North Clark Street, Chicago"). As in *Advice,* Bodenheim attempts to create a balance with occasional lyrical turns to nature in poems such as "Landscape" and "Country Girl"; but these poems are fewer in number and seem to be intended more as nostalgic excursions than effective antidotes.

Even as Bodenheim's poetry drifted further and further into well-wrought jeremiads relieved by occasional wit and lyricism, his finances improved and his alcoholic and sexual exploits began to give him that legendary aura Kreymborg spoke of. Contemptuous and arrogant for all his courtly polish, he took on the literary establishment in New York and elsewhere, and the results ranged from reluctant tolerance to outright ostracism by his fellow writers.

In the Village, there were wild parties where Bodenheim drank the Worcestershire sauce out of the bottle, finished off whole buffets by himself, and then would get drunk and make passes at the women. Never flush for very long, despite the success of his novels, he was known to depart with other guests' overcoats, which he would then pawn. An accomplished clog dancer, he was detained once by the police for dancing in the moonlight; but the women loved him. Two committed suicide over him; one made an attempt; a fourth was killed in a 1928 subway accident with an unpromising love note from Bodenheim in her pocket.

Amazingly, neither his novel writing—he had published all fourteen between 1923 and 1934— nor his poetry suffered as a result (though in 1929 Kreymborg belittled the novels as salacious acts of economic opportunism, and, indeed, *Replenishing Jessica,* 1925, about a nymphomaniacal young rich girl, would result in an obscenity hearing—and an acquittal).

By 1927, when *Returning to Emotion* was published, Bodenheim had, as his choice of title once more announced, taken another turn. At the height of his popularity among readers if not his fellow writers, he seemed a man willing to give a more exuberant vision a chance again. There are still poems such as "Through a Staten Island Ferry-Boat Window," in which "greenish black water, sinister pain . . . heaves against the sides"; or "Here Is Your Realism," which parodies the sordid love stories of pulp fiction—and Bodenheim's own novels as well. There is, nevertheless, a lightheartedness that belies the charged social criticism of the preceding volumes and that seems to be prompted by a new love, jazz. In "Jazz Music," he tries to approximate its syncopations orthographically— "Oh-h, you saxophone mo-o-oan. . . . Oh-h, you-u cra-zi-ly truthful flu-utes"—without noteworthy success; but he does capture the essence of jazz's chthonic powers:

> Oh, swing your legs and arms until they sing
> Religions into silence
> And improve the desecration
> Of all gods and chains—

verses which could be from Crane's "Voyages." There is as well a return to the less strident descriptiveness of the earlier imagist poetry: "Your fingers are flowers of motion" ("Poems to Minna"); "The moon has lost its necklace/And kneels in the grass blades, hunting for stray beads" ("Thoughts of a Precocious Child"). The social sense is not gone; "Lynched Negro" describes its subject's "downcast, harlequin, defenceless face" as "turned to ashen flakes," and "Cheap Dance Hall Girls" notes with "a sulky, dim, rebuked surmise/That nights, to them, are shoddy quips." In many ways, *Returning to Emotion* remains Bodenheim's most accomplished volume. As a foreword explains, "I have only written poems in which . . . emotion has been allowed to invade the colder processes of the mind."

That same foreword warns that " 'The Dial' will print a half sneering and half commending review"; and a poem in the volume is footnoted as having "had the honor of being rejected by 'The Dial.' " Those two literary swipes had unfortunate consequences; for, noting that reviewers had "objected to the 'irrelevant footnote' " in *Returning to Emotion*, Bodenheim announced that, in the spirit of "impish independence," his next volume, *The King of Spain* (1928), would not only continue but enlarge upon the practice. The poetry is as exacting in its devotion to craft and tone over theme and comment as that in *Returning to Emotion*. "Happi-

ness" compares the moon to "the ash-colored wraith of a candle-flame"; "Thoughts While Walking" compares the soul to "a large sapless park." "Suffering" describes how "the morning lowers its fire-veined back," and even "Street," with its social focus, renders an exquisite image of "Rows of exact, streaked faces,/Each afraid to be unlike the other." Had Bodenheim confined himself to poetry, *The King of Spain* might have been an admirable successor to the polished and assured touch achieved in *Returning to Emotion;* but throughout the newer volume are distracting, needling headnotes and footnotes. In them Bodenheim takes on *Poetry*, the *Nation*, the *Bookman*, Babette Deutsch, Burton Rascoe, and H. L. Mencken in particular and all poetry competitions in general.

In 1929, flush with his novel earnings, he spent a brief, unhappy sojourn on the Left Bank in Paris, where he had expected to be greeted as a visiting celebrity and was instead haughtily ignored, despite his flamboyant attire, which included a red beret.

Whether or not becoming the Peck's Bad Boy of American letters enhanced the already considerable Bodenheim legend, it did signal the beginning of his poetic decline. Perhaps the years of literary sniping and warfare had taken Bodenheim's heart out of the game. There would still be another half decade of moderate successes with his fiction, but *Bringing Jazz!*, Bodenheim's next volume, published in 1930, would be his last book of poetry until 1942. Artistically the poet had already entered his derelict phase. For *Bringing Jazz!* is a disappointment, and Bodenheim himself achieves a better rendering of the Jazz Age and Harlem speakeasies in his *Naked on Roller Skates*, which was published in 1931 and became popular for its daring sexuality. In *Bringing Jazz!* Bodenheim's concept of jazz is realized in singsong rhythms and verses with all the flair of strungout limericks. There are even directions on pacing for reading the poems aloud. Some of them, such as "Underworld Jazz I" and "Underworld Jazz II," do capture the sleazy flavor of the period; others, such as "Jazz Kaleidoscope," successfully imitate the lingo of black Harlem:

> Listen, you palm-scratchers,
> Lippy baby-snatchers—
> Stay 'way from mah Harlem chippy,
>   'less ah get mad!

Otherwise, the effort to be hip results in a second-rate poetry that, like the popular songs of the era, gives the surface textures but little else of a cultural phenomenon of the first order.

Perhaps Kreymborg had been correct, then, when he had written in 1929 that Bodenheim had sacrificed artistic integrity for the fast buck of popular fiction. In any case, even that bubble had burst by 1935. With the nation in the Depression, Bodenheim was back to sleeping regularly in doorways (a practice that led to his being called the "doorway poet") and cadging drinks and occasional meals from friends, acquaintances, and total strangers. He tried to have New York City provide for its poets with the municipal relief funds and took part in a march on City Hall. He did obtain relief through the Federal Writers' Project, but in 1940 hints of an earlier association with the Communist party took him off the public welfare dole for good. The summer trips to Cape Cod and wild Village parties stopped. While he continued to publish his poetry in *Esquire*, the *American Mercury*, and *New Masses* and in 1939 won *Poetry*'s Oscar Blumenthal Award, by 1942 he had written only enough poetry for one last, slim volume, *Lights in the Valley*.

The idyllic title is belied by much of the poetry. The first poem, "One Generation," begins "O volatile, distrustful, angry beast/Confronted now by vultures long unseen." The poet seems to have reverted to the Southern Gothicism of the Poe-like persona of his youth. He confesses in "Renunciation" that "I was a mystic once" and now claims to know "that this huge wistfulness dies slow." Other poems, such as "Home-Relief Bureau" and "Southern Labor Organizer," deal with the recent economic distresses and social turmoil, and there continue to be poems directed toward the literary life: "Sonnet to John Gould Fletcher," "Different Ivory-Tower," "To Maxwell Anderson," even one to "Dear Noel Coward" who knows "the men, deliberately gay." In the lengthy final poem, "Advice to a Man," with its title reminiscent of Bodenheim's youthful volume of 1920, the poet admits that this volume is very likely a final bow: "The formalized, secretly unmoving critics . . . will call you a failure, a talent dispersed in the lowlands," but

> The more slowly attained
> Friendship, understanding of scattered strugglers,
> Is a secretly tarrying tribute sometimes detected,
> Renewed in the rummage of posterity.

Bodenheim had been divorced by Minna in 1938, and he married Grace Finan in 1939; she would remain his wife until her death in 1950. Though he received occasional fees and royalty checks, Bodenheim suffered financially far more in the 1940s than he had in the 1930s. When word went out that he was dying of tuberculosis, fifty Village friends tried to start a relief fund; it raised twelve dollars. Diagnosed an alcoholic, he was in and out of Bellevue. In 1952 he was picked up for vagrancy in Brooklyn; a trip to Chicago later that same year with his third wife, Ruth Fagan (he claimed to have married her in 1952), for a reunion of the old Chicago crowd became a series of personal disasters and disgraces.

Selected Poems, 1914-1944 includes much of his previous work and a handful of poems published in periodicals subsequent to *Lights in the Valley*. The dust jacket described Bodenheim as "a stormy petrel in American literature, alternately praised and denounced by the critics" and called the book's publication "a literary event of importance." That it was; for with the exception of the posthumous *My Life and Loves in Greenwich Village* (1954), a series of loosely organized prose pieces which Jack B. Moore contends was penned more by its editors than by the ailing Bodenheim, *Selected Poems* was his last book-length publication. "The Village used to have a spirit of Bohemia, gaiety, sadness, beauty, poetry," he told *Time* in 1952. "Now it's just a geographical location." When Maxwell Bodenheim was brutally murdered there with Ruth in February 1954 by a psychopathic killer, its streets, doorways, run-down apartments, bars, and coffeehouses had been his only home for nearly forty years.

Scandal, literary enmities, and the specter of failure shadowed him all his life, yet it is clear that Maxwell Bodenheim remains a unique and ironically heroic figure in American letters because of his total devotion to the roles of iconoclast and drunken poet, roles he had created out of his first devotion, which was to literature. In the Village up to the time of his death, Bodenheim was still the bohemians' bohemian, buying drinks for himself and Ruth at the San Remo Bar and Grill on Bleecker Street by dashing off lyrics to sell to willing tourists; and Ben Hecht, the friend of his Chicago youth, would say of him that "he was the only poet I ever knew who lived only in the land of poetry and recognized words as the only riches there were." Bodenheim was a literary character, wholly in the American grain, taking a modernist's free-style approach to everything—and wholly out of it, an old-style Southern Gentlemen, and lover of periodic sentences.

As a character alone, Bodenheim should not be forgotten. As an impishly charming and elusive figure in American literary history, and as a writer whose poetry reveals sharp social insights, he cannot be forgotten. Yet only a handful of his books are currently in print. He was a species of literary genius who chose the path of eccentricity in his life rather than in his art, but the charade outstripped his career, which began to come to a faltering halt by the mid-1930s. Bodenheim was forced to live out the charade. Pictures of him in his final years show a gaunt, desiccated man, his face a hollow and shrunken death mask, his clothes the tattered remnants of a well-tailored respectability. He became the very image of an immense talent wasted by alcohol, bold irreverence, and insouciant lack of self-discipline. His life may yet prove to be his finest work of art. He died with an open copy of Rachel Carson's *The Sea Around Us* neatly placed over the .22 caliber bullet hole in his chest.

References:

Hugh Ford, *Published in Paris* (New York: Macmillan, 1975);

Stanley Kimmel, "R.I.P. Sadakichi," *Lost Generation Journal,* 6 (Winter 1980): 2-5;

Alfred Kreymborg, *Our Singing Strength: An Outline of American Poetry* (New York: Coward-McCann, 1929), pp. 494-500;

Kreymborg, *Troubadour: An Autobiography* (New York: Boni and Liveright, 1925);

Jack B. Moore, *Maxwell Bodenheim* (New York: Twayne, 1970);

D. D. Paige, ed., *Selected Letters of Ezra Pound, 1907-1941* (New York: New Directions, 1971);

Brom Weber, ed., *The Letters of Hart Crane, 1916-1932* (New York: Hermitage House, 1952);

William Carlos Williams, "Prologue to Kora in Hell," in his *Selected Essays* (New York: Random House, 1954), pp. 3-26.

Louise Bogan

(11 August 1897-4 February 1970)

Carol Shloss
Drexel University

BOOKS: *Body of This Death* (New York: McBride, 1923);

Dark Summer (New York: Scribners, 1929);

The Sleeping Fury (New York: Scribners, 1937);

Poems and New Poems (New York: Scribners, 1941);

Achievement in American Poetry, 1900-1950 (Chicago: Regnery, 1951);

Collected Poems, 1923-1953 (New York: Noonday Press, 1954);

Selected Criticism: Prose, Poetry (New York: Noonday Press, 1955);

The Blue Estuaries: Poems 1923-1968 (New York: Farrar, Straus & Giroux, 1968);

A Poet's Alphabet: Reflections on the Literary Art and Vocation, edited by Robert Phelps and Ruth Limmer (New York: McGraw-Hill, 1970);

Journey Around My Room: The Autobiography of Louise Bogan, A Mosaic, edited by Ruth Limmer (New York: Viking, 1980).

OTHER: Ernst Juenger, *The Glass Bees,* translated by Bogan and Elizabeth Mayer (New York: Noonday Press, 1961);

Johann Wolfgang von Goethe, *Elective Affinities,* translated by Bogan and Mayer (Chicago: Regnery, 1963);

The Journal of Jules Renard, translated by Bogan and Elizabeth Roget (New York: Braziller, 1964);

Johann Wolfgang von Goethe, *The Sorrows of Young Werther* and *Novella,* translated by Bogan and Mayer (New York: Random House, 1971).

In 1970, at a memorial service for Louise Bogan, W. H. Auden identified what he thought to be the most enduring qualities of her lyric poetry: "aside from their technical excellence, [what] is most impressive about her poems is the unflinching courage with which she faced her problems, and her determination never to surrender to self-pity, but to wrest beauty and joy out of dark places." Auden had first met Bogan in 1941 when she was well established as a critic of poetry at the *New Yorker* and had already written four of the six books

Louise Bogan

of verse on which her reputation as one of America's finest lyric poets was to rest. For almost thirty years, he had watched the unfolding of a talent. His appreciation of her gifts as poet, essayist, fiction writer, and autobiographer was shared by many of Bogan's friends, who also saw the violence of feeling which her work expressed and subdued through the regularities of form. Classical in their adherence to the laws of traditional poetic structure, romantic in their tendency to embrace the extremes of passionate experience, her best lyrics can stand with the work of the poets she most admired: Yeats, Rilke, and Auden. As Theodore Roethke had earlier written in honor of his friend, teacher, and mentor, "The best work will stay in the language as long as the language survives."

Bogan's journey to a place of prominence in American letters had been wrested from unpromising beginnings. Born on 11 August 1897, the daughter of Daniel Bogan, a clerk in a paper mill in Livermore Falls, Maine, and Mary Helen Murphy Shields Bogan, she was more properly destined

for married life in the mill towns of New England. Her mother was a reckless, violent, and undependable woman who handled the disappointments of her marriage through numerous love affairs. The Bogan children, Louise and her brother, Charles, were raised in a succession of rooming houses and exposed to an equally consistent succession of their mother's lovers. These childhood circumstances would never leave Bogan's memory, and they account for one of the predominant emotional constellations in both her life and art: the belief that love was inextricably bound with rage, guilt, and betrayal. By the age of six or eight she had become "what I was for half my life: the semblance of a girl, in which some desires and illusions had been early assassinated: shot dead."

If her parents served as the source of Bogan's early grief, they also provided her, indirectly, with the resources for coping with that sorrow. Eventually Daniel Bogan moved his family to Boston, where Louise was given piano lessons and then sent to Girls' Latin School. She was trained in Greek and Latin, and in the classical structures of versification. These few years were almost the whole of her formal education. Although she wrote constantly (by the age of eighteen, she "had a thick pile of manuscripts in a drawer in the dining room"), she chose not to pursue a full college career. After one year at Boston University (1915-1916), she abandoned plans to go on to Radcliffe in favor of marriage, on 4 September 1916, to a young soldier of German origin, Curt Alexander. In part she married as an escape from the domestic traumas of her parents' household, but she proved to be more of her mother's child than she could comfortably admit; for in later years, she reenacted the cycle of lust and betrayal that she so regretted in her parent. It was as if she were drawn to recapitulate her position as a helpless, violated child until, with the help of psychoanalysis, she broke through the cycle of damage to a superior awareness.

Nowhere does her poetry discuss these painful experiences; nonetheless they underlie and explain the dynamics of many of her early lyrics. Later in life, she was able to formulate a theory about the relationship between poetry and the experiences in life which empower it: in *Journey Around My Room* (1980) she said, "The poet represses the outright narrative of his life. He absorbs it, along with life itself. The repressed becomes the poem. Actually, I have written down my experience in the closest detail. But the rough and vulgar facts

Corporal Curt Alexander at about the time of his marriage to Louise Bogan (courtesy of Maidie Alexander Scannell)

are not there." Yet initially, in her poetry and in her life, she sought passion for its own sake and was dismayed when it offered her so little that she wanted.

On 19 October 1917 Mathilde (Maidie), her only child, was born; several months later, two of her first poems were published in *Others*, a little magazine edited by Alfred Kreymborg in New York City. By May 1918 she had left Alexander at his station in Panama and returned to the home of her parents. This, too, was a temporary move, a prelude to a life of uncommon transience in which moving represented or expressed an underlying restlessness of spirit. Years later, her emotions governed by a hard-won and mature perspective, she

wondered if she had eradicated the deepest sources of her own creativity in the course of mastering her otherwise self-destructive conflicts. To Morton Zabel she wrote in December 1935, "I don't recommend to you, this calm I have reached. It may be spiritual death or spiritual narcosis." But in the midst of young adulthood, she did not pause to analyze. She was pulled toward New York City, where she hoped to find a context for herself among the bohemians of Greenwich Village.

New York in 1919 did, in fact, nurture her talent and provide her with the friends who remained closest to her in later life: William Carlos Williams, Malcolm Cowley, Maxwell Bodenheim, Edmund Wilson, Léonie Adams, Margaret Mead, Ruth Benedict, and Rolf Humphries were among her earliest acquaintances. Leaving Maidie with her parents, she found a lover; she worked and wrote. In 1920 she learned of Curt Alexander's death. Whatever remorse she may have felt about their broken relationship and the temporary abandonment of their child was seasoned with the rewards of poetic achievement. By 1921 Harriet Weaver had published five of her poems in *Poetry;* by 1923 Bogan had found a publisher for her first book of verse. Robert M. McBride and Company brought out *Body of This Death.*

The title of the book is taken from Rom. 7:24: "O wretched man that I am! who shall deliver me from the body of this death?" Its themes are those that would absorb her for her entire career: the betrayal of beauty by the flesh, the antipathy between passion and wisdom, the tension between time and the "crystal clasp" of art. Strongly influenced by Yeats, Bogan found highly personal and deeply feminine ways to express the yearning for transcendence which must succumb to the limitations of time and human error. "Knowledge" can stand as an example of themes whose variations are worked out by "A Tale," "Medusa," "A Letter," "Sonnet," and the other poems of this collection: "Now that I know/Now passion warms little/Of flesh in the mould,/And treasure is brittle,—I'll lie here and learn/How, over their ground,/Trees make a long shadow/And a light sound."

When Robert Frost read "A Tale," the opening poem of *Body of This Death,* he remarked, "That woman will be able to do anything." Other critics shared his appreciation of Bogan's technical mastery and commented on the intensity, fierceness, and pride which seemed to motivate the writing. But not everyone was as discerning or generous. Often reviewers were puzzled, finding the language "only obscurely significant" (*Dial*). The worst review came from John Gould Fletcher, who considered the book to have "an emptiness of thought that is positively painful" (*Freeman*).

Bogan took what she could from both praise and blame. Her allegiance to the life of letters was too deeply ingrained to let adverse reactions discourage her. Among those whose opinions she valued, the book's publication established her as a serious new talent. She would continue to write and to grow closer to Wilson and Humphries and the small group of writers who published in the *Measure*, the *New Republic*, and the *Nation*.

In 1924 she met Raymond Peckham Holden, the son of a wealthy New York family, a man who aspired to the life of poet and novelist, and who

later became the managing editor of the *New Yorker*. On 10 July 1925 they were married; and after living briefly in Boston, New York, and Santa Fe, they bought a farmhouse in Hillsdale, New York. This house became for Bogan the place of harmony and abundance which her own childhood had denied her. Here she cooked, gardened, raised her child, and learned to see the patterns of nature which life in the city had rendered obscure. Here, too, she wrote most of the lyrics for *Dark Summer* (1929), sending them, finally, to Edmund Wilson for criticism and advice about publication.

By recommending that she forward a copy of *Body of This Death* to Charles Scribner's Sons, Wilson initiated the strongest and most enduring publish-

Raymond Holden and Maidie Alexander (left) and Louise Bogan (right) at their house in Hillsdale, New York, August 1928 (courtesy of Maidie Alexander Scannell)

ing relationship of Bogan's career. Maxwell Perkins was favorably impressed with her work and John Hall Wheelock even more so. He offered Bogan a contract, asked for more work, and eventually published her next three volumes of poetry.

With these prospects before her, Bogan settled into one of the still, certain interludes of her life. Domestic order mirrored a psychic order that was all too rare in her experience of intimate relationships. It was precisely the fragility of this balanced, pastoral life that made its subsequent destruction so grim. After Christmas 1929, the Holdens returned to Hillsdale only to see their house on fire, manuscripts and notebooks—indeed all their possessions—destroyed in the blaze. Posed as she was between desire and rage, Bogan could not help but read the fire emblematically; and in fact, the equanimity of her marriage seems to have dissipated along with her more tangible belongings. Although *Dark Summer* had come out the previous September, the pleasure of its publication could not offset another kind of interior disintegration.

The middle period of Bogan's creative life is marked by a dichotomy between the increasing solidity of her reputation as a poet and the seeming vulnerability of her emotions. Even as she received the accolades of critics, she lapsed into a deepening depression. In public life, Yvor Winters reviewed *Dark Summer*, singling out "Come, Break with Time" and "Simple Autumnal" for special praise. They could, he said, stand "with the best songs of the sixteenth and seventeenth centuries, whether one selects examples from Campion, Jonson, or Dryden." From a much later vantage point, Elizabeth Frank named "Simple Autumnal" "one of the great lyrics in American poetry." She saw it as the effort of a writer to ally herself with the seasonal cycles of ripening and decay that Bogan's earlier poetry had tried to escape. Like Hart Crane's "Voyages," it is a song of reconciliation and acceptance, which moves toward integration of the personal and natural worlds. "Summer Wish" is even more accomplished and brings Bogan's work into the company of Yeats's "The Tower" and Wallace Stevens's "Sunday Morning." It is a meditative eclogue, a dialogue in which two voices confront the problem of despair. Although the second voice overwhelms the first, offering it a vision of stasis ("See now/Open above the field, stilled in wing-stiffened flight,/The stretched hawk fly"), Bogan, in private life, was less and less able to find those quiet moments.

In April 1931 she submitted herself for a rest cure at the Neurological Institute in Manhattan.

Once again, her private struggle was carried on amid an otherwise flourishing career. In 1933 when she was awarded a Guggenheim Foundation grant for travel in Europe, Bogan seized the opportunity, for she sensed that distance and change would grant her a perspective valuable both to her craft and to her domestic situation. In the first goal, she succeeded, but her marital problems were not so easily resolved. Very shortly after she returned from Europe, she once again admitted herself to a hospital for rest and personal reflection. By 1935, when she divorced Raymond Holden, the period of greatest turbulence in Bogan's life was over.

It is probably not fortuitous that the 1930s were also the time of Bogan's greatest achievements in prose writing. The self-reflection required by psychoanalysis may have spurred her autobiographical trilogy: "Journey Around My Room" (*New Yorker*, 1932), "Dove and Serpent" (*New Yorker*, 1933), and "Letdown" (*New Yorker*, 1934). All of these pieces constitute Bogan's inquiry into those steps that "started me toward this point, as opposed to all other points on the habitable globe." Her *New Yorker* stories, influenced by Viola Meynell, Ivan Turgenev, and Anton Chekhov, often seemed to work through the issues that were most pressing in her actual experience—the destructiveness of romantic attachment, the need for private sources of strength and grace.

This belief in the value of turning inward can also explain Bogan's resistance to the social movements of the 1930s. She placed her faith in the lessons of psychoanalysis and in individual responses to fate; she gave no credence to solutions posed in terms of collective destiny. If one were "to lift the material world to the ideal," she said (*New Republic*, 1936), "it would be just as well to clear up the ideal, to know the human springs that feed it." Freud, with his discovery of the unconscious, was more important to her than Marx, with his belief in economic determinism; and as the 1930s passed, and as more and more of her intimate friends—Rolf Humphries, Léonie Adams, Edna St. Vincent Millay, and Edmund Wilson—came to sympathize with the Communist cause, Bogan found herself increasingly isolated.

To Rolf Humphries and Edmund Wilson she proposed a political truce, since she needed their help in preparing her next book of poems. *The Sleeping Fury*, once again published by Scribners, appeared in 1937. The title of the book is also the name of a relief sculpture Bogan had seen in Rome at the Museo Nazionale delle Terme, "L'Erinni Addormentata"; and to some extent, this im-

Louise Bogan, 1937 (courtesy of Maidie Alexander Scannell)

age of rage and grief, exhausted and given over to sleep, informs the entire collection of poems. Where Bogan's first two books had shown the influence of Yeats, *The Sleeping Fury* showed most clearly the influence of Rilke, whom she had been reading avidly for several years. When she had needed a language for anger, indignation, and bitter disappointment, Yeats's high blown rhetoric had been an adequate guide; now that she sought to transcend suffering and to express emotional equanimity, the German poet served her better. The most beautiful lyrics in this collection, "Henceforth from the Mind," "The Sleeping Fury," and "Song for a Lyre," have the quiet authority of a poet in full command of her art.

The Sleeping Fury was essentially Bogan's last full book of original verse; the books that followed it were collections of previously published works with new poems added to them. *Poems and New Poems,* which came out in 1941, was the last book Bogan published with Scribners before her break

with John Hall Wheelock. *Collected Poems, 1923-1953* was brought out by Cecil Hemley of Noonday Press in 1954. *The Blue Estuaries: Poems 1923-1968,* which Farrar, Straus, and Giroux published in 1968, served as a summary of her poetic achievement as it stretched from youth to age.

Although the years after 1937 were years of declining productivity, they were years when Bogan consolidated her reputation and reaped the fruits of an earlier devotion to letters. Others were anxious to know her opinions. If it was as a poet that Bogan made her reputation, it was as a critic that she made her living. Her work for the *New Yorker* continued until shortly before her death. Twice a year she provided the magazine with omnibus reviews of the most interesting poetry of the previous months, and she wrote countless brief notices. On her resignation from the magazine in 1969, William Shawn, then editor in chief, wrote, "for thirty-eight years we have been in the extraordinary position of knowing beyond all question that no other magazine's reviewing of poetry was as perceptive or trustworthy or intelligent as our own."

Awards and requests for readings, talks, and teaching posts started coming in the 1940s. In 1944 she became a Fellow in American Letters at the Library of Congress; in the same year, she gave the Hopwood Lecture at the University of Michigan. In 1945 she went to Washington, D.C., as the Consultant in Poetry to the Library of Congress. The year 1948 was filled with invitations to universities, and though she remained acutely aware of her own lack of formal education and convinced that the academy had slighted her, a catalogue of her activities in this one year alone belies her own assessment: she went to a poetry conference at Sarah Lawrence College, gave a reading at the New School for Social Research with Robert Lowell, Marianne Moore, and Allen Tate, taught summer school at the University of Washington, and spoke at Bard "On the Pleasures of Formal Verse."

In 1951 she was elected to the National In-stitute of Arts and Letters; in 1954 she was elected to the Academy of American Poets. In 1955 she shared the Bollingen Prize for poetry with Léonie Adams. In 1957 she was invited to the MacDowell Colony, and in the following year she participated in the Salzburg Seminar in American Studies. An award from the Academy of American Poets came in 1959, and she received the Creative Arts award from Brandeis University in 1962. In 1969, a year before her death, she was elected to the American Academy of Arts and Letters. On the more personal level, she had sustained the lifelong friendships of people she respected and had found room, at an age when other lives are often narrowing in scope, to admit new intimacies: William Maxwell, the new poetry editor for the *New Yorker;* Elizabeth Mayer, a German translator; and May Sarton, a younger writer and poet, are several examples.

Bogan's final years were lived in a kind of secular monasticism. Weaned from the destructive passions that had governed her youth, she lived alone and with the dignity of a hard-won victory over private terrors. To her lifelong friend, Morton Zabel, she wrote, "It is as though I had, after thirty years, really come into my whole being. . . . I can feel rage, but I am never humiliated, any more, and I am never lonely." Despite her brave words, her struggle was never simple and success never to be assumed. She could relapse into depressions until the end of her life. But she had, on the whole, found admission to the "temperate threshold" so avidly sought in and through her verse.

Poetry, to Bogan, was wrought from "rhythm as we first experience it . . . within the heartbeat, pulse and breath." Certainly, in her own case, it was an extension of self so vital that its excision would have left her vulnerable to inner demons and, as Stanley Kunitz put it, to "the deep night swarming with images of reproach and desire." But language did not fail her nor she it; and in her devotion to poetry she found forgiveness and personal reconciliation. To others she gave some of the most austere, searing, and beautiful lyrics written in America in this century.

Louise Bogan died on Wednesday, 4 February 1970. At her memorial service, Richard Wilbur, who spoke along with Auden, observed that "she remained faithful to the theme of passion." William Meredith, writing during her lifetime, was more encompassing in his praise: Louise Bogan was "one of the best women poets alive."

Louise Bogan, 1970 (photograph © Thomas Victor)

Letters:

What the Woman Lived: Selected Letters of Louise Bo-

gan: 1920-1970, edited by Ruth Limmer (New York: Harcourt Brace Jovanovich, 1973).

Bibliographies:

William J. Smith, *Louise Bogan: A Woman's Words* (Washington, D.C.: Library of Congress, 1971);

Jane Couchman, *Louise Bogan: A Bibliography of Primary and Secondary Materials, 1915-1975,* part 1, *Bulletin of Bibliography,* 33 (February-March

1976): 73-77, 104; part 2, *Bulletin of Bibliography,* 33 (April-June 1976): 111-126, 147.

Biography:

Elizabeth Frank, *Louise Bogan: A Portrait* (New York: Knopf, 1985).

Papers:

The Louise Bogan Papers are at Amherst College.

Van Wyck Brooks
(16 February 1886-2 May 1963)

Robert H. O'Connor
North Dakota State University

BOOKS: *Verses by Two Undergraduates,* by Brooks and John Hall Wheelock (Cambridge, Mass.: Privately printed, 1905);

The Wine of the Puritans: A Study of Present-Day America (London: Sisley's, 1908; New York: Kennerley, 1909);

The Soul: An Essay Towards a Point of View (San Francisco, 1910);

The Malady of the Ideal: Obermann, Maurice de Guérin, and Amiel (London: Fifield, 1913; Philadelphia: University of Pennsylvania Press, 1947);

John Addington Symonds: A Biographical Study (New York: Kennerley, 1914; London: Richards, 1914);

The World of H. G. Wells (New York: Kennedy, 1915; London: T. Unwin Fisher, 1915);

America's Coming-of-Age (New York: Huebsch, 1915);

Letters and Leadership (New York: Huebsch, 1918);

The Ordeal of Mark Twain (New York: Dutton, 1920; London: Heinemann, 1922; revised edition, New York: Dutton, 1933; London: Dent, 1934);

The Pilgrimage of Henry James (New York: Dutton, 1925; London: Cape, 1938);

Emerson and Others (New York: Dutton, 1927; London: Cape, 1927);

The Life of Emerson (New York: Dutton, 1932; London: Dent, 1934);

Sketches in Criticism (New York: Dutton, 1932; London: Dent, 1934);

Three Essays on America (New York: Dutton, 1934); revised as *America's Coming-of-Age* (Garden City: Doubleday, 1958);

The Flowering of New England, 1815-1865, volume 1 of *Makers and Finders* (New York: Dutton, 1936; London: Dent, 1936; revised edition, Cleveland: World, 1946);

New England; Indian Summer, 1865-1915, volume 2 of *Makers and Finders* (New York: Dutton, 1940; London: Dent, 1941);

On Literature Today (New York: Dutton, 1941);

Opinions of Oliver Allston (New York: Dutton, 1941; London: Dent, 1942);

The World of Washington Irving, volume 3 of *Makers and Finders* (New York: Dutton, 1944; London: Dent, 1946);

The Times of Melville and Whitman, volume 4 of *Makers and Finders* (New York: Dutton, 1947; London: Dent, 1948);

A Chilmark Miscellany (New York: Dutton, 1948);

The Confident Years; 1885-1915, volume 5 of *Makers and Finders* (New York: Dutton, 1952; London: Dent, 1952);

The Writer in America (New York: Dutton, 1953);

Van Wyck Brooks (photograph by Robert Gumpper)

Writers and the Future (New York: Spiral Press, 1953);

Scenes and Portraits: Memories of Childhood and Youth (New York: Dutton, 1954; London: Dent, 1954);

John Sloan: A Painter's Life (New York: Dutton, 1955; London: Dent, 1955);

From a Writer's Notebook (Worcester, Mass.: A. J. St. Onge, 1955; enlarged edition, New York: Dutton, 1958; London: Dent, 1958);

Helen Keller: Sketch for a Portrait (New York: Dutton, 1956; London: Dent, 1956);

Days of the Phoenix: The Nineteen-Twenties I Remember (New York: Dutton, 1957; London: Dent, 1957);

The Dream of Arcadia: American Writers and Artists in Italy, 1760-1915 (New York: Dutton, 1958; London: Dent, 1959);

Howells, His Life and World (New York: Dutton, 1959; London: Dent, 1959);

From the Shadow of the Mountain: My Post-Meridian

Years (New York: Dutton, 1961; London: Dent, 1962);

Fenollosa and His Circle, With Other Essays in Biography (New York: Dutton, 1962);

An Autobiography (New York: Dutton, 1965)—includes *Scenes and Portraits, Days of the Phoenix,* and *From the Shadow of the Mountain.*

OTHER: *The American Caravan. A Yearbook of American Literature,* edited by Brooks, Lewis Mumford, Alfred Kreymborg, and Paul Rosenfeld (New York: Macauley, 1927).

During his undergraduate years at Harvard, Van Wyck Brooks had ambitions of becoming a poet. His poetry appeared regularly in the *Harvard Advocate,* and in 1905, he and another aspiring writer, John Hall Wheelock, privately published a small volume of poems entitled *Verses by Two Undergraduates.* His poetic ambitions were soon superseded by his desire to be a critic, but he remained vitally interested in poetry and dedicated much of his criticism to commenting on the state of American verse. In particular, he campaigned vigorously against the desiccating influence on American poetry of certain nineteenth-century poets; he attempted to establish a sense of tradition and community among poets in this country; and he fought an unrelenting battle against what he considered to be the expatriate, nay-saying, elitist tendencies fostered in American verse by T. S. Eliot. For Brooks, the American poetic tradition centered on the expansive, democratic Walt Whitman, and Eliot was a destructive, misguided interloper.

Van Wyck Brooks, the second son of Charles Edward Brooks and Sarah Bailey Ames Brooks, grew up in Plainfield, New Jersey, a community with connections to America's literary past but dominated during Brooks's youth by Wall Street businessmen. His father was a stockbroker whose financial difficulties helped inspire his son's disdain for the American business mentality. Van Wyck was also put off by the obvious contradiction between the surface gentility of Plainfield and the aggressive acquisitiveness of many of its most prominent citizens. Brooks, the critic, was later to suggest that this split between "high brow" aspirations toward an ideal separate from mundane life and "low brow" gropings toward material success was a general malady of the American character, a malady that had stunted the development of many an American writer.

Brooks received his first formal schooling in

Plainfield, where he was quickly recognized as a student of great promise. His budding intellectual interests were further stimulated by a tour of Europe taken with his family in 1898 and 1899. He filled eight notebooks with his impressions of the cultural riches of the Old World, riches that emphasized the comparative cultural inadequacy of Plainfield and America. Most of his adult life was spent attempting to correct this inadequacy.

Brooks enrolled at Harvard University in 1904 and completed his undergraduate program in 1907. During this three-year period, he was elected to Phi Beta Kappa, joined The Stylus (a literary organization), and served as an editor of the *Harvard Advocate*. His Plainfield friend, Maxwell Perkins, assisted him in his introduction to literary Harvard, but it was his personal dissatisfaction with contemporary American culture and his fascination with Europe that contributed most to the ease with which he adjusted to his new surroundings. Although he sometimes felt uncomfortable with the dogmatic tone of Harvard's intellectuals, especially Irving Babbitt, he sympathized with many of their objections to things

American. However, this sympathy was to lead him in an entirely different direction from that taken by many of his fellow students, most notably, his future adversary, T. S. Eliot.

Brooks's literary efforts during his association with the *Harvard Advocate* included essays, short fiction, and poetry. One essay in particular, "The Poet Who Dies Young," contains an early statement of what Brooks saw as the antipoetic strain in the American character. The poet in us dies, he tells us, because we are lured toward a materialistic, insensitive masculinity. We give in to the "greatest fallacy in all the world," the assumption that our "duty leads" us "into material ways that leave no room for beautiful things." We "amuse ourselves with grosser joys" than poetry, and "we deliberately acquire our ungraceful ways in an effort to be manly."

At its worst, Brooks's own poetry sins in the opposite direction, toward a romantic prettiness and an adolescent hypersensitivity that betray its author's literary inexperience. "Humanities," for example, is a singsong attempt to express the privacy of human love and the separateness of human life from its cosmic environment. The final stanza, especially, slips into greeting-card awkwardness:

> What have gods and stars to do
> With *You love me* and *I love you?*
> Many things are deep and high
> That have no word for such as I.

Somewhat more accomplished is the poetic dialogue, "The Boy and the Others," a poem on the same theme as "The Poet Who Dies Young." The Boy is fascinated with natural beauty, with "The lichen" which "climbs upon the wall/To hear the hidden robins call," and he resists the materialistic urgings of the others to "Life give up and living get." But the urgings ultimately prove to be overpowering, and the poetic boy is metamorphosed into the philistine:

> Give back my stool—I ask no more,
> The desk, the pen I loathed before:
> The lichen climbs not on the wall
> To hear the hidden robins call.

The poem achieves a simplicity reminiscent of the poetry of the Pre-Raphaelites, but its didactic purpose considerably detracts from its appeal. Another of the *Harvard Advocate* poems that exhibits Brooks's incipient but imitative artistry and his youthful awkwardness is "To a Man of Pompeii."

Van Wyck Brooks, 1909 (pastel sketch by John Butler Yeats)

The poem is a ponderous, romantic meditation on the remains of a victim of Mount Vesuvius, whose petrified body becomes a symbol of stoic courage. The poem's tone is unpleasantly lugubrious, but a few of the lines, imagined to be spoken by the body, are surprisingly effective:

> I have lingered long
> With cymbals and sweet song,
> And I have wandered forth as yesternight.
> These days have been to me
> Between two screens as flecks of candle-light:
> And I discern the near and ultimate shade.

Brooks's other major creative venture during his Harvard years, his poetry in the privately printed *Verses by Two Undergraduates,* is also of uneven quality. Brooks had met Wheelock, his collaborator and lifelong friend, at a social gathering on his second evening at Harvard, and the two were soon working toward publication of the twenty-poem volume that was to be the first book for both of them. The book is really little more than a pamphlet, one hundred copies of which were printed in 1905. Brooks's ten poems appear on the right-hand pages, with Wheelock's on the left, but neither author's name occurs anywhere in the volume.

In general Brooks's contributions—"Each to Each," "Cui Fata Parent," "Sonnet," "They and Thou," " 'If We Wait till the Close?,' " "The Philosophers," "No longer I Exalted," "Amalfi," "The Cry from Galway," and "Autumn Leaves in June"—display a careful regularity of rhyme and meter, although "No Longer I Exalted" imitates the free-verse style of Walt Whitman. Several of them are about love, and most are touched with a yearning for the beautiful, the passionate, and the imaginative. The book of poems itself (according to "Each to Each")

> came to me from very far
> Over a spacious lake of dreams
> To this garish world that only seems,
> From the dim sweet hills that really are.

"They and Thou" compares friendship with love and concludes that friendship is a matter of circumstance but that no circumstance can conquer love:

> though preborn upon a glimmering star,
> Immeasurably far,
> I should have yearned across the infinite abyss,
> And spanned it with a kiss
> And grasped thy hand in mine.

"No Longer I Exalted" is also concerned with the human passions and claims that

> There is but one unpardonable sin—
> The permitting, the fostering of life without a passionate heart,
> Herein are all insincerities.

"Amalfi" is perhaps the most romantically passionate of all the poems, as the following stanza suggests:

> There we shall lie in the warm sand
>   Together lost in dreams,
> By orange-laden breezes fanned
>   And perfume from cool streams,
> And shall not care while hand in hand
>   What is and what but seems.

Brooks later repented these youthful excursions into poetry and would react with embarrassment to Wheelock's sudden recitation of one of them, but the tone of romantic intensity that characterizes Brooks's contributions to the volume, his concern for the beautiful and the imaginative and his hatred for the unimpassioned, can also be found throughout his critical writings.

Those critical writings began to appear very soon after his leaving Harvard. The first, *The Wine of the Puritans,* was written and published in 1908, during a stay in England. Although he had left America under the impression that his future lay in Europe, he quickly discovered that everything he wrote was obsessively concerned with his homeland. After writing various articles on America for British periodicals and then spending four months in a Sussex farmhouse composing *The Wine of the Puritans,* his first lengthy attempt to explain the malady at the heart of the American creative experience, he returned to the United States.

During the next several years, Brooks moved from coast to coast and continent to continent, working at various jobs which kept him in touch with literature and acquiring a wife and a family. For Doubleday and Page, he assisted in the editing of *Worlds Work,* a magazine for which he interviewed important writers of the day. He helped with the publication of the *Standard Dictionary* and *Collier's Encyclopedia* before moving to Carmel, California, in 1911. Eleanor Kenyon Stimson, who would bear him two sons, Charles Van Wyck and Oliver Kenyon, married Brooks on 26 April 1911, and during the fall, he began a two-year stint as an instructor in American literature at Stanford Uni-

Van Wyck, Eleanor, and Charles Brooks in 1912 or 1913 (courtesy of University of Massachusetts Press)

versity. Brooks spent part of 1913 teaching in England, after which he returned to the United States and translated several works from the French, including novels by Romain Rolland, for the Century Company.

Throughout these years, he continued working diligently at the craft of criticism and developed the ideas that had begun to crystalize in *The Wine of the Puritans.* He became more and more convinced that a sustaining national tradition is necessary to foster creative literature and that America lacked, or was insufficiently aware of, such a tradition. We had always had writers, but those writers, he believed, had been pulled in contradictory directions. They had either been drawn to ideals that had no relevance to life as it is actually lived, or they had written for the sake of money and popular acclaim, with aesthetically disastrous results. These writers were produced by and wrote for a society whose psyche was split, as the Puritan psyche had been split, between a bloodless spirituality and a crass materialism.

This summary of the ideas Brooks developed during the years preceding World War I is drastically simplified, but it is, nevertheless, a convenient starting point for discussing the impact he was soon to have on American literature in general and American poetry in particular. During the years up to and including 1915, Brooks sharpened his critical skills through the publication of *The Soul: An Essay Towards a Point of View* (1910), *The Malady of*

the *Ideal* (1913), *John Addington Symonds* (1914), and *The World of H. G. Wells* (1915). These works won him a reputation as one of this nation's significant young critics, but it was *America's Coming-of-Age* (1915) that made him a powerful spokesman for America's literary renewal.

Of greatest importance to understanding Brooks's concept of the poet are the book's two chapters entitled "Our Poets" and "The Precipitant." In "Our Poets," Brooks demolished the right of Henry Wadsworth Longfellow, James Russell Lowell, John Greenleaf Whittier, and others of the genteel tradition to continue their dominance of American verse. Even when they were alive, he asserted, they had done nothing "to move the soul of America from the accumulation of dollars. . . ." They were part of that "immense, vague cloud canopy of idealism which hung over the American people during the nineteenth century" and which "was never permitted, in fact, to interfere with the practical conduct of life." Of what significance, then, could such poets be for the twentieth century? Walt Whitman, on the other hand, was potentially "The Precipitant" of an effectual literature. He "laid the cornerstone of a national ideal capable . . . of releasing personality and of retrieving for our civilization, originally deficient in the richer juices of human nature, and still further bled and flattened out by the 'machine process,' the only sort of 'place in the sun' that is really worth having." Whitman was, perhaps, too uncritical of the mercenary aspects of the American character, but he had managed to fuse the ideal with the real, and that achievement could lead other writers to the production of works that would avoid both the bloodless idealism and the vulgar commercialism that had tainted the American literary past.

Inspired by *America's Coming-of-Age,* James Oppenheim and Waldo Frank founded *Seven Arts* magazine, a project to which Brooks was invited to contribute. The magazine's purpose, as one of Brooks's biographers, James Vitelli, describes it, was to proclaim "that a new day had come, that Americans could no longer indulge in the questionable luxury of cultural provincialism, and that the acquisitive impulse heretofore characteristic of American behavior would have to yield to the creative impulse. Henceforth art and artists would provide the leadership that would create a genuine civilization, a corporate community." The artist, whom America had paid scant attention to in the past, would become a public force for cultural improvement.

Some of Brooks's essays for *Seven Arts,* credited by Horace Gregory and Marya Zaturenska with helping to inspire the poetry of Hart Crane, were published in 1918 as *Letters and Leadership.* Two of the crucial ideas in that volume, suggested to Brooks by a remark Goethe had made about the literature of Germany, were that America had no cultural center to give purpose to the efforts of its writers and that for this very reason its writers had no sense of community. Brooks's search for America's cultural center, anticipated in his discussion in *America's Coming-of-Age* of the significance of Walt Whitman, was to be the laborious task of decades, culminating in the publication between 1936 and 1952 of the five volumes of *Makers and Finders: A History of the Writer in America, 1800-1915.* His attempt to give America's writers a sense of community was to occur much sooner, in 1927, with the publication of the first volume of *The American Caravan.* Edited by Brooks, Lewis Mumford, Alfred Kreymborg, and Paul Rosenfeld, the stated purpose of *The American Caravan* was to affirm "the health of the young American literature" and to act as "an earnest of the eventual formation of a guild for the cooperative publication of its works." Its contributors included William Carlos Williams, Mark Van Doren, Archibald MacLeish, John Dos Passos, Yvor Winters, Babette Deutsch, and Robert Penn Warren; and two of its inclusions were Allen Tate's "Ode to the Confederate Dead" and Hart Crane's "Ave Maria."

The volume also included an essay by Francis Fergusson entitled "T. S. Eliot and His Impersonal Theory of Art," which agreed entirely with one of Brooks's own objections to Eliot's aesthetic, that it failed "to take account of the relation between art and human life. . . ." Eliot's theories, he said, tended "to separate the man from the artist and humanity from the art," and for Fergusson and Brooks both, this division was an artistic error of the first magnitude. It led in the direction of coterie art, art that had lost its social roots.

Even before *The American Caravan* appeared, Brooks entered the darkest period of his life. From 1925 to 1931 he struggled with feelings of despair which threatened to destroy him. During the decade before his breakdown, his career and his personal life seemed to prosper. He made at least one visit to Carmel but spent much of his time in New York and in Westport, Connecticut, where he settled in 1920. He worked for four years as literary editor of the *Freeman* and read manuscripts for Harcourt, Brace while continuing to publish books of criticism. He won the *Dial* Award for 1923 but almost immediately began bending under the com-

bined effects of exhaustion and an insidious self-doubt. By 1927 he had experienced a complete psychological breakdown and was treated for his malady by some of the world's finest therapists, including Carl Jung. That he was able, during the period following his treatment, to complete the voluminous *Makers and Finders,* with its extraordinary overview of America's literary history, testifies to the completeness of his recovery.

Although much of what he wrote during the years following his successful treatment lacks the aggressive edge of his earlier work, his distaste for Eliot grew, and his attacks on Eliot's poetry and criticism became more and more rancorous. Brooks had begun his career as an expatriate but had repented his expatriatism and had emerged as the foremost defender of an American literature firmly rooted in the American soil. Brooks was drawn to poets such as Vachel Lindsay, Stephen Vincent Benét, Robert Frost, and Carl Sandburg. He loved the public poet who drew his inspiration from the people and spoke to the people, who trusted in the people's strength. He lauded poetry which showed a democratic faith in mankind's capacity for self-renewal, and he despised poetry like *The Waste Land* (1922) that expressed a fashionable despair. Nor did he care for poetry, like that in Eliot's later manner, that sought mankind's salvation in authoritarian ritual. Eliot was among those, referred to in *On Literature Today* (1941), who had "broken with their group-life, by choice, on grounds of taste and taste alone." He was one of those "adolescent minds" producing so much of present literature, minds which gave the world hopelessness despite its "hunger for affirmations." As Brooks expressed it in the final chapter of the concluding volume of *Makers and Finders, The Confident Years; 1885-1915* (1952), Eliot was the ultimate life-denier, the most powerful enemy in this century of the life-affirming tradition at the heart of the American experience.

Eliot was occasionally nettled into responding to Brooks's attacks; a thoroughly irritated Eliot, for example, published a letter in the April 1942 *Partisan Review* in which he suggested a strong similarity between Brooks's fervent nationalism and Nazism. Such responses were unnecessary, however, because Brooks's attacks on Eliot seem to have hurt his own reputation considerably more than they hurt Eliot's. Brooks's standing in American literature had been in decline since the 1930s, and his increasingly reactionary position on literary issues had lost him much of his following, at least among the literati. He was especially anathema

Van Wyck Brooks, Lewis Mumford, George Biddle, and Mark Van Doren at a party given by the American Academy of Arts and Letters to celebrate Brooks's seventy-fifth birthday

among the New Critics, who found his essentially sociological approach to criticism repugnant.

Nevertheless, for the general public, Brooks, who had won a Pulitzer Prize in 1936 and been elected to membership in the American Academy of Arts and Letters in 1937, was a certified literary sage to whom all respect was due. The two decades before his death in Bridgewater, Connecticut, on 2 May 1963, lacked the innovative adventurousness of the earlier years, but they were laden with honors. The one tragedy of those years, the death of his wife Eleanor in 1946, caused Brooks a temporary return to unhappiness, but he was soon remarried (to Gladys Rice on 2 June 1947), and he quickly reestablished his equilibrium. Dividing his time between residence in Connecticut and travel to California and Europe, Brooks spent his declining years enjoying recognition as one of America's most distinguished and influential men of literature.

Nor has his influence died. Brooks remains a significant figure in the history of twentieth-century American letters. In particular, he had a pro-

found effect on this nation's poetry. He swept away a great deal of the poetic debris that was hindering the development of a new poetry; he gave a whole generation of poets a sense that they were part of a great literary renewal; and he gave eloquent expression to the Whitmanesque aspects of the American literary tradition. If his chauvinism and his failure to appreciate the darker aspects of American literature were limitations on his critical outlook, those limitations at least did American poetry no lasting harm.

Letters:

The Van Wyck Brooks-Lewis Mumford Letters: The Record of a Literary Friendship, edited by Robert E. Spiller (New York: Dutton, 1970).

Biography:

James Hoopes, *Van Wyck Brooks: In Search of American Culture* (Amherst: University of Massachusetts Press, 1977).

Reference:

James R. Vitelli, *Van Wyck Brooks* (New York: Twayne, 1969).

Papers:

The Museum of the American Academy of Arts and Letters has a collection of Brooks's papers.

Bob Brown

(14 June 1886-7 August 1959)

Bruce Comens
State University of New York at Buffalo

See also the Brown entry in *DLB 4, American Writers in Paris, 1920-1939*.

BOOKS: *What Happened to Mary?* (New York: Clode, 1913);

The Remarkable Adventures of Christopher Poe (Chicago: F. G. Browne, 1913);

Tahiti (New York: Guido Bruno, 1915);

My Marjonary (Boston: Luce, 1916);

1450-1950 (Paris: Black Sun Press, 1929; enlarged edition, New York: Jargon Press, 1959);

The Readies (Bad-Ems: Roving Eye Press, 1930);

Globe-Gliding (Diessen: Roving Eye Press, 1930); revised as *Nomadness* (New York: Dodd, Mead, 1931);

Words (Paris: Hours Press, 1931);

Gems: A Censored Anthology (Cagnes-sur-Mer: Roving Eye Press, 1931);

Demonics (Cagnes-sur-Mer: Roving Eye Press, 1931);

Let There Be Beer! (New York: Smith & Haas, 1932);

You Gotta Live (London: Desmond Harnsworth, 1932);

Toward a Bloodless Revolution (Newllano, La.: Llano Publishing, 1933);

Houdini (New York: Modern Editions, 1933?);

The Wine Cook Book, by Cora, Rose, and Bob Brown (Boston: Little, Brown, 1934);

The European Cookbook for American Homes, by Cora, Rose, and Bob Brown (New York: Farrar & Rinehart, 1936; revised and enlarged edition, New York: Prentice-Hall, 1951);

The Country Cookbook, by Cora, Rose, and Bob Brown (Weston, Vt.: Countryman Press/New York: Farrar & Rinehart, 1937);

10,000 Snacks, by Cora, Rose, and Bob Brown (New York: Farrar & Rinehart, 1937);

Homemade Hilarity (Weston, Vt.: Countryman Press, 1938);

Most for Your Money Cookbook, by Cora, Rose, and Bob Brown (New York: Modern Age, 1938);

Salads and Herbs, by Cora, Rose, and Bob Brown (Philadelphia & New York: Lippincott, 1938);

The Wining and Dining Quiz: A Banquet of Questions and Answers from Soup to Nuts, by Cora, Rose,

and Bob Brown (New York & London: Appleton-Century, 1939);

The Vegetable Cook Book, by Cora, Rose, and Bob Brown (Philadelphia & New York: Lippincott, 1939);

Soups, Sauces and Gravies, by Cora, Rose, and Bob Brown (Philadelphia & New York: Lippincott, 1939);

The South American Cook Book, by Cora, Rose, and Bob Brown (New York: Doubleday, Doran, 1939);

Can We Co-operate? (Pleasant Plains, Staten Island, N.Y.: Roving Eye Press, 1940);

Outdoor Cooking, by Cora, Rose, and Bob Brown (New York: Greystone, 1940);

America Cooks, by Cora, Rose, and Bob Brown (New York: Norton, 1940);

Fish and Sea Food Cook Book, by Cora, Rose, and Bob Brown (Philadelphia & New York: Lippincott, 1940);

Look Before You Cook, by Rose and Bob Brown (New York: McBride, 1941);

Amazing Amazon, by Rose and Bob Brown (New York: Modern Age, 1942);

Hotell Skjaêrsilden (Oslo: Tiden, 1949);

The Complete Book of Cheese (New York: Random House, 1955);

Culinary Americana, by Eleanor and Bob Brown (New York: Roving Eye Press, 1961).

OTHER: *Readies for Bob Brown's Machine,* edited, with an appendix, by Brown (Cagnes-sur-Mer: Roving Eye Press, 1931).

PERIODICAL PUBLICATIONS: "I am Aladdin," *Others,* 1 (August 1915): 28-30;

"Experiment," *transition,* no. 18 (November 1929): 208;

"Overseas Americans," *American Mercury,* 19 (January 1930): 22-29;

"The Readies," *transition,* no. 19/20 (June 1930): 167-173;

"Sub-Tropical," *transition,* no. 21 (March 1932): 27-36;

"Pages from the Book of Beer," *American Mercury,* 26 (June 1932): 185-191;

"Drug-store in a Dry Town," *American Mercury,* 26 (August 1932): 405-411;

Contempo: A Review of Books and Personalities, special Brown issue, includes essays and poems by Brown, 2 (31 August 1932);

"Report of a Returned New Yorker," *American Mercury,* 27 (October 1932): 185-192;

"Swell Days for Literary Guys," *American Mercury,* 27 (December 1932): 480-485;

"Houdini," *Prairie Schooner,* 7 (Fall 1933): 156-158;

"Them Asses," *American Mercury,* 30 (December 1933): 403-411;

"Greenwich Village Gallops," *American Mercury,* 31 (January 1934): 103-111.

Bob Brown was successful in almost all his many and varied pursuits. Journalist, stockbroker, publisher, novelist, poet, editor, culinary authority, world traveler, and member of the avant-garde in Greenwich Village and Paris, he was a colorful and energetic figure who also developed a reading machine that he hoped would revolutionize reading and writing. His ideas on writing, together with his own optical poems, cast an interesting light on the modernist "Revolution of the Word."

Robert Carlton Brown was born in Chicago, Illinois, into a family that surrounded him with the printed word at an early age. His father, Robert Carlton Brown, published new books and collected rare ones; his mother, Cora Bracket Brown, later collaborated with her son on most of his culinary books. Bob Brown graduated from Oak Park High School and later attended the University of Wisconsin with the class of 1908, but neither experience affected him as much as his home environment: he lived with a publisher who "was almost a book," and thus, as Brown said, "I was almost a book myself." It was probably because of this background that, for Brown, the word was always the written word, primarily a visual rather than an aural object.

A curious split in his attitude toward the written word also showed itself early. On the one hand, he was fascinated by the word as such, as a concrete, visual thing. He traced the origin of his reading machine back to his eighteenth year, when, reading (and *seeing*) the title of Stephen Crane's poem "Black Riders," he "was struck with the idea that black printed words are romantic knights galloping across white pages, astride inky chargers." And at nineteen he wrote a short story that used dashes for swear words, or parts of words. He later gave "A------for Adam, --------espont of Hellespont" as an example of this technique and explained that he "played with the interior structure of words instinctively and got pleasure out of it." Yet that same story was sold to a newspaper for two dollars, inaugurating Brown's career as a very successful commercial writer, as a man who used words, and his extraordinary facility for producing them, in order to make a living. Writing was a vehicle of exchange:

through it he could transmit his ideas and receive money in return.

At twenty-one Brown's career as a journalist and pulp-fiction writer was well enough established to warrant a move to New York, "the very heart of success." The following year Frank Munsey suggested that he go to England to get "the English slant" into his stories, and Brown accordingly moved to London, continuing to write serials for Munsey and earning, as he put it, "big money." He was also living the good life, but that was not all that Brown wanted, and so he returned to New York after one year. There he married Rose Johnston, the couple having a son, Robert Carlton, in 1912. He continued to write prolifically for a living, including a best-seller, *What Happened to Mary?* (1913), which was made into one of the first successful movies, and a popular collection of detective stories, *The Remarkable Adventures of Christopher Poe* (1913). According to his own account, by the age of twenty-nine Brown had produced "jokes, poems, epigrams, novelettes, anecdotes, articles, jingles, sketches, monologues, serials, digests, slogans, advertisements, feuilleton, reports, memoirs, confessions, tales, narratives, guides, monographs, descriptions, obituaries, wisecracks, legends, journals, lives, plays, adventures, experiences, romances, fairy tales, parables, apologues, circulars, doggerel, sonnets, odes, episodes, lyrics, thrillers, dime novels, nickel novels, society verse, essays, rondelets, biographies and codexes"—in just that disorder, totaling some ten million words and earning him as much as $15,000 a year. The peak came in 1913, when the writing machine wrote of its own achievements: Brown published a long article on his own business and literary accomplishments, received $600 for it at ten cents a word—and found himself written out.

Earlier, though, Brown had at twenty-five "summed up" his life in an *Everybody* magazine article, in which he "proved that spiritual and material man are eternally duelling," and he had not entirely neglected the more spiritual side of literature. From 1913 to 1915 he was in fact close to the center of the avant-garde in New York. While his career as a commercial writer was peaking in 1913, he also associated with the Others group of poets, first in Grantwood, New Jersey, and later in Greenwich Village. The group was led by Alfred Kreymborg, with help from Walter Arensberg, and included Maxwell Bodenheim, Malcolm Cowley, Man Ray, William Carlos Williams, and Marcel Duchamp. Brown was probably something of a patron to the group: Williams called him Grantwood's own

plutocrat, since Brown had made enough money that he could now afford to write at leisure. In March 1915, immediately after he had published Kreymborg's *Mushrooms*, Guido Bruno published Brown's *Tahiti*, a collection of ten poems, in his chapbook series. Brown also contributed to the second issue of *Others* in August 1915, his five poems appearing alongside work by Williams, Kreymborg, Wallace Stevens, Skipwith Cannell, Amy Lowell, and Alanson Hartpence.

Despite his support and participation, Brown was not overly enthusiastic about the group. He later remarked that Mina Loy was the only one he could read, for the Others and imagist groups' interest in words generally "seemed sophomoric to me." He felt that he could not write any better, but that he could write differently—witness the striking poem he had produced in response to the 1913 Armory show, "Eyes."

Brown had spent part of 1913 in Spain on his profits from commercial writing, but the big event of the year was the Armory show. Like most who saw the exhibit, Brown was deeply affected by the recent developments in international modernism, and his conversations with Marcel Duchamp increased both his enthusiasm for and his understanding of the exhibits. The combination of words and pictures and the emphasis on spontaneity gave Brown an escape route from the excessively formulaic and pedestrian writing which made up the bulk of his work. Hugh Ford reports that it was "the morning after he had absorbed 'eyefuls of Armory pictures and a mindful of Marcel's exciting art talk' " that Brown began to experiment himself. Almost the first product was the "Eyes" poem. It was sparked by a visual rhyme, the similarity between his own eyes and the oysters on his plate, and it begins with drawings of four sets of eyes arranged vertically, each set progressively larger, with a caption below each set: "EYES/EYES/MY GODT/WHAT EYES!" Under the fourth caption is a circle of eyes, or oysters, with the caption "EYES ON THE HALF-SHELL." This "simple and direct" poem, which could be taken in "without moving an eye," became a symbol and a slogan for Brown. He felt that it carried him "safely through and past Cubism, Imagism, Dadaism, Surrealism, Humanism" and all the other art movements of the time. It announced his own program, which called for art that could be more immediately apprehended, almost directly imprinted on the mind's eye.

Another revelation was Gertrude Stein's *Tender Buttons*, published in 1914 by Brown's friend Donald Evans. Although he did not know "what it

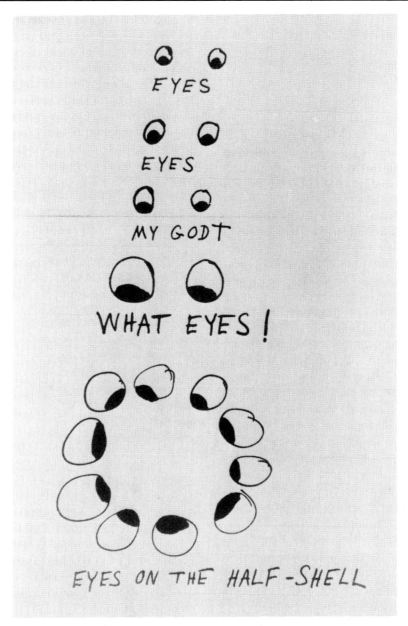

Brown's "Eyes" poem, as it appears in the 1959 Jargon Press edition of 1450-1950 *(courtesy of Jonathan Williams)*

was about," Stein's work also seemed to Brown to be "optical" poetry. Her "formula," precisely because it was new and unknown, gave "a great kick" to Brown's conception of writing: "I began to see that a story might be anything. Hurrah! . . . A story didn't have to be a tangible hunk of bread interest. Thank God for that. Thank God for Gert Stein. Thank God for everything."

Despite these spurs to his creativity, and despite Duchamp's publication of the "Eyes" poem in *Blindman,* Brown did little concerning his experimental impulses for more than a decade. A small

book of free verse, *My Marjonary,* was published in 1916 with the help of H. L. Mencken. The first, dedicatory poem ("aux mes frères") shows the gulf he felt between himself and other poets, referring to them as "you daredevil dilettantes/In vers libre." Brown links free verse to jazz rather than to Greek cadences and concludes by stressing the intimate connection between art and life:

You wretched rhymesters
Imaginary imagists!
Cut out your cant

About cadences;
Go back to rhyming
"Dear" with "tear"
As you were born to do.
To write free verse
You've got to
Be
Free verse.

But although the poems do not show an affiliation with any other movements, neither do they indicate a development of the revelation of the "Eyes" poem.

Meanwhile Brown had all but abandoned commercial writing for Wall Street, where he made and subsequently lost a fortune. He left Wall Street in 1916 "badly bent," but having learned that "writing for a living is the bunk." He dealt in rare books for a while, and then in 1919 he and his wife moved to Rio de Janeiro. There Brown founded the *Brazilian American* weekly, which began, as the Browns later stated, "a whole generation of goodwill" between Brazil and America. Brown published magazines in Rio, London, and Mexico City for a decade, earning between $15,000 and $30,000 a year—more than he had made on Wall Street—and at his peak producing a sixty-page magazine every six days. But he finally decided that he had had enough: he wanted to "do something of permanent value for reading or writing." In Brown's case, that meant trying to revolutionize "the reading half of literature" by finally transforming his reading machine from an idea to an actuality.

It had been the Wall Street ticker-tape machine that had finally given a positive direction to Brown's dissatisfaction with the book format. He wanted a similar machine to modernize reading, so that readers would apprehend words more directly and easily and so that writers might "approach closer the hieroglyphic mysteries that have streamed across the gossamer brain-tapes from the beginning of time to infinity." In his machine a roll of tape, on which could be printed in a single line an entire novel, would move under a magnifying glass. The reader would control the speed and could read the novel merely by looking through the magnifying glass, thus eliminating the wasted time and eye strain caused by moving the eyes back and forth from line to line. The machine would also eliminate such "useless" words as articles, prepositions, and grammatical connectors, words that Brown felt were invented solely for the ear: "Speech might go on the same, I didn't give a damn about that, but the written word would change.

Speech to me was unimportant, it had clogged the mechanism of writing and reading too long." He was determined to make the "Black Riders" of Crane's title a reality.

After a tour through the Orient, Brown and his wife moved to France (eventually settling in the artists' colony of Cagnes-sur-Mer), where Brown supported his family, according to Joseph Flora, by dealing in rare books. He immediately immersed himself in the avant-garde, and the years from 1929 to 1939 were to be his most productive of experimental literature. The year 1929 saw the publication in *transition* (at the end of the "Revolution of the Word" section) of an "Experiment" that marked a return to optical poems, and Harry Crosby's Black Sun Press published *1450-1950*, a book of such pieces (including "Eyes"). Although it is difficult to see how the reading machine could be used for these poems, the book is in part a celebration of Brown's machine. The title refers to five hundred years of printing—in the colophon the book is dated "in the year Gutenberg 479." And facing the first poem is a statement calling for reading to make a second great advance to "the speed of the day—1929—not 1450." To dramatize the point, this statement is reduced to the size of reading-machine print: a long page in ordinary print, here it occupies about one square inch of a page.

The poems themselves, "painfully hand-lettered" by Brown, are exuberant and playful. The first is an invitation and exhortation: "WIPE/ YOUR MUDDY MIND/BEFORE/ENTERING MY/MOSQUE/AND LEAVE YOUR/THICK/ CEREBRAL SHOES/OUTSIDE." The best poems are not simply illustrated verse but fuse together words and drawings into a single, and singular, artifact. William Carlos Williams, Marcel Duchamp, Gertrude Stein, H. L. Mencken—almost all who read the book responded enthusiastically. Williams contrasted it favorably to T. S. Eliot's work: it was "a million times more to the point than T. S. Eliot's scholasticism classicism or whatever it might be called. I enjoyed the reading and take the book seriously." The book was clearly not one of Brown's money-making projects, as only 150 copies were printed, and opposite the title page more than fifty names are listed as recipients of free copies. Partly because of its scarcity, *1450-1950* had become something of a legend by the time Jonathan Williams discovered and published (in 1959) an enlarged edition of what he called this "utterly charming and singular book."

The years 1930-1931 proved to be busy for Brown, largely in connection with his machine.

"The Readies," an essay explaining the machine and the new kind of writing ("readies") it would inspire, appeared in *transition* in June 1930. The title plays on "movies" and "talkies", two other revolutionary arts that were inspired by technological change. Brown then published an enlarged version of the essay, together with examples of "readies," in *The Readies* (1930). This was the first publication under Brown's own imprint, the Roving Eye Press, which he established to publish his own books and to publicize the reading machine. His second book of 1930 was *Globe-Gliding*, a collection of free-verse travel poems that describe various places Brown had seen on his journeys. (With very slight changes and a new title, *Nomadness*, the book was reprinted by Dodd, Mead in 1931, whereupon it gained a much greater audience.) The name of Brown's press was appropriate both to his ideas and to his life.

Four new books appeared in 1931. Under the Hours Press imprint Nancy Cunard published *Words*, a collection of poetry intended to publicize the reading machine's impact on printing. Brown's Roving Eye Press published three books, *Demonics, Gems: A Censored Anthology*, and *Readies for Bob Brown's Machine. Demonics*, as Hugh Ford says, contains some of Brown's best poems, at least his best nonoptical poems. The range of the book is quite extraordinary, from fairly serious poems for Stuart Davis (to whom the book was dedicated), Ezra Pound, and William Carlos Williams, to comic poems such as the "Report of a Meeting of the Olive Branch of the United Red-thumbed Writers Association":

Writers' rights	Hooray!
Writers' cramp	Boo!
Poet's license	Hip! Hip!
Royalties	Hurrah!

In the poem for Pound Brown states his preference for Pound's American Cantos over the "Graeco-Roman" ones, while the lyrical poem for Williams shows Brown's support of Williams's program for a new, American writing:

Fresh-hearted daisy boy sitting
self-sunlit
on the wistful weather-beaten
front porch of America
holding out a bouquet of
damp inward-eyed violets
offering a trembling fistful of
nervous Fourth-of-July electric sparklers
....

-------a spark-spraying bouquet
al que quiere.

Gems is an amusing attack on censorship and "bookleggers," those unprincipled and unread profiteers who print pirated editions of literary works in order to capitalize on the curiosity sparked by capricious censorship. Brown's argument, that censorship can make the most innocent literature appear pornographic, is supported by an anthology of censored classics, ranging from nursery rhymes—

Old Mother Goose, when
She wanted to ***
Would *** a fat goose
Or a very fine gander

—to Shakespeare, Tennyson, and Wordsworth:

She *** among the untrodden ways
Beside the springs of Dove;
A maid whom there were none to ***,
And very few to ****.

Brown apparently found Wordsworth particularly susceptible to this treatment, as some dozen "gems" are drawn from his poetry.

Brown had meanwhile made friends with two American artists in Cagnes-sur-Mer, Hilaire Hiler and Ross Saunders. Saunders and Hiler made a crude but working model of the reading machine, which spurred Brown to publish an anthology of "readies" by various contemporary writers. *Readies for Bob Brown's Machine*, Brown's last book in France, included a preface by Hiler describing the machine, some forty contributions, and an appendix by Brown that related the history of his idea. Contributors included Eugene Jolas, Alfred Kreymborg, William Carlos Williams, Gertrude Stein, Ezra Pound, Paul Bowles, and Kay Boyle. Dashes and equal signs between words or phrases were used to suggest the effect of words flowing by in a straight line. While some, such as Paul Bowles and Kay Boyle, clearly took Brown's invitation seriously, others seem to have been more amused by the experiment. Kreymborg's contribution in fact declines the invitation: "Old man Kreymborg has grown too seedy/To write Bob Brown a speedy readie." Pound's is a perfectly ordinary poem, with a few equal signs included—and these set off "useless" words such as the indefinite article. Williams wrote a sequence of rhymes such as "Grace-face: hot-pot: lank-spank." And although Stein's "We Came: A History" is extraor-

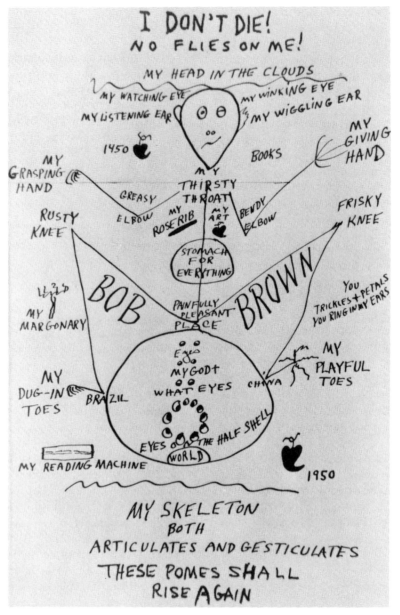

Brown's revised version of the last poem in 1450-1950, published in the 1959 Jargon Press edition (courtesy of Jonathan Williams)

dinary, it is quite typical of Stein's work, the only concession to the reading machine being the equal signs added to set off phrases.

Brown stayed in France until 1932, attempting to sell his machine to a manufacturer. (He was not so avant-garde as to scorn making money from his idea.) But publishers worried that the machine might damage their business, book lovers simply wanted to keep the traditional format, and, finally, there were several competing machines, the Fiskeoscope being the most prominent. Brown was forced to give up the idea. After his years in France, he

rarely attempted to publicize his machine in his publications.

His return to New York was heralded by a special Bob Brown issue of *Contempo: A Review of Books and Personalities* (31 August 1932), of which Brown was a contributing editor. The issue featured a story, an editorial, and a review of Kay Boyle, as well as essays and optical poems by Brown. In the same issue, Louis Untermeyer confessed that his enthusiasm for Brown was "almost unqualified" and declared, "if he has any god it is Gusto." Appropriate to this remark, the magazine also contained an advertisement for Brown's latest book, *Let There Be Beer!* (1932), "A History of beer from its Origins in 7,000 B. C. to date, and on into the future." The book was dedicated to H. L. Mencken, who published a series of Brown's reflective articles in his *American Mercury.* Of Brown's history of beer, Mencken said, "I hope every honest beer fanatic will buy two copies of *Let There Be Beer!,* one for himself and one for his pastor." Brown and his books always sparked enthusiasm.

Most of Brown's literary output in the years following France was devoted to his culinary interests. One exception was *You Gotta Live* (1932), a novel set during World War I and dedicated to Kay Boyle. Others were *American Mercury* articles, a poem, "Houdini," that was published in 1933 (and as a separate pamphlet), and *Amazing Amazon* (1942), which Brown wrote with his second wife to chronicle their five-month trip along the Amazon River. Most of the culinary books were also the product of the Browns' collaboration, often including his mother, as in the entertaining 1939 book, *The Wining and Dining Quiz: A Banquet of Questions and Answers from Soup to Nuts.*

In 1940 the Roving Eye Press, now based in New York, published *Can We Co-operate?,* in which Brown discussed Communism. Brown was interested in alternatives to capitalism, despite his own success as a capitalist. (There were also failures: in 1916 Brown lost the small fortune he had made in 1915, and in the 1930 he and Williams both lost money in an oil scheme.) Brown contributed to *New Masses* and had been a contributing editor of *Masses.* When *1450-1950* was being prepared for publication by Jargon Books, Brown related the meaninglessness of words to capitalism: "I think Coolidge (today: add Eisenhower) and Will Rogers have worn [words] as thin and mean meaningless as the dimes Rockefeller and Woolworth rub together between them." Many of Brown's earlier essays use economics to discuss writing, while in *Readies for Bob Brown's Machine* he had compared the "stories" told by the Wall Street ticker tape to novels. Since he lived in both worlds, Brown had a natural interest in, and keenly felt, their relation.

For the republication of *1450-1950,* Brown made two additions to the final poem, a self-portrait. Above it he wrote, "I DON'T DIE/NO FLIES ON ME!," and below, "THESE POMES SHALL RISE AGAIN." Brown was indeed energetic throughout his life, but after a brief illness he died in 1959, just before his optical poems reappeared. Since that reappearance, Brown's work has again lapsed into obscurity and the marginal status of the cult object. Yet his writing deserves another resurrection, for it instances a more exuberant and refreshing side of modernism than that to which we have grown accustomed. In all their variety, Brown's works testify to his zestful approach both to writing and to life. As Kay Boyle wrote in the *Village Voice,* "that verve and wit and virility which make his writing—poetry or prose—move rapidly across the page never faltered, never grew old." But Jonathan Williams captured more of Brown's own spirit: *"Prosit!* Let there be Brown!"

References:

Contempo: A Review of Books and Personalities, special Brown issue, 2 (31 August 1932);

Hugh Ford, *Published in Paris: American and British Writers, Printers, and Publishers in Paris, 1920-1939* (New York: Macmillan, 1975), pp. 302-311;

Bernard Harden Porter, *Robert Carlton Brown (Bob Brown)* (N.p.: Privately printed, 1956).

Kenneth Burke

(5 May 1897-   )

W. Ross Winterowd
University of Southern California

BOOKS: *The White Oxen and Other Stories* (New York: A. & C. Boni, 1924);

Counter-Statement (New York: Harcourt, Brace, 1931);

Towards a Better Life (New York: Harcourt, Brace, 1932);

Permanence and Change: An Anatomy of Purpose (New York: New Republic, 1935; revised edition, Los Altos, Cal.: Hermes Publications, 1954);

Attitudes toward History, 2 volumes (New York: New Republic, 1937; revised edition, Los Altos, Cal.: Hermes Publications, 1959);

The Philosophy of Literary Form: Studies in Symbolic Action (Baton Rouge: Louisiana State University Press, 1941; revised and abridged edition, New York: Vintage, 1957);

A Grammar of Motives (New York: Prentice-Hall, 1945; London: Dobson, 1947);

A Rhetoric of Motives (New York: Prentice-Hall, 1950; London: Bailey Bros. & Swinfen, 1955);

Book of Moments: Poems 1915-1954 (Los Altos, Cal.: Hermes Publications, 1955);

The Rhetoric of Religion: Studies in Logology (Boston: Beacon Press, 1961);

Perspectives by Incongruity [and] *Terms for Order*, edited by Stanley Edgar Hyman, with the assistance of Barbara Karmiller (Bloomington: Indiana University Press, 1964);

Language as Symbolic Action: Essays on Life, Literature, and Method (Berkeley & Los Angeles: University of California Press, 1966);

Collected Poems 1915-1967 (Berkeley & Los Angeles: University of California Press, 1968);

The Complete White Oxen: Collected Short Fiction (Berkeley & Los Angeles: University of California Press, 1968);

Dramatism and Development (Barre, Mass.: Clark University Press, 1972);

Representing Kenneth Burke, edited by Hayden White and Margaret Brose (Baltimore & London: Johns Hopkins University Press, 1982).

Known as a literary theorist and critic, Kenneth Duva Burke has written one novel—*Towards*

Kenneth Burke, 1935 (courtesy of Malcolm Cowley)

a Better Life (1932)—and has published poetry throughout a career that has been always controversial, always fascinating. Now in his late eighties, Burke is still active and is gaining increased recognition, not only for his work with literature but also for his epistemology and interpretive methods. *Representing Kenneth Burke* (1982), a volume edited by historian Hayden White and Margaret Brose, is evidence of Burke's growing influence throughout the humanities and social sciences.

Burke says in the preface to *Collected Poems 1915-1967* (1968) that the poems in *Book of Moments* (1955) are in a roughly backward chronological order, starting with late poems, going on to "some survivals from the Thirties," and ending with early work; but, he adds, "it would certainly not be worth while trying to get them in their exact chronological order. . . ." The poems in "Book of Moments," the first section of *Collected Poems*, cover the years 1915-1954; the volume also contains "Introduction to What, Poems 1955-1967" and "In Conclusion," twenty-five pages of undated jeux d'esprit.

In many senses the poems are a chart of Burke's intellectual development and gain their interest largely from what they say about their author, who is one of the most versatile and fertile thinkers of the twentieth century. It is reasonable to divide Burke's career into three phases: his student and wander years (until 1931), the first period of his theoretical work (1931-1944), and the years after the appearance of *A Grammar of Motives* (1945), the first volume in his massive project to do nothing less than explain the human condition.

Kenneth Duva Burke was born in Philadelphia to James Leslie and Lillyan Duva Burke. Enormously learned, he was a college dropout, having attended Ohio State for one semester in 1916-1917 and leaving Columbia University after the 1917-1918 academic year to devote himself to writing. Perhaps the first lasting influence on Burke's thought and method was the French symbolist poets, and early in his career he published a Baudelairean prose poem in the Ohio State University literary magazine the *Sansculotte* while he was a student at that institution in 1916. In 1918 he was established in Greenwich Village among a group of writers and intellectuals that included, at one time or another, his lifelong friend Malcolm Cowley, Hart Crane, Allen Tate, and Gorham B. Munson.

In 1919 he married Lillian Mary Batterham, by whom he ultimately had three daughters. Two years later, the couple purchased a farm near Andover, New Jersey, that is still Burke's residence. Of this establishment, Richard Kostelanetz recently wrote:

> His property stretches behind his house through the trees as far up the hill as the eye can see; beyond our sight is a little house that his second wife had built for herself. The trees are the descendants of those he chopped down to heat his houses. . . .
>
> Further on down the road, now renovated and enlarged, is the house that K. B. purchased in 1921. "It wasn't like it is now," he told me. "We had two rooms then. There was newspaper on the walls, and when we walked into it for the first time, the man who was renting it was butchering a live chicken." A safe distance from each house are the little sheds that still function, in K. B.'s phrase, as "Garden of Eden Plumbing."

In 1924 *The White Oxen,* a collection of Burke's short fiction, was published, and from 1923 to 1931 Burke was associated with three magazines: *Broom, Secession* (of which he was coeditor in 1923), and the *Dial*. The *Dial* published much of Burke's criticism and the first six chapters of his novel, *Towards a Better Life*. From 1927 until the demise of the magazine in the crash of 1929, Burke was its music critic. During the *Dial* period, Burke was closely associated with Marianne Moore, who became acting editor in 1925, and with one of the magazine's founders, J. S. Watson, to whom Burke dedicated one of his critical books, *The Philosophy of Literary Form* (1941).

Much of the early poetry is modernist, with overtones of T. S. Eliot and Ezra Pound. In *Kenneth Burke* (1969) Armin Paul Frank says the speaker "can easily be recognized as a not so distant nephew of J. Alfred Prufrock . . . ," a connection apparent in the following lines:

> Passed through the tunnelled length of corridor,
> Mounted the shaft of squarely winding stairs.
> (With each new floor ascended he could peer
> Down the dark well upon his increased absence,
> While episodes of undistinguished sound
> Grew into words or footsteps, purposes
> Unseen, and after having been such, faded.)
> Slowly, he said, I rise above the street—
> Until he stood beneath the milky dawn
> Of an internal, sunless, angled sky,
> Stood there and waited, asking—should he knock.

And surely "Eroticon: As from the Greek Anthology" could be mistaken for one of Pound's works:

> Lamp, when there is a faint shuffling of sandals
>   outside my door,
> And the odor of unguents and perfumes
> Calls me like a blare of trumpets, so that I
> Arise hastily from my table . . . go out, lamp.
> For tonight I shall be laying aside my text
> To become the grammarian of sweet Amyctis' body.

The young Kenneth Burke could, however, be not only a Pound or an Eliot but also a romantic dithyrambist, as suggested in these lines from "Rhapsody Under the Autumn Moon":

Dewy, perplexing, wide-eyed moon,
Tonight I suddenly awoke, and felt you—and your
  poem.
Here in my bed I understood the pagan moon.
With your Gothic savagery laughing at my furniture,
I understood you.

From the standpoint of his place as a critic, theorist, and philosopher, Burke's career began in 1931 with the publication of *Counter-Statement,* in which he starts to develop his most important theories about literature and language.

In the early 1930s Burke divorced his first wife and on 18 December 1933 married her sister, Elizabeth Batterham, by whom he had two sons.

Between 1932 and 1944 he published his novel, *Towards a Better Life* (1932), as well as important theoretical books: *Permanence and Change* (1935), *Attitudes toward History* (1937), and *The Philosophy of Literary Form* (1941). Moreover, in 1943 he began teaching at Bennington College, a position that he held intermittently until 1961.

His career has been amazingly diverse. He has done editorial work for the New York Bureau of Social Hygiene (1928-1929); was a music critic for the *Nation* (1934-1935); and has held various academic posts at the New School for Social Research (1937), the University of Chicago (1938), Princeton (1949), Kenyon College (1950), Indiana University (1953, 1958), Drew University (1962-1964), and Pennsylvania State (1963), among others. In 1949 he was a fellow at the Princeton Institute for Advanced Study, and in 1957-1958 he was a fellow at the Institute for Advanced Study in the Behavioral Sciences.

By 1955, when the collected poems of 1915-1954 were published as *Book of Moments, A Grammar of Motives* (1945) and *A Rhetoric of Motives* (1950) had appeared, and Burke's major philosophical and critical work had reached its pinnacle.

During this middle period and after, Burke's poetry takes on a new cast. The poems can fairly be divided into three groups: humorous verse, oratorical verse, and philosophical poetry mirroring the concerns of his books.

The roistering "Alky, Me Love" is typical of Burke when he pulls the stops:

Spirit of Alcohol,
Bejeez,
One by one we have failed you.

Jack's liver, Tom's kidneys,
Bill's pump, Howard's bean
(they took him off in a wagon)—
Always there was something or other
Just couldn't stand it.
. . . .
Well, damn it all:
Down the hatch, old man . . .
Bottoms up, old girl . . .
Here's to you—

And the wit of "The Momentary, Migratory Symptom" is worthy of an Ogden Nash. The "doc" attempts to track the symptom down "with every verb and adjective and noun," but failing to find the cause, he gives Burke this advice:

"All through your life," he said, "You'll have this
  trouble"—
And charged me double.

"If you would live as long as people can
Then simply die a very ancient man.

"This much at least about your aches is true:
If they last long enough, then so will you."

Burke the oratorical poet is apparent in this excerpt from "Neo-Hippocratic Oath":

Wherever I go, I'll go asseverating for love of the art
and not to the end of malice or sheerly venereal
  appetite.
And if I come upon unsavory private matters
I'll keep them to myself
except insofar as I noise them abroad to everyone
as observations about everyone.

If I live by these rules
may I deservedly prosper.
But if I break the rules
may any good that comes to me
come undeserved.

Burke's philosophical poetry is problematic in that it usually presents the skeleton of ideas that he has "fleshed out" in his other writings; the poems may seem cryptic to readers who cannot place them in the context of the prose works. For example, Burke argues that language develops both scientifically (in terms of exactitude and strict logic) and dramatistically (as an imprecise instrument of the drama of human relations and actions).

Science abstracts, but dramatism generalizes. It is the dramatistic generalization that yields the notion of right and wrong, for only acts can be right or wrong in the ethical sense.

As Burke explains in *Language as Symbolic Action* (1966), if your approach is "scientistic," then you say that the negative began in the indicative mood, "X is not Y." If your approach is dramatistic, you begin from the imperative mood: "Do not do that." When you use the negative with regard to actions, it contains the seeds of the hortatory. And the hortatory, "Thou shalt not," is the source of guilt. With this outline, which overlooks all but the most obvious routes in the map of Burke's intellectual territory, it may be possible to begin to see how much he packs into his philosophical poems, or, to state the matter differently, how much of himself Burke expects his readers to bring with them to poems such as "Creation Myth," from which the following lines are drawn:

In the beginning, there was universal Nothing.
Then Nothing said No to itself and thereby begat
    Something,
Which called itself Yes.

Then No and Yes, cohabiting, begat Maybe.
Next all three, in a ménage à trois, begat Guilt.

In 1961 Burke published *The Rhetoric of Religion*, a study not directly of theology but of logology, words about words. The concluding section of this book is one of the author's most dazzling performances: "Epilogue: Prologue in Heaven," a dialogue between the Lord and his son Satan regarding the nature of free will. In this tour de force, Burke manages to deal with both a major theological question and with speech act theory.

For more than half a century Burke has been honored as a man of letters, thinker, and great dissenter. Among his awards are: *Dial* award for distinguished service to American letters, 1928; Guggenheim Fellowship, 1935; D.Litt., Bennington College, 1966; Rockefeller Foundation Grant, 1966-1967; Brandeis University Creative Arts Award, 1967.

With "Introduction to What, Poems 1955-1967," Burke has largely abandoned his essayistic style, though, in poems such as "Apostrophe on Being Happy," he has not lost his wit. He is happy, he says, that he did not get to know a certain lady very well, but was with her for only an hour or two and merely touched her hand as a formality.

Happy am I in this frustrate design
Which I must bear as my good-fortuned cross.
Happy am I that you were never mine,
To make me dread the terror of your loss.

Primarily, however, in the later poems we find a mellowing, a richly autumnal quality, a Kenneth Burke looking back on an eventful life and forward to days full of vigor and doing. In his *Towards a Better Life* Burke had said, "If we must have a slogan, let that slogan be the present. To move vigorously through chill water, and stretch like a snake in the sun—to do this actually, and to do the equivalent as regards the subtler pleasures of the mind—such is gratitude to Makers. . . . Surely no flower protests at withering in the autumn; even subsidence can be a purpose—and days of gentle ecstasy might bring us to welcome our decline."

Sometime around 1978 or 1979, Burke was sitting in the California sun with a group of students and faculty. It was March and still winter in New Jersey. He told of awakening late one night, certain that he was dying. He decided, however, he would not die in bed. So he arose, dressed, and went outdoors into a gentle snowstorm. He began to shovel snow, and the more he shoveled the better he felt. Finally he was ready to get back into the warmth of his bed. As he lay under the covers, he said to himself, "Well, I'm through dying—this time, anyway."

The predominant mood of "Introduction to What" (the poems of 1955-1967) might be summed up as "Ripeness is all." Not that the poems—constituting the penultimate section of *Collected Poems*—are monotonic; there is great variety here. In the verse, we find no more essays and no more diatribes, but in poems such as "Here and Now," we see Kenneth Burke celebrating days of gentle ecstasy and dealing, in his own inimitably wry way, with decline.

While with my cane in hand
I gaze across the sand
As though within my reach
Spreads all that frames this beach.

My eyes were given me
To watch this tumbling sea
And thus to exercise
Most grandly with the eyes.

Personally a gentle and convivial soul, Burke has always been uncompromising in his work, to the point, some think, of idiosyncrasy. This independence has been his glory and his curse, making

Kenneth Burke (photograph by Betty Rueckert)

him unique as a thinker and creative artist but making him also vulnerable to criticism. In all of his poetry, but particularly in the collection "Introduction to What," Burke asks readers to take him on his own terms. He is an honest and forthright poet, not only publishing poems that he considers flawed but explaining the nature of the flaw, as he does with "Staircase as Renewal": "(Let's admit it: I got into this one, in trying to sneak the word 'renewal' enigmatically into the penultimate line.)"

When *Collected Poems* appeared, the reception was mixed. In the *Library Journal* (August 1968), M. M. Miller said, "Apparently Kenneth Burke has never discarded a thought, a phrase, a line, or a poem. They are all here—296 pages of bad verse." And in *Poetry* (February 1969), Richard Howard paid homage to the whole Burke edifice, in which the poems stand only as "a broken pillar . . . and were it not for the great prose which stands behind them, one would not linger here." In the *Saturday Review* (22 June 1968), however, M. L. Rosenthal celebrated the poems: "The great K. B. is a poet, too! Did you know that? Those of us who, smugly, have known it rejoice to see [this book]. . . . Burke

is one poet of a thinker and one thinker of a poet." In *The Nation* (7 July 1969), Alexander Laing made sympathetic, if not enthusiastic, comments, and in the *New York Review of Books* (11 July 1968), Denis Donoghue spoke of Burke's gift for transforming the everyday into the magical: "Most of Burke's poems sound as if they were written by a Wandering Scholar, a wordman sleepless in a motel between late night and early morning. The corresponding themes include these: first and last things, dreams, insomnia, traffic, money, politics, contamination . . . and Progress, hated for its siren songs."

However, almost inadvertently the anonymous reviewer for the *Times Literary Supplement* (19 December 1968) rendered the most Burkean verdict on the poems of Kenneth Burke, calling them "amateurish because his criticism is professional. With decorous prose he has bought the privilege of being somewhat gamy in verse, as if to remind himself that he is still, in some degree, Bohemian." The reviewer goes on to comment on the variety in the poems and concludes with the judgment, particularly felicitous, that "On the evidence of his recent poems, he is still perky."

The comparison of Kenneth Burke with Robert Frost is inevitable, those two completely American, one-hundred percent individualistic writers who, in so many ways, are so much alike. Frost ended "Birches" thus:

> I'd like to go by climbing a birch tree,
> And climb black branches up a snow-white trunk
> *Toward* heaven, till the tree could bear no more,
> But dipped its top and set me down again.
> That would be good both going and coming back.
> One could do worse than be a swinger of birches.

With Burke, the themes are sometimes the same, but the voice is quite different:

> Almighty God, last night I damn near died.
> A dream last night near threw me off the track.
> Took me too near the other side.
> O let me hurry back.

Burke will probably not rank with Frost as one of America's greatest poets, yet we must be thankful that one of our greatest original thinkers has given us a body of poetry that we can enjoy and that allows us better to understand a person well worth knowing.

References:

Wayne C. Booth, *Critical Understanding: The Powers and Limits of Pluralism* (Chicago: University of Chicago Press, 1979);

Armin Paul Frank, *Kenneth Burke* (New York: Twayne, 1969);

Stanley Edgar Hyman, "Kenneth Burke and the Criticism of Action," in his *The Armed Vision: A Study in the Methods of Modern Literary Criticism* (New York: Knopf, 1948);

Richard Kostelanetz, "About Kenneth Burke: A Mind that Cannot Stop Exploding," *New York Times Book Review*, 15 March 1981, pp. 11, 24-26;

William H. Rueckert, *Critical Responses to Kenneth Burke: 1914-1966* (Minneapolis: University of Minnesota Press, 1969);

W. Ross Winterowd, "Dramatism in Themes and Poems," *College English*, 45 (October 1983): 581-588.

Skipwith Cannell

(22 December 1887-15 June 1957)

Milne Holton
University of Maryland

BOOKS: *Regional Shifts in the Postwar Traffic of Class I Railroads*, by Cannell and Julian Smith Duncan (Washington, D.C., 1946);
Postwar Earnings of Class I Railroads, by Cannell, Spurgeon Bell, and Leroy E. Peabody (Washington, D.C., 1946).

OTHER: Ezra Pound, ed., *Des Imagistes*, includes poems by Cannell (New York: A. & C. Boni, 1914; London: Poetry Bookshop, 1914);
Alfred Kreymborg, ed., *Others: An Anthology of New Verse*, volumes 1 and 2, includes poems by Cannell (New York: Knopf, 1916, 1917).

PERIODICAL PUBLICATIONS: "A Sequence," *Poetry*, 2 (August 1913): 171-172;

"Nocturne in Pastels," *Poetry*, 2 (August 1913): 172;

"Nocturne Triste," *Poetry*, 2 (August 1913): 173;

"Nocturnes I-V," *Poetry*, 2 (August 1913): 174-176;

"The Dance," *New Freewoman*, 1 (1 September 1913): 114;

"The Ship of Dead Dreams," *New Freewoman*, 1 (1 October 1913): 150;

"Love," *Smart Set*, 41 (October 1913): 140;

"A Moon Song," *Smart Set*, 42 (January 1914): 95;

Letter in "Correspondence," *Egoist*, 1 (February 1914): 78;

"Ikons," *Poetry*, 4 (May 1914): 50;

"The Blind Man," *Poetry*, 4 (May 1914): 50-51;

"Epilogue to the Crows," *Poetry*, 4 (May 1914): 51;

"The Dwarf Speaks," *Poetry*, 4 (May 1914): 51;

"Wild Swans," *Smart Set*, 43 (May 1914): 141;

"Nocturnes," *Glebe*, 1, no. 5 (1914): 36-37;

"Fragment from the 'Song of Creation,' " *Poetry Journal*, 2 (June 1914): 246-248;

"Monoliths," *Poetry*, 4 (September 1914): 207-210;

"The Silver Ship," *Little Review*, 1 (October 1914): 20;

"The Butterfly," *Little Review*, 1 (October 1914): 20;

"The Tidings," *Little Review*, 1 (October 1914): 21;

"Wild Songs," *Little Review*, 2 (April 1915): 6-7;

"Songs of Hunger," *Poetry*, 6 (June 1915): 127-129;

"To England," *Others*, 1 (August 1915): 27;

"The Coming of Night," *Others*, 1 (August 1915): 26-27;

"Ikons," *Others*, 2 (February 1916): 156-166;

"A Diptych," *Little Review*, 3 (June-July 1916): 17-19;

"On a London Tennis Court," *Others*, 3 (July 1916): 9.

Humberston Skipwith Cannell established himself as one of the more promising of the early imagists sponsored by Ezra Pound before World War I. But Cannell's life as a poet was one of great promise followed by many disappointments. Although he lived sixty-nine years and his poems began to appear in print when he was twenty-four, his career as a publishing poet lasted only three years. Cannell's literary work did not end when his last published poem appeared in 1917, however, although he disappeared from the literary world for forty years. When he died in 1957, he left behind him other remarkable documents: the submission manuscript of a long dramatic poem (a characteristically "proletarian" work of the 1930s which was entitled "By the Rivers of Babylon"), a number of later poems, and fragments and an outline of an unfinished and untitled religious poem based on the Old Testament story of David and Jonathan. Yet, in spite of the quality of much of this later work, it remains unpublished, and Skipwith Cannell's name is hardly known.

Humberston Skipwith Cannell, Jr., was born on 22 December 1887, in Philadelphia, the third child of Humberston Skipwith Cannell, a merchant of rather distinguished Southern lineage. The Cannells were from Maryland, a prominent name on the Eastern Shore around Chestertown since the eighteenth century. The Skipwiths were descended from the Skipwiths of Prestwould in Leicestershire, and from Sir William Skipwith (died 1610), who had been eulogized by Sir John Beaumont. The Royalist Skipwiths came to Virginia during the protectorate and were established at Prestwould House, an elegant seventeenth-century manor which still stands near Clarksville, in the Roanoke River Valley. Skipwith Cannell's mother, Susan Ridgway Cannell, was born to a prominent Philadelphia Quaker family which had originally come to America in the seventeenth century. Although she listed herself as an artist in the 1900 census, after her husband's death, which occurred around 1910, and her retiring to Cape May, New Jersey, she was described as a "Philadelphia *grande dame*" by her daughter-in-law. Raised in the family house on proper Locust Street, Cannell attended local schools and was prepared for college at the Gymnase Scientifique in Lausanne, Switzerland, and at Lehigh University, where he took two French courses in the fall term of 1905. In 1906 he entered the University of Virginia and studied there for three years. He majored in chemistry but did not complete work for his degree.

In 1911 or shortly before, Skipwith Cannell went to live in France. By 1912 he was to be found in Paris, living on a barge on the Seine, with an allowance of thirty dollars per month from his family. Cannell was allegedly preparing himself for a career as an "artist," and his allowance was to continue if he showed success within three years. What particular art remained unspecified, although a twenty-year-old New York girl named Kathleen Eaton, in Paris since 1910, where she was studying French at the Sorbonne and training as a dancer, spoke of Cannell's original ambition to be a "singer." Cannell would marry her in February of 1913.

In the spring of 1913 Cannell, who was by then writing rhymed romantic verse, made the acquaintance of John Gould Fletcher, a fellow University of Virginia alumnus, recently arrived in Paris with five books of poetry already published in London. Cannell declared himself a "revolutionary anarchist" to Fletcher but also expressed a wish to return to the mountains of Virginia, where he would live like an Indian on wild game. However, it was at the Closerie des Lilas with Fletcher one spring day that he encountered (through John Duncan Fergusson, a painter) an American poet named Ezra Pound, then visiting in Paris.

Fletcher soon returned to London, and the Cannells followed him in early June for a fortnight's visit. During their stay Cannell called at Pound's rooms in Kensington to renew the acquaintance. Robert Frost happened to be on hand (*A Boy's Will* had been published in London earlier that year), and he later told of Pound's welcoming his fellow Philadelphian, encouraging him in his effort to "show results" of his artistic studies to his family, setting him an exercise in the writing of an imagist poem, and offering to help place the result of the exercise. By mid-June Pound had contacted Harriet Monroe in Chicago and proposed a set of Cannell's poems for publication in *Poetry* magazine.

Almost immediately the Cannells took the room below Pound's, at 10 Church Walk in Kensington, and remained there for a month. They dined with Ford Madox Hueffer (later Ford Madox Ford), Pound's employer on the *English Review*, and met Yeats, F. S. Flint, May Sinclair, and even H. G. Wells. By the time the Cannells had returned to Paris, at the end of the season, Cannell's poems were scheduled to appear in Harriet Monroe's *Poetry* (for which Pound was foreign editor) and in the *Smart Set*.

In the August 1913 issue of *Poetry* were two poetic sequences and a pair of prose poems by Skipwith Cannell. Two of the lined poems reappeared, together with two new poems in the September and the October issues of the *New Freewoman*, a London radical feminist journal funded by Fletcher and increasingly dominated by Pound (in the September issue Cannell's name was given as "Skipworth"). A new poem appeared in the October 1913 *Smart Set*, and another was printed there in January 1914. Two more poems, both previously published, were translated into French by Guillaume Apollinaire for inclusion in his *Les Soirées de Paris* of June 1914. Skipwith Cannell's career as a poet had begun.

The first of the *Poetry* sequences, "Poems in Prose and Verse," gives evidence of Cannell's belief, apparent in his remark to Pound upon their first meeting in Paris (reported by Fletcher), that "the best *vers libre* is still that of the King James version of the English Bible." For Cannell's set of poems, which describe impressionistically a crucifixion, have about them an incantatory and biblical quality. The prose-poems which follow are an exercise in metaphor-making, and the final sequence, entitled "Nocturnes," is much in the vein of Edwardian Pre-Raphaelitism. Yet all three are richly imagined and capably executed, certainly highly promising as the work of a novice poet.

If the poems in *Poetry* launched Cannell's brief career, the appearance of his work in Pound's anthology, *Des Imagistes* established his reputation. As early as the summer of 1913 Pound had proposed to Alfred Kreymborg and Man Ray a collection of poets to be printed together as "Des Imagistes" at their press in New Jersey; Cannell's work was to be included. Man Ray and Kreymborg accepted "Des Imagists" as the first issue of their nascent little magazine, to be called the *Glebe*. But

there was a delay; it was not until February 1914 that *Des Imagistes*, containing Cannell's "Nocturnes" sequence, appeared, first as the fifth issue of the *Glebe*, and then published separately by Albert and Charles Boni in Greenwich Village.

Cannell seems to have had an instinct for self-publicizing controversy, for in the February 1914 issue of the *Egoist* (the successor to *New Freewoman*) he offered himself as an expert on the joys of female sexual experience and provoked irate controversy. In the same journal Richard Aldington (Hilda Doolittle's husband) objected to the inclusion of Cannell's "Nocturnes" sequence in *Des Imagistes* and alleged that Cannell was no imagist. It was certainly the case that Cannell's poems lacked the concreteness and the classical allusions of those by the Oxonian Aldington and his Bryn Mawr wife, H. D., a fact apparent as Cannell's new poems appeared in 1914. When later in the year Amy Lowell planned her own collection of imagist poets, *Some Imagist Poets* (1915) to compete with Pound's, Skipwith Cannell's work was not included, nor was he represented in her collections of 1916 and 1917.

Yet Pound's new poet was productive and accomplished, and his poems continued to appear in print throughout 1914. Three new poems and a vers libre sequence entitled "Ikons" were in the May issue of *Poetry*, and another poem, called "Wild Swans" (presumably the fruit of the exercise to which Pound had set him that day in Church Walk), appeared in the May *Smart Set*. There was also "Fragment from 'The Song of Creation'" in the June issue of Richard Hunt's New York based *Poetry Journal;* here was a vigorous song to be sung by Jehovah in Cannell's familiar Old Testament cadences. In *Poetry* again, in September, a new set of three poems by Cannell appeared under the title of "Monoliths," and in the same month's issue of Margaret Anderson's *Little Review* there were two prose poems and one poem in verse. The 1914 poems seemed to move out of the early imagist mode; now Cannell was more enigmatic, more symbolist, and considerably more mature and "modernist." A collection, also to be called "Monoliths," was expected from Elkin Mathews, a London bookseller and publisher, a friend of Pound, and the publisher of several of Pound's early collections.

But war was upon Europe, and many Americans were returning home. By the time the Cannells sailed on a late ship in the fall of 1914, they had bid their last good-byes to Guillaume Apollinaire, who by then was bearing a stretcher during the German advance on the Channel ports and would shortly serve in the French artillery and die of war wounds in 1918. Back in the United States Cannell was to see more of his new poems appear in the *Little Review* in April 1915—a set of three "Wild Songs" from the anticipated "Monoliths"— and in *Poetry* in June—"Songs of Hunger," now cadenced and rhymed and among the most accomplished of his short lyrics. The Cannells settled in New York, and in midsummer they made the acquaintance of Alfred Kreymborg, who had recently published the first issue of a new poetry journal called *Others*. As Kreymborg described him, "the . . . gentleman was a sepulchral roundhead with round glasses who looked and talked like a Buddhist monk and wore the exotic name, Skipwith Cannell." In August the second issue of *Others* included two of Cannell's poems. Now Cannell was beginning to strike out on his own. The *Others* poems, especially "The Coming of Night," were in contemporary settings, and the "Songs of Hunger," committed to more objective, more social concerns, were all rhymed, some rather Yeatsian, none imagist. As Kenneth Wiggins Porter, in an unpublished essay on Cannell, has said, "Songs of Hunger" could have appeared in the highly political *Masses* as well as in the more purely literary *Poetry*. Yet these poems retained their symbolical, enigmatic qualities. One of the more remarkable was "The Lean Gray Rats."

> The lean gray rats of hunger
> Have gnawed my heart in twain;
> Till cursing the God that made it,
> The good half died in pain.
>
> The ill half lived and prospered,
> Waxed brutal and strong and fat;
> But the good half died and was eaten
> In hell by a lean, gray rat.

By 1916—even as the new directions which marked this poem and others of the new poems seemed to be increasingly manifest—Cannell became more and more prominent among the new poets of Greenwich Village. He was now working for John Wanamaker, and along with William Carlos Williams he became a significant presence in *Others;* as Marianne Moore put it, "*Others* was Alfred Kreymborg and Skipwith Cannell, Wallace Stevens, and William Carlos Williams." Now Cannell was independent of Pound; apparently their relationship was to cool in 1916 and 1917. New interests and Amy Lowell's aggressive and well-funded presence turned Pound away from imagism and to a rather single-minded sponsorship of

T. S. Eliot as a major poet, and Cannell nursed some offense, real or imagined, which Pound had committed against him. Pound's former disciple figured prominently at a party given by Williams in the spring of 1916, when he tried to leap on the running board of an automobile and barely escaped serious injury. His poems continued to appear in *Others*, of course, in the February and July issues, and in the *Little Review* in July. A new work with an old title, "Ikons," a sequence of five self-revaluations in three free-verse strophes each, was featured in the first annual *Others* anthology for the year.

The new "Ikons," Cannell's longest poem to date, brought considerable attention. Certainly less finished than the 1915 lyrics, "Ikons" represented poetic intentions which were—much later—to take Cannell considerably beyond the lyric, in the direction of extended and reflective evaluations of his time and place. But "Ikons" would also be Cannell's last new poem to see print. "Monoliths," the first collection of poems which Cannell had announced a year before, had failed to materialize. In 1916 another was planned, to appear in a series to be published by John Marshall of The Little Bookshop Around the Corner.

Again nothing came of it: By the end of the year Kreymborg was off to Chicago; Cannell would serve as his stand-in as secretary to a prominent Democrat who was a leader in the Hungarian community in New York, and John Marshall assumed responsibility for *Others*. Cannell did not last long in the job; he had been fired, and the politician, fed up with poets, had filled the job with another person when Kreymborg returned in 1917. Now *Others* was not regularly published, and Cannell's poems did not appear in it for that year, although, in the annual *Others* anthology, three old poems— "The King," from *Poetry* (1914), "The Coming of Night," from *Others* (1915), and "Fragment from 'The Song of Creation,'" from the *Poetry Journal* (1914)—were included. Indeed, although there was still talk with Kreymborg about a book of Cannell's poems, and a manuscript collection was prepared with an eye toward this publication, no new Cannell poems appeared in print in 1917. Skipwith Cannell, apparently already estranged from Kitty Cannell, volunteered for military service and was inducted into the army on 20 April. He then embarked upon what was to be an entirely new life.

Cannell's first military duties . . . supposedly because of his background in French and his chemistry major at Virginia—were as a cook to German prisoners. He was in France by May 1917, and there

At William Carlos Williams's Others *group party, 1916: (front) Alanston Hartpence, Alfred Kreymborg, William Carlos Williams, Skipwith Cannell; (back) Jean Crotti, Marcel Duchamp, Walter Arensberg, Man Ray, R. A. Sanborn, Maxwell Bodenheim*

he was assigned to military intelligence (in its "police," according to Cornell alumni records) and rose to the rank of sergeant.

Kitty Cannell had hardly secluded herself in grief during his absence. She had had ambitions for a theatrical career as a dancer as early as 1915, when Skipwith had attempted to encourage Kreymborg to establish The Others Playhouse. Late in 1916 she had appeared with John Reed and William Zorach in the Playwrights Theater's production of *The Game*. By early 1918 Kitty Cannell, performing under the stage name of "Rihani," was presenting her modernist "Static Dances" in various Village clubs and ultimately in The Other Players production (The Other Players were an offshoot of the Provincetown Players) of three plays by Alfred Kreymborg. Kitty remained very much a part of the *Others* crowd; she was often seen in the company of Julian Freedman, an impecunious composer from Vienna.

In Paris in 1918 Skipwith Cannell met Marie Juliette Del Grange, a French bookkeeper at the Dunlop Tire Company. She was the daughter of a Parisian seamstress and a cello player at the Opera Comique, and before long the soldier and the bookkeeper were deeply involved. Before his return to the States in early 1919 Cannell presented Juliette with an engagement ring and promised to come back to her in France. Skip and Kitty Cannell had obviously grown apart; they were separated upon his return to the United States.

Discharged from the army on 17 March 1919, Skipwith Cannell settled for a time on East 29th Street in Manhattan, then went off to Ithaca, New York, where in April he enrolled at Cornell as a special student in agriculture and took a course in beekeeping. Cannell's manuscript of prewar poems was now lost; (much later it would fall into Kitty's hands, but by then she did not know where to find him). Skipwith was, presumably, embittered by the war and by what he perceived to be the disloyalties of Pound, Kitty, and the *Others* crowd. He left poetry behind him and anticipated a bucolic future with his Juliette. At the conclusion of his beekeeping course he returned to France and Juliette Del Grange, and, joined by her brother Emil, the three settled in Menton, on the Mediterranean at the Italian border, as beekeepers.

Kitty Cannell also returned to France in 1919 but hers were quite different circumstances. After a brief flirtation with Robert McAlmon in 1921, she obtained a divorce from Cannell in 1921, became the mistress of Harold Loeb, with whom she shared adjoining apartments in Paris, and worked on his magazine, *Broom*. She was seen in the company of Malcolm Cowley, Flossie Williams, and other expatriate literati in 1923 and 1924, and in 1924 she and Loeb met Ernest Hemingway and earned immortality as Frances Clyne and Robert Cohn in *The Sun Also Rises* (1926). Kitty Cannell published her own short stories in *transition* and in the *Americans Abroad* anthology of 1932. She was a friend of Pauline Pfeiffer, Hemingway's second wife and the Paris *Vogue* correspondent, and between 1931 and 1941 Kitty Cannell herself served as fashion correspondent for the *New York Times*. She remained in Paris during World War II and covered German press conferences there for the *Times*, until she was exchanged by the Nazis and returned to the United States in 1944. Then she settled in Boston, wrote a book of childhood reminiscences (*Jam Yesterday*, 1945), became dance critic for the *Christian Science Monitor*, and taught a course in "Books and Authors" at the Cambridge Center for Adult Education. Upon her death in 1974 her papers were installed at Harvard's Widener Library.

Skipwith Cannell was living in Digne with Juliette and Emil Del Grange and the bees in 1921 when the divorce was granted. He married Juliette, and their first child, May Jeanne, was born in May of that year. They moved to Laragne (also in Haute Provence) in 1922 and in 1923 sold the bees and undertook a new venture in the resort town of Beaulieu near Menton, where the couple sold candy and cheeses in a small shop above which they lived.

The new venture was none too successful, and Juliette Cannell was again pregnant, so in 1924 they removed to Paris and thence to Cherbourg, where they set sail for New York on 21 February 1925. They proceeded to Cape May, New Jersey, where Cannell's widowed and wealthy mother had retired and his married sister lived, owned, and operated the Stockton Villa, a fashionable resort hotel. Their second child, Sarah, was born in Cape May on 23 March 1925. In August the Cannells set out for Florida (Skip's mother often passed her winters there) and settled in Coconut Grove. Now times were hard for Skip Cannell, who offered few useful skills. He took work of a menial nature—first as an

automobile parking lot watchman—and he and his family endured the devastations of a serious hurricane. Soon he was selling real estate in Coconut Grove and in Coral Gables, but again he was not successful, and in 1927 he returned with his family to Cape May. Now they had been reduced to the position of family dependents. Cannell taught bridge and Juliette Cannell gave French lessons at the Stockton Villa for the season, but when the hotel closed for the winter, the family returned south, this time to St. Petersburg, where Cannell became a salesman for Singer sewing machines.

Cannell continued this occupation for more than two years. The Great Depression was upon them. The family lived in a succession of boardinghouses and rented rooms, and often Cannell was forced to accept clothes made upon his sewing machines as payment for them. In 1931 the Cannells were again in Cape May, again supported by the generosity of Cannell's mother. Cannell was once more employed by Singer during his mother's final illness. Cannell lost his inheritance in the stock market almost immediately upon receiving it in 1932, and in that year the family removed to Philadelphia.

Needless to say, there was no poetry. Skipwith Cannell's own daughter, May, had no awareness of her father writing until the mid-1930s. William Carlos Williams had kept in touch with Cannell until 1925, and had been aware of his return to the United States, but no one else seemed to know of his whereabouts. Cannell's name was included in a "Supplementary List of Poets" in John Manly and Edith Rickert's *Contemporary American Literature* of 1929, but in 1930 Richard Aldington (who had had a change of heart) was unable to include poems by Cannell in his *Imagist Anthology* because he could not make contact with him. To the literary world, as William Carlos Williams would describe it in his *Autobiography* (1951), Skipwith Cannell, talented and significantly published early imagist poet who seemed in 1916 to have brought his lyric talent well beyond the mere fashion of imagism, was truly *disparu*.

But if Cannell was no longer a practicing poet, there were other intellectual commitments. There had been within him radical impulses even before World War I, and the hard years in Florida and the bitterness of the Depression had left their mark. Like many Americans, by the 1930s Cannell had developed a social conscience. He was committed to various proletarian causes, not the least of which was the organization of the Pennsylvania contingent of the Bonus Expeditionary Force, the largest of the state "bonus armies" which camped in Washington in June and July of 1932. Cannell was one of the leaders of the Pennsylvania group; he visited encampments and assisted with arrangements in the Philadelphia area. And his commitment to the cause of the working man would not fade in later years. It would become the dominant theme of his next poetry.

In late 1932 Cannell went to Washington, first to receive medical treatment at Walter Reed Hospital, later to seek work in the government. His search was not spectacularly successful at first; his first position was as a messenger. But he soon found a bureaucratic position in the Department of Agriculture, later in the Interstate Commerce Commission, where he was employed as an economist and statistician. Cannell was quite successful in his career in government, and he established his family in a comfortable house in the District of Columbia, near Silver Spring, Maryland.

By 1935 Cannell's poetic ambitions were rekindled. He began to undertake a study of the Old Testament as preparation for the writing of an extended poem, and before long he was writing again. In the summer of 1937 he was ready with a group of poems. Using the pseudonym of David Ruth, he sent them to his old friend, William Carlos Williams.

Williams, who made a point of always answering his mail, responded to his unrecognized correspondent with care and tact; he admired some of the love lyrics but was put off by biblical analogies. Cannell replied with a defense and to his correspondent revealed his identity. As the correspondence continued, the friendship was warmly renewed. By 18 November of the next year a "long poem" had arrived at 9 Ridge Road in Rutherford, and by the next day Williams had read it, marked it, and was ready to recommend publication. Cannell revised and placed the manuscript in Williams's hands on 14 February 1939.

The manuscript entitled "By the Rivers of Babylon" and still bearing the pseudonym of David Ruth, was unlike anything Cannell had previously written. "By the Rivers of Babylon" is most distinctly 1930s poetry—socially oriented rather than subjective, leftist, polemic in intent, and rough-hewn rather than finely turned. Yet, for all its vigor, its language is abstract and rhetorical, its diction of a kind long since put aside by Williams, its allegorical and allusive procedures of a kind long disdained.

"By the Rivers of Babylon" inveighs against the corruption, injustice, and economic inequality in "Babylon," a modern American city. Its poet-protagonist "tunes his lyre" and, like his Old Testament predecessor of Psalm 137, finds himself in a decayed and corrupted land. In six parts the poem combines polemical attacks on capitalism and predictions of its demise with Old Testament allegories—perhaps the most notable being an incident in which Sampsonoff, a worker machine-gunned by company finks in a strike, manages as his dying act to overturn a cement truck on his tormentors and save his comrades. Then there are accounts of a corrupt senator and his victim-prostitute, a bittersweet love sequence (which may be autobiographical), and a conclusion centering around a bank failure in a small American town named Bethlehem and coinciding with the death by cardiac arrest of John J. Mammon, capitalist. In the last narrative section there is set forth a faintly autobiographical narrative, describing the career of one Moses Wyefield, a labor organizer of aristocratic origins, his beating at the hands of company goons, his plans for a John Brown-like raid on Mammon's arsenal, his capture and commitment to a psychiatric hospital. In a conclusion the poet, David Ruth, looks out upon the landscape before him and imagines how, once the river is crossed, the hill before him can be a Hill of Zion, the city a New Jerusalem.

In late April of 1939 Williams journeyed south to visit Cannell and his family, Ezra Pound (who was then on his self-appointed mission to Washington to set things straight in American diplomacy and economics), and the Dorsey Hydes (old friends of Cannell and Pound from 1913 Kensington). Out of this meeting emerged Williams's commitment to undertake an introduction to "By the Rivers of Babylon." The introduction, which was carefully revised through four quite different drafts, seems an important document, for in it Williams set forth ideas concerning the long poem which would apply not only to "By the Rivers of Babylon" but to his own forthcoming *Paterson*.

But Williams's introduction would not see print until 1977, and Cannell's "By the Rivers of Babylon" remains unpublished. For, although Williams arranged with Coley Taylor's Gotham House for publication, and a typescript of poem and introduction were duly submitted and marked up, Gotham House failed before the book was published. Cannell's subsequent efforts to find a publisher, one as late as 1940, all failed, and today the poem languishes in typescript in the Skipwith Cannell Papers at the Library of Congress.

Again disappointed, Cannell turned away

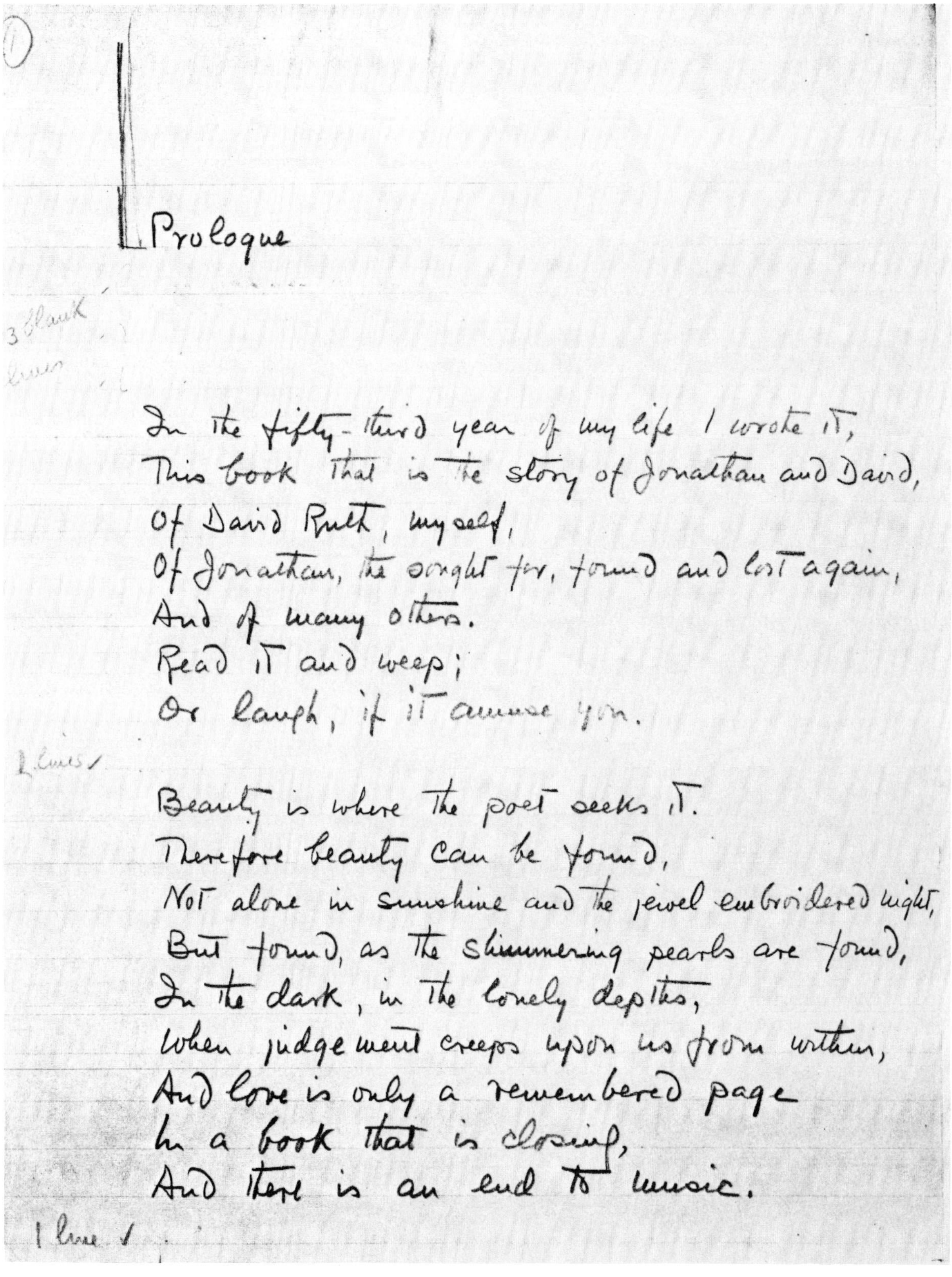

Prologue

3 blank
lines

In the fifty-third year of my life I wrote it,
This book that is the story of Jonathan and David,
Of David Ruth, myself,
Of Jonathan, the sought for, found and lost again,
And of many others.
Read it and weep;
Or laugh, if it amuse you.

2 lines

Beauty is where the poet seeks it.
Therefore beauty can be found,
Not alone in sunshine and the jewel embroidered night,
But found, as the shimmering pearls are found,
In the dark, in the lonely depths,
When judgement creeps upon us from within,
And love is only a remembered page
In a book that is closing,
And there is an end to music.

1 line

Pages from a draft for "By the Rivers of Babylon" (by permission of Dr. John Cannell, courtesy of the Library of Congress)

(2).

Do not be astonished that my verse is harsh,
Halting and maimed,
For it treats
Of monstrous things and sad,
Of broken things within a broken world.
It moves,
Not as the bright breasted swan that moves
Rythmic, among ~~bright~~ lillies,
But rather as the graceless loon that darts,
Hungry and intent, among the scattering fish,
Or flings herself in arrowed flight,
Purposeful and swift, upon her small occasions,
Or, wailing, drifts beneath a hostile moon.

2 lines /
         /

from his poetry and his marriage. He had met a young woman from Idaho, Catherine Pettigrew, at a labor meeting in 1939. She had served as typist for "By the Rivers of Babylon," and by 1940 she and Cannell were in love. After his marriage with Juliette was dissolved, Skip and Catherine Pettigrew were married in 1941. They remained in Washington, where Skipwith Cannell continued to pursue a successful career in the federal bureaucracy.

As a statistician, H. Skipwith Cannell was the author of "A Method of Multiple Correlation," a much-used statistical study, and in 1946 he coauthored two government studies—*Regional Shifts in the Postwar Traffic of Class I Railroads* (with Julian Smith Duncan) and *Postwar Earnings of Class I Railroads* (with Spurgeon Bell and Leroy E. Peabody)—but in the 1940s he wrote no poetry. There were five children by his third marriage—David Skipwith Cannell in 1943, Mary Catherine in 1944, Michael John in 1945, John Jacob in 1948, and Susan Ann in 1950. The family moved to Jessup, Maryland, in 1947 (where Cannell was hospitalized for a time) and in 1950 to Annapolis.

For Cannell the 1950s were marked by illness. He contracted cancer and in 1956 retired from government service. In that year, the dying bureaucrat undertook a final effort in the realization of his ambitions as a poet. He made an unsuccessful attempt to trace the whereabouts of the manuscript of his first collection, left behind with an acquaintance upon his induction into the army in 1917. And he undertook a third book-length poem, this no longer pseudonymously authored by the socially aware David Ruth, but now by the pious Jonathan Small (the Old Testament was with Cannell until the end). It seems to have been intended as a religious work. Shortly before his death, Cannell described it as "a pilgrimage in search of a shrine" and as "a Requiem High Mass composed by a bad Quaker." And he went on to say, "It may be better than either [of his other works], if I can finish it—or at least, leave it in some publishable form." But he did not even settle on a title. Only an outline and a single finished section, entitled "The House on the Hill," remain in his papers. Skipwith Cannell died on 15 June 1957 at Fort Howard Veterans' Hospital in Maryland. He is buried in Virginia in Arlington Cemetery.

Also among his papers is another poem,

prophetically entitled "Arlington," and certainly written with the end in view. "Arlington" can be read as Cannell's epitaph for himself. It concludes,

> But let these trees bear witness how
> Your manhood might have stood,
> Tall, strong and green, the years endowed
> With more than marble monuments.

Skipwith Cannell, a poet of capability and varied talents, a dark presence in many of the literary celebrations of the first half of his century, reflects light on the writers and writing of his time. A poet whose almost totally unpublished writing is shaped by the sensibilities of three different decades, the imagist experiments of the second decade of the twentieth century, the disillusion and radicalism of the 1930s, and the spirituality and conservatism of the 1950s, Cannell was a child of his time. Caught as he was in the crosscurrents of its conflicted values and loyalties, he was its victim as well.

References:
Stanley K. Coffman, Jr., *Imagism: A Chapter for the History of Modern Poetry* (New York: Octagon Books, 1972), pp. 15, 17, 18;

John Gould Fletcher, *Life is My Song* (New York: Farrar & Rinehart, 1937);

Milne Holton, "Prolegomenon to *Paterson:* William Carlos Williams's Introduction to *By the Rivers of Babylon,*" PROOF 5 (1977): 147-170;

Alfred Kreymborg, *Troubadour* (New York: Sagamore Press, 1957);

Marianne Moore, *A Marianne Moore Reader* (New York: Viking, 1961), p. 269;

Charles Norman, *Ezra Pound*, revised edition (New York: Minerva, 1969);

Ezra Pound, *Selected Letters, 1907-1941* (New York: New Directions, 1971), pp. 21, 37, 64, 88, 124;

Noel Stock, *The Life of Ezra Pound* (New York: Pantheon Books, 1970), pp. 136, 138;

William Carlos Williams, *The Autobiography of William Carlos Williams* (New York: New Directions, 1951).

Papers:
The papers of H. Skipwith Cannell, including the manuscript for "By the Rivers of Babylon," are on deposit at the Library of Congress. The papers of Kathleen Eaton Cannell are at the Widener Library of Harvard University.

Robert P. Tristram Coffin

(18 March 1892-20 January 1955)

Berkley Peabody

BOOKS: *Christchurch* (New York: Seltzer, 1924);

Book of Crowns and Cottages (New Haven: Yale University Press, 1925);

Dew and Bronze (New York: A. & C. Boni, 1927);

Golden Falcon (New York: Macmillan, 1929; London: Macmillan, 1929);

An Attic Room (Garden City: Doubleday, Doran, 1929);

Laud, Storm Center of Stuart England (New York: Brentano's, 1930);

The Dukes of Buckingham, Playboys of the Stuart World (New York: Brentano's, 1931);

Portrait of an American (New York: Macmillan, 1931; London: Macmillan, 1931);

The Yoke of Thunder (New York: Macmillan, 1932; London: Macmillan, 1932);

Ballads of Square-toed Americans (New York: Macmillan, 1933);

Lost Paradise, A Boyhood on a Maine Coast Farm (New York: Macmillan, 1934);

Strange Holiness (New York: Macmillan, 1935; London: Macmillan, 1935);

Red Sky in the Morning (New York: Macmillan, 1935);

John Dawn (New York: Macmillan, 1936);

Kennebec, Cradle of Americans (New York & Toronto: Farrar & Rinehart, 1937);

Saltwater Farm (New York: Macmillan, 1937; London: Hutchinson, 1937);

Maine Ballads (New York: Macmillan, 1938; London: Macmillan, 1938);

New Poetry of New England: Frost and Robinson (Baltimore: Johns Hopkins Press, 1938);

Collected Poems of Robert P. Tristram Coffin (New York: Macmillan, 1939; London: Macmillan, 1939);

Captain Abby and Captain John; An Around-the-world Biography (New York: Macmillan, 1939);

Thomas-Thomas-Ancil-Thomas (New York: Macmillan, 1941);

Christmas in Maine (Garden City: Doubleday, Doran, 1941);

Book of Uncles (New York: Macmillan, 1942);

The Substance That Is Poetry (New York: Macmillan, 1942);

Robert P. Tristram Coffin

There Will Be Bread and Love (New York: Macmillan, 1942);

Primer for America (New York: Macmillan, 1943);

Mainstays of Maine (New York: Macmillan, 1944);

Poems for a Son with Wings (New York: Macmillan, 1945);

People Behave like Ballads (New York: Macmillan, 1946);

Yankee Coast (New York: Macmillan, 1947);

Collected Poems of Robert P. Tristram Coffin, New and Enlarged Edition (New York: Macmillan, 1948);

One-horse Farm: Down-East Georgics (New York: Macmillan, 1949);

The Third Hunger, & The Poem Aloud (Denton: Texas State College for Women, 1949);

Coast Calendar (Indianapolis: Bobbs-Merrill, 1949);

Maine Doings (Indianapolis: Bobbs-Merrill, 1950);

Apples by Ocean (New York: Macmillan, 1950);

On the Green Carpet (Indianapolis: Bobbs-Merrill, 1951);

Life in America: New England (Grand Rapids: Fideler, 1951);

Sir Isaac Coffin, bart., 1759-1839: Admiral and Prophet (New York: Newcomen Society in America, 1951);

Hellas Revisited (Athens: Icaros, 1954);

Selected Poems (New York: Macmillan, 1955).

OTHER: *A Book of Seventeenth-century Prose*, selected and edited by Coffin and Witherspoon (New York: Harcourt, Brace, 1929);

Seventeenth-century Prose and Poetry, selected and edited by Coffin and Witherspoon (New York: Harcourt, Brace, 1946).

In 1955, when Robert P. Tristram Coffin was stricken in the chapel at Westbrook Junior College, he was one of America's busiest, most loved, and most successful poets. The Pulitzer Prize winner had just returned from a week at Macalester College to his regular teaching at Bowdoin College in Maine; but typically he was spending that particular evening giving a public lecture in nearby Portland. That the *New York Times* had printed his poem "The Wisdom of Forgetting Mortal Things" three days before was only an ironic coincidence, because Coffin had had at least one work accepted for publication every month since Bowdoin had given him a doctor of letters degree in 1930. His *Selected Poems* (1955) was well into production with the Macmillan Company, which had already published nearly thirty volumes of his works; and the same issue of the *New York Times* that gave his death front-page notice told elsewhere that at the forty-fifth annual dinner of the Poetry Society of America, which he had been too busy to attend, Coffin had been awarded a Borestone Mountain Award. In its editorial the following day, the *Times* said, it "must not be thought that Mr. Coffin was a local rustic bard."

Robert Peter Coffin was born across College Street from Bowdoin College in Brunswick, Maine. His mother, Alice Mary Coombs Coffin, was the second wife of James William Coffin, a Civil War veteran and jack-of-all-trades, who raised two families, and who, when he died in 1908, left a skill and a house of some kind to each of the ten children in his second brood. Although Coffin's early years were spent on island farms far to the south

of town, he was sent to school in Brunswick in the seventh grade and, according to his father's plan, entered Bowdoin in 1911, where he was Alfred Kinsey's roommate. He made Phi Beta Kappa as a junior, graduated summa cum laude in 1915, took his master's degree in English at Princeton on a graduate scholarship in 1916, and went on as a Rhodes Scholar to Trinity College, Oxford. His years there were interrupted by service as an American artillery officer in World War I and by his wedding back home to Ruth Neal Phillip on 22 June 1918. He returned to Oxford, however, and was awarded a B.A. in 1920 and, with Robert Bridges and Walter Raleigh as examiners, a B.Litt. in 1921. He joined the faculty of Wells College in upstate New York the same year, introduced Oxford's teaching style to that school, and was named to an endowed chair there in 1928. After a sabbatical spent in Oxford, he became chairman of Wells's English department. By the time Bowdoin gave him an honorary doctorate at his fifteenth reunion in 1930, he had published seven books. In 1934 he moved back to Bowdoin as Pierce Professor of English and, in 1955, was at the peak of a distinguished academic career, when suddenly he died.

Coffin's father had marked him to be the family's man of letters. Brunswick's vast Carpenter-Gothic First Parish Church, where Harriet Beecher Stowe once had her vision of Uncle Tom's death, also marked him. The same year his father died, the sixteen-year-old Coffin made a pilgrimage to the dying Sarah Orne Jewett in South Berwick, who predicted that he would be a great poet. Coffin unquestioningly accepted this aegis, assuming as his own poetic mark a family name, Tristram. As Robert P. Tristram Coffin he was to become the covenanted epic voice of Puritan America.

All Coffin's work—verse, essays, fiction, criticism, history, biography, lectures, drawings—is of one piece. Everything he wrote—and there is probably as much material unpublished, or at least uncollected, as is available between hard covers—celebrates life from the biblical creation to apocalypse, catching, preserving, and displaying the glorious and infinitely recurring epiphanies of the living God. Coffin's voice, even at its most personal, is always a public voice revealing God to his people.

Coffin honored the divine gift of epic song in his account of "Caedmon," which with other tales from the religious background of his New England ancestors appeared in *Christchurch* (1924). In *Dew and Bronze* (1927), however, heroic poems such as "Crecy" and "Dawn at Ashdown" are mixed with

Maine poems such as "Cranberryhorn School" and "Snoozer." The great Puritan sacrifice is a feast of celebration and thanksgiving, and, like a chef in the kitchen, Coffin said of *Dew and Bronze,* "I put in one part Maine country and my boyhood and another part English countryside where I lived for three years."

A scholastic syllogism in the title poem of *Golden Falcon* (1929) sums up Coffin's understanding of his poetic role and illuminates the significance he found in his heroic name, Tristram: "Living things are lovely things,/And lovely things must die." The couplet, now on his gravestone in the Cranberryhorn Cemetery, closes this book: "I have kept the ancient law,/I have written what I saw." These are the words of a covenanted New England Puritan.

Coffin certainly wrote what he saw, but his Puritan eyes looked over the Kantian half-glasses of a secular literary tradition that stretched from Homer to Thomas Hardy and Robert Frost. "Rura Cano," which opens *The Yoke of Thunder* (1932), may suggest a turning away from the European scene (though adopting, as he does, the language and pose of a Roman elegiac poet), and Coffin did say he owed a great deal to Robert Frost for opening his eyes to the poetry in common speech, people, and usual sights; but Wordsworth, Horace, Aristophanes, and the gamut of European literature inform his work. Like Milton, Coffin was a learned, authoritative, and consummate assimilator, enriching his own work with refractions of the past. Yet he was not a classicist, nor a romantic. If, on occasion, he called himself a romantic, he was only separating himself from a new literary formalism that was being hailed as classicism at the time. His true role was that of the traditional epic poet who gives living voice to the past in the context of the immediate present.

Ballads of Square-toed Americans (1933) established Coffin's choice of the Border Ballad as his own narrative verse form. In this book he also presented his father as his Beowulf and his own family and people as his Vergilian Trojans driven by fate. He took a panoramic look at America from "John Brown" to the "Mormons" and "Henry Hudson"; but in his long, earlier 1932 Harvard Commencement Phi Beta Kappa poem, "Prologue: the Strange Children," he had already settled squarely on his own people as the chosen people of the new creation, a new nobility in homespun.

Coffin's biography of his father, *Portrait of an American* (1931), had won him an honorary life membership in the National Arts Club, but the chauvinist vigor of his vision seems not to have found much favor at Harvard, which had embarked on a more international course.

In 1934 Bowdoin called Coffin home. He was named Outstanding Poet of the Nation at the Ninth Annual Poetry Week observances at the RCA Building in New York in 1935 and given a gold medal. When *Strange Holiness* (1935) won the Pulitzer Prize for poetry in 1936, Robert Frost spoke for him at the presentation ceremonies. Typically, all but four of the sixty-one poems in that collection had already appeared in various periodicals; and, also typically, such a poem as "The Haters," seemingly about raspberries in a cellar hole, is informed by the medieval epic theme of *Gawain and the Green Knight.*

Coffin was awarded the Golden Rose of the New England Poetry Society that same year, but the local coloring of his next collection, *Saltwater Farm* (1937), is cleverly deceptive, for it masks the skill for mixing diverse ingredients that he learned from Horace and John Donne. Coffin also mastered their art of selecting instances as tokens of universals, and he developed Maine as a microcosm of the universal macrocosm. As he told the Catholic Poetry Society of America, speaking to them in the Starlight Room of the Waldorf Astoria in 1937, "When I began to write poetry, I had the mistaken idea that a poet must always be on the mountain top. Only in maturity did I learn to come down upon the plain and chose for my poems the simple subjects of everyday." Percy Hutchinson said of *Saltwater Farm,* "Seldom will one run across lines so indigenous to a locale as these, yet so universal in human significance."

At Johns Hopkins University Coffin said in the Percy Turnbull Memorial Lectures, *New Poetry of New England: Frost and Robinson* (1938), that older American poets were orators of truth, prophets; Frost and Robinson looked at things in a new way. Coffin's own way, however, was very New England and very old. Although William Rose Benét called him "our most pictorial poet," Coffin was not an impressionist, or a describer of things, so much as he was a descrier of God's presence. In this respect his style was medieval; and, because of its antiquity, his way of displaying meaning, rather than stating it, is, ironically, perhaps his most provincial characteristic. His is the pristine, epic, sparkling, pied voice of divine epiphany; but Coffin never confused epiphany, a Puritan concern, with appearances, which are at best genteel.

Coffin's University of Maine commencement address in 1937 found "Maine—a State of Grace";

but, because he proclaimed the virtue of maintaining independence by one's own foresight and thrift, he unexpectedly found himself hailed as a Republican poet in a country swept by the New Deal. Unfortunately, the few Republicans with whom he was thrown were largely people concerned with genteel appearances, people with whom he had little in common. Coffin found increasingly that "a poet works by himself. He keeps no good hours. He knows loneliness and he comes to believe in it. He comes to believe in himself most of all."

Coffin's Puritanism had little to do with self-denial or sin and everything to do with truth, honesty, and direct, naked dealing, like Blake's Job, with God. Political parties and intellectual postures were not important; it was the degree to which individuals face God directly that distinguished people for Coffin. It is these people, those who do and those who do not, that inhabit the world of his *Maine Ballads* (1938).

Coffin's preface to his *Collected Poems* (1939) hailed the old unified vision of the Elizabethan poet who thought and felt in whole designs. Writing in *The Substance That Is Poetry* (1942), he again emphasized the importance of the permanent and the universal as well as the central role of the poet's selectivity in displaying them. Coffin had no use for esoteric logics or for idioms having nothing in common with the reader; nor did he respect the difficulties of modern verse. His concern for simple, direct public communication was as much a feature of his traditional-epic calling as it was of the Platonic transcendentalism of his thought.

Mary M. Colum in her *New York Times* review of *There Will Be Bread and Love* (1942) recognized in Coffin the "breath of the divine afflatus that gives him the rare power of revelation. . . . More than anyone except de la Mare, Coffin can touch people and things with mystery and strangeness." She sensed, too, his orphic vitalizing capacity: "his animals are always alive."

Coffin knew well what Homer had done for ancient Greece. He believed the poet to be the best teacher, and he championed American education when he shared the podium with Fiorello La Guardia at the dedication of the Hunter College tower on Park Avenue in the fall of 1940. He gave over his sabbatical at the start of World War II to visiting and teaching at Indiana University, where his old roommate, Alfred Kinsey, was also teaching.

In Indiana Coffin was excited to find himself at the heartland of America, with different people, yet with people who were still his people, people who thought as he did. A surge of patriotism

poured out in his *Primer for America* (1943), in which he presented the "first lessons in the first principles of being American; the primary stages of the American myth."

These primary stages included Coffin's faith in the liberating power of intellectually independent education and in his undialectic belief that every son must rise above his father, a belief that found ironic expression in *Poems for a Son with Wings* (1945), where Coffin, in Miltonic fashion, mixed Hermes with the cherubim as his older son flew away to war.

Coffin's family survived World War II intact, and his joy spilled over in his mythically titled *People Behave like Ballads* (1946). Some of these poems are hauntingly poignant, but others roar with a hearty humor that runs back through Mark Twain and a thousand Yankee yarn tellers to Chaucer's "Miller's Tale" and beyond. This fierce Olympian laughter belongs to those who speak directly with the gods and who observe those who do not. This open, uncompromising American laughter, which the genteel sometimes think in bad taste, resounds through Coffin's work.

After his wife's death in 1947, Coffin took time out to prepare the enlarged edition of his *Collected Poems* (1948) with its elegiac close. His work showed increasing attention to large cosmic patterns, as in the Vergilian *One-horse Farm: Down-East Georgics* (1949), which explores the cycle of the year, and his beautifully illustrated *Coast Calendar* (1949), which is informed by Edmund Spenser's *The Shepheardes Calender* (1579).

Coffin's physical speaking voice gave his verse magical and immediate impact. Literary critics such as Robert Hillyer faulted the prosody of *Apples by Ocean* (1950) and elsewhere; but, as tens of thousands who listened spellbound to his readings could attest, Coffin's verse is highly dramatic and varied: epic, not sweet; and it is always supple. Coffin is not primarily a lyric poet. He does not maintain a lyric cry like his friend and neighbor, Edna St. Vincent Millay. His verse shifts modes constantly from comment to statement, from refrain to opinion, from dialogue to aside, from reflection to keening and lament; and it makes these shifts with the dramatic clarity and deliberate skill of a Shakespeare. The formal irregularities that critics noted mark these dynamic shifts in his poems. Read aloud properly, Coffin's verse is always smooth; and its aural contours cue a host of semantic dimensions unrealized in silent perusal. When his poems are heard, a rich, epic polyphony emerges without need for explication and with compelling clarity.

A page, with Coffin's illustration, from the 1949 book in which the poet explores the seasonal cycle much in the manner of Edmund Spenser's The Shepheardes Calender *(1579)*

America's postwar role as a low-profile world superpower was alien to the patriotic Puritan poet. As he said in *Yankee Coast* (1947), "Maine never has put much stock in those un-American, imported, European, fighting, hateful words—capital and labor." But the tradition of intellectually independent American education was not, he believed, immune from politicization. Coffin worked harder and spent more and more time lecturing off campus. He inaugurated a poetry chair at the University of Cincinnati in 1951. He had finished his unpublished epic, "VIP," when he left for a sabbatical in Greece in 1953. He brought home a slender book of verse, *Hellas Revisited* (1954), for his friends, but Bowdoin, under a new administration,

was unsympathetic to Coffin's vision of America. When Coffin died suddenly, the Coffin room in the college union was soon dismantled. The Pierce chair was filled by someone with different tastes. Macmillan, which held copyrights on most of his works, did little more than see through the production of *Selected Poems* (1955), those poems his countless audiences had most often asked him to read. The rest was sudden silence.

Robert Frost had said of Coffin, "He may, in time to come, since he will probably outlive me, stand a head taller than I in the world of poetry." Good New England friends that they were, the two men were quite different. If there is a list to which Coffin belongs, it would read something like this:

Charles Ives, Frank Lloyd Wright, William Faulkner, Thomas Hart Benton, and perhaps a lyric poet whom Coffin did not appreciate but should have,

E. E. Cummings—all first-rate and wildly American.

S. Foster Damon
(22 February 1893-25 December 1971)

Alice Hall Petry
Rhode Island School of Design

BOOKS: *William Blake: His Philosophy and Symbols* (Boston & New York: Houghton Mifflin, 1924; London: Constable, 1924);

A Note on the Discovery of a New Page of Poetry in William Blake's Milton (Boston: Club of Odd Volumes, 1925);

Astrolabe: Infinitudes and Hypocrisies (New York & London: Harper, 1927);

Tilted Moons (New York & London: Harper, 1929);

Thomas Holley Chivers, Friend of Poe (New York & London: Harper, 1930);

The Day After Christmas (New York: A. & C. Boni, 1930);

Some American References to Blake Before 1863 (N.p., 1930);

Amy Lowell, a Chronicle (Boston & New York: Houghton Mifflin, 1935);

The History of Square Dancing (Barre, Mass.: Barre Gazette, 1957);

Yankee Doodle (Meriden, Conn.: Privately printed, 1959);

Nightmare Cemetery, A Hallowe'en Frolic, as Samuel Nomad (Providence: Privately printed, 1964);

A Blake Dictionary: The Ideas and Symbols of William Blake (Providence: Brown University Press, 1965; London: Thames & Hudson, 1973);

The Fig Tree: A Fragment (Newport, R.I.: Third & Elm Press, 1966);

Elegy for Abigail (Providence, R.I.: Hellcoal Press, 1969);

The Moulton Tragedy: A Heroic Poem with Lyrics (Boston: Gambit, 1970);

Selected Poems of S. Foster Damon, edited by Donald E. Stanford (Omaha: University of Nebraska at Omaha, 1974);

Heaven & Hell, edited by Catherine Brown (Providence: Copper Beech Press, 1978).

S. Foster Damon

OTHER: *Eight Harvard Poets*, includes poems by Damon (New York: Gomme, 1917);

Oluf Friis, ed., *A Book of Danish Verse*, translated by Damon & Robert Hillyer (New York: American-Scandinavian Foundation, 1922; London: Oxford University Press, 1922);

Eight More Harvard Poets, edited by Damon and

Hillyer (New York: Brentano's, 1923);
"S. Foster Damon (1893-1971): Selections from His
Personal Journal," edited by Catherine
Brown, *Books at Brown*, 28 (1981): 1-57.

Myriad-minded: to those who knew S. Foster
Damon as a friend and colleague, that felicitous
Coleridgean adjective best describes a man whose
kaleidoscopic talents and interests—William Blake,
cooking, Punch and Judy, fencing, book collecting,
square dancing, the occult—made him one of the
most remarkable individuals in academe for half a
century. But if any one pursuit may be singled out
as most illustrative of the man and his mind, it
would probably be his writing poetry. By the end
of the 1920s, Damon had so established himself
with two slim volumes of verse that he was widely
regarded as one of the most promising young poets
in the United States. Although his poetic reputation
diminished somewhat after 1930, he continued to
write, and in 1964 he produced, under the pseudonym Samuel Nomad, what Malcolm Cowley has
aptly termed Damon's epitaph: *Nightmare Cemetery,*
a remarkable sonnet sequence which continues to
be admired by Damonites and which may yet enjoy
the critical attention it deserves.

Samuel Foster Damon's poetic talents were
not immediately apparent in his youth. The son of
Joseph Neal and Sarah Wolf Pastorius Damon, he
was born into comfortable circumstances in Newton, Massachusetts, and received an orthodox late-
Victorian upbringing to which his voluminous journals bear eloquent and moving testimony. He was
educated in local schools and at the public library,
and in 1910 he matriculated at Harvard, where he
majored in music. At about this time—"My developments were always late"—he composed his first
poem to fulfill an assignment in English class.
Then, inspired by the example of his friend and
classmate E. E. Cummings, Damon in late 1913
began "to write poetry furiously" and continued to
do so virtually until his death. These early efforts
in verse were published in the *Harvard Monthly* and
the *Harvard Advocate* beginning in 1915 (Damon
had graduated cum laude with a B.A. degree in
1914), and he so distinguished himself as a writer
in the Cambridge community that his poems were
included in the anthology *Eight Harvard Poets*
(1917), along with poems by Cummings, John Dos
Passos, and Robert Silliman Hillyer. Having made
a postgraduation tour of Europe with his older sister, and then having been twice rejected by the
armed forces, Damon spent the years of World War
I diffusing his literary talents and energy—an un-

*S. Foster Damon and E. E. Cummings during their Harvard
years (Moses Photo Studio, Boston)*

fortunate tendency which would become most apparent in a scholarly career that included, for
example, five years dedicated to a critical biography
of the minor poet Thomas Holley Chivers. From
May to August 1917 Damon was a bayonet instructor with the Harvard ROTC; from July to September 1918 he taught French to soldiers stationed in
Boston; and from October to May 1919 he "polished gadgets" in an airplane factory in New York.

In 1918 Damon and Cowley perpetrated the
hoax of Earl Roppel, "the plowboy poet of Tioga
County," whose crude verses were intended to further the cause of modernism in poetry. They sent
the poems to Witter Bynner, Amy Lowell, and Conrad Aiken—who all responded, with varying degrees of enthusiasm, and did not detect the hoax.
This predilection for literary hoaxes, games, and
personae was also apparent in Damon's composition of *Kiri nō Meijiyama*, published in the *Dial* in
February 1920 and identified by Arthur Waley as
an authentic Japanese Nō drama of the sixteenth
century, as well as in the creation of the pseudon-

ymous *Nightmare Cemetery;* and it serves as an unexpected counterpoint to Damon's distinguished career as a meticulous and authoritative scholar, editor, and library curator.

At about the time of the Nō drama hoax, Damon became a traveling fellow of the American-Scandinavian Foundation, and spent a year in Copenhagen with Hillyer translating the poems in *A Book of Danish Verse* (1922). While in Denmark, he also worked on a Persephone trilogy. Portions began to appear in poetry magazines at that time, but it was not published in book form until it appeared in *Heaven & Hell* in 1978. Having returned to Harvard for graduate work (1921-1927), Damon began publishing poems in such journals as the *Bookman, Harper's,* the *Nation,* and *Poetry,* and by 1927, when he received his M.A., his poetic canon and reputation had grown to the point where he was able to publish his first book of verse, *Astrolabe: Infinitudes and Hypocrisies. Astrolabe* was warmly received, not only because three years earlier its young author had established himself as the world's foremost Blakean with *William Blake: His Philosophy and Symbols,* but also because the little volume is an unusually fine first effort. As might be expected, it echoes (and anticipates) a variety of poets. Blake permeates "Bridge" ("I turn my eyes away—and stare/Astounded at the curious tactics/Of certain angels high in air"). The remarkable "Dusk: N.Y.C.," a lament for faith usurped by commercialism, is reminiscent of both T. S. Eliot's *The Waste Land* (1922) and Hart Crane's poem "To Brooklyn Bridge"; and a notable number of the poems, including "Conversation" and "Mechanical Devices," clearly show the influence of Stephen Crane's poetry. *Astrolabe* also established the various themes, motifs, and techniques which would preoccupy Damon for his entire writing career. "Epitaph on an Invalid" and "Atlantic Garden" show his interest in the warping or blurring of time. "Dialogue," in which a firefly mistakes a rose for the moon, demonstrates Damon's fondness for manipulating perspective. "Last Supper: Jesus to Judas" reveals his tendency to assume personae (in this case, Jesus) and to present biblical incidents in verse. "A House" reflects his passion for the macabre, and "Epitaph on a Poem" anticipates by forty years *Nightmare Cemetery*'s concern with the writing process. The *Saturday Review* termed *Astrolabe* "fitfully brilliant, glittering with individuality," as indeed it is; and the New York *Bookman* spoke for many in calling it "exceedingly promising." Harvard was less impressed: despite Damon's success with *William Blake* and *Astrolabe,* he was not granted a doc-

torate, and he was brought to Brown University to teach in the fall of 1927 by his cousin, Lindsay Todd Damon. In the following year, on 29 April, he married Louise Wheelwright of Boston.

Damon's second volume of poetry, *Tilted Moons* (1929), is a curiously lackluster performance compared to *Astrolabe.* There are a few bright moments: "Insomnia" presents an intriguing blurring of birth, sleep, and death; and Damon shows his characteristic interest in narcissism (as in "Passion") and in dramatic renderings of biblical incidents ("Magdalene Festival"). But generally speaking the little book is so full of platitudes about flowers and lovers that it is difficult not to concur with the appraisal of the critic for the *Wheeling Register* that *Tilted Moons* would "be enjoyed by many readers who like a sugary volume, full of prettiness." Its oddly Victorian air, which led the *New York World* to describe Damon as "the contemporary Tennyson," makes it a far less mature work than *Astrolabe.*

It would be thirty-five more years before Damon would publish his next volume of verse, *Nightmare Cemetery* (1964); but in the meantime he was active in literary circles. In 1932 he was awarded the Golden Rose of the New England Poetry Society, and in 1934 he was elected a fellow of the American Academy of Arts and Sciences. Having been appointed curator of the Harris Collection of American Poetry and Plays at Brown in 1929, he enlarged the manuscript holdings tremendously while simultaneously demonstrating his love of American poetry, drama, and folksongs; and as offshoots of his career as a poet/scholar, he prepared critical biographies of Thomas Holley Chivers (1930) and Amy Lowell (1935). Damon's book on Lowell is still the most definitive study of her life and work. Its insights are a tribute to his scholarly abilities, but they also owe much to the deep and genuine friendship he shared with Lowell. He was a frequent guest at her Brookline estate, Sevenels, and was devastated by her unexpected death in 1925.

All the while, fragments of his longer efforts at versification appeared in poetry journals; but too often these fragments are more impressive than the finished works. For example, *The Moulton Tragedy* (1970), written over the course of forty years and completed in the summer of 1967, is an overly long (250 pages) and surprisingly dry narrative dealing with Jonathan Moulton (1726-1787), the "Yankee Faust." The story had exceptional potential: Damon always was fascinated by the occult, and the idea of a New Hampshireman's bargain with the devil—a theme handled so memorably by

S. Foster Damon

Stephen Vincent Benét—provided an ideal opportunity for him to indulge his interest in New England folklore, character, and values. The topic also gave Damon the chance to engage in technical experimentation, a tendency quite evident in *Astrolabe;* and in fact *The Moulton Tragedy* consists of a remarkable variety of soliloquies, narratives, elegies, and dramatic scenes interspersed with prose passages and occasionally enlivened by dialect and rhythm reminiscent of Oliver Wendell Holmes's "The Deacon's Masterpiece." But despite the story's intrinsic interest and the technical variety displayed, *The Moulton Tragedy* does not materialize; Moulton himself is surprisingly wooden for a central character; the portions of the book dealing with his family members and neighbors contribute little to the atmosphere, plot, and setting; the background material about the American Revolution is so intrusive that the book's focus is seriously blurred; and those "eerie moments" which Cowley praises are rare indeed. There are memorable fragments, including "Nancy Moulton and John Mar-

ston" and "Prologue," but generally speaking *The Moulton Tragedy* is not one of Damon's better efforts.

The same may be said of his Persephone trilogy. Damon had worked on this long verse drama (80 pages) while living in Denmark, and portions of it had begun to appear in periodicals as early as the 1920s; but it was not until 1978 that it was published (along with a fragment of "Christ in Hell") under the rather misleading Blakean title of *Heaven & Hell.* The trilogy—"Persephone in Eden," "Persephone in Hell," and "Persephone in Eternity"—is a curious amalgam of Blakean symbolism and Jungian motifs; and Damon's editor and literary executor, Catherine Brown, is probably correct in perceiving it as a sort of allegory of sexual initiation. In several respects this verse drama is typically Damonesque. One finds the narcissism motif so characteristic of his poetry in the 1920s, and the assignment of speaking parts to flowers perhaps reflects his interest in writing from unusual perspectives; but it also is typical inasmuch as it reveals Damon's incapacity for presenting a series of poems in a single volume as an emotionally, intellectually, and technically satisfying unit. The happy exception to this is his masterpiece, *Nightmare Cemetery, A Hallowe'en Frolic.*

The physical appearance of *Nightmare Cemetery* signals its special place in Damon's poetic canon: a small book (ninety pearl-gray pages) in paper covers, it was handprinted and illustrated with woodcuts by Ilse Buchert at the Rhode Island School of Design in a limited edition of 200 copies. It is characteristic of Damon's sense of irony that this most personal of his books appeared under a pseudonym, Samuel Nomad; but it is likewise characteristic of his love of literary games that the surname is an anagram of Damon, and that Samuel is his first name. It is unclear whether he sincerely expected readers to decipher the code. True, the poem entitled "The Frost will Fill it in" mentions "the clumsy letters of my name reversed," but it is doubtful how many potential reviewers bothered to read that far into the volume (page ten): one can well imagine their being cooled either by the note facing the verso of the title page ("All the characters in this book/are entirely imaginary/including the Author") or by the "Prelude," so clearly written within the outmoded tradition of the Graveyard School. A quick glance at the book, in other words, would suggest that it was either the work of an amateur given to "poetic" Gothic poses, or some sort of elaborate joke. The volume was ignored, and in 1966 Damon wrote Cowley a "mildly querulous" letter which lamented the dearth of notice accorded the dozens of review copies he had diligently sent out. Even so, the book did gain acceptance among Damonites, and with good reason. Technically speaking, the book is a stunning achievement. It consists of approximately seventy poems, each of them a sonnet—the one verse form which, thirty-five years earlier, Theodore Spencer in the *New Republic* had singled out as ideal for Damon because the "strictness sharpen[s] his thought and its expression," and which reveals itself amenable to extraordinary complexity and flexibility in Damon's capable hands. In keeping with his lifelong interest in the occult, the conscious and subconscious, and the extent to which the body and spirit are separate, Damon investigates in *Nightmare Cemetery* whether it is feasible—or, for that matter, desirable—to be immortalized in one's work. The volume is transparently an attempt to communicate with the living after Damon/Nomad's death, for he notes that the "Dear Reader" is "the non-existent purpose of my verse . . . and yet its Final Cause." But the volume is far less ghoulish than one might expect: thanks to Damon's wit and imagination, there is just enough self-deprecation and literary burlesque to render the book simultaneously sobering and exhilarating, thought provoking and entertaining. The "Prelude" is a case in point: it is a seriocomic parody of the romantic poses and motifs of the Graveyard School, wherein bats ("foul mosquitos") search for a new grave to have "their feast of dead blood." The focus shifts to "a youth alone,/cloaked and with harp half-strung" who sees in the grave "his own dead face, which also happens to be mine"; and upon this note of narcissism and blurred personae, Damon/Nomad begins the sonnet sequence itself, each poem dealing with some facet of his demise, the likelihood of his verse surviving him, and the problems of a postmortem literary reputation—not only for Damon, but also for other writers and even for such fictional characters as Pandarus, Troilus, and Cressida. In a typically Damonesque blurring of time and space, he points out to his reader: "I look to the future; you to the past," and yet both share "the present"—the words on the pages of *Nightmare Cemetery*. Although the reader may be a bit startled to find the poet speak directly to him from beyond the grave, as it were, he feels neither fear nor pity nor melancholy. Damon's powerful personality and imagination are responsible for this, as he looks forward to being reunited with his beloved dog Sambo, who died in 1949 ("Sambo Psychopompos"); he wonders how people will react to the news

of his demise ("No Buddy Knows de Trubble"); and he even entertains the possibility that a nuclear holocaust might annihilate all future readers, an event to be blamed not on the bomb itself, but on the mind that created it—that "bone-bubble blown upon the human spine/by Nature some half-million years ago" (*Thy* Hand, Great Anarch . . ."). Damon/Nomad's conclusion, in the aptly titled "Inconclusive Epilogue," is that it is impossible to know if one will be immortalized in one's work; quite simply, the creation of *Nightmare Cemetery* had served as what he terms his "catharsis." If indeed the book is a game, a "Hallowe'en Frolic," it is so only in the sense that religious meditations upon "last things" were games to Donne and his contemporaries. The writing of *Nightmare Cemetery* was intellectually, emotionally, and spiritually cleansing for Damon, and in the final analysis it is rather touching to find him wishing a comparable "good, healthy, Aristotelian purge" for the reader who has accompanied him through his "frolic."

S. Foster Damon was seventy-one years old when *Nightmare Cemetery* appeared; within seven years he was dead, the highlights of his last years having been Brown's awarding him an honorary Litt.D. and giving him a two-day birthday celebration in 1968. He will always be remembered as a Blake scholar; but whether his poetry (and in particular *Nightmare Cemetery*) attains the critical recognition it so clearly deserves remains to be seen.

Bibliography:

Ernest D. Costa and Elizabeth C. Wescott, "S. Foster Damon: A Bibliography," in *William Blake: Essays for S. Foster Damon*, edited by Alvin Rosenfeld (Providence: Brown University Press, 1969), pp. xxix-xlvi.

References:

Malcolm Cowley, "The New England Voice," in his —*And I Worked at the Writer's Trade* (New York: Viking, 1978), pp. 35-50;

Laurence Goldstein, "Damon's Poetic Testament," *Michigan Quarterly Review*, 16 (Summer 1977): 323-329;

Alvin Rosenfeld, "Samuel Nomad, *Nightmare Cemetery*," *Books at Brown*, 21 (1966): 207-210;

Donald E. Stanford, Introduction to *Selected Poems of S. Foster Damon*, edited by Stanford (Omaha: University of Nebraska at Omaha, 1974);

Barton Levi St. Armand, "S. Foster Damon: Demonologist," *Michigan Quarterly Review,* 16 (Summer 1977): 308-314.

Papers:
The major depository of Damon's manuscript material is at the John Hay Library, Brown University.

Donald Davidson
(18 August 1893-25 April 1968)

Robert W. Hill
Kennesaw College

BOOKS: *An Outland Piper* (Boston & New York: Houghton Mifflin, 1924);

The Tall Men (Boston & New York: Houghton Mifflin, 1927);

The Attack on Leviathan: Regionalism and Nationalism in the United States (Chapel Hill: University of North Carolina Press, 1938);

Lee in the Mountains and Other Poems, Including The Tall Men (Boston: Houghton Mifflin, 1938);

American Composition and Rhetoric (New York: Scribners, 1939); revised edition, by Davidson and Ivar Lou Myhr (New York: Scribners, 1953);

The Tennessee, volume 1: The Old River, Frontier to Secession, The Rivers of America Series (New York: Rinehart, 1946);

The Tennessee, volume 2: The New River, Civil War to TVA, The Rivers of America Series (New York: Rinehart, 1948);

Why the Modern South Has a Great Literature (Nashville: Vanderbilt University Press, 1951);

Singin' Billy, libretto by Davidson, music by Charles F. Bryan (N.p, 1952);

Twenty Lessons in Reading and Writing Prose (New York: Scribners, 1955);

Still Rebels, Still Yankees and Other Essays (Baton Rouge: Louisiana State University Press, 1957);

Southern Writers in the Modern World, Lamar Memorial Lecture (Athens: University of Georgia Press, 1958);

The Long Street: Poems (Nashville: Vanderbilt University Press, 1961);

The Spyglass: Views and Reviews, 1924-1930, edited by John Tyree Fain (Nashville: Vanderbilt University Press, 1963);

Poems: 1922-1961 (Minneapolis: University of Minnesota Press, 1966).

OTHER: *Fugitives: An Anthology of Verse,* edited by Davidson (New York: Harcourt, Brace, 1928);

"A Mirror for Artists," in *I'll Take My Stand: The South and the Agrarian Tradition, by Twelve*

Southerners (New York & London: Harper, 1930);

"That This Nation May Endure—The Need for Political Regionalism," in *Who Owns America?—A New Declaration of Independence,* edited by Herbert Agar and Allen Tate (Boston & New York: Houghton Mifflin, 1936);

British Poetry of the Eighteen-Nineties, edited by Davidson (Garden City: Doubleday, Doran, 1937);

Readings for Composition from Prose Models, edited by Davidson and Sidney Erwin Glenn (New York: Scribners, 1942; revised, 1957);

Selected Essays and Other Writings of John Donald Wade, edited by Davidson (Athens: University of Georgia Press, 1966);

Voltmeier, or The Mountain Men, volume 1 of *The Writings of William Gilmore Simms,* introduction and notes by Davidson and Mary C. Simms Oliphant (Columbia: University of South Carolina Press, 1969).

Best known for his membership in the group of Fugitive poets, who gathered in Nashville during the 1920s, Donald Grady Davidson was born in Campbellsville, Tennessee, to William Bluford and Elma Wells Davidson in 1893. In 1909, graduated from Branham and Hughes School in Spring Hill, Tennessee, Davidson entered Vanderbilt University, with which he was to remain intimately identified for most of his life. Unfortunately, in 1910, inadequate finances forced his withdrawal after only one year in attendance, and he taught in small town schools until he could return in 1914 to Vanderbilt, where he attended classes taught by Edwin Mims, John Crowe Ransom, and Walter Clyde Curry. While a student, he also taught at Wallace University School and attended summer school for two summers at George Peabody College. He had not quite finished his course work when he entered officer's candidate school at Fort Oglethorpe, Georgia, in 1917, but he was granted his A.B. degree in absentia from Vanderbilt that same year. After he was commissioned a second lieutenant in August, he reported to the 81st Infantry Division at Camp Jackson in Columbia, South Carolina.

In June 1918 Davidson married Theresa Sherrer of Oberlin, Ohio, and in August he sailed for Europe, where, as a first lieutenant, he saw combat in Vosges, Meuse-Argonne, and elsewhere in France. Davidson's daughter, May Theresa, was born in March 1919, and in June he was able to leave the Continent, later to be discharged at Camp Sherman, Ohio. In September 1919 he began

teaching at Kentucky Wesleyan College in Owensboro as head of the English department.

After his re-entry into Vanderbilt University in 1914, Davidson had quickly formed friendships with William Yandell Elliott and Stanley Johnson, Nashvilleans who led Davidson into discussions and meetings with the Jewish intellectual and mystic Sidney Mttron Hirsch, at whose father's apartment Davidson, Elliott, Johnson, John Crowe Ransom, and Alec Stevenson gathered. Barely twenty-one years of age, he was at first timid about engaging in the erudite, indeed esoteric, disquisitions of Hirsch and his disputatious guests. In 1919, when he returned, the Nashville discussion group—which by then consisted of Ransom, Hirsch, Walter Clyde Curry, William Frierson, and others, meeting at the home of Hirsch's brother-in-law, James M. Frank—had turned to literary discussions. In June 1920, when Davidson took summer work with the *Evening Tennessean,* he began attending meetings regularly, and he continued to attend after taking an instructor's job at Vanderbilt that same year and starting work on his M.A., which he received in 1922.

Soon their debates grew into formulations, and they came to speak of themselves as the Fugitives, eventually publishing a poetry magazine called the *Fugitive* (April 1922-December 1925), whose credo was concisely delivered by John Crowe Ransom in the first issue: "*The Fugitive* flees from nothing faster than from the high-caste Brahmins of the Old South." It is commonly thought that the Fugitives strongly resisted the tenets of modern poetry, when in fact they sought to understand and to apply the best of the modernist principles; they were particularly intrigued by, if not entirely approving of, the poetry of T. S. Eliot.

Later many of these same thinkers exercised themselves in matters of politics or social criticism, particularly in espousing programs to get Americans back on small farms. As Edmund Wilson observed in the *New Republic* (27 July 1931), "Cousin Charles' feeling about the depression is that it serves the 'industrialists' right." The impulse of the Agrarians, as they came to be known after they entered the realm of economic theory, was mostly moral, in that they felt that America's founding fathers, particularly Jefferson, had counted on the virtues of the subsistence farm to promote economic stability and personal integrity. In particular, the Agrarians urged a renewed dedication to the concept of regionalism in the face of national policies and widespread attitudes which they saw as a threat both to individualism and to national

A Fugitive reunion, 1956: (first row) Allen Tate, John Crowe Ransom, Donald Davidson; (second row) Milton Starr, Alec Stevenson, Robert Penn Warren; (third row) William Y. Elliott, Merrill Moore, Jesse Wills, Sidney Mttron Hirsch (courtesy of Joint University Libraries, Nashville)

stability. Unfortunately, for the credibility of the Agrarians, much of what they said was published in magazines that also published neofascist materials, and the Tennesseans were sometimes tarred with the same brush.

In 1924 Davidson became an assistant professor at Vanderbilt and book-page editor for the *Nashville Tennessean.* His first volume of poetry, *An Outland Piper,* appeared in the same year, and the *Fugitive* expired in December 1925. By 1928 Davidson's book page had begun to appear in the *Memphis Commercial-Appeal* and the *Knoxville Journal,* and *Fugitives: An Anthology of Verse,* which he edited, was published. Following the appearance of his second book of poetry, *The Tall Men* (1927), he was promoted to associate professor. In 1930 his essay "A Mirror for Artists" was published in *I'll Take My Stand,* and he gave up his book-page editorship. Beginning in 1931 he taught during summers at Bread Loaf in Middlebury, Vermont (now far be-

yond having to sell wall maps in Alabama, as he had done in the summer of 1921).

Because of a disruptive fire at Wesley Hall in February 1932, Davidson spent a year on leave at Marshallville, Georgia, at the home of John Donald Wade—influential teacher, editor, author of *John Wesley* (1930), and founder in 1947 of the *Georgia Review.* In 1936 Davidson wrote "That This Nation May Endure—The Need for Political Regionalism" for *Who Owns America?—A New Declaration of Independence,* edited by Herbert Agar and Allen Tate; and in 1937, the year he was promoted to full professor, he edited *British Poetry of the Eighteen-Nineties.*

Two more books were published in 1938, *Lee in the Mountains and Other Poems, Including The Tall Men* and *The Attack on Leviathan: Regionalism and Nationalism in the United States. American Composition and Rhetoric* appeared in 1939, with *Readings for Composition from Prose Models* in 1942. The first volume of his monumental study of the Tennessee

River came out in 1946; the second, in 1948.

In 1952 Davidson collaborated as librettist with Charles F. Bryan in writing and rather successfully staging the opera *Singin' Billy*, and in 1955 he returned to his early interest in writing pedagogy with *Twenty Lessons in Reading and Writing Prose*, and he served as state chairman for the Tennessee Federation for Constitutional Government. The largest collection of Davidson's essays is *Still Rebels, Still Yankees and Other Essays* (1957), in which the whole spectrum of Davidson's ideology is spread. With specific attention given to the Fugitives, Faulkner, John Gould Fletcher, Thomas Wolfe, Jesse Stuart, Elizabeth Spencer, Madison Jones, and Walter Sullivan, *Southern Writers in the Modern World* (1958) reiterates the tone and message that Davidson firmly established decades earlier. In 1961 another volume of poetry, *The Long Street*, appeared, and in 1963 John Tyree Fain edited a collection of Davidson's book reviews and essays, *The Spyglass: Views and Reviews, 1924-1930;* in 1966 *Poems: 1922-1961* presented the final verse of Davidson's long and distinguished career, and in 1974 Fain and Thomas Daniel Young's edition of *The Literary Correspondence of Donald Davidson and Allen Tate* set a personal and distinctive seal upon one of the most significant group endeavors in Southern literature.

Davidson's first book of poems, *An Outland Piper* (1924), is not a great treasure waiting to be discovered by a contemporary critic with hitherto unknown powers of percipience and appreciation. Many commentators find *An Outland Piper* simply embarrassing. The book does, however, have considerable charm. The poems are obviously influenced by William Blake, at least in their simple desire to clarify lyric impressions. The meters and diction are familiar even if Blake's passionate vision is not in evidence. "I heard strange pipes when I was young,/Piping songs of an outland tongue" is an opening very like Blake's in "Introduction" to *Songs of Innocence* ("Piping down the valleys wild,/ Piping songs of pleasant glee"), but some of the distinctive pathos of Davidson's early poetry is in the melancholy distance between the speakers of the poems and the possible enactment, or fulfillment, of their visions. In his most romantic lyrics Davidson often sees himself as one who views the romantic figure from some distance, either in time or space: "Roofs clapped, and windows blazed to see/That alien piper, so like me." Other poems, often cited for their kinship with visionary romantic poetry, deal with a lady and a tiger in a deep wood; in one poem at least, they are explicitly in society

with the Natural Deity. One of Davidson's several mystic seekers who has become "weary of toiling" pursues the "long-lost Queen of the Faëries" until she is found in a house in the woods, where she "smiled down from the window/And opened the casement bars." When she "the latchstring lifted,"

> There were the lovely three,—
> God, and the Queen, and the Tiger,
> And God's hand welcomed me.
> The Tiger slept on the hearthstone.
> The Faëry gave me her ring.
> My rose began to blossom;
> My lute began to sing.

Davidson himself was obviously aware of the dangers of such flimsy romanticism, however gracefully and charmingly it is set forth. In "A Dead Romanticist" he displays a fairly sure satiric sense that carries into several poems in *An Outland Piper*, including the last, "The Man Who Would Not Die."

Several of Davidson's poems in *An Outland Piper* are similar in tone to the more painfully skeptical verses of Edwin Arlington Robinson. "Variation on an Old Theme" laments the bitter truths of life that make music seem too incongruous for any reasonable poet to embrace as a means of dealing with this world, especially in view of the difficult terms under which past sinners and victims have had to sustain themselves:

> Must I have done with music?
> These things would have it so.
> But there is certain magic
> For those who walk in woe.
> The apple Eve has bitten
> Is mortal sweet within,
> And Cain was not quite smitten
> To earth, because of sin.

But Davidson's narrator is willing to make some effort to enliven this fatal world; it is feeble, no doubt, but the effort apparently satisfies the young poet:

> Then if, upon my roof-tree,
> The raven croaks too long,
> I'll sing a stave of Heaven
> And put him in my song.

Other poems in the volume are less reconciled and find their satisfaction in satiric portrayals, though not with high skills and trenchant insights. These poems include "Corymba," the tale of an exotic dancer who "has not rejected/Familiarities," and

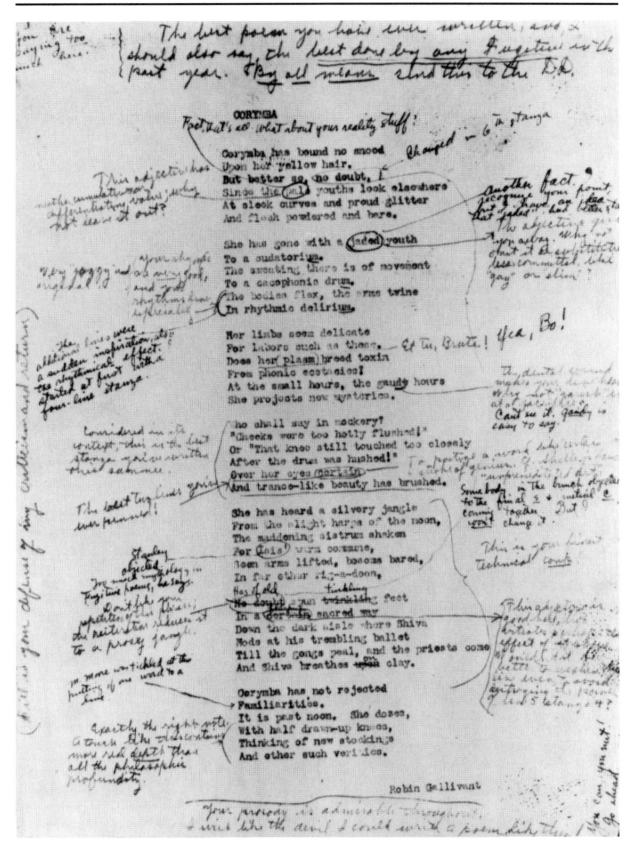

Draft of a poem by Davidson, with comments by Allen Tate and Davidson's responses (in darker ink) (by permission of the Estate of Donald Davidson)

"Naiad," about a woman who envisions herself in an ancient, lusty woods-and-water scene but who drowns in an ecstatic illusion of mythic participation, her body discovered most ordinarily by "A rustic, stumbling in a sandy bight,/[who] Gloated upon the dead with obscene woe." "Voice of the Dust," Davidson's version of "Ozymandias," lacks an overwhelming central image such as Shelley mustered for his service. Perhaps the most unsympathetic portrait of all is "The Wolf," whose subject is a sort of small-businessman cross between Robinson's husband in "Eros Turannos" and Frost's male suitor in "The Subverted Flower," not to mention Yeats's unsavory shopkeepers in "Easter 1916":

> The flour-barrels, cracker-boxes, cans
> Of lard and coffee hem the live beast in,
> Who jingles furtive fingers through the till,
> Dropping delicious coins with snap and grin.

One of the most completely realized of these satiric poems is "The Man Who Would Not Die." With skillful lineation and deft control of meter, enjambment, and rhyme, Davidson creates a fairly strong image of a man whose will to live has even the local parson somewhat in awe. At first, Evan Thane seems to be only a tough old braggart who chooses to astonish his neighbors and to assert his own strengths by denying any strength to death, at the same time being rather condescending to other, mortal, persons:

> He said he was no rotten Jericho
> To shake for village prophets' reputations,
> And scorned the bench where others whittled out
> Their easy days with amiable discourse
> Of usual death,—until at last they died.
> Grimly he watched them coward it away;
> Glowered contempt beneath the funeral cedars.

The parson is in some ways afraid of Thane for his unwillingness to trust religion, and Davidson is quite explicit as he tells of Thane's dedication to mortal life, not to death or to any promises that death might be construed to hold:

> Then Parson knew that death was not a friend
> To this old man who hailed the growing corn,
> Germinant, like its grains,—in love with time
> Because it gave expectancy of dawns
> And fervor for to-morrow and live hope
> That something might be better than before.

It is the sustaining power of Thane's faith in "coming men/Plying the tangled threads of world desire/

To some dim ever far-off unity" that keeps the old man's spirit up, not any future, eternal goal. And it is this fierce old man who alters and reinvigorates the parson's sermons: "So he preached/Most on the Resurrection and the Life,/And preached for one wild face of all the faces. . . ." For this parson—and, it seems, for Davidson—the power of the romantic Evan Thane is worth remembering, even worth (cautiously) assimilating into oneself. Seeming to fear the consequences of hopelessness, the repercussions upon one's soul, Davidson's parson somewhat envies and somewhat avoids the heroic posture of this rustic modern who, by denying death, so dangerously concurs in Satan's pronouncement, *"non serviam."*

In a letter to Davidson (20 January 1927) Allen Tate's magnanimous and sensible judgment of Robert Penn Warren makes a distinction that has persisted throughout the careers of these closely associated poets: "He is the only one of us who has *power*." In fact, it is the dominance of ideas over distinctive imagery that relegated the Fugitives to the categories of "distinguished" and "pretty good" rather than "great." Again and again their interest in clarity, logic, and order creates the impressions of nicety rather than passion; or, when passion should rise to defend a strongly held principle, the tone seems to go shrill, with its audience only the already converted.

In his books of poetry after *An Outland Piper*, Davidson's clarity has little strain, few hints of effort. Perhaps as the Fugitive-Agrarian philosophy took the pressure out of the rhetoric, verse became, in Yeats's words, "a comfortable kind of old scarecrow." That is, having written and discussed these ideas so clearly for so long, Davidson—surely more than Ransom, Tate, and Warren—proved less subject to the struggles of language with imagination and more susceptible to the accommodation of verse form to prosaic materials. Clarity and certainty rendered poetry bland at last by the ideological homogeneity of literary intellectuals so convinced of their tenets that the conflicts and subsequent resolutions usually prized in poetry are less fiery, less generative, than they are nicely anticipated, conventionally poised.

This is not to say that there are no pleasures or excellences in Davidson's poetry. Quite to the contrary, the deliberately satisfying cadences and careful rhetorical image-making work less to blur difficult distinctions in the modern world than to establish beyond caviling a particular position, even a sensibility.

The epigraph to part one of *The Long Street*

(1961), drawn from the first poem, "The Ninth Part of Speech," displays the classical (almost classical prose) poise and counterpoise evident throughout this volume and typical of the books published after *An Outland Piper:*

> For those who like their walking rough
> Up trails that slip around technology
> To gulfs of fern and banks of memory.

The reference to rough walking seems a little out of place, except that Davidson's idea of rough is not to be felt only in stumbling, shocking rhythms; rather, he intends "rough" also to convey "tough," even "toughening," as in the muscular effort much climbing takes, not just the halting and sliding of distorted meters. This sort of poetic roughness does not convey merely physical, onomatopoeic jaggedness; it also conveys the deliberateness of effort to good purpose, working hard both to accomplish a present task and to build capacity for similar, future accomplishment. That is the sort of effort one senses throughout Davidson's kind of grace; his effort is rarely to be graceful for its own

sake. There persists a feeling of moral muscle-building, of being in vigorous training for the battle to come (even a probably lost battle).

But Allen Tate's letter of 20 February 1927 makes quite obvious the younger man's irritation at his colleague's narrowness in meditating on science and art/poetry: "you speak of the battle between poetry and science, and the limitations of poetry such as I write for the purposes of victory by the former. The term battle gets you into a metaphor which destroys you. There is no battle. As for the rigidity of science, and the participation of my poetry in that rigidity, this is another metaphor. Art is just as rigid as science. The implications of your remark might lead me to suspect that for you art is vague and science exact. Art, in a sense, is more 'exact' than science, and in what sense is clear. . . ." "Cantankerous" is a word that crops up occasionally in the criticism of Davidson's writings, but it mostly applies to his essays, reviews, and his personal contentiousness in behalf of ideals about which he felt strongly. In his poetry, however, one senses not so much crankiness as the strength of a genuinely able and civilized man to confront and to explain significant issues of his day and his region, issues in fact that one might be hard pressed to deny are issues of national import, as well.

In a poem dedicated to his parents—*The Tall Men,* first published in 1927, with a revised version in *Lee in the Mountains* (1938)—Davidson sometimes borders on mystico-genetics as he speaks in awe of the moral and physical courage of the great men (including the great average men) of the South: "Tallness is not in what you eat or drink/ But in the seed of man." However, it is clear from the rest of this title poem that the reference to "seed of man" implies both spiritual seed and physical, that the permanent mystery about mankind at its best—or worst—lies in some vast context to which the human rational mind has only the most limited access but to which thoughtful (or prayerful) human beings may refer for strength. Part of the access lies simply in the examples of grand persons who have gone before: John Sevier, Andrew Jackson, David Crockett, Robert E. Lee; children and grandparents who fought their fierce, single battles against the Yankees or the Axis; sarcastic poets who write to deflate the current puffery of self-important mystics, satyrs, and expatriates: "Until I visited Oxford I never knew/What was wrong with me. Then I adopted/The Oxford accent, and became a gentleman." Finally, these poems are oratorical rather than lyric, calling for human values against the inhumanity of machine and system, as in these

Donald Davidson (photograph by Fletcher Harvey)

General Lee Remembers

Walking into the shadows, walking alone
From the hitching-rock under the shadow of the locusts.
Up to the President's office. Hearing the voices
whispering, Hush, it is General Lee. Boys,
Face if you into to General Lee.
And the soldiers' faces under the gleam of flags
Lifting, no more on any road or field
Where is Virginia still, Though lost and gone
Sunken, and lost, and perished, remembering, waiting bugles.
Walking the rocky path; and the column old
Where the paint cracks and the grass grows in the stones plank
It is Robert Lee in his dark, certain, suit who walks who walking
Lost in the shadow of elms where no flag flies

My father's house is taken and his hearth
Cold as a sword that
Left to the candle-drippings, sown with ashes
Moverless as are the dreams, no more renewed

I cannot remember my father's hand, I cannot
Answer his voice as he calls from the misty
Mounting where riders gather at gates.
And they have come too far away.
Even He was old, then, I knew him not, His hand
Was stretched for
Put down to mine, at daybreak snatched away
As he rode out and came no more. The grave
Lies in a far land and keeps the vow
I made there, once, in better days, yet knew
The savor of my fortune even then
As a man beholds with certain eyes, the drift
Of time, and tongues of men, and a sacred cause.
The fortune of the Lees is with the land

Beginning of the first draft for "Lee in the Mountains" (by permission of the Estate of Donald Davidson)

lines from "Epilogue: Fire on Belmont Street":

> But who will stand tonight,
> Holding this other door against the press
> Of brazen muscles? Who can conquer wheels
> Gigantically rolled with mass of iron
> Against frail human fingers? Who can quench
> The white-hot fury of the tameless atoms
> Bursting the secret jungle of their cells?

On 25 April 1968, having stood tall and sometimes cantankerously for what he believed, Donald Davidson died in Nashville, Tennessee.

Letters:

The Literary Correspondence of Donald Davidson and Allen Tate, edited by John Tyree Fain and Thomas Daniel Young (Athens: University of Georgia Press, 1974).

References:

Richmond Croom Beatty, "Donald Davidson as Fugitive-Agrarian," *Hopkins Review,* 5 (Winter 1952): 12-27;

Lawrence E. Bowling, "An Analysis of Davidson's 'Lee in the Mountains,'" *Georgia Review,* 6 (Spring 1952): 69-88;

M. E. Bradford, "A Durable Fire: Donald Davidson and the Profession of Letters," *Southern Review,* 3 (Summer 1967): 721-741;

Thomas Lawrence Connelly, "The Vanderbilt Agrarians: Time and Place in Southern Tradition," *Tennessee Historical Quarterly,* 22 (March 1963): 22-37;

Louise Cowan, "Donald Davidson: The 'Long Street,'" in *Reality and Myth: Essays in Memory of Richmond Croom Beatty,* edited by William E. Walker and Robert L. Welker (Nashville: Vanderbilt University Press, 1964);

Cowan, *The Fugitive Group: A Literary History* (Baton Rouge: Louisiana State University Press, 1959);

Charles Edward Eaton, "Donald Davidson and the Dynamics of Nostalgia," *Georgia Review,* 20 (Fall 1966): 261-269;

Marion Montgomery, "Bells for John Stewart's Burden," *Georgia Review,* 20 (Summer 1966): 145-181;

William Pratt, ed., *The Fugitive Poets: Modern Southern Poets in Perspective* (New York: Dutton, 1965);

Rob Roy Purdy, ed., *Fugitives' Reunion: Conversations at Vanderbilt, May 3-5, 1956* (Nashville: Vanderbilt University Press, 1959);

John Crowe Ransom, "The Most Southern Poet," *Sewanee Review,* 70 (Spring 1962): 202-207;

Louis D. Rubin, Jr., *The Wary Fugitives: Four Poets and the South,* The Walter Lynwood Fleming Lectures in Southern History (Baton Rouge: Louisiana State University Press, 1978);

Randall Stewart, "Donald Davidson," in *South: Modern Southern Literature in Its Cultural Setting,* edited by Louis D. Rubin, Jr., and Robert D. Jacobs (Garden City: Doubleday, 1961);

Allen Tate, "The Gaze Past, The Glance Present," *Sewanee Review,* 70 (Autumn 1962): 671-673;

John Donald Wade, "Oasis," *Sewanee Review,* 70 (Spring 1962): 208-212;

Robert Penn Warren, "A Note on Three Southern Poets," *Poetry,* 40 (May 1932): 103-113;

Joseph Williams, "Donald Davidson: Agrarian and Poet," M.A. thesis, University of South Carolina, 1957;

Thomas Daniel Young and M. Thomas Inge, *Donald Davidson* (New York: Twayne, 1971);

Young and Inge, *Donald Davidson: An Essay and a Bibliography* (Nashville: Vanderbilt University Press, 1965).

Papers:

The Joint University Libraries in Nashville have the largest collection of Davidson's papers.

Babette Deutsch

(22 September 1895-13 November 1982)

Edna Cunningham White

SELECTED BOOKS: *Banners* (New York: Doran, 1919);

Honey Out of the Rock (New York & London: Appleton, 1925);

A Brittle Heaven (New York: Greenberg, 1926);

In Such a Night (New York: John Day, 1927; London: Secker, 1927);

Potable Gold: Some Notes on Poetry and This Age (New York: Norton, 1929);

Fire For the Night (New York: Cape & Smith, 1930);

Epistle to Prometheus (New York: Cape & Smith, 1931);

Mask of Silenus: A Novel about Socrates (New York: Simon & Schuster, 1933);

This Modern Poetry (New York: Norton, 1935; London: Faber & Faber, 1936);

One Part Love (New York: Oxford University Press, 1939);

Heroes of the Kalevala, Finland's Saga (New York: Messner, 1940; London: Methuen, 1941);

Walt Whitman: Builder for America (New York: Messner, 1941);

It's a Secret! (New York & London: Harper, 1941);

Rogue's Legacy: A Novel about François Villon (New York: Coward-McCann, 1942);

The Welcome (New York & London: Harper, 1942);

Only the Living (New York: Emergency Committee to Save the Jewish People of Europe, 1943);

Take Them, Stranger (New York: Holt, 1944);

The Reader's Shakespeare (New York: Messner, 1946);

Poetry in Our Time (New York: Holt, 1952; revised and enlarged edition, Garden City: Doubleday, 1963);

Tales of Faraway Folk, by Deutsch and Avrahm Yarmolinsky (New York: Harper, 1952);

Animal, Vegetable, Mineral (New York: Dutton, 1954);

Poetry Handbook: A Dictionary of Terms (New York: Funk & Wagnalls, 1957; London: Cape, 1958; revised and enlarged edition, New York: Funk & Wagnalls, 1962; London: Cape, 1965; revised again, New York: Funk & Wagnalls, 1969; revised again, 1974);

Coming of Age; New and Selected Poems (Blooming-

ton: Indiana University Press, 1959; London: Oxford University Press, 1960);

More Tales of Faraway Folk, by Deutsch and Yarmolinsky (New York: Harper & Row, 1963);

Collected Poems 1919-1962 (Bloomington: Indiana University Press, 1963);

I Often Wish (New York: Funk & Wagnalls, 1966);

The Collected Poems of Babette Deutsch (Garden City: Doubleday, 1969).

OTHER: Alexander Blok, *The Twelve*, translated

108

by Deutsch and Avrahm Yarmolinsky (New York: Huebsch, 1920);

Modern Russian Poetry, edited and translated by Deutsch and Yarmolinsky (New York: Harcourt, Brace, 1921; London: John Lane, 1923); revised as *Russian Poetry* (New York: International, 1927); republished as *A Treasury of Russian Verse* (New York: Macmillan, 1949);

Contemporary German Poetry, edited and translated by Deutsch and Yarmolinsky (New York: Harcourt, Brace, 1923; London: John Lane, 1923);

K. I. Chukovsky, *Crocodile*, translated by Deutsch (Philadelphia: Lippincott, 1931);

Solomon Blumgarten and Leo Low, *Rosh Hashanah L'Ilanoth (The Trees' New Year's)*, translated by Deutsch (New York: Transcontinental Music Corp., 1940);

Rainer Maria Rilke, *Poems from "The Book of Hours,"* translated by Deutsch (New York: New Directions, 1941; London: Vision, 1947);

Alexander Pushkin, *Eugene Onegin*, translated by Deutsch, edited by Deutsch and Yarmolinsky (New York: Limited Editions Club, 1943; Harmondsworth: Penguin, 1965);

Nicholas Leskov, *The Steel Flea*, translated by Deutsch and Yarmolinsky (New York & London: Harper, 1943; revised edition, New York: Harper & Row, 1964);

Selected Writings of Boris Pasternak, verse translated by Deutsch (New York: New Directions, 1949);

Ivan Goll, *Jean sans Terre*, translated by Deutsch, Lionel Abel, and others (New York & London: Yoseloff, 1958);

Goll, *Elegy of Ihpetonga*, translated by Deutsch (Kentfield, Cal.: Allen Press, 1962);

Two Centuries of Russian Verse, translated and edited by Deutsch and Yarmolinsky (New York: Random House, 1966);

Poems of Samuel Taylor Coleridge, edited by Deutsch (New York: Crowell, 1967);

Elizabeth Borchers, *There Comes a Time*, translated by Deutsch (Garden City: Doubleday, 1969).

In her later years, Babette Deutsch told Jean Gould of an incident which obviously gave her great personal pleasure and also summarized the pivotal concern of her artistic life. She returned to pick up a pair of shoes left far too long at a shoe shop, and, when asked for them, the cobbler immediately handed them over. Even though he said he did not remember her name, he had penciled the word POET in large letters on the paper sack. A doyenne among established twentieth-century poets and a mentor to many beginners, Deutsch wrote verse that was a matchless blend of emotion and intellect, and her critical studies *Poetry Handbook* (1957) and *Poetry in Our Time* (1952) are standard sources for students of poetic craft and technique.

Of German-Jewish descent, Babette Deutsch was born in New York City on 22 September 1895 to Michael Deutsch and Melanie Fisher Deutsch. Her literary interest and verbal skill had manifested themselves by age five when she wrote:

> I knew that the sky was blue,
> And I knew that the sun was gold,
> But I never knew that the earth was round
> Until I was told.

Even though Deutsch chose not to include in either edition of her *Collected Poems* such critically acclaimed poems as the book-length *Epistle to Prometheus* (1931), "Coming of Age" (a sonnet sequence presented as a portion of the Phi Beta Kappa poem at Columbia University), or "Thoughts at the Year's End" (winner of the *Nation*'s 1926 poetry prize), she allowed this verse to remain.

From early in her life Deutsch was surrounded and nurtured by her native city's rich cosmopolitan ferment and liberal-minded intelligentsia. After finishing her elementary and secondary education at the Ethical Culture School, she entered Barnard College and studied under such notable members of the Columbia University faculty as anthropologist Franz Boas and the historians Charles A. Beard, James Shotwell, and James Harvey Robinson. During her college years she also had contact with Randolph Bourne, a well-known liberal journalist who was a regular contributor to the *New Republic* and whose socialist sympathies had been influential on the youth of the day.

While still an undergraduate, Deutsch began publishing poems in periodicals such as the *North American Review* and the *New Republic*. After graduating with an honors B.A. in 1917, she was briefly *associated with the Political Science Quarterly*. William Reedy, who also granted space to her verses in his *Reedy's Mirror*, asked her for articles as well, and she responded with one about economist and educator Thorstein Veblen, then at the peak of his career. Much impressed with her clear grasp of his ideas, Veblen asked Deutsch to be his secretary while he taught at the New School for Social Research (around 1920), and she accepted.

While Deutsch continued to publish poems in the *Dial*, the *Liberator*, *Lyric*, the *Nation*, the *New Republic*, *Poetry* and other periodicals, she received attention in the literary world with the appearance of *Banners*, her first volume of verse, in 1919. The title poem, composed in March 1917 to celebrate the beginning of the Russian Revolution on which so many young, liberal intellectuals had pinned their hopes for a new order, speaks of the plain red flag adopted as the banner of the long, evolutionary trek "to the red dawn, to the light." The contents, written for the most part in rhythmic free verse, were grouped under five headings: "The Dancers," "Ephemeris," "Songs and Silences," "Sonnets," and "Banners." One remarkably perceptive poem, "To an Amiable Child," was inspired by the inscription on a funerary urn at a Riverside Drive gravesite and reflects a deep sympathy for infants and children that would remain a prominent theme in her work:

> I see you stilly radiant,
> And—like delicious food, delicious play—
> Loving music and motion and
> Pleasure you did not understand
> In voice or face or golden weather;
> But sometimes for whole hours together
> Hooding yourself in silence;
> And when you were tired of being good,
> Driving them wild.

Virtually all the reviewers of this first volume, many of whom were writing for journals in which Deutsch's poetry had already appeared, recognized and praised her poetic achievement and her potential for development, even if reviewers such as C. H. Towne (*Bookman*, 19 July 1919) faulted her for such shortcomings as being "too serious," "too deadly in earnest." They particularly noted the fresh imagery with which she described concrete details and her rigorous idealism. The reviewer for the *Dial* (9 July 1919) observed that her verses "reveal a subtle sense of the contrasts which lie in crowds, and the contradictions between . . . modern life and the verities of nature. Pessimism is in the roots of many of them, but pessimism without bitterness."

The following year Robert Frost recommended to his publishers, Henry Holt and Company, that they include Deutsch's poetry in a young poets series they were contemplating, an endorsement she did not know of until much later. In 1960

Frost said that he had always been proud of having "discovered" her among the poets he read for Holt's consideration. Even though Holt did not publish a volume of her verse at that time, they later published *Poetry in Our Time* (1952).

On 28 April 1921 Babette Deutsch married Avrahm Yarmolinsky, head of the Slavonic Division at the New York Public Library. The union was an eminently congenial one of intellectual equals and was destined to produce a number of outstanding translations of German and Russian verse. They had already translated Alexander Blok's *The Twelve* (1920), and by the end of the year they had completed *Modern Russian Poetry*, a selection of lyrics from the previous century. Many were appearing in English for the first time and had been translated expressly for this volume. (Because Deutsch did not know Russian, her husband, of Russian as well as German heritage, rendered the Russian into English; she polished the final version.) This anthology was followed in 1923 by *Contemporary German Poetry* which, according to William Rose Benét, displayed "the skill of an able linguist and the inspiration of a fine poet."

After the birth of their first child, Adam (later followed by a second son, Michael), Deutsch and Yarmolinsky traveled extensively in western and eastern Europe, touring Berlin, Riga, Moscow, Leningrad, Warsaw, Florence, Paris, and London. Upon returning, Deutsch settled into the routine of writing, teaching (at the New School for Social Research, 1933-1935, and at Columbia University, 1944-1971), and occasional lecturing that she would follow from then on alongside her domestic obligations.

Honey Out of the Rock (1925) contains short, imagistic poems on marriage and motherhood as well as those reflecting her continuing concern for children and the elderly and her fervent interest in the arts. Titles such as "Eros," "Ballet School," "To a Lady Painted by Holbein," and "Biblical Ballads" display the influence of imagism, the Japanese haiku, and Greek and Jewish culture. Critics agreed that in this second volume the poet's expressive skills had matured and acquired a new resonance and timbre, but two reviewers, Marcia Nardi of the *New Republic* and Arthur Guiterman of *Outlook*, commented on the cold intellectuality and lack of warmth belied by the book title.

In the 10 February 1926 issue, the *Nation* published Deutsch's "Thoughts at the Year's End" and announced that from over three thousand entries it had been chosen as the winner of that magazine's annual poetry prize. When she gathered the first collected edition of her poems in the 1960s, Deutsch did not include this one, saying simply that it was no longer acceptable to her and could not be reworked to her satisfaction.

Deutsch tried her hand at another genre with *A Brittle Heaven* (1926), a barely disguised autobiographical novel. Having little plot, the novel is peopled with believable characters, one of whom, Mark Gideon, was modeled on Randolph Bourne. The book covers the events in the life, to the age of twenty-five, of Bianca Ernestis, who grows up in a middle-class home, attends college, experiences normal sexual emotions, endorses socialism for a time, writes a book, marries, and has a child. At the book's close the main character appears to be at the beginning of a new phase of existence, one in which she is struggling to reconcile the demands of being a professional writer and a wife and mother.

Deutsch's *In Such a Night* (1927) was the least-well received of her four novels. The book examines the reactions of a group of jaded sophisticates when one of the women gives birth to a daughter at a housewarming they are attending. Showing the influence of Virginia Woolf's stream-of-consciousness technique, the novel was evidently intended, by means of a series of psychological snapshots, to take a mildly satirical poke at gentility, but reviews regarded it as thin and inadequate in result, if not in intent.

In 1929, for her role as Phi Beta Kappa poet at Columbia University, Deutsch wrote a sonnet series, and she published *Potable Gold*, which was followed in 1930 by *Fire For the Night*. Consistently intellectual and modern in tone, the poems in *Fire For the Night* nonetheless revealed the influence of tradition and of the questions arising from the ancient conflicts of flesh and spirit, of the sense of time's brevity with the dreams of eternity.

Irwin Edman of *Books* observed, "More than any other poet of our time, Miss Deutsch moves with passion and deftness in the complex world of contemporary attitudes and ideas," and Granville Hicks of the *New York World* said, "Miss Deutsch has accepted a definite range of thought and emotion, and has explored and mastered it. Within that range, her insight is impressively sure. . . . She does not suppress or evade her emotions, but she does hold them in subjection to her sense of proportion. . . . The result is a peculiar poignancy which a more abandoned display of feeling could not give."

Deutsch's first book-length work of criticism, *Potable Gold*, consists of five essays on poets and

poetry, in which she discusses the reasons for writing and reading poetry, poets and their audiences, poetry and the modern machine age, the future of poetry, and poets such as William Butler Yeats, John Millington Synge, Jules Laforgue, T. S. Eliot, and Robinson Jeffers. *Potable Gold* was the kernel which, over the next two and one-half decades, would grow into *Poetry in Our Time*.

A long, philosophical poem regarded by some as Deutsch's finest work, *Epistle to Prometheus* (1931) was another of the poems she did not allow to be collected; yet she initially said that it was the poem for which she hoped to be remembered. Primarily in free verse, it is a letter to Prometheus, the mythical patron of the human race. In search of the Promethean spirit, the poet surveys human history from creation to the twentieth century and finds this prized quality in Socrates, Christ, Voltaire, Lenin, and Gandhi. The book's reception was gratifying, with critics such as J. N. North (*Poetry*, June 1931) emphasizing that the loosely structured free verse (interspersed with regular rhymed poems) was undeniably the author's best medium and that it revealed the author's scholarship and disciplined, symphonic expression.

Mask of Silenus (1933), a novel about Socrates, was reviewed widely and, almost without exception, more favorably than *In Such a Night*. Beginning at a colloquy with Xanthippe, Socrates' shrewish wife, the action moves on to the philosopher's influence on the youth of Athens and ultimately to his trial. Deutsch employed her considerable inspirational abilities in such passages as the speech Socrates made in his defense: "I tell you, men of Athens, that while I have life and strength I will go on doing the bidding of the gods and speaking as I have always spoken. The fishermen know that the sea is dangerous, but they have never found danger a good reason for staying safe at home. And I think, too, that danger is not so bad as the fear of danger. So though you threaten me with death if I go on— fishing, as you may say, for your souls, and not yours only, but the soul of every man I meet—why, I must put to sea just the same." Deutsch based her portrait on Plato's *Dialogues*, setting for herself the task of separating the human side of Socrates from the dialectic, a task that she accomplished admirably. Deutsch's knowledge of Greek art and life, long a theme in her poetry, was recognized by critics as the basis of the clear, lifelike pictures that emerged of Socrates, Plato, Crito, and Phaedo and of the ease with which the salient points of Socratic philosophy were conveyed.

This Modern Poetry (1935) was the next in the

series of critical writings that would culminate in *Poetry in Our Time.* Tracing the development of verse in the previous two decades, the book focuses on American writers such as W. H. Auden, E. E. Cummings, Ezra Pound, Walt Whitman, Carl Sandburg, Hart Crane, Edgar Lee Masters, Archibald MacLeish, and Edgar Allan Poe and includes suggestions for understanding modern poetry. E. L. Watson of the *New York Times* pointed out that such a survey, with its outlines of the various schools of thought represented by the different poets, had long been needed and that Deutsch's book had filled the void. In addition to collecting materials that had formerly been available only in anthologies, the book also includes critical essays and separate studies of individual authors.

By 1939, when *One Part Love* was published, it had been eight years since Deutsch had produced a volume of poetry. A number of the book's fifty-three poems on contemporary subjects, especially peace or its absence, had previously appeared in the *New Yorker.* "To a Friend Who Fears Revolution" displays effective imagery to juxtapose the irreconcilable opposites of peace, represented by the home, and the destructiveness of war:

The fragile penates are threatened, the porcelain, the
  blown
Glass, and the box of sweet sounds, and satiny woods,
Lares lovingly wrought, worshiped as gods and goods,
These may be ravished, dismembered, overthrown!
And these gone, what goes too? The hearth is shaken
By no violence native to earth or air,
But by the mob, the arch-Goth, that cannot care
For an image smashed, an idolatrous heart forsaken.
These propped, these sheltered you, powerful though
  frail
These magnified your house, miraculously
Extended time. Are they endangered? You see
Life shrink, peace fly, animal strength prevail.

Her finer moments, ones in which she is at her most personal, are also evident in her poems about animals. In the series called "Zoo" the creatures are presented in all their picturesque oddities, as in "Ape":

His eyes are mournful, but the long lined palm
He thrusts between the bars expects the best.
His old man's face as innocent as calm,
The beggar puts compassion to the test
And fails. He grips the bars; his pained stare grows
To a brown study framed in dusty fur
. . . .
The fingers, strong to clutch, quick to explore,
Again extended, are again refused.

The eyes, poor sorrow's jewels, seldom wink,
But to his grinning public, as before,
show endless patience, endlessly abused.

In 1941 Deutsch's *Walt Whitman: Builder for America,* a biography for children, won the Julia Ellsworth Ford Foundation for Children's Literature annual contest for the best children's book manuscript. A Spanish translation, sponsored by the American Council of Learned Societies, was published in Mexico in 1942. In her book Deutsch stressed the influences that made Whitman the poet of democracy: his seafaring ancestors, the friends he made in all walks of life, his struggle to earn a living, and his physical handicaps. Approximately one-half of the book consists of selections of the Whitman poems most likely to be enjoyed by young people. A. M. Jordan, writing in the highly respected *Horn Book,* said that it was "a clearly written, direct biography, not so filled with side issues that essential things lose their proper weight."

A fictionalized account of the life of fifteenth-century poet François de Montcorbier, better known as François Villon, was the subject of Deutsch's fourth novel, *Rogue's Legacy* (1942). A mixture of fact and fiction, the novel made use of all available bits of historical information about this thief and wastrel whose poems are still read and remembered. The central theme of Villon's work had been the transiency of youth and worldly glory, and Deutsch's novel highlights the reasons for his focus. Critics agreed that Deutsch's extensive knowledge of the details of medieval life was sound and that the resulting portraits of Villon's relatives and cronies and the fevered, lusty life of mid-fifteenth-century France are convincing and vivid. Deutsch presented as one the life and poetry of a man who killed a priest, loved Katherine de Vauselles, robbed the College of Navarre, matched rhymes with the Duc d'Orleans, and reputedly died miserably in a ditch far from his beloved Paris.

Deutsch continued to write books for young readers. *The Welcome* (1942) is the tale of a little German refugee, Ernst, whose friendship with an American boy becomes a source of happiness for both. A plea for democracy and tolerance at a time of great persecution, the story provides authentic glimpses of life at a refugee center. *Tales of Faraway Folk* (1952) and *More Tales of Faraway Folk* (1963) are stories from the folklore of Russia, Central Asia, Karelia, and Lithuania retold by Deutsch and Avrahm Yarmolinsky.

Take Them, Stranger (1944) and *Animal, Vegetable, Mineral* (1954) contain poems voicing the author's rage at the destruction of war. One of her two sons served on a distant front, and in "To My Son" (published in *Take Them, Stranger*) she asks:

> How shall we talk
> To you who must learn the language
> Spelled on the fields in famine, in blood on the sidewalk?
> Child (shall I say?)
> When the night roars, remember
> The songs we sang, lapped in the warmth and bright
> Of the nursery.

F. C. Flint of the *New York Times* observed that this maternal concern and perspective express themselves as touchingly personal references in some of the poems and as an interest in wider, more impersonal issues in others. In either case the focus is on the change from what is past, remembered, and domestic to the harsh contingencies of what is unexperienced, remote, and yet to come.

Poetry in Our Time (1952) assembled and expanded commentary by Deutsch on poets such as Gerard Manley Hopkins, A. E. Housman, W. H. Auden, William Butler Yeats, T. S. Eliot, Wallace Stevens, Thomas Hardy, Allen Tate, Dylan Thomas, Karl Shapiro, and Randall Jarrell. Incorporating new material with discussions that had already appeared in essays, book reviews, and *This Modern Poetry*, the book discusses not only British and American poetry but also that of other English-speaking countries, including Canada, South Africa, and Australia. The book is organized thematically, not chronologically, with chapters such as "The Earthly and the Definite," "Wars and Rumors of Wars," and "Science and Poetry." As a consequence, older and newer poets are discussed together.

Critical reception of *Poetry in Our Time* was gratifying. Reviewing the book for the *New York Herald Tribune*, Kenneth Rexroth said, "If I were a student in a French lycee, starting to read contemporary English and American poetry, or a civilized attorney or doctor in Grand Rapids, who had just decided to catch up on the stuff he had missed in college, or even that amorphous being, the cultivated general reader, this would be the book for me." L. L. Martz of the *Yale Review* concurred, praising Deutsch's "deft control" and the "consistent vigor, clarity and pungency" of her writing. "Most remarkable," he added, was "the critical poise, the judicious tone, the analytic fairness," and he called *Poetry in Our Time* "a book which everyone concerned with modern literature will find rewarding."

Deutsch's criticism had long been preoccupied with the correlation between modern poetry and modern society. *Potable Gold* focuses on the influence of technology on poetry and the poet's relationship to his public. *Poetry in Our Time*, like *This Modern Poetry*, studies the interrelationship between poetry and politics. According to Deutsch, the modern poet, in order to become a genuine revolutionary, must create a mythology powerful enough to transcend the power of men.

Cited for its thoroughness, technical knowledge, intuition, native poetic sensibility, and intellectual vigor when it first appeared, *Poetry in Our Time* was later faulted by Jean Gould for the scant attention it gave female poets. Gould pointed out that of the 226 poets selected by Deutsch for discussion, only eighteen were women. No mention was made of Sara Teasdale or Genevieve Taggard, a former colleague of Deutsch's and founder of *Measure*, a magazine of which Deutsch was once editor. Muriel Rukeyser merited only three lines, though, Gould believed, her output had by 1950 rated more extensive treatment. Deutsch placed Edna St. Vincent Millay in the chapter called "A Look at the Worst," dismissing her in a single paragraph and crediting her with "no more than a handful of touching songs on the transience of love and the shortness of life...." Among those she did discuss at more length were Louise Bogan, Elinor Wylie, Elizabeth Bishop, Marianne Moore, Jean Garrigue, and Léonie Adams.

Poetry Handbook: A Dictionary of Terms (1957), a lexicon of alphabetically arranged poetic terms, draws on the work of many poets for illustrations of the definitions and was aimed largely at students and beginning poets. W. H. Auden called it "an excellent job in judgment, insight and presentation" and once told Deutsch that he withdrew from a contract to write a book on prosody because she had already said everything necessary. Her purpose evidently was to be useful rather than exhaustive, and she eliminated certain more obscure terms.

Between 1959 and 1969 many of the poems from Deutsch's previous volumes of poetry and translations were published with some new verses in three collections: *Coming of Age; New and Selected Poems* (1959), *Collected Poems 1919-1962* (1963), and *The Collected Poems of Babette Deutsch* (1969). Their contents are a refined summary of her themes and talents. Her compassion for the elderly, apparent in such previously published poems as "Distance" and "Late Reflections" (*Collected Poems*, 1963), is combined with her admiration for Robert Frost in

"Heard in Old Age" (*Coming of Age*, 1959). In it she asks, "Is there a song left, then, for aged voices?" and in the final three lines replies:

> Till the Enigma, in a wandering phrase
> Offers a strain never audible before:
> Immense music behind a closing door.

The resolution implies that not only is there indeed a song for the aged, but it is one not possible for the younger voice, one "never audible before" which can only be expressed after having passed through the portals of later life. A few years later she memorialized Frost, Wallace Stevens, Robinson Jeffers, E. E. Cummings, Kenneth Fearing, William Carlos Williams, Theodore Roethke, W. B. Yeats, and Louis MacNeice—all of whom died at about the same time—in "Lament for the Makers." With the type of philosophical conclusion for which so many of her poems are noted, she observes that "There is no end to grief. Nor no end to poetry," a declaration of love for her calling and for those others who also served.

Deutsch's continuing acute concern for infants and children, especially for those who do not live to adulthood, is evident in poems such as "Small Colored Boy in the Subway," "Urban Pastoral," "Feeding the Chickens" (winner of the 1957 William Rose Benét Memorial Award), "Afternoon with an Infant," "Entertainment in the Parlor at 8:30," and "Death of a Child." Her love of music is revealed in extraordinarily witty, memorable, and instructive images, as in "At the Green Grocer's," where she speaks of pears "Shapely as violins" and states that "like the 'cello/The eggplant's note is resonantly low." In "String Quartet" she notes,

> The serious 'cello's blond body glows.
> How faithful are the dog-eared scores, and how
> The bows lift, scenting music!

"Piano Recital," "The Prepared Piano," "Three Nuns Listening to Chopin," and "The Belvedere: Mozart's Music" are other pledges of affection for traditional musical forms, and in "Electronic Concert" she delivers her verdict of this newer sound:

> Hurricane winds sweep through the skyscrapers,
> Their shrieks of destruction cannot
> Confound like the following silence.
> Some demon's child is running, is banging on giant,
>   invisible, impalpable iron railings.

New York, where Deutsch lived all her life, is the locale of many poems, including "Barges on

Babette Deutsch (Gale International Portrait Gallery)

the Hudson," "NY *December *1931," and "Voices on Riverside." In these and other poems she has memorialized the city with numerous references to its characteristic scenes: rivers, water, boats, parks, subways, concerts, museums, and, of course, Riverside Drive. Throughout, affection is tempered with reservation. The eye of a seasoned city dweller such as Deutsch cannot miss the waste and pathos existing side by side with the ceaseless activity and rich diversity of opportunity.

By the time *Collected Poems* (1963) appeared, Deutsch's stature had long since been recognized, and her poetry had been praised on all sides for its lucidity, sense of color, balance, compassion, and perfection of technique. Reviewing the book for the *Virginia Quarterly Review*, George Garrett called *Collected Poems* "the harvest of half a century of continuous creativity, . . . one which dazzles the reader with its virtuosity and at the same time defies him to remark any lessening of the essential vigor and energy of the artist. This is the voice not just of a poet, but of an artist in exactly the same sense that Picasso is an artist or Stravinsky." Louise Bogan aptly summarized Deutsch's poetic gifts: "Miss Deutsch's lyrics are dramatically pictorial; she presents moments of everyday reality that turn out to be mirrors of her informed convictions."

In her lifetime Deutsch supported liberal politics and causes, although she was not formally aligned with any party. At one time she belonged to the Civic Club, a forerunner of the American Civil Liberties Union, and she was active in the Committee for Cultural Freedom headed by John Dewey. For many years she was a member of the International P.E.N. Club, an organization of writers advocating universal freedom of expression for all writers, with special attention to those jailed as political prisoners. She disaffiliated herself from the League of American Writers because of that group's partisan character. The National Institute of Arts and Letters elected her to its ranks, and she served on the Board of Chancellors of the Academy of American Poets.

After Deutsch's husband retired from his post at the New York Public Library in 1955, the two of them undertook the massive task of compiling a new anthology, *Two Centuries of Russian Verse*, published in 1966. Their accomplishment was a fitting culmination of a harmonious, forty-five-year partnership as editors and translators. Devoted to her husband in private life as well, Deutsch had dedicated more than one of her books to him, and his death on 28 September 1975 was a deep loss not only for Deutsch personally but for literature.

Barnard College, Deutsch's alma mater, an-

nounced in 1976 that a scholarship was being established in her name. Until 1971 she had taught at Columbia University, where her wit and invigorating presentations made her popular with students. Despite ill-health in her later years, she continued to write (as yet uncollected) poems for periodicals, carrying on with what Kenneth Rexroth called her "special calm . . . in the face of terror and mystery and miscellaneous excitements of life. This evenness of temper is very valuable, as it is an extremely rare quality in modern verse."

On 13 November 1982 Deutsch died in her sleep at her Manhattan apartment. She was eighty-seven.

References:

George Garrett, "The Naked Voice," *Virginia Quarterly Review*, 40 (Spring 1964): 326-329;

Jean Gould, *American Women Poets: Pioneers of Modern Poetry* (New York: Dodd, Mead, 1980), pp. 293-301;

Louis L. Martz, "The Grace of Modern Poetry," *Yale Review*, 42 (September 1952): 135-139;

Louis Untermeyer, "Three Notable Collections," review of *Collected and New Poems: 1924-1963*, by Mark Van Doren; *Collected Poems: 1919-1962*, by Deutsch; and *Caged in an Animal's Mind*, by Stanley Burnshaw, *Poetry*, 103 (March 1964): 382-385.

Hilda Doolittle
(H. D.)

Susan Stanford Friedman
University of Wisconsin-Madison

See also the Doolittle entry in *DLB 4, American Writers in Paris, 1920-1939*.

BIRTH: Bethlehem, Pennsylvania, 10 September 1886, to Dr. Charles Leander and Helen Eugenia Wolle Doolittle.

EDUCATION: Bryn Mawr College, 1905-1906.

MARRIAGE: 18 October 1913 to Richard Alding-

ton, divorced 1938; child: Frances Perdita.

AWARDS AND HONORS: Guarantors Prize (*Poetry* magazine) for "The Wind Sleepers," "Storm," "Pool," "The Garden," and "Moonrise," 1915; Vers Libre Prize (*Little Review*) for "Sea Poppies," 1917; Levinson Prize (*Poetry* magazine) for "Sigel XV" and "Callypso Speaks," 1938; Harriet Monroe Memorial Prize for "In Time of Gold," "Nails for Petals," and "Sometimes and After," 1958; Bran-

Photograph inscribed to Marianne Moore, circa 1921 (courtesy of the Beinecke Rare Book and Manuscript Library, Yale University)

deis University Creative Arts Award for Poetry, 1959; Citation for Distinguished Service, Bryn Mawr College, 1960; Award of Merit Medal for Poetry, American Academy of Arts and Letters, 1960.

DEATH: Zurich, Switzerland, 27 September 1961.

BOOKS: *Sea Garden* (London: Constable, 1916; Boston & New York: Houghton Mifflin, 1916);

The Tribute and Circe: Two Poems (Cleveland: Clerk's Private Press, 1917);

Hymen (London: Egoist Press, 1921; New York: Holt, 1921);

Heliodora and Other Poems (Boston: Houghton Mifflin, 1924; London: Cape, 1924);

Collected Poems of H. D. (New York: Boni & Liveright, 1925);

H. D., edited by Hughes Mearns (New York: Simon & Schuster, 1926);

Palimpsest (Paris: Contact Editions, 1926; Boston: Houghton Mifflin, 1926);

Hippolytus Temporizes (Boston: Houghton Mifflin, 1927; revised edition, Redding Ridge, Conn.: Black Swan Books, 1985);

Hedylus (Boston: Houghton Mifflin, 1928; Oxford: Blackwell, 1928; revised edition, Redding Ridge, Conn.: Black Swan Books, 1980);

Borderline—A Pool Film with Paul Robeson (London: Mercury, 1930);

Red Roses for Bronze (London: Chatto & Windus, 1931; Boston & New York: Houghton Mifflin, 1931);

Kora and Ka (Dijon: Darantière, 1934; Berkeley: Bios, 1978);

The Usual Star (Dijon: Darantière, 1934);

Nights, as John Helforth (Dijon: Darantière, 1935);

The Hedgehog (London: Brendin, 1936);

The Walls Do Not Fall (London & New York: Oxford University Press, 1944);

What Do I Love? (London: Brendin, 1944);

Tribute to the Angels (London & New York: Oxford University Press, 1945);

The Flowering of the Rod (London & New York: Oxford University Press, 1946);

By Avon River (New York, London & Toronto: Macmillan, 1949; revised edition, Redding Ridge, Conn.: Black Swan Books, forthcoming, 1986);

Tribute to Freud (New York: Pantheon, 1956; enlarged edition, Boston: Godine, 1974);

Selected Poems of H. D. (New York: Grove, 1957);

Bid Me to Live (A Madrigal) (New York: Grove, 1960; enlarged edition, Redding, Conn.: Black Swan Books, 1983);

Helen in Egypt (New York: Grove, 1961);

Hermetic Definition (unauthorized edition, West Newberry, Mass.: Frontier Press, 1971; authorized edition, New York: New Directions, 1972; Oxford: Carcanet, 1972);

Temple of the Sun (Berkeley: ARIF Press, 1972);

Trilogy: The Walls Do Not Fall, Tribute to Angels, The Flowering of the Rod (New York: New Directions, 1973; Cheadle: Carcanet, 1973);

The Poet & the Dancer (San Francisco: Five Trees Press, 1975);

End to Torment: A Memoir of Ezra Pound, edited by Norman Holmes Pearson and Michael King (New York: New Directions, 1979);

HERmione (New York: New Directions, 1981); republished as *Her* (London: Virago, 1984);

The Gift (New York: New Directions, 1982);

Notes on Thought and Vision & the Wise Sappho (San
   Francisco: City Lights Books, 1982);
Collected Poems, 1912-1944, edited by Louis L. Martz
   (New York: New Directions, 1983);
Priest and A Dead Priestess Speaks (Port Townsend,
   Wash.: Copper Canyon, 1983).

RECORDING: *Readings from Helen in Egypt*, Watershed Tapes, 1982.

OTHER: "Sitalkas," "Hermes of the Ways," "Pria-
   pus," "Acon," "Hermonax," and "Epigram,"
   in *Des Imagistes: An Anthology*, edited by Ezra
   Pound (New York: A. & C. Boni, 1914; Lon-
   don: Poetry Bookshop, 1914), pp. 20-30;
"The Pool," "The Garden," "Sea Lily," "Sea Iris,"
   "Sea Rose," "Oread," and "Incantation," in
   Some Imagist Poets: An Anthology, edited by
   Amy Lowell (Boston: Houghton Mifflin,
   1915; London: Constable, 1915), pp. 21-30;
"Sea Gods," "The Shrine," "Huntress," and "Mid-
   Day," in *Some Imagist Poets: An Anthology*, ed-
   ited by Lowell (Boston: Houghton Mifflin,
   1916; London: Constable, 1916), pp. 17-31;
"The God," "Adonis," "Pygmalion," and "Euryd-
   ice," in *Some Imagist Poets: An Anthology*, edited
   by Lowell (Boston: Houghton Mifflin, 1917),
   pp. 19-34;
*Choruses from the Iphigenia in Aulis and the Hippolytus
   of Euripides*, translated by Doolittle (London:
   Egoist, 1919);
"Narthex," in *The Second American Caravan*, edited
   by Alfred Kreymborg, Lewis Mumford, and
   Paul Rosenfeld (New York: Macauley, 1928),
   pp. 225-284;
"In the Rain," "If You Will Let Me Sing," and
   "Chance Meeting," in *Imagist Anthology 1930*,
   edited by Richard Aldington (New York: Covici, Friede, 1930; London: Chatto & Windus,
   1930), pp. 85-105;
Euripides' Ion, translated by H. D. (London: Chatto
   & Windus, 1937; Boston: Houghton Mifflin,
   1937; revised edition, Redding Ridge, Conn.:
   Black Swan Books, 1985);
Vale Ave, in *New Directions in Poetry and Prose*, no.
   44 (New York: New Directions, 1982), pp. 18-
   167.

H. D.'s life and work recapitulate the central
themes of literary modernism: the emergence from
Victorian norms and certainties, the entry into an
age characterized by rapid technological change
and the violence of two great wars, and the development of literary modes which reflected the dis-

integration of traditional symbolic systems and the
mythmaking quest for new meanings. H. D.'s
oeuvre spans five decades of the twentieth century,
1911-1961, and incorporates work in a variety of
genres. She is known primarily as a poet, but she
also wrote novels, memoirs, and essays and did a
number of translations from the Greek. Her work
is consistently innovative and experimental, both
reflecting and contributing to the avant-garde milieu that dominated the arts in London and Paris
until the end of World War II. Immersed for decades in the intellectual crosscurrents of modernism,
psychoanalysis, syncretist mythologies, and feminism, H. D. created a unique voice and vision that
sought to bring meaning to the fragmented shards
of a war-torn culture. The development of H. D.'s
increasingly complex and resonant texts is best
understood when placed in the context of other
important modernists, many of whom she knew
intimately and all of whom she read avidly—especially poets such as Ezra Pound, T. S. Eliot, William Butler Yeats, William Carlos Williams,
Marianne Moore, Wallace Stevens, and the Sitwells;
and novelists such as D. H. Lawrence, Dorothy
Richardson, Virginia Woolf, James Joyce, Gertrude Stein, Colette, May Sinclair, Djuna Barnes,
and William Faulkner. Within this modernist tradition, H. D.'s particular emphasis grew out of her
perspective as a woman regarding the intersections
of public events and private lives in the aftermath
of World War I and in the increasingly ominous
period culminating in the Atomic Age. Love and
war, birth and death are the central concerns of
her work, in which she reconstituted gender, language, and myth to serve her search for the underlying patterns ordering and uniting
consciousness and culture.

Following in the footsteps of Henry James
and Mary Cassatt and paralleling the paths of
Pound, Eliot, and Stein, H. D. lived as an expatriate
in England and Europe from 1911 until her death
in 1961. Her roots, however, were fully American
and provided a heritage that permeated her later
life and art. It is well worth knowing about her
early life and the meanings she discovered in it
because these clusters of associations appear repeatedly not only in memoirs such as *The Gift*
(1982), *Tribute to Freud* (1956), and *End to Torment*
(1979), but also in much of her poetry and fiction.

H. D.'s childhood began on Church Street in
Bethlehem, Pennsylvania, in the close-knit Moravian community in which her mother's family had
been influential since its founding in the eighteenth
century by a small band of people persecuted for

their membership in the Unitas Fratrum, a mystical Protestant sect. Her grandfather, a noted biologist, was the director of the Moravian Seminary; her mother's brother was a musician, the founder of the well-known Bethlehem Bach Festivals. Also an artist, her mother taught music and painting to the seminary children. Something of an outsider, H. D.'s father was a professor of astronomy at Lehigh University. To H. D. he was always the calm, detached scientist whom she characterized as "pure New England," descendant in spirit as well as fact from the Puritan fathers who "burned witches and fought the Indians." When she was nine, her father became professor of astronomy at the University of Pennsylvania and director of the Flower Observatory in Upper Darby, near Philadelphia. Into this different world dominated by the upper-middle-class conventions of university life and Main Line society, H. D. brought her rich Bethlehem memories, which blended the warmth of her large extended family, the omnipresent art of her mother's family, the vivid imagery and melodies of Moravian hymns, and the familiar but mysterious rituals of the Unitas Fratrum—the love feasts, the kiss of peace, and candlelight processions on Christmas Eve.

Hilda was the sixth child and the only daughter to survive in the professor's large family. From his first marriage, there were Alice (who died in infancy), Alfred, and Eric (H. D.'s favorite half brother and her father's assistant). With Helen Wolle there were five more children: Gilbert, Edith (who died as a baby), Hilda, Harold, and Melvin. Always feeling "different" as the only girl among five brothers, H. D. remembered asking, "Why was it always a girl who had died?" She later decided that her survival was linked to her "gift," the combined capacity for artistic and religious inspiration that came from her mother's family.

Hilda was her austere father's favorite child. Only she was allowed to play quietly in his study and cut the pages of his new books. As a child, she associated the fables and myths she loved to read with her father's stars and the astrological symbols filling the pages of his work. Influenced by feminism's advocacy of the "new woman," the Professor was ambitious for his daughter. He wanted her to be a second Marie Curie, but his efforts to tutor her in math led to the now familiar syndrome of math anxiety. "The more he explained," H. D. recalled, "the less I understood." Eric, to whom she was very close, was more successful, helping Hilda with math and providing her with books by writers such as Louisa May Alcott, Jane Austen, and the

Hilda Doolittle, 1904 (courtesy of the Beinecke Rare Book and Manuscript Library, Yale University)

Brontës. William Carlos Williams remembered the Professor as a very distant man whose eyes did not focus on anything nearer than the moon, and Sigmund Freud told H. D. that he was "cold."

Hilda was drawn to her more spontaneous, artistic mother but was repeatedly hurt by her mother's open favoritism of Gilbert. Trying to get close to her mother, Hilda identified with Gilbert, the prototype of the many brother figures who people her later novels and poems. It was to her mother that she expressed excitement at a performance of *Uncle Tom's Cabin* which prompted her to ask, " 'Can ladies write books?' 'Why, yes,' her mother replied, 'lots of ladies write very good books.' " Hilda wanted to be an artist like her mother. But her father forbade art school, and her mother's self-effacement and conventional devotion to the Professor's work provided a problematic model for her aspiring daughter. H. D. recalled that as a child her mother had loved to sing, but she never once sang after her father complained of the "noise." "I wanted to paint like my mother," H. D. wrote in her Freud journals, "though she laughed at her pictures that we admired so. . . . My mother was morbidly self-effacing." As a wife in the world of Upper Darby, Helen Doolittle was known for silencing all talk when her husband signaled his desire to speak. Williams remembered her as a bustling, warmhearted matron always busy with children or her beautiful garden and well-known for her midnight missions to the Flower Observatory with hot water to thaw out the Professor's frozen whiskers, stuck to the telescope. As Hilda became a young woman, her mother increasingly represented the confines of feminine conventionality from which she had to escape in order to become an artist. But this belief in her artistic destiny did not come easily. The difficulty H. D. experienced in creating an identity that incorporated the various forms of her art and her womanhood is evident in her lifelong fascination with names as "signs" of an underlying self-creation. Not only H. D. but also Edith Gray, J. Beran, Rhoda Peter,

Helga Dart, Helga Dorn, John Helforth, D. A. Hill, and Delia Alton were to appear as "signatures" on her published and unpublished work.

The years from 1905 to 1911 were critical for H. D.'s later artistic development, not only because she experienced her first real intellectual and poetic awakenings, but also because as a woman she faced questions of identity revolving around the conflicting demands of sexuality, gender, and vocation. College did not provide the hoped-for environment for rebellion and growth. In 1905 she enrolled at Bryn Mawr College, well-known among women's colleges for its difficult "men's curriculum." In the following year she withdrew from college at mid-year, having done poorly in both math and English. "My essays were held up, as samples of the very worst description," she recalled years later. In her roman à clef *HERmione* (1981), written in 1927 and based on her life from 1905 to 1911, H. D. vividly described the crisis of identity she felt at age twenty: "I am Hermione Gart, a failure," which "meant fresh barriers, fresh chains." Cut off

The Doolittles, circa 1910: Charles Leander, Hilda, Melvin, Gilbert (wearing glasses), Helen, Harold, Eric, and Alfred (courtesy of the Beinecke Rare Book and Manuscript Library, Yale University)

from earning a teaching salary and being an "O.M., Old Maid precisely," she felt she was only "a disappointment to her father, an odd duckling to her mother, an importunate over-grown, unincarnated entity that had no place here."

H. D. found the stimulation that led to an artistic identity in her personal relationships, outside the family and classroom. Most important among her friends were Ezra Pound, William Carlos Williams, and Frances Josepha Gregg. She met Pound when she was fifteen. By 1903, Pound and Williams, both students at the University of Pennsylvania, visited the observatory on Sunday afternoons. What comes through Williams's ambivalent descriptions of Hilda in his *Autobiography* (1951) is the image of an intense young woman seeking to step outside the confinement of Victorian conventions. Williams found her angular beauty "bizarre," but was fascinated by her "provocative indifference to rule and order." She started to write poems, she told him, by splashing ink from her pen all over her clothes "to give her a feeling of freedom and indifference." Careless about her clothes, she wandered in the woods and fields, climbed fences, and once startled Williams by the ecstatic abandon with which she embraced a summer storm.

Pound, however, was H. D.'s first love and the one she returned to in memory and letters during the last years of her life, as recorded in her memoir *End to Torment* and her long poem *Winter Love* (1972). Together they shared their early poems and read William Morris, Algernon Swinburne, Henrik Ibsen, George Bernard Shaw, Yogi books, and Honoré de Balzac's *Seraphita* (1835). Pound named her Dryad, the wood spirit muse of his. earliest poems, especially those in the handmade volume now published as *Hilda's Book* (1979). In 1906 and 1907 Pound was a dashingly disreputable poet, but the professor's disapproval did not halt their developing "understanding" and final engagement. This engagement survived the Professor's disgust at finding them embracing, the scandal that followed Pound's resignation from his teaching position at Wabash College in 1907, the consequent need to meet secretly, and the rumors of Pound's "engagements" to other women. But their plans to marry gradually faded with the continued opposition of her family, the aftereffects of Pound's sudden trip to Europe in 1908, and Hilda's increasing discomfort with the idea of marriage. She had dreamed of a bohemian life with Pound, but the more their courtship progressed, the more conventional the romance became. In *HERmione*, H. D. wrote about feeling "smothered," "smudged out" by Pound,

whose kisses presaged a suffocation of the spirit in which she feared that she would become the object of his poem rather than the poet. "You are a poem, though your poem's nought," Pound apparently told her. In *End to Torment*, H. D. wrote that "Ezra would have destroyed me and the center they call 'Air and Crystal' of my poetry."

H. D.'s love for Pound, but disenchantment with her role as his muse, paralleled a deepening involvement with Frances Josepha Gregg, an intense young woman she met through her college friend Mary Herr, probably in 1910. Gregg wrote poetry and was something of a mystic, whose psychologically difficult childhood led to psychic abilities that entranced H. D. She found in Gregg the lost sister, the "twin soul" whom she described in *HERmione* as an "alter ego" who could "run, would leap, would be concealed under autumn sumac or lie shaken with hail and wind, lost on some Lacedaemonian foot-hill." The refrain from Swinburne's "Itylus," "*O sister, my sister, O fleet sweet*

A 1912 photograph of Frances Gregg, whom H. D. would later describe as her "twin soul"

swallow," which refers to the forbidden love between women, is the line that echoes through much of H. D.'s writings about Gregg—especially in the unpublished novels "Paint It Today" (written in 1921) and "Asphodel" (written in 1921-1922), and in *HERmione*. Both Pound and Helen Doolittle regarded their intimacy as "unwholesome," but with Gregg, H. D. felt freed from being the "decorative" object inspiring Pound's poems. In her unpublished "Autobiographical Notes" (written in 1949) H. D. described 1910 as the "Frances Gregg period" and noted that her first published work appeared in New York syndicated newspapers during that year. However, the first poems which fully pleased her were the lyrics she wrote for Gregg. She modeled these love poems on the pastorals of Theocritus that Pound had brought her. As Barbara Guest has shown, however, her relationship with Gregg was not without its problems. Gregg was not only possessive, but she engaged in a secret liaison with Pound which left H. D. feeling doubly betrayed when she found out. This erotic triangle complicated the poetic one. Pound hurt H. D. again by favoring Gregg's conventional lyrics over her own poems in the fall of 1911. Breaking the traditional patterns of both creativity and love proved to be a difficult task.

Whatever the stresses in the threesome, H. D.'s relationships with Pound and Gregg succeeded in loosening the control of her family and initiating her life as an artist. Loving both, H. D. was torn in two directions, between heterosexual love and lesbian love, each of which presented its own dynamic fusion of the visionary, the erotic, and the aesthetic. This bisexual pull remained one of the central patterns of H. D.'s later life, one which she discussed extensively with Freud and encoded in much of her writing.

In the summer of 1911, Hilda set off for a short visit to Europe in the company of Frances and Mrs. Gregg. In Paris she saw the musician Walter Rummel frequently, but London and Pound's literary circle offered the artistic stimulation she had sought for years. With some difficulty she convinced her parents to let her stay, and she returned to the United States for visits only four or five times until her death. Through Pound, H. D. met many of the writers who became her community of friends and fellow artists until 1919—especially people such as Richard Aldington, Yeats, Eliot, F. S. Flint, John Gould Fletcher, Ford Madox Hueffer (later Ford Madox Ford), Violet Hunt, May Sinclair, John Cournos, Wyndham Lewis, Brigit Patmore, Arthur Waley, George Plank, and Oli-

via and Dorothy Shakespear. H. D. was upset when she failed to convince Frances to stay with her in London (1911) and later devastated by Frances's sudden letter from the United States announcing her marriage to Louis Wilkinson (1912). In "Asphodel," part one of which deals with H. D.'s early London years, H. D. described the letter as "vitriolic blue acid" and recalled their earlier pact to be "modern women," never to marry. Gregg planned for H. D. to join her on her honeymoon trip to Europe, but Pound intervened and convinced H. D. to remain in London. The two women were never again so intimate, although Gregg published poems and fiction in the same journals as H. D., and they met and corresponded sporadically until 1939.

Pound's own engagement to Dorothy Shakespear also came as a shock to H. D., but increasingly the persistent attention of Aldington began to fill the emotional gap left by Pound and Gregg. They studied Greek together at the British Museum, wrote poetry, and read widely in French and English poetry. From the first, Aldington greatly admired H. D.'s talent and dedication, both of which he believed would lead to important achievements. Aldington, Pound, and H. D. frequently met for tea to discuss life and art, chiefly, Aldington later wrote, to establish "a comraderie of minds" and to laugh until their sides ached. They spent the spring of 1912 in Paris together, and after the arrival of her parents, Aldington and the Doolittles toured Italy, occasionally joined by Pound. Florence and Venice in particular always carried associations of this early companionship with Aldington, the idyllic quality of which H. D. celebrated in *Bid Me to Live (A Madrigal)* (1960), her roman à clef drafted in 1939 about the years 1912-1919. In October of 1913, Aldington and H. D. were married in the presence of her parents and Pound. H. D. had high hopes that their intimate companionship, based on mutual respect and love for poetry, would lead to a new kind of marriage, one which would foster the creative work of both partners.

By the time she married Aldington, H. D.'s literary career was already underway, her reputation as the best of the imagists well-established, thanks to the efforts of Pound and her own hard work. Imagism, the short-lived but influential movement officially in existence from 1913 until 1917, was launched in the tea shop of the British Museum in September of 1912. H. D. had given Pound three new poems, "Epigram," "Hermes of the Ways," and "Priapus" (later titled "Orchard"), and he was impressed with their hardness, clarity, and intensity—the very qualities he associated with the best of poetic tradition and advocated for modern poetry. In *End to Torment* H. D. recalled the scene: " 'But Dryad,' (in the Museum tea room), 'this is poetry.' He slashed with a pencil. 'Cut this out, shorten this line. "Hermes of the Ways" is a good title. I'll send this to Harriet Monroe of *Poetry*. Have you a copy? Yes? Then we can send this, or I'll type it when I get back. Will this do?' And he scrawled 'H. D. Imagiste' at the bottom of the page." H. D.'s recollection almost fifty years later captures the contradictory but crucial role Pound played in the construction of modern poetry. Ever the impresario, Pound was domineering, but generous; blunt, but fair; free with his editing pen, but unerringly sharp in his advice, as he later was in drastically cutting Eliot's draft of *The Waste Land* (1922). No longer her fiancé entangling poetry with the demands of a lover, Pound was her greatest promoter. "The strangest thing," H. D. later wrote, "is that Ezra was so inexpressibly kind to anyone who he felt had the faintest spark of submerged talent." She was delighted to abandon her surname, which seemed, she later reflected, to mock her aspirations; "Do-little" was hardly an encouraging name for an ambitious young woman. However, the violence of his slashing pen in her description of his naming "H. D. Imagiste" suggests an ominous undertone in his support, as Sandra Gilbert, Susan Gubar, and Janice Robinson have suggested. His power to name, upon which her new identity depended, carried with it a threat to her autonomy as a creative artist, as she was later to explore in *HERmione*.

Pound believed that she had more than a faint spark of talent, and he wrote to Monroe in October of 1912: "am sending you some *modern* stuff by an American, I say modern, for it is in the laconic speech of the Imagistes. . . . Objective—no slither; direct—no excessive use of adjectives, no metaphors that won't permit examination. It's straight talk, straight as the Greek!" The opening lines of "Hermes of the Ways" bear out Pound's praise of a poetic language cleansed of Victorian and Georgian excesses:

> The hard sand breaks,
> and the grains of it
> are clear as wine.
>
> Far off over the leagues of it,
> the wind,
> playing on the wide shore,

> piles little ridges,
> and the great waves
> break over it.

Monroe published "Epigram," "Hermes of the Ways," and "Priapus" in the January 1913 issue of *Poetry* under the signature of H. D., Imagiste. More poems by H. D. and others rapidly appeared in subsequent issues of *Poetry* with the imagist label. Although Pound and Aldington had used the term *imagist* before the publication of H. D.'s poems, H. D.'s three poems were the first fully imagist poems, according to Cyrena Pondrom, who argued that Pound's poetry changed dramatically after he saw "Hermes of the Ways" and "Priapus."

Many writers and literary historians have speculated that Pound created the imagist movement to describe and promote the poems that H. D. was writing. While her innovative and influential role in the history of modern poetry should be recognized, imagism was not synonymous with H. D. It was a genuine movement, held together by personal ties and a loose consensus of principles, magnetically drawing many diverse poets who later constituted the modernist poetic mainstream. Its roots went back to the Poet's Club of 1908 whose members (including Pound and T. E. Hulme) developed a theory of "the image," but wrote little poetry that embodied its doctrine. Pound edited the first imagist anthology, *Des Imagistes* (1914), having selected poems from eleven poets (including the four charter imagists, H. D., Aldington, Flint, and himself, as well as Amy Lowell, Joyce, Williams, Hueffer, and Cournos). With publication arranged by Lowell, three more imagist anthologies followed. *Some Imagist Poets* (1915, 1916, 1917) drew in a wider circle of poets, including D. H. Lawrence, whom H. D. met through Lowell in August 1914. The story of Pound's break from the imagists has been frequently told: the poets advocated a democratic selection process and a more inclusive definition of imagist principles while Pound wanted to maintain his exclusive editorial power and a narrow doctrine. Avoiding an open fight with Pound, H. D. and Aldington nonetheless supported Lowell and the idea of democratic decision making for the anthology. The poets published in nonestablishment journals like *Poetry*, the *Little Review*, and the *New Freewoman* (a feminist journal controlled by Dora Marsden and Rebecca West, for which Pound and Aldington served as literary editors; in 1914 the journal's name changed to the *Egoist*, but it continued to publish feminist articles). Although the imagists were frequently attacked, imitators sprang up everywhere, and their anthologies sold extremely well (Aldington's later estimate was 20,000 copies). The devastating impact of World War I and a growing diversity of the imagist poets led to the official abandonment of the annual anthologies by 1918. In 1930 Aldington organized a final imagist anthology, but the group had effectively disbanded by the end of the war.

The imagist principles which H. D.'s poems epitomize had their roots in the prewar intellectual crosscurrents that mingled the ideas of Henri Bergson and T. E. Hulme, the art of the Postimpressionists and cubists, the new Freudian psychoanalysis filtered through the work of Bernard Hart, and the poetic forms of the Japanese haiku, Greek lyrics, French symbolism, vers libre, and troubadour poetry of medieval Provence. In the March 1913 issue of *Poetry* Pound and Flint published two articles on imagist "rules" for the production of poems "in accordance with the best tradition . . . in Sappho, Catullus, Villon." Flint specified the three rules: "1. Direct treatment of the 'thing,' whether subjective or objective. 2. To use absolutely no word that did not contribute to the presentation. 3. As regarding rhythm: to compose in sequence of the musical phrase, not in sequence of a metronome." Pound expanded by defining the "Doctrine of the Image" to which Flint had enigmatically alluded: "An 'Image' is that which presents an intellectual and emotional complex in an instant of time. I use the term "complex" rather in the technical sense employed by the newer psychologists, such as Hart. . . . It is the presentation of such a "complex" instantaneously which gives that sense of sudden liberation. The poets of the 1915 imagist anthology expanded the "rules" to six principles in their preface, stressing that the language of poetry should be the language of "common speech," that poems should avoid "vague generalities," and that "concentration is the essence of poetry." "We oppose the cosmic poet," they wrote. Free verse was not an absolute prescription, but the influence of French vers libre on the individualized music of the imagist poets was apparent to critics and proponents alike. "Oread," H. D.'s most frequently anthologized poem, which was first published in 1914, demonstrates why poets regarded her as the quintessential imagist and a master craftsman:

> Whirl up, sea—
> Whirl your pointed pines,
> splash your great pines
> on our rocks,

> hurl your green over us,
> Cover us with your pools of fir.

H. D.'s ability to concentrate language, construct a musical line, and project intensity through the crystalline image gave poetic flesh to imagist doctrine. But she did not write poetry to fit the theory, nor did she contribute in print to the doctrinal debates about imagism. Rather, she was "true to" her personal *daemon*, as she described her muse to Cournos and Lawrence. It is probably more accurate to say that imagist doctrine was developed to describe the poetry she wrote. Her importance to the development of modern free verse is evident in the awards she won from *Poetry* magazine in 1915 and the *Little Review* in 1917. According to the reviewers and scholars who wrote about her work in the 1910s and 1920s (such as Flint, Lowell, Sinclair, Eliot, Pound, Monroe, Williams, H. P. Collins, Alfred Kreymborg, and Marianne Moore), her work was very influential in the legitimization of the "modern" style of poetry.

H. D.'s very perfection as an imagist poet, however, has tended to obscure what was unique in her early poetry, qualities that reflected her American background, encoded her gender-related attempts to escape from the confines of Victorian femininity, and prefigured the prophetic voice of her work in the 1940s and 1950s. Pound was no doubt correct in writing to Monroe that H. D.'s poems were as concrete and direct as those of the Greeks. *Sea Garden*, her first volume, published in 1916, evokes a generalized Greek landscape, with its naming of various gods and shrines. However, this landscape of rocky shore, forest, and flowers came not from Greece, as her readers often assumed, but from her American childhood, as she later told Norman Holmes Pearson, the Yale professor who became her close friend, adviser, and literary executor in the 1940s and 1950s. While the urban world of London gave H. D. the freedom to write, the natural world of *Sea Garden* was rooted in her mother's garden, the fields and woods of Upper Darby, and the shorelines of Maine, New Jersey, and Rhode Island. Her rhythmic lines, with their unconventional patterns of resonant and dissonant sound, were her mother's musical gift transposed to language.

The natural world of *Sea Garden* is not itself the subject of any given poem, as objects often are in Williams's imagist poems such as "Poem" or "The Red Wheelbarrow." Rather, nature serves as the vehicle that objectifies consciousness in H. D.'s early work. Creating a modernist version of American transcendentalism, for which "nature is a symbol of spirit," H. D. uses the natural world to explore the subjectivities of consciousness. The wind, the sand, the sea iris become what Eliot was to call the "objective correlative" for the poet's emotion in his essay "Tradition and the Individual Talent" (1919). Some poems, such as the well-known "Heat" or "Pear Tree," convey the poet's sensations in experiencing heavy summer heat or bursting pear blossoms. Others rely on objects from nature to incarnate human subjectivity, as in "Mid-Day": "a split leaf crackles on the paved floor." Still others, such as the often-anthologized "Storm," are influenced by the Japanese haiku and use nature to suggest fleeting human perception of life's evanescence, as in "The Pool":

> Are you alive?
> I touch you.
> You quiver like a sea-fish.
> I cover you with my net.
> What are you—banded one?

H. D.'s construction of the image, based in nature, to explore subjectivity accounts for the paradoxical tension in her imagist lyrics between what some of her critics called "fire" and "ice"—that is, between a cold objectivity and a fiery passion. The poet Robert Duncan, who regards H. D. and Pound as his poetic mother and father, identifies this quality in H. D.'s early lyrics as her "animism" or "sense of the sacred," which prefigures the hermeticism of her later work. The ecstatic intensity that underlies these poems evokes both Sappho and Euripides, the two Greek poets to whom she most often turned. As Susan Gubar has argued, H. D. identified deeply with Sappho, the woman who was both mother and lover of women, the woman poet who shone so brilliantly out of a largely male poetic tradition. Like Sappho's passionate lyric, Euripides' exploration of Dionysian and Eleusinian mysteries attracted H. D. Their controlled and concrete images for disruptive and forbidden desire served as a linguistic model for her poems of ecstatic abandon. Williams's memory of her youthful passion in the fields and shores removed from the proper drawing rooms of her home found chiseled expression in her imagist lyric, poems such as "Acon," "Sea Gods," "Pursuit," "Wind Sleepers," "Orchard," "The Gift," and "Huntress." The crashing waves of "Oread," for example, match Williams's memory of Hilda's walking straight into dangerous breakers and appearing "entranced" as the waves knocked her flat and finally unconscious. In the

words of Adalaide Morris, H. D.'s imagist poems are "bridges to the sacred."

The objectification of human passion in H. D's imagist poems highlights another quality that distinguishes them from other imagist poems. Taken as a whole, *Sea Garden* is a volume that indirectly explores the unnamed, impersonal identity of the poet. The poet appears before the reader enigmatically hidden behind initials. Anticipating Eliot's ideal of the "impersonal poet" in "Tradition and the Individual Talent," the early imagist "H. D." was a disembodied figure, taken out of time, out of history, out of gender. The anguish of a poem like "Mid-Day," the loss of "Loss," the prostration of "Orchard," the ecstasy of "Hermes of the Ways" were all undoubtedly emotions anchored in historical self, in events with a place, time, and circumstance. But H. D.'s presentations of these emotions deliberately removed them from any historical reference, unlike, for example, Lawrence's intensely autobiographical lyrics in *Look! We Have Come Through!* (1918), some of which also appeared in imagist anthologies. When Amy Lowell published a photo of H. D. without her permission in *Tendencies in Modern American Poetry* (1917), H. D. was furious: "It's not that picture, but any picture! The initials, 'H. D.,' had no identity attached; they could have been pure spirit. But with this I'm embodied."

As disembodied as the *Sea Garden* poems appear, they are nonetheless poems about identity. Removed from the confines of respectability, the natural world of *Sea Garden* is a kind of pastoral realm imaginatively existing outside culture, what Louis Martz aptly called "borderline." "Sheltered Garden" serves as a kind of touchstone for the volume, highlighting the poet's desire to escape from the suffocating "border-pinks" of the domestic garden into the "coarse weeds" of "some terrible/wind-tortured place." Read as a coded poem about the female self, "Sea Rose" opens *Sea Garden* with an expression of the poet's simultaneous vulnerability as a woman, rejection of conventional femininity, and defiant celebration of her difference. She is unlike the beautiful domestic rose, but nonetheless more precious for her wildness:

> Rose, harsh rose,
> marred and with stint of petals,
> meagre flower, thin,
> sparse of leaf,
>
> more precious
> than a wet rose

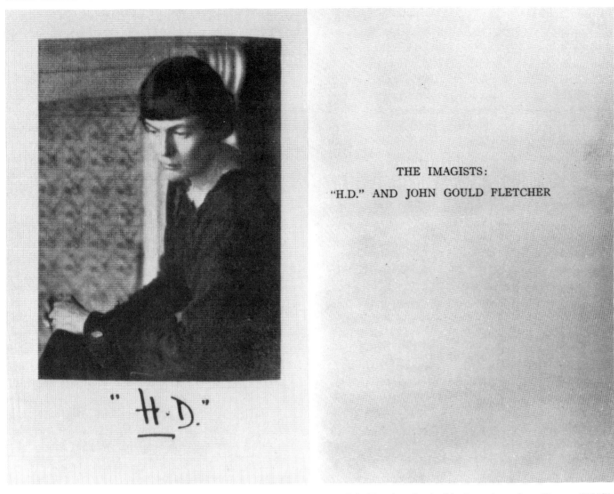

THE IMAGISTS:

"H.D." AND JOHN GOULD FLETCHER

When Amy Lowell published Doolittle's picture over the signature "H. D." in Tendencies in Modern American Poetry *(1917), Doolittle was furious because, she explained, "The initials, 'H. D.,' had no identity attached; they could have been pure spirit. But with this I'm embodied." Nonetheless, she later referred to herself as H. D.*

single on a stem—
you are caught in the drift.

Many of the moderns condemned Victorian sentiment and clichéd beauty, but H. D.'s celebration of the wild and the harsh carries overtones of her denial of traditional femininity. Many of her imagist poems implicitly question culturally prescribed gender and advocate an androgynous identity, as in "Oread," with the fusion of land and sea, masculine and feminine; or in "The Huntress" and "The Shrine," with their worship of Artemis and approving portraits of strong women; or in "The Contest," which presents three different modes of masculinity. These patterns reflect H. D.'s emergence from a Victorian past and anticipate the revision of conventional gender that characterizes her great epics.

Permeating H. D.'s early revisionary exploration of female identity is an austere sensuality, an erotic dimension of repressed yet explosive sexuality that is nonreferential in nature. Like the potent flowers in Lawrence's early novels and Georgia O'Keeffe's paintings, H. D.'s flowers indirectly suggest an intense eroticism, whose power comes precisely from its elusive, nonhuman expression. Related to her animistic sense of the sacred, H. D.'s objective correlatives for the self often radiate erotic energy and rhythms. In particular, the five flower poems of *Sea Garden* ("Sea Rose," "Sea Lily," "Sea Poppies," "Sea Violet," and "Sea Iris") structure that volume and underline its revisionary treatment of the sentimental Victorian language of flowers. They also contrast sharply with the sexuality of Moore's poems (which H. D. nonetheless greatly admired) and the direct "wantoness" of Aldington, who wrote for example: "The moon/with a rag of gauze about her loins/Poses among them [chimneys], an awkward Venus—/And here am I looking wantonly at her/Over the kitchen sink."

To explore the nature of her difference in her imagist lyrics, H. D. repeatedly established dualisms that paralleled the fundamental polarity of male and female, masculine and feminine, another aspect of her imagist poems that is both unique to her work and continuous with her later development. Her imagist poems are often linguistically and thematically structured on polarities such as land and sea, hard and soft, ripe and unripe, wild and sheltered, swift and slow, stunted and lush, torn and whole, pointed and round, positive and negative, salt and sweet, and so forth. Prefiguring the philosophic dualisms and dialectics of her *Trilogy* (*The Walls Do Not Fall*, 1944; *Tribute to the Angels*, 1945; and *The Flowering of the Rod*, 1946) and *Helen in Egypt* (1961), these oppositions reflect the divisions H. D. always felt, what she called the "two's and two's and two's in my life," ultimately "this unsatisfied duality," "this mother-father" that "tears at our entrails." Reflecting in part her pride in her difference, and her separation from the conventional or sentimental, H. D. always rejected the ripe for the unripe, the lovely for the harsh, the soft for the hard. At the same time, however, her representation of polarity became the first step in a dialectical process moving toward synthesis.

As poems deliberately removed from the historical moment, few of H. D.'s imagist lyrics deal directly with World War I, which was gradually engulfing the personal moment of her success as well as a whole historical era, but "Loss" (*Sea Garden*), "Prisoners" (*Sea Garden*), and "The Tribute" (*Egoist*, November 1916), highly ritualized and distanced poems, are indirectly about the war that was destroying a generation. The four and a half war years left H. D.'s life and relationships shattered, permanently scarred by the intersecting catastrophes of public and private worlds. Against a backdrop of mindless patriotism and omnipresent death in a trench war for blasted territory, a series of events fragmented the poetic identity forged in imagist successes and the balance of woman-poet she had achieved with Aldington. The first trauma was the stillbirth of her child in 1915, a loss she believed was brought on by the news of the *Lusitania*'s sinking. With Britain reeling under the shocking army casualties, H. D. suppressed her private grief and found that her new friend D. H. Lawrence was the only one who seemed to understand her loss. Her friendship with Lawrence grew

rapidly, and by 1916 they were regularly exchanging drafts of poems by mail, a fact that made Aldington jealous because of the intensity of their bond.

The second event that ultimately resulted in the dissolution of her marriage was Aldington's entrance into the army in 1916. He enlisted to avoid conscription into a war he despised, and his experiences at the front understandably produced a profound change in his outlook. For all his cynicism about the war, H. D. found him transformed into a soldier, insensitive and mocking about their prewar dedication to poetry. She took over his post as literary editor for the *Egoist* and worked hard to keep the flame of poetry alive, her way of countering the nihilism of the war years; he continued to be involved in literary plans but was unable to write much poetry. Paralyzed by the smell of gas on his breath, by her fear for his death, and by her doctor's orders not to get pregnant, H. D. began to associate his frequent sexual demands during his leaves with death; as she later wrote, "the War was my husband." By mid-1917 his leaves had become nightmares. Aldington's brief affairs with other women (most hurtfully with H. D.'s close friend Brigit Patmore) may well have begun during her pregnancy in 1915. But by 1917, he began an extended affair with Dorothy Yorke, an American H. D. was sheltering at the request of Cournos. Aldington wrote H. D. from the front in 1918, "I love you, but desire *l'autre*." Both agreed that she should leave London, enjoy an affair with music historian Cecil Gray in Cornwall, and return to Aldington at the end of the war. Her resulting pregnancy upset Aldington, as the affair did not; but H. D. refused to abort the child or to marry Gray, and Aldington's promises to care for her and the child were reassuring.

The third distressing event was the "loss of the friendship with Lawrence." In the fall of 1917 H. D. sheltered the Lawrences at 44 Mecklenburgh Square after they had been expelled from Cornwall because of Frieda Lawrence's German citizenship. There had been some tensions in their relationship—H. D. had not liked his manuscript of *Women in Love* (1920). She rejected his "blood-stream, his sex-fixations, his man-is-man, woman-is-woman" and was angry when he told her that she should stick to the "woman-consciousness" and not try to write about men. But in *Bid Me to Live* she wrote about Lawrence as her twin, her equal in "cerebral" intensity. Frieda Lawrence may well have set them up for an affair, but according to H. D., Lawrence rejected her and then later abruptly brought their relationship to an end when he learned of her affair with Gray. H. D.'s portrait of their intense artistic communion, but aborted affair, is consistent with references to Lawrence in her letters. In 1935 she wrote after reading Frieda Lawrence's *Not I, But the Wind . . .* (1934), "how grateful I am . . . that I never slept with D. H. L.; it makes my hair stand on end—his talk of men being 'morphia' to her." The importance of the relationship between H. D. and Lawrence is evident in the number of allusions each made to the other in such works as Lawrence's *Aaron's Rod* (1922), *Kangaroo* (1923), and *The Man Who Died* (1929) and H. D.'s *Bid Me to Live, Tribute to Freud* (1956), the unpublished novel "Pilate's Wife" (written in 1924, 1934), and the unpublished memoir "Compassionate Friendship" (written in 1955).

The fourth trauma H. D. suffered during World War I was a series of blows initiated by the death of her brother Gilbert in France and the subsequent death of her father from shock early in 1919. When she first got the news of her father's death, she was nearly ready to deliver. Suddenly she caught the deadly influenza of 1919 and was not expected to survive. Pound visited the nursing home to say, "My only real criticism is that this is not my child." The landlady demanded burial money from H. D.'s new friend Bryher (Winifred Ellerman), daughter of shipping magnate Sir John Ellerman. But H. D. and her daughter Perdita, born 31 March 1919, miraculously survived, and she decided to return to Aldington, as he had requested. When she arrived at his hotel, however, he told her he could not give up Yorke and threatened that if she registered Perdita in his name, he would have her thrown in jail and subjected to penal servitude. Defiantly, H. D. registered the child as Frances Perdita Aldington, but remained frightened for years that Aldington would carry out his threat. In her divorce papers (1937) and a number of memoirs, H. D. referred to March of 1919 as a "psychic death" from which she really did not recover until World War II. As a friend told her, an "asbestos curtain" dropped between H. D. and her pre-March self. She survived to begin a new life with Bryher and Perdita by repressing the interlocking events of love and betrayal, pregnancy and war, poetry and the loss of her male lover-poet companions. The result was what she called her personal "War Phobia," whereby the threat or reality of war triggered the associations of personal and historical catastrophe and the resultant breakdown.

Bryher's love and promise of a trip to Greece

H. D. and Perdita, 1919 (courtesy of the Beinecke Rare Book and Manuscript Library, Yale University)

saved H. D.'s life. They had met in July of 1918, when Bryher's request for a meeting with the mysterious "H. D.," whose poems she had memorized, resulted in an invitation to tea and a lifelong relationship. H. D. later wrote that Bryher took "the place of Frances." Fiery yet sturdy, deeply troubled yet steadily loyal and practical, Bryher was nothing like the "fey," psychic Frances. Herself a writer, she changed her name to Bryher (after one of the Scilly Isles), her declaration of independence from the demands of her wealthy family and the constrictions of a feminine destiny. The poem to Bryher which opens *Palimpsest* (1926) describes the role she played in H. D.'s life: "when all the others, blighted, reel and fall,/your star, steelset, keeps lone and frigid trist/to freighted ships baffled in wind and blast." During this period, however, Bryher was herself suicidal, confused about her sexual identity, angry at the patriarchal system, and yearning to be a boy. The two women sustained each other, with Perdita providing a compelling reason to survive.

Bryher in Capri, 1922 (courtesy of Perdita Schaffner)

Thought and Vision (1982), an experimental prose meditation about the interconnections between the conscious and unconscious, creativity and procreativity, gender and the imagination. No description of her "jelly-fish" vision has survived, although she wrote and rewrote about this and other psychic phenomena she had felt chosen to witness. But the word "Fish" hereafter served as her overall code word signifying the messages that come from the unconscious or the supernatural as hieroglyphs of hermetic wisdom.

The most important trip, however, was the journey to Greece that Bryher had promised H. D. In the spring of 1920 they set off with Ellis on the *Borodino* on a still-dangerous tour through the mine-infested seas to Greece and Crete. On board ship H. D. experienced a strange alteration of space and time that seemed to transform the choppy sea into a timeless Botticelli painting of dancing dolphins and the handsome Peter Rodeck at her side into an ideal lover. Rather than destroy that ideal by having a real affair with Rodeck, as she had been about to do, she let him remain in the realm of the imagination as an archetypal lover who informed the figure of the male lover in later works such as "Pilate's Wife," *Palimpsest*, and *Helen in Egypt* (1961). On the island of Corfu H. D. saw what she called the "writing-on-the-wall," a series of flickering light pictures mysteriously projected onto her wall, whether from her subconscious mind or some other source, she did not know. Each picture was like a Tarot card whose translation might reveal future pathways for healing and renewed creativity: first, a soldier's head; then a mystic chalice; next a spirit lamp like the sacred tripod at Delphi; then tiny people at the base of the tripod; then a ladder of light leading to her own special sign, the image of Niké (Victory) flying free; and finally a sun disk from which a man beckoned to draw the Niké into the circle of light. Waiting patiently at her side, Bryher saw nothing until H. D. dropped her face in her hands as the image of Niké's flight faded. It was Bryher who "read" the final picture script. "Perhaps," H. D. later wrote, "we were 'seeing' it together, for without her, admittedly, I could not have gone on."

The trip to Greece was for H. D.; Bryher herself yearned for the imagined freedom of the "New World," from which H. D. herself had had to flee. Hoping to immigrate to America in 1921, Bryher took H. D. to New York in the fall of 1920. After meeting Marianne Moore, with whom H. D. had corresponded since 1916, H. D. and Bryher headed out to Hollywood and the California coast. They

As Bryher later wrote, "H. D. had a great gift for friendship." During the spring and summer of 1919 they saw a great deal of Havelock Ellis, whose progressive ideas seemed to validate both their anger and love.

A series of journeys from 1919 to 1923 brought both H. D. and Bryher back to a productive, creative life and gave H. D. many of the fundamental motifs and symbols of her later work. They also set the scene for a number of H. D.'s visionary experiences, moments of altered consciousness that she regarded as a kind of personal oracle whose enigmatic messages she must learn to translate. In July 1919 they spent an idyllic month in the Scilly Isles off Cornwall, where H. D. had what she later termed her "jelly-fish" and "bell-jar" experiences. Anticipating Sylvia Plath's metaphor in *The Bell Jar* (1963), H. D. at one point felt enclosed in a "double globe" from which she safely regarded the world as if she were seeing through water. She wrote about the experience in *Notes on* were disappointed with commercialized cinema but delighted with the wild shores of the Pacific, where they experimented with their cameras by taking nude photos of each other on the isolated coast, as Diana Collecott has discovered. After returning to New York, Bryher abruptly proposed marriage to the writer Robert McAlmon, a liaison which she hoped would provide her with freedom from her family and him with money to promote the arts. All three returned to Europe, where their residences, both separate and together, shifted rapidly between London, Paris, and Switzerland. One of their first activities was to publish a volume of Moore's poetry without her permission (*Poems*, 1921). H. D.'s and Bryher's friendship with Moore remained an important source of creative and emotional support for all three women. H. D. and Moore, in particular, remained enthusiastic admirers of each others' work. After H. D.'s mother

H. D. in Egypt, 1923 (courtesy of the Beinecke Rare Book and Manuscript Library, Yale University)

joined them in 1922, H. D. went to Greece with her mother, stopping briefly on the island of Lesbos, where H. D. felt empowered by the spirit of Sappho. Finally, in 1923, H. D., Bryher, and Mrs. Doolittle went to Egypt, where they chanced to be present at the opening of King Tut's tomb. The hieroglyphs and treasures of a world more ancient than Greece fascinated H. D., who turned repeatedly to Egypt as a symbol for the sacred, in works such as *Palimpsest*, "Pilate's Wife," *Trilogy*, and *Helen in Egypt*.

These journeys with Bryher were indicative of the direction of H. D.'s life and art for the next two decades. The years between the two world wars were for H. D. decades of search, quests for selfhood and direction that led to extensive experimentation in her writing, voracious reading in wide areas of research, involvement in cinema, the creation of a new community of artists, and immersion in both psychoanalysis and the occult. Imagism as a poetic prescription was inadequate to deal with the events of history, with the violence of war, and with the fragmentation of belief that affected a whole generation. The dissolution of symbolic systems unveiled as grand illusions impelled a literature centered on quest, art whose epic forms and cosmic themes were consistent with the search for new patterns of meaning. Imagism began as a philosophy of art but evolved into a craft that served the larger explorations of the modernist poets. In the postwar years, H. D.'s former writing companions abandoned the short lyric to engage in the cosmic quests that underlay works such as *The Cantos*, *Paterson*, and *The Waste Land*. The development of H. D.'s poetry from imagist to epic art follows this modernist path, but while Pound and Williams had their life works well underway in the 1920s, she took a more indirect route to find what she called her "true direction." She often imaged the period between the wars in terms of the life cycle of the butterfly. She was Psyche, the soul wrapped in the chrysalis, the shroud spun by the disasters of the war. The result of this gestation was an explosion of creativity in the midst of World War II and the major modernist achievements of her mature poetic voice in the 1940s and 1950s.

In the decade following World War I H. D. wrote constantly, publishing a few volumes and piling up stacks of manuscripts that she left unpublished for a variety of reasons. As she wrote her American friend Viola Jordan, "I sit at my typewriter until I drop. I have in some way, to justify my existence, and then it is also a pure 'trade' with me now. It is my 'job.' " Perdita, later remembering the precious but rationed hours with her mother, recalled H. D. telling her that her steady disciplined writing was "like working on a sampler. So many stitches and just so many rows, day after day. If I miss even one day, I drop a stitch and lose the pattern and I feel I'm never going to find it again."

H. D. felt trapped by the imagist label, by the expectations of her critics who held up to her what they thought "H. D. ought to be like. . . . I say WHO is H. D.? They all think they know more about what and why she should or should not be or do than I." She later said that the imagist term could not be used to describe her work since World War I, but actually her growth beyond imagist constraints began to be evident in the 1917 imagist anthology. Between 1921 and 1931 H. D. published four full-length volumes of poetry and one verse drama, all of which demonstrate the difficult transition for H. D. between imagism as aesthetic into imagism as craft: *Hymen* (1921), *Heliodora and Other Poems* (1924), *Hippolytus Temporizes* (1927), and *Red Roses for Bronze* (1931). Her *Collected Poems* appeared in 1925 and received generally good reviews, especially from her fellow poets Moore and Williams, who agreed on the importance of her body of work for modern poetry. Although these volumes were quite widely and positively reviewed in the literary journals of England and America and although a number of the poems such as "Helen" (*Nation and Athenaeum*, 27 January 1923), have been frequently anthologized, they have yet to receive sustained criticism in the scholarly literature, perhaps since no one volume stands out with the innovative sharpness of *Sea Garden* or the comprehensive vision of her later work.

Many of the poems in these volumes, however, are brilliant, both revealing central conflicts in her identity as a woman poet and anticipating the revisionary direction of *Trilogy* and *Helen in Egypt*. Poems such as "Eurydice" (*Collected Poems*), "Helen" (*Heliodora*), "Leda" (*Hymen*), "At Ithaca" (*Heliodora*), "Heliodora" (*Heliodora*), and "Pygmalion" (*Collected Poems*) demonstrate how H. D. began to move in simultaneously opposite but reinforcing directions after her success with *Sea Garden*: the revisionary re-creations of myth and the autobiographical use of mythic masks. She increasingly used the lyric form to explore various classical myths as the texts of culture, as the largely masculine words that have told women's stories and constructed the meaning of woman's nature. Eliot, Pound, Yeats, and Williams were also engaged in this period with mythology, whose stories they hoped might contain shards of meaning which

could help heal the fragmented modern world. Like them, H. D. read widely in the current anthropological and classical research, books such as James Frazer's *The Golden Bough* (1907-1915), Jane Harrison's *Prolegomena to the Study of Greek Religion* (1903), Jessie Weston's *The Quest of the Holy Grail* (1913), and Louis Farnell's *Cults of the Greek States* (1896-1909). But unlike her fellow poets, H. D.'s transformation of myth involved a critique of classical tradition from a woman's perspective.

Most brilliantly in "Eurydice" (*Egoist*, May 1917) and "Helen," H. D.'s myth poems in general give speech to the silent women of mythology, whose stories have been overwhelmingly told by a male literary and religious tradition. As Rachel Blau DuPlessis pointed out, H. D.'s "Eurydice," for example, reverses the traditional lament of Orpheus for his lost love by presenting a defiant Eurydice who angrily condemns her husband: "So for your arrogance/and your ruthlessness/I have lost the earth/and the flowers of the earth." Eurydice then transforms her bondage in hell into a celebration of autonomy: "At least I have the flowers of myself,/and my thoughts, no god/can take that;/ I have the fervour of myself for a presence/and my own spirit for light." As an answer to the representations of Helen in Homer, Poe, and Yeats, H. D.'s "Helen" is an ominous poem about the paralyzing misogyny at the heart of male worship of woman's beauty: "All Greece hates/the still eyes in the white face/ . . . /could love indeed the maid,/ only if she were laid,/white ash amid funeral cypresses." "Cassandra" (*Rhythmus*, June-July 1923) is a poem about gynophobia, particularly male fear of woman's potent speech, which in this poem makes a woman unmarriageable. The highly encoded "Demeter" (*Collected Poems*) carries lesbian overtones in its suggestion that Demeter's passionate kiss of Koré is greater in love than her rough rape by Hades. H. D.'s brilliantly erotic "Leda" (*Monthly Chapbooks*, July 1919) reverses centuries of literary and artistic tradition, which usually features Zeus in the shape of a swan raping Leda. There is no rape or violence in H. D.'s poem, in which the red swan and the gold lily commingle in the gold-red sunset, "Where tide and river meet." An objective correlative for Leda, the lily is an image whose traditional associations with female genitalia demonstrate how H. D.'s imagist craft was becoming inseparable from her revisionary stance toward mythology. These poems anticipate the feminist revisionary nature of "Callypso Speaks" (written in the 1930s, partially published in *Poetry*, June 1938) and the poems of the 1940s and 1950s.

They are also important precursors for the reinterpretations of classical mythology common in the work of later women poets such as Muriel Rukeyser (who knew and admired H. D.), May Sarton (who also knew H. D.), Louise Bogan, Mona Van Duyn, Denise Levertov, Margaret Atwood, Anne Sexton, Adrienne Rich, and Judy Grahn.

H. D.'s poems of the late war years and the 1920s not only reinterpret myth, but they also sometimes use myth as a distancing mask for her own life. Generally more autobiographical than the "impersonal" poems of *Sea Garden*, specific situations and relationships can be identified in some of these poems with the help of biographical clues. Louis Martz, for example, has discovered that H. D. masked three important poems about her disintegrating relationship with Aldington ("Amaranth," "Eros," and "Envy," not published in their original form until *Collected Poems, 1912-1944*, 1983) as expansions of fragments of Sappho. "Fragment Forty" (*Heliodora*) and "Fragment Forty-one" (*Heliodora*) include slightly altered and disguised portions of these poems about herself and Aldington. The deserted women of "Circe" (*Egoist*, December 1916) and "Toward the Piraeus" (Heliodora) are disguised versions of H. D., addressing Aldington about his affairs and desertion. "At Baia" (*Poetry*, 1921), *"They said"* (*Hymen*), "We Two" (*Poetry*, 1921), "Stars Wheel in Purple" (*Palimpsest*), and "I Said" (written in 1919, first published in *Collected Poems, 1912-1944*) are about Bryher. In her verse play *Hippolytus Temporizes* (1927) and the Phaedra poems ("Phaedra," *Dial*, November 1920; "She Contrasts Herself with Hippolyta," *Hymen;* "She Rebukes Hippolyta," *Dial*, November 1920), H. D. explored her own bisexuality as well as the myth of the Amazon Hippolyta. Standing behind the personal and mythic dimensions of these poems is the lyric voice of Sappho, whose influence on H. D. in the 1920s is evident in H. D.'s translations of Sappho, her re-creations of full-length poems from extant fragments, and her essay on Sappho, written about 1920 and first published as "The Wise Sappho" in *Notes on Thought and Vision* (1982). Influenced as well by her reading of Colette and Emily Dickinson in the 1920s, H. D.'s poetry weaves the personal and mythic into a tapestry that recreates from a woman's perspective the connections between identity, love, and poetry.

Red Roses for Bronze (1931), a volume with which H. D. herself was dissatisfied, demonstrates that the vein she mined in the earlier volumes was petering out. However, the title poem, "Red Roses

for Bronze," is an important, highly coded poem about her relationship with the famous Afro-American singer and actor Paul Robeson. Like her earlier myth poems and the prose of the 1920s, it examines the connection between passion and poetry. "Halcyon" (first published in *Poetry*, June 1927), a lovely poem about her relationship with Bryher, has the interestingly different conversational tone of an intimate, realistic portrait. "Triplex" is an important poem about the conflict of identities women face in a culture which divides the feminine into the images of Artemis, Athene, and Aphrodite: "Let them not war in me," the poet prays. The volume also contains the beautiful "Epitaph" that was later placed on H. D.'s headstone in Bethlehem. But taken as a whole, the volume has little drive and direction. During the 1930s H. D. wrote little poetry compared to her previous production. A collection of nine poems significantly entitled "The Dead Priestess Speaks" was never published in her lifetime, and only occasional poems (including "The Poet," "Sigil," "Callypso Speaks") came out in journals.

H. D.'s vigorous experimentation in the 1920s went into her fiction. Interested greatly in the work of Joyce, Stein, Woolf, William Faulkner, and Dorothy Richardson, H. D. developed her own techniques of altering conventional narrative and rendering consciousness in modernist transformations of marginal prose genres: the roman à clef—"Paint It Today," "Asphodel," *HERmione,* "Narthex" (in *The Second American Caravan*, 1928), *Nights* (1935), *Kora and Ka* (1934)—and the historical novel—"Pilate's Wife" (written in 1924 and 1934), *Palimpsest* (1926), and *Hedylus* (1928). All texts represent her attempt to retell, reorder, and thereby re-create her own "legend." This work represents the reconstitution of the self in the modern world, based on but not equivalent to her life from 1905 to the present. H. D.'s achievement in prose needs assessment separate from her poetry, but such a systematic study has yet to be made, particularly since she left so many of these texts unpublished (some because they were genuinely unfinished, others because of their openly lesbian content or their revelation of Perdita's parentage). *HERmione* is generally recognized as the most important of these texts. Adopting imagist technique and cinematic montage to the needs of narrative and interior monologue, H. D. broke down syntax and words much like Stein and used images in a way that anticipated Woolf's *The Waves* (1931).

Like her poetry, H. D.'s efforts in prose began to displease her by the early 1930s. She particularly liked *Nights* and *Kora and Ka,* but she described them as "born from the detached intellect," even as "'hallucinated writing.'" She completed *The Hedgehog* (1936), a fascinating fable begun in 1924 as a pacifist tract in the guise of a children's tale, but wrote no more prose. During the 1930s she experienced a writing block that made her writing labored, painful, often obscure, and relatively scant compared to her productivity in subsequent decades. Given the return of creative energy in the 1940s, however, it is evident that the late 1920s and 1930s were a period of regenerative latency in which her involvement in areas seemingly extraneous to her own poetry laid the foundation of what was to come. First of all, H. D. gained greatly from the circle of avant-garde artists she and Bryher attracted to their residences in London, Paris, Berlin, and Switzerland. During the early 1920s her close friendship with McAlmon (renewed during the 1950s) introduced her to the artists of his circle and press, Contact Editions, especially Stein, Toklas, Hemingway, Joyce, Nancy Cunard, Man Ray, Berenice Abbott, and Mary Butts. Marianne Moore, Sylvia Beach, Adrienne Monnier, and Dorothy Richardson were intimate friends, each providing important emotional and aesthetic support for the others. Bryher not only gave McAlmon large sums of money for his press, but she also set up trust funds which yielded £250 a year for both H. D. and Richardson (these funds were renegotiated in 1933 after the death of Sir John Ellerman, but they provided the same annuity to both; H. D. used the money to supplement her inheritance from her father in 1919 and from her mother, who died in 1928).

In 1926 Frances Gregg sent a young artist, Kenneth Macpherson, to meet H. D. Again H. D. felt she had met a soul mate, a twin in psychic intensity and vision much as Gregg and Lawrence had been. They were lovers for a time, living in a highly charged household along with Bryher and Perdita. After her divorce from McAlmon in 1927, Bryher married Macpherson to help screen H. D.'s affair, according to her report to Pearson. When Aldington told H. D. that he wanted to marry Brigit Patmore, H. D. feared once again that he would charge her with false registration of Perdita, and she arranged for the Macphersons to adopt Perdita officially in 1928. Also in 1928, at the age of forty-two, H. D. had an abortion in Berlin. The three adults and a child, whom Bryher refused to send to school (except for one brief period in the 1930s) continued living and working together mainly in Switzerland (with brief stays in London and Berlin)

until Macpherson's involvement with other men in the early 1930s gradually dissolved this unusual family. H. D.'s "Narthex," *Nights,* and *Kora and Ka* are representations of this household.

Cinema, psychoanalysis, and literature dominated the intellectual life of Fido (Bryher), Rover (Macpherson), Cat (H. D.), and Pup (Perdita), as they called one another. Cinema was the special focus of their joint work. They started the film journal *Close Up,* widely known as the first journal to take cinema seriously as an art form. During its publication from 1927 to 1933, H. D., Bryher, Macpherson, Richardson, and many others reviewed films from all over the world, including especially Germany, France, Russia, Japan, Mexico, and the United States. Sergei Eisenstein's theory of montage as a dialectic first appeared in English in *Close Up* (1930) and may well have influenced H. D.'s own dialectical vision and narrative technique. In addition, Macpherson directed three films for which H. D. acted and participated in the editing: *Wing Beat* (1927), *Foothills* (1928), and *Borderline* (1930). Testifying to the influence of the Harlem Renaissance on H. D., *Borderline* is a full-length feature film about interracial sex and violence, starring Paul and Essie Robeson, along with H. D. and Bryher. The essay entitled *Borderline* that H. D. published about the film demonstrates how important issues of racial discrimination and Afro-American culture were to the formation of her postwar modernist vision. Identifying with the Robesons' status as outsiders, H. D. defined modernism in this essay as the experimental disruptions of time and space related to the borderline existence of all outsiders existing at the margins of culture. "Two Americans" (written in 1934), her short story about her relationship with Robeson, further develops the connections between his racial and her gender marginalities.

German film director G. W. Pabst thought highly of their work and became a close friend, along with the actress Elizabeth Bergner (with whom Bryher was in love) and the silhouettist Lotte Reiniger. Using the name "Helga Dorn" for her films, H. D. thought seriously of going into acting. Bergner, Greta Garbo, and above all the androgynous Marlene Dietrich were women with whom H. D. deeply identified. With the rise of fascism in Berlin, however, her film community scattered and *Close Up* stopped publication. Macpherson lost interest in making films, and the advent of soundtracks spoiled what was for H. D. the cinema's most avant-garde potential: the pure play of light and images on a screen, like the "writing-on-the-wall"

Robert Herring, Kenneth Macpherson, and Bryher in Switzerland, 1929 (courtesy of the Beinecke Rare Book and Manuscript Library, Yale University)

in Corfu. As Morris, Friedberg, and Mandel have argued, H. D.'s fascination with silent film was a key influence on the thematic and formal aspects of her work. Her poems "Projector" and "Projector II," first published in *Close Up* in 1927, explore the connection between film and her concept of creativity.

At least as important as cinema, however, were the twin influences that directly restored H. D.'s sense of poetic destiny and direction: psychoanalysis and syncretist hermetic tradition, especially various branches of the occult. These two sources of inspiration—science and religion—appeared to many, including Freud, as antithetical, but H. D. experienced them as parallel forms of spiritual quest. After Ellis gave Bryher an article by Freud in the early 1920's, Bryher subscribed to psychoanalytic journals, met Freud in 1927, and began analysis with Hanns Sachs in 1928. Donating time and money, Bryher became a tireless advocate of psychoanalysis and even planned for a time to become an analyst. As early as the mid-1920s H. D. began reading widely in Bryher's psychoanalytical

library. In addition to Sachs, the analysts Walter and Melitta Schmideberg, Barbara Low, Stephen Guest, and Mary Chadwick were close friends. H. D. took the plunge into analysis with Chadwick in the spring of 1931 and then again with Sachs in the winter of 1931-1932. Sachs recommended her to Freud, and in March of 1933 H. D. began the daily sessions with the "Professor," "Papa," or "Master," as she variously called him.

Psychoanalysis was a pivotal experience in H. D.'s artistic development. She went to Freud as a student in the hopes that he could help her clear out the "psychic weeds" cluttering the well-springs of inspiration and making her writing difficult and sterile. She saw Freud in Vienna from 1 March to 12 June 1933, when her analysis was cut short by the violence related to the spread of Nazism into Vienna. She returned to work further with Freud from 31 October to 2 December 1934, after having suffered from a brief breakdown when she heard about the sudden death of Dr. J. J. Van der Leeuw, another of Freud's analysands, whom she associated with her brother Gilbert. She sought healing through self-knowledge, but she was also Freud's student and disciple. He pronounced her analysis "finished," and with his permission she held informal "hours" with several people in the 1930s. In sifting through her memories, dreams, and psychic experiences with Freud, who behaved more like a kindly old hermit than a severe classical analyst, H.D. believed she found the patterns shaping her past, directing her future, and connecting the personal to the universal. Psychoanalysis took H. D. inward in a way that systematized and expanded her early fascination for intense, subjective experience. At the same time, this journey inward taught her to relate the personal to the universal. As Pearson has said, Freud showed her "the relationship between the individual dream and the myth as the dream of the tribe."

In her memoir *Tribute to Freud* (1956; written in the fall of 1944 and first published in serial form—as "Writing on the Wall" in *Life and Letters Today*, 1945-1946), H. D. singled out as highpoints their discussions of the "writing-on-the-wall" at Corfu and her dream of a princess discovering a baby floating in a basket. With Freud's help she translated these psychic Tarot cards to mean that she should become a poet-prophet, a Moses for the modern world who would fuse in her work the fragmented arts of religion, healing, and poetry into a single stream. She regarded the unconscious as a personal Delphi, an oracle that could nourish her art and religion. Freud's enormous influence on her sense of artistic destiny, however, took place within a dialogue in which disagreement was as fundamental as agreement. "About the greater transcendental issues, we never argued," H. D. wrote, "but there was an argument implicit in our very bones." To gain what she wanted from Freud, H. D. had to transform the scientific, rationalist, materialist, and androcentric sides of Freud into something quite different. *Tribute to Freud* is a brilliant modernist memoir, which demonstrates this dialogue and metamorphosis, offers a profound interpretation of Freud's place in the history of ideas, and (like Yeats's *A Vision*, 1925) offers a key to understanding the religious aesthetic of her mature poetry.

In the memoirs, letters, and poems about Freud that she chose not to publish, H. D. was much more explicit about her explorations with him on questions of sexual identity, especially her bisexuality and its relationship to her writer's block. "Advent," published in the 1974 edition of *Tribute to Freud*, is a memoir about analysis written in 1948 and based heavily on the journal she kept during

the first weeks of analysis until Freud asked her to stop. "The Master" (probably written in 1935, suppressed by H. D., and published in *Collected Poems, 1912-1944*, 1983) is centrally important to her later work. It records not only her reverence for Freud, but also her anger at his theories of "man-strength." For his theory of women's penis envy, she substituted an assertion that *"woman is perfect"* and celebrated woman's erotic and spiritual power. Echoing her early flower poems in *Sea Garden* and anticipating the goddesses of her later epics, the goddess of "The Master" is the "Lord become woman," "is a woman,/yet beyond woman,/yet in woman":

> there is a purple flower
> between her marble, her birch-tree white
> thighs,
> or there is a red flower,
>
> there is a rose flower
> parted wide,
> as her limbs fling wide in dance
> ecstatic
> Aphrodite,
> there is a frail lavender flower
> hidden in grass;
>
> O God, what is it,
> this flower
> that in itself had power over the whole earth?
> for she needs no man,
> herself
> is that dart and pulse of the male,
> hands, feet, thighs,
> herself perfect.

As she also explored in "The Master" and reported to Bryher in her daily letters about analysis during 1933 and 1934 (now in the Beinecke Library at Yale), H. D. found comfort and healing in Freud's view that she was that "all-but extinct phenomena, the perfect bi-[sexual]," that her discomfort with her bisexuality was causing the creative block, and that her psychic experiences represented a "mother-fixation," a lesbian desire to reestablish the pre-Oedipal bond between mother and daughter. Having reawakened rich memories of her Moravian-artist mother and scientist father, he suggested that she could break through her block by telling her story of the war years "straight," with no Greek frills. H. D., who had always felt "caught like a nut between two rocks," found in Freud's psychoanalysis the means to transcend the duality represented by her father's science and her to open a tiny bank-account for her n.e. ?

They have them for children, under" guardian" .

If you could let me know her NAME, I mean for

pass-port purposes- her legal name, ad give me a

little note - or I could arrange through my lawyer .

What do you think ?

I am very proud and happy that the "fleece of gold"

continues.

I will write again. I dash off letters, after my own

bad typing.

I have no good poems by the way.

The youth you seek of, is I presume L. 3rd ? I had a

note from Merrill Moore saying he might be in V.rd or

in London. Do you know if he is likely to come

here ? There seems very little to offer- but if I know in

time, I might dig up one or two "contacts" for him.

I presume he will go direct, Elliot.

So let me hear again.

Lore

"Dryad"

Page from a 1938 letter from H. D. to Ezra Pound, signed with the name he had given her more than thirty years earlier (by permission of Perdita Schaffner; courtesy of the Beinecke Rare Book and Manuscript Library, Yale University)

mother's art. But her sensitivity to his situation as a Jew during the rise of Nazism led her to suppress discussion of her "War Phobia," the psychic element she desperately needed to bring to a consciousness because of her sense of the impending war caused by "man's growing power of destruction and threat of racial separateness." Like Bryher, who helped more than one hundred—mostly Jewish—refugees escape (between 1933 and 1939), H. D. was deeply anti-Fascist, finally cutting off all ties with Pound because of his pro-Fascist stance. She saw psychoanalysis as a means to fortify herself against the coming war. But understanding the psychic patterns which led her to link love and war came from later analysis, with Schmideberg (1935-1937) and Erich Heydt (1953-1961).

Paralleling and reinforcing H. D.'s experience of psychoanalysis was her extensive research into hermetic tradition. Alienated from orthodox religion and feeling chosen for esoteric tradition by her Moravian heritage, H. D. found in the many shapes of the occult and syncretist mythologies the "tribal myths" that reproduced her personal dreams on a cultural level. Astrology, numerology, Tarot, and crystal balls provided access to the unconscious, a structure for meditation and self-discovery. The more philosophical forms of hermeticism that she found particularly in the books of Denis de Rougemont, W. B. Crow, Jean Chaboseau, and Robert Ambelain introduced her to the dialectics of the Kabbalah and the syncretism of ancient mystical traditions. In all of these traditions she found a concept of the Divine which incorporated woman as symbol and thereby validated the matriarchal goddesses with whom she identified herself and her mother (as in "Pilate's

Wife"). H. D.'s stance in regard to the occult included a strong component of skepticism. She avoided occult organizations, joining only the Society for Psychical Research of which Freud himself had been an honorary member. She regarded herself as her father's daughter as she carried out her "religious research," especially the hidden mysteries encoded in the numbers and stars she had failed to understand as a child. As in psychoanalysis, she sought to integrate the mother-father duality, to balance reason and inspiration. The androgynous One of esoteric tradition held out for her an important image of transcendant Wholeness which paralleled the integration she sought with Freud.

The violence of war jolted H. D. out of a decade of relative latency and led her to weave the science and religion of the psyche together to produce an art that was both deeply personal and broadly based in esoteric traditions. Destruction paradoxically brought, in Pearson's words, "an astonishing revitalization," functioning for her much as World War I had for writers such as Pound and Eliot. Impelled by the finalization of her divorce in 1938 as well as the outbreak of fighting, the first text to emerge was *Bid Me to Live* (1960), the "straight" story about the first war that Freud told her to write (it was drafted rapidly in 1939 and completed in 1949). She wrote *The Gift* (1982), a memoir of her mother's Moravian past and her own inheritance of the Moravian "gift," from 1941 to 1943. An exploration of her matrilineal heritage, it led directly into the matriarchal goddess of *Trilogy* (written in 1942-1944). Along with *Tribute to Freud*, she began writing the three volumes of this epic, which serves as both primer and profound expression of modernism.

The starting point of modernism is the crisis of belief that pervades twentieth-century Western culture: loss of faith, experience of fragmentation and disintegration, and shattering of cultural symbols and norms. War for H. D., as for Woolf, was the "hideous offspring" of the modern age and the central expression of this crisis. Dispelling the frequent critical notion, expressed by Douglas Bush and others, that she was essentially escapist in her art, H. D. squarely confronted the worst of the war by living in London and by beginning *The Walls Do Not Fall* (1944) with the concrete horror of war, rendered by concise imagist craft that now serves a philosophical purpose. Walking through the bombed-out streets of London, the poet's task is to determine what, if any, meaning lies beneath the chaos of rubble. As a poet-prophet tied to an evolving hermetic tradition of initiates, she finds at the heart of destruction a larger apocalyptic pattern that incorporates regeneration, a sign of a "spiritual realism" by which the Divine incarnates itself in the empirical reality of war. The poet's task is to ignore the mocking utilitarian voices and push beyond materialist nihilism to define the transcendent reality inaccessible to science or "sterile logic, trivial reason." Like Eliot's quest through the wasteland and on to religious epiphany in *Four Quartets*, H. D.'s walk through the "city of ruin" ultimately requires an existential leap of faith in the transformative power of Logos, the poet's Word:

> we are powerless
> and
> dust and powder fill our lungs
> our bodies blunder
> ....
> we walk continually
>
> on thin air
> that thickens to a blind fog,
>
> ....
>
> we know no rule
> of procedure,
>
> we are voyagers, discoverers
> of the not-known
>
> the unrecorded;
> we have no map;
>
> possibly we will reach haven,
> heaven.

Unlike Eliot's quest, however, H. D.'s quest through the shards of culture did not end in the established Church and State, as *Tribute to the Angels* (1945) and *The Flowering of the Rod* (1946) make clear. Symbols of salvation appear to the poet in the form of a Lady, who is both the same as and different from the holy mother portrayed by male artists. H. D.'s Lady is herself the incarnation of the Divine as she reveals herself through dream and in the charred, but still flowering, may-apple tree. The poet is a modern John, whose revelations subject the biblical text of both *Genesis* and *Revelation* to an essentially feminist revisionary process. The Lady is "Love, the Creator," who appears without the Child, carrying a blank book whose pages await the poet's Word. She is "not-fear, she is not-war," the Bona Dea; "she is Psyche, the butterfly/ out of the cocoon." Here, the process begun in poems such as "Eurydice" and "Helen" takes on the broader philosophical parameters of what Susan Gubar has called a "feminist revisionary theology," replete with female iconography. Poetry is an alchemy of the Word, whereby culture itself is purified of misogyny. In her crucible, the "venery" of Venus becomes once again "veneration," and the bitter jewel "marah" becomes her philosopher's stone, pulsating gem of the Goddess, "Star of the Sea,/Mother." The mother-symbol restored to consciousness by Freud merges with the matriarchal goddesses who embody rebirth, resurrection, and the potent force of Love.

The *Flowering of the Rod* contains the "tale of jars," the narrative the poet writes on the Lady's blank pages of the new. At the heart of the tale is the witty and dramatic confrontation between Kaspar, an Arab merchant soon to be one of the Wise Men, and Mary Magdalene, the adulteress who comes to buy the myrrh which will be her gift to the Christ child. He finds her presence annoying, "unseemly" in a woman, until suddenly a fleck of light in her hair reveals a glimpse of the lost Atlantis, the Hesperides, the power of Love embodied in woman and falsely desecrated by orthodox religious tradition.

H. D.'s *Trilogy* is a celebration of survival against the forces of death. "Remember, O Sword," she wrote in *The Walls Do Not Fall*, "you are the younger brother, the latter-born//your Triumph, however exultant,/must one day be over,//*in the beginning/was the Word.*" The "Word" or "logos" of the Christos—image, of the Lady, and of the poet— withstands and transcends the power of the Sword. "Let us leave/The-place-of-a-skull/to those who have fashioned it," the poet concluded about those who would make war. Her poem celebrates the mystical power of Love as a spiritual force for peace. Many writers, friends, and reviewers were enthusiastic about H. D.'s new prophetic voice. Marianne Moore and May Sarton wrote strong praise from the United States. Edith Sitwell sent glowing letters of praise, while Osbert Sitwell arranged for the publication of the first volume and wrote a positive review that asked for more volumes. Bryher, Robert Herring, and Pearson (who visited H. D. weekly and arranged for Perdita's job) were equally as enthusiastic. H. D. had gained much publicity by being one of the poets at the "Reading of Famous Poets," a group including Eliot, the Sitwells, and Vita Sackville-West that read before the Queen and her daughters on 14 April 1943. Elizabeth Bowen and Sackville-West also became important supporters and friends during the war years. There were, however, some reviewers,

such as Babette Deutsch, who complained that H. D. had abandoned pure imagism, a criticism that particularly annoyed H. D., who regarded imagism as "something that was important for poets learning their craft early in this century." Resenting the reviewers who did not want her work to change, she later described her early work as a "little sapling, which in the intervening years, has grown down into the depths and upwards in many directions."

H. D.'s firmest anchor in the face of imminent death was also the one which led to her most severe breakdown at the end of the war. First through Arthur Bhaduri, a half-Indian medium, and then Hugh, Lord Dowding (Chief Air Marshal at the Battle of Britain, who was relieved of his command in 1941 and became well-known during the war for his lectures on spiritualism), H. D. became involved in weekly spiritualist séances around a table that once belonged to William Morris, a poet whom she regarded as her spiritual father. "Majic Ring," an unpublished novel written in 1943-1944, is about

Hugh, Lord Dowding, who shared H. D.'s interest in spiritualism (courtesy of the Imperial War Museum, London)

these séances. At the Morris table, H. D. experienced a number of visions that became major motifs in *Helen in Egypt,* as her reflections on this period in her unpublished novel "The Sword Went Out to Sea (Synthesis of a Dream)" (1946-1947) and her unpublished journal "Hirslanden Notebooks" (1957-1959) reveal. At one séance on 29 October 1943, for example, she had a vision of a Viking ship far at sea that began to approach her at the shore. Gradually she could see at the prow of the ship the commanding presence of a man who finally stepped off to meet her. This vision served as the basis for the image of Achilles, the dead hero of *Helen in Egypt,* whose shade is drawn to the shores of Egypt in an Egyptian death caravel by the "magic" of Helen, who restores Achilles to a new kind of life just as Isis did for Osiris in Egyptian religion. At another important séance on 3 September 1945, just a few weeks after the atomic bombs were dropped on Hiroshima and Nagasaki, H. D. heard urgent messages tapped out on the Morris table from some of Dowding's dead RAF pilots. They told her to contact Dowding to warn the world that another terrible war was imminent because of the atomic bomb. Whether they were projections of her own unconscious or visitations from an astral realm was irrelevant, she believed, as she once again fused psychoanalytic and occult traditions. These RAF pilots and their warnings about future wars are transformed in *Helen in Egypt* into the dead soldiers of Achilles whose fate Helen must learn to interpret as she tries to understand the meaning of war. The RAF pilots also stand behind H. D.'s pacifist message in "The Sword Went Out to Sea." She later told Aldington that she wrote the novel as an antiwar statement, "the 'Message' being simply, that the world was, perhaps is and possibly will be 'crashing to extinction,' if those in authority, no matter where or who, don't stop smashing up things with fly-bombs, V2 and the ubiquitous (possibly) so-called 'atom.' They could do something with the atom—better than smashing cherry orchards." Deeply disturbed by the atomic bomb, H. D. recorded information about its development at Los Alamos in her notebooks for *Helen in Egypt.*

When Lord Dowding (whom she regarded as a version of Aldington raised to a psychic level) dismissed H. D.'s message from the RAF pilots as inferior to those from his own séances in February of 1946, H. D.'s mental and physical condition deteriorated, much as it had at the end of World War I. Suffering from anemia and meningitis, H. D. finally lost touch with reality and believed that

World War III had begun, that another atomic bomb had been dropped. Bryher and Schmideberg took her in May of 1946 to Seehof, Klinik Küsnacht in Switzerland, where she recovered after six months. As with the shorter breakdown of 1919, H. D. emerged from the "beehive," as she called it, to begin another fourteen years of extraordinary creative productivity. As an artist, she recognized that the unconscious could produce madness as well as inspiration, "the dregs of the dreariest symptoms of mental unrest and disease" as well as "creative idea." Like Woolf, who believed that her "voices" were linked to her creative powers, H. D. regarded her war-related breakdowns as the price of a creativity nourished by the transrational.

Art was both a sign and agency of reestablished control. In the fall of 1946 H. D. completed *By Avon River* (1949), her tribute to Shakespeare and the Elizabethan poets who lived in an age which H. D. found similar to the modern period. Setting prose and poetry voices side by side in the interesting, two-pieced text, H. D.'s tribute showed the same revisionary impulse apparent in *Tribute to Freud* and served both formally and thematically as a real transition between *Trilogy* and *Helen in Egypt.* As poet, she did not identify with Shakespeare's resourceful women, but instead with Claribel, a minor character existing only offstage as Alonso's daughter, who marries in Tunis in *The Tempest.* "Why did I choose/the invisible, voiceless Claribel," she asks. "She never had a word to say,/An emblem, a mere marriage token." H. D. gives this silent woman speech by imagining this mere "shadow on his page" as a questor who breaks out of her token status through her discovery of the Cathar heresy and courtly-love tradition introduced in England by Eleanor of Aquitaine. The poem is followed by a prose-essay on the "gentle Shakespeare," who contrasts to the swashbuckling Christopher Marlowe and political hero Sir Walter Raleigh. She suggests that Shakespeare was an androgynous artist who loved the "her-his face" of his daughter Judith and associated either consciously or unconsciously with the tradition dedicated to the Cathar Lady. Like Freud, Shakespeare ultimately represented the union of the mother-father duality which she attempted to reproduce through her art.

H. D.'s fascination with mysticism and the role of woman as symbol within its traditions grew steadily in the late 1940s and early 1950s. Reading with great interest such diverse authors as Robert Graves (*The White Goddess*), Dante, Henry James, Dickinson, Lawrence, Pound, Ambelain, E. M. Butler, Margaret Murray, and the Pre-Raphaelites, she wrote three lengthy, still unpublished novels about different flare-ups of the impulse: "The Sword Went Out to Sea"; "White Rose and the Red" (written in 1948), about the poet Elizabeth Siddall in Pre-Raphaelite tradition; and "The Mystery" (written in 1949-1951), her re-creation of early Moravian family history. Less interesting than the novels of the 1920s, this prose told in more or less indirect form versions of her own story. The results were not works of distinction in themselves but nonetheless important preparation for her "cantos," her term for the sequences about Helen which she began scribbling in faint pencil in her old school copybooks, with scarcely a change, from 1952 to 1956.

Helen in Egypt (1961) weaves together in ex-

traordinary fashion the various strands of H. D.'s imaginative and relational life for the previous forty years. Along with *Trilogy*, it is recognized by many as her greatest achievement, the culmination of the broad-ranging philosophical and aesthetic concerns that had consumed her after World War I. The epic, based on obscure variants of Greek myth, is unconventional in its handling of chronology, situation, and narrative. It takes place shortly after the end of the Trojan War and centers on the postwar destinies of Helen and Achilles, but in the palimpsest of history (H. D.'s favorite metaphor for time), the epic is about all-time, all-war, all-love. Like "Eurydice," the epic takes culture as recorded in myth for its subject, but embodies also

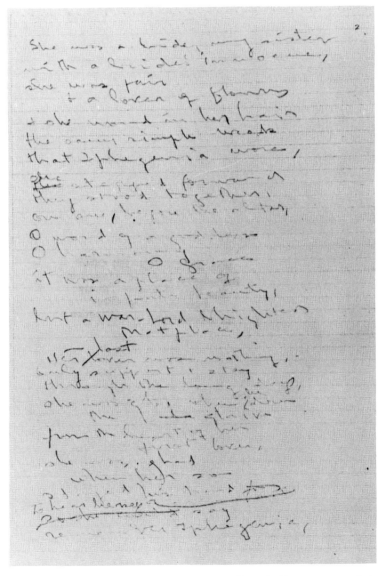

Page from the manuscript for Helen in Egypt *(by permission of Perdita Schaffner; courtesy of the Beinecke Rare Book and Manuscript Library, Yale University)*

the patterns of H. D.'s life—the Dryad's early love for Pound (Helen Dendritis and Paris); H. D.'s soldier-lovers Aldington and, on another level, Dowding (Achilles); the shattering impact of war; and her androgynous analyst Freud (Theseus). As DuPlessis and Gelpi have shown, H. D.'s memoirs of the 1950s, such as the unpublished "Thorn Thicket" (written in 1960) and "Hirslanden Notebooks," identify the casts, but it is essential to avoid biographical reductionism and to focus instead on the creative mind of the artist who transforms the raw material of her personal life and cultural myth into a unique text.

Echoing Homer's *Iliad* and *Odyssey*, H. D.'s text both uses and dramatically revises the masculine epic tradition. Her epic is also about the Trojan War and its aftermath. However, H. D. moves the epic's traditional focus of the masculine hero by making Helen the center of consciousness. Helen's meditative quest for identity through the fragments of memory, dream, and occasional conversation constitutes the epic's action. Adapting the associational processes of both psychoanalysis and the modernist novel of consciousness, H. D.'s epic creates a multilayered narrative whose emphasis is on an inner journey, not on external action. The epic's free associational movement is carefully structured, however. There are three main parts to Helen's story: "Pallinode [*sic*]" "Leuké," and "Eidolon." The first two parts each contain seven "books," while the last part has six books. Each book in turn contains eight sections. As the key unit of the epic's organization, each section consists of a prose introduction and a differing number of mainly three-line unrhymed, but musically resonant stanzas. Rhyme appears occasionally with an incantational effect for special emphasis. The prose interludes, written in 1955 to 1956 after she finished all the verse sections in 1954, comment on the poetry and contribute brilliantly to the multilayered form of the epic. This weaving of poetic and prose voices also brings to completion a form she had first explored in "Hymen" (1921), returned to in *Ion* (1937), and used in *By Avon River* (1949). Although she had the idea for prose notes on the verse in *Helen in Egypt* as early as 1953, she did not begin to write these notes until the verse was completed. When Pearson arranged for her to record parts of the verse sections in 1955, she developed prose introductions for each section. At Pearson's urging, she wrote prose introductions for all the remaining sections and incorporated them into the final text. These double voices linguistically highlight a philosophical pattern in her whole oeuvre:

the desire to explore, represent, and ultimately transcend duality.

Helen in Egypt begins with the image of "Helena, hated of all Greece," a Pandora who has brought death and destruction to victors and victims alike in the Trojan War. According to tradition, as the prose voice reminds us, Stesichorus and Euripides were punished by the gods for their early portraits of this evil, hated Helen and subsequently wrote palinodes affirming her innocence. Zeus, as the variant myth has it, placed a phantom Helen upon the ramparts of Troy and kept the faithful wife safe in Egypt until Menelaus retrieved her. H. D.'s "Pallinode" revises the myth yet again by redefining the nature of Helen's innocence. H. D.'s Helen did indeed leave her husband and child and go to Troy with her lover Paris. But the weight of male hatred has caused her to repress the memory of her rebellion. Like the free associational, reflective, and interpretive structure of H. D.'s analysis with Freud, Helen gradually peels back the layers of memory and family history to answer the question, "Helena? Who is she?"

The epic begins with Helen in Egypt searching the sacred hieroglyphs of the Amen temple to understand why Zeus brought her to Egypt and to clarify her relation to the hated phantom of Helen. In the action that sets the epic in motion, Helen's power draws the dead Achilles to her for the answers he might provide. Shipwrecked, lost, and limping from the fatal wound in his heel, Achilles shatters Helen's peace of certain innocence. When he recognizes the woman he used to watch in fascination and anger, he calls her "Hecate," "witch," and tries to strangle her. She appeals desperately to his mother Thetis, the goddess of the sea. The name of the goddess recalls Achilles to a former self that knew nothing of killing, and his violence turns to love. The two lovers meet again to decipher their memories and the meaning of the past. "Pallinode" is a love story of sorts, but before the lovers can be united on the island of Leuké, as the variant myth has it, each must undertake a separate quest for identity. Achilles reflects on how his fatal glance at Helen of Troy led to his unfastened ankle greave and subsequent rebirth as the "new Mortal" who has renounced the death cult of war. Helen learns that "she herself is the writing," the hieroglyph that must be deciphered if she is to remember earlier selves. Her meeting with Achilles, in which violence became love through the agency of Thetis, is the central hieroglyph to which she returns in reflection as the embodiment of fundamental truths about Love and War, L'Amour and La Mort, Eros and Eris.

"Leuké" and "Eidolon" are structured primarily by Helen's inner confrontation with the past. Narrative based on identifiable action is scanty and often like a dream sequence in its shifting time and locale. As "Leuké" opens, a skiff brings Helen to the island where she awakens not to Achilles but to the memory of laughing joyfully with Paris. The alchemy of her memory draws Paris to her, and together they relive the years of their springtime love and the Trojan War. Helen refuses Paris's demand that she renounce Achilles but is still torn by the conflict of selves. This suffering brings her baffled and tired to the home of Theseus, her first lover. Now an old man, he kindly helps Helen sort through the past to reconcile her fragmented selves. "Eidolon" records Helen's slow process of synthesizing dual selves in the search for wholeness. Her identification with Thetis, who embodies the mystical Love of the Cathar heresy and Moravian mysticism, is key, as is her attempt to understand the dialectical interactions of Love and War. Her union with Achilles and the birth of their androgynous child Euphorian take place "off stage" and do not serve as the climax of the epic. Instead, the emphasis is on Helen's own sense of who she is. Helen, whether the hated phantom of Troy or the repressed woman of Egypt, has become the Helen of Troy, Egypt, and Greece who is at peace with a fully healed, conscious self.

Helen's self-acceptance and self-creation are made possible by a series of reflections on Love and War as embodied in myth and history, ideas which taken together constitute a critique of patriarchy. Aware of Pound's fascism in *The Cantos*, H. D. created a counter voice in her cantos that saw the world divided into the forces of Love and Life in opposition to the forces of War and Death. As H. D. revised both Freud and esoteric tradition, Eros is the intangible power of life represented in myth through the protean forms of the matriarchal goddesses and incarnated in reality by Helen and all the other women in her family. Thanatos is the force of death epitomized by the fascistic "Command" under Achilles' leadership and the death cult at the heart of the "purely masculine 'iron-ring' " of war. Once Helen understands this dualism, she is able to remember and reinterpret her past and the Trojan War in the context of this opposition between matriarchal and patriarchal forces. From this revisionary perspective, the image of "hated Helen" is indeed a phantom created by the divine patriarch Zeus, but the real Helen is the human incarnation of the Goddess, of Love, of the potent maternal principle she finds in the eidolon of Thetis and the hieroglyphs of Isis. The "Pallinode," Helen's defense or "apologia," concludes with Helen's understanding that her flight with Paris was a justifiable act of rebellion against a patriarchal mythos by which the woman was either chaste wife or illicit lover.

Helen's redefined innocence is only the first step, however, in understanding the central Mystery, the dialectical interactions of Love and War. Helen released the warrior Achilles from the "icy fortress of the soul" to become the "new Mortal," but the agency of her power was Death, "Love's arrow." Love becomes death, violence becomes love in the Mystery of the Trojan War, in the hieroglyphic meeting of Helen and Achilles on the shores of Egypt. "Leuké" and "Eidolon" take Helen not only along the paths of memory, but also into the mysteries which lead into transcendence of all dualisms revealed in the epiphany of the moment. Heavily influenced by Ambelain's writings on the Kabbalah, de Rougemont's interpretation of the Cathar heresy, and the Moravian Mystery of Zinzendorf, H. D.'s transcendent moment embodying the healing synthesis of opposites joins other modernist myths of wholeness, especially the Woolfian moment and the vision of "the still point of the turning world" in Eliot's *Four Quartets*.

The extraordinary burst of creative energy that produced *Helen in Egypt* took place in an environment quite different from the communal households of the 1920s and 1930s. Living together in a small flat during World War II had put a great strain on H. D.'s and Bryher's relationship, particularly because Bryher became increasingly hostile to the occult. In 1946 they decided not to live together again, although they visited frequently and their near-daily correspondence for the next fifteen years attests to their continued intimacy. H. D. lived alone for the rest of her life, mainly in Swiss or Italian hotels until she returned to Küsnacht Klinik for an operation in 1953. After she broke her hip in 1956 and underwent a slow recovery, she remained at Küsnacht, where she continued her esoteric researches, became involved in the lives of the Küsnacht patients, and wrote *End to Torment* (1979), as well as *Sagesse, Winter Love*, and *Hermetic Definition*, all published under the title *Hermetic Definition* in 1972. She lived just a few houses away from Jung, whom she undoubtedly read, but never met because of her loyalty to Freud and her preference for "taking mysticism straight" from writers such as Ambelain. Her important relationship with

her existentialist analyst Erich Heydt was both col-
leagial and therapeutic. With him she discussed the
cases of the neurotic patients at Küsnacht, and in
their "tea sessions," she reviewed the patterns underlying her past experiences with Pound, Aldington, Lawrence, and Dowding. Heydt, as a sort of
double for first one then another of these men,
stimulated her to relive her past and then transform those experiences into art.

Perdita, who had driven an ambulance and
then worked with Pearson in the OSS during the
war, had immigrated to the United States and in
1949 married John Schaffner, with whom she had
four children. H. D., whose own mothering of Perdita had been shared with Bryher and checkered
by the conflicts of her life, was greatly moved by
the births of her grandchildren, whom she repeatedly compared to the books she was writing in
the 1950s. These overlapping creativities of mother
and daughter may well have been the source for
H. D.'s important fusion of artistic creativity and
procreativity in *Hermetic Definition* and *Winter Love*.
Twice H. D. went to the United States to see the
children, once in 1956 when Pearson arranged a
special exhibit of her work at Yale in honor of her
seventieth birthday and once in 1960 when she was
the first woman to receive the poetry award from
the American Academy of Arts and Letters. This
award gave her great satisfaction, as did the "radiant maturity" of her daughter, whose fourth
child was born around the same time.

Pearson's importance to H. D.'s artistic productivity in the 1950s should not be underesti-
mated. He had written to her as early as 1937, but
this friendship with yet another "Professor" became significant during the war when Pearson
came to tea every Sunday and finally a critical life-
line to the outside world during the 1950s. Pearson
arranged with Beinecke Library for the preserva-
tion of her papers and manuscripts, encouraged
her in frequent letters to prepare her huge stacks
of manuscripts for publication, suggested that she
write memoirs, and served as the important liaison
between the private world of creative production
and the public world of publishing. By the mid-
1950s Pearson had clearly become an important
sounding board for H. D., for she regularly sent
him drafts of her novels and sequences from *Helen
in Egypt*. She greatly valued his advice, followed his
suggestion about the prose introductions for *Helen
in Egypt*, and responded eagerly to his encouragement that she expand her early notes on Pound
into *End to Torment*. But she nonetheless maintained
her artistic autonomy, rejecting some of his sug-

*H. D., Norman Holmes Pearson, and Bryher at Yale University,
1956 (courtesy of the Beinecke Rare Book and Manuscript
Library, Yale University)*

gestions for *Helen in Egypt* and refusing to allow
him to publish *Winter Love* as a coda to *Helen in
Egypt*.

Pearson's other important contribution was to
put H. D. and Pound in touch once again. Although
H. D. abhorred Pound's fascism and anti-Semitism,
she was very upset by his confinement in St. Elizabeths, a kind of imprisonment which she increasingly regarded as a symbol for her own specific
"confinements" and for the general position of the
poet in the modern world. They began corresponding once again, both clearly reflecting in old age
on their early love. Some of Pound's Pisan Cantos,
which H. D. found "heartbreaking," directly allude
to those times, to the Dryad of his youth. H. D. in
turn wrote *End to Torment* and *Winter Love* about
Pound. The renewal of her relationship with
Pound paralleled a somewhat less intense, but
nonetheless warm and important friendship with

Aldington carried on by correspondence. They wrote extensively about their daughters, their daily lives, their health, and their creative work. The final outpouring of H. D.'s poetry and prose took place within the context of a renewal of her ties with the two men who had been crucial to her early literary development. It is not surprising that, as DuPlessis has pointed out, the patterns of those early relationships reappear in her final works in variously encoded and transposed forms.

After reading Nikos Kazantzakis's epic poem *The Odyssey—A Modern Sequel* (1938), H. D. wrote *Winter Love* in the spring of 1959 as an epilogue to her own epic. Much more evidently autobiographical than *Helen in Egypt, Winter Love* presents an aging Helen once again in love with Odysseus, who in a variant myth was an early lover. She is the poet H. D. reliving and reconstituting her love for Pound in sequences that climax in the birth of the child-poem Espérance. In *Sagesse* and *Hermetic Definition*, the bed-ridden poet abandons all mythic masks to speak in her own voice. Written in the summer and fall of 1957, *Sagesse* begins with the image of the caged Scops owl whose photo H. D. saw in the *Listener* and transformed into a symbol of the divine which is mocked and misunderstood by the utilitarianism and materialism of the modern world. Through an identification with a little girl half-crazed and inspired during the London Blitz—a figure that represents the child yet alive in the aging woman—the white-haired poet seeks to penetrate the mysteries revealed through the Kabbalistic angels of the hours in "le Grand Arbre Kabbalistique" pictured in Ambelain's *La Kabbale Pratique* (1951). Once again the Goddess is the agency of revelation as she whispers the "simple mystery" of Love to her child, the poet, through the echo of a seashell.

With the first letters of the words in its title ("H. D.") signalling its significance, *Hermetic Definition* serves as a brilliant culmination of her earlier poetic quests for self-definition as a woman poet. Written over a seven-month period from August 1960 to February 1961, this three-part long poem takes as its subject H. D.'s own obsessions with the archetypical male lover-poet and her search for autonomy which can only be achieved through the (pro)creation of her poem. In "Red Rose and a Beggar," part one of the poem, the bed-ridden poet falls in love with the young reporter who comes to interview her for a magazine review of her new book. After a short exchange of letters, she is crushed when he stops writing. Equally devastating is his dismissal of her art in the review—"fascinat-

H. D., 1956 (courtesy of the Beinecke Rare Book and Manuscript Library, Yale University)

ing . . ./if you can stand its preciousness." In its outline, the poem is directly autobiographical. Lionel Durand, the Haitian head of *Newsweek*'s Paris Bureau, visited H. D. in April and May 1960; shortly thereafter a condescending review of *Bid Me to Live* appeared in *Newsweek*. H. D.'s Durand diary records her passion for him and her pain at his double rejection. In the poem, H. D. presents Durand as the archetypally masculine Lover, who embodies the personal and mythic male lovers with the amber-eyed Paris (or Bar-Isis, son of Isis according to Ambelain) as the prototype. In the fervor of her love, she seeks to be absorbed into his being, thus enacting a loss of self which DuPlessis has called the sexual politics of "romantic thralldom." In the personal palimpsest of love and victimization, Durand has taken the place of Pound and Aldington; the "reddest rose" of unfolding passion reduces the poet to "beggar."

In "Grove of Academe," part two of the poem, H. D. gratefully leaves the intoxication of passion and the "abasement" of femininity behind as she becomes absorbed in the poetry of St.-John Perse, one of the other poets at the awards ceremony at the American Academy of Arts and Letters in May of 1960. Perse's steadying gesture when H. D. nearly fell on her way to the podium at the awards ceremony becomes in the poem a symbol of his acceptance of her as his colleague in poetry. Leaving behind the paralyzing sexual politics of part one, she finds a validation of her artistic identity emanating from his action: "our curious preoccupation with stylus and pencil,/was re-born at your touch." But "swept away/in the orgy of your poetry," H. D. begins to experience a different kind of thralldom, a paralyzing intellectual absorption that threatens her self-esteem and capacity to write autonomously.

"Star of Day," part three of the poem, narrates her struggle to free herself from the obsessions with the two men who symbolize the male lover and the male literary tradition. To succeed, she must affirm her creative center as female. Once again H. D. turns to her personal and mythic mother symbol for inspiration. Isis is her patron and muse: "She draws the veil aside,/unbinds my eyes,/commands,/write, write or die." News of Durand's death in January 1961, just nine months after their meeting, leads H. D. to regard that period as a "pregnancy" which will result in the "birth" of her completed poem and Durand's "rebirth" as a resurrected being. Just as Isis bore Paris according to the hermetic tradition encoded in Notre Dame, H. D. will "give birth" to Durand in the world of the poem. Because her poem incorporates the "human" passion of the "reddest rose" as well as Perse's abstract *"unalterable law,"* it also establishes her independence from the dominance of masculine "intellect and achievement." Indeed, her final act of poetic motherhood allows her to transcend in her "own way" the many dialectical polarities in the poem's imagery and structure.

After a brief illness, H. D. died in Zurich on 27 September 1961, just a few hours after her first copy of *Helen in Egypt* had been placed in her hands. An earlier poem serves as a fitting epitaph on her grave in Bethlehem, Pennsylvania:

So I may say,
"I died of living,
having lived one hour";

So they may say,
"she died soliciting
illicit fervour,"

So you may say,
"Greek flower; Greek ecstasy
reclaims forever

one who died
following
intricate song's lost measure."

Critical assessments of H. D.'s poetry have exhibited the kind of shifts that demonstrate the relative nature of all literary criticism and epitomize the problems many women writers have faced in gaining admission to the established canons of literature. Jackson Bryer's "H. D.: A Note on Her Critical Reputation" (*Contemporary Literature*, 1969) ably summarizes the early evolution of her reputation in both reviews and scholarship. On the whole, H. D.'s work in the 1910s and 1920s was highly praised and widely anthologized. Pound, Eliot, Aldington, Moore, Amy Lowell, F. S. Flint, May Sinclair, Conrad Aiken, Bryher, Louis Untermeyer, and Mark Van Doren were among the many prominent authors who praised H. D.'s work. But beginning with the publication of *Red Roses for Bronze*, reviews tended to be mixed. The publication of *Trilogy* during the war led to some enthusiastic reviews, some complaints about her abandonment of imagism, and some negative reviews, with Randall Jarrell's brief and disparaging review of *Tribute to the Angels* being the most damaging. Ignoring the later development of H. D.'s fellow imagists, Jarrell argued that "imagism was a reductio ad absurdum upon which it is hard to base a later style."

During the 1960s, two books on H. D. appeared, but in all her *Helen in Egypt* received only five reviews, the least number for any volume she had published. The publication of Thomas Burnett Swann's *The Classical World of H. D.* (1962) and Vincent Quinn's *Hilda Doolittle* (1967) did little to stem the tide of neglect. A few of her imagist poems (such as "Oread," "Heat," "Helen," and "Orchard") continued to be anthologized, but her long poems were out of print, seldom taught in the universities, and rarely given the serious critical attention they deserve. L. S. Dembo's *Conceptions of Reality in Modern American Poetry* (1966) was an important exception, and his assessment of H. D.'s "neo-epics" as significant contributions to modernist poetry led ultimately to his editing of a special issue of *Contemporary Literature* devoted to H. D. (1969). This superb issue, which reflected the range and complexity of H. D.'s poetic achievements, has proved to be the turning point in the return of H. D. to a central place in the history of twentieth-century American poetry. Pearson's prediction in Dembo's important interview with him in the issue "that the next half-dozen years will see H. D. discovered" has proved correct.

The critical climate was ripe for this discovery. The explosion of feminist criticism in the 1970s combined with the revival sparked by *Contemporary Literature* to produce the kind of extended, serious critical examination that H. D.'s modernist work demands. Feminist critics in particular have created a body of theoretical and practical criticism that illuminates the anomalous position of the woman writer in the largely male literary tradition, the thematic and formalist aspects of the female literary tradition, and the androcentric lens of established critical traditions that has led to the undervaluation of many important women writers. The revival of interest in women writers accomplished by feminist criticism led to renewed attention to H. D.'s entire oeuvre among readers and scholars of widely varying perspectives.

Many of these readers and critics have recognized that certain common assumptions about H. D. have inhibited a full-scale comprehension of her work and a knowledgeable assessment of her achievement. The first assumption that led to misapprehensions of her work has emerged from the tyranny of the imagist label. H. D.'s justified reputation as the greatest and purest imagist paradoxically led to a critical cage whose perpetrators either lamented the fact that she stopped writing perfect gems or persisted in discussing five and ignoring forty-five years of poetic development ("as though five of the shortest pieces in 'Harmonium' were to stand for the life's work of Wallace Stevens," Hugh Kenner complained in his review of *Hermetic Definition*). The second misleading assumption has been the charge that H. D.'s classical masks and mythmaking methods constitute escapism, the inability of a fragile consciousness to confront the modern world. The third tendency has been the subtle operation of a double standard, whereby H. D.'s religious, philosophical, or linguistic explorations are dismissed as abstract, unstructured, and difficult while similar qualities in male modernist poetry have been praised as challenging and profound. The fourth problem has been the persistence of the treatment of H. D. in terms of the famous men she knew—Pound, Aldington, Lawrence, Freud. This approach is particularly ironic because the influence of these men threatened to subsume her own creative drive, and the very measure of her achievement was her ability to resist the male-centered ideologies and interactions that each variously represented. Feminist critics have led the way in critiquing such assumptions and argued that H. D.'s poetry represents a profound exploration of the situation of the woman as writer, lover, and seeker of redemptive realities in a male-dominated world that is perpetually at war.

The revival of interest in H. D. during the 1970s and 1980s has made possible the publication of a number of her unpublished works and the republication of many of her out-of-print volumes, mostly with the prestigious publisher of modernist and postmodernist avant-garde work, New Directions. Before his death in 1975, Pearson brought out most of H. D.'s unpublished poetry written in the late 1950s and early 1960s in the volume *Hermetic Definition* (1972). He published the three volumes of World War II poems under the title *Trilogy* (1973), thereby fulfilling H. D.'s wish and making her first epic available to the poetry-reading public. Hoping to convince readers of the scope of H. D.'s achievement, Pearson then republished the 1956 edition of *Tribute to Freud* and included the unpublished "Advent" in 1974. At his death, he was preparing H. D.'s memoir of Pound, *End to Torment*, a project that Michael King ably completed in 1979. Perdita Schaffner, now her mother's literary executor, carried on in Pearson's footsteps and has written profoundly perceptive portraits of her mother as introductions to newly published and republished volumes: *Hedylus* (1980), *HERmione* (1981), *The Gift* (an abridged edition, 1981), and *Bid Me To Live (A Madrigal)* (1983). John Walsh, editor of Black Swan Books, has supplemented the work of New Directions by publishing beautiful, revised editions of unavailable volumes that incorporate the corrections H. D. made in the 1950s and some of her unpublished journal material related to these works: *Hedylus* (1980), *Bid Me to Live (A Madrigal)* (1983), *Hippolytus Temporizes* (1985), *Ion* (1985), and *By Avon River* (forthcoming 1986). *Notes on Thought and Vision and The Wise Sappho* appeared in 1982 from the City Lights Book Store in San Francisco, testifying to the West Coast interest in H. D. Unpublished poems and short prose selections began to appear with some regularity in a wide range of journals, including *Feminist Studies, Southern Review, Yale Review, Iowa Review, Montemora, Ms. Magazine,* and *Copper Canyon.* "Vale Ave," written in 1957 and the last of H. D.'s unpublished long-sequence poems, appeared in the New Directions annual anthology (1982). Masterfully edited by Louis Martz, H. D.'s *Collected Poems, 1912-1944* appeared in 1983. The volume includes some two-hundred pages of previously unpublished poetry.

Stimulated by this publication of H. D.'s unavailable work, scholars covering the spectrum of critical perspectives and methodologies began writing about H. D. Books and book chapters, special issues of journals, critical articles, scholarly papers, convention panels, and dissertations have begun to proliferate, gathering momentum and depth from the increasing availability of H. D.'s voluminous papers in the Beinecke Library at Yale. Feminist critics have pioneered in this work, but the multiple dimensions of H. D.'s life and work require and are receiving scholarship from other critical perspectives. A critical study and two biographies appeared in the 1980s to stimulate further teaching and research: Susan Stanford Friedman's *Psyche Reborn: The Emergence of H. D.* (1981); Janice S. Robinson's *H. D.: The Life and Work of an American Poet* (1982); and Barbara Guest's *Herself Defined: The Poet H. D. and Her World* (1984). Two more books on H. D. are forthcoming in 1986, and several others are in process. Centennial celebrations of H. D.'s birth in 1886 are underway at Bryn Mawr College, the Modern Language Association Convention, and a National Poetry Foundation conference. Special issues of *Contemporary Literature* (1986), *Poesis* (1985), and *Iowa Review* (1986) are being devoted to H. D.

While the H. D. revival has gathered great momentum, the reassessment of her work is still in the process of change. Some critics, such as Hugh Kenner and Alfred Kazin, still consider H. D. a minor chapter in literary history, notable for her contributions to imagism. But a growing chorus of critics—including, for example, Pearson, Louis Martz, Sandra Gilbert, Albert Gelpi, Susan Gubar, Denis Donoghue, Susan Stanford Friedman, Rachel Blau DuPlessis, Alicia Ostriker, Adalaide Morris, Sherman Paul, Carroll Terrell, Cyrena Pondrom, Diana Collecut, and Paul Smith—consider H. D. a major poet belonging both to the modernist mainstream and the tradition of women's writing. This assessment of her importance is symbolically evident in the full title of a new journal: *Sagetrieb—Poetry in the Tradition of Pound, H. D., and Williams;* it is also clear in the selections from H. D. and introductory material included in the *Norton Anthology of Literature by Women: The Tradition in English* (1985), edited by Sandra Gilbert and Susan Gubar.

From many other poets, however, H. D. has consistently received high praise, so much so that she may be considered above all a "poet's poet."

Pound, Marianne Moore, Amy Lowell, Williams, Conrad Aiken, Aldington, Flint, Merrill Moore, Muriel Rukeyser, and May Sarton (as well as writers such as Ford, Sinclair, Richardson, and Horace Gregory) always considered her poetry supreme. Jarrell may have rejected her, but beginning in the 1950s a group of younger poets began reading her poetry, writing to her while she was alive, traveling to the Beinecke Library to read her unpublished work, and then circulating copies among one another (a pirated edition of *Hermetic Definition* appeared before Pearson brought out the legitimate text). Robert Duncan is the most important of these poet-admirers—he met with her several times; there is an extended correspondence between them; she figures in a number of his poems; and she serves as the significant medium of his own aesthetic philosophy in his *The H. D. Book* (parts of which have appeared in various periodicals since 1963). But the group also includes Denise Levertov (who also corresponded with H. D.), Allen Ginsberg, Robert Creeley, Robert Kelly, and Tram Combs. With the explosion of women's poetry and culture in the 1970s, H. D. acquired a new and avid audience of poets whose work she nourished. Adrienne Rich is the most important of these, but the group also includes Marilyn Hacker, Kathleen Fraser, Judy Grahn, Diane di Prima, Alicia Ostriker, Rachel Blau DuPlessis, Sandra Gilbert, Norman Weinstein, Barbara Guest, Ann Stanford, and many others. Pearson believed that her appeal to poets began with the "open line which she so magnificently and unflatteringly renders." But beyond the music and clarity of her line is a vast vision of search in which many poets and readers alike have found mirrors to their own desire.

Letters:

"Selected Letters from H. D. to F. S. Flint: A Commentary on the Imagist Period," edited by Cyrena N. Pondrom, *Contemporary Literature*, 10 (Autumn 1969): 557-586;

"H. D.: A Friendship Traced: Letters to Silvia Dobson and a Poem," edited by Carol Tinker, *Conjunctions*, 2 (Spring-Summer 1982): 115-157.

Bibliography:

Jackson R. Bryer and Pamela Roblyer, "H. D.: A Preliminary Checklist," *Contemporary Literature* 10 (Autumn 1969): 632-675.

Biographies:

Janice S. Robinson, *H. D.: The Life and Work of an*

American Poet (Boston: Houghton Mifflin, 1982);

Barbara Guest, *Herself Defined: The Poet H. D. and Her World* (Garden City: Doubleday, 1984).

References:

Marilyn Arthur, "Psycho-Mythology: The Case of H. D.," *Bucknell Review*, 28 (1983): 65-79;

Louise Berkinow, *Among Women* (New York: Harmony Books, 1980), pp. 155-192;

Winifred Bryher, *The Heart to Artemis—A Writer's Memoirs* (New York: Harcourt, Brace & World, 1962);

Claire Buck, "Freud and H. D.—bisexuality and a feminine discourse," *M/F*, 8 (1983): 53-65;

Douglas Bush, *Mythology and the Romantic Tradition in English Poetry* (Cambridge: Harvard University Press, 1937), pp. 497-506;

Hayden Carruth, "Poetry Chronicle," *Hudson Review*, 27 (Summer 1974): 52-65;

Stanley K. Coffman, Jr., *Imagism—A Chapter for the History of Modern Poetry* (Norman: University of Oklahoma Press, 1951);

Diana Collecott, Introduction to *The Gift* (London: Virago, 1984), pp. vii-xix;

Collecott, "*Remembering oneself: the reputation and later poetry of H. D.,*" *Critical Quarterly*, 27 (Spring 1985): 7-22;

L. S. Dembo, *Conceptions of Reality in Modern American Poetry* (Berkeley: University of California Press, 1966), pp. 20-47;

Dembo, ed., *H. D.: A Reconsideration, Contemporary Literature*, 10 (Autumn 1969);

Robert Duncan, *The H. D. Book:* "From the Day Book," *Origin*, 10 (July 1963): 1-47; "Beginnings: Chapter 1 of the H. D. Book, Part 1," *Coyote's Journal*, 5/6 (1966): 8-31; "The H. D. Book, Part I: Chapter 2," *Coyote's Journal*, 8 (1967): 27-35; "Rites of Participation," *Caterpillar*, 1 (October 1967): 6-34; "Rites of Participation, II," *Caterpillar*, 2 (January 1968): 125-154; "Two Chapters from *H. D.*," *Tri-Quarterly*, 12 (Spring 1968): 67-98; "From the H. D. Book: Part 1: Beginnings, Chapter 5: Occult Matters," *Stony Brook Review*, 1/2 (Fall 1968): 4-19; "Nights and Days," *Sumac*, 1 (Fall 1968): 101-146; "The H. D. Book, Part 2, Nights and Days: Chapter 2," *Caterpillar*, 6 (January 1969): 16-38; "The H. D. Book, Part 2, Nights and Days: Chapter 4," *Caterpillar*, 7 (April 1969): 27-60; "The H. D. Book, Part 2, Nights and Days: Chapter 9," *Io*, 6 (Summer 1969): 117-140; "From the H. D. Book, Part II, Chapter 5," *Stony Brook Review*, 3/4 (Fall 1969): 336-347; "Glimpses of the Last Day: from Chapter 2 of the H.D. Book," *Io*, 10 (1971): 212-215; "From the H. D. Book: Part 2, Chapter 5," *Credences*, 2 (August 1975): 50-95; "The H. D. Book: Part 2: Nights and Days, Chapter 9," *Chicago Review*, 30 (Winter 1979): 37-88; "From the H. D. Book," *Montemora*, 8 (1981): 79-116; "LThe H. D. Book: book II, Chapter 10," *Ironwood*, 22 (Fall 1983): 47-64; "H. D. Book: Book II, Chapter 6," *Southern Review*, new series 21 (January 1985): 26-48;

Rachel Blau DuPlessis, "Family, Sexes, Psyche: An Essay on H. D. and the Muse of the Woman Writer," *Montemora*, 6 (1979): 137-156;

DuPlessis, *H. D.: The Struggle of That Career* (Brighton: Harvester, forthcoming, 1986);

DuPlessis, "Romantic Thralldom in H. D.," *Contemporary Literature*, 20 (Summer 1979): 178-203;

DuPlessis, *Writing Beyond the Ending: Narrative Strategies of Twentieth-Century Women Writers* (Bloomington: Indiana University Press, 1985), pp. 66-83, 116-121;

DuPlessis and Susan Stanford Friedman, " 'Woman Is Perfect': H. D.'s Debate with Freud," *Feminist Studies*, 7 (Fall 1981): 417-430;

Kenneth Fields, Introduction to *Tribute to Freud* (Boston: Godine, 1974), pp. xvii-xliv;

Peter E. Firchow, "Rico and Julia: The Hilda Doolittle-D. H. Lawrence Affair Reconsidered," *Journal of Modern Literature*, 8 (1980): 51-76;

Lucy Freeman and Herbert Stream, *Freud and Women* (New York: Ungar, 1981), pp. 117-120;

Lucy Freibert, "Conflict and Creativity in the World of H. D.," *Journal of Women's Studies in Literature*, 1 (Summer 1979): 258-271;

Freibert, "From Semblance to Selfhood: The Evolution of Woman in H. D.'s Neo-Epic *Helen in Egypt*," *Arizona Quarterly*, 36 (Summer 1980): 165-175;

Anne Friedberg, "Approaching *Borderline*," *Millenium Film Journal*, no. 7/8/9 (Fall-Winter 1980-1981): 130-139;

Susan Stanford Friedman, "Creating a Woman's Mythology: H. D.'s *Helen in Egypt*," *Women's Studies*, 5 (1977): 163-198;

Friedman, "Ghost Stories: H. D.'s *Hedylus*," *Sagetrieb*, 5 (forthcoming, Spring 1986);

Friedman, " 'I go where I love': An Intertextual Study of H. D. and Adrienne Rich," *Signs*, 9(Winter 1983): 228-246;

Friedman, "A Most Luscious Vers Libre Relationship: H. D. and Freud," in *The Annual of Psy-*

choanalysis, 14 (New York: International Universities Press, 1986);

Friedman, *Psyche Reborn: The Emergence of H. D.* (Bloomington: Indiana University Press, 1981);

Friedman, "Psyche Reborn: Tradition, Re-Vision, and the Goddess as Mother-Symbol in H. D.'s Epic Poetry," *Women's Studies*, 6 (1979): 147-160;

Friedman, " 'Remembering Shakespeare always, but remembering him differently': H. D.'s *By Avon River*," *Sagetrieb*, 2 (Summer-Fall 1983): 45-70;

Friedman, "Who Buried H. D.? A Poet, Her Critics and Her Place in 'The Literary Tradition,' " *College English*, 36 (March 1975): 801-814;

Friedman and DuPlessis, " 'I had two loves separate': The Sexualities of H. D.'s *Her*," *Montemora*, 8 (1981): 3-30;

Friedman and DuPlessis, eds., *H. D.: Centenary Issue, Contemporary Literature*, 27 (forthcoming, Winter 1986);

John T. Gage, *In the Arresting Eye: The Rhetoric of Imagism* (Baton Rouge: Louisiana State University Press, 1981);

Albert Gelpi, "Hilda in Egypt," *Southern Review*, 18 (Spring 1982): 233-250;

Gelpi, "The Thistle and the Serpent," in *Notes on Thought and Vision* (San Francisco: City Lights, 1983);

Kathryn Gibbons, "The Art of H. D.," *Mississippi Quarterly*, 15 (Fall 1962): 152-160;

Sandra M. Gilbert, "H. D.? Who Was She?," *Contemporary Literature*, 24 (Winter 1983): 496-511;

Jean Gould, *American Women Poets: Pioneers of Modern Poetry* (New York: Dodd, Mead, 1980), pp. 151-176;

Judy Grahn, *The Highest Apple: Sappho and The Lesbian Poetic Tradition* (San Francisco: Spinsters, Ink, 1985);

E. B. Greenwood, "H. D. and the Problem of Escapism," *Essays in Criticism*, 21 (October 1971): 365-376;

Horace Gregory, Introduction to *Helen in Egypt* (New York: New Directions, 1974), pp. vii-xi;

Susan Gubar, "The Echoing Spell of H. D.'s *Trilogy*," *Contemporary Literature*, 19 (Spring 1978): 196-218;

Gubar, "Sapphistries," *Signs*, 10 (Autumn 1984): 43-62;

J. B. Harmer, *Victory in Limbo: Imagism, 1908-1917* (London: Secker & Warburg, 1975);

Norman Holland, *Poems in Persons* (New York: Norton, 1973), pp. 4-163;

Glenn Hughes, *Imagism & The Imagists* (Stanford: Stanford University Press, 1931);

Thomas H. Jackson, ed., *Marianne Moore and H.D., Poesis*, 6 (Fall 1985);

Nora Crow Jaffe, " 'She herself is the writing': Language and Sexual Identity in H. D.," *Literature and Medicine*, 4 (Fall 1985);

Peter Jones, *Imagist Poetry* (Harmondsworth: Penguin, 1972);

Jeanne Kerblat-Houghton, " 'The Rose Loved of Lover' or the Heroines in the Poems of the Twenties," *GRENA* (1982): 45-64;

Michael King, Foreword to *End to Torment* (New York: New Directions, 1979), pp. vii-xii;

King, ed., *H. D.: Woman and Poet* (Orono, Maine: National Poetry Foundation, forthcoming, 1986);

Deborah Kelly Kloepfer, "Flesh Made Word: Maternal Inscription in H. D.," *Sagetrieb*, 3 (Spring 1984): 27-48;

Peggy A. Knapp, "Women's Freud(e): H. D.'s *Tribute to Freud* and Gladys Schmitt's *Sonnets for an Analyst*," *Massachusetts Review*, 24 (Summer 1983): 338-352;

Denise Levertov, "H. D.: An Appreciation," *Poetry*, 100 (June 1962): 182-186;

Amy Lowell, *Tendencies in Modern American Poetry* (New York: Macmillan, 1917), pp. 235-243;

Beverly Lynch, "Love, Beyond Men and Women: H. D.," in *Lesbian Lives: Biographies of Women from The Ladder*, edited by Barbara Grier and Colletta Reid (Baltimore: Diana Press, 1976), pp. 259-272;

Charlotte Mandel, "Garbo/Helen: The Self-Projection of Beauty by H. D.," *Women's Studies*, 7 (1980): 127-135;

Robert McAlmon, "Forewarned as Regards H. D.'s Prose," in *Palimpsest* (Carbondale: Southern Illinois University Press, 1968);

Adalaide Morris, "The Concept of Projection: H.D.'s Visionary Powers," *Contemporary Literature*, 25 (Winter 1984): 411-436;

Morris, "Reading H. D.'s 'Helios and Athene,' " *Iowa Review*, 12 (Spring-Summer 1981): 155-163;

Morris, ed., *Special Issue on H. D.*, *Iowa Review* (forthcoming, Winter 1986);

Margaret Newlin, " 'Unhelpful Hymen': Marianne Moore and Hilda Doolittle," *Essays in Criticism*, 27 (July 1977): 216-230;

Alicia Ostriker, "The Thieves of Language: Women Poets and Revisionist Mythmaking,"

Signs, 8 (Autumn 1982): 68-90;

Ostriker, *Writing Like a Woman* (Ann Arbor: University of Michigan Press, 1983), pp. 7-41;

Norman Holmes Pearson, Foreword to *Hermetic Definition* (New York: New Directions, 1972), pp. v-viii;

Pearson, Foreword to *Trilogy* (New York: New Directions, 1973), pp. v-xii;

John Peck, "Passio Perpetuae H. D.," *Parnassus,* 3 (Spring-Summer 1975): 42-74;

Cyrena N. Pondrom, "H. D. and the Origins of Modernism," *Sagetrieb,* 4 (Spring 1985): 73-100;

William Pratt, ed., *The Imagist Poem* (New York: Dutton, 1963), pp. 11-39;

Vincent Quinn, *Hilda Doolittle* (New York: Twayne, 1967);

Quinn, "H. D.'s 'Hermetic Definition': The Poet as Archetypal Mother," *Contemporary Literature,* 18 (Winter 1977): 51-61;

Peter Revell, *Quest in Modern American Poetry* (New York: Barnes & Noble, 1981), pp. 171-198;

Joseph N. Riddel, "H. D.'s Scene of Writing—Poetry as (AND) Analysis," *Studies in the Literary Imagination,* 12 (Spring 1979): 41-59;

Alfred Satterthwaite, "John Cournos and 'H. D.,'" *Twentieth-Century Literature,* 22 (December 1976): 394-410;

Perdita Schaffner, "Merano, 1962," *Paideuma,* 4 (Fall/Winter 1975): 513-518;

Schaffner, "Pandora's Box," in *HERmione* (New York: New Directions, 1981), pp. vii-xi;

Schaffner, "A Profound Animal," in *Bid Me to Live (A Madrigal)* (Redding Ridge, Conn.: Black Swan Books, 1980), pp. 185-194;

Schaffner, "Unless a Bomb Falls . . . ," in *The Gift* (New York: New Directions, 1984), pp. ix-xv;

Heather Rosario Sievert, "H. D.: A Symbolist Perspective," *Comparative Literature Studies,* 16 (March 1979): 48-57;

Paul Smith, *Pound Revised* (London: Croom Helm, 1983), pp. 110-133;

Thomas Burnett Swann, *The Classical World of H. D.* (Lincoln: University of Nebraska Press, 1962);

John Walsh, Afterword to *Bid Me to Live (A Madrigal)* (Redding Ridge, Conn.: Black Swan Books, 1983), pp. 195-203;

Walsh, Afterword to *Hedylus* (Redding Ridge, Conn.: Black Swan Books, 1980), pp. 147-156;

Walsh, Afterword to *Hippolytus Temporizes* (Redding Ridge, Conn.: Black Swan Books, 1985);

Walsh, Afterword to *Ion* (Redding Ridge, Conn.: Black Swan Books, 1985);

Emily Stipes Watts, *The Poetry of American Women from 1632-1945* (Austin: University of Texas Press, 1977), pp. 152-158;

Harold H. Watts, *Hound and Quarry* (London: Routledge & Kegan Paul, 1953), pp. 209-222;

Eric Walter White, *Images of H. D./From The Mystery* (London: Enitharmon Press, 1976);

Francis Wolle, *A Moravian Heritage* (Boulder, Colo.: Empire Reproduction & Printing Co., 1972), pp. 55-60.

Papers:

Manuscripts for H. D.'s published and unpublished works are in the Collection of American Literature, Beinecke Rare Book and Manuscript Library, Yale University. Most of H. D.'s correspondence is at the Beinecke Library, but letters can also be found at the Houghton Library (Harvard University); the Berg collection (New York Public Library); Lockwood Library (State University of New York at Buffalo); Rosenbach Collection, Rosenbach Foundation in Philadelphia; The Huntington Library (San Marino); and the libraries of the University of Texas at Austin, Bryn Mawr College, and Southern Illinois University. Part of H. D.'s library is at the Beinecke Library.

T. S. Eliot

Jewel Spears Brooker
Eckerd College

See also the Eliot entries in *DLB 7, Twentieth-Century American Dramatists,* and *DLB 10, Modern British Dramatists, 1900-1945.*

BIRTH: St. Louis, Missouri, 26 September 1888, to Henry Ware and Charlotte Chauncy Stearns Eliot.

EDUCATION: A.B., 1909; A.M., 1910; Harvard University; University of Paris (Sorbonne), 1910-1911; Harvard University, 1911-1914; Oxford University, 1914-1915; Ph.D. dissertation accepted by Harvard University, 1916.

MARRIAGES: 26 June 1915 to Vivien (Vivienne) Haigh-Wood; 10 January 1957 to Esme Valerie Fletcher.

AWARDS AND HONORS: Sheldon Traveling Fellowship (Harvard), 1914; *Dial* Award for *The Waste Land,* 1922; Litt. D., Columbia University, 1933; LL.D., University of Edinburgh, 1937; Litt. D., Cambridge University, 1938; Litt. D., University of Bristol, 1938; Litt. D., University of Leeds, 1939; Litt. D., Harvard University, 1947; Litt. D., Yale University, 1947; Litt. D., Princeton University, 1947; D. Litt., Oxford University, 1948; Nobel Prize for Literature, 1948; Order of Merit of the British Empire, 1948; Honorary Fellow, Magdalene College, Cambridge University, 1948; Honorary Fellow, Merton College, Oxford University, 1949; Commander, Ordre des Arts et des Lettres, 1950; Officier de la Légion d'Honneur, 1950; D. Litt., University of London, 1950; New York Drama Critics Circle Award for *The Cocktail Party,* 1950; Litt. D., Washington University (St. Louis), 1953; LL. D., St. Andrews University, 1953; Hanseatic Goethe Prize (Hamburg), 1954; Litt. D., University of Rome, 1958; Dante Gold Medal (Florence), 1959; Litt. D., University of Sheffield, 1959; D. ès L., University of Paris (Sorbonne), 1959; D. ès L., University of Aix-Marseille, 1959; D. ès L., University of Rennes, 1959; Orden Pour le Merite (West Germany), 1959; D. Philos., University of Munich, 1959; Emerson-Thoreau Medal of the

T. S. Eliot in Stockholm, May 1942 (courtesy of the Hayward Collection, King's College Library, Cambridge)

American Academy of Arts and Letters, 1959; Honorary Citizen, Dallas, Texas, 1959; Honorary Deputy Sheriff, Dallas County, Texas, 1959; Campion Medal of the Catholic Book Club, 1963; U.S. Medal of Freedom, 1964; Litt.D., University of Bologna, 1967.

DEATH: London, England, 4 January 1965.

BOOKS: *Prufrock and Other Observations* (London: The Egoist, 1917);
Ezra Pound: His Metric and Poetry (New York: Knopf, 1918);
Poems (Richmond: Leonard & Virginia Woolf at The Hogarth Press, 1919);
Ara Vos Prec (London: Ovid Press, 1920); republished with one substitution and one title change as *Poems* (New York: Knopf, 1920);

The Sacred Wood: Essays on Poetry and Criticism (London: Methuen, 1920; New York: Knopf, 1921);

The Waste Land (New York: Boni & Liveright, 1922; Richmond: Leonard & Virginia Woolf at The Hogarth Press, 1923);

Homage to John Dryden: Three Essays on Poetry of the Seventeenth Century (London: Leonard & Virginia Woolf at The Hogarth Press, 1924);

Poems 1909-1925 (London: Faber & Gwyer, 1925; New York & Chicago: Harcourt, Brace, 1932);

Journey of the Magi (London: Faber & Gwyer, 1927; New York: Rudge, 1927);

Shakespeare and the Stoicism of Seneca (London: Oxford University Press, 1927);

A Song for Simeon (London: Faber & Gwyer, 1928);

For Lancelot Andrewes: Essays on Style and Order (London: Faber & Gwyer, 1928; Garden City: Doubleday, Doran, 1929);

Dante (London: Faber & Faber, 1929);

Animula (London: Faber & Faber, 1929);

Ash-Wednesday (London: Faber & Faber, 1930; New York & London: Putnam's, 1930);

Marina (London: Faber & Faber, 1930);

Thoughts After Lambeth (London: Faber & Faber, 1931);

Triumphal March (London: Faber & Faber, 1931);

Charles Whibley: A Memoir (London: Oxford University Press, 1931);

Selected Essays 1917-1932 (London: Faber & Faber, 1932; New York: Harcourt, Brace, 1932);

John Dryden: The Poet The Dramatist The Critic (New York: Terence & Elsa Holliday, 1932);

Sweeney Agonistes: Fragments of an Aristophanic Melodrama (London: Faber & Faber, 1932);

The Use of Poetry and The Use of Criticism: Studies in the Relation of Criticism to Poetry in England (London: Faber & Faber, 1933; Cambridge: Harvard University Press, 1933);

After Strange Gods: A Primer of Modern Heresy (London: Faber & Faber, 1934; New York: Harcourt, Brace, 1934);

The Rock: A Pageant Play (London: Faber & Faber, 1934; New York: Harcourt, Brace, 1934);

Elizabethan Essays (London: Faber & Faber, 1934); republished, with omission of three essays and addition of one, as *Essays on Elizabethan Drama* (New York: Harcourt, Brace, 1956); republished as *Elizabethan Dramatists* (London: Faber & Faber, 1963);

Words for Music (Bryn Mawr, Pa., 1934);

Murder in the Cathedral, acting edition (Canterbury: H. J. Goulden, 1935); complete edition (London: Faber & Faber, 1935; New York: Harcourt, Brace, 1935);

Two Poems (Cambridge: Cambridge University Press, 1935);

Essays Ancient & Modern (London: Faber & Faber, 1936; New York: Harcourt, Brace, 1936);

Collected Poems 1909-1935 (London: Faber & Faber, 1936; New York: Harcourt, Brace, 1936);

The Family Reunion (London: Faber & Faber, 1939; New York: Harcourt, Brace, 1939);

Old Possum's Book of Practical Cats (London: Faber & Faber, 1939; New York: Harcourt, Brace, 1939);

The Idea of a Christian Society (London: Faber & Faber, 1939; New York: Harcourt, Brace, 1940);

The Waste Land and Other Poems (London: Faber & Faber, 1940; New York: Harcourt, Brace, 1955);

East Coker (London: Faber & Faber, 1940);

Burnt Norton (London: Faber & Faber, 1941);

Points of View (London: Faber & Faber, 1941);

The Dry Salvages (London: Faber & Faber, 1941);

The Classics and the Man of Letters (London, New York & Toronto: Oxford University Press, 1942);

The Music of Poetry (Glasgow: Jackson, Son & Company, Publishers to the University, 1942);

Little Gidding (London: Faber & Faber, 1942);

Four Quartets (New York: Harcourt, Brace, 1943; London: Faber & Faber, 1944);

What Is a Classic? (London: Faber & Faber, 1945);

Die Einheit der Europäischen Kultur ["The Unity of European Culture"—bilingual] (Berlin: Carl Habel, 1946);

A Practical Possum (Cambridge: Harvard Printing Office & Department of Graphic Arts, 1947);

On Poetry (Concord, Mass.: Concord Academy, 1947);

Milton (London: Geoffrey Cumberlege, 1947);

A Sermon (Cambridge: Cambridge University Press, 1948);

Selected Poems (Harmondsworth: Penguin/Faber & Faber, 1948; New York: Harcourt, Brace & World, 1967);

Notes Towards the Definition of Culture (London: Faber & Faber, 1948; New York: Harcourt, Brace, 1949);

From Poe to Valéry (New York: Harcourt, Brace, 1948);

The Undergraduate Poems of T. S. Eliot published while he was in college in The Harvard Advocate, unauthorized publication (Cambridge, 1949);

The Aims of Poetic Drama (London: Poets' Theatre Guild, 1949);

The Cocktail Party (London: Faber & Faber, 1950; New York: Harcourt, Brace, 1950; revised edition, London: Faber & Faber, 1950);

Poems Written in Early Youth (Stockholm: Privately printed, 1950; London: Faber & Faber, 1967; New York: Farrar, Straus & Giroux, 1967);

Poetry and Drama (Cambridge: Harvard University Press, 1951; London: Faber & Faber, 1951);

The Film of Murder in the Cathedral, by Eliot and George Hoellering (London: Faber & Faber, 1952; New York: Harcourt, Brace, 1952);

The Value and Use of Cathedrals in England Today (Chichester: Friends of Chichester Cathedral, 1952);

An Address to Members of the London Library (London: London Library, 1952; Providence, R.I.: Providence Athenaeum, 1953);

The Complete Poems and Plays (New York: Harcourt, Brace, 1952);

Selected Prose, edited by John Hayward (Melbourne, London & Baltimore: Penguin, 1953);

American Literature and the American Language (St. Louis: Department of English, Washington University, 1953);

The Three Voices of Poetry (London: Cambridge University Press, 1953; New York: Cambridge University Press, 1954);

The Confidential Clerk (London: Faber & Faber, 1954; New York: Harcourt, Brace, 1954);

Religious Drama: Mediaeval and Modern (New York: House of Books, 1954);

The Cultivation of Christmas Trees (London: Faber & Faber, 1954; New York: Farrar, Straus & Cudahy, 1956);

The Literature of Politics (London: Conservative Political Centre, 1955);

The Frontiers of Criticism (Minneapolis: University of Minnesota Press, 1956);

On Poetry and Poets (London: Faber & Faber, 1957; New York: Farrar, Straus & Cudahy, 1957);

The Elder Statesman (London: Faber & Faber, 1959; New York: Farrar, Straus & Cudahy, 1959);

Geoffrey Faber 1889-1961 (London: Faber & Faber, 1961);

Collected Plays (London: Faber & Faber, 1962);

George Herbert (London: Longmans, Green, 1962);

Collected Poems 1909-1962 (London: Faber & Faber, 1963; New York: Harcourt, Brace & World, 1963);

Knowledge and Experience in the Philosophy of F. H. Bradley (London: Faber & Faber, 1964; New York: Farrar, Straus, 1964);

To Criticize the Critic and Other Writings (London:

Faber & Faber, 1965; New York: Farrar, Straus & Giroux, 1965);

The Waste Land: A Facsimile and Transcript of the Original Drafts Including the Annotations of Ezra Pound, edited by Valerie Eliot (London: Faber & Faber, 1971; New York: Harcourt Brace Jovanovich, 1971);

Selected Prose of T. S. Eliot, edited by Frank Kermode (New York: Harcourt Brace Jovanovich/Farrar, Straus & Giroux, 1975).

OTHER: Charlotte Eliot, *Savonarola: A Dramatic Poem*, introduction by Eliot (London: Cobden-Sanderson, 1926);

Edgar Ansel Mowrer, *This American World*, preface by Eliot (London: Faber & Gwyer, 1928);

Ezra Pound, *Selected Poems*, edited, with an introduction, by Eliot (London: Faber & Gwyer, 1928);

Charles Baudelaire, *Intimate Journals*, translated by Christopher Isherwood, introduction by Eliot (London: Blackamore Press/New York: Random House, 1930);

St.-J. Perse, *Anabasis a Poem*, translated, with an introduction, by Eliot (London: Faber & Faber, 1930; New York: Harcourt, Brace, 1938; revised edition, New York: Harcourt, Brace, 1949; London: Faber & Faber, 1959);

Pascal's Pensées, translated by W. F. Trotter, introduction by Eliot (London & Toronto: Dent/New York: Dutton, 1931);

"Donne in Our Time," in *A Garland for John Donne, 1631-1931*, edited by Theodore Spencer (Cambridge: Harvard University Press, 1931), pp. 1-19;

"Address by T. S. Eliot, '06, to the Class of '33, June 17, 1933," *Milton Graduates Bulletin*, 3 (November 1933): 5-9;

Harvard College Class of 1910. Seventh Report, includes an autobiographical note by Eliot (June 1935), pp. 219-221;

Marianne Moore, *Selected Poems*, edited, with an introduction, by Eliot (New York: Macmillan, 1935; London: Faber & Faber, 1935);

Alfred Tennyson, *Poems of Tennyson*, introduction by Eliot (London, Edinburgh, Paris, Melbourne, Toronto & New York: Nelson, 1936);

Djuna Barnes, *Nightwood*, introduction by Eliot (New York: Harcourt, Brace, 1937); introduction and preface by Eliot (London: Faber & Faber, 1950);

Rudyard Kipling, *A Choice of Kipling's Verse*, edited, with an introduction, by Eliot (London: Faber & Faber, 1941; New York: Scribners, 1943);

Samuel L. Clemens (Mark Twain), *The Adventures of Huckleberry Finn*, introduction by Eliot (London: Cresset Press, 1950);

"Ezra Pound," in *Ezra Pound: A Collection of Essays*, edited by Peter Russell (London & New York: Peter Nevill, 1950), pp. 25-36;

Joseph Chiari, *Contemporary French Poetry*, foreword by Eliot (Manchester: Manchester University Press, 1952);

Pound, *Literary Essays*, edited, with an introduction, by Eliot (London: Faber & Faber, 1954; Norfolk, Conn.: New Directions, 1954);

Chiari, *Symbolisme from Poe to Mallarmé*, foreword by Eliot (London: Rockliff, 1956);

Paul Valéry, *The Art of Poetry*, translated by Denise Folliot, introduction by Eliot (New York: Pantheon, 1958);

From Mary to You, includes an address by Eliot (St. Louis: Mary Institute, 1959), pp. 133-136;

"The Influence of Landscape upon the Poet," *Daedalus*, 89 (Spring 1960): 420-422;

The Criterion 1922-1939, 18 volumes, edited by Eliot (London: Faber & Faber, 1967).

T. S. Eliot is one of the giants of modern literature, highly distinguished as poet, literary critic, dramatist, and editor/publisher. In 1910-1911, while still a student, he wrote "The Love Song of J. Alfred Prufrock" and other poems which are landmarks in the history of literature. In these college poems, written with virtually no influence from his contemporaries (William Butler Yeats was well-known, but not yet modern; Ezra Pound at this time was neither well-known nor modern), Eliot articulated distinctly modern themes in forms which were both a striking development of and a striking departure from those of nineteenth-century poetry. Within a few years, he had composed another landmark poem, "Gerontion" (1920), and within a decade, the century's most famous and influential poem, *The Waste Land* (1922). While the origins of *The Waste Land* are in a sense personal, the voices projected are universal. Perhaps without having intended to do so, Eliot diagnosed the malaise of his generation and indeed of Western civilization in the twentieth century. In 1930 he published his next major poem, *Ash-Wednesday*, written after his conversion to Anglo-Catholicism. Conspicuously different in style and tone from his earlier work, these confessional lyrics chart his continued search for order in an age of chaos. The culmination of this search as well as of Eliot's poetic writing is his great meditation on the nature of time and of human history, *Four Quartets* (1936-1942).

With *Four Quartets*, Eliot virtually concluded his career as a poet.

Eliot was almost as distinguished a literary critic as he was a poet. From 1916 through 1921, he contributed approximately one hundred reviews and articles to perhaps a dozen periodicals. This early criticism was produced at night under the pressure of supplementing his meager salary, first as a teacher, then as a bank clerk; and not, as is sometimes suggested, under the compulsion to rewrite literary history. He did much, it is true, to generate a revolution in literary taste, but this was not part of his intention. Possessing a special critical intelligence and superb training in philosophy and literature, he wrote with such elegance and incision that his essays, however hastily written and for whatever motive, had an immediate impact. His ideas quickly solidified into doctrine and became, with the early essays of I. A. Richards, the basis of the most influential school of literary criticism in this century, the so-called New Criticism. Three of these essays—"Tradition and the Individual Talent," "Hamlet and His Problems," and "The Metaphysical Poets"—outline in canonical form such modern critical doctrines as "tradition," "impersonality," "irrelevancy of belief," "objective correlative," and "unified sensibility."

Through half a century of critical writing, Eliot's concerns remained more or less constant; his position regarding those concerns, however, was frequently refined, revised, or, occasionally, reversed. He discovered, though, that those early and tentative formulations had taken on a life of their own. Even today, most commentators seem to be unaware of the complexity of Eliot's developing critical mind and of the distortion which results from the assumption that those well-known phrases do justice to that mind. Beginning in the late 1920s, Eliot's literary criticism was supplemented by, at times supplanted by, religious and social criticism. Some of these writings, such as *The Idea of a Christian Society* (1939), are interesting as social commentary and elucidative in regard to his plays and to *Four Quartets*.

As a dramatist also, Eliot is an important figure in the twentieth century. He was inclined from the first toward the theater—his early poems are essentially dramatic; many of his early essays and reviews are on drama or dramatists. By the mid-1920s, he was writing a drama, *Sweeney Agonistes;* in the 1930s he wrote *The Rock* (1934), *Murder in the Cathedral* (1935), and *The Family Reunion* (1939); in the 1940s and 1950s, he devoted himself almost exclusively to plays, of which *The Cocktail Party*

(1950) has been the most popular. His goal, realized only in part, was the revitalization of poetic drama in terms which would be consistent with the modern age. He experimented endlessly with language which, though close to contemporary speech, is essentially poetic and thus capable of extraordinary spiritual, emotional, and intellectual resonance. He did more, perhaps, than any other person to reestablish poetic drama and to create an audience for it. His work has influenced a number of important twentieth-century dramatists, including W. H. Auden and Harold Pinter.

Eliot also made significant contributions as an editor and publisher. From 1922 to 1939, he was the editor of a major intellectual journal, the *Criterion,* and from 1925 to 1965, an editor/director in the publishing house of Faber and Faber. In both capacities, he worked tirelessly behind the scenes to nurture the intellectual and spiritual life of his time.

Because Eliot's definitive biography is unwritten and his letters are unpublished, any discussion of his life must be tentative. A number of basic facts, of course, are part of the public record, and others have been revealed in occasional remarks by the poet himself. Thomas Stearns Eliot was born 26 September 1888; he was the second son and seventh child of Charlotte Stearns and Henry Ware Eliot, members of a distinguished Massachusetts family recently transplanted to Missouri. Eliot's family tree includes settlers of the Massachusetts Bay Colony, prominent clergymen and educators, a president of Harvard University (Charles William Eliot), and three presidents of the United States (John Adams, John Quincy Adams, and Rutherford B. Hayes). The move from Boston to St. Louis had been made by the poet's grandfather, William Greenleaf Eliot, a Unitarian minister and educator. In St. Louis, he established the first Unitarian church and founded both Smith Academy and Washington University. His grandson grew up in an old house at 2635 Locust Street in an old section of St. Louis, graduating from Smith Academy in 1905. Never entirely at home in the Midwest, the Eliot family carefully maintained the Massachusetts connection. From 1896, they summered on Cape Ann on the Massachusetts coast; and when their sons graduated from Smith Academy, they sent them to Massachusetts to continue their education.

From these few facts, several points emerge as relevant to Eliot's future mind and art. First, he was to become extremely conscious of history—his own, that of his family, his civilization, his race—

T. S. Eliot, 1896, in the schoolyard at Mary Institute, the St. Louis girls' school founded by his grandfather, William Greenleaf Eliot (courtesy of the Hayward Collection, King's College Library, Cambridge)

and of the ways in which the past constantly impinges on the present and the present on the future. Second, he was early possessed by a sense of homelessness. As he explained in a 1928 preface, "The family guarded jealously its connections with New England; but it was not until years of maturity that I perceived that I myself had always been a New Englander in the South West, and a South Westerner in New England." He might have added that in England, he was an American, and in America, a European. His poetry is haunted by a feeling of homelessness, of being everywhere in exile.

Third, as he himself revealed in a 1930 letter quoted in an appendix to *American Literature and the American Language* (1953), "St. Louis affected me more deeply than any other environment has done." His most powerful and typical images—city streets and city slums, city rivers and city skies— (though eventually mediated through such literary sources as Charles Baudelaire's images of Paris) were etched on his mind in the streets of St. Louis. In Eliot's childhood, his widowed grandmother lived around the corner, and out of respect for her wish to continue living in the house her husband had built, the family resisted the flight to the suburbs. In "The Influence of Landscape upon the Poet" (1960), he explained that they chose to stay in "a neighborhood which had become shabby to a degree approaching slumminess.... for nine months of the year my scenery was almost exclusively urban, and a good deal of it seedily, drably urban at that. My urban imagery was that of St. Louis, upon which that of Paris and London had been superimposed." He might have inserted Boston between St. Louis and Paris, for he spent most of his college years there. The littered labyrinthine streets, the faint stale smells of beer, and the yellow fog that rubs its muzzle on the window panes, that lingers, leaps, slips, falls, and curls up for a nap—these now well-known images are inseparable, then, from the city of St. Louis. The river imagery which pervades his poetry from beginning to end also comes from St. Louis, from the great Mississippi. In the 1930 letter just quoted, Eliot says "Missouri and the Mississippi have made a deeper impression on me than any other part of the world." The early poems are strewn with images of city rivers—the Mississippi, the Charles, the Seine, and the Thames—rivers littered with "empty bottles, sandwich papers—Silk handkerchiefs, cardboard boxes, cigarette ends/Or other testimony of summer nights." And one of his last major poems, *The Dry Salvages,* evokes the river known from the nursery bedroom, the implacable unpropitiated brown god with its cargo of dead Negroes and chicken coops.

Eliot was educated at Smith Academy in St. Louis (1898-1905), at Milton Academy in Massachusetts (1905-1906), at Harvard University (A.B., 1909; M.A., 1910; Ph.D. courses, 1911-1914), at the University of Paris (Sorbonne, 1910-1911), and at Oxford University (1914-1915). He devoted a further year (1915-1916) to a doctoral dissertation on the philosophy of F. H. Bradley. Although he was prevented by World War I travel restrictions from returning to Harvard for his doctoral defense, the dissertation was accepted by the philosophy department, with Josiah Royce calling it the work of an expert.

The first two decades of the twentieth century were golden years for the Harvard University philosophy department. During his time there, Eliot had some of the century's most distinguished philosophers as teachers, including George Santayana, Josiah Royce, and Bertrand Russell. As an undergraduate, Eliot emphasized language—Latin, Greek, German, and French; as a graduate student,

T. S. Eliot at Harvard, 1907 or 1908 (courtesy of the Hayward Collection, King's College Library, Cambridge)

he emphasized philosophy. One of the distinctive traits of his poetry can be directly associated with his splendid education. His early masterpieces are distinguished by a curious combination of sensuous imagery and intellectuality; in his mind, the smell of cooking and the philosophy of Spinoza meet and form new wholes. This combination, which he was later to remark in the metaphysical poets, derives in part from his decade-long immersion in philosophy and language. Eliot's most fruitful extracurricular activity at Harvard was his association with the college literary magazine, the *Harvard Advocate.* Many of his earliest poems were first published by the *Advocate,* and at least one of his lifelong friendships, that with fellow poet Conrad Aiken, was formed in this well-known nursery of writers and poets.

The most far-reaching consequence of Eliot's

The Harvard Advocate *staff for 1910: Eliot is seated third from the left in the first row; Conrad Aiken is standing fourth from the left in the second (courtesy of the Houghton Library, Harvard University)*

undergraduate career at Harvard was his accidental discovery of Arthur Symon's *Symbolist Movement in Literature* (1899), a book which Eliot later said had changed the course of his life. Symons introduced him to the poetry of Jules Laforgue, and Laforgue, Eliot claimed, helped him to discover himself as a poet, to find his own voice. Reading Laforgue taught him how to handle emotion in poetry, through irony and through a quality of detachment which enabled him to see himself and his own emotions essentially as objects for analysis. By feeding his increasing Francophilia, Symons also led Eliot in 1910 to take a course in French literary criticism from Irving Babbitt. Babbitt became perhaps the single most important influence on Eliot's mind. Babbitt's antipathy toward romanticism and his advocacy of tradition, for example, are cornerstones of Eliot's later criticism. And finally, at least indirectly, Symons led Eliot to spend the academic year 1910-1911 reading literature and philosophy

at the Sorbonne in Paris, immeasurably augmenting his indebtedness to France. In rereading Baudelaire, whom he had discovered before he read Symons, Eliot perceived how to transform the sordid images of quotidian urban life into art; in reading Mallarmé, how to gain the collaboration of his readers by impregnating the blank spaces between words and by underpinning poetic structures with ritualistic ones; and in listening to Henri Bergson, whose lectures he attended at the Sorbonne, Eliot began to ponder the questions on time and consciousness which are at the center of *Four Quartets*, and which hover just above and just below everything he wrote.

Eliot's career as a poet can be divided into three periods—the first coinciding with his studies in Boston and Paris and culminating in "The Love Song of J. Alfred Prufrock" in 1911; the second coinciding with World War I and with the financial and marital stress of his early years in London, and culminating in *The Waste Land* in 1922; and the third coinciding with his melancholy and alarm at the economic depression and the rise of Nazism, and culminating in the wartime *Quartets* in 1942. The poems of the first period were preceded only by a handful of schoolboy exercises, clever after a fashion, but in no way suggestive of the creative intelligence which was to manifest itself in 1910-1911, when with four poems—"Portrait of a Lady," "Preludes," "Rhapsody on a Windy Night," and "The Love Song of J. Alfred Prufrock"—Eliot virtually invented modern English poetry. In the earlier poems, he had been concentrating on form. As he told Donald Hall in a 1959 interview, "My early *vers libre* . . . was started under the endeavor to practice the same form as Laforgue . . . merely rhyming lines of irregular length, with the rhymes coming in irregular places." In the four greater poems, he told Hall, he was burdened with material which had been incubating in his mind for years, and was not concerned with form *per se*: "There were things in the next phase which were freer, like 'Rhapsody on a Windy Night.' I don't know whether I had any . . . model . . . in mind . . . It just came that way." And until the form "just came," he said in *The Use of Poetry and The Use of Criticism* (1933), he himself was unable to understand the material to which it gave birth. These poems perfectly illustrate his idea, not articulated until years later, of tradition and the individual talent, in that they issue from a marriage of the classics of the Western past—that which educated Westerners have in common—and the experience of a unique mind of the present. In these early poems, Homer, the Greek dramatists, the biblical writers, Dante, Shakespeare, even Alfred Tennyson and Rudyard Kipling, meet the fastidious and sensitive youth from St. Louis, producing totally new works of art which modify and reshape the tradition from which they sprang.

The early poems introduce themes to which, with variation and development, Eliot was to return time and again. These themes are all related in one way or another to the problem of isolation, and to the causes and the consequences in the contemporary world of isolation. In a minor poem of 1909, "Conversation Galante," a man and a woman speak to each other, but neither comprehends what the other is saying. In "Portrait of a Lady," a man and woman meet, but the man is inarticulate, imprisoned in thought. In this ironic dramatization of a "conversation galante," the woman speaks without thinking and the man thinks without speaking. Her words are juxtaposed against his thoughts—an "in-

sistent out-of-tune/Of a broken violin" juxtaposed against "a dull tom-tom . . ./Absurdly hammering a prelude of its own" inside his brain.

The profound isolation of the lady in "Portrait of a Lady" who decorously extends her hand across the abyss becomes in "The Love Song of J. Alfred Prufrock" an isolation which is absolute. The specific lady is succeeded by generalized women; the supercilious youth by the middle-aged intellectual he will become, for whom women and indeed the entire universe exist as abstractions. The poignance of this superb poem derives in part from a tension between Prufrock's self-generated isolation and his obsession with language. Although he is afraid to speak, he can think only in the language of dialogue. This dialogue with himself, moreover, consistently turns on the infinite possibilities (or impossibilities) of dialogue with others. The tension created by this obsession with language is reinforced by another quality which implies the real existence of other people—fear. Interestingly, though, he is not so much afraid of other people as of other people's language. These women who (simply by talking) can transform the greatest of artists, Michelangelo, into a meaningless, tea-party abstraction will have no trouble with Prufrock. His anguished refusal to be formulated and pinned (wriggling) to the wall is one of the greatest expressions of isolation in modern European literature. In "Preludes" and "Rhapsody on a Windy Night," the lady and Prufrock's women are succeeded by a woman who exists only as one of "the thousand sordid images/Of which [his] soul [is] constituted." And his sordid image of her includes the sordid image of himself that she sees flickering on the ceiling.

In these early poems, the progression from a feeble attempt to build a bridge in "Conversation Galante" to a failure in "Portrait of a Lady" to an impossibility in "The Love Song of J. Alfred Prufrock" is paralleled on other levels, and understanding these levels is crucial in getting to the heart of Eliot. The isolation of man from woman is paralleled by the isolation of man from man, of man from God, and of poet from reader; isolation is sexual, human, religious, and since Eliot is a poet, vocational. In "Conversation Galante" and "Portrait of a Lady," other people and perhaps God exist, but they are unreachable; in "The Love Song of J. Alfred Prufrock," they exist, but only as aspects of Prufrock's mind; in "Preludes" and "Rhapsody on a Windy Night," the other, whether human or divine, has been so thoroughly assimilated that it can no longer be defined. This situation is explicitly aesthetic. The poet-persona of "Conversation Galante" bores his companion with baffling metaphors. The protagonist of "Portrait of a Lady" is paralleled by an artist in the concert room, and both the suitor and the pianist fail to reach their listeners. In both cases, this failure is described in ceremonial terms which act to superimpose the religious on the sexual and aesthetic. J. Alfred Prufrock—as lover, as prophet, as poet—also fails to reach his audience. These failures are skillfully layered by the use of imagery which defines Prufrock's problem as sexual, as religious (how to raise himself from the dead, how to cope with his own flesh on a platter), and as rhetorical (how to sing, how to say, how to revise). And as "The Love Song of J. Alfred Prufrock" shows most clearly, the horizontal and vertical gaps mirror a gap within, a gap between thought and feeling, a partition of the self.

The techniques of Eliot's early poems owe something to the Jacobean dramatists and to Robert Browning, but these essentially dramatic ancestors have been transformed in his mind by an encounter with the French symbolist poets and by his own impulse toward idealism. Browning's dramatic monologue, a recognizable ancestor, becomes in "The Love Song of J. Alfred Prufrock" interior monologue. Formally, Browning's logical and psychological continuity gives way to Eliot's systematic juxtapositions, both linear and vertical. In part, the form in these early poems is a protest against the immediate past; in part (and more important), an attempt to solve a very practical problem. Because art is at bottom a collaborative achievement which the artist initiates and the audience completes, it becomes virtually impossible unless the artist and his audience have enough in common to permit communication on some level. The early-twentieth-century shattering of shared meanings puts the artist in a situation analogous to that of Prufrock. Prufrock can never get beyond the corridors of his own mind, can never speak to the chattering abstractions who convert him into an abstraction. But Eliot did reach beyond his own mind. By using formal techniques which force the reader to do his part of art's labor, he has spoken to and has moved countless readers. The once shocking techniques of these early poems—deliberate open-endedness, concentrated allusiveness, juxtaposition, irony—all work to gain the creative collaboration of readers with whom Eliot had almost nothing in common. Of reader collaboration, he had learned much from the symbolists, whose methods were especially contrived to generate poems in the minds of readers.

Between the great poems of 1910-1911 and *The Waste Land*, Eliot lived through a number of experiences which are crucial in understanding his development as a poet. First, from 1911 to 1916, he studied for a Ph.D. in philosophy—from 1911 to 1914 at Harvard; in the 1914-1915 academic year at Oxford; and in 1915-1916 in London working on his dissertation. Eliot's 1911-1914 work at Harvard included serious study of both Eastern and Western philosophy. His Indic studies (two years of Sanskrit and of Indian philosophy) abetted his innate asceticism and provided a more comprehensive context for his understanding of culture. Inevitably, these studies entered his poetry. The Indian myth of the thundergod, for example, provides the context for section five ("What the Thunder Said") of *The Waste Land*, and Buddha's fire sermon the context for section three ("The Fire Sermon"). In his study of European philosophy, Eliot concentrated on problems in contemporary epistemology. His immersion in the neo-idealism of F. H. Bradley and the neorealism of Bertrand Russell had many effects, of which two proved especially important. Positively, these studies suggested methods of structure which he was able to put to immediate use in "Gerontion" and *The Waste Land*. Negatively, these studies convinced him that the best and most sophisticated answers to the cultural and spiritual crisis of his time were finally inadequate. This conclusion contributed to his decision to abandon the career for which his education had prepared him. To the great disappointment of his family, he chose not to return to America and settle down as a professor of philosophy, but rather to remain in England and follow a literary career.

Eliot's decision to put down roots, or to discover roots, in Europe stands, together with his first marriage and his conversion, as the most important of his entire life. With the original intention of staying for one year, Eliot left Boston in June 1914 for the University of Marburg in Germany. He was forced by the outbreak of war to abandon his fellowship, and in August arrived in London, an intellectual hothouse with "isms" proliferating in every field, especially the arts.

He had been preceded by his Harvard friend Conrad Aiken, who had come to London with the idea, as he put it in a letter of June 1914, of doing a little "self-advertising," and with the secondary intention of helping his friend Tom Eliot. Aiken had seen a longer early version of "The Love Song of J. Alfred Prufrock," had made suggestions, which Eliot accepted, about dropping part of it, and in the summer of 1914, carried it and another Eliot poem, "La Figlia che Piange," with him to London. Either on this occasion or an earlier one, he tried unsuccessfully to interest Harold Munro in Eliot's work. He also showed "The Love Song of J. Alfred Prufrock" to the American Ezra Pound and left Eliot an introduction to Pound. In September, Eliot called on Pound, a meeting with enormous consequences for modern poetry. Pound discovered that Eliot had modernized himself by himself and immediately adopted him as a cause, peddling his poetry, introducing him to the in-crowd, convincing him to settle in London, writing soothing letters to Eliot's disappointed father. At a time when Eliot was close to giving up, Pound arranged in 1915 for the publication of "The Love Song of J. Alfred Prufrock" in *Poetry,* and in 1917 for the publication of *Prufrock and Other Observations.*

The impact of Ezra Pound, however, pales beside that of Vivien Haigh-Wood, the pretty but nervous English girl Eliot married in June 1915. The marriage, however lovingly begun, was in most respects a disaster. "She is a person who lives on a

knife-edge," Bertrand Russell observed a few months after the marriage, "and will end as a criminal or a saint." In fact, she ended in madness, a development which in retrospect seems inevitable but for which Eliot felt partially responsible and for which he forgave himself only in old age, if ever. This burden is the biographical shadow behind a motif recurrent in the poems and plays—the motif of "doing a girl in," of wife murder. The struggle to cope emotionally and financially with Vivien Eliot's illness almost, in truth, did Eliot in, leading him first to exhaustion, and then, in 1921, to collapse. His conscientious effort between 1915 and 1922 to build a bridge across the gulf which separated them, reflected most conspicuously in part two of *The Waste Land,* is a lived experience behind all of his subsequent work.

Eliot's marriage and his determination to make it as a literary man in London had two other immediate, and far-reaching, consequences. The first was estrangement from his family, particularly his father. For the rest of his life, Eliot deeply regretted that his father did not live to see him make a success as a poet. This lingering regret can be seen, perhaps, in the persistent but ambiguous interest in father death which appears in *The Waste Land* and in the plays. The second consequence of his decision was severe financial distress. To support himself and his chronically ill wife, he took a job as a teacher—in the fall of 1915 at High Wycombe Grammar School, and throughout 1916 at Highgate Junior School. Finding the teaching of young boys extremely draining work, he gave it up at the end of 1916 and in March of 1917 began work in the Colonial and Foreign Department of Lloyds Bank. Although he was to stay with Lloyds for the next nine years, he discovered that banking, like teaching, did not produce nearly enough income to cover his expenses and Vivien's medical bills. He was thus forced to supplement his duties as a teacher, as banker, and as nurse to his wife with a great deal of night work as lecturer, reviewer, and essayist. Working from 1916 to 1920 under incredible pressure (a fifteen-hour work day was common for him), he wrote the essays, published in 1920 as *The Sacred Wood,* which reshaped literary history.

The focus in Eliot's early essays is essentially the same as in the poetry—the problem of isolation, its causes and its consequences. In the poems, the emphasis is on man's isolation from man (from woman, too, of course) and his related isolation from God. In the literary criticism, the emphasis is on the artist in isolation, cut off from his audience,

T. S. and Vivien Eliot, 1919 (courtesy of Simon & Schuster)

and from great artists and thinkers of both the present and the past. In "Tradition and the Individual Talent" (1919), one of this century's most celebrated essays, Eliot attempts to cope with the isolation of the artist resulting from the early-twentieth century's massive repudiation of the past, a repudiation which severed man's intellectual and spiritual roots. Eliot deals with the implications of this disaster by defining "tradition" as an ideal (that is, mental) structure in which the "whole of the literature of Europe from Homer and within it the whole of the literature of [the artist's] own country has a simultaneous existence and composes a simultaneous order." To put it more simply, he defines tradition not as a canon, but as an ongoing relationship of Western masters, living and dead, within the mind and bones of the contemporary poet. Eliot's reaction against romanticism, similarly, is related to the fact that romanticism celebrates the artist in isolation; his dedication to order, to the fact that order by definition is an organized assembly of what otherwise would be isolated fragments. Eliot's notion that modern poetry should be complex derives in part from his attempt to overcome his isolation from his readers by forcing them to become involved as collaborators in his poetry. When he began to turn, a decade later, to religious and social criticism, he explored in new areas the same problem and suggested tentative solutions.

In regard to poetry, the decade between the Harvard poems and *The Waste Land* is for the most part a long dry stretch. Although Eliot had written a few short pieces at Oxford in 1915, he was afraid by 1916 that "The Love Song of J. Alfred Prufrock" was his swan song. And by 1917, he had become, by his own testimony, quite desperate. To get going again, Eliot wrote a handful of poems in French, one of which, "Dans le Restaurant," in a truncated English version, ended up in *The Waste Land.* Eliot and Pound were at their closest during these years, and some of the impetus for Eliot's revival as a poet came from his flamboyant friend. Both felt that the freedom achieved in the previous decade of revolution in the arts had degenerated to license, and they decided to move back toward more precise forms, a move analogous to Picasso's move a few years later from Cubism to neoclassicism. In Eliot, the result was the quatrain poems, so-called because they were modeled, at Pound's suggestion, on the quatrains of Théophile Gautier's *Emaux et Camées* (1852). These Gautier-inspired poems, all highly polished satires, include "The Hippopotamus," "Sweeney Erect," "Sweeney among the Nightingales," "Burbank with a Baedeker," "Mr. Eliot's

Sunday Morning Service," "Whispers of Immortality," and "A Cooking Egg." The themes of the French poems and of the quatrain poems are those of Eliot's great poems of 1910-1911 and of the criticism—the absence of a common ground, isolation, consequent sterility, death which is final, death which leads to regeneration. Largely as a result of World War I, Eliot's focus—international, cultural, institutional—is broader than in the earlier poems. Prufrock is primarily an individual; Burbank and Sweeney are primarily types.

The difference between the "The Love Song of J. Alfred Prufrock" and the Sweeney poems, however, is only partially due to expanded focus; much more important is enlarged technique. For Eliot, the quatrain poems were experiments; for the critic, they are a laboratory for studying his developing poetic. Form rather than content is uppermost. He settled on the quatrain form, in fact, before he had any idea of what he was going to say. The form of the stanza is Gautier's; in every other way, though, the form is Eliot's—a natural development of his inclusive and systematic mentality. In the 1910-1911 poems, Eliot had used allusions as a means of layering texts and of forcing the reader to reevaluate (and thus reinvigorate) the entire Western tradition. For example, beneath Eliot's ironic love song, the perceptive reader cannot but hear the sentimental love songs of the nineteenth century; beneath Prufrock's debate with himself, the reader may discover the medieval debate of body and soul; beneath Prufrock's paralysis, that of Hamlet; beneath Prufrock's burial, that of Lazarus; beneath Prufrock's hell, Dante's inferno. The careful reader not only sees this complex layering of texts, but is literally forced to see with new eyes the entire tradition in which these texts exist.

In the quatrain poems, allusions are used in much the same way, but in much greater density, becoming a means for remarkably intricate, highly systematic intellectual gymnastics. William Arrowsmith, one of Eliot's most perceptive critics, aptly dubs this highly deliberate and systematic layering of texts "the poem-as-palimpsest." The poem-as-palimpsest, although never again used as conspicuously as in these poems, is basic to *The Waste Land.* Eliot continued to use allusions to layer texts in a complex way, but beginning with "The Hollow Men," he used them more sparingly. In that it requires special knowledge and much work from the reader—at least as much work, Eliot wryly notes, as would be required of a barrister preparing a difficult court case—the poem-as-palimpsest enables the poet to gain from his audience the sort of creative co-labor without which the greatest art cannot exist.

Eliot's most important single poem between 1911 and 1922 is "Gerontion." Important in itself, it also serves as a transition to *The Waste Land,* to which, for thematic reasons, Eliot considered it an appropriate prelude, and to which, until dissuaded by Pound, he considered attaching it. The emphasis in the early poems had been on the isolation of the individual (Mr. Prufrock and company), on its causes and consequences. In "Gerontion" and *The Waste Land,* the individual crisis is seen as part of a cultural crisis; the causes and consequences are seen to be embedded in contemporary history. On all levels, the causes are more or less the same. Isolation is produced, first, by the collapse of common ground in culture, the loss of that mythic substructure which enables man to understand his relatedness to anyone or anything, to place himself in his world. In the early part of the twentieth century, the collapse of shared assumptions in many fields—religion, physics, philosophy, art—produced a crisis in epistemology, in knowing, and this crisis is basic to all of Eliot's work. The second cause is related to the first. To Eliot and to many intellectuals, the villain is knowledge; or from a slightly different angle, the villain is human intelligence. Knowledge, in leading modern man to know that he cannot know anything, in robbing him of shareable assumptions about reality, has banished his brothers and maimed his gods and condemned him to solitary confinement within himself.

Among the special ironies of literary history is the fact that Eliot, his fine intelligence burnished to a rare brilliance, was always painfully aware of intelligence as destroyer. The villain in all of his poems through *The Waste Land* is thinking, intellection. From "Conversation Galante" through "Portrait of a Lady" to "The Love Song of J. Alfred Prufrock" and "Preludes," the persona moves into increasingly purer realms of abstraction, and consequently into deeper and deeper isolation. It is "thinking" that dissolves the unity of felt thought or thought feeling, producing the divided self; thinking that first generates and then perpetuates self and other. The young man in "Portrait of a Lady" is encased in silence by "thinking"; Prufrock is etherized upon the table of his mind by continuous thinking and rethinking. Gerontion and the inhabitants of the waste land are also thought-trapped creatures, sealed in the prison of solipsism, in which thinking, particularly thinking of the key with which to break out, only confirms the prison. That no lover, human or divine, that no friend can

reach through the wall of thought is one of Eliot's special themes. The consequences of isolation—fragmentation, sterility, and death—are parallel on all levels: sexual, cultural, religious, and aesthetic. The cure for isolation similarly is parallel. Generation and renewal are contingent on transcendence of the self, on collaboration between human beings.

In the early poems, then, Eliot's great themes had been established. Preeminent is the profound isolation of modern urban man, isolation from friends, enemies, lovers, gods, readers. The cause is the collapse of the common ground—in language, in culture, in religion, in art—which serves as a bridge, as a means of self-transcendence. And the consequences of isolation are sterility and death. This accounts for Eliot's perennial preoccupation in life and in art with the necessity for and, in the early poems, the impossibility of resurrection or regeneration. In "Gerontion" and *The Waste Land,* Eliot begins to explore possibilities for overcoming the consequences of isolation. In "Gerontion," he experiments with a solution suggested by his readings in philosophy; in *The Waste Land,* with solutions suggested by his readings in anthropology.

T. S. Eliot and Virginia Woolf

"Gerontion" is the most negative of all Eliot's major poems, reflecting among other things his melancholy over the war; his conclusion that philosophy and religion, like sexual love, promise more than they deliver; his fear that great art is impossible in the twentieth century; his conviction that Western civilization is, in Pound's well-known line, "an old bitch gone in the teeth" ("Ode pour l'Election de Son Sepulchre"). Civilization in Eliot's poem is a shrivelled old man, not only gone in the teeth, but also gone in the eyes, gone in the head, gone in the groin. His name, a transliteration of the Greek word for "little old man," is also a description. The poem is a representation of the state of this old man's mind; and his mind, consisting of bits and pieces of floating cultural, intellectual, spiritual, and sexual debris, is an image of contemporary civilization. Here displayed in all their horror are the consequences of that isolation Eliot had been brooding on and living in for years.

In the opinion of most critics, "Gerontion" is Eliot's most difficult poem. The difficulty derives not so much from content as from form, or as some would have it, from absence of form. What appears at first to be a Prufrockian interior monologue proves to be totally lacking in psychological coherence. In truth, the structure of "Gerontion" is far more complex than that of "The Love Song of J. Alfred Prufrock," due in part to Eliot's assimilation of the idealism of F. H. Bradley, on whose epistemology he had recently completed a dissertation. An understanding of one of Bradley's basic ideas, the systematic nature of truth and judgment, makes "Gerontion" far more accessible. (See Jewel Spears Brooker, "The Structure of Eliot's Gerontion," *ELH*, Summer 1979.)

Common to all absolute idealists and endorsed in Eliot's thesis, the doctrine, simply stated, is that reality consists of parts which are all interconnected in a single system. On the intellectual level, Bradley's doctrine explains away the fragmentation and chaos which seem to characterize contemporary culture. Everything that exists, simply by virtue of existing, is included in the Absolute, which is an over-arching, all-inclusive whole. From the fact that the Absolute is all-inclusive, it follows that every perception, every object, every thing in the universe, is a part rather than a whole. Any fragment, no matter how isolated it may appear, is connected to other fragments; every fragment is self-transcendent, that is, it reaches beyond itself and participates in successively greater fragments until it reaches the all-inclusive whole. More simply, every fragment has a context which in turn has a context which in turn again has a context which finally is the Absolute. Because these fragments are all part of one single thing, they are necessarily and systematically related. No fragment has its meaning alone; it exists as part of a unitary and timeless system. Most of Eliot's criticism, including his notion of "tradition," is rooted in this Bradleyean doctrine, and most of his poetry, "Gerontion" noticeably, takes it as a structural principle.

In "Gerontion" the dynamic controlling movement from one part to another is not the flow of an old man's consciousness, but the expansion and contraction of the contexts of fragments. The poem is arranged into an almost endless number of superimposed contexts by using the image of houses within houses. By placing houses within houses within houses, Eliot is able to show that every fragment is part of a context which is itself part of a larger context. The objects contained within the houses become less inclusive houses which in turn contain other houses; at the same time, all of the houses are included in more inclusive houses. The house which serves as the model for all of the others is Gerontion's literal house. In the first stanza this house, its tenants, and its surroundings are described. In subsequent stanzas other major houses are superimposed. Although the house image appears at the beginning of the poem, its function as a structural element is not clear until one has read the entire poem and then returned to the beginning. The coda of the poem—"Tenants of the house,/Thoughts of a dry brain in a dry season"—becomes a structural key when it is in the mind of a reader who is re-reading the poem.

As Gerontion describes his literal house and its desiccated tenants, the reader who has the final image in his mind will immediately perceive that Gerontion is more than a tenant in this old house. Gerontion himself, his body, is also an old house with dying tenants, one of which, his brain, is another ruined house with diseased tenants, his thoughts. The idea that all fragments exist necessarily within more inclusive contexts is perfectly illustrated by these images, because a brain can only exist as part of a more inclusive whole. In that the crucial clue is placed at the end of the poem, "Gerontion" illustrates the point made long ago by Joseph Frank: modern literature cannot be read; it can only be re-read, because the whole, of which the last lines are a part, must be in the reader's mind throughout.

The house in which Gerontion lives, clearly on the edge of doom, is old, decayed, brittle, windowless, drafty; it is located in a neglected yard filled with rocks, moss, excreta. The tenants—Gerontion and a woman—are old and sick, and they are transients in a rented house. The owner, a depraved contemporary Jew, squats on the window sill. The "dry season" is upon them all, and wind batters the house. From this house, there is a proliferation of houses in many directions, and all of them are replicas of the first one. All of the houses are, from a larger point of view, tenants; all of the tenants, from a smaller point of view, are houses. In the first stanza alone, there is a series of houses (tenants): Gerontion's thoughts, his brain, his body, his house, the yard, the field, and Europe. All of these tenants are dying transients in houses rented from a predator who represents both Western religion and modern capitalism.

To these doomed houses are added in subsequent stanzas the houses of history and of hell; the houses of David (Israel) and of Lancelot Andrewes (the Christian church); of the whore's womb and the messiah's tomb; and many more, all precisely modeled on the first one. The cause of ruin in all is related to a loss of feeling, a decay of religion, and an expansion of knowledge. United in decay, the houses are also to be united in judgment. The coda of the poem returns the reader to the house which, though small, includes all of the others: the arid brain of the withered intellectual whose memories and thoughts, visions and revisions, furnished Eliot with a perfect metaphor for his vision of postwar civilization.

Eliot's first years as a literary man bore tangible fruit in 1920 with the publication of *Ara Vos Prec* (American title, *Poems*), collecting most of his poetry through the quatrains and "Gerontion," and the publication of the best of his literary essays, including "Tradition and the Individual Talent," in *The Sacred Wood*. As Eliot wrapped up the details surrounding these projects, he moved on to what was to prove a watershed experience not only in his life as a poet but also in the history of European poetry. In December 1919 he wrote his mother in America that his New Year's resolution was "to write a long poem I have had on my mind for a long time." That long poem, *The Waste Land*, continues Eliot's exploration of what he saw as the decay of European civilization. In "Gerontion" Eliot had managed to impose order on the chaos by seeing all fragments as part of a system. In the last analysis, however, this purely philosophic solution, even if true, is woefully inadequate. Gerontion's ruined houses, even if seen as parts of a whole, are still ruined. That all the fragments are ordered may be great comfort for the philosopher,

or even to the artist, but it is little comfort to the individual who must live and work in the ruins. Bradley's notion was pushed into the background because Eliot's long poem is much more than an account of the breakdown of civilization; *The Waste Land*, unlike "Gerontion," is an account of a breakdown in the poet's personal life.

In the five years between his marriage and composition of *The Waste Land*, Eliot had suffered continuously from overwork, financial strain, and marital anxiety; and he lost in these years two men he especially loved, his friend Jean Verdenal and his father. Verdenal, whom Eliot had met in Paris in 1910-1911, fell in the war late in 1915. Eliot was deeply moved by Verdenal's death, so moved that he dedicated his first two volumes of poems to his friend's memory. In January 1919 Eliot's father died, still believing that his youngest son had made a mess of his life. Eliot's plan for regaining his father's esteem had been to get his poems published in America and then follow up with a visit home. His father died, however, just before the poems went to press. By 1919, furthermore, it had become all too clear that Thomas and Vivien Eliot were not good for each other. His comments about her in the letters that have surfaced are in no way disrespectful (they reflect, mainly, concern for her health and respect for her resourcefulness), but if the poems "Hysteria" (written in 1914-1915) and "Ode" (written in 1918) are any indication, his feelings were more negative than he could admit to his family or friends, or even to himself.

These years of unmitigated anxiety culminated, finally, in serious illness. In 1921, on the verge of a nervous breakdown, he was forced to take a leave from the bank. For rest, he went in October for a month to Margate; and then, leaving Vivien Eliot in Paris, he went to a sanatorium in Switzerland. From Lausanne, he wrote his brother that he was trying to learn "to use all my energy without waste, to be *calm* when there is nothing to be gained by worry, and to concentrate without effort." In this protected environment, he devoted himself to writing the "long poem" that had been on his mind, a work in which his illness is included as part of the material. "On Margate Sands/I can connect nothing with nothing." "By the waters of Leman [Lake Geneva] I sat down and wept." In the original typescript, there is a reference to leaving Vivien: "I left without you/There I left you/Clasping empty hands."

In January 1922 Eliot returned to London, stopping briefly in Paris, where he left the manuscript of *The Waste Land* with Ezra Pound. Pound

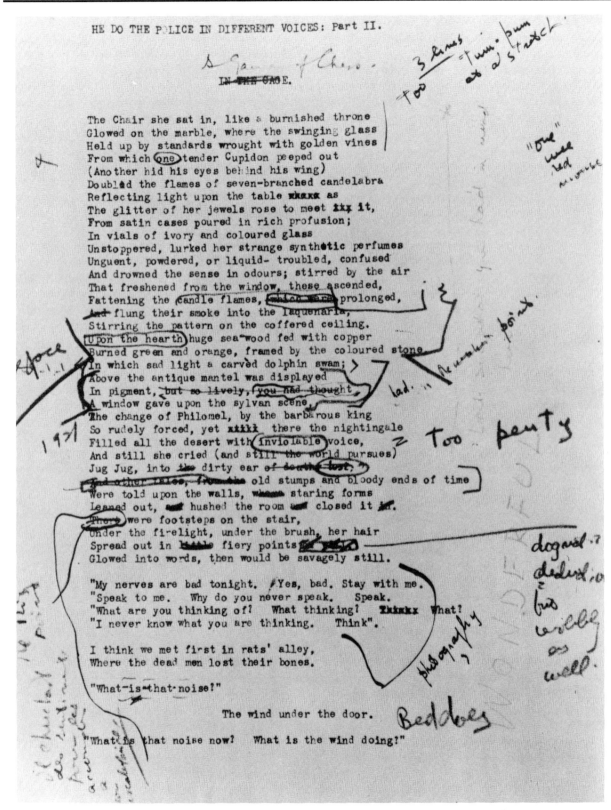

Page from the original draft for part two of The Waste Land, *with Eliot's revised title. Most of the comments and revisions are by Ezra Pound. The remarks lightly penciled in the right margin are by Vivien Eliot (by permission of Valerie Eliot; courtesy of the Henry W. and Albert A. Berg Collection, New York Public Library, Astor, Lenox and Tilden Foundations, and Harcourt Brace Jovanovich).*

immediately recognized it as a work of genius ("About enough, Eliot's poem, to make the rest of us shut up shop"), but he thought it needed cutting and suggested revisions to bring it down to size. Eliot accepted most of Pound's suggestions and later testified that Pound was "a marvelous critic because he . . . tried to see what you were trying to do." In October 1922 *The Waste Land* appeared in England in the first issue of the *Criterion*, the journal Eliot was to edit for most of the next two decades; three weeks later, on 5 November, it appeared in America in the *Dial*, with Eliot receiving the *Dial* award of $2,000.

The Waste Land was taken by some critics as a tasteless joke, by others as a masterpiece expressing the disillusionment of a generation. As far as Eliot was concerned, it was neither. He needed, he explained in the *Paris Review* interview, to get something off his chest, adding, "one doesn't know quite what it is that one needs to get off the chest until one's got it off "; or as he put it in the conclusion to *The Use of Poetry and The Use of Criticism*, he did not know until the shell broke what sort of egg he had been sitting on. In a lecture at Harvard, quoted in *The Waste Land* facsimile, he gave another explanation, astonishing in its simple honesty, its humility. Responding to those who considered *The Waste Land* "an important bit of social criticism," he remarked, "To me it was only the relief of a personal and wholly insignificant grouse against life; it is just a piece of rhythmical grumbling." The grumbling is personal, of course, which is why he calls it insignificant, but in that its causes are inseparable from those that set a generation or more of intelligent and talented Westerners to grumbling, it is more than personal. Eliot's "grouse against life," certainly, is part of a larger and shared discontent about the decay of the West and the conditions of modern urban life.

Another aspect of Eliot's "grumbling" which is more than personal is his anxiety about possibility in art. A major theme in his poetry and prose from 1910 had been the situation of the artist who is isolated from his audience by a collapse of common ground in culture. Deprived of a shared mythic or religious frame, the modern artist was forced to come up with other means of unity, other grounds for collaboration with an audience. He had to find, as Eliot put it in "*Ulysses*, Order, and Myth" (*Dial*, November 1923), his review of James Joyce's *Ulysses* (1922), "a way of controlling, of ordering, of giving a shape and a significance to the immense panorama of futility and anarchy which is contemporary history." The "narrative method," rooted in se-

quence, in continuity, in an orderly flow of life (and stories) from beginning to end, had been rendered obsolete by modern science and by conditions of history. The philosophic method, Eliot had concluded, was an elusion. Consequently, in *The Waste Land,* he experimented with a new method which he hoped was "a step toward making the modern world possible for art." This method, "already adumbrated by Mr. Yeats," Eliot called the "mythical method." He defined it as the manipulation of a continuous parallel between an ordered world of myth (an abstraction) and a chaotic world of history, contemporary or otherwise. In keeping the chaos of his own time on the surface, the artist is being true to history; in referring this chaos to a timeless order, he is being true to art. And in forcing the reader to know (or to learn) the myth, to hold it in his mind as a reference point, and to manipulate the parallel between the world of myth and the world of time, the modern artist is forcing the reader into a collaborative role. This reader must be competent and active, for he is the cowriter in whose mind works such as *Ulysses* and *The Waste Land* take their shape and find their meaning.

Eliot claimed that the mythical method would have been impossible a few years earlier, and had become possible only because of recent work in psychology and ethnology, and because of Sir James Frazer's *The Golden Bough* (1890-1915). (See Jewel Spears Brooker, "The Case of the Missing Abstraction: Eliot, Fraser, and Modernism," *Massachusetts Review*, Winter 1984.) Frazer's monumental twelve-volume work is an attempt to interpret the history of religion in terms consistent with Darwinian science. As Darwin had attempted to discover the origin of species and chart the descent of man, anthropologists attempted to discover the origin of religion and chart the descent of the gods. The controlling idea, consistent with the Newtonian/Darwinian assumption of continuity, was that all religions, all myths, originated from a single parent myth. And by examining literally thousands of myths, anthropologists were able to reconstruct this parent myth. To artists trying to find a genuine common ground upon which to unify their art, these ideas proved invaluable. Theoretically, the monomyth is a perfect common ground in that it is shared by all. Religion in the modern world exists only in fragments, but if all of the fragments have a common parent, they can be unified by reference to this Urmyth. All beliefs, no matter how bizarre, are part of one belief; all believers, part of one family.

Eliot saw in this thesis a solution to his problem as an artist—how both to respect and to transcend not only his own isolation, but also the chaos of contemporary history. In the notes to *The Waste Land*, he acknowledged his general debt to Frazer; and his specific debt to Jessie Weston, who in 1920 had published a book called *From Ritual to Romance*, in which she tried to find the origin of all stories having to do with the Holy Grail. Some scholars had postulated a Christian origin, others a folk origin; Weston traces both Christian and folk elements to a common parent, in her words, to "an ancient Ritual, having for its ultimate object the initiation into the secret of the sources of Life, physical and spiritual." In other words, she tried to find the monomyth for the Grail legends. Most important, the monomyth itself exists only as an abstraction, a mental reconstruction made up from many surviving fragments. As a reconstruction in the mind of Frazer or Weston, it serves to structure and unify all fragments of religion and myth; in the mind of the poet, it serves to unify all fragments of religion and culture in twentieth-century Europe; in the mind of the reader of *The Waste Land*, it serves to structure the religious and cultural fragments which make up the poem.

The fragments of myth and religion in *The Waste Land* come from all over the globe and from all periods of history. Christianity in this poem is just one more religion, and fragments of it exist side by side with fragments of Buddhism, ancient fertility cults, contemporary fortune-tellers. All derive ultimately from and find their unity in the Urmyth. One myth, however, has special importance for the poem because it supplied Eliot with the title and much of the symbolism of his poem. That myth, found in *From Ritual to Romance*, tells of a kingdom in which the vitality of the king and that of his kingdom are mysteriously intertwined. The king has suffered a wound (from war, sickness, old age, or whatever) in his genitals, and this sexual wound affects his entire kingdom, depriving it of regenerative power, turning it into a waste land. The land may be restored by a hero who undergoes certain trials and asks certain questions. In Eliot's poem, this myth exists in the same form as it exists in the modern world, that is, in fragments which in the mind of a Jessie Weston or a T. S. Eliot or an intelligent reader may be reconstructed into a whole. As structural principle, then, the monomyths of Weston and Frazer enable the informed reader to unify all fragments in Eliot's poem. As symbol, Weston's myth enables Eliot to construct parallels between contemporary civilization and the mythic waste land; between diseased religion in his-

tory and the sexually wounded god-king; and it enables the poet to suggest that, in history as in myth, the wounding of god and the decay of culture are interrelated.

In *The Waste Land*, then, as in "Gerontion," the overall theme is the breakdown of contemporary civilization. In *The Waste Land*, this theme is illustrated and reinforced by juxtaposition to breakdown in Eliot's personal life on the one hand, and on the other to the repeated breakdowns of many, perhaps all, temporal civilizations. Also as in "Gerontion," the structural method is spatial rather than narrative: meaning does not emerge from the sequential arrangement of parts on a page, but from the spatial arrangement of parts in the mind of the reader. In neither poem, however, does the insistence on spatiality amount to a denial of temporality. The poem in the mind is *in time*—it is not given all at once and not given once for all; and it is dynamic rather than static.

The major differences in "Gerontion" and *The Waste Land* are related to point of view. In "Gerontion," unity is inextricable from the consciousness of a single narrator. His mind is an image of civilization. In *The Waste Land*, there is no single narrator, but a multiplicity of super-imposed minds, one of which, that of the blind and impotent prophet Tiresias, has a special status. Far more important than the mind of Tiresias, however, is the mind of the reader. The basic structural principle, learned from Bradley, of the systematic nature of reality is modified as Eliot moves from "Gerontion" to *The Waste Land*. In "Gerontion," unity is achieved by referring fragments to ever more inclusive houses or contexts until the Absolute, in which all contexts are systematically contained, is reached. In *The Waste Land*, unity is achieved by referring all fragments to increasingly inclusive parents until the original is reached. There are several important groups of fragments, each leading to its own parent, for example, linguistic fragments leading to Indo-European or some parent language. But the most important group of fragments is the religious or mythic, and the most important parent, the monomyth. The origin of all fragments, even of those seemingly most unconnected to religion, is ultimately religious. The fragments of art, for example, descend from ritual; this, of course, is the meaning of Weston's title, *From Ritual to Romance*.

The Waste Land consists of five parts which, by traditional standards, seem unrelated. In each part, Eliot's own verse is mixed with fragments of the verse of others, all joined without transitions. This montage includes fragments from several languages and allusions to hundreds of other texts. On one level, these fragments refer primarily to contemporary civilization; on another level, to other temporal civilizations; on the deepest level, to a world of myth. The meaning of the poem exists in all of the fragments taken together, as a whole. The emergence of order and simplicity from this bewildering complexity can perhaps be suggested by a brief survey of the poem.

The primary subject of the first section of the poem—"Burial of the Dead"—is death; death which is just a problem in waste disposal, death which is part of a natural cycle, death as a prelude to life, death as a part of life, life which is a death-in-life, death as an end, death as a beginning. Eliot's montage includes the death of the year, death of individuals, of cities, of civilizations. The title of the first section is a fragment of the title of the majestic burial service in the *Book of Common Prayer*, "The Order for the Burial of the Dead." This service affirms the belief that the burial of the dead is a prelude to the resurrection of the body and to everlasting life. The Anglican church is a descendant of medieval Catholicism, nurturer of the Grail legends, and medieval Catholicism, in turn, descends from first-century Christianity, which has for its major doctrine the death and resurrection of Christ. All of these go back in Frazer's genealogy to primitive rituals in which burial is a ritualistic "planting" intended to insure a rich harvest. Eliot refers specifically to such rituals in the lines "That corpse you planted last year in your garden/'Has it begun to sprout?" The ritualistic planting, in April, of a male corpse (or part of one, usually the genitals) in mother earth is at the center of many ancient fertility ceremonies. But Eliot's lines refer also to the contemporary world, where planting the corpse insures harvest by acting as organic fertilizer, and where April is cruel because, in "breeding/Lilacs out of the dead land," it promises what it does not deliver, new life.

The last line of "Burial of the Dead" is a quotation from the prefatory poem of Baudelaire's *Fleurs du Mal*, and may be translated "You! Hypocrite reader!—my double—my brother!" In this poem, entitled "Au Lecteur" ("To the Reader"), Baudelaire addresses his reader directly and indicts him as a fellow sinner. In appropriating Baudelaire's line, Eliot indicts his reader not only as a fellow sinner, but also as a partner in the wasting of the land and of civilization. This is so because in his "menagerie of vices," Baudelaire ranks sins, placing at the top, as the most hideous and most evil, the very sin which in Eliot's view swallows up

all meaning and turns the world into a waste land. The deadliest sin to Baudelaire and to Eliot is not pride, not greed or rape or murder. The vice of all vices which Baudelaire and Eliot discern both in their readers and in themselves is *ennui*, an inability to invest everyday life with meaning and structure. This monster, the hound devouring the inhabitants of the contemporary waste land, makes a grand entrance in section two of Eliot's poem.

The underlying subject of the second section—"A Game of Chess"—is sex, in myth part of a larger interest in life and life-giving forces. In history, though, as Eliot shows, sex is often not associated with life at all. He juxtaposes two "love" scenes—minidramas from opposite ends of the social scale, both displaying sterile and meaningless relationships. The relationship of the upper-class couple is structured by a game of chess, and that of the Cockney couple by visits to the pub. The title of the section alludes to the origin of the game of chess in Hindu agrarian ritual, a context emphasizing enrichment of life for the individual and the community. The original meaning of the game of chess is lost, but the game itself survives, a remnant of a lost and barely glimpsed whole. In this part of *The Waste Land*, Eliot focuses on two relatively modern uses of the game of chess, both related to sexual rituals, but neither to life enhancement. The first modern use of the game is introduced by an allusion to two seventeenth-century plays by Thomas Middleton—*A Game of Chess* and *Women Beware Women*. In *Women Beware Women*, a chess game is used to structure a seduction which is also a betrayal and a rape. The second modern use of a game of chess is introduced in the nonconversation between the upper-middle-class couple. Finding themselves totally bored, they play a game of chess to structure (and to kill) time. Through allusion, other sterile sexual situations—Ophelia's, Cleopatra's, Philomela's—are superimposed. In Philomela, sex is associated with brutality; in Cleopatra, with passion; in Ophelia, with betrayal; in Eliot's characters, with boredom. All of these situations involve sex and sexual games. Sex is not associated with regeneration in any of the situations, but only in the contemporary situation is it associated with the ultimate evil of *ennui*.

The underlying subject of section three—"The Fire Sermon"—is again the sexual wound behind civilization's decay. As in "A Game of Chess," there are two contemporary sexual situations—one, a homosexual proposition; the other, a mechanical sexual transaction between a typist and a clerk. Both situations issue from boredom; both, obviously, are loveless and fruitless. The theme is enlarged by including references to loveless couples through the centuries, and to fallen gods in Wagner's *Gotterdammerung*. The title—"The Fire Sermon"—refers to the sermon in which Buddha urges men to extinguish the fires of lust. In the contemporary world Buddha's admonition has been fulfilled in a most ironic way. There is no lust because there is no feeling.

The underlying subject in the short fourth section—"Death by Water"—is again death. The drowning of a sailor, followed by dissolution of his body, is juxtaposed, through allusion, to the death by water of Christian baptism and of Frazer's vegetation myths, both of which are ritualistic preludes to rebirth. The ritualistic death by water involves purification; the contemporary death by water is also, ironically, a purification, a cleansing of bones.

The underlying subject of the fifth section of *The Waste Land*—"What the Thunder Said"—is restoration, not as a fact, but as a distant possibility. The previous images of desolation and drought and sterility reappear, but now accompanied by images suggesting the possibility of revitalization. Thunder sounds in the distance; Christ, the slain and resurrected hero whose death effects restoration, walks in the land; the mythic questor whose personal trials can secure communal blessing approaches the Chapel Perilous. The title of this section refers to an Indian legend in which men, gods, and devils listen to the thunder and then construct from that sound the positive message which can restore the waste land and make its inhabitants fruitful again. The poem ends, however, not with restoration, but with an avalanche of fragments, the most concentrated in the entire poem. Two are questions indicating a desire for purification and rebirth; they are answered, unfortunately, with a fragment indicating the persistence of violence, madness, and death. The last fragment, by chance a benediction, is the cruelest in that, like April, and perhaps like thunder, it awakens expectations that it does not satisfy. In conclusion, restoration remains only as a possibility; it all hinges, finally, on man's willingness to take the given—thunder, for example—and to construct something which will enable him to reclaim structure and meaning. The waste land is not a result of the lack of water, but of the lack of belief. The waste land is filled with water, but it is demythologized water, water that drowns. All of the mythic acts—such as burial in the earth, immersion in water, sexual intercourse— are practiced in the waste land. But they have all been demythologized by the absence of belief.

What is needed to restore the waste land is a re-mythologizing of the events of everyday life, a re-sacramentalization which will reinvest life with structure and meaning. The last lines seem to make a distinction which will become crucial in Eliot's own life: it is probably impossible to refresh the waste land which is Western civilization, but it may be possible to restore order in the waste land of one's personal life.

The Waste Land was both an end and a beginning; it was also a continuation. The distance traveled in the following decade can be gauged by the fact that in 1932, Eliot, now a world-famous poet, returned to Harvard as Charles Eliot Norton Professor of Poetry. Three events of the intervening decade are important in following the shape of his life and art. First, his financial and in a sense his

T. S. Eliot outside Faber & Gwyer, 1926 (photograph by the poet's brother, Henry Eliot)

vocational situation was resolved when, in 1925, he left Lloyds Bank for the publishing house of Faber and Gwyer (later Faber and Faber). Second, his marital situation continued to deteriorate, ending with his permanent separation from Vivien Eliot in 1932; and third, his spiritual odyssey culminated in 1927 in baptism into the Anglican church and in naturalization as a British subject. The financial nightmare had begun to fade in 1922 when he launched the *Criterion*. When, on the eve of World War II, a weary Eliot announced that he was bringing the *Criterion* to a close, he was able to look back with considerable pride on the quality and range of its accomplishments. By publishing such distinguished writers as Paul Valéry, Marcel Proust, James Joyce, Virginia Woolf, D. H. Lawrence, W. H. Auden, Jacques Maritain, Charles Maurras, and Wilhelm Worringer, he had greatly enhanced intellectual fellowship in Europe *l'entre deux guerres*. At Faber, Eliot found a congenial and enduring group of associates, a community. And through Faber, he was able to be a mentor and friend to younger writers. Stephen Spender reports that Eliot, in his dealings with younger poets, was "gentle, helpful, and tolerant, and never expressed disapproval of their politics." W. H. Auden, according to Spender, claimed "that of all the older writers with whom we had dealings, Eliot was the most consistently friendly, the least malicious, envious, and vain." The reciprocally rewarding relationship with Faber continued for the rest of Eliot's life.

The community of intellectuals and artists of which, through the *Criterion* and Faber, Eliot became a part assuaged somewhat the sense of fragmentation which had always haunted him. The sexual and the religious aspects of his isolation, however, proved resistant to transcendence. He and Vivien Eliot were unable to forge any sort of unity, and, as their relationship and her health continued to deteriorate, he suffered in ways which could not help but surface in his poetry. Inseparable from his realization that human love, and in particular, sexual love, had failed is his turn toward God and the church. The emptiness and desolation of this period are perfectly caught in a poem thought by I. A. Richards to be Eliot's most beautiful, "The Hollow Men."

"The Hollow Men," composed in fragments over a two- or three-year period, appeared as a single poem in *Poems 1909-1925* (1925). Written in the style of what Eliot once said was the best part of *The Waste Land,* the water dripping song in "What the Thunder Said," "The Hollow Men" is based on four main allusions—to Dante's *The Divine Comedy,* to Shakespeare's *Julius Caesar,* to Joseph Conrad's *Heart of Darkness,* and to an event in English history, the Gunpowder Plot of 1605. Dante, Shakespeare, and Conrad are arguably the most important writers in the background of Eliot's art, and *Heart of Darkness* is probably second only to *The Divine Comedy* as an intellectual/spiritual resource. Conrad's hero, Mr. Kurtz, a cultivated European idealist and carrier of civilization to dark places, glimpses as he dies a vision which he expresses as "The horror! The horror!" These words, included in Eliot's original epigraph for *The Waste Land*, describe the vision both Conrad and Eliot saw beneath the veneer of European civilization. And they describe what Conrad probably and Eliot certainly saw beneath the veneer of modern idealism.

In "The Hollow Men" Eliot focuses on the idealism shared by such figures as Brutus, Guy Fawkes, and (as in *The Waste Land*) Mr. Kurtz, and in an epigraph which is also a conclusion, he quotes from *Heart of Darkness* the simple announcement by a jungle boy—"Mistah Kurtz—he dead." The death of Mistah Kurtz and all that he stands for is, of course, at the center of the meaning of this poem. From one point of view, however, the most interesting of the disillusioned and defeated idealists is not Mistah Kurtz, but Mistah Eliot, who in 1925 wrote to Bertrand Russell "I am quite desperate." Physically and spiritually worn out, Eliot presents an unforgettable picture of exhaustion and emptiness. The "Old Guy" of the epigraph is not only Guy Fawkes, but also "the old man" whose death, according to St. Paul, is the condition of new life. Many figures in Eliot's early poems, including all the gods and semi-gods from Frazer, have to die or be put to death as the condition for the continuation of life. Those who cannot die cannot really live. The most striking of these death-in-life figures, of course, is the Sibyl of Cumae who presides over *The Waste Land.* In "The Hollow Men," Eliot does not go beyond a presentation of emptiness, but in presenting it, he seems to accept the death that is the essential step toward his own *vita nuova.* In "Gerontion" and *The Waste Land,* Eliot had seen the death-in-life figures as primarily other than himself. But in "The Hollow Men," in trying to articulate his own inarticulate emptiness, he numbers himself among the living dead. His idealism, like that of Brutus, Fawkes, and Kurtz, has led him to the cactus land.

The way out of the cactus land led Eliot to his own "death by water" in a small church at Finstock near Oxford where on 29 June 1927 he was baptized into the Anglican Communion. In November, in what seemed to him part of the same ritual, he was naturalized as a British citizen. Many of Eliot's contemporaries, having adopted him as a sort of spokesman, felt that in embracing traditional Christianity he had abandoned them in the desert. He gently explained that he had never intended to be the spokesman for a generation; that he had been trying all along to work out his own salvation; and that, for "powerful and concurrent reasons," he had been drawn inexorably toward Christianity. As he said in "Christianity and Communism" (*Listener*, March 1932), "In my own case, I believe that one of the reasons was that the Christian scheme seemed to me the only one which would work . . . the only possible scheme which found a place for values which I must maintain or perish." Like Pascal, Eliot had proceeded to the Christian position by a careful process of rejection and elimination. He had tried schemes from philosophy and from anthropology, and he discovered that in the end these schemes failed to account for the world as he saw it and were a less-than-satisfactory basis for order in life and in art.

The Christian scheme, at once personal and communal, which Eliot chose for a basis of order carries as its first condition death and rebirth. The truth that rebirth involves its own pain can be seen in retrospect as a major theme of *The Waste Land*, caught in the opening line, "April is the cruelest month." The painful journey through death into new life is dealt with explicitly in *Journey of the Magi*, a dramatic monologue published as a pamphlet a month after Eliot's baptism. "A cold coming we had of it," say the wise men. In coming to this birth, the incarnation of Christ, they come also to the crucifixion, and to something bitter, "like Death, our death." Eliot's coming, his turning, forms the material for *Ash-Wednesday*, his main poem between *The Waste Land* and *Four Quartets*.

The second poem in the *Ash-Wednesday* sequence appeared in the *Saturday Review of Literature* (10 December 1927) a few months after Eliot's baptism. Titled "Salutation," it demonstrates that the old guy, in the pun of "The Hollow Men," is dying, the new guy coming to life; and it introduces not only the new man, but also the new style. The scene of "Salutation" is the waste land, the cactus land of his earlier work; the subject is certain death and possible new life. The fact that the setting and subject are the same only serves to underscore the great difference in tone and general import. "Lady, three white leopards sat under a juniper-tree/In the cool of the day, having fed to satiety/On my

T. S. Eliot and George the cat, 1928 (courtesy of the Houghton Library, Harvard University)

legs my heart my liver and that which had been contained/In the hollow of my skull. And God said—shall these bones live?" Allusions to the Garden of Eden, to Ezekiel's Valley of Dry Bones, to Saint Paul, and to Dante show that the old man has been dismembered, that his now clean dry bones patiently await oblivion or resurrection. The bones sing a litany celebrating the "End of the endless/Journey to no end" and the arrival at "the Garden/Where all love ends." The resonance of these lines derives in part from the religious and philosophic richness of Eliot's use of the word "end." An "end" is a cause or source, a purpose or raison d'être, a cessation, a logical conclusion, and a fulfillment. An "end" is also the place where the "end" happens. Thus the endless (unceasing, unfulfilling, pointless, placeless) journey through the dark wood of his life with and to no end (purpose, conclusion, haven) finds an end (conclusion, purpose, and thus a beginning and a cause) in the Incarnation, and in the Garden where all love ends (meets its source and cause, finds its fulfillment, ceases in itself to become part of larger love).

Eliot uses the word "end" with similar richness

in *Four Quartets*, his most magnificent meditation on beginnings and ends. A major theme of *East Coker*, for example, is carried in the lines: "In my beginning is my end . . . In my end is my beginning." And the aesthetic and the theodicy of *Little Gidding* culminate in "What we call the beginning is often the end/And to make an end is to make a beginning./The end is where we start from." and "We shall not cease from exploration/And the end of all our exploring/Will be to arrive where we started/And know the place for the first time." The exploration of ends and beginnings which came to dominate his later poetry and his plays had its beginning in this first poem of *Ash-Wednesday*, "Salutation," a poem that "ends" with "This is the land. We have our inheritance." In that this "ending" echoes the "end" of *The Waste Land*—"Shall I at least set my lands in order?" and the fragment from Nerval's "El Desdichado" ("The Disinherited")— "Salutation" constitutes an important bridge between the two major parts of Eliot's career as a poet.

Ash-Wednesday is composed of six parts, three of which had been published separately before the 1930 publication of all six under one title. The title refers to the first day of Lent, a day of repentance and fasting in which Christians acknowledge their mortality and begin the forty-day period of self-examination leading to the new life of Easter. The structure of this sequence comes from Eliot's new principle of order, the Christian scheme which for him had subsumed both Bradley and Frazer. In place of the monomyth as a reference point, Eliot now uses the Incarnation of Christ—not only in *Ash-Wednesday*, but also in *Four Quartets* and the plays. The Incarnation represents a unique intersection of the human and the divine, of time and the timeless, of movement and stillness. Eliot's earlier schemes had been a means of making art possible in the chaos of contemporary history; his new scheme, however, is a means of making life, of which art is only a part, possible. The integration of life and art can be seen in the fact that *Ash-Wednesday* is at once more personal, confessional even, and at the same time more formal and stylized than the earlier work.

The *Ash-Wednesday* sequence as a whole celebrates the turning point in Eliot's life—turning from one blessed face to a higher one, from fragmentation to unity, from a world of ambition to a God of peace. The personal and the universal turning which is the poem's major subject—the "unstilled world still whirled/About the centre of the silent Word"—is also the basis of structure. The first lines circle and hover as they introduce the

theme of turning—"Because I do not hope to turn again/Because I do not hope/Because I do not hope to turn." The circling continues in line after line as the penitent turns in his attempt to stay still and to build something upon which to rejoice. The turning of the first poem is followed in the second by stillness—the bright vision of the leopards who have fed on the dry bones of the penitent's former self. Then in the third poem, the turning resumes as the penitent ascends a spiral staircase, leaving his previous self to struggle with the devil of the stairs. The fourth poem, like the second, is a vision, but the desert has been succeeded by a garden, the stillness by movement, and death by life. The fifth is a meditation on the still point, the Word, which is the source and end of all turning. The last poem circles back on the first, but with a slight advance— "Because I do not hope to turn again" has become "Although I do not hope to turn again." The poem returns at last to its opening prayer, "Teach us to care and not to care./Teach us to sit still."

For all its brightness, *Ash-Wednesday* remains a poem about twilight, about "the time of tension between dying and birth." The tension is resolved in *Marina* (published as a pamphlet in 1930), frequently regarded as Eliot's most beautiful short poem. It consists of an interior monologue spoken by Pericles, the Prince of Tyre, who in Shakespeare's play sails the seas in search of his beloved wife, lost after giving birth at sea to an infant daughter, also lost and presumably dead. Eliot's monologue, inspired by Shakespeare's recognition scene, conveys the wonder and awe the old prince experiences in realizing that the beautiful girl standing before him is Marina, his daughter. What "Gerontion" is to *The Waste Land*, this joyous celebration of new life is to *Four Quartets*.

The decade inaugurated with *Ash-Wednesday* was an eventful one for Eliot. In 1932 he published *Selected Essays*, a collection of his literary journalism through the 1920s; in 1933, *The Use of Poetry and The Use of Criticism*, his lectures as Charles Eliot Norton Professor of Poetry at Harvard in 1932-1933. In the spring of 1933, he gave lectures at the University of Virginia, which were published in 1934 as *After Strange Gods*. He also lectured at Edinburgh and at Cambridge; the Cambridge lectures were later collected as *The Idea of a Christian Society* (1939). Also in the 1930s, he realized his longstanding ambition of becoming a dramatist, finishing both *Murder in the Cathedral* (1935) and *The Family Reunion* (1939). Eliot also published *Old Possum's Book of Practical Cats* (1939), light poems composed for his godchildren. This book became, some fif-

Robert Speight as Becket (seated) in a scene from the first production of Murder in the Cathedral

teen years after Eliot's death, the text for a spectacular rock opera, with music by Andrew Lloyd Webber. Having loved the English music hall, Eliot would have been delighted with *Cats*.

Eliot's major poetic achievement during the 1930s was *Burnt Norton*, composed in 1935, initially considered as an independent work—and included as such in *Collected Poems 1909-1935* (1936)—but becoming during the war the first of four comparable works which together are known as *Four Quartets*. This magnificent sequence—*Burnt Norton* (1936), *East Coker* (1940), *The Dry Salvages* (1941), and *Little Gidding* (1942)—is widely regarded as Eliot's masterpiece. He himself thought *Four Quartets* his greatest achievement, and *Little Gidding* his best poem.

Burnt Norton originated from some lines Eliot cut from *Murder in the Cathedral*. In the play, Becket is confronted by a tempter who suggests a return to the past as a way to escape the dangerous present: "The Chancellorship that you resigned/When you were made Archbishop—that was a mistake/On your part—still may be regained." In this scene,

requiring a reexamination of the whole of life in the light of the present moment, a priest originally responded with the following words: "Time present and time past/Are both perhaps present in the future./Time future is contained in time past. . . . What might have been is a conjecture/Remaining a permanent possibility/Only in a world of speculation. . . . Footfalls echo in the memory/Down the passage which we did not take/Into the rose-garden." These beautiful lines, only slightly modified, now form the opening section of *Burnt Norton*. The temptation to try to go back and take a different road, to cancel history and create an alternative present, constitutes an intersection where the lives of Becket, of Christ, and of Eliot come together. This intersection generated Eliot's meditation on time and timelessness, on history and consciousness, on life and art, and on God.

Eliot's exploration of these great subjects is resumed and completed in the other three *Quartets*, written some five years after *Burnt Norton*. Whereas his earlier poems had been centered on the isolated individual, *Four Quartets* is centered on the isolated

Drained pools at Burnt Norton: "the pool was filled with water out of sunlight, / And the lotos rose, quietly, quietly, / . . . . / Then a cloud passed and the pool was empty." (photograph by Jewel Spears Brooker)

moment, the fragment of time which takes its meaning from and gives its meaning to a pattern, a pattern at once in time, continuously changing until the supreme moment of death completes it, and also out of time. Since the individual lives and has his being only in fragments, he can never quite know the whole pattern, but in certain moments, he can experience the pattern in miniature. These timeless moments in time—"the moment in the rose-garden,/The moment in the arbour where the rain beat,/The moment in the draughty church at smokefall" (*Burnt Norton*)—provide for Eliot the means of conquering time. This moment of sudden illumination, in and out of time, Eliot associates with the Word-made-flesh, the Incarnation; and also with the word-made-art, poetry. The part-pattern configuration, especially in these three dimensions, is both the main subject and the main principle of form in *Four Quartets*. Both idea and form issue ultimately from Eliot's new "scheme," the Christian religion; and his masterpiece, like Milton's, is a theodicy, a vindication of the ways of God to man. "Love is the unfamiliar Name/Behind the hands that wove/The intolerable shirt of flame/Which human power cannot remove./We only live, only suspire/Consumed by either fire or fire"; "All manner of thing shall be well/When the tongues of flame are in-folded/Into the crowned knot of fire/And the fire and the rose are one" (*Little Gidding*).

The fact that *Four Quartets* is a meditation on time and a celebration of pattern points to a secondary principle of form, albeit the one usually mentioned first by literary critics. From the title and from a lecture called *The Music of Poetry* (1942), delivered early in the year he finished *Little Gidding*, it is clear that Eliot was working with a musical analogy throughout *Four Quartets*, especially in regard to structure: "There are possibilities for verse

which bear some analogy to the development of a theme by different groups of instruments; . . . possibilities of transitions . . . comparable to the different movements of . . . a quartet, . . . possibilities of contrapuntal arrangement of subject-matter." There can be no doubt that Eliot is here describing his own composition of *Four Quartets*. The most conspicuous analogies to music include statement and counterstatement, theme and variation, tempo variation, and mood variation. By using the musical analogy, Eliot was able to avoid monotony, the plague of long and complex philosophical poems. He is returning, furthermore, to his beginnings as a poet and thus demonstrating one of the themes of *Four Quartets:* "We shall not cease from exploration/And the end of all our exploring/Will be to arrive where we started/And know the place for the first time" (*Little Gidding*). In three of his four early masterpieces, "The Love Song of J. Alfred Prufrock," "Preludes," and "Rhapsody on a Windy Night," an analogy with music is established in the title (in the fourth, "Portrait of a Lady," an analogy is established through imagery). The analogy with music is useful in clarifying the nondiscursive nature of *Four Quartets*, but as Eliot warns in *The Music of Poetry* and in essays on the symbolists, it should not be pushed too far.

One other major aspect of form in *Four Quartets* is noteworthy in view of the status of this sequence as both the pinnacle of Eliot's achievement and also a pinnacle of modern art. In *Four Quartets*, Eliot brilliantly solved a problem at the core of most modern art, a problem which could be called the case of the missing abstraction. (See Jewel Spears Brooker, "The Case of the Missing Abstraction," *Massachusetts Review*, Winter 1984.) In a 1924 essay, "Four Elizabethan Dramatists," written a year or so after he completed *The Waste Land*, Eliot explained

T. S. Eliot, 1938; portrait by Wyndham Lewis (courtesy of the Durban Municipal Art Gallery)

that great art always consists of a relationship between actual life, which is its material, and an abstraction, which is its basis of form. And because great art is always a collaboration between an artist and his audience, this abstraction must be common; that is, it must exist (or be capable of existing) not only in his mind, but in his reader's. Yeats solved the case of the missing abstraction by making up an elaborate system and publishing it as a sort of mythic handbook for his readers. Eliot solved it in *The Waste Land* by giving his readers the fragments from which they could construct (or reconstruct) the missing abstraction, the Urmyth; and then by referring them to Frazer and Weston, whose work provides a precise model for do-it-yourself mythmakers.

In *Four Quartets* Eliot solved the case of the missing abstraction by allowing the poem itself to generate the pattern which undergirds it and gives

it meaning. On the simplest level, the abstraction is born of the fact that there are *four* meditations, all different, and yet obviously all of a kind. Just as from many myths, Frazer abstracted one myth; just as from forty-one symphonies, the listener abstracts a Mozartian symphony, heard only in the mind's ear; just as from six tragedies, the theatergoer or reader abstracts a Shakespearean tragedy, performed only in the theater of the mind; so the reader of *Four Quartets* inevitably if unconsciously abstracts an Eliotian quartet. This poem in the mind is private to each reader, but because it is generated by the text all readers share, it agrees to a remarkable extent with the abstractions constructed by other readers. The poem in the mind is at once spatial (it exists all at once in mental space) and temporal (it is always changing): "The knowledge imposes a pattern, and falsifies,/For the pattern is new in every moment/And every moment is a new and shocking/Valuation of all we have been" *(East Coker)*. In order to perceive the pattern, one must temporarily spatialize it. Such spatialization inevitably falsifies, but it is necessary because it is the only way of glimpsing the still point at the center of all movement: "Only by the form, the pattern,/Can words or music reach/The stillness, as a Chinese jar still/Moves perpetually in its stillness" *(Burnt Norton)*.

The Quartet in the mind, the pattern, emerges automatically from the fact that each of the *Four Quartets* explores the same general subject; each is named for a place; and each has approximately the same form. The subject—the intertwined mysteries of part-pattern and of movement-stillness—has many faces and can be viewed from many angles. The meaningfulness of Eliot's treatment is immeasurably enriched by the fact that the form of the sequence is itself a perfect illustration of the twin mysteries.

The title of each meditation refers to a specific place important to the poet. Burnt Norton is the name of a country house in Gloucestershire, which Eliot visited in the summer of 1934 in the company of his American friend Emily Hale, an amateur actress and a professor of drama whom Eliot had known well during the Harvard years (after he had settled in England, he asked Conrad Aiken to dispatch flowers to her on opening night). Pending the availability of Eliot's many letters to this friend of more than half a century (letters sealed at Princeton University until the year 2020), the details of their relationship cannot be known. But it seems likely that on this summer day in the rose garden, Eliot, guilt-torn and exhausted from his disastrous

The church at East Coker (photograph by Jewel Spears Brooker)

marriage and recent separation, experienced a temptation to deny the present by returning to the road not taken in 1914, a temptation exactly analogous to that of Thomas Becket which generated the lines which now open *Burnt Norton.*

The title of the second Quartet, *East Coker,* refers to the village in Somersetshire from which in the seventeenth century Eliot's family had immigrated to America, and to which, after his death, Eliot's own ashes were to be returned. The mystery of man's beginnings and his ends—"In my beginning is my end"—"In my end is my beginning"—in and out of history is explored in this Quartet. The third Quartet takes its title from a small but enormously treacherous group of rocks, the Dry Salvages, located off the coast of Cape Ann, Massachusetts, where Eliot had passed his childhood summers. These rocks, the cold and seemingly limitless ocean in which they are anchored, and the great Mississippi River of his childhood are the major symbols in this meditation.

The last Quartet takes its title from a tiny village in Huntingdonshire, Little Gidding, which in the seventeenth century had been a community of dedicated Christians under the leadership of Nicholas Ferrar. Eliot, who visited Little Gidding in 1936, admired the example of this small group who had renounced position and wealth for a life of work and prayer. Each of these four places is associated with Eliot's part-pattern, stillness-movement theme. He insists on the importance of specific places as he does of specific moments. The timeless moment, in fact, can only occur in a specific place—a rose garden, a drafty church, a rain-washed arbor. The places are only fragments of the pattern; they constitute, nevertheless, the only way to transcendence. "Only through time time is conquered" (*Burnt Norton*); only through place place is conquered.

As all the Quartets explore the same theme, as all point to a specific place, so all have the same general form. The first part of each consists of a meditation on time and consciousness, arranged as statement-counterstatement-recapitulation. The second consists of a highly structured poetical passage followed by a relatively prosaic passage, both on the general subject of being trapped in time. The third explores implications of the first two in terms of a journey metaphor, of some concept of movement of the self in and out of time. The fourth is a brief lyric treating of death and rebirth. The fifth begins with a colloquial passage and then ends with a lyric which secures closure by returning to the beginning and by gathering the major images. This fifth section in each Quartet also incorporates a meditation on the problem of the artist who must still move in stillness, keep time in time (both continuously move in step, and continuously be still).

In "Four Elizabethan Dramatists" Eliot had argued that the greatest artists have achieved consistency not by copying life, but by anchoring their work in an abstraction from life. Eliot's remarkable achievement in *Four Quartets* is that he simultaneously anchored his work and generated the abstraction in which to anchor it. As an individual, he accepted the Christian religion, but as an artist, he accepted the limitations posed by a post-Christian civilization. He therefore eschewed anchoring his art in the Christian myth, or as Yeats had done, in a private myth, choosing the more difficult way of anchoring it in an abstraction rising from its own creation. That he created *Four Quartets* within these limitations places him among the greatest artists to have ever written in English.

Eliot's career as a poet virtually ends with *Four Quartets.* The remainder of his creative energy was put into his comedies and his many public ad-

The Dry Salvages, off the coast of Cape Ann, Massachusetts (photograph by Samuel Eliot Morison)

dresses. His long-standing despair over Western civilization, at the heart of "Gerontion" and *The Waste Land,* still conspicuous in 1939 in his farewell editorial for the *Criterion,* was modified by the onset of World War II. He suddenly realized that there were traditions and principles worth dying for, and he did what he could to help preserve them. In January 1947 the most painful chapter in his personal history came to an end when Vivien Eliot, after years of madness, died in an institution. Ezra Pound, the old friend who had urged him to marry the vivacious English girl, was himself confined in a mental hospital, St. Elizabeths in Washington, D.C., charged with treason for the radio speeches he had made during the war. With other concerned friends of letters, Eliot did what he could to improve the situation of his old benefactor. Against these shadows, Eliot must have experienced some pleasure in his growing reputation as the world's greatest living poet and the century's most-distinguished man of letters.

Beginning in the mid-1940s, he received almost every accolade the West had to offer a poet. The world's oldest and most prestigious universities, including his alma mater, bestowed honorary doctorates. In 1948, he received England's most exclusive and prestigious civilian prize, the Order of Merit, and, in the same year, the Nobel Prize for Literature. In subsequent years, he was awarded the most coveted international prizes in the humanities. The superstar status of this most private and difficult poet is indicated by other awards (for example, he was made an "Honorary Deputy Sheriff " of Dallas County, Texas); by coverage in popular magazines (for example, in March 1950 *Time* did a cover story on him); and by the size of his audiences (for example, nearly 15,000 came to his 1956 lecture in Minneapolis). Eliot accepted all of this attention with characteristic grace and good humor. "He was, above all, a humble man; firm, even stubborn at times, but with no self-importance; quite unspoilt by fame; free from spiritual or intellectual pride"—this quotation from his obituary in the *Times* (London) is substantiated by the testimony of those who knew him as a person rather than as a monument.

The most important event in Eliot's later life was his second marriage. In his sixty-ninth year (1957), he married Esme Valerie Fletcher, his devoted secretary at Faber since 1949, and almost forty years his junior. By all accounts, this happy marriage rejuvenated the poet. His obvious con-

T. S. Eliot receiving the Nobel Prize for Literature, 10 December 1948 (courtesy of Keystone Press Agency)

tentment may seem to contradict all or most of his earlier references to sexual love. In fact, the marital bliss reveals with special clarity a larger pattern in his life and art. That pattern involves a continuous dissatisfaction with brokenness, a continuous quest for wholeness. His early obsession with brokenness and isolation can easily be seen in retrospect as the negative expression of a quest for wholeness and communion. Such a quest is religious in the most radical sense, for "religion" (*re* "again"; ligare "to tie or bind") is literally a reconnecting of pieces into a whole, a rebinding of fragments. Religion begins with an awareness of brokenness, of isolation from something or someone; religious activity by definition is motivated by dissatisfaction with isolation, with partness. Eliot's universality (the quality he admired most in Vergil and Dante) is inseparable from the fact that, both in poetry and in life, he represents a man of great feeling and intelligence

in quest of wholeness. The quest for unity in art was realized in different ways in different periods, with "The Love Song of J. Alfred Prufrock," "Gerontion," *The Waste Land*, *Ash-Wednesday*, and *Four Quartets* representing various solutions. Inseparable from the quest for unity in art is the quest for a system or an abstraction which would allow for philosophical wholeness, a quest which includes encounters with Bradley, Frazer, Saint Paul, and others. Inseparable too is the quest for self-transcendence through human love. For most of his life, he believed that this sort of transcendence was a chimera ("April is the cruellest month"). His second marriage is important because it is the complement in his personal life of the religious unity he found through commitment to the Incarnation, and of the aesthetic unity he achieved in *Four Quartets*. The personal unity, the "new person/Who is you and me together," is celebrated in his last play,

Valerie and T. S. Eliot, 1957 (photograph by Angus McBean)

The Elder Statesman (1959), and in the last poem in his *Collected Poems 1909-1962*, "A Dedication to My Wife." Eliot's last years, though happy, were darkened by illness. He died in London of emphysema and related complications on 4 January 1965. The *Times* (London) obituary was entitled "The Most Influential English Poet of His Time." And the long obituary in *Life* magazine concluded with "Our age beyond any doubt has been, and will continue to be, the Age of Eliot." Such claims inevitably provoke reaction and reevaluation. In Eliot's case, the reevaluation, well under way even before his death, has reaffirmed his stature as a great poet and a central figure in the European tradition.

Letters:

D. D. Paige, *The Letters of Ezra Pound 1907-1941,* includes a letter from Eliot (New York: Harcourt, Brace, 1950), pp. 170-171;

A. Sheekman, ed., *The Groucho Letters; Letters from and to Groucho Marx,* includes six letters from Eliot (New York: Simon & Schuster, 1967), pp. 154-162;

The Autobiography of Bertrand Russell, volume 2, in-

cludes four letters from Eliot (London: Allen & Unwin, 1968), pp. 58, 173, 174;

B. L. Reid, *The Man from New York: John Quinn and His Friends,* includes letters and excerpts from letters from Eliot (New York: Oxford University Press, 1968);

Valerie Eliot, *The Letters of T. S. Eliot,* 4 volumes forthcoming, volume 1 (London: Faber & Faber, forthcoming 1986; San Diego, New York & London: Harcourt Brace Jovanovich, forthcoming 1986).

Interviews:

M. W. Childs, "From a Distinguished Former St. Louisan," *St. Louis Post-Dispatch,* 5 October 1930;

"Inquiry into the Spirit and Language of Night," *transition,* no. 27 (April/May 1938): 236;

Desmond Hawkins, "The Writer as Artist: Discussion between T. S. Eliot and Desmond Hawkins," *Listener,* 24 (28 November 1940): 773-774;

Ranjee Shahani, "T. S. Eliot Answers Questions," *John O'London's Weekly* (London), 19 August 1949, pp. 497-498;

John Lehmann, "T. S. Eliot Talks About Himself and the Drive to Create," *New York Times Book Review,* 29 November 1953, pp. 5, 44;

" 'The Confidential Clerk' Comments by T. S. Eliot," *New York Herald Tribune,* 7 February 1954, IV: 1;

"T. S. Eliot Gives a Unique Photo-Interview ... Stepping Out a Little? I Like the Idea," *Daily Express* (London), 20 September 1957, p. 6;

Donald Hall, "The Art of Poetry, I: T. S. Eliot," *Paris Review,* 21 (Spring/Summer 1959): 47-70; republished in *Writers at Work,* second series (New York: Viking, 1963), pp. 91-110; and in Donald Hall, *Remembering Poets* (New York: Harper & Row, 1977), pp. 203-221;

Tom Greenwell, "Talking Freely: T. S. Eliot and Tom Greenwell," *Yorkshire Post* (Leeds), 29 August 1961;

Donald Carroll, "An Interview with T. S. Eliot," *Quagga,* 2, no. 1 (1962): 31-33;

"T. S. Eliot ... An Interview," *Granite Review,* 24, no. 3 (1962): 16-20;

Leslie Paul, "A Conversation with T. S. Eliot," *Kenyon Review,* 27 (Winter 1964/1965): 11-21.

Bibliographies:

Donald C. Gallup, *T. S. Eliot: A Bibliography,* revised and extended edition (New York: Harcourt, Brace & World, 1969);

Bradley Gunther, *The Merrill Checklist of T. S. Eliot* (Columbus: Merrill, 1970);

Mildred Martin, *A Half-Century of Eliot Criticism: An Annotated Bibliography of Books and Articles in English, 1916-1965* (Lewisburg: Bucknell University Press, 1972);

Richard M. Ludwig, "T. S. Eliot," in *Sixteen Modern American Authors: A Survey of Research and Criticism,* edited by Jackson R. Bryner (Durham: Duke University Press, 1973);

Beatrice Ricks, *T. S. Eliot: A Bibliography of Secondary Works* (Metuchen, N.J.: Scarecrow Press, 1980).

Biographies:

William Turner Levy and Victor Scherle, *Affectionately, T. S. Eliot: The Story of a Friendship, 1947-1965* (Philadelphia & New York: Lippincott, 1968);

Robert Sencourt, *T. S. Eliot: A Memoir,* edited by Donald Adamson (New York: Dodd, Mead, 1971);

T. S. Matthews, *Great Tom: Notes Toward the Definition of T. S. Eliot* (New York: Harper & Row, 1974);

Joseph Chiari, *T. S. Eliot: A Memoir* (London: Enitharmon Press, 1982);

Caroline Behr, *T. S. Eliot: A Chronology of His Life and Works* (London: Macmillan, 1983);

Peter Ackroyd, *T. S. Eliot: A Life* (New York: Simon & Schuster, 1984).

References:

Mowbray Allan, *T. S. Eliot's Impersonal Theory of Poetry* (Lewisburg: Bucknell University Press, 1974);

Keith Alldritt, *Eliot's Four Quartets: Poetry as Chamber Music* (London: Woburn Press, 1978);

Charles Altieri, "Steps of the Mind in T. S. Eliot's Poetry," *Bucknell Review,* 22, no. 2 (1976): 180-207;

William Arrowsmith, "The Poem as Palimpsest: A Dialogue on Eliot's 'Sweeney Erect,' " *Southern Review,* 17 (January 1981): 17-69;

Bernard Bergonzi, *T. S. Eliot* (New York: Macmillan, 1972);

Bergonzi, ed., *T. S. Eliot, Four Quartets: A Casebook* (London: Macmillan, 1969);

Staffan Bergsten, *Time and Eternity: A Study in the Structure and Symbolism of T. S. Eliot's Four Quartets* (Stockholm: Bonniers, 1960);

Harry Blamires, *Word Unheard: A Guide Through Eliot's Four Quartets* (London: Methuen, 1969);

Anne C. Bolgan, *What the Thunder Really Said: A Retrospective Essay on the Making of The Waste Land* (Montreal: Queen's University Press, 1973);

George Bornstein, *Transformations of Romanticism in Yeats, Eliot, and Stevens* (Chicago: University of Chicago Press, 1977);

Neville Braybrooke, ed., *T. S. Eliot: A Symposium for His Seventieth Birthday* (New York: Farrar, Straus & Cudahy, 1958);

Jewel Spears Brooker, "The Case of the Missing Abstraction: Eliot, Frazer, and Modernism," *Massachusetts Review,* 25 (Winter 1984): 539-552;

Brooker, "Common Ground and Collaboration in T. S. Eliot," *Centennial Review,* 25 (Summer 1981): 225-238;

Brooker, "F. H. Bradley's Doctrine of Experience in T. S. Eliot's *The Waste Land* and *Four Quartets,*" *Modern Philology,* 77 (November 1979): 146-157;

Brooker, "The Structure of Eliot's 'Gerontion': An Interpretation Based on Bradley's Doctrine of the Systematic Nature of Truth," *ELH,* 46 (Summer 1979): 314-340;

Brooker, "Substitutes for Christianity in the Poetry of T. S. Eliot," *Southern Review,* 21 (Autumn 1985): 899-913;

Brooker, ed., *Approaches to Teaching the Poetry and Plays of T. S. Eliot* (New York: Modern Language Association, forthcoming 1987);

Cleanth Brooks, *"The Waste Land:* Critique of the Myth," in his *Modern Poetry and the Tradition* (Chapel Hill: University of North Carolina Press, 1939), pp. 136-172;

Ronald Bush, *T. S. Eliot: A Study in Character and Style* (New York: Oxford University Press, 1984);

C. B. Cox and A. P. Hinchcliffe, eds., *The Waste Land: A Casebook* (London: Macmillan, 1968);

Elizabeth Drew, *T. S. Eliot: The Design of His Poetry* (London: Eyre & Spottiswoode, 1950);

Joseph Frank, "Spatial Form in Modern Literature," *The Widening Gyre: Crisis and Mastery in Modern Literature* (Bloomington: Indiana University Press, 1968), pp. 2-63;

Northrop Frye, *T. S. Eliot* (Edinburgh: Oliver & Boyd, 1963);

Helen Gardner, *The Art of T. S. Eliot* (London: Cresset Press, 1949);

Gardner, *The Composition of Four Quartets* (London: Faber & Faber, 1978; New York: Oxford University Press, 1978);

Gardner, *T. S. Eliot and the English Poetic Tradition*

(Nottingham: University of Nottingham Press, 1966);

Lyndall Gordon, *Eliot's Early Years* (Oxford & New York: Oxford University Press, 1977);

Michael Grant, ed., *T. S. Eliot: The Critical Heritage*, 2 volumes (London: Routledge & Kegan Paul, 1982);

Piers Gray, *T. S. Eliot's Intellectual and Poetic Development, 1909-1922* (Atlantic Highlands, N.J.: Humanities Press, 1982);

Donald Hall, "Notes on T. S. Eliot," in *Remembering Poets* (New York: Harper & Row, 1977), pp. 77-110;

Nancy Duvall Hargrove, *Landscape as Symbol in the Poetry of T. S. Eliot* (Jackson: University Press of Mississippi, 1978);

William Harmon, "T. S. Eliot: Anthropologist and Primitive," *American Anthropologist*, 78 (1976): 797-811;

Herbert Howarth, *Notes on Some Figures Behind T. S. Eliot* (Boston: Houghton Mifflin, 1964; London: Chatto & Windus, 1975);

Genesis Jones, *Approach to the Purpose: A Study of the Poetry of T. S. Eliot* (London: Hodder & Stoughton, 1964);

Hugh Kenner, *The Pound Era* (Berkeley & Los Angeles: University of California Press, 1971);

Kenner, *T. S. Eliot: The Invisible Poet* (New York: McDowell, Obolensky, 1959);

Kenner, ed., *T. S. Eliot: A Collection of Critical Essays* (Englewood Cliffs, N.J.: Prentice-Hall, 1962);

Russell Kirk, *Eliot and His Age: T. S. Eliot's Moral Imagination in the Twentieth Century* (New York: Random House, 1971);

Robert E. Knoll, ed., *Storm Over The Waste Land* (Chicago: Scott, Foresman, 1964);

Jacob Korg, "Modern Art Techniques in *The Waste Land*," *Journal of Aesthetics and Art Criticism*, 18 (June 1960): 453-463;

Harry Levin, *Ezra Pound, T. S. Eliot, and the European Horizon* (Oxford: Oxford University Press, 1975);

A. Walton Litz, ed., *Eliot in His Time: Essays on the Occasion of the Fiftieth Anniversary of The Waste Land* (Princeton: Princeton University Press, 1973);

Edward Lobb, *T. S. Eliot and the Romantic Critical Tradition* (London: Routledge & Kegan Paul, 1981);

Richard March and Thurairajah Tambimuttu, eds., *T. S. Eliot: A Symposium from Conrad Aiken and Others* (London: Editions Poetry, 1948; Chicago: Regnery, 1949);

John D. Margolis, *T. S. Eliot's Intellectual Development*

1922-1939 (Chicago & London: University of Chicago Press, 1972);

Jay Martin, ed., *A Collection of Critical Essays on The Waste Land* (Englewood Cliffs, N.J.: Prentice-Hall, 1968);

Timothy Materer, *Vortex: Pound, Eliot, and Lewis* (Ithaca & London: Cornell University Press, 1979);

F. O. Matthiessen, *The Achievement of T. S. Eliot: An Essay on the Nature of Poetry* (London & New York: Oxford University Press, 1935; revised and enlarged, 1947);

D. E. S. Maxwell, *The Poetry of T. S. Eliot* (London: Routledge & Kegan Paul, 1952);

James E. Miller, Jr., *T. S. Eliot's Personal Waste Land: Exorcism of the Demons* (University Park, Pa. & London: Pennsylvania State University Press, 1977);

A. D. Moody, *Thomas Stearns Eliot: Poet* (Cambridge & New York: Cambridge University Press, 1979);

Moody, ed., *The Waste Land in Different Voices* (New York: St. Martin's Press, 1974);

James Olney, "Four Quartets," in his *Metaphors of Self: The Meaning of Autobiography* (Princeton: Princeton University Press, 1972), pp. 260-316;

Olney, ed., *Southern Review: An Anniversary Issue: T. S. Eliot*, 21 (Autumn 1985);

Gertrude Patterson, *T. S. Eliot: Poems in the Making* (Manchester: University of Manchester Press, 1971; New York: Barnes & Noble, 1971);

Jeffrey M. Perl and Andrew P. Tuck, "Foreign Metaphysics: The Significance of T. S. Eliot's Philosophical Notebooks," *Southern Review*, 21 (January 1985): 79-88;

Raymond Preston, *Four Quartets Rehearsed* (London: Sheed & Ward, 1946);

Balachandra Rajan, *The Overwhelming Question: A Study of the Poetry of T. S. Eliot* (Toronto: University of Toronto Press, 1976);

Rajan, ed., *T. S. Eliot: A Study of His Writing By Several Hands* (London: Dobson, 1947);

M. L. Rosenthal, *Sailing into the Unknown: Yeats, Pound, and Eliot* (New York: Oxford University Press, 1978);

Elisabeth W. Schneider, *T. S. Eliot: The Pattern in the Carpet* (Berkeley: University of California Press, 1975);

Ronald Schuchard, "Eliot and Hulme in 1916: Toward a Revaluation of Eliot's Critical and Spiritual Development," *PMLA*, 88 (October 1973): 1083-1094;

Schuchard, " 'First-Rate Blasphemy': Baudelaire

and the Revised Critical Idiom of T. S. Eliot's Moral Criticism," *ELH*, 42 (Summer 1975): 276-295;

Schuchard, "'Our mad poetics to confute': The Personal Voice in T. S. Eliot's Early Poetry and Criticism," *Orbis Litterarum*, 31 (1976): 208-223;

Kristian Smidt, *Poetry and Belief in the Work of T. S. Eliot* (Oslo: J. Dybwad, 1949; revised: London & New York: Humanities Press, 1961);

Smidt, *The Importance of Recognition: Six Chapters on T. S. Eliot* (Tromso: Peter Norbye, 1973);

Grover Smith, *T. S. Eliot's Poetry and Plays: A Study in Sources and Meanings*, enlarged edition (Chicago: University of Chicago Press, 1974);

Smith, *The Waste Land* (London: Allen & Unwin, 1983);

B. C. Southam, *The Student's Guide to the Selected Poems of T. S. Eliot* (New York: Harcourt, Brace & World, 1968);

William V. Spanos, "Hermeneutics and Memory: Destroying T. S. Eliot's *Four Quartets*," *Genre*, 11 (Winter 1978): 523-573;

Spanos, "Repetition in *The Waste Land:* A Phenomenological De-struction," *Boundary 2*, 7 (Spring 1979): 225-285;

Stephen Spender, *T. S. Eliot* (New York: Viking, 1975);

Sheila Sullivan, ed., *Critics on T. S. Eliot* (London: Allen & Unwin, 1973);

Allen Tate, ed., *T. S. Eliot: The Man and His Work* (New York: Delacorte, 1966; London: Chatto & Windus, 1967);

Marianne Thomrahlen, *The Waste Land: A Fragmentary Wholeness* (Lund: C. W. K. Gleerup, 1978);

Derek Traversi, *T. S. Eliot: The Longer Poems* (London: Bodley Head, 1976);

Leonard Ungar, *T. S. Eliot: Movements and Patterns* (Minneapolis: University of Minnesota Press, 1966);

Linda Wagner, ed., *T. S. Eliot: A Collection of Criticism* (New York: McGraw-Hill, 1974);

Helen Williams, *T. S. Eliot: The Waste Land* (London: Edward Arnold, 1968);

George Williamson, *A Reader's Guide to T. S. Eliot* (New York: Noonday Press, 1966).

Papers:
The most valuable collections of Eliot's papers are located in the Eliot Collection of Houghton Library at Harvard University; the Berg Collection of the New York Public Library; the Hayward Collection of King's College Library at Cambridge University; and the Princeton University Library. Many of these papers are restricted, and one major collection (the Emily Hale papers at Princeton) is sealed until the year 2020. Smaller collections are located in numerous universities around the world.

John Gould Fletcher

(3 January 1886-10 May 1950)

Meredith Yearsley

See also the Fletcher entry in *DLB 4, American Writers in Paris, 1920-1939.*

BOOKS: *The Book of Nature* (London: Constable, 1913);

The Dominant City (1911-1912) (London: Goschen, 1913);

Fire and Wine (London: Richards, 1913);

Fool's Gold (London: Goschen, 1913);

Visions of the Evening (London: Macdonald, 1913);

Irradiations, Sand and Spray (Boston & New York: Houghton Mifflin, 1915; London: Constable, 1915);

Goblins and Pagodas (Boston & New York: Houghton Mifflin, 1916);

Japanese Prints (Boston: Four Seas, 1918);

The Tree of Life (London: Chatto & Windus, 1918; New York: Macmillan, 1919);

Some Contemporary American Poets, Chapbook, 2, no. 11 (1920);

Breakers and Granite (New York: Macmillan, 1921);

Paul Gauguin: His Life and Art (New York: Brown, 1921);

Preludes and Symphonies (Boston: Houghton Mifflin, 1922)—includes *Irradiations, Sand and Spray* and *Goblins and Pagodas;*

Parables (London: Kegan Paul, Trench, Trubner, 1925);

Branches of Adam (London: Faber & Gwyer, 1926);

John Smith—Also Pocahontas (New York: Brentano's, 1928);

The Black Rock (London: Faber & Gwyer, 1928; New York: Macmillan, 1928);

The Crisis of the Film (Seattle: University of Washington Book Store, 1929);

The Two Frontiers: A Study in Historical Psychology (New York: Coward-McCann, 1930); republished as *Europe's Two Frontiers: A Study of the Historical Forces at work in Russia and America*

as they will Increasingly Affect European Civilization (London: Eyre & Spottiswoode, 1930);

XXIV Elegies (Sante Fe: Writers' Editions, 1935);

Life Is My Song: The Autobiography of John Gould Fletcher (New York & Toronto: Farrar & Rinehart, 1937);

Selected Poems (New York & Toronto: Farrar & Rinehart, 1938);

South Star (New York: Macmillan, 1941);

The Burning Mountain (New York: Dutton, 1946);

Arkansas (Chapel Hill: University of North Carolina Press, 1947; London: Oxford University Press, 1947).

OTHER: "Trees" and "Lunch," in *Some Imagist Poets: An Anthology,* edited by Amy Lowell (Boston: Houghton Mifflin, 1915), pp. 53, 55;

"Arizona," "The Unquiet Street," "In the Theatre," "Ships in the Harbour," "The Empty House," and "The Skaters," in *Some Imagist Poets: An Anthology,* edited by Lowell (Boston: Houghton Mifflin, 1916), pp. 35, 42-45, 48;

"Lincoln" and "Black-berry Harvest," in *Some Imagist Poets: An Anthology,* edited by Lowell (Boston: Houghton Mifflin, 1917), pp. 39, 44;

Edgar Allan Poe, edited by Fletcher (New York: Simon & Schuster, 1926);

John Smith, *The True Travels, Adventures, and Observations of Captaine John Smith . . . ,* introduction by Fletcher (New York: Rimington & Hooper, 1930);

"Education, Past and Present," in *I'll Take My Stand: The South and the Agrarian Tradition, by Twelve Southerners* (New York: Harper, 1930), pp. 92-121.

TRANSLATIONS: Elie Faure, *The Dance Over Fire and Water* (New York & London: Harper, 1926);

Jean Jacques Rousseau, *Reveries of a Solitary* (New York: Brentano's, 1927);

Yvan Goll, *Jean Sans Terre/Landless John,* translated by Fletcher, Lionel Abel, William Carlos Williams, and Clark Mills (San Francisco: Grabhorn Press, 1944).

John Gould Fletcher was associated with two major groups of poets: Amy Lowell's imagists and the Southern renaissance group The Fugitives. He was, however, a rugged individualist, who believed that as a modern writer he must be open to every kind of experiment. His innovations with poetic form, based on painting, music, and French symbolism, along with the innovations of his associates under the banner of imagism, were an important force in the breakdown of the rigid conventions that they felt had dominated verse composition for at least two hundred years.

Like Ezra Pound and T. S. Eliot, Fletcher fled as a young man from the barren materialism of America to the cultural oasis of Europe. Later he became friends with Pound, and it was Fletcher's library and his practice of French symbolist ideas that introduced Pound to modern French poetry. Fletcher and Lowell, too, borrowed extensively from each other; as Lowell's right-hand man, Fletcher made key decisions in the publication of her three imagist anthologies (*Some Imagist Poets*, 1915, 1916, 1917). And Conrad Aiken found in Fletcher both a friend and a literary stimulus.

On 3 January 1886, John Gould Fletcher was born in Little Rock, Arkansas, the only son of John Gould Fletcher (a banker, cotton broker, and Confederate veteran, of Scotch-Irish descent) and Adolphine Krause Fletcher (a musically and artistically inclined woman of German-Danish descent, with a passion for literature). John Fletcher senior was fifty-five and his wife was twenty-four years younger. There were two other children, both girls: Adolphine and Mary.

In 1889 the family moved into the Albert Pike Mansion in Little Rock—a large square white house with a pillared front, built by an Arkansas settler. The house, in which Fletcher lived until preparatory school, made a deep impression on him, which he recorded after a visit in 1915 in a series of twenty-four poems called "The Ghosts of an Old House." "No sun ever seeks/Its six white columns,/ The nine great windows of its face," he wrote. The house faced north and his descriptions emphasize its gloomy eeriness. The poems do not suggest a happy childhood: "I cannot go to this room,/Without feeling something big and angry/Waiting for me/To throw me on the bed,/And press its thumbs in my throat," he says of the room where his father died; the nursery brings memories of "A boy crying"; and the back stairs remind him of his mother who would "sit all day and listlessly/Look on the world that had destroyed her." Images of death, decay, anger, and sadness predominate.

A lonely, sheltered child, taught by his mother and by private tutors, he was early an avid reader. Always a loner, he went to private school in 1896, and Little Rock High School from 1899 to 1902; he read Longfellow, Scott, and Tennyson, and he read Poe from cover to cover. In 1903, after a year at Phillips Academy, he entered Harvard, where he read French, German, Latin, and English lit-

erature, including Théophile Gautier, Charles Baudelaire, the Pre-Raphaelites (especially Dante Gabriel Rossetti and William Morris), Walter Pater, Oscar Wilde, and James Thomson (1834-1882), and he began writing poetry. But he remained a misfit who did not understand the northern atmosphere, and who often skipped classes to pursue his own reading instead of what had been assigned. He spent most of his time outside of classes in the Harvard library or on the occasional trip to the symphony or the Boston Museum of Fine Arts. Van Wyck Brooks describes him as "the most forlorn and hopeless individual at Harvard," "an old man's son" who "seemed to have been born old himself, stiff-jointed, with big angular bones and stooping shoulders." Lyman Willet Rogers seems to have been the only close friend at Harvard with whom Fletcher could discuss his enthusiasms for poetry and Christianity. In 1907 he quit, just before final exams, and in 1908, when he inherited an income (his father had died in 1906), he sailed for Italy. His mother did not approve of his literary career: like his father, she insisted that Fletcher go into banking or the law. In a letter to Amy Lowell in 1917, Fletcher confided that he believed his moodiness and mistrust of people were caused by his parents' opposition. His mother's lack of encouragement, when he desperately needed it, he said, made him insecure about his vocation. Mrs. Fletcher died in 1910.

During his first year in Europe (he arrived in Italy the same year as Pound), Fletcher stayed in Venice and Rome, soaking up culture and history, reading John Keats, Percy Bysshe Shelley, and Robert Browning, and almost converting to Roman Catholicism. Then in 1909, like Pound, Fletcher moved to London, where he lived in Adelphi Terrace. He met T. E. Hulme and A. R. Orage (who ran the *New Age*), read Walt Whitman, whom Orage had praised, discovered William Blake, and, through a poem by Emile Verhaeren in the *Little Review*, he discovered the French symbolists.

He went to every art exhibition and concert of any importance, developing an interest in painting and music that would profoundly influence his own poetry and lead him to become a regular publisher of art criticism. By 1912 he had collected a large number of poems about his travels and experiences, but these were consistently rejected by publishers and literary magazines.

Eventually, in May 1913, he financed their publication himself; five volumes were published at the same time from four publishing houses. Edna Stephens describes them as follows: "*Fire and*

Wine, about poetry and imaginary loves; *Fool's Gold,* concerning his personal experiences and disillusionments; *The Book of Nature,* in imitation of the Georgians; *The Dominant City,* showing the influence of Charles Baudelaire and Emile Verhaeren; and *Visions of the Evening,* the latest work, showing the influence of French symbolism."

During the war, Fletcher pulped all unsold copies of these "wild oats" volumes. But although the poems were often juvenile, derivative, and clumsy, they were innovative in their use of French symbolist techniques. "Mr. Fletcher's 'music' is more comparable to that made by a truck-load of iron rails crossing a cobbled pavement than to a wailful sound of violins," Pound says of them, remarking that "He has such distinction as belongs to a man . . . who prefers his own [faults] to those of anyone else." He noted that Fletcher was one of the few men in touch with current French poetry. Fletcher was, he said, a poet who "has an art that dares to go to the dust-bin for its subjects," and who "shows . . . a determination to fight out his own rhythms."

Fletcher had already met Pound in May or June 1913 in Paris, where he had traveled to see impressionist art. Feeling he had failed as a poet, he thought he might take up painting instead. But already he was at work on "Irradiations," a new series of poems in which he departed from the bounds of meter and rhyme, and instead improvised freely with splashes of color and sound. This sudden modernization of his style and subject matter was Fletcher's response to the Postimpressionist exhibition of Gauguin, Cézanne, Matisse, Picasso, and van Gogh, and the performances of Nijinsky and the Russian Ballet. Music and painting were breaking conventional bonds, so why not poetry? He wrote the first three "Irradiations" in London and the rest in Paris during May 1913.

Also during the spring and summer of 1913 he began making friends in literary circles: Horace Holley, Skipwith Cannell, Ford Madox Hueffer (who later changed his name to Ford Madox Ford), William Butler Yeats, H. D. (Hilda Doolittle), Richard Aldington, and F. S. Flint were among those he met. Pound persuaded Fletcher to give financial support to Harriet Weaver's *Egoist,* and back in London in July Pound introduced him to Amy Lowell. But when Fletcher showed Pound "Irradiations" he was shocked at the detailed criticism Pound returned. Ultimately, he was unable to separate the criticism of his work from criticism of himself, even though Pound clearly admired "Ir-

radiations" and sent them along to Harriet Monroe, who published them in *Poetry.*

Fletcher also became irritated with Pound when, after perusing several of Fletcher's volumes of French poetry and hearing Fletcher discuss his use of French techniques in "Irradiations," Pound decided to write an article on the French poets for *New Age,* thus taking credit that Fletcher thought should be his. The result of their differences was that he refused to let Pound include his work in Pound's anthology *Des Imagistes* (1914). Forming a lasting distrust of Pound, Fletcher turned away from what could have been a valuable friendship, and began with Amy Lowell the most significant literary relationship of his career. Whereas Pound preferred the pared-down, highly visual, intense lyric, Lowell was less exacting in her demands of poetry. She was also a less talented and more sentimental writer. But with her Fletcher could talk as an equal; with Pound he would always be treated as a disciple. Similarities in their wealthy backgrounds and careers also drew them together. Both had served long, isolated apprenticeships, using conventional forms and, as recent converts to experimental free verse, were eager for stimulation and encouragement from fellow artists.

Within a week of their first meeting Fletcher had read her his "Irradiations." She liked them so much that she immediately offered to help him get them published just as they were, without the changes suggested by Pound. She quickly became an ardent believer in Fletcher's poetics, consistently applying them in her own writing after that time.

Meanwhile, Fletcher had become involved with an older, married woman, Florence Emily (Daisy) Arbuthnot—an affair which between the fall of 1913 and the fall of 1914 changed him from eager buoyant youth to resigned middle age. They met when her husband invited Fletcher down to their summer beach house. Here he began his "Sea Symphony" and during the fall, when the two frequently met at the beach house, he began a series of love poems that eventually formed book one of *The Tree of Life* (1918).

Early in 1914 Fletcher agreed to support Daisy and in April moved in with her and her two children in her suburban house in Sydenham. Here Fletcher worked on more love poems and his series of color symphonies. But he kept his domestic life carefully separate from the literary contacts he maintained in London. For a time he had a renewed friendship with Pound, whom he openly admired and emulated, and who sent off his "Blue Symphony" to *Poetry* with high praise.

Meanwhile, Amy Lowell was taking over the imagist movement—which Pound thereafter called "Amy-gism"—and planning her series of imagist anthologies. "Fletcher became an Imagist under Miss Lowell," Edmund de Chasca remarks, "because they shared similar attitudes toward poetry and sympathized with each other's work. . . . Fletcher felt important in her presence, not diminished and on his guard as with Pound. Nor did he believe that the new arrangement would restrict the kind of poetry he could write. . . . As her ally . . . he could write as he pleased without too much dogmatic carping about abstractions and rhetoric. Imagism with Miss Lowell, he felt, would be liberating, not confining. Moreover, Amy Lowell had just taken his 'Irradiations' manuscript in order to find a publisher for it in Boston."

After World War I broke out Fletcher sailed in November 1914 for America, where, for the next year and a half he helped Amy Lowell produce the three editions of *Some Imagist Poets.* Houghton Mifflin published the 1915 volume and Fletcher's *Irradiations, Sand and Spray* on the same day in 1915, which led reviewers to see Fletcher's book as an imagist collection, when in fact his poetry depends more for its effect on onomatopoeia and a muted mood created by abstract phrases than on the hard impact of concrete images: innovative though it was, it is closer to symbolist or decadent verse than to imagism.

As soon as Fletcher got back to America in 1914, he began writing poems about his homeland, experimenting with a prose-poem form he had borrowed from Amy Lowell. "Out of the black granite she is rising surprising as sunrise over the head of the Sphinx," begins the piece "New York." He called it "Polyphonic Prose," which Lowell defined as "polyphonic because it makes use of all the voices of poetry: . . . metre, *vers libre,* assonance, alliteration, rhyme and return." His best piece in this genre is "Clipper Ships," written in March 1915.

From December 1914 to February 1915 Fletcher visited his old home at Little Rock and wrote "The Ghosts of an Old House" and several poems about the South. On his way back to Boston, he stopped at Chicago, where he saw an exhibition of Japanese prints at the Art Institute. This along with his recent rediscovery of the Oriental wing at the Boston Museum of Fine Arts prompted him to write a series of epigrammatic pieces in which he experimented with haiku- and tanka-like forms. Published in 1918 under the title *Japanese Prints,* they were not very successful, suffering in spite of their brevity from Fletcher's habitual wordiness,

abstract diction, and, sometimes, downright banality.

However, this exposure to the Orient brought about a major shift in Fletcher's philosophy. He saw the importance of man's connection to nature and of an intuitive Eastern perception of the world. He decided his purpose as an artist should be to criticize America's aggressive materialism by affirming this Eastern vision. One of the most urgent tasks of the twentieth century, he thought, was to remold the world by bringing Eastern and Western philosophies together. Thus Fletcher's concern shifted from the craft of his poetry to its message.

The poems in *Goblins and Pagodas* (published in April 1916), however, were still highly experimental and improvisational in form. The book contained "The Ghosts of an Old House" (the goblins) and "Symphonies" (the pagodas), the latter reflecting Fletcher's reading of such poets as Li-Po, Wang-Wei, Tu-Fu, and Po Ch'u-I. His aim was to "narrate . . . phases of the emotional and intellectual development . . . of an artist" in terms of colors, "the imaginative phantasmagoria of landscape" which they evoke, thereby creating "the dominant mood of each poem."

Contributing regularly to the *Egoist, Dial, Poetry,* and the *Little Review,* Fletcher continued work on the love poems; on a steamboat trip down the Mississippi and travels through Texas and Arizona to the West Coast, he rediscovered the American landscape and wrote such poems as "Down the Mississippi," "Grand Canyon of the Colorado," and "Arizona Poems." In Boston, he visited Amy Lowell at Sevenels at least once or twice a week and became her closest friend in the world of poetry. They discussed plans for her lecture on French poets; they shared poetic techniques; and they praised each other's work in *Poetry* and the *Egoist.* He also became close friends with Conrad Aiken, who lived next door to him on Walnut Street. Aiken disliked the "Amygists" (he had called them "a very loud-mouthed mutual-admiration society") but had singled out Fletcher's work; he adopted Fletcher's symphony concept in *The Charnel Rose* (1918) and *The Jig of Forslin* (1916).

Lowell disliked Aiken, and she objected to Fletcher's friendship with him. Other irritations grew up between Lowell and Fletcher as well. Fletcher did not like her politicking with writers and editors and her aggressive publicity campaigns of lectures and appearances. Increasingly domineering, she was becoming a celebrity who traveled up and down the country, while he sat in Boston, alone and unnoticed. At the same time, he became steadily more indebted to her, both financially and otherwise, for it was she who saw that Houghton Mifflin published *Goblins and Pagodas*. Lowell helped get Fletcher published, but she also tried to control his artistic identity. She objected strongly, for instance, when he published a poem in Alfred Kreymborg's *Others* because it might suggest that *Others* writers were imagists (her territory). In fact, Fletcher had been invited to contribute to what was billed as a special number, edited by William Carlos Williams, containing work by the fifteen best poets in America—a very desirable group, indeed, for him to belong to.

The final blow to Fletcher's friendship with Lowell came after he returned to England in June 1916. That fall Houghton Mifflin turned down "Love's Tragedy," his love poems. And when Fletcher discovered that, while he had been reviewing Lowell's *Men, Women, and Ghosts* (1916) with the highest praise, it was Lowell herself who was responsible for the rejection, he felt utterly betrayed.

Fletcher's morale sank, and the incident marked the beginning of a long, fallow period in his career, which was further aggravated by Houghton Mifflin's rejection in 1917 of three more collections of poems: "Under the Guns," "A Boy's World," and "Elements." They never were published. His domestic circumstances did little to cheer him. On 5 July 1916 he had married Florence Emily Arbuthnot and settled in at Sydenham. But there were differences between them they had overlooked. Although they shared a love of music, Daisy Fletcher found his speculative mind and moody temperament baffling. She was a conventional woman, whose life centered around home and family. Her hobby was raising canaries, some fifty of which she kept in a converted billiard room in the basement. By the winter of 1916-1917 Fletcher knew the marriage was not a success.

Nor did he find much inspiration or support in his literary contacts. The work of Aldington and H. D., he felt, had flagged badly during the war and for the first time he began to see how his own work differed from imagist concepts. "I do not believe that a poem should present an 'image,'" he wrote to Lowell in September 1916, "I believe it should present an emotion. I do not believe in 'clear, hard and definite presentation.' I believe in complete, that is to say, shifting and fluid presentation. . . . I do not believe that the 'exact' word is possible. I do not believe in 'cadence,' but in rhythm." Thus he shunned most of Pound's original tenets of imagism. And he urged her to dis-

continue the imagist anthologies, since the group's interests had become very divergent.

When the last imagist anthology was published in the spring of 1917, it included Fletcher's "Lincoln," in which, he says in his autobiography, "the technique of Imagism was complemented by stanzas expressive of nothing but plain, unabashed, didactic purpose." This reflects his shift to a new aesthetics of simplicity, majesty, and austerity, where the craft of poetry must serve a higher purpose. It marked the beginning of a period in which he attempted to write more about mankind and less about nature.

In 1919 Fletcher made new friends—John Cournos, who shared his rather gloomy outlook, Edward O'Brien, Robert Graves, and Van Wyck Brooks. He was contributing regularly to the *Freeman* but was apparently writing very little new verse, apart from the collection of poems based on his travels in America. The poems published in 1918 (*Japanese Prints* and *The Tree of Life*) were all written before 1916. He would publish no new verse until 1925.

The Tree of Life (which he called in draft "Love's Tragedy") records the joys, sorrows, and frustrations of his romance with Daisy, many of the scenes and images suggesting the beach and summer house where they met. The poems also record their separation during Fletcher's trip to America and his isolation and depression in Boston during the breakdown of his friendship with Amy Lowell. The book was not well received, which caused him much pain, as he had poured his soul into its pages. Like most of his work it is marred by his inability to select the genuinely effective from awkward inversions and vague, overly adjectival diction. In spite of its subject matter it is cold and detached, another persistent problem in Fletcher's work.

In July 1920 he wrote "The Great River," reaffirming the dream of freedom he saw in the quest of La Salle and de Soto, and contrasting the noble purpose of the Mississippi, as "it flows/. . . . For ever in its splendid onward march," with the factories which were built "till the air is grimed with dust." Like Edwin Arlington Robinson, Fletcher saw nothing but decay and destruction ahead for a United States devoted to materialism. He heard the river saying to him, "Endure, and in your constant daily striving,/Carve out somewhere the stuff of new-made kingdoms,/Though no man heeds them, though hopes turn to dust." This was Fletcher's raison d'être and the purpose that informed the collection of American poems *Breakers and Granite* (1921). Fletcher warns of the gluttonous, machine-ridden hordes and the ugly factories; he reaffirms the values suggested by an unravaged landscape and by the harmonies of plantation life. It has been described as a Whitmanesque salute to America.

The publication in 1920 of *Some Contemporary American Poets*, a book of criticism, was followed the next year by the appearance of *Paul Gauguin*, the first biography of the painter in English. Fletcher was attracted to Gauguin as a fellow exile from and rebel against industrial civilization. The biography reveals much of Fletcher's own personality, as well as his revolt against the machine age and his consequent search for meaning in Christianity, Buddhism, and mysticism. He could well identify with an artist who struggled for years without encouragement.

Although 1922 saw Houghton Mifflin's republication, with Amy Lowell's encouragement, of *Irradiations* and *Goblins and Pagodas* under the title *Preludes and Symphonies*, and although the avant-garde magazine *Broom* published some of his work, the most significant event in terms of Fletcher's later career was when, challenged by a listener at his Oxford lecture on American poetry, he heard about the Fugitives. Finding their agrarianism and distrust of the city congenial, he soon began contributing to their magazine, the *Fugitive*, himself.

Over the next four to five years Fletcher traveled back and forth to Paris and other parts of the Continent and made many new literary friends, including T. S. Eliot, I. A. Richards, and C. K. Ogden (the editor at Kegan Paul who published *Parables*). And he regularly contributed to the *Criterion*. Fletcher admired Eliot's use of musical structures and, like Eliot, came to affirm man's search for God; this he expressed in a religious phase that included *Parables* (1925), *Branches of Adam* (1926), *The Black Rock* (1928), and *XXIV Elegies* (1935).

In 1923 when Edward O'Brien left Oxford to form a new "Franciscan" order of "holy fools," Fletcher responded by writing *Parables*—a collection of verse, prose poems, and prose parables. Man's search for God and salvation is overtly the theme of this book and of *Branches of Adam*, both of which he wrote to counter Joyce's *Ulysses* (1922), which he saw presenting man as motivated by lust and greed. *Branches of Adam*, published only in England and hence little known in the United States, is a long Blakean poem whose object, says Fletcher's preface, is to show "that good in fact depends upon evil and evil on good" in retelling the stories of Creation, The Fall, Cain and Abel, and The Flood. Ben Kimpel suggests that it fails because in seeking consciously to create a myth Fletcher created only

a symbol inadequate for the abstract message; yet, he says, "for a poem which had to make its own technique unlike anything other poets at the time were interested in making, *Branches of Adam* is an amazing achievement." The title poem of *The Black Rock* is dedicated to Thomas Hardy, whom Fletcher admired for his stoic resignation and agnosticism—the wave-battled black rock. *XXIV Elegies* concludes Fletcher's religious phase, expressing the poet's grief over man's spiritual loss in the mechanized world. Though some critics thought highly of the elegies, R. P. Blackmur identified their weakness: "At his best he does not put much meaning into his words . . . ; hence it takes a great many words piling up, clattering, singing, to collect a semblance of the meaning that was in him."

Meanwhile, in the spring of 1927, Fletcher made a lecture tour of the South; his theme was that the future of American poetry would be epic rather than analytical. He expected to be challenged by the Fugitives, but instead he met both Donald Davidson and John Crowe Ransom on friendly terms and looked up Allen Tate when he got to New York. In 1929 Tate invited Fletcher to contribute to *I'll Take My Stand* (1930), which became the Fugitive/Agrarian manifesto. In 1931 he took Tate's place at a conference on regionalism at the University of Virginia and argued for an anti-industrialist, antimechanical culture based on the rural life found in the South. His poetry, however, never resembled that of the Fugitives.

Throughout this period Fletcher's interest in French culture had not abated. In 1926 and 1927, respectively, his translations of Elie Faure and Jean Jacques Rousseau appeared and in 1930 he contributed an article on French painting to *This Quarter*. He was highly regarded by such French contemporaries as Paul Fort and Jean Catel.

Glenn Hughes describes Fletcher in 1931 as "an energetic, genial man of many friends and many interests" who knows London "from one end to the other, and is a marvellous guide to its wonders. He is fairly tall, [with] a high forehead, a long face, and dreamy grey eyes. His voice is pleasant and low-toned. . . . He talks easily on any subject, and when he talks he does nothing else. If he is dining with you, he forgets to eat, particularly if the conversation is on poetry or painting. His pockets are always bulging with books."

One would not guess from this description that a year later, in 1932, Fletcher would suffer a nervous breakdown and spend five months in a hospital. The following year he returned to America to settle in Little Rock for good, his London life and his first marriage completely ended. The University of Arkansas gave him an honorary doctorate and he began devoting himself to bringing the best music, art, and literature to the state. "Fletcher was almost the first strong intellectual to which Arkansas had been exposed," notes Kimpel, "and the state owes him a considerable debt." In 1935 he organized the Arkansas Folk Lore Society, and in 1936 he was commissioned to write for the state centenary "The Story of Arkansas," an epic poem which appeared in the *Arkansas Gazette*'s State Centennial Supplement on 15 June 1936. Earlier that same year his divorce from Daisy Fletcher was finalized, and on 18 January he had married Charlie May Hogue Simon, an author of children's books.

Fletcher's last two books of poetry, *South Star* (1941) and *The Burning Mountain* (1946), represent his regional phase. *South Star*, the title suggesting Fletcher's belief that the South could lead the country, includes "The Story of Arkansas" and a collection of lyrics under the headings "Echoes of Arkansas," "Upper South," and "Deep South." Fletcher's primitivism, which he had found in Rousseau and Gauguin, is reflected in his Ozark Farmer—a figure of simple, proud endurance. In his descriptive poems, Fletcher is at his best; landscape, clouds, and weather had always inspired him. The sense of craft sharpened during his imagist days served him well in parts of "The Story of Arkansas," but his regionalism led to some of his worst work. His attempt at a simple style, Kimpel notes, "often fell into flat oratorical prose broken up into functionless lines and tagged with stale rimes." Kimpel calls *Arkansas* (1947), the prose version of "The Story of Arkansas," "a masterpiece" of its type, far more successful than the centenary poem.

Fletcher's last book of poems, *The Burning Mountain*, reflects both his identification with the South and his recurrent theme that modern culture is trapped by materialism, neglecting nature, the spiritual, and the unconscious. "In both his occasional hope and his frequent despair," Harvey Webster said, reviewing the book for *Poetry* (March 1947), "Fletcher is in accord with the insights of such poets as Auden, Eliot, and Yeats. Unfortunately, . . . [he] does not phrase his intelligent convictions as vividly as these poets did." The problem in this book, as in others, Webster noted, is that "Fletcher's best and most concentrated writing is often lost in the wide reaches of a diffuse whole." The best fragments, such as the following lines from "August 1940," are surrounded by didactic cliché-ridden verbiage:

Scatter the talking leaf, be swift and harry
The air with dying words. The word that will not die
Is silenced now. Let lies as rain fall down
From Heaven, as manna dew. Truth is yet quiet.
Truth need not speak; let her be still as stone.

And there is no doubt about the excellence of the opening of "Symphony of Snow."

By the time *The Burning Mountain* appeared, Fletcher's wanderings had come to rest in a period of peace and harmony which Charlie May Simon describes in her book *Johnswood* (1953), named after the house Fletcher built on a ridge outside Little Rock. Donald Davidson calls the house, its site, its furnishings, its rugs, its fine library of modern works, "beautiful."

In 1935 Fletcher wrote *Life is My Song* (1937), his autobiography, at the McDowell Colony in Peterborough, New Hampshire. Norreys Jephson O'Connor calls it a valuable "picture of the poetic renaissance and of the temper of literary life in London and in the United States, before, during and after World War I." The following year, 1938, saw the publication of his *Selected Poems*, which includes most of *The Black Rock*. It won him the 1939 Pulitzer prize, but he remained, though established, an uncelebrated poet.

In 1941 Fletcher told Kunitz and Haycraft that, "Apart from poetry my chief interests are painting and music. Someday I would like to show the parallel lines of development on which painting and poetry travel." He said he was writing a novel and that he expected to live another 20 years, having "long since lost the feeling that I will die young." But on 10 May 1950 the mental illness that he had struggled with earlier caused him to drown himself in a pool near his home. In *Johnswood* Charlie May Fletcher described his suicide as the result of the rage and despair felt by a sensitive man confronted with the machine age and its wars. At the time of his death Fletcher was working on an anthology of Southern poetry and was planning a historical project with his wife.

Noting that Fletcher was "unflinching in his individualism," Donald Davidson has called him "an extraordinary, almost unique example of the isolated artist." Fletcher forged his own symbolist poetry from what he later called the triple influence of Mallarmé, Gauguin, and Debussy; then he turned to a new theme: man's search for God. In doing so, he said, in *Life is My Song*, he was "committing myself to an anachronism, greater even than the anachronism I had committed myself to by becoming primarily a poet." But Fletcher's individualism made him unreceptive to criticism that would have tightened his writing, helped him to discriminate. Pound had objected to obviousness in his poetry; "Pound would still be right," Kerker Quinn says, reviewing *South Star* for *Poetry* (September 1941); "obviousness remains central in the inadequacy of Fletcher's expression." In 1919 Conrad Aiken commented that "Mr. Fletcher is his own implacable enemy" and thought it unlikely that Fletcher's poetry would receive the eminence it deserves, for "readers who would like Mr. Fletcher at his best cannot muster the patience to read beyond his worst." Fletcher's chief problem, Aiken saw, was his inability to see how the language-play that he had developed had become habitual "verbal reflexes" and had ceased to be conscious art. Although the poetry was like the symbolism of Mallarmé, he said, in Fletcher's work the symbols had no meaning: it is "a poetry of detached waver and brilliance . . . as if the language were fertilized by itself rather than by thought or feeling."

Sixteen years later R. P. Blackmur made a similar comment: "His poems . . . do not modify and compose, do not share and discover and brim over with an inner light; they make a light-shot procession, almost a mob, that cannot be added up." Yet, as Blackmur says, "we have again and again to recognize, strikingly deployed, the elements of poetry presided over by a genuinely poetic figure. . . . there is always the possibility, the suggestion, the fragment—if never the achieved composition." Fletcher's *Selected Poems* (1938) did little to gather such fragments together, and a new collection of his best work would gain him the readership he deserves.

References:

Conrad Aiken, *Skepticisms: Notes on Contemporary Poetry* (New York: Knopf, 1919);

R. P. Blackmur, "Versions of Fletcher," review of *XXIV Elegies, Poetry*, 47 (March 1936): 344-347;

Van Wyck Brooks, *Scenes and Portraits* (New York: Dutton, 1954), pp. 227-229;

Stanley K. Coffman, *Imagism: A Chapter for the History of Modern Poetry* (Norman: University of Oklahoma Press, 1951);

Richard Crowder, "John Gould Fletcher as Cassandra," *South Atlantic Quarterly*, 52 (January 1953): 88-92;

S. Foster Damon, *Amy Lowell: A Chronicle* (Boston: Houghton Mifflin, 1935);

Donald Davidson, "In Memory of John Gould Fletcher," *Poetry*, 77 (December 1950): 154-161;

Edmund S. de Chasca, *John Gould Fletcher and Imagism* (Columbia: University of Missouri Press, 1978);

Alice Corbin Henderson, "Two Books by John Gould Fletcher," review of *Japanese Prints* and *The Tree of Life, Poetry*, 13 (March 1919): 340-341;

Glenn Hughes, *Imagism and the Imagists: A Study in Modern Poetry* (Palo Alto: Stanford University Press, 1931);

Ben Kimpel, "John Gould Fletcher in Retrospect," *Poetry*, 84 (August 1954): 284-296;

Amy Lowell, *Tendencies in Modern American Poetry* (New York: Macmillan, 1917), pp. 235-343;

Harriet Monroe, "Comment: John Gould Fletcher," *Poetry*, 27 (January 1926), 206-210;

Noreys Jephson O'Connor, "Impressions of John Gould Fletcher," *Southwest Review*, 38 (Summer 1953): 238-243;

David Perkins, *A History of Modern Poetry from the 1890s to the High Modernist Mode* (Cambridge: Harvard University Press, 1976), pp. 341-343;

Ezra Pound, "In Metre," *New Freewoman*, 1 (15 September 1913): 131-132;

Kerker Quinn, "Story of an Arkansas Poet," review of *South Star, Poetry*, 58 (September 1941): 334-336;

Charlie May Simon, *Johnswood* (New York: Dutton, 1953);

Edna B. Stephens, *John Gould Fletcher* (New York: Twayne, 1967);

Hyatt H. Waggoner, *American Poets from the Puritans to the Present* (New York: Dell, 1970), pp. 341-343;

Harvey Curtis Webster, "Music vs. Eloquence," review of *The Burning Mountain, Poetry*, 69 (March 1947): 353-356.

Papers:

Fletcher's papers are housed in the University of Arkansas Library, Fayetteville; his correspondence with Harriet Monroe is in the *Poetry* collection at the University of Chicago Library; and his correspondence with Amy Lowell is at the Houghton Library, Harvard University.

DuBose Heyward

(31 August 1885-16 June 1940)

Harlan Greene
South Carolina Historical Society

See also the Heyward entries in *DLB 7, Twentieth-Century American Dramatists,* and *DLB 9, American Novelists, 1910-1945.*

BOOKS: *Carolina Chansons: Legends of the Low Country,* by Heyward and Hervey Allen (New York: Macmillan, 1922);

Skylines and Horizons (New York: Macmillan, 1924);

Porgy (New York: Doran, 1925; London: Hodder & Stoughton, 1926);

Angel (New York: Doran, 1926);

Porgy: A Play in Four Acts, by Heyward and Dorothy Heyward (Garden City: Doubleday, Doran, 1928);

Mamba's Daughters: A Novel of Charleston (Garden City: Doubleday, Doran, 1929; London: Heinemann, 1929);

The Half Pint Flask (New York: Farrar & Rinehart, 1929);

Brass Ankle (New York: Farrar & Rinehart, 1931);

Jasbo Brown and Selected Poems (New York: Farrar & Rinehart, 1931);

Peter Ashley (New York: Farrar & Rinehart, 1932; London: Dickson, 1934);

Porgy and Bess, libretto by Heyward, lyrics by Heyward and Ira Gershwin, music by George Gershwin (New York: Gershwin Publishing Corporation, 1935);

Lost Morning (New York & Toronto: Farrar & Rinehart, 1936; London: Dickson, 1936);

Fort Sumter, by Heyward and Herbert Ravenel Sass (New York & Toronto: Farrar & Rinehart, 1938);

The Country Bunny and the Little Gold Shoes: As Told to Jenifer (Boston & New York: Houghton Mifflin, 1939);

Mamba's Daughters: A Play, by Heyward and Dorothy Heyward (New York & Toronto: Farrar & Rinehart, 1939);

Star Spangled Virgin (New York & Toronto: Farrar & Rinehart, 1939).

SCREENPLAY: *Emperor Jones,* adapted by Hey-

DuBose Heyward (photograph by the Marion Studio, courtesy of the South Carolina Historical Society)

ward from Eugene O'Neill's play, United Artists, 1933.

OTHER: *Year Book of the Poetry Society of South Carolina,* foreword by Heyward and Hervey Allen (Charleston: Poetry Society of South Carolina, 1921);

Year Book of the Poetry Society of South Carolina, foreword by Heyward and Allen (Charleston: Poetry Society of South Carolina, 1922);

Year Book of the Poetry Society of South Carolina, foreword by Heyward (Charleston: Poetry Society of South Carolina, 1923);

"Beatrice Ravenel," in *Library of Southern Literature*, supplement no. 1, edited by Edwin A. Alderman and Charles A. Smith (Atlanta: Martin & Hoyt, 1923), pp. 473-475;

Year Book of the Poetry Society of South Carolina, foreword by Heyward (Charleston: Poetry Society of South Carolina, 1924);

Samuel Gaillard Stoney and Gertrude Mathews Shelby, *Black Genesis: A Chronicle*, foreword by Heyward (New York: Macmillan, 1930);

"The Negro in the Lowcountry," in *The Carolina Low-Country*, edited by Augustine T. Smythe and others (New York: Macmillan, 1932);

E. T. H. Shaffer, *Carolina Gardens*, foreword by Heyward (New York: Huntington Press, 1937).

PERIODICAL PUBLICATIONS: "Poetry South," by Heyward and Hervey Allen, *Poetry*, 20 (April 1922): 35-48;

"And Once Again—the Negro," *Reviewer*, 4 (October 1923): 39-42;

"The New Note in Southern Literature," *Bookman*, 61 (April 1925): 153-156;

"The MacDowell Colony," *Southwest Review*, 11 (January 1926): 162-168;

"Contemporary Southern Poetry," *Bookman*, 62 (January 1926): 561-564; 63 (March 1926): 273-312;

"A New Theory of Historical Fiction," *Publishers Weekly*, 122 (13 August 1932): 511;

"Porgy and Bess Return on Wings of Song," *Stage*, 13 (October 1935): 25-28;

"Dock Street Theatre," *Magazine of Art*, 31 (January 1938): 10-15;

"Charleston: Where Mellow Past and Present Meet," *National Geographic*, 75 (March 1939): 273-312;

"The American Virgins," by Heyward and Daisy Reck, *National Geographic*, 78 (September 1940): 273-308.

It was in the late 1910s and early 1920s that DuBose Heyward seriously began to pursue writing poetry and having it published. By the time of his death in 1940, however, he had given it up for novels and playwriting. Today, despite the fact that his poems have all been forgotten (a fate not entirely merited), his novels are mostly unread, and his plays remain unstaged, he has gained worldwide renown for his role in the writing of the opera *Porgy and Bess*.

Born in Charleston, South Carolina, on 31 August 1885, the poet was christened Edwin

DuBose Heyward, although DuBose, an inheritance from his Huguenot ancestor Isaac DuBose, was the sole name by which he was known. His parents were Jane Screven DuBose Heyward and Edwin Watkins (Ned) Heyward, great-grandson of Thomas Heyward, signer of the Declaration of Independence. Had he been born earlier, Heyward would have been born into wealth as had his grandparents; but their families fell from plenty to near penury in the catastrophe of the Civil War and its aftermath.

The poet's early life was marked with tragedy. On his first birthday, Charleston was rocked by a devastating earthquake from which his father barely escaped with his life. The reprieve, however, was only temporary. On 21 May 1888 Ned Heyward was killed in an accident in the rice mill where he worked. The young man left behind a son not quite three, a widow in her early twenties, and a daughter, Jeannie DuBose Heyward, who had just celebrated her first birthday. So it was in a house of women (including his maternal grandmother) that Heyward grew up; he took his position as the only male and the chivalric tradition of his city very seriously. Even as a child, he worked part-time, turning over his earnings to his mother, who supported the family by taking in boarders, accepting sewing, and writing poetical advertisements for a local printing company. Heyward himself turned early and facilely to poetry, but his poems were a child's efforts, displaying none of his later maturity. His mother, with a slender poetic gift of her own, would render many episodes from Heyward's youth in her verse; her first volume, *Wild Roses*, was published in 1905 by the Neale Company.

Although bright, Heyward was absentminded and did poorly at his studies. There apparently were no objections on his mother's part (she had been catered to by her husband) when he dropped out of school at fourteen to work full-time in a hardware store to support his family. A few years later, he was stricken with infantile paralysis that went undiagnosed until a wealthy kinswoman paid for his visit to a Philadelphia hospital. His right arm was affected, and although he was fortunate enough to be left-handed, he would never have full use of that limb again. It was characteristic of Heyward's modesty that he would rarely ever mention that illness to anyone. In 1906 he developed pleurisy and went to recuperate in Arizona. When the disease recurred in 1917, he went to what would become his habitual summer retreat, the mountains of North Carolina, where he briefly took up painting. But he concentrated most seriously on supporting his dependent family.

For a while around 1905-1906 he had been a cotton checker on the wharves, where he came into contact with the characters and life-styles he would later work into his fiction, plays, and poetry. By 1910, however, he had become half-partner in an insurance company and had taken his expected place in Charleston society. He wrote and acted in amateur theatricals and the local press praised his efforts extravagantly.

In the summer of 1914, when nearing thirty, Heyward visited Europe with an older friend of the family, but their visit was cut short by the invasion of France and the outbreak of World War I, which was also to change Heyward's native city. The activity at its naval base, the enlistment of native sons, the immigration of blacks to higher paying jobs in the North, and the "discovery" of Charleston by tourists who could no longer visit Europe all had radical effects. Charleston belatedly entered the twentieth century; and it was at this point, in this collision of two cultures and two centuries, that Heyward began writing. One of his main themes would be celebration of the city that "time had forgotten before it destroyed," as he was to write in his novel *Porgy* (1925).

He first turned to poetry, however; and it seems doubtful that he would have ever become a professional writer at all if not for the presence in Charleston of two outsiders. One was the older John Bennett, who had resided in Charleston since 1902; and the other was the younger Hervey Allen, a wounded war veteran who found a job teaching in Charleston a year or two after the Armistice. From Bennett, an author of children's books, an artist, and an often-anthologized poet, Heyward was to receive much-needed criticism and the advice to write about that which he knew—the Carolina lowcountry. From Allen, soon to be published in the Yale Series of Younger Poets (and eventually to make publishing history with his phenomenally successful novel *Anthony Adverse,* 1933) Heyward was to learn the enthusiasm and dedication of a young professional. It was in a meeting of the three that Heyward first proposed to found a state poetry society and in 1920 he became its first secretary. As the society's representative, Heyward took to the lecture circuit to promote his and other Southern poetry.

In 1922 he published his first book, a collaboration with Hervey Allen called *Carolina Chansons: Legends of the Low Country.* Working along preconceived plans, Allen wrote mood poems and verses

of the picturesque. Heyward, who contributed only eight of the approximately thirty poems, wrote mostly of dramatic episodes from local history.

In 1924 Heyward published his first solo effort, *Skylines and Horizons,* poems of the South Carolina lowcountry, the North Carolina mountains, and a few others of a more general nature and theme. Critics felt that Heyward had just found his voice; and a cautious but enthusiastic Allen Tate said that "Mr. Heyward may justly rank as the most important autochthonous poet in the South at the present time." Others, more glibly, called Heyward the best poet of the South and one of the better in the country. Having reached this point, however, instead of solidifying his position, Heyward virtually gave up poetry for prose. It was not until 1931 (by that time he was a new father, his play *Brass Ankle* had just failed on Broadway, and he was in dire need of money) that he brought out a final volume of poetry. *Jasbo Brown and Selected Poems* contained just four new poems, and it functioned both as a selection of his best works as well as his farewell to poetry.

Heyward was neither a deep nor an original thinker; yet in the few prefaces and essays he wrote on the subject, he in effect formulated his poetic theory. He rejected most of the experiments in form and content prevalent in the 1920s and instead chose simple words to portray his grand, although uncomplicated subjects, including the beauty, quaintness, grandeur, and tragedy of the Southern landscape and inhabitants as he knew them. Poetry, he said, was not to be introspective, subjective, or obscure; it was to provide the common man an access to beauty. As Frank Durham, William Slavick, and Morris Coxe have noted, all his poems fall into one of four categories.

As a group, his mountain poems are the strongest and most deserving of remembrance. Among the earliest he wrote, they were the most anthologized in his lifetime. Typically, they depict in dramatic vignettes the life and spirit of the Carolina mountain people. "The Mountain Woman," perhaps his best, tells the tale, in four stanzas of six lines each, of an unnamed woman: "At first youth left her face, and later, hope." She loses all her battles with life, yet remains stoic, until one afternoon her drunken husband finds her tending "with reverent touch" a scarlet flower that he snatches from her and crushes in the dust. At the end of the poem, where she is crying "away the afternoon," Heyward extracts the best of melodrama and avoids the weaknesses of mere sentimentality.

Also notable is "A Yoke of Steers," which contains such vivid lines as "Uncouth and primal, on and up they sway,/Taking the summit in a drench of day," and "They will arrive in their appointed hour/Unhurried by the goad of lesser wills,/Bearing vast burdens on." Less effective is the ending: *"They are the great/Unconquerable spirit of the hills."*

Of nearly equal interest and merit are Heyward's four poems on the Negro, including "Porgy," which first served as an epigraph to his novel, "Modern Philosopher" or "Philosopher" ("whose future is today!"), "Gamesters All," and "Jasbo Brown." "Gamesters All," a narrative of more than one hundred lines, won the *Contemporary Verse* Prize for 1921 and was included in *Carolina Chansons*. It relates the story of a black gambler named Joe, caught shooting craps. The white policeman who captures him is also something of an odds man; he gives Joe a fighting chance of escape but eventually guns him down rather ruthlessly, as if Joe's life had no other value than a game of chance, a thematic statement that many tried to interpret as Heyward's stand on the "Negro Question"; but Heyward, like the narrator in the poem, was an observer only and would not burden his lines with a political statement. The poem is successful in parts; the black rhythms and spiritual cadences definitely foreshadow *Porgy and Bess;* but the flat narrative voice that relates the story deadens its total effectiveness. "Jasbo Brown," another narrative of approximately 175 lines, is discursive and does little else than allow the title character, who would eventually give his name to jazz music, to state his fate: his life is his music and very little else. It was a very popular work in its day, however, being twice broadcast nationally on the radio to the musical accompaniment of George Gershwin's *Rhapsody in Blue.* The character Jasbo would later reappear, to be cut from and finally restored, in the opening of the opera *Porgy and Bess.*

Heyward's poems on the Carolina lowcountry vary widely in theme and quality. The short poems are often colorful and even moving. "The Equinox" compares a hurricane to a muscled, sweating prizefighter demolishing the city; "Buzzard Island" likens a local rookery to a place of lost hopes, stillborn dreams, and bitter memories; "Dusk" is a stately song of praise and gratitude to his city. Less successful are his long narratives celebrating episodes in Charleston's history, such as "The Last Crew," Heyward's longest poem (approximately 250 lines), memorializing Civil War battles in the harbor, and "The Pirates," a loose and episodic description of the expedition against Stede Bonnet. There is

something too self-concious in both poems—and too self-congratulatory in the proud and quaint nature of Charleston's history. The main nemesis that plagued Heyward's poetry was his too-frequent lapse into mere celebration of local color rather than using it to illuminate a broader or more universal theme, as Robert Frost and Carl Sandburg were doing.

Heyward's more general poems are effective, if not original, expressions of emotions such as love, resignation, and devotion. All are competently written and include a few good lines with those characteristic touches of grace and dignity that the public grew to expect from Heyward. His total poetic output was not great—only fifty or so published poems; and except for one or two which stand with no apology, they are more interesting in retrospect, poetry having been for Heyward an apprenticeship for his other writing.

In 1924 Heyward gave up poetry for prose, and he also gave up his insurance company to devote all his time to his writing. The first result was his best-known novel, *Porgy* (1925), the tale of a crippled beggar and Bess, the woman he came to love and to lose in one summer of passion and violence. A year later, in 1926, came *Angel*, a tale of the North Carolina mountains that incorporates some of the themes and situations of his mountain poetry. In 1929 he published *Mamba's Daughters*, an ambitious, complex, and very nearly successful novel about blacks and whites in Charleston from the turn of the century to the 1920s. *Peter Ashley* (1932), Heyward's tribute to Civil War Charleston, was followed by *Lost Morning* (1936), a study of an artist who had given up integrity for commercial success. A year before his death he finished a humorous novel about the New Deal era in the Virgin Islands, *Star Spangled Virgin* (1939). During these years he also produced a classic ghost story, a children's book, and several articles and essays.

On 22 September 1923 DuBose Heyward married the playwright Dorothy Hartzell Kuhns (1890-1961), whom he had met at the MacDowell Colony in Peterboro, New Hampshire. They had one daughter, Jenifer DuBose Heyward (1930-1984). At Dorothy Heyward's insistence, and with her skills as a playwright to guide them, the husband and wife team turned two of Heyward's novels into Broadway successes, *Porgy* in 1927 and *Mamba's Daughters* in 1939. (*Brass Ankle*, the only play that Heyward wrote on his own, was a melodrama of mixed blood and was not successful.) It was the play *Porgy*, itself based on Heyward's novel, that was to become the basis for the opera *Porgy*

Working draft for "Dusk" (by permission of the DuBose and Dorothy Heyward Memorial Fund; courtesy of the South Carolina Historical Society)

*DuBose Heyward (courtesy of the South Carolina
Historical Society)*

not a commercial success; as an investor in it, Heyward lost money. He died of a heart attack in the North Carolina mountains in 1940 and was buried in Charleston in St. Philip's Episcopal Church cemetery, so he did not live to witness its eventual success. It was the longest-running American opera presented at La Scala, and in the 1950s it toured the world in a cultural exchange financed by the State Department. It was later produced in Russia. In 1985, in its fiftieth year, the opera was finally produced in New York's Metropolitan Opera House, thus being assured of a place in the august company of the other great operas of the centuries.

Perhaps there is some justice in Heyward's immortality being assured by an opera; for although he had given up poetry, most of the best elements in his poems—their color, their depiction of blacks, their drama, and their lowcountry settings—are all present in the work that seems destined to take Heyward's name down to posterity.

References:
Hervey Allen, *DuBose Heyward, a Critical and Biographical Sketch, Including Contemporary Estimates of His Work* (New York: Doran, 1927);

Emily Clark, "DuBose Heyward," *Virginia Quarterly Review*, 6 (October 1930): 546-556; reprinted in her *Innocents Abroad* (New York: Knopf, 1931), pp. 235-250;

Frank Durham, *DuBose Heyward: The Man Who Wrote Porgy* (Columbia: University of South Carolina Press, 1954);

Durham, "DuBose Heyward's 'Lost' Stories," *Short Fiction Studies*, 2 (Winter 1965): 157-163;

Durham, *DuBose Heyward's Use of Folklore in His Negro Fiction*, The Citadel Monograph Series, no. 2 (Charleston, S.C.: The Citadel, 1961);

Durham, "The Rise of DuBose Heyward and the Rise and Fall of the Poetry Society of South Carolina," *Mississippi Quarterly*, 19 (Spring 1966): 66-78;

Harlan Greene, ed., "Charleston Childhood: The First Years of DuBose Heyward," *South Carolina Historical Magazine*, 83 (April 1982): 154-167;

Anthony Harrigan, "DuBose Heyward: Memorialist and Realist," *Georgia Review*, 5 (Fall 1951): 335-344;

Josephine Pinckney, "Charleston's Poetry Society," *Sewanee Review*, 38 (January 1930): 50-56;

William H. Slavick, *DuBose Heyward* (Boston: Twayne, 1981);

and Bess, written by Heyward, George Gershwin, and Ira Gershwin. It is unfortunate that, over the years, Heyward's contribution to the opera has been misunderstood and overlooked. Beginning no doubt with Heyward's habitual modesty, the lack of attention to Heyward's role in composing the opera continued unabated after his death, his name falling lower and lower in (and sometimes disappearing from) the credits. The name Heyward could not compete with the glamour of Gershwin.

Responsible for the libretto, lyrics for many of the best arias and much of the recitative, often lifted verbatim from the play or novel, Heyward was active in every stage of the collaboration. With only one or two exceptions the lyrics were written first, either by Heyward himself or by Ira Gershwin who often took his starting point from Heyward's text; then they were set to music. While Heyward contributed in some fashion to many of the arias, some, such as "Summertime," "A Woman is a Sometime Thing," and "I Got Plenty o' Nuttin'," as well as other verses set to music, are nearly all his work. The opera premiered in 1935 but was

Slavick, "Going to School to DuBose Heyward," *Studies in the Literary Imagination*, 7 (Fall 1974): 105-129.

Papers:
Most of DuBose Heyward's papers are part of the collections of the South Carolina Historical Society, Charleston.

Robinson Jeffers

Robert Ian Scott
University of Saskatchewan

BIRTH: Pittsburgh, Pennsylvania, 10 January 1887, to Annie Robinson Tuttle and William Hamilton Jeffers.

EDUCATION: University of Western Pennsylvania (now University of Pittsburgh), 1902-1903; B.A., Occidental College, 1905; University of Southern California, 1905-1906, 1907-1910; University of Zurich, 1906-1907; University of Washington, 1910-1911.

MARRIAGE: 15 August 1913 to Una Call Kuster; children: Maeve, Donnan Call, and Garth Sherwood.

AWARDS AND HONORS: D.H.L., Occidental College, 1937; D.H.L., University of Southern California, 1939; Levinson Prize (*Poetry* magazine), 1940; Chancellor, American Academy of Poets (1945-1956); Eunice Tietjens Memorial Prize (*Poetry* magazine), 1951; Union League Civic and Arts Foundation Prize (*Poetry* magazine), 1952; Borestone Mountain Poetry Award, 1955; Academy of American Poets Fellowship, 1958; Shelley Memorial Award (Poetry Society of America), 1961.

DEATH: Carmel, California, 20 January 1962.

SELECTED BOOKS: *Flagons and Apples* (Los Angeles: Grafton, 1912);
Californians (New York: Macmillan, 1916);
Tamar and Other Poems (New York: Peter G. Boyle, 1924);
Roan Stallion, Tamar, and Other Poems (New York: Boni & Liveright, 1925; London: Leonard & Virginia Woolf at the Hogarth Press, 1928; enlarged edition, New York: Modern Library, 1935);

The Women at Point Sur (New York: Boni & Liveright, 1927); enlarged as *The Women at Point Sur and Other Poems* (New York: Liveright, 1977);
Poems (San Francisco: Book Club of California, 1928);
An Artist (Austin: Privately printed by John S. Mayfield, 1928);
Cawdor and Other Poems (New York: Liveright, 1929; London: Leonard & Virginia Woolf at the Hogarth Press, 1929);
Dear Judas and Other Poems (New York: Liveright, 1929; London: Hogarth Press, 1930);
Stars (Pasadena: Flame Press, 1930);
Descent to the Dead (New York: Random House, 1931);
Thurso's Landing and Other Poems (New York: Liveright, 1932);
Give Your Heart to the Hawks and Other Poems (New York: Random House, 1933);
Return, An Unpublished Poem (San Francisco: Gelber, Lilienthal, 1934);
Solstice and Other Poems (New York: Random House, 1935);
The Beaks of Eagles (San Francisco: Printed for Albert M. Bender, 1936);
Such Counsels You Gave to Me & Other Poems (New York: Random House, 1937);
The Selected Poetry of Robinson Jeffers (New York: Random House, 1938);
Two Consolations (San Mateo: Quercus Press, 1940);
Be Angry at the Sun (New York: Random House, 1941);
Medea: Freely Adapted From the Medea of Euripides (New York: Random House, 1946);
The Double Axe & Other Poems (New York: Random House, 1948; enlarged edition, New York: Liveright, 1977);

photograph by Horace Lyon

Robinson Jeffers.

Poetry, Gongorism and A Thousand Years (Los Angeles: Ward Ritchie Press, 1949);

Hungerfield and Other Poems (New York: Random House, 1954);

The Loving Shepherdess (New York: Random House, 1956);

Themes in My Poems (San Francisco: Book Club of California, 1956);

The Beginning & the End and Other Poems (New York: Random House, 1963);

Selected Poems by Robinson Jeffers (New York: Random House, 1963);

Cawdor: A Long Poem, Medea, after Euripides (New York: New Directions, 1970);

The Alpine Christ & Other Poems, edited by William Everson (Monterey: Cayucos Books, 1973);

Tragedy Has Obligations (Santa Cruz: Lime Kiln Press, 1973);

Brides of the South Wind: Poems 1917-1922, edited by Everson (Monterey: Cayucos Books, 1974);

What Odd Expedients and Other Poems, edited by Rob-

ert Ian Scott (Hamden, Conn.: Shoe String Press, 1981).

PLAY PRODUCTIONS: *Medea*, New York, National Theatre, 20 October 1947;

The Tower Beyond Tragedy, New York, ANTA Playhouse, 26 November 1950.

OTHER: "Mirrors" [short story], *Smart Set*, 40 (August 1913): 117-118.

Because he thought "poets lie too much," Robinson Jeffers said in his foreword to *The Selected Poetry* (1938) he decided "not to pretend to believe in . . . irreversible progress; not to say anything because it was popular . . . unless I myself believed it; and not to believe easily." Such skepticism antagonizes some, but Jeffers's descriptions of human misery and unimportance in a divinely beautiful universe have won a remarkably large audience. His 1938 volume, *The Selected Poetry of Robinson Jef-*

William, Annie, and Robinson Jeffers in Pittsburgh, 1893

fers, had eleven printings, and the 1935, Modern Library edition of *Roan Stallion, Tamar, and Other Poems* had seventeen (some 40,000 copies); his *Medea* (1946), with Judith Anderson in the title role, became a success on Broadway in 1947 and then an international success.

John Robinson Jeffers's education began early, before he was three and a half, with tutoring by his mother and then by his father, the Professor of Biblical and Ecclesiastical History and the History of Doctrine at the Western Theological Seminary, a Presbyterian institution in Pittsburgh. Jeffers then attended private schools in Pittsburgh, Germany, and Switzerland; by age twelve he had read widely in English, French, German, Latin, and Greek. In 1902, when he was fifteen, he entered the University of Western Pennsylvania (now the University of Pittsburgh), but transferred to Occidental College in 1903 when his father's health prompted a move to Los Angeles. At Occidental, Jeffers studied astronomy, geology, ethics, history, economics, rhetoric, biblical literature, and Greek, among other subjects, and edited the college's literary magazine. In 1905-1906, he took graduate

courses in literature at the University of Southern California, and fell in love with a student in one of his classes, Una Call Kuster, then twenty and already married; Jeffers was eighteen. After spending the 1906-1907 academic year at the University of Zurich, where he studied literature, history, and philosophy, Jeffers studied medicine for three years at the University of Southern California (including a semester when he taught physiology) not to become a doctor but to continue preparing himself as a poet.

Jeffers went to the University of Washington in Seattle in 1910, thinking that this time separation might end the affair with Una Kuster, and that as a forester he could both save trees and have time to write. But in 1912, he inherited $9,500 and had no sooner gone home to Los Angeles than he met Una Kuster again. She got an amicable divorce, which the Los Angeles newspapers considered a scandal and gave such misleading headlines as "Parents Wash Hands of It." Jeffers married Una in August of 1913; their first child, Maeve, was born 5 May 1914 and died the next day. They had planned to live in Europe, but the outbreak of

*Robinson and Una Jeffers, shortly after their marriage
in August 1913*

make for the rest of his life. In June 1904 Jeffers
first received payment for a poem, twelve dollars
for "The Condor," by winning a contest sponsored
by the *Youth's Companion*. It was the first of Jeffers's
many poems admiring condors, vultures, eagles,
hawks, pelicans, and gulls, all capable fliers (in
1899, when twelve years old, Jeffers had tried to
fly with homemade wings).

When he inherited money in 1912, Jeffers
paid a Los Angeles printer to publish his first book,
Flagons and Apples, which no one reviewed; its
thirty-three embarrassingly naive and stilted love
poems later made Jeffers wish that he had destroyed the whole edition. His marriage and his
move to the Sur coast ended such foolishness; there
for the first time he saw "people living—amid magnificent unspoiled scenery—essentially as they did
in Homer's Ithaca," he said, and he made those
people and that coast his subject for the rest of his
life, setting most of his long narratives in actual
places there (see the map at the end of Robert
Brophy's *Robinson Jeffers, Myth, Ritual and Symbol in
His Narrative Poems* or the earlier, less complete
map at the end of Lawrence Clark Powell's *Robinson
Jeffers, The Man and His Work*).

Jeffers first began describing that coast and
its people in his second book, *Californians,* published by Macmillan in 1916. In the introduction
to his 1974 edition, William Everson argues that
Jeffers could not feel free to express his view of
the universe as God and of humanity as tragically
foolish until his father died in December 1914. The
violence, insanity, and sex in Jeffers's narratives
might have shocked his father—they have certainly
shocked some reviewers—but Jeffers did not begin
to write these narratives until his mother had died,
in 1921, and after he had discovered the universality of human suffering and conceived of the universe as the God which both creates us and saves
us from such suffering. *Californians* shows little sign
of either discovery; Jeffers's realization of the suffering in World War I apparently came suddenly,
between the summer of 1916 and the spring of
1917, provoking his next and longest poem, the
long-lost "The Alpine Christ." Ten years afterward, Jeffers called it "useless and absurd," naive
in its "use of Christian mythology," and refused to
permit the publication of even a part of it, but with
this poem his later success began. He wrote the
poem before the United States had entered the
war, but after the miseries of trench warfare and
the German invasion of Belgium had become
widely known. Jeffers reacted with horror, pity,
and disgust, a mixture of feelings which helped

World War I and the advice of a friend, poet Frederick Mortimer Clapp, led them instead to Carmel
at the northern end of the Sur coast of California
that September, and there they stayed, apart from
vacations in Ireland and in Taos, New Mexico, and
one lecture tour around America, until Una Jeffers
died in Carmel in 1950, and Jeffers died in 1962.

Jeffers wrote his first poem when he was ten.
A cousin who lost it years later remembered that
it concerned a snake—perhaps the garden snake
which the first letter in *The Selected Letters of Robinson
Jeffers, 1897-1962* (1968) says he killed that year.
At fourteen he read and imitated the poems of
Thomas Campbell and Dante Gabriel Rossetti, and
at sixteen he first had his poems published—two
in the December 1903 issue of *Aurora,* Occidental
College's literary magazine. One of them, the sonnet "The Measure," concludes that compared to
the immensity of the universe, only space, eternity,
and God are "truly great," a point he continued to

provoke what Jeffers later called "the accidental new birth" of his mind. As his wife explained it, "The conflict of motives on the subject of going to war or not was probably one of several factors that, about this time, made the world and his own mind much more real and intense to him. Another was building Tor House [the Jeffers's home]. As he helped the masons shift and place the wind and water-worn granite I think he realized some kinship with it and became aware of strengths in himself unknown before. Thus at the age of thirty-one there came to him a kind of awakening such as adolescents and religious converts are said to experience." Jeffers became thirty-two on 10 January 1919 and helped build his house the following summer.

In the winter of 1971-1972, William Everson found 147 of the 227 typed pages of "The Alpine Christ" in the collection of Jeffers's papers at the Humanities Research Center of the University of Texas at Austin; Jeffers had used the blank sides of those pages for later poems. That find reveals what seems to be Jeffers's first written response to

Tor House and Hawk Tower

the universality of human suffering. Unlike his later poems, "The Alpine Christ" (which Everson included in *The Alpine Christ & Other Poems*, 1973) accepts Christianity as literally true. The poem begins with a conference in heaven in which Satan congratulates God for having had World War I make life on earth worse than Hell. God cannot disagree, so Christ returns to earth to save mankind from itself again, only to vanish at the end, having accomplished nothing as the war continues. Jeffers seems to have written the poem because the suffering distressed him, turned to Christianity for some help or explanation, but found in writing the poem that Christianity could not help or explain away the misery for him. The poem remains naive and much too long, but it was a fortunate failure because from it Jeffers learned to become an original poet. In just four years, the deaths of his first child, of his father, and then of millions in World War I had led him from imitating Rossetti (while writing about himself in *Flagons and Apples*) to imitating Wordsworth (while writing about ranch families and hermits in *Californians*) to imitating "Prometheus Unbound" and *Paradise Lost* (while writing about whole countries suffering in "The Alpine Christ"). He apparently took the next step —to writing tragedies that consider the human species and the universe as a whole— because, unlike Shelley, Jeffers could not believe any revolution would end human suffering and because, unlike Milton, Jeffers did not think Christianity could justify it. As a result, Jeffers found an unchristian way in which mankind might suffer less by learning more.

Jeffers's concern with suffering began his conversion in 1916-1917, but it remained distractingly incomplete until he helped build his home in the summer of 1919. Then, as he came to admire its granite and the rest of the universe for their unhuman beauty and permanence, he gained a peaceful self-surrender and increased awareness. By so expanding his awareness beyond himself and humanity, he had made his troubles seem vanishingly small, and had found the detached yet compassionate awareness which makes the poems he wrote from that summer on unlike anyone else's. He went on to write more than three hundred poems, almost all of them praising what he repeatedly called "the enormous beauty of the universe." As he explained to a reader years later, "When you are excited by something that seems beautiful or significant, you want to show it to others." He had discovered for himself the basic point of Buddhism—that selfishness blinds us, causing misery which we can and should avoid—and that he could transcend that selfishness by looking beyond himself to suffering humanity, as he did in his tragedies, and to the universe.

Jeffers said that he rejected Buddhism as well as Christianity, apparently because the misleading descriptions of Buddhism then available in the European languages made Jeffers think of Buddhism as self-centered. In "Theory of Truth," the poem with which Jeffers chose to end *The Selected Poetry of Robinson Jeffers*, he describes Buddha as "willing to annihilate Nature . . . to annul the suffering" of mankind, as if Buddha thought that he could make the universe not exist, a delusion which Jeffers understandably rejected. In "Credo," with which Jeffers ended the Modern Library edition of *Roan Stallion, Tamar, and Other Poems,* he made that contrast clearer still. His "friend from Asia . . . believes that nothing is real except as we make it," but Jeffers believed (as he also said in *Themes in My Poems,* 1956) exactly the opposite: the world makes us, and its "heartbreaking beauty will remain when there is no heart to break for it." Jeffers's misunderstanding of Buddhism was apparently caused by Western mistranslations of the Buddhist term *nirvana,* the state of mind which Buddhists want to achieve. Despite such translations, nirvana does not mean oblivion or any annihilation of the universe; it means a detached yet compassionate awareness of much more than the self, much like the cosmic perspective which Jeffers's poems advocate and display.

William Everson also recovered parts of Jeffers's next book, *Brides of the South Wind* (1974), which several New York publishers had rejected in 1921-1922. Not even Jeffers seems to have kept a copy of it, perhaps because he used much of it in later books. Apparently it contained Jeffers's earliest tragic narratives, in which unbridled selfishness brings misery to families on the Sur coast, thus demonstrating how not to behave, or so some of the fragments and Jeffers's later tragedies suggest. In both his tragedies and his short poems, Jeffers suggested that seeing the world's enormous beauty and our own unimportance should console us, and keep us from the mistakes which cause so much misery. Radcliffe Squires has claimed that Jeffers's view echoes that of Arthur Schopenhauer's *The World as Will and Idea* (1819), which expresses precisely that Western misunderstanding of Buddhism which Jeffers explicitly rejects in "Credo" and "Theory of Truth," among other poems, and in his comment in *Themes in My Poems.* Arthur Coffin and others have seen Jeffers as following Friedrich Nietzsche's philosophy, though apparently only the

comment in *Thus Spake Zarathustra* (1883-1892)—that poets lie too much—had much effect on Jeffers. His awareness of the cycles of life, including the decline and extinction of whole cultures and species, ours included, came not from Nietzsche, but from his knowledge of archaeology, history, and evolution. Jeffers seems to have been most influenced by scientific discoveries from Copernicus on, by Greek tragedy, by the bitingly realistic early Greek lyric poet Archilochus, and by the philosophies of Lucretius and Baruch Spinoza. Like Lucretius, Spinoza, and many scientists, Jeffers described the universe as one interconnecting, infinite, and eternal system which we can and need to understand. He believed, as Stuart Hampshire has said Spinoza did, that "If we would improve human beings, we must study the natural laws of their behavior as dispassionately as we would study the behavior of trees and horses. . . ." Hampshire adds that in the seventeenth century only Spinoza "seems somehow to have anticipated modern conceptions of the scale of the universe, and of man's relatively infinitesimal place within the vast system . . ." while other philosophers and literary people, except perhaps Pascal, "still implicitly thought in terms of a man-centered universe. . . ." Hampshire concludes that "To Spinoza it seemed that men can attain happiness and dignity only by identifying themselves . . . with the whole order of nature, and by submerging their interests in this understanding. . . . it is this aspect of Spinoza's naturalism, the surviving spirit of Lucretius against a greater background of knowledge, which most shocked and baffled his contemporaries and successors."

Such factually accurate humility still shocks and baffles many. Jeffers expressed this cosmic perspective in vividly sensed metaphors and examples, rather than in the abstractly logical language of Spinoza's philosophy, but the moral remains the same despite the difference in methods. As Bertrand Russell noted when writing about Spinoza during World War II, "it is comforting to reflect that human life, with all that it contains of evil and suffering, is an infinitesimal part of the life of the universe. Such reflections . . . may not constitute a religion, but in a painful world . . . [they] are a help toward sanity and an antidote to the paralysis of utter despair." Such reflections may not constitute a supernatural religion, but like Lucretius and Spinoza, Jeffers made them the basis for a more modestly matter-of-fact religion which notices and tries to do something to alleviate human suffering; because he mentions evil and suffering, however, some critics called Jeffers a sadist. Near the end of his life, in *Hungerfield and Other Poems* (1954), he recapitulated his view in "De Rerum Virtute," a title that emphasized its resemblance to the world view Lucretius had expressed in *De Rerum Natura*. Both Jeffers and Lucretius believed that virtue comes from an accurate knowledge of the world, including an unflattering recognition of human mistakes, their causes and their results, and not from pious ignorance, no matter how good we may think our intentions.

Jeffers saw his poems as expressing not just a scientifically accurate knowledge of the universe (as they do), but also a mystical experience of the universe as God, appreciating its size and beauty and our unimportance—a view he felt humanity in general needs. As he said in *Themes in My Poems*, his poems "also express a protest against human narcissism. . . . If a person spends all his emotions on his own body and states of mind, he is mentally diseased. . . . It seems to me . . . that the whole human race spends too much emotion on itself. The happiest and freest man is the scientist investigating nature, or the artist admiring it; the person who is interested in things that are not human. Or, if he is interested in human beings, let him regard them objectively, as a very small part of the great music. Certainly humanity has its claims, on all of us; we can best fulfill them by keeping our emotional sanity; and this by seeing beyond and around the human race" to the universe which Jeffers thought "so beautiful that it must be loved." Jeffers used the clinical term *narcissism* accurately here, perhaps as a result of his medical training; and, according to Christopher Lasch's *The Culture of Narcissism* (1978), this emotional affliction is becoming increasingly common in our culture.

Perhaps because no publisher had accepted *Brides of the South Wind,* the book he wrote before *Tamar,* Jeffers had *Tamar and Other Poems* published at his own expense in April 1924 by the New York City printer Peter G. Boyle; Jeffers had noticed Boyle's advertisement in the *New York Times Book Review.* Six months later, enthusiastic reviews by Babette Deutsch, James Rorty, and Mark Van Doren suddenly made Jeffers famous, leading Boni and Liveright to publish a larger volume, *Roan Stallion, Tamar, and Other Poems,* in 1925. These reviewers hardly mentioned Jeffers's cosmic perspective and his protest against narcissism, but they did admire his ability to tell a story vividly. "Tamar" retells chapter thirteen of the second book of Samuel, setting the title character's story on the California coast by Point Lobos, two miles south of

Jeffers's home, from December 1916 to the following August.

Jeffers's version begins when Tamar's brother drunkenly rides his horse over a cliff; she nurses and then seduces him, becomes pregnant, seduces a neighbor to force a marriage, and then in her disgust with everyone involved, provokes a confrontation which ends when her family's farmhouse burns, killing them all. In his foreword to *The Selected Poetry of Robinson Jeffers,* the poet says the poem grew from the biblical story, from Shelley's "The Cenci," and from the "introverted and storm-twisted beauty of Point Lobos," presumably including the burned-out house which actually stood where the poem ends; the owner reputedly read the poem and said it was "a hell of a thing to write about a fellow's ranch!" The places and local legends of the Sur coast suggested many of Jeffers's poems. The isolation of its people made destructive emotional behavior easy, and the wilderness and weather provided metaphors and a backdrop for those emotions.

The seductions, incest, insanity, and violence of "Tamar" horrified some readers. An anonymous editorial writer for the 9 January 1926 issue of the *San Francisco Monitor* complained that "Jeffers has the power of Aeschylus, the subtlety of Sophocles," and so is "intrinsically terrible," without seeming to notice that terror may have a moral purpose and result. Not until Robert Brophy's *Robinson Jeffers, Myth, Ritual and Symbol in his Narrative Poems* appeared in 1973 did a critic show just how closely Jeffers had followed Aeschylus, Sophocles, and Euripides. Jeffers's long poems repeatedly use the five-part plot structure of Greek tragedies (introduction, complication, crisis, catastrophe, denouement) and their seasonal metaphors; both describe suffering and death as necessary for knowledge and new life. Jeffers divided "Tamar" into seven numbered sections: one and two introduce Tamar's brother's fall and recovery; three through five present the complicating seductions; six describes the crisis and catastrophe in which Tamar symbolically dies to be reborn as a willfully selfish child, who bullies her family until she indirectly causes their death by fire in part seven, the denouement which completes the plot and solves their problems by ending the characters. The poem dates these stages of its plot by the moon and tides, stars and weather, to show its characters' lives as both parts and products of the world's much larger cycles, cycles Jeffers repeatedly called "the great music" we need to hear. Tamar's loves begin in spring and end in a fire in the sterile heat of August, the dead season in California's Mediterranean climate. That end seems both the epitome and the result of reckless passions in a situation so corrupt that perhaps only fire could purify it and so let new lives start. As Gilbert Murray explained in the second chapter of *The Classical Tradition in Poetry* (1927), tragedies celebrate the cycle of the seasons and sacrifice human scapegoats to ensure the continued survival of life in general, and so does "Tamar."

With this poem, Jeffers began a series of experiments with tragedy. Five years after "Tamar" appeared, Joseph Wood Krutch claimed in *The Modern Temper* (1929) that the scientific discoveries which diminish our sense of our own importance make any modern tragedy impossible; but Jeffers's tragedies repeatedly mention these discoveries: his characters' tragic mistakes result from selfishly ignoring the human unimportance these discoveries reveal, and the misery these mistakes cause shows how dangerous ignorance can prove to be.

In 1925 Jeffers's tragedy "Roan Stallion" made that unimportance more explicit, but it became notorious for another reason: some misread it as describing a sexual relationship between a horse and a woman. In fact, it does not; it describes her glimpse of the more than merely human beauty of the universe which the horse exemplifies, as she realizes when she briefly escapes the degrading circumstances of her life. When her husband tries to abuse her again, she runs to the horse for protection; the horse has become her god. It kills the husband, and then, moved by "some obscure human fidelity," she shoots the horse, only to realize too late that she has destroyed what had meant god and power, glory and freedom, to her. As the poem suggests in an often noticed but generally misunderstood reference to releasing energy by splitting atoms, she has had her chance to learn and change by suffering, to grow beyond her depressingly human limitations, but like most of us, she wastes that chance, a point Jeffers went on to make again.

Also in *Roan Stallion, Tamar, and Other Poems,* in "The Tower Beyond Tragedy," Jeffers rewrote a Greek tragedy for the first time, to show how to escape tragedy. Tamar's narcissism kills her and five others; the woman in "Roan Stallion" survives, but without the liberation she might have had. In "The Tower Beyond Tragedy," his version of Aeschylus's *Oresteia,* Jeffers has his Orestes grow beyond the blind emotions which cause such tragedies. He begins with Agamemnon's triumphal return from the Trojan War, a situation Agamemnon's wife Clytemnestra complicates by killing him, causing her son Orestes to kill her, a crisis resolved

by a catastrophe. Orestes then regains his sanity by realizing that his feelings do not matter. He escapes what might otherwise have become an endless and pointless cycle of tragedy after tragedy by learning from tragedy, and giving up the political power he won by killing his mother and her lover. Jeffers's Cassandra foresees not just individuals but whole cultures caught in such cyclic tragedies. If we have such a cosmic perspective, we might avoid the delusions of importance which cause tragedies, or might learn from tragedies not to repeat such mistakes, or so Jeffers kept suggesting, a hope apparently provoked by World War I, and made to seem more desperate by World War II. Jeffers had not intended "The Tower Beyond Tragedy" for the stage, but it appeared with some success on Broadway in 1950, with Judith Anderson as Clytemnestra. Apparently the granite tower Jeffers built next to his house in 1920-1924 provided the title and central metaphor of the poem, which suggested that a selfless sense of kinship with the universe, which includes granite and stars, birds, and the ocean (what Jeffers saw from his tower), can help us escape the all-too-human emotional blindnesses which cause so much misery. So Jeffers found, as he built and lived in his house and tower, and wrote about those subjects. His house and tower still stand, a national literary historical monument defying the real estate developers who have planned to demolish the house and tower and subdivide what little remains of Jeffers's property.

In 1927 Jeffers's next book, *The Women at Point Sur,* confused even his friends. This 175-page poem concerns a Reverend Dr. Barclay, whose name and delusion seem a parody of Bishop George Berkeley (whose name is pronounced "Barclay") and his philosophy that the world exists only as and because God perceives it. Jeffers's Barclay is so upset by his only son's death in World War I that he renounces his country and Christianity. Failing to notice anyone else's suffering, he comes to think of himself as the prophet of some new religion, and then as God. When an earthquake shakes him, it surprises him, but he claims that he created it and controls the world, when, in fact, he cannot control anything, himself included. When he looks at the universe of millions of galaxies which astronomers were then just beginning to photograph, Barclay sees all that immensity as only his own eye reflected, looking back at itself. Like Narcissus, he thinks the world exists only as his mirror when in fact, like an eye, he exists only as a dependent part which cannot survive alone; he dies because he will not learn that lesson. He behaves so immorally because he cannot imagine how anyone else might feel. He rapes his daughter—Jeffers repeatedly used incest as a metaphor and example of narcissism—and wanders off into the wilderness, hopelessly lost, to die of exhaustion while claiming that he is God, and inexhaustible, as if his words could cause miracles. Like the logical positivists, semanticists, C. S. Peirce (but very few other poets apart from Lucretius and the German Christian Morgenstern), Jeffers regarded words as only words, inevitably abstract, at best approximate, and quite unmagical, a skepticism which seems a part of his humility for himself and mankind in general.

Apparently to avoid the confusion caused by *The Women at Point Sur,* Jeffers promptly made his next tragedy, "Cawdor," shorter and simpler, using the plot of Euripides' already proven *Hippolytus* (he used it again for his play "The Cretan Woman," published in 1954 in *Hungerfield and Other Poems*). In its first section, the poem "Cawdor" introduces the dangerously beautiful and resentful Fera, first seen emerging from a range fire leading her blind and dying father; they have nowhere to go and no money. Her name means "wild," and she is: she cynically marries the smugly self-confident fifty-year-old rancher Cawdor to save her father, and proceeds to complicate Cawdor's life disastrously when her father dies. Cawdor's son (Jeffers's Hippolytus) will not let Fera seduce him (parts two through seven), and, in a spiteful refusal to accept such limitations or to consider anything but her own emotions, she provokes a crisis by claiming the son has raped her. In his bewildered innocence, he flees from his father's anger only to fall to his death in the dark (parts seven through ten). Fera then provokes a catastrophe by telling the truth (parts eleven through fifteen); like Oedipus, Cawdor then blinds himself when he realizes how blind he has been (part sixteen). The poem celebrates the world's cycles by depicting fires that destroy old lives to make new life possible—as in "Tamar," a metaphor suggested perhaps by the fires California ranchers used to set, burning the old grass each fall to make more new grass grow the next spring, as at the beginning of "Cawdor"; Fera's emotions obviously resemble that fire.

The poem's fire metaphors also include two descriptions of dreams caused by death. In section seven, Fera's father's remembered failures produce a series of increasingly self-indulgent and simple-minded fantasies as his brain cells decompose, disconnecting first from the world and then from one another, a process Jeffers compares to the slow fire of decaying wood as it shines weakly in the dark; the process soon ends in a numb dark silence. In section fifteen, a caged eagle dies, and dreams of soaring up as the earth dwindles beneath it—a remarkable anticipation of the view astronauts began having as their rockets took off some forty years later—until it finds its peace in the very heart of light and fire, the source of life, the sun. The bird's dream explodes outward, making it more aware of the universe beyond itself; the man's fantasies collapse inward, ignoring everything but his own self-pity and the contemptibly petty greediness which his life kept frustrating. Like many of Jeffers's other women, Fera proves fearlessly emotional, and spectacularly destructive as a result; though Jeffers deplores the misery they cause, he seems to admire such characters, as well as finding the misery they cause morally instructive.

As Jeffers told his bibliographer S. S. Alberts, the title poem of his next book, *Dear Judas and Other Poems* (1929), "was written in 1928, with the thought of presenting the only divine figure still living in the minds of people of our race, as the hero of a tragedy. The Japanese Nō plays, in which the action is performed by ghosts revisiting the scenes of their passions, no doubt influenced my conception."

In this poem, the ghosts of Judas, Jesus, and the Virgin Mary comment on what happened almost twenty centuries ago, just before and after the Crucifixion, giving the audience the benefit of their hindsight and three firsthand points of view. Their comments make Judas's behavior seem understandably human, and perhaps even admirable: Judas prudently and compassionately foresaw that any attempt at rebellion against the occupying Romans would cause widespread misery, and so tried to prevent it by having its most probable leader detained. In this attempt to avoid still worse oppression, Judas succeeds disastrously well: he becomes a tragic fool as his well-meaning mistake makes possible not just the human sacrifice with which Christianity began, but also the misery which Christianity has helped cause since then, a mistake Jesus forgives because it made his glorification possible. Judas remains unconsoled, because his mistake has consequences which go on for centuries, consequences he did not want and cannot prevent. His betrayal is an impressive example of how good intentions can lead straight to Hell, when a seemingly small act has enormous and mostly unexpected consequences. Jeffers had not imagined that anyone would ever produce "Dear Judas" as a play, and seemed quite unsurprised when a production of it was banned in Boston in 1947 because, the mayor said, it might stir up religious feelings.

Jeffers's success with an unchristian view of the world and humanity predictably offended some critics, most notably Yvor Winters, who wrote that because Jeffers saw the world as God, and in terms of a textbook in physics, Jeffers had "abandoned narrative logic" as well as ethics. Winters seems to have meant that nothing which did not agree with his own view could make sense. He claimed that Jeffers's poems are "defective" because they have no rational plots or structures, and so cannot be paraphrased, though Winters did paraphrase two of them, both inaccurately. Winters claimed that Jeffers's poems only repeat images, "with no rational necessity for any order . . . the order being determined wholly by the author's feeling about the graduation of importance or intensity." Such a comment may describe *The Waste Land* accurately, but not any of Jeffers's more than 440 poems except one twenty-line lyric Winters did not mention, "The Maid's Thought," which first appeared in *Tamar and Other Poems* in 1924. That poem begins with the girl saying, "listen, even the water is sobbing for something"; seventeen lines later she says what she wants, having progressed step by step from the ocean to plants to animals to herself, with each example of longing more intense and important to her than the one before. The whole series neatly recapitulates the evolution of life which she epitomizes, and which will continue if she gets what she wants, not an act without consequences despite Winters's claim that none of Jeffers's characters do anything that has any meaning or consequence. Winters said literature should be judged by the accuracy of its perceptions, a principle which may also apply to the criticism of literature. Winters claimed Jeffers used "the terminology of modern physics" but mentioned no examples, perhaps because Jeffers used so few such terms, and he seemed unable to admit how vividly and accurately Jeffers described the world, a point Horace Lyon documented in *Jeffers Country* (1970), a collection of some of Jeffers's previously published poems illustrated by Lyon's photographs. Though Winters says Jeffers does not describe the world as a botanist would, "The Maid's Thought" mentions precisely what a botanist would notice in that particular place and season: the "sulphury pollen dust" of the pines, the broom, deerweed, wild iris, globe tulips, and bronze bell in blossom, and all referred to by nontechnical names.

Though Winters managed to ignore them almost totally in his survey of the methods of organizing poetry, Jeffers used the rhetorical structures—tragic plots and other sequences, seasonal metaphors and other comparisons—which have been basic to poetry at least since Aeschylus. Winters's argument that Jeffers's poems have no moral meaning or coherence depends upon the curious assumption that because scientific discoveries reveal the causes, results, and circumstances of what we do, such knowledge leaves us unable to make choices or to understand anything, as if we can be free, moral, and intelligent only when ignorant. From "Tamar" on, Jeffers's poems say and show why we need to escape such self-pitying and irresponsible ignorance, and to know what misery it causes, a matter-of-fact morality Winters ignored. For instance, he called such plots as that of "The Loving Shepherdess" in *Dear Judas and Other Poems* "non-narrative" because "reversible," and paraphrased that poem as about "a girl who knows herself doomed to die . . . in childbirth . . . [who] wanders over the countryside . . . turned cruelly from door to door . . . until finally the girl dies. . . ." The plot depends on two obviously irreversible changes, pregnancy and death, and shows that the girl dies as a result of her self-centered ignorance, including the delusion that her baby is the world and God, so she thinks that she contains it rather than it containing her. The result seems the opposite of the *Odyssey.* The male Odysseus returns home with great success by cheating and killing others; the shepherdess wanders from her home to her death alone, hurting no one but herself and failing at everything she tries, which makes her delusion of importance as the creator of the world and God pathetically understandable but no less dangerous as a compensation for her failures. As Aristotle said of the *Odyssey*, the rest is anecdote. In both cases, all the anecdotes describe and explain the central character's behavior, and help to determine what happens next in memorably vivid ways.

Jeffers wrote little criticism, but as *The Selected Letters of Robinson Jeffers* shows, he answered questions from readers. He wrote a helpful foreword to *The Selected Poetry* (1938), as well as *Themes in My Poems* (1956) for his only lecture tour, and *Poetry, Gongorism and A Thousand Years* for the 18 January 1948 *New York Times* (republished as a book in 1949). As his poem "Self-Criticism in February" shows, he knew what critics said, and why he thought them wrong:

> *And now*
> *For the worst fault: you have never mistaken*

Demon nor passion nor idealism for the real God.
Then what is most disliked in those verses
Remains most true. *Unfortunately. If only you could sing*
That God is love, or perhaps that social
Justice will soon prevail. I can tell lies in prose.

The "more massive violence" he had predicted promptly came in World War II. While much modern poetry became notorious for its obscurity and its retreat from public subjects, Jeffers apparently thought he had something important to say to mankind about mankind and the world we inhabit, and so tried to say it clearly, offending some.

By 1929 Jeffers had written nine tragedies in seven years and thirty or more shorter poems, establishing himself as one of the most widely read and discussed American poets. He was the first to appear on the cover of *Time*, the 4 April 1932 issue, some twenty years before T. S. Eliot did. As Jeffers later said, he felt tired by 1929 and wanted to rest

by "playing dead for a few months. Foreign travel is like a pleasant temporary death; it relieves you of responsibilities and familiar scenes and duties." Jeffers and his wife and twin sons went to Ireland and Britain for the second half of 1929; the result was *Descent to the Dead*, sixteen short poems about the dead of those islands, published as a separate book in 1931 and included in *Give Your Heart to the Hawks* in 1933.

Once home again in 1930, Jeffers began a series of narratives whose painful ends still demonstrate the need for an unselfish detachment from otherwise blinding emotions. Most of them are without the plot structure of Greek tragedy, as if he had decided to avoid repeating himself and to find new forms for tragedy by writing something like naturalistic novels in verse. In "Thurso's Landing," published in 1932, a stupidly jealous husband and a resentfully unfaithful wife destroy each other. His strength and courage and her passion prove worse than useless without some detached intelligence, a moral point obscured by so much misery and their confusion.

In "Margrave," also in *Thurso's Landing and Other Poems*, Jeffers contrasts the useless self-pity of a condemned medical student's last hours with the outward-looking discoveries about the universe which astronomers make. The student's consciousness only makes him more miserable—he knows precisely what hanging will do to him—and more pathetic as well as despicable; he kidnapped a little girl to get money to continue his education, and then killed her, a plot suggested by the then famous but now forgotten Hickman case. Considering how miserably we behave, Jeffers said, no wonder the whole universe seems to be recoiling from us as if in horror. Astronomers had then just discovered the red shift in the light from galaxies which indicates that other galaxies are moving away from us as the universe expands—a staggering metaphor, but readers may refuse to consider so depressing and despicable a character as the medical student a representative example of humanity, and may not appreciate Jeffers's disgust as a result of a long-tried compassion.

In "Give Your Heart to the Hawks," Jeffers seems less exasperated, perhaps because he has made his characters more likable. The poem presents a family on the Sur coast destroyed by their reactions to a single disastrously emotional moment, and here Jeffers at least began with a Christian organizing archetype to replace the plot structure and seasonal metaphors of Greek tragedy. The poem begins with Michael Fraser's play-

The Jeffers family in Ireland, 1929

fully putting a harmless snake up his sister-in-law's leg as she picks apples, as if they were Adam and Eve in Eden, and Jeffers meant to invite Freudian interpretations. Their happy time soon ends: in the next scene, at a drunken party on the beach below, her husband kills a rattlesnake and then either jealously kills his brother Michael or helplessly watches him fall from the cliff (in emotional moments he cannot distinguish between his guilty fantasies and fact). Because he cannot "give his heart to the hawks" (cannot detach what he sees from his blindly human emotions), he loses his sanity and then his life while trying to escape from his fantasies. His pregnant wife survives because she can and does love unselfishly, caring for others while knowing that the world does not depend on her. Her husband had thought his guilt ruined everything, making the whole world hate him, and so he slaughtered the cattle he thought were pursuing him. His wife has only one such self-important delusion, that the child she carries "will change the world," and so the tragedy may happen again.

In 1933 Jeffers returned to Greek plots: "At the Fall of an Age," in *Give Your Heart to the Hawks and Other Poems*, shows the dead of the Trojan War come back from Hades to take Helen of Troy to the woman with whom she grew up. Blaming Helen for the war, in which the woman's husband died, that woman has Helen killed, and kills herself, the last of Helen's many victims. In "Resurrection," in *Solstice and Other Poems* (1935), a soldier who died in World War I temporarily returns from death to haunt the guilty, a dramatic device Jeffers used again in "The Love and the Hate," the first half of the title poem about World War II in *The Double Axe & Other Poems* (1948). Jeffers wrote about ghosts as early as 1924, in "Tamar," and seemed to like to think of his ghost haunting his granite home for centuries to come. Despite Yvor Winters's claims, Jeffers was not altogether a determinist; he had his inconsistent and often moving moments of belief in the supernatural.

In the title poem of *Solstice and Other Poems* Jeffers also used a Greek plot, retelling Euripides' *Medea* as he would again more successfully in his *Medea* (1946). After his successes from "Tamar" to "The Loving Shepherdess" in 1924-1929, Jeffers seemed to need to find new sources and forms for tragedy, and he used the supernatural more often in his narrative poems, as if he had begun to find a strictly naturalistic world view too bleak, or too limiting for what he wanted to say.

Solstice and Other Poems also includes "At the Birth of an Age," Jeffers's one tragedy using a Teutonic legend. It describes a stupidly petty and suicidal squabble between three brothers, leaders of a minor Germanic tribe, and their sister, who became Attila's consort because they had murdered her husband. The squabble has results they cannot even imagine: because it also kills the general who might otherwise have conquered the disintegrating Roman empire, Attila suffers his only defeat (as in fact he did, near Châlons, a hundred miles east of Paris, in the year 451) and Europe remains Christian. The victims seem dwarfed by the enormous consequences of their passionate ignorance, and at the end of the poem Jeffers makes them seem still smaller, still more pathetically limited and foolish in their pride, by contrasting them with the universe as a whole, as personified by Odin (the god of wisdom, conflict, and death in Teutonic and Norse mythology), who tortures himself in order to discover everything, which is to say, his own identity. Here Jeffers restates the traditional moral of Greek tragedies—to know who you are by knowing your limits, and so to do nothing excessively—not just in terms of another mythology, but also in terms of scientific discoveries about the universe that limits and creates us. He seems to suggest that if we discover enough we may save ourselves from the often miserable effects of ignorance. As scientists have from Newton or Galileo on, Jeffers sees the universe as one totally interconnecting network of forever-changing yet forever-balancing forces; he also sees those changes as producing not just the consciousness of his universe-as-God, but ours as well. At its most intense, consciousness becomes painful, but without it we cannot learn, so like Jeffers's Odin we must keep on balancing between opposing forces to survive.

Jeffers's view parallels the Buddhist and Taoist view of the universe as yin and yang, a perpetual balancing of mutually dependent opposites, and the Buddhist and Hindu metaphor of the universe as Indra's net (Indra is the Hindu god of the heavens). In his net, every part of the universe reflects and affects every other. Jeffers never mentions Indra, and may have independently rediscovered the world-as-God-as-net metaphor which he used at least sixty times. He might also have borrowed it from Newton's law of gravitational attraction, in which every particle of the universe reflects every other, a point made clear in the astronomy textbook which Jeffers read at Occidental. As the physicist Fritjof Capra has since said in *The Tao of Physics* (1975), apparently without knowing about Jeffers, this view is basic to physics and astronomy, and to both Eastern and Western mys-

Letter from Jeffers to Edwin Arlington Robinson. Jeffers thanks Robinson for sending him a copy of Talifer (1933) *and mentions having earlier sent one of his own books to the older poet (by permission of the Estate of Robinson Jeffers; courtesy of the E. A. Robinson Papers, Manuscript Division, New York Public Library).*

ticism, as in William Blake's "Auguries of Innocence," which starts

> To see a World in a grain of sand
> And a Heaven in a wild flower,
> Hold Infinity in the palm of your hand,
> And Eternity in an hour.

The net metaphor and Newton's law suggest that every part of the universe is what it is, does what it does, because of all the rest, and so (as these lines may say) each part in part reflects the whole universe. These lines also seem a recipe for mystical experience; *innocence* may mean that selflessly detached compassionate awareness which Jeffers and Buddhists advocate. Jeffers saw the sheer size and beauty of the universe as both revealing our unimportance and consoling us: see the planet as a grain of sand or as an eyeball (as Jeffers did in "The Eye," 1948) and mankind becomes too small to see and our individual troubles vanish—a liberation resented by those who prefer to cling to their self-important miseries, and misunderstood by critics who called Jeffers nihilistic, inhuman, and immoral. But if we see the universe as a net of cause—result relationships, as Jeffers did, we may choose what we do much more carefully, knowing that every act has its consequences, some of them irreversible, and so become more morally and ecologically responsible. The word *ecology* means the net of relationships between each species or individual and his environment, and, as with a net, disturbing any part inevitably affects all the rest. Thus, for Jeffers, if we see our feelings as only our feelings, and relatively unimportant, and as often misleading distractions, we may become less selfish, less harried by such misery-causing emotions as ambition and greed, and so become more compassionate and responsible because more aware of individuals and of the universe beyond ourselves.

In 1937 Jeffers continued his experiments with sources and forms for tragedy by writing one based on the old Scots border ballad "Edward," whose last line gave Jeffers his title for the poem and for the book containing it: *Such Counsels You Gave to Me*. In the ballad, a man with wife and children takes his mother's counsels and kills his father but is then forced to go into exile and curses her. Jeffers makes the young man an unmarried medical student whose health and sanity break down from overwork after his father refuses to go on paying for his education. He murders his father, but refuses to avoid punishment or to let his mother seduce him. Like many of Jeffers's tragic fools, he

seems haunted by a ghostly counterpart of himself which tells him what he could have done, increasing his anguish without helping him succeed; he cannot see beyond that projection of himself to see anything objectively.

In 1938 Jeffers put together *The Selected Poetry of Robinson Jeffers* and then, just before flying over the Sierra Nevada to Death Valley that Easter as the passenger in an open cockpit biplane with his younger (and only) brother Hamilton, left his wife a note in which he anticipated his possible death on that flight. He included his will and directions for his funeral, asking "to be cremated as cheaply, quickly, and quietly as possible, no speech, no meeting nor music, no more coffin than may be necessary, no embalming, no flowers . . . Put the ashes a few inches deep . . . near our little daughter's ashes" in the yard by the house. Meanwhile, he said that he had "no desire to die before writing another poem or two," and that he "should love to know" his wife and sons "for hundreds of years," but he neither shrank from nor welcomed death. When

Robinson Jeffers on Hawk Tower, 1939

he did die, in 1962, his directions were followed.

In the summer of 1938, perhaps because he would not become Mabel Dodge Luhan's pet poet in Taos to replace D. H. Lawrence, Luhan encouraged a younger woman to try distracting Jeffers. Una Jeffers shot herself, perhaps by accident, and not seriously; the Jeffers avoided Luhan after that. The incident had its aftermath, as Jeffers's note later that year reveals. It begins,

Una, *I can't write* . . . and writing—during the past 30 years—has become one of the conditions of life for me. . . .
I believe I'll have a new birth . . . something will happen, and *life through this hell come home to me.* . . .

as it had in 1917-1919 in "the accidental new birth" of his mind which made his original poetry possible.

Apparently Jeffers turned to Buddhism for that rebirth, because his next long narrative, "Mara" in *Be Angry at the Sun* (1941), is named for the temptress who tried unsuccessfully to distract Buddha from enlightenment. With Jeffers's tragic fool, she succeeds, and his self-pity and disgust with World War II drive him to suicide. Jeffers's Mara may owe something to Sir Edwin Arnold's best-selling biography of Buddha, *The Light of Asia*, first published in 1879. Buddha's distractions begin with

The Sin of Self, who in the Universe
As in a mirror her fond face shown,
And crying "I," would have the world say "I"

—the narcissistic mistake Jeffers's tragic fools, especially Barclay and the loving shepherdess, repeatedly make.

In his foreword to *Be Angry at the Sun,* Jeffers apologized for his "obsession with contemporary history" before and during World War II. It threatened his detachment and his patience, and left many of his poems from 1939 on pinned to particular events and dated. In one, "The Day is a Poem (September 19, 1939)," Jeffers calls Hitler

A man of genius: that is, of amazing
Ability, courage, devotion, cored on a
        sick child's soul
. . . .
                a sick child
Wailing in Danzig; invoking destruction and wailing
    at it.

Hostile reviewers sometimes quoted "genius"

out of context while calling Jeffers a fascist, and not adding that *genius* can mean "the evil spirit dominating a situation" or that Jeffers also described Hitler as a dangerous and contemptible psychotic. Hitler disgusted but also interested Jeffers as a spectacular example of the sort of delusion best avoided. In poem after poem, Jeffers tried to make such delusions unattractive by showing their ignoble causes and painful results.

"The Bowl of Blood," the other long poem in *Be Angry at the Sun*, shows Hitler in April 1940 consulting a fortune-teller because his invasion of Norway seems about to fail and he does not know what to do next (it is now known that Hitler did consult an astrologer then for that reason). But as a compulsive talker, Hitler tells his own fortune only to ignore it, thus helping make it come true. He says he will not repeat Napoleon's mistake of getting trapped by invading Russia before finishing England and will shoot himself rather than surrender as Napoleon did. Hitler did shoot himself

Jeffers and his twin sons, Donnan and Garth, 1944

in April 1945 just as Jeffers predicted in May or June 1941, when or just before Hitler invaded Russia. The popular impression of Jeffers as a misanthropic hermit hiding in his tower has misled many a hostile critic; in fact, few other poets in America have taken such risks to comment on current public events to predict the culture's future in order to warn and help their readers, or been so resented for trying.

Jeffers could neither ignore the war nor suppose his warnings could prevent it. He regarded it as a "tragic farce," with millions of victims but no heroes. Any tragedy he might have written about the whole war would have been bewilderingly long and complicated, and worse, might have made Hitler seem sympathetic as its central figure and victim. "The Bowl of Blood" solves both problems: it concentrates on a few minutes in which Hitler seems contemptible in his stupidity and self-pity while so many others die, and doomed because he will not learn even when he unwittingly happens to tell the truth, a poetically just fate for so compulsive and lavishly rewarded a liar.

As the poems about the war which Jeffers left out of his books show even more clearly (see the posthumous collection *What Odd Expedients*, 1981), the war left Jeffers often more disgusted and despairing than detached because mankind suffers so much, while learning so little. Many of his poems of 1933-1961 read like choruses for a tragedy never written, a tragedy he might have felt no one would want to read, because the tragic fools and victims are whole countries and cultures, the readers included. He spent the war years writing shorter

Robinson Jeffers (photograph by Leigh Wiener)

poems and smaller tragedies, including the adaptation of Euripides' *Medea* Judith Anderson requested.

Medea made Jeffers wealthy enough to keep his house as Carmel's taxes kept increasing; the play opened on Broadway on 20 October 1947 with Judith Anderson as Medea, and has since been produced in Scotland, England, Denmark, Italy, France, Portugal, Australia, and on Broadway again in 1982, and translated into four languages. Jeffers had seen only five plays before he wrote it, one of them his own *The Tower Beyond Tragedy*, but he made *Medea* move quickly from the first speech, in which Medea's nurse wishes Medea had never met the Greek adventurer Jason, to Jason's utter humiliation an hour later. As in Euripides' tragedy. Jason plans to marry a princess and exile his first wife, Medea, and their two sons, although he knows she killed members of her family to save him and so cannot go home. She arranges for sanctuary elsewhere, gives the princess a golden robe which burns her and her father alive, and kills Jason's sons. In Euripides' version, the gods then carry Medea away; in Jeffers's, she walks away, leaving an utterly defeated Jason to live on in misery, forever discredited for having so violated her love and trust.

With *The Double Axe & Other Poems* (1948), Jeffers offended the patriotic by describing World War II as a slaughter best avoided, and possibly also by his "rejection of human solipsism and recognition of the transhuman magnificence" of the universe on which our lives depend. He said we need his "philosophical attitude," which he unfortunately called Inhumanism, because "It seems time that our race began to think as an adult does, rather than like an egocentric baby or insane person. This manner of thought and feeling is neither misanthropic nor pessimist, though two or three people have said so and may again. It involves no falsehoods, and is a means of maintaining sanity in slippery times. . . . It offers a reasonable detachment instead of love, hate and envy" which cause tragedies, including "The Love and the Hate," the first half of the title poem. The second half shows how to survive by having so skeptical a detachment. Like Bodhidharma (470-543), who began Zen Buddhism, Jeffers's Inhumanist lives alone in the mountains and turns away would-be disciples by challenging them with riddles to make them think and to make them see the beauty of the universe beyond themselves.

In the summer of 1948 Jeffers and Una made their third trip to Ireland, where Jeffers nearly died of pleurisy; they got back to California to find that Una had cancer. She died in his arms in September 1950, leaving Jeffers desolate. He survived to write *Hungerfield and Other Poems*, published in 1954, and the poems his son Donnan and his biographer Melba Berry Bennet collected in *The Beginning & the End and Other Poems*, published in 1963, the year after Jeffers's death. He began "Hungerfield" by hoping that somewhere, somehow, Una might still live, but he admits in a few lines that he knows she has died, so he thinks of Hungerfield, the man who temporarily defeated death. Watching his mother die of cancer, Hungerfield decides to wrestle with death, and stop him, as Hungerfield thinks he did when wounded in World War I. He does, and, for a few agonizing hours no one appreciates, no one dies. Then the dam bursts: Hungerfield's wife, child, and brother die, and Hungerfield burns his house, killing himself, but his mother escapes to live two more years. The poem portrays death as a needed mercy, as Jeffers apparently needed to think then; he also thought of Una living serenely on as a part of the lovely natural world. After 1958, he suffered illness after illness and died in his sleep on 20 January 1962.

Letters:

The Selected Letters of Robinson Jeffers, 1897-1962, edited by Ann N. Ridgeway (Baltimore: Johns Hopkins Press, 1968).

Bibliographies:

S. S. Alberts, *A Bibliography of the Works of Robinson Jeffers* (New York: Random House, 1933);

Alex A. Vardamis, *The Critical Reputation of Robinson Jeffers* (Hamden, Conn.: Shoe String Press, 1972).

Biography:

Melba Berry Bennett, *The Stone Mason of Tor House: The Life and Works of Robinson Jeffers* (Los Angeles: Ward Ritchie Press, 1966).

References:

Newton Arvin, "The Paradox of Jeffers," *New Freeman,* 1 (17 May 1930): 230-232;

Joseph Warren Beach, *The Concept of Nature in Nineteenth Century Poetry* (New York: Macmillan, 1936), pp. 542-546;

Robert Boyers, "A Sovereign Voice: The Poetry of Robinson Jeffers," *Sewanee Review,* 77 (Summer 1969): 487-507;

Robert J. Brophy, afterword to *Dear Judas and Other*

Poems (New York: Liveright, 1977), pp. 131-153;

Brophy, *Robinson Jeffers, Myth, Ritual and Symbol in His Narrative Poems* (Cleveland: The Press of Case Western Reserve University, 1973);

M. Webster Brown, "A Poet Who Studied Medicine," *Medicine Journal and Record,* 130 (6 November 1929): 535-539;

Frederic Ives Carpenter, *Robinson Jeffers* (New York: Twayne, 1962);

Carpenter, "The Values of Robinson Jeffers," *American Literature,* 11 (January 1940): 353-366;

Arthur B. Coffin, *Robinson Jeffers: The Poetry of Inhumanism* (Madison: University of Wisconsin Press, 1971);

James Daly, "Roots Under the Rocks," review of *Tamar and Other Poems, Poetry,* 26 (August 1925): 278-285;

Babette Deutsch, "Brains and Lyrics," review of *Tamar and Other Poems, New Republic,* 43 (27 May 1925): 23-24;

James Dickey, "First and Last Things," *Poetry,* 103 (February 1964): 320-325;

Fraser Bragg Drew, "The Gentleness of Robinson Jeffers," *Western Humanities Review,* 12 (Autumn 1958): 379-381;

William Everson (Brother Antoninus), foreword to *The Double Axe and Other Poems* (New York: Liveright, 1977), pp. vii-xix;

Everson, Introduction to *Californians* (Monterey: Cayucos Books, 1974), pp. vii-xxvi;

Everson, Introduction to *Cawdor: A Long Poem, Medea after Euripides* (New York: New Directions, 1970), pp. vii-xxx;

Everson, Preface, Introduction, and Afterword to *Brides of the South Wind* (Monterey: Cayucos Books, 1974), pp. ix-xxxiii, 119-137;

Everson, *Robinson Jeffers: Fragments of an Older Fury* (Berkeley: Oyez, 1968);

Horace Gregory, "Poet Without Critics: A Note on Robinson Jeffers," *New World Writing: Seventh Mentor Selection* (New York: New American Library, 1955), pp. 40-52;

"Harrowed Marrow," *Time,* 19 (4 April 1932): 63-64;

William Savage Johnson, "The 'Savior' in the Poetry of Robinson Jeffers," *American Literature,* 15 (May 1943): 159-168;

Benjamin Miller, "The Demands of the Religious Consciousness," *Review of Religion,* 4 (May 1940): 401-405;

William H. Nolte, "Robinson Jeffers as a Didactic Poet," *Virginia Quarterly Review,* 47 (Spring 1966): 257-271;

Nolte, *Rock and Hawk: Robinson Jeffers and the Romantic Agony* (Athens: University of Georgia Press, 1975);

"Pagan Horror from Carmel-by-the-Sea," *San Francisco Monitor,* 9 January 1926, p. 8;

Lawrence Clark Powell, *Robinson Jeffers, The Man and His Work* (Pasadena: San Pasquel Press, 1940);

Robinson Jeffers Newsletter (1962-   );

James Rorty, "In Major Mold," review of *Tamar and Other Poems, New York Herald and Tribune Books,* 1 March 1925, pp. 1-2;

Robert Ian Scott, "Robinson Jeffers' Tragedies as Rediscoveries of the World," *Rocky Mountain Review of Language and Literature,* 29 (Autumn 1975): 147-165;

Radcliffe Squires, *The Loyalties of Robinson Jeffers* (Ann Arbor: University of Michigan Press, 1956);

Mark Van Doren, "First Glance," review of *Tamar and Other Poems, Nation,* 120 (11 March 1925): 268;

Hyatt H. Waggoner, *The Heel of Elohim: Science and Values in Modern American Poetry* (Norman: University of Oklahoma Press, 1959), pp. 74-180, 201-202;

Yvor Winters, *In Defense of Reason* (New York: Swallow Press/William Morrow, 1947), pp. 30-74;

Winters, "Robinson Jeffers," *Poetry,* 35 (February 1930): 279-286.

Papers:

The bulk of the Jeffers papers are at the Humanities Research Center of the University of Texas at Austin.

Fenton Johnson

(7 May 1888-17 September 1958)

Shirley Lumpkin
University of Tennessee

BOOKS: *A Little Dreaming* (Chicago: Peterson Linotyping Co., 1913);
Visions of the Dusk (New York: Fenton Johnson, 1915);
Songs of the Soil (New York: Fenton Johnson, 1916);
For the Highest Good (Chicago: Favorite Magazine, 1920);
Tales of Darkest America (Chicago: Favorite Magazine, 1920).

OTHER: "Children of the Sun," "The New Day," "Tired," "The Banjo Player," and "The Scarlet Woman," in *The Book of American Negro Poetry*, edited by James Weldon Johnson (New York: Harcourt, Brace, 1922), pp. 117-123; enlarged edition, adds "Lines from 'The Vision of Lazarus'" (New York: Harcourt, Brace, 1931), pp. 141-146;
"The Lost Love," "How Long, O Lord," and "Who Is That A-Walking in the Corn?," in *The New Poetry: An Anthology of Twentieth-Century Verse in English*, edited by Harriet Monroe and Alice Corbin Henderson (New York: Macmillan, 1923);
"The Banjo Player," "The Drunkard," and "The Minister," in *An Anthology of American Poetry: Lyric America, 1630-1930*, edited by Alfred Kreymborg (New York: Tudor Publishing, 1930), pp. 537-538;
"Rulers," "The Banjo Player," "The Scarlet Woman," "Tired," "Aunt Annie Allen," "When I Die," "The Lonely Mother," and "Who Is That A-Walking in the Corn," in *The Poetry of the Negro, 1746-1949*, edited by Langston Hughes and Arna Bontemps (Garden City: Doubleday, 1949), pp. 61-64;
"The Daily Grind," "The World Is a Mighty Ogre," "A Negro Peddler's Song," "The Old Repair Man," and "Counting," in *American Negro Poetry*, edited by Bontemps (New York: Hill & Wang, 1963), pp. 25-28.

PERIODICAL PUBLICATIONS: "The Last Love," "How Long, O Lord," and "Who Is

Fenton Johnson

That A-Walking in the Corn?," *Poetry*, 11 (June 1918): 136-137;
"Tired," *Others*, 5 (January 1919): 8;
"Aunt Hanna Jackson," "Aunt Jane Allen," "The Gambler," "The Barber," and "The Drunkard," *Others*, 5 (February 1919): 17-18;
"The Artist" and "Dreams," *Others*, 5 (April-May 1919): 20;
"A Dream" and "The Wonderful Morning," *Poetry*, 19 (December 1921): 128-129.

Publishing his own work after the death of the popular Negro poet Paul Laurence Dunbar in 1906 and before the emergence of the new Negro voices of Claude McKay, Jean Toomer, Langston Hughes, and Countee Cullen in the decade between 1917 and 1927, Fenton Johnson experienced a continual struggle, as he put it, to maintain his idealism and "to obtain a foothold in literature." Although the poems in his self-published books of poetry (1913, 1915, and 1916) were primarily written in artificial and imitative plantation dialect and genteel, imitative Victorian diction, his continuing struggle to present the life of his race in his work resulted in a handful of poems, published in anthologies and magazines from 1919 through the early 1930s, that sounded a new stylistic and thematic note in black poetry. Yet these poems failed to bring Johnson any recognition or any real possibility for the publication of another volume of poetry during his lifetime. His early description of his endeavor in literature as like "trying to walk the Atlantic ocean" turned out to be correct. His published books remain unimportant, and the poems written during World War I and his period on the Federal Writers' Project, free verse depictions of urban despair and of human destruction by inhuman forces, remain unpublished as a volume but form the basis of his reputation as a poet.

A factual recitation of Fenton Johnson's career reflects, as it did in his own view, a downward spiral. The son of Elijah H. and Jesse Taylor Johnson, he spent a relatively comfortable youth in Chicago, where, according to Arna Bontemps's biographical note, he was "once a dapper boy who drove his own electric automobile around Chicago at the end of the first decade of this century." The only child in a middle-class black family of moderate means, Johnson had the opportunity to pursue his interests in the arts by writing plays that were produced at the Pekin Theater when he was nineteen, attending the University of Chicago (and later Northwestern University), and composing poems. Through the generosity of others, he was able to publish his first book of poems privately in 1913 in Chicago, after he had returned from a year of teaching in the South. Entitled *A Little Dreaming*, the volume was dedicated to his grandmother, who might have been the helpful patron he mentions in that book. The generosity of others also allowed him to move to New York after its publication and to attend the Pulitzer School of Journalism at Columbia University. While writing for the Eastern Press Association and serving as the acting dramatic editor of the *New York News*, Johnson was able to finance the publication of two more books of his poetry, *Visions of the Dusk* (1915) and *Songs of the Soil* (1916), before returning to Chicago to take up the life of a magazine editor. He edited the *Champion* in 1916-1917, and in February 1918 he founded the *Favorite Magazine* and managed to

keep it going until the spring of 1920, when he began the descent into the poverty and oblivion which silenced his voice, except for occasional anthology and magazine appearances. The last twenty-eight years of his life, before his death in 1958, were lived in almost total literary obscurity.

While these misfortunes adversely affected Johnson's personal life, ironically the experiences seemed to strengthen his poetry. His contact with poverty, his unsuccessful literary ventures, his attempts to found a movement to reconcile the races, and his work with the WPA writers' project in Chicago, as well as his contact with the emerging Chicago new poetry school between 1917 and 1919 (including *Poetry* magazine editor Harriet Monroe and poets Edgar Lee Masters, Carl Sandburg, and Vachel Lindsay) gave new vigor and direction to his writing, as did his association with Alfred Kreymborg, editor of the New York little magazine *Others*. From 1916 to the mid-1930s came his free-verse poems which present a number of powerful speakers and explore the harsh working and living conditions of ordinary urban black Americans "tired" of struggling to live in an American "civilization" that oppressed them racially, economically, and culturally. These poems were never published in book form. He could find no publisher for the first group, which were reportedly part of a manuscript he called "African Nights." This manuscript, from which Alfred Kreymborg may have selected some of Johnson's poems for publication, is now lost. "The Daily Grind: 41 WPA Poems," written when Johnson was working for the Federal Writers' Project in Chicago, also remains unpublished in book form (a copy of the entire manuscript is in the Fisk Library). Some of the poems in these two groups were published individually in magazines and anthologies; ironically this highly selective body of approximately fifteen poems forms the basis for the critical respect and public recognition accorded Johnson's poetry.

In this work his style had changed from the use of American poetic diction or the local-color dialect best represented by Paul Laurence Dunbar and James Whitcomb Riley to the use of a concrete, free verse which created powerful speakers and explored the harsh working and living experiences of ordinary, primarily black, Americans struggling to get along in the city and tired of the battle. While both dialect and genteel poetic styles were inherently incapable of effectively representing Afro-American experience in memorable poetry, Johnson's reversals and his reflections upon them had turned him in the more fruitful direction of employing concrete, spoken expression to describe common, ironic experiences. Despite what must have been profound discouragement about his waning fortunes and his increasingly limited possibilities, Johnson recognized and created more powerful poetic language during his later years than during his more buoyant and successful youth.

Johnson introduced his first book of poetry, *A Little Dreaming*, with a foreword written in the "high poetic" diction he used in most of the poems, calling himself "the poor minstrel, wandering through the maze of time, come to thy palace, O my King the Reader, with naught save my little lyre upon which I play my feeble strain." He closed the volume in the same vein by saying, "And now my chord is silent. The night has come upon the land, and I fain would rest. Perhaps I have pleased thee, perhaps I have not. There are many minstrels, O my King the Reader, and I am the humblest in all thy realm." Conceiving of himself and his poetry in such archaic, clichéd, pseudoromantic terms in 1913 did not, however, mean that Johnson saw himself as separate from other black people. In that same foreword he hoped that his songs not only pleased and cheered the reader but also gave the reader "sympathy for my people."

The majority of the poems in *A Little Dreaming*, including an apt tribute to Paul Laurence Dunbar, whose poetic style and interests had obviously influenced him, are in this Victorian/romantic diction, which was characteristic of the popular public "cultivated" Anglo-American poetry of the early twentieth century; but Johnson's subjects, like Dunbar's, are not only generalized sentiments about love, loss, dreaming, and death but also praise for the beauty of Afro-Americans, as in "To An Afro-American Maiden" (in whom "All the world romantic" lived) and in "The Ethiopian's Song." Also included in his "high" or cultivated poetry was another atypical theme most apparent in "The Plaint of the Factory Child" that would come to the fore in the works of his later poetry-writing years. Another work, "The Vision of Lazarus," was praised by anthologists and critics as an ambitious treatment of religious vision in blank verse, a theme that had never been successfully captured in Dunbar's high-literary style with its overly simplistic versification.

While Johnson was not purely pedestrian in his self-consciously literary work, his representations of his people in the plantation dialect style of poems such as "Mistah Witch" and "Uncle Isham Lies A-Dyin," in dignified lyrics for "coon songs"

such as "Kentucky Moon" in the manner of James Weldon Johnson, and poems in other popular dialects—such as the "Jewish" dialect of "Mine Rachel" and "Scottish" dialect of "When I Speak of Jamie"—are more obviously competent but undistinguished imitations of popular conventions.

Sufficiently encouraged by the reception of *A Little Dreaming*, Johnson continued to publish his own poetry in New York, bringing out *Visions of the Dusk* in 1915 and *Songs of the Soil* in 1916. A favorable review of his first volume in the 2 April 1914 *Literary World* (London) noted his use of two distinct styles of poetry, one in "formal cultivated English" and one in "the corrupted language of the American negro [*sic*]," and the reviewer for the January 1914 issue of the *American Review of Reviews* praised his poetry as the result of "a natural spontaneous lyricism with the same distinguishing racial qualities that characterize the work of Paul Laurence Dunbar" and the "primitive" and "plaintive" effectiveness of his chant form, comparing it to the spirituals. Employing this chant form in the opening to *Visions of the Dusk* and continuing to use two distinct styles, Johnson emphasized in "Prelude" that it was neither the "broken Afric tongue" of plantation dialect nor the "classic mould" of the English tongue, but his vision of the beauty of his people that made his poetry important: "The vision is the thing, and not the word." He was turning more to the plantation-dialect style in this collection, although in poems such as "Singing Hallelujah (A Negro Spiritual)" he also experimented with nondialect diction and versification that depended upon simple, concrete images and repeated refrains and interjections as a form for poetic versions of Negro spirituals. Realizing that the rhymed couplet and tight metrical systems, deliberately grotesque misspellings and the overly contrived, naive misuses of English words which created dialect's effect were inappropriate to capture the essence of the spirituals, Johnson tried to develop a new style. As he said in a preface to a group of three "Negro Spirituals"—"Jubal's Free," "Song of the Whirlwind," and "My God in Heaven Said to Me"— "These songs we offer not as genuine Negro spirituals, but as imitations. We attempt to preserve the rhythm and the spirit of the slaves, and to give a literary form and interpretation to their poetic endeavour. Here and there we have caught a phrase the unlettered minstrels used; here and there we have borrowed of that exquisite Oriental imagery the Africans brought with them." Neither dialect nor transcriptions of folk spirituals, Johnson's poetic imitations use rhythmical arrangements, imagery, and repetition to catch the pattern of the spirituals successfully enough to interest many future anthologists and editors such as Harriet Monroe and Alfred Kreymborg, who later chose to publish these and other poems in the same style. While he did, in other poems, adopt the popular plantation-dialect entertainment style, Johnson never used it to maintain plantation stereotypes. His black speakers, most of them old and rural, sing of genuine aspects of Afro-American life, of the conjure man, of loneliness, of love, of old age and death, and of washing day. Their language may be quaint, misspelled, and rhymed, but it is never an evocation of the "good old days of slavery" when master and mistress took loving care of their "ignorant lazy darkies" who laughed away their days lounging on the levee and in slave quarters, a stereotype often perpetuated in plantation-dialect literature by white Southern writers of the late-nineteenth and early-twentieth centuries, and even by some black plantation-dialect writers. Nor were his speakers ever the foolish, sentimental, or undignified caricatures associated with minstrel characterizations of blacks. Despite the limitations and the lack of originality in Johnson's use of the dialect style, his speakers all have human dignity, as one would expect from a poet who in *Visions of the Dusk* used his cultivated English to praise men's dreaming, men's strength, and religious love clearly reflected, to him, in black heroes such as Frederick Douglass. His linguistic styles might be imitative and reflective of the tastes of his age, but his attitudes and ideas are not sentimental nor are they molded by the stereotypical expectations of a white audience.

Johnson deliberately tried to devote almost all of *Songs of the Soil* to his people by representing "the Negro life in the rural districts of the South." He considered this volume a distinct departure from his previous books, which he called "attempts at versification in the language of the academies and colleges." In *Songs of the Soil* he said he "cast aside the English of the Victorians and assume[d] the language of the plantation and levee." Unfortunately he incorrectly associated this language with the literary plantation dialect, failing to see, as James Weldon Johnson, Countee Cullen, Langston Hughes, and Sterling Brown did later, that this style was not truly representative of Negro speech but was a limited entertainment style with what James Weldon Johnson was to call only two stops—pathos and humor—a style conditioned by the minstrel stage rather than shaped by the hand of the poet. Dunbar's employment of the form had not

been able to inject the true accents of Negro speech and experience, or to stretch its emotional expressiveness beyond those two flat emotions.

For whatever reasons—perhaps lack of sustained contact with folk speech, ways, and music—Fenton Johnson did not discover the limitations of plantation dialect until later in his career. Instead he sought to combine the plantation-dialect style with the concerns of Georgian poets, who, according to Johnson, were seeking romance in their environment. Johnson found a wealth of such romance in the traditions and emotions of his people and prefaced this volume about his people with an analysis of their characteristics. To Johnson his people experienced sorrow and humor more powerfully than others and experienced religion with a particular intensity which made God and the devil actual beings and the vision of the judgment day real. As he would try to do in this volume and through his spiritual poems, Johnson insisted that a writer who wanted to sing of Negroes had to do so by drawing his inspiration from the soil of their religious sensibility.

The introduction to *Songs of the Soil* revealed more than Johnson's new poetic deliberation about rooting his songs in his people's sensibilities; it revealed growing critical and social pressures on Johnson. While acknowledging again the kind reviews of critics who had remarked upon his double language, his introduction indicates his awareness that his dual style had become controversial by late 1915. More and more black poets and readers were beginning to consider so-called poetic language restrictive and the dialect representation of blacks degrading. Johnson refused to bow to that pressure, although he admitted its power, saying that, while some "bitterly oppose the writing of dialect," he believed "unless one gains inspiration from the crudest of his fellows, the greatest of his kind cannot be elevated." Yet, he added, "I do not hope to complete my career as merely a singer of the plantation." Johnson hoped to unearth what he called the "wealth of buried Negro tradition" and to present it in a form so attractive that people would realize that the Negro had a history and was something more than a peasant. Perhaps his fervent desire to prove that, despite their unlettered speech, black people close to the soil had a noble tradition blinded Johnson to the limitations of the plantation-dialect style and its true origins. Nonetheless he never created the sentimental nostalgia which so weakens much dialect poetry. What he did want to believe was that "Race prejudice is not a product of the soil but of propagandists who attempt to keep a political balance in the South." Believing that the black and white masses would love one another but were being manipulated by Southern politicians and propagandists, Johnson trusted the language of the dialect style and the academies of his time perhaps because he, at this point, trusted the basic motivations of all mankind.

While, according to Johnson, the primarily plantation-dialect poems in *Songs of the Soil* were successful with reviewers, none of his dialect poems ever reached a wider audience or achieved the reputation of those by Dunbar or the "coon lyrics" of James Weldon Johnson. Fenton Johnson's spiritual poems (some of which were included in *Songs of the Soil* and reached a broader audience through Monroe's *Poetry* magazine, her anthologies, and later anthologies of black poetry) were the first genuinely powerful attempts to communicate some of the essence of spirituals in a purely literary form. Increasingly the public was interested in the truth about people's folkways; and these nondialect poems caught more of the flavor of the images, the repetitions, the vivid living faith, and the dramatic personages from the oral tradition of black spirituals and sermons than Johnson's deliberately misspelled, pseudofolksy, rhymed dialect poems. Only about four poems in *Songs of the Soil* succeeded in giving beautiful form to the treasures of his people's heritage.

Returning to Chicago in 1916, Johnson was affected by World War I (in "The Story of Myself," published in *Tales of Darkest America*, 1920, he keyed events in his life to important battles). He tried to break new ground with his writing and to change the popular conception of literature by founding and publishing several magazines, the most important of which was the *Favorite Magazine*. He tells of writing almost all the stories and poems in that periodical, as well as supporting it financially, with the assistance of his friend James Moody. While he had personal good fortune in meeting and marrying a woman he loved, Johnson was ultimately unable to sustain his magazine ventures. The times, marked by virulent racism in an era often referred to as the nadir of black American experience (the government's repressive attitude is apparent in documents such as the Hoover Report on Negro Radicalism of 1919), as well as Johnson's lack of adequate financial resources, contributed to the demise of his magazine. Trying to save the *Favorite Magazine* he had an unforgettable personal experience with racism. He could not get a surety bond on his aunt's estate to keep the magazine going because, in the firm's words, "colored people's es-

tates were too risky." In addition, he seemed to feel pressured to become a radical if he were to retain his and his magazine's reputation with some of his audience. He remarked that his refusal "to sell his soul" to the "agitators of Bolshevism" had "brought unpopularity to the magazine among a certain class." Having worked so hard and failed for reasons which seemed unrelated to his literary expertise, Johnson turned to politics himself, trying to help alleviate the effects of racism by acting upon his ideas about how a proper relationship among the races might solve the problem of law and order. In late 1919 or early 1920 he went to New York briefly to found the Reconciliation Movement, based on the idea of the cooperation of all races. In those heated days, with widespread paranoia about radicals and black Americans living in cities (expressed in a wave of white violence directed against them which reached its height in the "Red Summer riots of 1919") there seemed to be little audience among blacks or whites for Johnson's approach.

As he wrote "The Story of Myself," the introduction to his last self-published book, a volume of short stories titled *Tales of Darkest America* (1920), Johnson depicted himself in a far different light from the optimistic, strong, if humble man presented in his previous volumes. He described himself as an idealist in despair. In 1920, he wrote, he faced ruin and starvation, the death of his magazine because of debt, the death of his dream of a reconciliation movement because Americans had no desire to reconcile the races, and the death of his dream of success in literature because all his work was rejected by standard magazines and because he always had to "climb over the barrier of race" to even begin to have his work considered. Johnson sounded like a defeated man. Concluding this introduction to a small group of literarily undistinguished short stories, Johnson said that he had lived for the highest good, had injured no man, woman, or child, and prayed that his wife and James Moody would not suffer if his struggle should end in his death. Such a conclusion makes Johnson sound almost suicidal, but he had enough personal and literary resources to continue the struggle, even though he published no more books after 1920.

After Johnson's return to Chicago in 1916, Harriet Monroe had published five of his spiritual poems in *Poetry* and she and Alice Corbin Henderson included three of these poems in the 1923 and 1932 editions of their anthology *The New Poetry*. In January and February 1919 *Others*, edited by Alfred Kreymborg, published some of Johnson's free-verse poems on urban life, which represented his absorption of some of the stylistic innovations introduced by Masters and Sandburg and his adaptation of these techniques to black urban life. In the January issue Kreymborg included Johnson's "Tired," now his best-known poem, in which a man fed up with living according to other people's sense of "civilization" comes to life in authentic accents. Published in the next issue were other memorable poetic portraits of characters in various stages of defeat: "Aunt Hannah Jackson," "Aunt Jane Allen," "The Gambler," "The Barber," and "The Drunkard." Written in a powerful free-verse style that dramatically recreated the voice of black people more appropriately than dialect, these poems struck a note of weariness and despair, a despair echoed in "The Artist," which appeared in the April-May 1919 issue of *Others*. Johnson might have been using his own fatigue and despair in writing these lines from "The Artist": "Who cares to hear my song of this wonderful world?/Who cares?" Still, he was pressing on, just as some of his characters were still struggling and living.

After 1920, without financial resources, Johnson continued to have his work published by attracting the notice of others. James Weldon Johnson included "Tired" along with the new poems "Children of the Sun," "The New Day," "The Banjo Player," and "The Scarlet Woman" in his *The Book of American Negro Poetry* (1922), observing that Johnson had turned effectively to "formless forms" and was striking a powerful new note of "fatalistic despair" with "tremendous power." Lamenting Johnson's ten-year silence in the 1931 revised edition, to which he added "Lines from 'The Vision of Lazarus,'" James Weldon Johnson also suggested that this "fatalistic despair" was "in some degree" "foreign to any philosophy of life the Negro in America had ever preached or practiced." These later poems, then, which might have been part of the lost "African Nights" manuscript, were written between about 1917 and the late 1920s but never published in a collected form. Other anthologies of the 1920s, such as Robert Kerlin's *Negro Poets and Their Poems* (1923), White and Jackson's *An Anthology of Verse by American Negroes* (1924), and Countee Cullen's *Caroling Dusk* (1927), included poems from *A Little Dreaming* or the *Favorite Magazine*, or unpublished earlier poems rather than these free-verse pieces. In a statement for Cullen's anthology, Johnson continued to sound a note of discouragement with his personal and literary fortunes: "My complete autobiography I promise to the world when I am able to realize that I have done something."

Like James Weldon Johnson, Alfred Kreymborg found that Fenton Johnson's best poems come from his later rather than his earlier work and included some in his *An Anthology of American Poetry* (1930). But after the appearance of James Weldon Johnson's revision of his anthology in 1931, publication of Fenton Johnson's work essentially ceased until the surge of interest in collecting the work of black poets began in the late 1940s. Johnson worked for the Federal Writers' Project in Chicago during the Depression and completed another unpublished collection of poems, "The Daily Grind: 41 WPA Poems," a copy of which is held by Fisk University, and then disappeared entirely from the literary scene. He died in 1958, having apparently written no poetry since the 1930s. Arna Bontemps, author, editor, collector of black cultural memorabilia, and the head of the Fisk library, published some of the previously unpublished poems in Fisk's collection *American Negro Poetry* (1963), making available for the first time some of the 1930s WPA works, including "The Daily Grind," "The World Is a Mighty Ogre," and "A Negro Peddler's Song" (in an authentic folk voice), "The Old Repair Man," and "Counting."

Fenton Johnson remains a rather obscure poet, overshadowed by earlier poets such as Paul Laurence Dunbar and by later poets such as James Weldon Johnson, Langston Hughes, and Sterling Brown. Johnson is almost entirely known for about fifteen anthologized poems; in fact, "Tired" is the single poem by which many readers know him. On that basis he is usually considered a minor poet, someone who responded, somewhat tardily, to the spirit of the times among the black urban poor, but lacked the ability to turn that response into sustained poetic achievement. Considering the times during which he tried to make his way as a poet who sang of his people, times which included the most virulent expressions of racial hatred and the Great Depression, and considering his own reversals of fortune, it seems remarkable that Johnson was able to write even a handful of living poems, poems that continue to strike the hearts of poets and readers. All his critics, even the most severe, agree that "Tired" and "The Scarlet Woman" powerfully embody an archetypal Afro-American urban experience in a language that recreates its intensity and uniqueness and moves the reader to feel the bleak despair of being trapped inside a dream that is not deferred but dead. That achievement is not what Johnson envisioned for himself, but his accomplishment is nonetheless significant.

References:
Sterling A. Brown, *Negro Poetry and Drama* (Washington, D.C.: Associates in Negro Folk Education, 1937), pp. 61-62;
James P. Hutchinson, "Fenton Johnson: Pilgrim of the Dusk," *Studies in Black Literature*, 7 (Autumn 1976): 14-15;
Jay Saunders Redding, *To Make a Poet Black* (Chapel Hill: University of North Carolina Press, 1939), pp. 85-88;
Eugene B. Redmond, *Drumvoices: The Mission of Afro-American Poetry, A Critical History* (Garden City: Anchor/Doubleday, 1976), pp. 165-168;
Jean Wagner, *Black Poets of the United States from Paul Laurence Dunbar to Langston Hughes*, translated by Kenneth Douglas (Urbana, Chicago & London: University of Illinois Press, 1973), pp. 179-183.

Papers:
The Negro Collection at Fisk University Library has copies of manuscripts for unpublished poems, including "The Daily Grind: 41 WPA Poems."

Eugene Jolas
(26 October 1894-26 May 1952)

Stephen Scobie
University of Victoria

See also the Jolas entry in *DLB 4, American Writers in Paris, 1920-1939.*

BOOKS: *Cinema* (New York: Adelphi, 1926);
Secession in Astropolis (Paris: Black Sun Press, 1929);
Epivocables of 3 (Paris: Editions Vertigral, 1932);
Hypnolog des Scheitelauges (Paris: Editions Vertigral, 1932);
The Language of Night (The Hague: Servire, 1932);
Mots-déluges: Hypnologues (Paris: Editions des Cahiers Libres, 1933);
Vertigralist Pamphlet (Paris: Transition Press, 1938);
I Have Seen Monsters and Angels (Paris: Transition Press, 1938);
Planets and Angels (Mount Vernon, Iowa: English Club of Cornell College, 1940);
Vertical: A Yearbook for Romantic-Mystic Ascensions (New York: Gotham Bookmart Press, 1941);
Words from the Deluge (New York: Distributed by Gotham Bookmart, 1941);
Wanderpoem; or Angelic Mythamorphosis of the City of London (Paris: Transition Press, 1946).

OTHER: *Transition Workshop*, edited by Jolas (New York: Vanguard, 1949).

As the editor of *transition*, the most important and influential of the expatriate magazines of the 1920s and 1930s, Eugene Jolas must be accounted a major figure in the literary history of the modernist period. As a poet, Jolas is of considerably less importance, though still of some interest. In his writing he attempted to provide examples of the kind of poetry he called for in his editorials and manifestos; he wished in fact to be the kind of writer published in *transition*. But his earnest efforts to experiment with poetic language and form remained too often at the level of surface imitation.

Jolas's parents came from Lorraine, an area whose ownership was disputed, and frequently fought over, between France and Germany; the split was reflected within the family itself, Jolas's mother speaking German and his father speaking French. They had immigrated to America, where Jolas was born, in Union-Hill, New Jersey, but they returned to Lorraine when Jolas was only two. This divided national and linguistic inheritance was to be of supreme importance to Jolas's later views. His most important statement on the topic comes from his widely quoted preface to *I Have Seen Monsters and Angels* (1938):

> I did not see my native America again
> until I was almost seventeen years old, and

Eugene Jolas, 1915

I had to learn my native language paradoxically in the diaspora-wilderness of the legendary immigrant.
....
     Twice, within half a century, my childhood-town has changed hands politically.
     The frontier-fear is a primordial emotion in the unconscious of my people.
     This history-haunted region . . . was, for many years, the source of many of my dreams.

The young Jolas briefly considered the priesthood, and, though he was not an orthodox believer, a religious sense permeates his writings. Instead, in 1910 he returned to America; he served in the army from 1916 to 1920 and then resumed an intermittent career as a journalist in Pittsburgh, in New York, and in Waterbury, Connecticut. At this time he was beginning to write poems, many of which appeared in his first collection, *Cinema*, published in New York in 1926. One of the best poems in this first book, "Reporters," reflects his newspaper experience. Much of it consists of fast, collagelike flashes of newspaper headlines:

    a maniac kills detectives
    Maine elects a new governor
    an aviator crashes to death
    Hollywood scandals
    five are killed
    by zero weather in New Hampshire.

Yet a fantastic or religious tone alternates with the realism: "Christ wanders through the editorial rooms," and the reporters are described as "evangelists of misery . . . cynical father confessors."

    By the time *Cinema* came out, Jolas had returned to Europe, and in 1924 he began his association with the Paris *Tribune* (the European edition of the *Chicago Tribune*), for which he worked as city editor, also contributing many articles on art and literary topics, including interviews and reviews that introduced the paper's American readers to French writers such as Jean Giraudoux, André Gide, Philippe Soupault, and André Breton. Jolas also promoted the works of American authors such as Sherwood Anderson, Ezra Pound, and Eugene O'Neill.

    In January 1926 Jolas married Maria McDonald, who had been born in Louisville, Kentucky, and had gone to Europe to study voice. The marriage took place in New York, but the couple soon returned to France; in 1927 they moved into a house outside Paris, in Colombey-Les-Deux-Eglises, a house later to be occupied by Charles de Gaulle.

    Meanwhile, in the autumn of 1926, Jolas had begun the magazine on which his reputation chiefly and deservedly rests. The first twelve numbers of *transition* were coedited by Jolas and Elliot Paul, who also worked for the *Tribune*. Together Paul and Jolas sought out distinguished contributors for their first issue and scored something of a coup in securing material from both James Joyce and Gertrude Stein. Indeed, *transition* was for several years one of the few forums in which these two loftily distant giants appeared together—at least until Jolas's major falling out with Stein after the publication of *The Autobiography of Alice B. Toklas* (1933), which resulted in the special supplement to *transition* 23, "Testimony Against Gertrude Stein."

    The magazine *transition* (the lower case "t"

used as a deliberate provocation to conservative critics) published important work by the finest writers of the age—including Joyce, Stein, Hart Crane, Samuel Beckett, and Dylan Thomas—as well as photographs of an impressive selection of art works by equally eminent painters—such as Juan Gris, Kurt Schwitters, Man Ray, Hans Arp, Pablo Picasso, and Georges Braque. But it was also, and became increasingly, a platform for Jolas's views on culture and poetry. These views were expressed through editorials and manifestos; through his own poems; and through several special "Inquiries," in which a wide array of writers were asked to answer loaded questions such as "Do you believe that, in the present world crisis, the Revolution of Language is necessary in order to hasten the re-integration of human personality?"

Jolas's position may be defined broadly as visionary and neo-Romantic. "In its eternal essence," he wrote in 1940, "poetry draws from the same sources as the mystic experience. It is a psychic operation with aerial projections. It tends towards a cosmic consciousness. It wants a transcendental awareness in an ultimate illumination" ("Verticalism," foreword to *Planets and Angels*). He believed passionately in the importance of dreams as a key to mystical insight and poetic inspiration. Yet he distrusted Freud, though he was attracted to and published works by Jung. He despised many aspects of modern society—its soulless mechanization, its industrial drabness—yet he eagerly embraced the new and the experimental in literature. An editorial statement in the third issue proclaims that "*transition* will attempt to present the quintessence of the modern spirit in evolution. . . . We believe in the ideology of revolt against all diluted and synthetic poetry, against all artistic efforts that fail to subvert the existing concepts of beauty. . . . We believe that there is no hope for poetry unless there be disintegration first. We need new words, new abstractions, new hieroglyphics, new symbols, new myths."

Such "new words" were to be found, most obviously, in Joyce's *Work In Progress* (published as *Finnegans Wake* in 1939), episodes of which appeared regularly in *transition*. Jolas, with his own multilingual background, was especially sympathetic to this form of linguistic experimentation. The most famous (or infamous) summation of the *transition* ideology is to be found in the "proclamation" of the "Revolution of the Word," which appeared in *transition* 16/17, in 1929.

The language of Jolas's manifestos and theoretical proclamations—lofty, rhetorical, abstract,

and vague—is also, all too often, the language of his poetry. The characteristic quality of "Reporters"—imagery, however surrealistic, grounded in the observed details of a particular situation—is not a recurring feature of Jolas's writing. The title poem of *Cinema* is full of passages such as:

night thoughts hungered
blossoms fluttered into your hair
a moon stood in a static trance
hallucinated we gazed into delirious eyes
pity shook enigmas

Not much had changed by 1938, as Jolas's major collection of poetry, *I Have Seen Monsters and Angels*, shows:

we drink wine to the midnight of our laughter
and our heads sink into the whiteness of our stars
that are full of tears
our pilgrimage ends in the yellow valley where
strangers wait with blinded eyes and with hands
shaking
in hunger for golden lunacies dark sounds float
into our throats with strange dynamoes

Not much is to be gained from such writing except a generalized impression of surrealistic incongruency, impassioned obscurity, and a willed determination to appear profound. The young Canadian writer John Glassco, who arrived in Paris in 1928 with Jolas and *transition* among his gods, soon confessed to disillusionment with surrealism, in terms which remain a damning indictment of what happens when a vision becomes a fashion: "I was struck by a certain sameness and monotony of treatment and even of syntax, above all by the reiteration of the heavy mallet-like grammatical constructions . . . where an endless number of out-of-the-way objects were placed in apposition to adjectives and verbs to which they had no relation but that of surprise."

Jolas's poetry becomes more interesting, however, in form at least, when he pushes his experimentation to deeper, more radical linguistic levels. *I Have Seen Monsters and Angels* contains, in the section entitled "Logos, Poetry of the Night," a variety of experimental poems under such headings as "Hypnologues," "Neo-Logos," "Incantations," and "Trilingual Poems."

In "Hypnologues" and "Neo-Logos" Jolas experiments with coinages, new words formed by compounding old ones or by juxtaposing familiar forms with nonsense syllables. In "Magna Mater,"

PROCLAMATION

TIRED OF THE SPECTACLE OF SHORT STORIES, NOVELS, POEMS AND PLAYS STILL UNDER THE HEGEMONY OF THE BANAL WORD, MONOTONOUS SYNTAX, STATIC PSYCHOLOGY, DESCRIPTIVE NATURALISM, AND DESIROUS OF CRYSTALLIZING A VIEWPOINT...

WE HEREBY DECLARE THAT :

1. THE REVOLUTION IN THE ENGLISH LANGUAGE IS AN ACCOMPLISHED FACT.

2. THE IMAGINATION IN SEARCH OF A FABULOUS WORLD IS AUTONOMOUS AND UNCONFINED.
(*Prudence is a rich, ugly old maid courted by Incapacity...* Blake)

3. PURE POETRY IS A LYRICAL ABSOLUTE THAT SEEKS AN A PRIORI REALITY WITHIN OURSELVES ALONE.
(*Bring out number, weight and measure in a year of dearth...* Blake)

4. NARRATIVE IS NOT MERE ANECDOTE, BUT THE PROJECTION OF A METAMORPHOSIS OF REALITY.
(*Enough ! Or Too Much !...* Blake)

5. THE EXPRESSION OF THESE CONCEPTS CAN BE ACHIEVED ONLY THROUGH THE RHYTHMIC " HALLUCINATION OF THE WORD ". (Rimbaud).

6. THE LITERARY CREATOR HAS THE RIGHT TO DISINTEGRATE THE PRIMAL MATTER OF WORDS IMPOSED ON HIM BY TEXT-BOOKS AND DICTIONARIES.
(*The road of excess leads to the palace of Wisdom...* Blake)

7. HE HAS THE RIGHT TO USE WORDS OF HIS OWN FASHIONING AND TO DISREGARD EXISTING GRAMMATICAL AND SYNTACTICAL LAWS.
(*The tigers of wrath are wiser than the horses of instruction...* Blake)

8. THE " LITANY OF WORDS " IS ADMITTED AS AN INDEPENDENT UNIT.

9. WE ARE NOT CONCERNED WITH THE PROPAGATION OF SOCIOLOGICAL IDEAS, EXCEPT TO EMANCIPATE THE CREATIVE ELEMENTS FROM THE PRESENT IDEOLOGY.

10. TIME IS A TYRANNY TO BE ABOLISHED.

11. THE WRITER EXPRESSES. HE DOES NOT COMMUNICATE.

12. THE PLAIN READER BE DAMNED.
(*Damn braces ! Bless relaxes !...* Blake)

— *Signed* : KAY BOYLE, WHIT BURNETT, HART CRANE, CARESSE CROSBY, HARRY CROSBY, MARTHA FOLEY, STUART GILBERT, A. L. GILLESPIE, LEIGH HOFFMAN, EUGENE JOLAS, ELLIOT PAUL, DOUGLAS RIGBY, THEO RUTRA, ROBERT SAGE, HAROLD J. SALEMSON, LAURENCE VAIL.

The "Revolution of the Word" proclamation in transition 16/17. *Jolas included his pseudonym "Theo Rutra" among the signators. The Blake quotations were provided by Stuart Gilbert.*

for instance, the combinations are fairly obvious and easy to follow:

> I saw the lustreyes upon her shineface moongleam-
> glowing
> nearer she came snowthudding through the quarter-
> light
> love-palsied shook the olivetrees the pneumawoman
> stopped.

"Earthgore" takes the technique much farther:

> Globes concussdance in mist. The sparklers
> flook and flake. A motor gurrs. Flimgored the
> comets zish in brail.

. . . .
> A revoluzzing glout. The storm in stala grims.
> Halt flows the singer's ring and bant. Space gloo-
> gloos catastrafing cassocked breasts of bray.

If the influence of Joyce is obvious here, in "Incantations" Jolas follows the example of Hugo Ball (whose "Lautgedichte" he had published in *transition*) and moves completely into the realm of invented, nonsense, or "abstract" neologisms, as in "Mountain Words":

> mira ool dara frim
> oasta grala drima
> os tristomeen.

Eugene Jolas and James Joyce (photograph by Giselle Freund). Jolas is holding the last issue of transition, *published in 1938.*

ala grool in rosa
alsabrume
lorabim
masaloo
blueheart of a

roolata gasta
miralotimbana
allatin
juanilama

Such incantations of pure sound, bypassing the rational levels of discourse to appeal directly to the emotions, form part of a continuing tradition of sound poetry, which was to be strongly revived in the 1960s and 1970s, long after Jolas's death, in the context of the international concrete poetry movement.

The "Trilingual Poems" are more straightforward. Jolas's three languages—English, French,

and German—are used in alternation, paragraph by paragraph, sentence by sentence, or word by word: "c'est le moment when l'opulence der liebessuechte finds its firegrammar sans les entraves des discours." The final poem in the book, "Planets and Angels," runs for three pages in French, then two in German, then three in English. The final lines, however, show that the linguistic experimentation of the surface form has not altered the rhetoric (insofar as it is comprehensible) of the content:

We grow huge and visionary
We play with spiral nebulae
With the angelic spheres
And ride upward
In a vertigo of fire-streams

We swarm in stellar dew
We are racing through burst-flames
Into a time without frontiers.

The final issue of *transition* appeared in 1938 and was followed in 1939 by the greatest exemplar of its aesthetic, Joyce's *Finnegans Wake*—whose final title Jolas had correctly guessed. In 1940 Jolas returned to America and worked during the war for the United States Office of War Information. Although he returned to Europe after the war and was associated with the publication of *Transition Forty-Eight*, which was edited by Georges Duthuit, there was no question of reviving the magazine, and his last publication of his own poetry was in 1946. He was working on his autobiography and on translations of Novalis when he died in Paris in 1952.

References:

John Glassco, *Memoirs of Montparnasse* (Toronto: Oxford University Press, 1970);

Dougald McMillan, *transition 1927-38: The History of a Literary Era* (New York: Braziller, 1976).

Joyce Kilmer
(6 December 1886-30 July 1918)

James A. Hart
University of British Columbia

BOOKS: *Summer of Love* (New York: Baker & Taylor, 1911);

Trees and Other Poems (New York: Doran, 1914; London: Duckworth, 1941);

The Circus, and Other Essays (New York: L. J. Gomme, 1916); enlarged as *The Circus, and Other Essays and Fugitive Pieces*, edited by Robert Cortes Holliday (New York: Doran, 1921);

Literature in the Making, by Some of Its Makers (New York & London: Harper, 1917);

The Courage of Enlightenment: An Address (Prairie du Chien, Wis., 1917);

Main Street, and Other Poems (New York: Doran, 1917);

Joyce Kilmer, two volumes, edited by Robert Cortes Holliday (New York: Doran, 1918).

OTHER: *Dreams and Images: An Anthology of Catholic Poets*, edited by Kilmer (New York: Boni & Liveright, 1917);

Francis P. Duffy, *Father Duffy's Story*, includes Kilmer's unfinished history of the 165th Regiment (New York: Doran, 1919).

The immediate reception and the subsequent treatment of Joyce Kilmer's poem "Trees" show to an extreme and disturbing degree the twentieth century's widening gulf between popular and academic tastes. While it is true that "Trees" first

Joyce Kilmer

appeared in *Poetry: A Magazine of Verse* (August 1913), a magazine acclaimed for its early publication of many noteworthy modern poems (including Carl Sandburg's "Chicago" and T. S. Eliot's "The Love Song of J. Alfred Prufrock"), Kilmer's work has never gained the esteem of leading literary critics. Its immense and world-wide popularity has been with more ordinary, less exalted readers. Still recollected fondly seventy years after its publication, it appears in textbooks and anthologies—if it appears at all—only to be ridiculed. Fortunately, Kilmer was a more interesting and accomplished writer than "Trees" suggests.

Alfred Joyce Kilmer spoke of himself as half-Irish, perhaps seeing his natural exuberance and love of food and company as manifestations of the Celtic spirit, but his ancestry was predominantly English and German. His father, Frederick Barnett Kilmer, was a professional chemist, his mother, Annie Kilburn Kilmer, a minor writer and composer. Born in New Brunswick, New Jersey, Joyce Kilmer attended Rutgers College (1904-1906) and Columbia University (A.B., 1908). Upon graduation in June 1908, he married Aline Murray, stepdaughter of Henry Mills Alden, the editor of *Harper's Monthly*, and earned his livelihood for a year as a Latin teacher at the Morristown, New Jersey, high school.

Attracted to New York City, he developed his skills as a magazine writer, particularly as a reviewer and editor. From 1909 to 1912 he was on the staff of the *Standard Dictionary*, involved in preparing new and revised definitions, a task which he did with gusto and proficiency. During the same period he was writing his early verse, much of which appeared in his first volume, *Summer of Love* (1911). In later years, he regretted the absence of the Catholic spirit in these poems and recognized their technical weaknesses. The sonnets, ballades, and lyrics have a sweet sensuousness, but often they will not bear analysis. In poems such as "Ballade of My Lady's Beauty" sound and fondness for the "poetic" phrase and reference dominate:

> To Venus some folk tribute pay
> And Queen of Beauty she is night,
> And Sainte Marie the world doth sway
> In cerule napery bedight.

The influence of William Butler Yeats and the Celtic Revival was obvious in many of the poems.

In 1912 he was literary editor for the Episcopal magazine *Churchman*, but the following year he obtained a more lucrative position with the Sun-day magazine and book-review sections of the *New York Times*.

National recognition came in August 1913 with the publication of "Trees" in *Poetry*. The combination of sweet sentiment and simple philosophy expressed in apparently pellucid language (characteristic of many of his poems) made the poem memorable and widely quoted. After it was set to music by his mother and published in her *Whimsical Whimsies* (1927), it became dear to millions.

The opening lines—"I think that I shall never see/A poem as lovely as a tree"—launched Kilmer on his metaphorical voyage, which continued with: "A tree whose hungry mouth is prest/Against the earth's sweet flowing breast. . . ." Kilmer doggedly kept to his metaphor, describing the tree's leafy, upraised arms, its robin-nested hair, and finally its snow-covered bosom. One need not be a rigid New Critic demanding cohesive analogy to be discomfited (or amused) by the anatomical absurdities of Kilmer's tree. The final lines are so unwittingly apt that one may fleetingly think the author is playing a joke: "Poems are made by fools like me,/But only God can make a tree."

With "Trees" Kilmer became a well-known poet and journalist. In a practiced, lively, and fluent style, he wrote reams of journalism. He managed the poetry sections of the *Literary Digest* and *Current Literature*, lectured on literature (there was something of the actor in his make-up), and wrote essays and prefaces on various authors.

In the fall of 1913, deeply moved by the infantile paralysis of his daughter Rose, he became a fervent convert from Episcopalianism to Roman Catholicism. Thereafter his writings—letters, essays, and poems—have frequent references to his new faith. He seemed, indeed, to desire an old form of Catholicism, as is shown in his 9 January 1914 letter to Father James Daly: "I need some stricter discipline, I think, and it's hard to get it. I enjoyed Father Cullen's direction very much, he is a fine Irishman with no nonsense about him. . . . And I wish I had some medieval confessor—the sort of person one reads about in anti-Catholic books—who would inflict real penance. The saying of Hail Marys and Our Fathers is no penance, it's a delight."

His fervent, often joyous Catholicism is apparent in many of his poems; and in his letters he worries—not always with full seriousness—about the offense a priest might receive from the language in some of his poems: "I've written to my long-suffering confessor to ask whether or not I can let characters in my plays and poems 'cuss,' " humorously calling it "vicarious profanity."

Trees and Other Poems (1914) demonstrates some advance in Kilmer's poetic skills, though the poems reflect the influence of earlier writers, such as the seventeenth-century poets George Herbert, Henry Vaughan, and Richard Crashaw (another convert to Catholicism), as well as the more recent A. E. Housman, Edwin Arlington Robinson, and Coventry Patmore (also a convert). Indeed Kilmer's debt to these poets is so noticeable that his poetry has been labeled "a broken bundle of mirrors," a phrase that implies not only a multiplicity of influences but also a failure to develop his own style and personality. Some of the echoes were unconscious, but Kilmer deliberately patterned works on Patmore's.

Despite Kilmer's outward bonhomie, he was occasionally intolerant, even inhumane, in his poems. His reaction to the suicide of a young poet is vividly, but callously, conveyed in these lines from "To a Young Poet Who Killed Himself," put into the mouths of grave worms:

> The fight was on—you ran away.
>   You are a coward and a craven.
>
> The rug is ruined where you bled;
>   It was a dirty way to die!

He closes with: "Then don't you feel a little shame?/ And don't you think you were an ass?" In "To Certain Poets" Kilmer expresses scorn for contemporary poets with "aesthetic" or too-delicate natures:

> You little poets mincing there
> With women's hearts and women's hair!
> . . . .
> Your tiny voices mock God's wrath
> You snails that crawl along his path!
> Why, what has God or man to do
> With wet, amorphous things like you?

Kilmer's next book of poems was preceded by a collection of previously published essays, *The Circus, and Other Essays* (1916), and a series of inter-

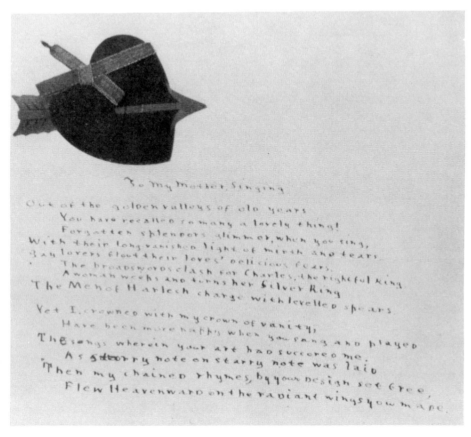

A 1915 Valentine from Kilmer to his mother, the composer who later set "Trees" to music (Annie K. Kilmer,
Memories of My Son, *1920)*

Joyce Kilmer in France, May 1918

enlisted as a private in the 7th Regiment of the New York National Guard and later transferred to the 165th Regiment. (He began writing a historical account of his regiment in France, but it was unfinished when he was killed.) Unwilling to take time to undergo officer training, he was proud of his rise to the rank of sergeant. His letters show him to be an earnest and enthusiastic soldier, welcoming new experiences. There is sadness but also acceptance in the declamatory lines of "Rouge Bouquet":

> There is on earth no worthier grave
> To hold the bodies of the brave
> Than this place of pain and pride
> Where they nobly fought and nobly died.

His Catholicism and painful wartime experiences combined to produce some of his best verse in "Prayer of a Soldier in France," a poem through which the reader may painfully stagger with Kilmer and Christ along the *via dolorosa* of World War I:

> My shoulders ache beneath my pack
> (Lie easier, Cross, upon His back).
>
> I march with feet that burn and smart
> (Tread, Holy Feet, upon my heart).
>
> Men shout at me who may not speak
> (They scourged Thy back and smote Thy cheek).

Volunteering to take the place of a slain officer during an attack on the hills above the Ourcq, Kilmer went out to scout machine-gun nests. On 30 July 1918, he was found dead with an enemy bullet through his head. For his bravery he was buried beside officers, mentioned in dispatches, and posthumously awarded the Croix de Guerre. He was survived by his wife, Aline (who became a minor poet), and four children.

The memory of Kilmer's ebullient personality and his courage has dimmed as the decades have gone by, and much of his verse is forgotten and derided; but he merits some remembrance for his idealism and valor and for one or two significant poems.

views with literary personages, such as William Dean Howells, Amy Lowell, and Edwin Arlington Robinson, *Literature in the Making* (1917). The verse in *Main Street, and Other Poems* (1917) is mellower and more varied. Readers sympathetic to his moral and religious preoccupations (such as Father Daly and the reviewer in *Catholic World*) praised his warmth and versatility, but there were others, such as Conrad Aiken, who still thought his verse facile and his ideas secondhand.

He wrote about contemporary events in "Easter Week" (in memory of Irish patriot Joseph Mary Plunkett, executed for his part in the Easter Week Rebellion of 1916) and in the few World War I poems. The interestingly varied lines of "The Cathedral of Rheims" probably owe much to Émile Verhaeren; and "The White Ships and the Red" was written in response to the sinking of the *Lusitania*, an event that made Kilmer—like so many of his countrymen—more sympathetic toward the cause of the Allies.

When the United States entered the war, Kilmer went to an officers' training camp, but he soon

References:

Katherine M. C. Brégy, *Poets and Pilgrims, from Geoffrey Chaucer to Paul Claudel* (New York: Benziger, 1925);

Harry J. Cargas, *I Lay Down My Life* (St. Paul, Minn.: St. Paul Editions, 1964);

James J. Daly, *A Cheerful Ascetic and Other Essays* (Milwaukee: Bruce Publishing, 1931);

Robert Cortes Holliday, "Memoir," in *Joyce Kilmer*, edited by Holliday (New York: Doran, 1918), I: 17-101;

Annie Kilburn Kilmer, *Memories of My Son, Sergeant Joyce Kilmer* (New York: Brentano's, 1920).

Papers:
The Alderman Library at the University of Virginia, the Houghton Library at Harvard University, and the Manuscripts Division of the Library of Congress have collections of Kilmer's papers.

Haniel Long

(9 March 1888-17 October 1956)

Shelley Armitage
West Texas State University

BOOKS: *Poems* (New York: Moffat, Yard, 1920);

Notes for a New Mythology (Chicago: Bookfellows, 1926);

Atlantides (Santa Fe: Writers' Editions, 1933);

Pittsburgh Memoranda (Santa Fe: Writers' Editions, 1935);

Interlinear to Cabeza de Vaca: His Relation of the Journey from Florida to the Pacific, 1528-1536 (Santa Fe: Writers' Editions, 1936); republished as *The Power Within Us: Cabeza de Vaca's Relation of His Journey from Florida to the Pacific, 1528-1536* (New York: Duell, Sloan & Pearce, 1944; London: Drummond, 1946); republished, with an abridged version of *Malinche*, as *The Marvelous Adventure of Cabeza de Vaca also Malinche* (London: Souvenir Press, 1972; New York: Ballantine, 1973);

Walt Whitman and the Springs of Courage (Santa Fe: Writers' Editions, 1938);

Malinche (Doña Marina) (Santa Fe: Rydal Press, 1939);

Piñon Country (New York: Duell, Sloan & Pearce, 1941);

French Soldier (Santa Fe: Santa Fe Press, 1942);

Children, Students, and a Few Adults (Santa Fe: Santa Fe Press, 1942);

The Grist Mill (Santa Fe: Rydal Press, 1945; revised, 1946);

A Letter to St. Augustine after Re-reading His Confessions (New York: Duell, Sloan & Pearce, 1950);

Spring Returns (New York: Pantheon, 1958);

If He Can Make Her So, edited by Ron Caplan (Pittsburgh: Frontier Press, 1968);

My Seasons, edited by James H. Maguire (Bonse: Ahsahta Press, 1977).

PERIODICAL PUBLICATIONS:
POETRY

"The Ides of March," *Poetry: A Magazine of Verse,* 7 (December 1915): 133;

"On the Road," *Poetry: A Magazine of Verse,* 12 (May 1918): 83, 89;

"The Four Girls of Zuni" and "An Indian," *Southwest Review,* 11 (October 1925): 69;

"To a Friend," *Nation,* 122 (6 January 1926): 14;

"Letter After a Visit," *Nation,* 125 (6 July 1927): 18;

"The Heart is a Vine," *New Mexico Quarterly,* 3 (1933): 222;

"Easter 1933," *Poetry: A Magazine of Verse,* 43 (December 1933): 138-140;

"Midnight Talk," *Space,* 1 (September 1934): 62;

"Gust of Wind," *New Mexico Quarterly,* 5 (1935): 96;

"Letter," *New Mexico Quarterly,* 5 (1935): 160;

"Web of Dew," *New Mexico Quarterly,* 5 (1935): 93;

"The Sexes" and "Into Delphiniums," *New Mexico Quarterly,* 7 (1937): 189;

"Another Harvest," *New Republic,* 92 (25 August 1937): 77;

"Hall of Mirrors," *Survey Graphic,* 28 (May 1939): 337;

"New Mexico Fire Place," *Southwest Review,* 28 (Autumn 1942): 201;

"The Green Gate," *Southwest Review,* 30 (Summer 1946): 292.

NONFICTION

"The Passing of George Meredith," *Harvard Monthly,* 48 (June 1909): 135-139;

"Young Heart," *New Mexico Quarterly,* 3 (1933): 256-257;

"Sonata of the Heart," *Space,* 1 (May 1934): 1-3;

"Sketch Book, *Space,* 1 (June 1934): 16-17;

"Sonata of the Waters," *Space,* 1 (August 1934): 37-40;

Review of *Texas Legacy: Anthology of Texas Poetry,* compiled by Lois Boyle, *New Mexico Quarterly,* 5 (1935): 216-217;

"Decentralization of Publishing," *Southwest Review,* 21 (October 1935): 89-95;

"The Whole Duty of a Young Poet," *Shards: the Poetry Quarterly* (1935);

"The Poets' Round-up," *New Mexico Quarterly,* 6 (1936): 223-225;

"Sandburg," *New Mexico Sentinel,* 20 July 1937;

"Thought and Feeling," *New Mexico Sentinel,* 17 August 1937;

"Robert C. Walker," *New Mexico Sentinel,* 24 August 1937;

"Mr. Merrild on D. H. Lawrence," *New Mexico Sentinel,* 14 September 1937;

"Corn Maiden," *Forum,* 98 (October 1937): 200-202;

Review of *Plays About the Theatre in England from the Rehearsal in 1671 to the Licensing Act in 1737,* by Dane Farnsworth Smith, *New Mexico Quarterly,* 7 (1937): 70-72;

"Thoreau and Friendship," *New Mexico Sentinel,* 27 October 1937;

"Facing Two Ways," *New Mexico Sentinel,* 8 December 1937;

"Recognition of Robert Frost," *New Mexico Sentinel,* 12 January 1938;

"Clinic for Writing," *New Mexico Sentinel,* 19 January 1938;

"Editorial Jottings," *New Mexico Sentinel,* 23 February 1938; 2 March 1938; 20 March 1938; 17 April 1938; 24 April 1938; 8 May 1938; 29 May 1938;

"Editor's Postscript," *New Mexico Sentinel,* 13 April 1938;

"Jottings," *New Mexico Sentinel,* 12 June 1938;

"Letters on Our Birthday," *New Mexico Sentinel,* 24 July 1938;

"Towards the Twentieth Century," *New Mexico Sentinel,* 13 November 1938;

"Fletcher," *New Mexico Sentinel,* 4 December 1938;

"Things on My Mind," *New Mexico Sentinel,* 18 December 1938;

"Jottings in Farewell," *New Mexico Sentinel,* 1 January 1939;

"Printing in the Southwest," *Southwest Review,* 26 (Autumn 1940): 37-49;

"That Man Coronado," *New Mexico Quarterly,* 10 (1940): 87-94.

Because Haniel Long is outside mainstream literary movements and cults, he traditionally is viewed as a minor poet and essayist, whose best-known work, *Interlinear to Cabeza de Vaca* (1936), while it received international attention, further cast him as a regional writer and critic. At least a decade younger than Carl Sandburg, Edgar Lee Masters, and Robert Frost, Long was a contemporary of T. S. Eliot and Ezra Pound. Yet, Long ignored the experimental movement in modern poetry, even though he shared the classical enthusiasms of Eliot and the Chinese interests of Pound. Reviewed retrospectively, Long's poetry—merely out of step with poetic modes considered superior by the New Critics of his time—stands up remarkably well as the chronology of a writer whose work grew out of and matured with his friendships and intellectual background and reflected the influence of his region. Moreover, regionalism, often a disparaging tag attached to would-be major writers, returned Long to sources whose traditions and mythology paralleled some of the most respected intellectual traditions in world literature.

Born in Rangoon, Burma, on 9 March 1888, the son of May Clark Long and Samuel Parker Long, a Methodist missionary, Haniel Clark Long returned to the United States with his parents in 1891. Settling in Pittsburgh and living, by choice, among the poor, the Longs continued to minister to the needs of the indigent and miserable. In Anton Long's words, Haniel as a child "saw Homestead strikers and their families housed and fed in his father's church, saw victims of panic and hard times fed and sheltered there in the middle 1890s, saw his father called by the men of the 18th Regiment, Pennsylvania Volunteers, to be their chaplain in 1898." Later, the family moved to Duluth and Minneapolis, where his father also held pastorates. Long's childhood was traditional. He enjoyed family life with his parents and sisters, and friendships with his cousins, most of whom were girls. In 1903 he was at Exeter; and in 1907, when his family moved to Minneapolis, he entered Harvard.

Long served on the *Advocate* staff with T. S. Eliot, but at the time when T. S. Eliot was busy reading the French symbolists and Ezra Pound was exploring Provençal poetry, Long was forming what was to be the beginning of a lifelong acquaintance with the writings of George Meredith. His memorial essay, "The Passing of George Meredith," won the *Harvard Monthly* Medal in 1909. This essay and a short poem, "The Swimmers," published the same year in the *Youth's Companion*, were Long's first publications. Although its prose style is neither so strong nor rich as Long's later style, the essay is important for his early view of the woman-soul, and it indicates Long's understanding of Meredith's thought. "To me," he wrote, "and I cannot but think to all them who read George Meredith and love him, the greatness of the man lies in his idea of woman." As in Meredith, the spirit of woman is central to Long's work. The following passage from his essay, therefore, is prophetic: "Woman relies on instinct and intuition; she is close to Nature's bosom. It is not surprising, therefore, that she always has been and will be man's inspiration and illumination. The 'democratic virus' is secret in her. Give her free rein, and

the true woman will recognize the rights of individual manhood in defense of station, of reason, of all the ideas inculcated by education and society."

Long also harkened to the wealth of great minds at Harvard; he attended lectures under William James, Josiah Royce, and George Santayana. Perhaps most important, he met Witter Bynner there in the home of Mrs. Celia Mitchell-Keays, a novelist whose sons were friends and classmates of Long's.

After a tenure as editor of *McClure's Magazine*, Bynner had returned to Harvard to begin his writing career. Bynner and Long's friendship grew at three crucial stages of Long's development as a poet: first at Harvard, later in Long's home in Pittsburgh, where Bynner was a frequent guest from 1913 to 1920, and finally in Santa Fe. From 1923 on, Long spent his winters in Pittsburgh and his summers in New Mexico, until in 1929 he permanently settled at the Santa Fe home he had bought in 1924.

In 1909-1910 Long did some of his course work at Harvard in absentia while he worked as a reporter on the *New York Globe and Commercial Advertiser;* after his graduation in 1910 he joined the faculty of the newly opened Carnegie Technology School (now the Carnegie Institute of Technology) in Pittsburgh as an instructor in English. Though plagued by ill health (and especially with eye trouble) he would teach there for nearly thirty years, becoming an assistant professor in 1915, an associate professor in 1920. From 1926 on, for reasons of health, he was a part-time professor. He retired in 1929. Pittsburgh was to become for him what Brooklyn had been for Walt Whitman, or London for Charles Lamb. Slowly it helped to strengthen his poetic being, revealing to him the soul of man in its weary struggle against the forces of industrialism and big business. Pittsburgh became the immediate inspiration for at least two of his books—*Notes for a New Mythology* (1926) and *Pittsburgh Memoranda* (1935). Long knew and loved Pittsburgh intimately and deeply; humanity was his subject. He found it among the furnaces and steel mills of this great soot-stained city of the East.

The years between Long's Harvard days and the publication of *Poems* in 1920 were largely devoted to teaching. Long had little time for writing, often working at it in the earliest hours of the morning, after grading papers and preparing lectures. Other responsibilities had accumulated also. On 12 August 1912 he married Alice Lavinia Knoblauch of Minneapolis and their son, Anton (Tony), was born in 1914. Long's teaching activities brought him many friendships with his students, including Frank Hogan, whose memory has been preserved in the *Pittsburgh Memoranda.*

Witter Bynner's friendship also deeply affected Long during the years from 1913 to 1920 when Bynner frequently stayed at Long's home in Pittsburgh. Here he revised many of the drafts of his translations of Chinese poems for his forthcoming anthology, *The Jade Mountain* (1929).

In 1920 *Poems,* Long's first book, was published. The notebooks Long kept prior to the publication of *Poems* reveal the wide extent of his reading. He refers to Catullus, Whitman, Marlowe (*Dr. Faustus*), William James (*The Varieties of Religious Experience*), Emerson, Bergson, Burns, and Ovid. But, in particular, the presence of William Blake and Goethe indicate fundamental influences on Long's first collection.

Thus, in his first published book, which Louis Untermeyer described as "one of the shyest volumes ever issued," Long exhibits both romanticism and classicism, traditions which Goethe had attempted to reconcile in *Faust.* More specifically, these are poems of an innately romantic spirit, with an acquired classical overtone. Subjectivism, naturalism, and mysticism are the specific expressions of this romantic spirit. Almost every poem is centripetal in its development. External presences are meaningful only in terms of their influence on the individual intelligence of each poem. Natural forms represent peripheral influences converging upon the single mind at the center of the poetic landscape. It is the convergence of these peripheral influences that establishes the emotional context of the poems, whose nebulous natural imagery relates them more closely to the poetry of Blake and Shelley; seldom do they reveal any of the concrete natural detail that characterizes the poetry of Wordsworth and Keats. This vagueness of imagery is exemplified in the following poem, where "The night came softly to the sea;/And they, the seven stars, to me." The sea and the stars are significant only as reflections of the speaker's emotional state, as they and he "Gave an involuntary cry" for which only he and the woman he has told know the reason. The poem ends with the speaker's pulling away from the natural landscape, which has finished serving its symbolic purpose: "But stars are strange, the sea is deep/And you were lovely, in your sleep."

The tendency of these poems, then, is toward the abstract, disembodied, imaginative nature of Blake. Similarly, the personalities of these poems are essential rather than substantial. For example,

in "The Water-Sprite," the essential personality of the poem is portrayed in relation to the imagination of the poet, who sees her as "Luminous, opaque," yearning "for young men's limbs to wind,/For young men's hearts to break." Yet she also "has weeds to wreathe their brows," and the poet imagines that "Some midnight" at the full moon,

> I shall walk slowly down to her,
>   Under the lake, alone,
> Bearing a cluster of land-flowers
>   And an agate stone.

Both imagery and emotion in this poem are diffused rather than concentrated. Fundamentally, the poem represents a mystical experience in the realm of nature, with the natural essence predominating over the mystical one. The mystical experiences of all these poems are esoteric in the romantic sense of nineteenth-century Gothicism, particularly that of the Pre-Raphaelites, rather than in the medieval sense of Catholic mysticism. Their mysticism is that of natural beauty, pagan rather than Christian, discursive rather than directive. The mystical experience of *Poems* is little more than an experience of beauty, demanding in its childlike whimsy nothing beyond the play of the imagination. As imaginative creations of a young poet, they most frequently lack, or imperfectly contain, depths of feeling and thought; but at the same time they are unquestionably fine for their imaginative sensitivity.

Because the early poems of a poet are more often derivative than original, it is not surprising to discover clear traces of other poetic influences, besides Blake, in Long's early poems. It is of more than casual significance that *Poems* was dedicated to Witter Bynner, whose *Grenstone Poems* (1917) were dedicated to Long in memory of Mrs. Celia Mitchell-Keays. Bynner's *A Canticle of Pan* (1920) mingles, like the Ionic caryatides, the spirits of orientalism and classicism. Both books, *A Canticle for Pan* for its classical tone, and *Grenstone Poems* for its nebulous intensity, compare closely with *Poems.* Unlike Bynner, however, Long blends his voice imperfectly with the voices of his predecessors. Thus *Poems* fails to integrate successfully thought, feeling, and imagination. But *Poems* is consistent in its lyricism, in the basic sense of songs: the majority of the poems are composed in stanza forms, usually the quatrain, the commonest lyrical form. Long's poetry was never more lyrical than when it was most deeply influenced by Bynner's poetry. Some of his later books, mainly *Atlantides* (1933), contain lyrics of splendid grace, but their merit, as with *Poems*, is never based solely on their lyricism. In the love lyrics of *Atlantides*, a note of sexuality exists, bringing to their emotional context a form of passion conspicuously absent from Bynner's poetry. The lack of sexuality in Long's early poems is both an indication of his youth and Bynner's temporary influence.

Although Long continued teaching on a full-time basis until 1926, poor health necessitated frequent leaves of absence. Long and his family were in Europe in 1923, returning in December. Witter Bynner, who had gone to Santa Fe on vacation in 1922 and decided to remain, persuaded Long to come there for his health in 1924. The Longs lived for a year in Santa Fe, and their stay had meaning beyond the improvement of Long's health. In 1938 Long remembered the writers' group that he was part of that year: "Witter Bynner, Spud Johnson, Lynn Riggs, and I would go up to Alice Corbin Henderson's on the Camino once every week after supper and spend three or more hours with that hospitable poet in the discussion of one another's verse and of verse in general."

Between 1924 and 1929 the Longs made their home in Santa Fe, but lived a large part of the time in Pittsburgh, where Long continued his teaching duties, after 1926 as a part-time professor. In 1926 he published his second book, *Notes for a New Mythology*, which laid out the concerns and themes which would be central to much of his subsequent career as a writer. "We are tired of being strangers in our own landscape," he wrote; "is it any wonder that we begin to take seriously those primitive interpreters of our land, the Indians?" He focused on the essential capacity of men and women to survive under the greatest of hardship and privation; on the forgotten yet still latent resources of the human spirit to renew itself in contact with the land, with the primitive, with the intuitive, to live in active cooperative harmony and delight with one another and with the world of nature. "The terror of Spring," he wrote in *Notes for a New Mythology*, "is the fear that this . . . gaiety, license, loveliness, these sudden visions of a change happening to human life to lift us from an age of enormous and terrible cities, . . . are but fairy tales, mirages, unrelated to our fate, idle incidents of the vernal season." And he affirmed, against that fear, a vision of human aspiration and accomplishment in which the sensual and intellectual interdependence of men and women as equals is utterly central.

The permanent move to Santa Fe at the end of 1929 marked the beginning of Long's richest literary period, for he was able to devote full time to writing. Almost all of his books were published after his move to New Mexico. His presence in Santa Fe, however, had more than a personal significance. He contributed much to the growth of Santa Fe as a literary place. In 1933 he helped organize Writers' Editions, Inc. (he was its executive director from 1935 to 1939): a cooperative publishing house, founded with the idea of decentralizing the publication of poetry and thus making each region a center in its own right, Writers' Editions saw itself as fostering a resurgence of American literature and was indeed influential in establishing a literature of the American Southwest. Annually during the 1930s Long and his friends organized "The Poets' Round-up," when local poets gathered to read their poems, stepping into the ring as if at a rodeo, in friendly competition.

In 1933 Long published *Atlantides*, the first of his five books printed at the Writers' Editions press. He published *Pittsburgh Memoranda* in 1935, and in 1936 he published the first book in which he employed regional material, *Interlinear to Cabeza de Vaca*. This nonfiction account of a sixteenth-century journey from Florida to the Pacific Ocean has probably been Long's most successful and most widely distributed book. Harry Sylvester notes that "the book has attracted and deeply interested people as various as Harvard professors and Benedictine nuns; Presbyterian ministers and grammar school teachers; historians and novelists."

On 20 July 1937, twenty-seven years after his brief apprenticeship on the *New York Globe*, Long again ventured into the field of journalism, this time as editor of the "New Mexico Writers" section of the *New Mexico Sentinel*, "a weekly page of prose and verse contributed by New Mexicans, at home or abroad." The page was a literary success, if not a financial one; Long contributed many editorials, and was instrumental, with Witter Bynner, in publishing for the first time the verse of Franciscan muralist Fray Angelic Chavez. Paul Horgan's novel, *Habit of Empire*, was serialized in the section. Other New Mexico writers, both part-time and full-time residents, such as Arthur Davison Ficke, Lynn Riggs, William Pillin, Raymond Otis, Spud Johnson, and Harvey Fergusson, contributed to this section. But on 1 January 1939 the page was discontinued because the expense of producing it had far exceeded its profits. As a literary venture, however, the section had been successful, publishing, through Long's efforts, the work of many unknown, but talented, writers.

Long's *Walt Whitman and the Springs of Courage,* published in 1938, was followed in 1939 by *Malinche (Doña Marina),* an on-the-whole powerful and successful fictional account of the Oluta Indian who, as Cortes's interpreter, made the conquest of Mexico possible; who, as his mistress, bore him a son; and whom Cortes later gave in marriage to one of his lieutenants. In a commentary which appears as epilogue to the first edition but which has been omitted from subsequent printings (though it appears in the Italian and French translations) Long relates her story to the archetypes of religion and literature, emphasizes the mythic qualities of Malinche's story, and expands further the views he adumbrated in *Notes for a New Mythology* on the proper relationship between man and woman.

In 1941 he contributed a volume to the American Folkway series, *Piñon Country,* dealing with the regional personality of the Southwest, particularly New Mexico and Arizona.

Though it was published after *Atlantides, Pitts-*burgh *Memoranda* was actually written while Long was still in Pittsburgh. In fact, Long sent a blank verse version to a publisher twenty years before it was published. After it was rejected, Long reconsidered its form and decided, he told Bynner, that it was "necessary to come as close as possible to the actual scene and use actual words from the people engaged in the different actions. This meant goodbye to all the blank verse. Then it seemed necessary for me to use terse pieces of prose along with the passages of poetry. One of my great aims was to save the reader as much time as possible in traversing a region full of high voltage wires and infinite detail. I wanted also to make the greatest possible effect on him in the few moments." *Pittsburgh Memoranda* tightly integrates narrative prose passages with poetry, generally unrhymed and irregular iambic lines. Long reserves poetry for his comments on the facts of the prose narrative, which is most often the actual words of individuals. The spirit and the vital essence of the book are contained in the poetry, as in these flowing lines from the "Prologue":

> They knew the mountains and the midnight skies.
> We know the chambers filled with talk and silence,
> Ghosts and hallucinations. We have come
> Under roofs to a fantastic air, somehow.
> Our father died victorious over the outward.
> Peace to them. Courage to us,
> Who fight not Indians but insanity.

Such lines are an attempt to write poetry that will be distinct from the prose passages, yet at the same time commingle with them smoothly. This integration succeeds in varying degrees throughout the book.

In *Atlantides,* written after Long had moved to Santa Fe, he made the transition from public poet to private poet. In *Pittsburgh Memoranda,* public events are shown in operation on the particular personality of the poet; but in *Atlantides,* particular experience directs itself toward the universal, the personal being a priori to the public.

It is particularly upon *Atlantides* and *The Grist Mill* (1945) that Long's right to a place in contemporary lyric poetry is based. As John Gould Fletcher said of *Atlantides,* "And all this range of effect, rich and dazzling, is used to illuminate a theme no male American poet, has dared to attack—the theme of sexual love. As a set of studied variation on this theme, ranging from accomplishment to despair, and not indulging in self-pity by the way that seems to haunt our women poets, this

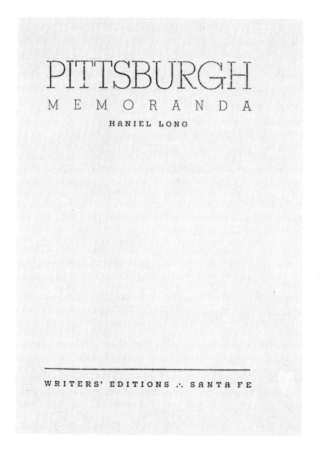

Title page for the poem in which Long found it "necessary to come as close as possible to the actual scene and use actual words from the people engaged in the different actions"

book is noteworthy." This theme links Long with the spirits of Goethe, Catullus, and Sappho rather than to the traditions of eighteenth- and nine-teenth-century poetry. "Song," one of the best of Long's personal lyrics, mingles these intensities with an artless perfection that belies the technical acumen behind it. Addressing the woman, the poet calls himself "hushed" by her gift to him and unable to shout like spruce trees "along the crest of the world/in a great wind." And, he speculates,

> You must have brushed
> the portals of the moon
> as you came out—

because her body still exhibits "A bewildering glow" that blinds him. In this poem the imagery is graphic, almost palpable, rather than nebulous and abstract, as in *Poems.*

It is this organic tie between nature and hu-man emotion that established Long's connection with Chinese poetry. Many poems in *Atlantides* and *The Grist Mill* are perfect reflections of the spirit of Chinese poetry. These lines from an untitled poem demonstrate Long's intrinsically Chinese reverence for nature, in their gentle ardor and quiet respect:

> Pussey-willows and bronze apple-trees
> Are portions of the sky, and high above them
> And towards the East, floats a great autumn cloud.

The poems in *The Grist Mill* are those of an older poet. While *Atlantides* contains poetry of love, both sexual and romantic, this later book contains poetry of thought and meditation. In its diminished sensual intensity, it brings forth another spirit, a sense of serenity gained from the peace of ripened relationship, of accepted triumphs and defeats, of remembered joys. The tone of *The Grist Mill* sug-gests that its poet has established a vantage point in his career and that his reflections represent judg-ments as well as a harmonizing of the discords of experience. Thus the love poems of this book are quieter in their passion, slower in their currents. In one poem the speaker asks rhetorically if a man is not "what he loves"—or if at least he does not grow toward it—"Becoming what to begin with/He was not?" His beloved is the embodiment, he says, of the beauty for which he has lived and fought. Yet, he ends the poem paradoxically:

> I touch my wish
> And I am young again;
> I long to have it always
> And I am old.

Title page for the book that John Gould Fletcher praised for a "style that goes deceptively deep despite its stark simplicity of surface"

In his review of *The Grist Mill,* John Gould Fletcher alluded to its spirituality, mysticism, in-stinctiveness, and its "style that goes deceptively deep despite its stark simplicity of surface." In de-fending the book, Fletcher opposed the modernism of T. S. Eliot and other "difficult" poets. For it is soon apparent to the reader of *The Grist Mill* that Long is everything the modernists are not. He fol-lows with great devotion Keats's dictum that "po-etry should be great and unobtrusive, a thing which enters the soul, and does not startle it or amaze it with itself—but with its subject." This is precisely what the poetry of *Atlantides* and *The Grist Mill* is—unobtrusive and soul-penetrating.

Though *Atlantides* and *The Grist Mill* reveal subjective differences of tone and mood, they dif-fer little in technique, the later book incorporating many of the poetic forms of the earlier one. John Gould Fletcher's statement regarding the technical nature of *Atlantides* is thus applicable to *The Grist Mill* as well: "Few if any present-day American poets could surpass the range of lyrical effects that Mr. Long shows in this volume. He tackles every possible form known to English verse, from the seventeenth-century echo of 'Butterflies,' through Heine-like song, Parnassian sonnet, down to Rupert Brooke ('Pool in the Desert'), Robert Frost, and the Imagists, and finally, 'Cobweb,' something like the palimpsest-technique invented by Ezra Pound." Fletcher's view, intended primarily as a rebuttal to a review by Robert Penn Warren that had criticized *Atlantides* for its "lack of tension or concentration" and its "poverty of metaphor and simile," ignores, however, the Chinese elements of the book. All but six or seven of the poems have the sort of natural setting characteristic of Chinese poems. As these lines from "Day and Night" demonstrate, the poems interpret life through images of nature, expressed in the Chinese manner:

All the flowers by the lake
are for your shadow;
red hibiscus for your heart,
zuchil with golden centre and ivory petals
for your body,
and a flower I do not know
for the thought of you which haunts me.

In December 1940 the young May Sarton (she was then twenty-eight) went to Santa Fe at last to meet Haniel Long (he had written to her when her first novel came out). They became fast friends. Alice and Haniel Long, she recalled some years later, "at first sight resembled an early American painting; he spare, tall, with lean high cheekbones and a wide mouth; she, plump as a tea cozy, with a light child-voice, soft vague hands, altogether absurdly like a dove." Sarton found in "these two remarkable natures who had created of their differences a marriage as whole as the two 'Philips' in a double almond" a deep source for her own writing, especially for her poetry, and judged that although Long was a true poet, no poem of his could reach the depth and intensity of his personal relationships. And the marriage was of course central: "he and Alice each knew that he was safely centered in her and their marriage. They were as different as night and day: she moved entirely from intuitive wisdom, . . . and was rooted entirely in him; he, hungry for knowledge, a man compelled to reach out constantly, to experience to the full

everything that came his way, . . . attracted people like a magnet, and then had to learn how to fend them off. Often a visitor to their house must have wondered at first what this intellectual being could see in what appeared to be a retarded child; on his second visit, eating homemade bread and butter, he might hear one of Alice's casual pronouncements and find himself turn to her in surprise; and by his third visit he could see. Women of Alice's kind are rare in America, as unpretentious as the morning sun, as ingenuous as the dove, as wise as the serpent."

As they grew older Haniel and Alice grew more dependent on each other. After two excruciatingly painful eye operations, he went partially blind, and depended on her for all reading. She began to grow deaf. In 1956 she became seriously ill, so Haniel went to the Mayo clinic for a heart operation, in the hope of gaining enough strength to nurse her; she was in the hospital in Santa Fe, and while Haniel was in surgery she died. Three days later, on 17 October 1956, alone in Minnesota, he too died; life without Alice would have been intolerable.

That Haniel Long was not a major writer is a result at least in part of his subordination of his writing to the business of living, to his insistence that men live in an immediate world of the emotions and the senses rather than in the world of books; in part it results from his determination, outlined in his three central books (*Notes for a New Mythology, Interlinear to Cabeza de Vaca, Malinche*), to retrieve for modern and urbanized man the world of mythology which lies under his nose. He recognized the importance of form and technique, but he perceived them as subordinate factors in his art. Despite his technical versatility, he never regarded experiment with technique as an end in itself. His poetry is the receptacle for large and sensitive intelligence, expressing a wisdom that comes from companionship with nature, from a natural humility that saw the essential equality of all mankind, and a marriage remarkable for the closeness of its mutual interdependence. Among his contemporaries, he is perhaps closest in his poetry to Robert Frost in his apparent artlessness and simplicity, and to Witter Bynner in the delicacy of his treatment of nature.

References:

Bert Almon, "Woman as Interpreter: Haniel Long's *Malinche*," *Southwest Review*, 59 (Summer 1974): 221-239;

Robert Burlingame, "Haniel Long and His Work,"

M.A. thesis, University of New Mexico, 1947;

Mabel Major, Rebecca W. Smith, and T. M. Pearce, *Southwest Heritage: A Literary History with Bibliography* (Albuquerque: University of New Mexico Press, 1938), pp. 128-129, 149;

Howard McCord, "The Existence of Augustine: A Counterplaint with Haniel Long," *whe're/1* (Spring 1966): 39-43;

Lester Raines, *More New Mexico Writers and Writings* (Las Vegas: New Mexico Normal University, 1935), p. 49;

Raines, *Writers and Writing of New Mexico* (Las Vegas: New Mexico Normal University, 1934), p. 88;

May Sarton, "The Leopard Land: Haniel and Alice Long's Santa Fe," *Southwest Review*, 57 (Winter 1972): 1-14;

Elizabeth Shepley Sergeant, "The Santa Fe Group," *Saturday Review of Literature*, 11 (8 December 1934): 352;

Harry Sylvester, "Cabeza de Vaca and Haniel Long," *Commonweal*, 38 (12 February 1943): 414-416;

Marta Weigle and Kyle Fiore, *Santa Fe and Taos: The Writer's Era* (Santa Fe: Ancient City Press, 1982).

Archibald MacLeish

(7 May 1892-20 April 1982)

Victor H. Jones
Indiana State University

See also the MacLeish entries in *DLB 4, American Writers in Paris, 1920-1939, DLB 7, Twentieth-Century American Dramatists,* and *DLB Yearbook: 1982.*

SELECTED BOOKS*: *Class Poem 1915* (New Haven: Yale University, 1915);

Songs for a Summer's Day (New Haven: Yale University Press, 1915);

Tower of Ivory (New Haven: Yale University Press, 1917; London: Milford, 1917);

The Happy Marriage and Other Poems (Boston & New York: Houghton Mifflin, 1924);

The Pot of Earth (Boston & New York: Houghton Mifflin, 1925);

Nobodaddy (Cambridge, Mass.: Dunster House, 1926; London: Jackson, 1926);

Streets in the Moon (Boston & New York: Houghton Mifflin, 1928);

The Hamlet of A. MacLeish (Boston & New York: Houghton Mifflin, 1928);

Einstein (Paris: Black Sun Press, 1929);

New Found Land (Paris: Black Sun Press, 1930; Boston & New York: Houghton Mifflin, 1930);

Housing America, anonymous (New York: Harcourt, Brace, 1932);

Conquistador (Boston & New York: Houghton Mifflin, 1932; London: Gollancz, 1933);

Poems, 1924-1933 (Boston & New York: Houghton Mifflin, 1933); abridged as *Poems* (London: Boriswood, 1935);

Archibald MacLeish, 1938

*This list omits government publications.

Frescoes for Mr. Rockefeller's City (New York: John Day, 1933);

Panic (Boston & New York: Houghton Mifflin, 1935; London: Boriswood, 1936);

Jews in America, anonymous (New York: Random House, 1936);

Public Speech (New York: Farrar & Rinehart, 1936; London: Boriswood, 1936);

The Fall of the City (London: Boriswood, 1937; New York & Toronto: Farrar & Rinehart, 1937);

Land of the Free (New York: Harcourt, Brace, 1938; London: Boriswood, 1938);

Air Raid (New York: Harcourt, Brace, 1938; London: John Lane/Bodley Head, 1939);

America Was Promises (New York: Duell, Sloan & Pearce, 1939; London: John Lane/Bodley Head, 1940);

The Irresponsibles: A Declaration (New York: Duell, Sloan & Pearce, 1940);

A Time to Speak: The Selected Prose of Archibald MacLeish (Boston: Houghton Mifflin, 1941; London: Allen & Unwin, 1941);

The American Cause (New York: Duell, Sloan & Pearce, 1941);

American Opinion and the War: The Rede Lecture (Cambridge: Cambridge University Press, 1942; Cambridge: Cambridge University Press/New York: Macmillan, 1942);

A Time to Act: Selected Addresses (Boston: Houghton Mifflin, 1943; London: Allen & Unwin, 1945);

The American Story: Ten Broadcasts (New York: Duell, Sloan & Pearce, 1944);

Actfive and Other Poems (New York: Random House, 1948; London: John Lane/Bodley Head, 1950);

Poetry and Opinion: the Pisan Cantos of Ezra Pound (Urbana: University of Illinois Press, 1950);

Freedom Is the Right to Choose (Boston: Beacon Press, 1951; London: John Lane/Bodley Head, 1952);

Collected Poems, 1917-1952 (Boston: Houghton Mifflin, 1952);

The Trojan Horse (Boston: Houghton Mifflin, 1952);

This Music Crept by Me Upon the Waters (Cambridge: Harvard University Press, 1953);

Songs for Eve (Boston: Houghton Mifflin, 1954);

Art Education and the Creative Process (New York: Museum of Modern Art, 1954);

J.B. (Boston: Houghton Mifflin, 1958; London: Secker & Warburg, 1959);

Poetry and Experience (Boston: Houghton Mifflin, 1961; London: John Lane/Bodley Head, 1961);

Three Short Plays (New York: Dramatists Play Service, 1961);

The Collected Poems of Archibald MacLeish (Boston: Houghton Mifflin, 1963);

The Dialogues of Archibald MacLeish and Mark Van Doren, edited by Warren V. Bush (New York: Dutton, 1964);

The Eleanor Roosevelt Story (Boston: Houghton Mifflin, 1965);

An Evening's Journey to Conway, Mass. (Northampton, Mass.: Gehenna Press, 1967);

Herakles (Boston: Houghton Mifflin, 1967);

A Continuing Journey (Boston: Houghton Mifflin, 1968);

The Wild Old Wicked Man and Other Poems (Boston: Houghton Mifflin, 1968; London: W. H. Allen, 1969);

Scratch (Boston: Houghton Mifflin, 1971);

Champion of a Cause: Essays and Addresses on Librarianship, edited by Eva M. Goldschmidt (Chicago: American Library Association, 1971);

The Human Season: Selected Poems 1926-1972 (Boston: Houghton Mifflin, 1972);

The Great American Fourth of July Parade (Pittsburgh: University of Pittsburgh Press, 1975);

New and Collected Poems: 1917-1976 (Boston: Houghton Mifflin, 1976);

Riders on the Earth: Essays and Recollections (Boston: Houghton Mifflin, 1978);

Six Plays (Boston: Houghton Mifflin, 1980).

"Ars Poetica" and Archibald MacLeish are inextricably bound for most readers of modern American poetry, but neither this poem nor "The End of the World" (both first collected in *Streets in the Moon,* 1928) nor MacLeish's other heavily anthologized poems, such as "You, Andrew Marvell" (*New Found Land,* 1930), begin to capture the range and variety of his work. For in addition to these and other excellent lyric poems, he wrote an epic (*Conquistador,* 1932), several effective satires, and no fewer than ten verse plays for radio and stage. He was also a lawyer, an editor, a Librarian of the Congress, an Assistant Secretary of State, one of the founders of UNESCO, a teacher, and a literary critic. Through nearly all of the phases of his career, MacLeish urged understanding (awareness) and love as necessary to the human revolution (the beginning of which he associated with the American Revolution) for which he so consistently and persuasively spoke. MacLeish should be remembered for this humane voice through the several decades of the twentieth century where there appeared to be little to be optimistic about; he should also be remembered for his virtuosity in lyric poetry and verse plays and for his contribution to the development of the modern verse play for stage and radio.

MacLeish was born in Glencoe, Illinois, "in a wooden chateau" overlooking Lake Michigan, the son of Andrew MacLeish and his third wife, Martha Hillard MacLeish, Andrew was a Glasgow Scot, Martha a Connecticut Yankee. The young MacLeish attended public schools in Glencoe and the Hotchkiss School in Lakeville, Connecticut (1907-1911), a preparatory school which he hated but which prepared him for Yale. At Yale he wrote poetry and short stories for the *Yale Literary Mag-*

azine, swam for the swimming team, and played center on the freshman football team. MacLeish later remembered the Harvard coach called him the "dirtiest little sonofabitch of a center to visit Cambridge, Massachusetts." The poet wittily noted that he really did not deserve the "honor" because he was not all that little. He completed his degree in 1915 and was elected to the Phi Beta Kappa Society, but he says his education did not really begin until he entered Harvard Law School in 1915. At Harvard, he began to study that profession whose business it is "to make sense of the confusion of what we call human life." Eventually, he would turn from law to poetry because the business of poetry was likewise to "make sense of our lives. To create an understanding of our lives. To com-

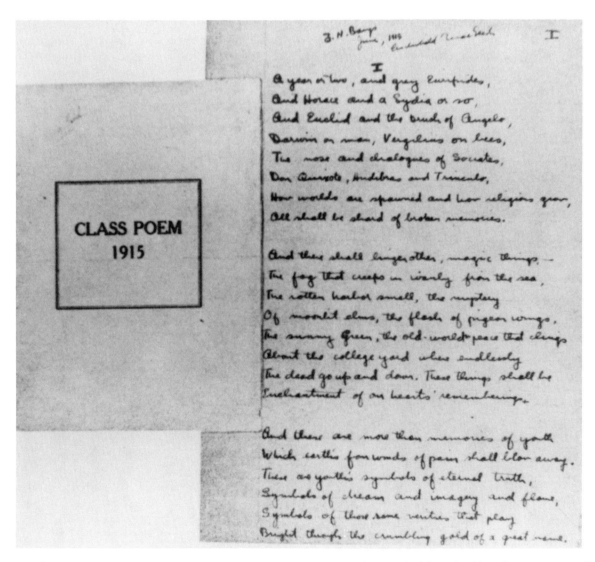

Cover and fair copy of the beginning of MacLeish's first separate publication, the poem he delivered at his Yale commencement (in their time/1920-1940, *1977*)

pose an order which the bewildered, angry heart can recognize. To imagine man." Before MacLeish earned his law degree, he married Ada Hitchcock of Farmington, Connecticut, on 21 June 1916. A gifted singer, Ada MacLeish supported the young poet's desire to master his craft. Their marriage would last until his death. In 1917 MacLeish entered the U.S. Army in World War I as an ambulance driver, "so as to do the right thing and not be hurt. In France got shifted to the Field Artillery out of shame." He advanced to the rank of captain by the end of the war. The poet's younger brother, Kenneth, was a Navy flyer; he was shot down and killed in 1918. MacLeish never forgot this death and wrote several poems about it.

Tower of Ivory (1917), MacLeish's first full-length volume of poetry, was seen through publication by Lawrence Mason (a Yale English instructor) while MacLeish was in the army. According to the reviewer for the *New York Times Book Review*, the poems in the volume are better "than the average run of minor verse." They are technically good but are conventional in form, the poetry of a young man. "Our Lady of Troy," however, merits comment. A blank-verse play in which Faustus evokes Helen of Troy for the students at the inn in Rimlich, it is important for Faustus's notion that "There's nought to fear from Heaven through to Hell;/Nothing that mind can't solve. Mind is the king." Later Faustus says that he, like Eve, has digressed somewhat from Eden: "Man must ever set his face/Toward the sunset, make his pilgrimage/Into the West. There is no pause for dream/With all the shining kingdom of the mind,/All truth, all science, all the stars to reap/And time forever clattering at heel/Like bone the children tie to yelping curs./So then, our true mathesis, next and next!"

In this brief play MacLeish first introduces the idea of man searching, fearing nothing, trying to shape his life through his own efforts. He has departed from the Garden of Eden and must forever move westward. The reference to Eve may be ironic, but eventually MacLeish employed the Eve-like woman to accompany the searcher and to keep him in touch with the natural world. This play and MacLeish's other plays exhibit in one way or another most of the themes that MacLeish dealt with in his lyric poetry.

Seven years passed before MacLeish published another volume of poetry. After World War I, he returned to Harvard and, leading his class in his senior year, took his LL.B. degree in 1919. For the next two years he was a successful trial lawyer in the firm of Choate, Hall, and Stewart of Boston.

His well-known decision to leave the firm, ironically, occurred on the very same day the senior partner invited him into the firm. MacLeish later recounted the process of reaching the decision, one of the more difficult in his life: it was "a cold, clear, winter evening in February of 1923 when I was five years out of the Great War and four years out of Harvard Law School and trying to support myself and my wife and two small children by practicing law in a Boston office and teaching a course in Legal Procedure in a night school—trying to find time to write on Saturday afternoons and Sunday mornings." Frustrated, MacLeish walked home that evening instead of taking his usual transportation. He had "Only one desire," he wrote, "to write the poems I wanted to write and not the poems" he was writing. In his debate with himself under the new moon, MacLeish realized that he had prepared for art but had not practiced it—that he owed art. He arrived home, his wife having anticipated what had happened, and together they discussed the matter through the night, deciding at last to go to France on what little resources they had. MacLeish dated the beginning of his adult life from this moment.

The decision made, the rest was not easy. MacLeish had to catch up—on reading Jules Laforgue, Arthur Rimbaud, St. John Perse, Paul Valery. He had to understand what T. S. Eliot, James Joyce, and Ezra Pound had discovered—that an era had ended and that in poetry, Rimbaud and the Chinese poets such as Li Po were good models for modern poetry. He had to reschool himself; he had to work to learn the craft of poetry, just as his friends (Ernest Hemingway, F. Scott Fitzgerald, and John Dos Passos) were working to learn the craft of fiction.

Early products from the beginning of his "adult life" were *The Happy Marriage and Other Poems* (1924) and *The Pot of Earth* (1925). *The Happy Marriage* is a book of traditional poetry, containing, among a number of lyrics, a sonnet cycle that Harriet Monroe admired. She marveled at the young poet's virtuosity with the "sonnet instrument, playing it to soft violin-like cadences." *The Pot of Earth*, written under the influence of Eliot, is about the death and renewal in a wasteland where life inexplicably and mysteriously goes on. Yvor Winters noted that both books were "not overly happy dilutions of Eliot, Swinburne, and anything else that came in handy."

In 1926 MacLeish wrote *Nobodaddy*, another play in blank verse. The play, which derives its title from one of Blake's names for God, depicts Adam

Archibald and Ada MacLeish with American expatriates Sara and Gerald Murphy in Vienna. MacLeish was later to dedicate his poem "American Letter" to Murphy.

and Eve emerging from the sleep of Eden, a state or condition in which they had lived in ignorant and unconscious harmony with their surroundings and in obedience to the will of God. When Adam chooses to know, he chooses consciousness and so separation from God and from Eve as well. This choice requires that he make his way in the desert, Eve by his side. In the second act the conflict continues, Cain representing the forces of consciousness and Abel of unconsciousness. Abel would return to the garden, to sleep, to total reliance on the will of God. When he kills Abel, Cain chooses the desert, the world where he will have to imagine his world and work to bring it into being. The play, then, is a twentieth-century interpretation of the Cain-Abel myth, in which the Adam/Cain figure rejects God's inexplicable and arbitrary ways and chooses the world. It is this figure (Adam/Cain) who is capable of knowing himself (of knowing his separateness from others and from the garden) who can know both good and evil. He would not return to the garden if he could.

The reviews of *Nobodaddy* were mixed. R. P. Blackmur, for instance, saw the conflict between Cain and Abel (reason and nature) as powerful and effective but argued that MacLeish did not handle Eve effectively, that she should have been able to understand her creations and so to have reconciled the opposites they imply.

If *Nobodaddy* states an important theme in MacLeish's work, *Streets in the Moon* (1928) is his first truly important collection of poetry. Indeed, two of MacLeish's most severe critics—Winters and Morton Zabel—found several good poems in the collection. In the fifty-two poems in the volume MacLeish's technique has changed. He can still write in traditional rhymed verse forms, as sonnets such as "Chiaroscuro" and "Conversation Balnweáire" and as the seemingly simple iambic tetrameter quatrains of *L'an trentiesme de mon eage* show. But he was developing his own line of poetry, too, lines such as those in "Ancestral," which experiments with sonnet form. But the lines only suggest rhymes and illustrate what John Ciardi called MacLeish's "chop line," seen in this excerpt, where the speaker recalls falling asleep beneath the stars:

Gathering darkness:
                    I was small.
                              I lay
Beside my mother on the grass, and sleep
Came—

MacLeish had reschooled himself well; he had learned to render experience (Pound's term), rather than to describe it. "Reading Opposite the Lamp," for instance, renders the physical movements of the eye in reading as well as the understanding of the experience that is the purpose of reading poetry in the first place.

But *Streets in the Moon* is much more than testimony to MacLeish's changed technique. Most of the speakers or characters in the poems are related to the Adam/Cain figure. Each is forced to make his way in the world without any apparent help from God. Thus the characters speak to the human situation of those residing in a wasteland. The light for the speakers is only dim moonlight, but it is there. To some of them the light reveals only death, as in "No Lamp Has Ever Shown Us Where to Look" and "Interrogate the Stones"; to others it reveals nothingness, as in "The End of the World." For all, the way is difficult to read, as in *Le seul malheur est que je ne sais pas lire";* for many there is a sense of having lost something, as in "Ancestral." Some of the poems ("Selene Afterwards") reveal the isolation so many people in the twentieth century have felt. The attitudes of the speakers toward their situation in the "desert" vary, but irony (more or less grim) in poems such as "Some Aspects of Immortality," "The End of the World," and "Man" is common. Many of the poems in the second part of the book, "Several Shadows of a Skull," speak to man's awareness of and behavior in the face of his certain death. Noteworthy is "Einstein" (also published separately, in 1929), a long blank-

verse poem in which the central character refuses to stop his search for understanding in the face of his inability to understand. Always flung back at him is "himself to answer him." That is to say, he is the answer to his own fate.

Einstein, like MacLeish's Faustus, Adam, and Cain, seeks answers to his questions. Such seeking exists in MacLeish's work in many variations, one important variation being through poetry (art), as in "Ars Poetica." A poem, as "Ars Poetica" makes clear, captures a human experience, an experience of grief, or of love, or of loneliness, or of memory. Thus a poem becomes a way of knowing, of seeing, albeit through the senses, the emotions, and the imagination. MacLeish often said that the function of a poem is to trap "Heaven and Earth in the cage of form."

If it is true, as MacLeish thought, that an era had ended after World War I and that a new era (the "wasteland" era) was upon us, there were still moments when nature seemed to provide comfort. MacLeish tries to capture this feeling in "Memorial Rain," the end of which permits the reader to forget from time to time the bad that is apparent when one chooses consciousness and to hold dear the good—beauty, courage, and love.

Generally speaking, MacLeish did not dwell too long on the lost paradise. He accepted the new era and, confident that man controlled his own destiny, saw promise in America, that continent in the West where the desert might be conquered. MacLeish as teacher, politician, and poet spent the remainder of his life trying to help man realize the promise of America, that promise having begun, in his mind, with the American Revolution.

In 1928 MacLeish returned to America, settling on Uphill Farm in Conway, Massachusetts. In "Conversations with MacLeish at Eighty-three" MacLeish told Bill Moyers that he and his wife loved the house for its beauty and simplicity. It had been "improved," MacLeish noted, but he and his wife restored it by removing the improvements. At the same time he was unsuccessfully trying to get Houghton Mifflin to change the way *The Hamlet of A. MacLeish* appeared on the printed page. This poem, an interior monologue after the manner of "The Love Song of J. Alfred Prufrock," is MacLeish's version of the Hamlet story. The speaker, identified as "MacLeish," ruminates on the difficulty of accepting the pain and suffering in his life, and while he knows that he must accept these conditions of life, he ends by echoing Hamlet: *"Thou wouldst not think/How ill all's here about my heart!"*

MacLeish's first collection of poetry published

Death" the speaker sees that life is more than death; it "is a haft that has fitted the palms of many,/Dark as the helved oak, with sweat bitter,/Browned numerous hands: Death is the rest of it." In the new found land, then, a man can make his life. This new found land, MacLeish wrote in "American Letter," is "Neither a place . . . nor a blood name." It is "West and the wind blowing." It is a shining idea in men's minds, and much as the speaker yearns for the lost world (the world of the garden), MacLeish knows there is no turning back for Americans. They must accept their land and the people on it:

> Here we must eat our salt or our bones starve.
> Here we must live or live only as shadows.
> This is our race, we that have none, that have had
> Neither the old walls nor the voices around us,
> This is our land, this our ancient ground—

Appropriately enough the collection ends with a celebration of American life in New York City in ". . . . . & Forty-Second Street."

Before MacLeish took permanent root in Conway, Massachusetts (his own little piece of the new found land), he wrote *Conquistador* (1932), another poem of discovery. The poem was generated by MacLeish's reading of Bernál Diaz del Castillo's *True History of the Conquest of New Spain* (1632) and of his having followed the route of the Conquistadors himself in Mexico during February of 1929. The epigraph to the poem, from canto twenty-five of Dante's *Inferno*, explains the nature of Bernál's discovery in New Spain; it is a discovery made by the senses of the common man, whom Bernál represents. The epigraph is also important because it is written in the terza-rima form, a variation of which MacLeish uses in the epic itself. That the speaker in the poem is a common soldier is also important because MacLeish had become interested in the fate of the individual without a race or without, really, a country or language; in short, the typical American. This man, like Bernál, is tied to the natural world through his senses, his emotions, his imagination. The beginning of the seventh book shows Bernál's connections with his world:

> *To the place called the Red Land. . . .*
>   and between the
> Fields valleys of great depth: and went down and
> Marched in the valleys:
>   and the pools were green a
> Copper water: and stank: the earth powder:
> No stalk of leaf in all those valleys:

Archibald MacLeish at Uphill Farm

after his return home was *New Found Land* (1930, published earlier the same year in Paris), the title being descriptive of MacLeish's belief about the promise of America. The speakers in the poems are initially torn between the values of Europe and those of America, but ultimately they choose the latter. In making this choice, already anticipated in *Streets in the Moon*, MacLeish wished to help shape the land of his birth, acknowledging human mortality but putting it in perspective through the joy he finds in life—in friends, in loved ones, in the beauty of the natural world, and in the recollection of people who settled the continent. In "Salute" he praised the sun, "symbol of the West," as Grover Smith put it, instead of the moon. In the light of the sun man can see more clearly that he is mortal, and this knowledge may help him to choose his life more consciously, should he be willing to accept the responsibility of consciousness. In "Tourist

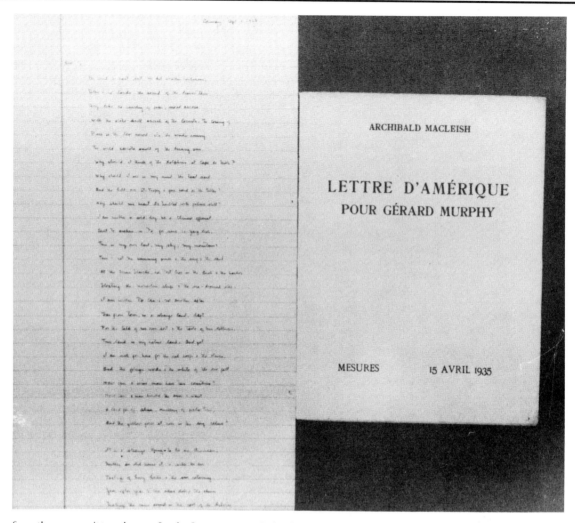

Page from the manuscript and cover for the first separate printing in French and English of MacLeish's poem for Gerald Murphy, an offprint from Adrienne Monnier's little magazine, Mesures. *The translation is by Germaine Landier* (in their time/1920-1940, *1977).*

We alone there and the whispering ground.

The great heat of the sun on us: neither shadow:
Neither shade of the cracked rock in that cañon:
The tree of the sun on our necks: the burning saddle:

So we came to strath's end: lanterns:
Cricked walls: heaped plaster: smell of the
Old men: of the straw: the dogs scattering.

Bernál's world contained few abstractions. The reader's senses of sight, touch, hearing, and smell are all appealed to in this passage. Through these senses Bernál learns; through the senses, MacLeish seems to suggest, most of us learn.

This passage also demonstrates MacLeish's modified terza rima, which relies primarily on as-sonance near or at the end of the line rather than end rhymes for linkage: for example, "between the" in the first line links to "green a" in the third; "down" in the second links to "powder" in the fourth and "ground" in the sixth. This subtle pattern is carried through the fifteen books of the poem, unifying the lines of the stanzas in the ear (often unconsciously) of the reader and testifying to MacLeish's technical virtuosity. The assonance MacLeish employs in *Conquistador* is a common feature in much of MacLeish's poetry, although he employed end-rhymed lines and free verse as well.

MacLeish was awarded his first Pulitzer Prize for *Conquistador,* and Harriet Monroe's positive response to his efforts with the form and with the epic theme might be taken as representative. She said that MacLeish had written in a subtly "adroit terza-rima of assonances" that "ambush and conquer" the reader with their "half-tones and strangely varied harmonies." There were dissenters, of course. Blackmur found it and *The Hamlet of A. MacLeish* "unintegrated, fragmentary, disjunctive, . . . failing of the purpose they manifest so well in detail."

Back in the United States permanently, MacLeish accepted a position on the editorial staff of *Fortune Magazine,* a job he would hold from 1928 to 1938. MacLeish wrote about present, past, and future life in the United States, revealing some of his preoccupations: Diego Rivera murals, Rockefeller Theatre, Roosevelt, the Secretary of State, the Securities Act, skyscrapers, Social Security, South America, Soviet art, and taxation. Given MacLeish's interests in American life in the modern world and given his belief that the "end and purpose" of the poet is "to serve the time; to write, whatever comes of it," as a child of his age, it is little wonder that the voice in his poetry became more and more public and more and more American. And in *Frescoes for Mr. Rockefeller's City* (1933) MacLeish's public voice, larded with irony, begins to emerge.

MacLeish's frescoes begin with the beauty of the land itself in "Landscape as a Nude," where the natural beauty of America is contrasted with the cultivated beauty of England and Italy; it is a western beauty. "Wildwest" pictures those who first loved the land, the American Indians. Certainly Crazy Horse fought for his land, asserts the speaker; it was his land, and when he "was there by the Black Hills/His heart would be big with the love he had for that country/And all the game he had seen and the mares he had ridden/And how it went out from you wide and clean in the sunlight." In "Burying Ground by the Ties" MacLeish honors the builders of modern America, the common man from all parts of the world. In "The Empire Builders," however, MacLeish harshly charges Josiah Perham, Jay Cooke, J. P. Morgan, William Averell Harriman, Cornelius Vanderbilt, Andrew Mellon, and Bruce Barton with betraying the promise of the land. At the end of an imagined tour of frescoes portraying the achievements of the empire builders, the tour guide concludes:

> You have just beheld the Makers making America:
> They screwed her scrawny and gaunt with their seven year panics:
> They bought her back on their mortgages old-whore-cheap:

> They fattened their bonds at her breasts till the thin blood ran from them:
> Men have forgotten how full clear and deep
> The Yellowstone moved on the gravel and grass grew
> When the land lay waiting for her westward people!

MacLeish's frescoes provided the reader with images of the promises that had been lost and of the current dangers that were. Chief of these were the unbridled economic greed of the empire builders and communism, which he attacks in "Background with Revolutionaries." Both capitalists and communists abandoned the pursuit of the human revolution in this country, the first unaware of or indifferent to the natural world, the second fearful of it. Both take refuge behind inhumane and fatalistic abstractions ("laissez faire" economics and "dialectical materialism") which free them from the burden of responsibility for themselves and for their fellow men.

There may have been another danger, too, this one for the artist, and in "Oil Painting of the Artist as the Artist," MacLeish attacked the "plump Mr. Pl'f" who had washed his hands of America, "an émigré from his own time." The target of this satire is in part expatriates. MacLeish has observed that such writers as Fitzgerald, Hemingway, Dos Passos, Pound, Cummings, and Eliot were not among them. In fact, he said that in his six years in Paris he never met an expatriate. The "lost generation" was not lost, he said; "the world out of which that generation came was lost. And it was not a generation of expatriates who found themselves in Paris in those years but a generation whose *patria,* wherever it may once have been, was no longer waiting for them anywhere." These so-called expatriates, then, were among those who first realized and captured in their work the lost age in which they lived. Each of them, as has often been noted, saw different solutions to the same basic problem, MacLeish's solutions being the application of consciousness and love to mankind's efforts to continue the revolution of man. Expatriates, the Mr. Pl'fs in the world of art, found that "The dead are excellent hosts" and so rejected the present and the possibilities of the people in their native land.

Frescoes for Mr. Rockefeller's City was the first of MacLeish's volumes of poetry to be heavily attacked on political grounds. Michael Gold in particular took exception to "Background with Revolutionaries," the last of six poems in the collection, charging MacLeish with holding Marxists, Jews, and socialist intellectuals in contempt; Gold thought the poet an "unconscious fascist." At the other extreme of critical response was Theodore Morrison's view that the collection was nationalistic, patriotic verse that ought to be savored.

MacLeish's next book was another verse play—*Panic* (1935). Always interested in verse form, MacLeish tried in this play to use a rhythm that captured American English as opposed to English English. In his preface to the first version of the play, MacLeish explained that American speech, to his ear, was in falling rather than rising rhythms and that it was more sharply accented than English English. For this reason, blank verse was unsuitable for American verse drama. The best solution, he thought, was "in the direction of a prosody frankly built upon accents without regard for syllabic interval." For the principal speakers, he wrote in a five-stress line without regard for the number of syllables in the line; for the minor characters, he chose a three-stress line, also without regard for the number of syllables. Both lines are in essentially falling rhythms and in both lines the stresses fall on the words "suggested by the sense."

The play had a three-day run in New York's Phoenix Theatre, was directed by Jimmy Light, and starred Orson Welles. About the Great Depression, then in "its sixth unendurable year," the play involves the bankruptcy and suicide of McGafferty, one of the nation's leading and wealthiest industrialists and bankers. McGafferty fails not through historical necessity, the charge of the Communists, but through a loss of vision, courage, and love. McGafferty, speaking about the suicide of his colleague Shelton, might well have been speaking about himself. Shelton had believed in the capacity of the American to build his republic, to "shape his world."

Now there was no future: only fate.
(*pause*)
Our fathers forged their destiny themselves like men . . .
We take it, spoon-fed, from the prophets, priests, who know the age of man is done, the age of faceless masses is beginning . . .
(*pause*)
Necessity has murdered time. . . .

Preoccupied with the abstractions of economic theory, McGafferty has also lost his capacity to love. Ione, his mistress, tries to help him recover his feeling for life but knows that she has failed: "You're gone and when I call to you it's someone/else turns back to speak. (*silence*) I do not/know you. . . ."

By far the most interesting response to *Panic* came from the exchange between the poet and the "editors of *The New Masses* and some of their Marxist friends." MacLeish met with these critics after the third performance, their debate taking place on stage. His critics believed in historical determinism; he did not. They, MacLeish said in the new preface to *Panic* in *Six Plays* (1980), "believed that history was made by immutable laws divulged by suitable oracles while the author continued to put his trust in the Jeffersonian doctrine that History is made by men. And this difference . . . affected their respective views of the Great Depression." For them "the Great Depression proved the truth of historical determinism: the Pytho of London had foretold the inevitable collapse of capitalism and here it was collapsing, taking self-government and the private activities of human beings with it." For MacLeish the Great Depression was caused by "human stupidity and cowardice and greed," and he quoted "Roosevelt's observation that we had nothing to fear but fear itself, meaning that men, as they had caused the Depression, could put an end to it themselves if they could find the courage."

MacLeish's desire to capture his era in the cage of form and to help shape his times sometimes went beyond poetry to something approaching political rhetoric, as he himself recognized. Some of his poems, he told Mark Van Doren, "were filled with political passion either berating the Marxists or berating their opposites. . . . Something, something went wrong there." Although MacLeish does not mention any specific poems that suffer in this way, he may well have had in mind some of the poems from *Public Speech* (1936). "Speech to Those Who Say Comrade" attacks Marxists, for instance, pointing out that shared experience rather than words makes brotherhood; "Speech to the Detractors" attacks those who detract from the pursuit and love of excellence, "Whether of earth or art,/Whether the hare's leap or the heart's recklessness." "Speech to a Crowd" chides those who do not use their eyes to see (understand) their reality and indicates that in worshiping too long the murdered gods (the past) they have missed their chances. Leave the dead (those who do not understand the possibilities of life) to lament their fate and "Laugh at them!," he advises: "But we who work have end of work together./Tell yourselves the earth is yours to take!/Waiting for messages out of the dark you are poor./The world was always yours: you would not take it."

In "The German Girls! The German Girls!"

the speaker addresses the German girls who, having been betrayed by romantic and militaristic notions about reality, are brought to their senses by a questioning voice, an inner voice. Theirs, finally, is the responsibility for having been deceived. It was they who acceded to the wishes of the men, who gave themselves to the "mounted men." Unconsciously the girls know one of the worst of all paradoxes: "Only by a woman's tenderness can come/The midnight volley and the prison drumbeat." The Eve figure has a responsibility in the fate of man, too.

In "Pole Star," the first poem in *Public Speech*, the pole star symbolizes that love may still guide when liberty, pride, and hope (other guides) have vanished. "Love's star will not" vanish; "Love is that waking light/That leads now when all others darken." But this guide, too, is difficult to see and easily missed. In fact, this guide is the one most missing for all the characters depicted in *Public Speech*. It is missed largely through commitments to abstractions or to the past.

About half of the poems in the volume are love lyrics (private speech), most notable of these being the ten poems comprising "The Woman on the Stair." This sequence is about the betrayal of love, the isolation that follows therefrom, and the difficulty that the young man in particular has in forgetting what has happened. In the last poem, "The Release," the young man manages to remember her as she was when they were in love. In that memory she is still perfect.

Eugene Davidson found the poems of this volume direct, honest, deriving from no political party; he concluded that the perception and imagery were good and that "the poems ought to confuse no one but the critics who have called Mr. MacLeish a fascist." Signi Falk marked this collection as the beginning of MacLeish's efforts to become the poet of American democracy.

In 1937 MacLeish wrote *The Fall of the City*, his first verse play for radio. With Orson Welles playing the role of a radio announcer reporting on and interpreting the actions and words of other characters, the play dramatizes the thoughts and actions of the citizens of the free city of Tenochititlàn, before the conquest. Before the historical fall of the city, a dead woman allegedly "appeared at noon at the tomb's door to prophesy: 'The city of masterless men will take a master.' " In the play MacLeish uses this legend near the opening:

> The city of masterless men
> Will take a master.

There will be shouting then:
Blood after!

Members of the crowd and the announcer try to interpret the meaning of her words but fail. A messenger arrives, warning that the conqueror has landed and is marching toward the city:

> beware of him!
> All doors are dangers.
> The warders of wealth
> Will admit him by stealth.
> The lovers of man
> Will invite him as friend.
> The drinkers of blood
> Will drum him in suddenly.
> Hope will unlatch to him:
> Hopelessness open.

The conqueror has wide appeal, reminiscent of the appeal of Lenin, Hitler, and Mussolini, leaders MacLeish surely had in mind, for he charged them with betraying the revolution of man. The Orator speaks, telling the people not to fear and to resist tyranny by refusing to take up weapons. To live by arms is to invite death by arms: "Force is a greater enemy than this conqueror—/A treacherous weapon."

The argument of the pacifistic Orator seems to prevail and the Announcer, functioning like a Greek chorus, approves the Orator's words:

> Men forget these truths in passion:
> They oppose the oppressors with blind blows:
> They make of their towns tombs: of the roofs burials:
> They build memorial ruins to liberty:
> But liberty is not built from ruins:
> Only in peace is the work excellent. . . .

A second messenger interrupts the celebration following the Orator's words with the news that the conqueror has arrived. Duty-bound to warn the people, the Messenger explains the conqueror's motives—fame, ambition, glory—and his technique: "He brings his own enemy," a scapegoat whom he sets up at every opportunity and characterizes as bloody and vicious. He then attacks the scapegoat, "knocking him down/In every town square/Till hair's on his blade/and blood's all about." The second messenger seems to prevail, but the Priests appear and urge the people to abandon the world and to place all trust in the gods, a position not unlike Abel's in *Nobodaddy*. The crowd wavers in its support of the messenger and turns to the gods. A General reminds the people of what they all should have known, that

> Freedom's the rarest bird!
> You risk your neck to snare it—
> It's gone while your eyeballs stare!

The General appeals to their love for family and freedom and urges them to resist the tyrant lest their children crawl for their failure to fight. But the people are too fearful; they see their city, what they had built with their own lives, as doomed:

> Let the conqueror have it! It is his!
> The age is his! It's his century!
>
> Our institutions are obsolete.
> He marches a mile while we sit in meeting.
> ....
> The age demands a made-up mind.
> The conqueror's mind is decided on everything.

The people succumb, bowing to the conqueror as soon as he appears. But the Announcer, standing to report the events, sees the conqueror raise his visor and whispers that "The helmet is hollow!" The cowering people do not see; they "invent their oppressors: they wish to believe in them/ They wish to be free of their freedom: released from their liberty:—/The long labor of liberty ended!" The play concludes with the Citizens saying, in joy: "The city of masterless men has found a master!/The city has fallen!/The city has fallen!" The Announcer adds in "*flat*" voice his agreement: "The city has fallen," and the play ends.

In *The Fall of the City* MacLeish again showed himself a child of his era by attempting to dramatize a major trend of thought that he fears; he tried to help shape the era by pointing out its faults and implicitly urging their correction. He did not want the Americans to give up the freedom to govern themselves as he thought the Europeans (especially the Germans) were then doing.

Most critics commended MacLeish's efforts, both for the play's opposition to blind acceptance and for the poet's attempt to use a verse form that would appeal to a mass audience. Malcolm Cowley thought the emptiness of the conqueror effective and said that it reminded him of Hitler and Mussolini. Only one critic, Randall Jarrell, censured the play severely; he believed it was an oversimplified, false interpretation of reality that was filled with "useless sensationalism and exoticism" and that it was "internally inconsistent."

Air Raid (1938) has its origin in MacLeish's response to Picasso's *Guernica*. Like *Fall of the City*, *Air Raid* is a verse play for radio. It features an announcer describing what he sees and hears as the people (mostly women) go about their lives, ignoring the threat of the air raid. They do not understand at first that modern war has arrived, that they will be attacked as though they were soldiers, that the conqueror's army has been modernized, and that it arrives over the city in dive bombers. MacLeish captures the horror of their growing realization.

Air Raid received less comment than *Fall of the City*, most of it, however, being favorable: John Brooks Wheelwright thought it MacLeish's best effort to that time. Falk later commented on MacLeish's effective handling of the contrast between life in the small Spanish town and the devastation of the air raid and noted that the announcer's objectivity was a comment on the callousness of our times toward suffering.

In 1938 MacLeish left his editorial post at *Fortune* to become curator of the Nieman Foundation of Journalism at Harvard, and the next year he became Librarian of the Congress (1939-1944). In addition to this service MacLeish was director of the U.S. Office of Facts and Figures (1941-1942), Assistant Director of the U.S. Office of War Information (1942-1943), and Assistant Secretary of State (1944-1945). He wrote many essays during these years, his voice powerful and eloquent in its support of the human revolution and fervent and effective in its opposition to political indifference and totalitarianism. The poetry he published between 1938 and 1948 was nationalistic and patriotic.

America Was Promises (1939) reflects MacLeish's abiding love of the land and of the American continent's promise for its inhabitants. Like so many of his poems, this one presents a speaker who reminds Americans of what they have lost or are in danger of losing. "America was promises to whom?," the speaker asks; then he answers that Jefferson, Adams, and Paine knew. The answer is: "the promises are theirs who take them!/Believe unless we take them for ourselves/Others will take them for the use of others!"

The title of "Colloquy of the States" (first published in the October 1929 issue of *Atlantic Monthly*), accurately describes the action presented—voices of the various states of the union commenting on alleged impurities in Americans because they, unlike those living near the Rhine (the Germans, of course, and Hitler's notion of Aryan supremacy) are of mixed blood or mixed nationalities. The voices refute the argument of Hitler, pointing out that his argument is the sort that Americans, choosing freedom, abandoned at the beginning of the American Revolution. Hitler's argument is atavistic, relieving the individual of responsibility for himself.

After the war MacLeish served his country and the world in helping to found UNESCO, participating in this endeavor throughout 1945 and 1946. And not until 1948 did another collection of his poetry appear, a collection called *Actfive and Other Poems.* "Actfive" is a dramatic poem in three parts. Part one opens with *"the King unthroned, the God/Departed with his leopards serpents/Fish, and on the forestage Man/Murdered."* The question asked is, who will be the "hero in the piece?" MacLeish imagines the aftermath of a totally destructive war and wonders what has happened to humanity. Part two is a masque of mummers, who trace various heroes through history up to "The Crowd" as hero. The third part of the poem announces that "Every age must have its hero:/Even the faint age of fear—/Even here, in this belated place/Deserted by the God, wherein the King/Abandons, and the shape of Man/Lies murdered in his deeds of grace." But in the end,

> The heart persists. The love survives.
> The nameless flesh and bone accepts
> Some duty to be beautiful and brave
> Owed neither to the world nor to the grave
> Nor to the stone God nor the exiled King
> Nor Man, the murdered dream, nor anything
> But only to the flesh and bone.

As in *Nobodaddy* the central character, knowing good and evil, continues; he endures and he loves, without a god, without a king. Man would keep trying because the heart (love of life itself) persists.

Selden Rodman and Hayden Carruth judged this collection too public and propagandistic. Among later critics, Falk thought it revealed "MacLeish's belief that a country reflects the image it worships," while for Grover Smith it clarified what MacLeish had been trying to say in his poetry.

While MacLeish was Boylston Professor of Rhetoric and Poetry at Harvard (1949-1962), he became interested in the cause of Ezra Pound, and in 1950 he delivered *Poetry and Opinion: the Pisan Cantos of Ezra Pound* as a lecture at the University of Illinois. This work supported the right of the poet (including Ezra Pound) to present the world as he saw it, without fear of critics who objected to the poet's work on any grounds other than those

of the art itself. MacLeish was instrumental in getting Pound released from St. Elizabeths Hospital in Washington, D.C., where he had been placed in 1948 because he was judged mentally deranged and thus unable to stand trial for his treasonous statements in support of Mussolini during World War II. MacLeish's willingness to defend Pound's poetry is important, for in the United States McCarthyism was on the rise. McCarthyism took advantage of the Americans' desire for security, for an end to World War II and to the Cold War which followed. But if gaining that security meant the loss of individual freedom of expression, MacLeish was opposed, and the threat of McCarthyism surely meant such a loss to the poet. It was McCarthyism, in fact, that MacLeish had in mind when he wrote *The Trojan Horse* (1952).

Again, MacLeish sought to warn Americans of the dangers in their world. The action of this verse play for radio begins when the Trojans find the wooden horse left outside the walls of Troy, the Greeks having apparently departed. The basic conflict in the play is between those who wish to tear down the walls to bring the horse (a material sign from the gods, they argue) into the city and those who wish the walls to stand, thinking that the signs from the gods are internal and heart-felt, not material. Their god is something to be loved, not feared, and, they argue, it was this love—freely given by the Trojans—which caused the citizens to defend Helen and Paris's right to choose each other in the first place.

Laocoön, opposing the idol-worshiping faction, recommends shoving the wooden horse over the cliff and into the sea. Although the people hear Laocoön's words they do not understand them, just as they do not understand the prophetic question of Cassandra: "Who rides the horse that has no rider?" When Laocoön and his sons are killed offstage by the serpents, the case against his argument is even stronger. When Helen approaches the horse and calls to the Greeks hidden inside, they do not answer, but she senses that they are there and flees. The people do not understand, still, and they breech their own walls. At the end of the play, Cassandra weeps, prophetically seeing the burning and sacking of the city.

MacLeish's concern is clear enough: there was a danger in the United States that people would accept the hypocrisy of McCarthyism, unwittingly participate in the destruction of the principles the republic was built on, and so destroy their own nation. In *The Trojan Horse* the causes of the people's failure are again lack of awareness of the truth and the loss of faith in the principles of the human revolution. More than anything else, MacLeish wanted Americans to pursue and to perpetuate the revolution, begun in this country, but having its roots in the Adam/Cain choice to leave the garden.

Collected Poems, 1917-1952 (1952) added some forty-one new poems to MacLeish's lyric output. Although he was still writing some public poetry, MacLeish's voice in most of the new poems is less public than in any volume since *Frescoes for Mr. Rockefeller's City*. Most public of the poems is "At the Lincoln Memorial," a poem that asks the reader to reflect on Lincoln's struggle to save the union and "To renew/That promise and that hope" with which the nation began but which are in jeopardy. The theme of the westward journey away from paradise is developed in the poet's favorite terza-rima form in "Calypso's Island," where the speaker chooses the real world and his Penelope over the paradise and the enchantress. He would leave the garden, longing "for the cold, salt,/Restless, contending sea and for the island/Where the grass dies and the seasons alter:/Where that one wears the sunlight for a while."

Several poems in the new group speak to MacLeish's efforts as poet. In "A Man's Work" MacLeish laconically notes that the wild apple tree and the wild oak tree thrive in the world, while his tree, the cedar, is "silent with its fruit to bear." "Hypocrite Auteur," recalling Eliot's "hypocrite lecteur" in *The Waste Land* (1922), shows again the function of the poet—to capture his era. "An age becomes an age, all else beside," says the poem, "When sensuous poets in their pride invent/Emblems for the soul's consent/That speak the meanings man will never know/But man-imagined images can show:/It perishes when those images, though seen,/No longer mean." It is the poet, the artist, deserted by the world, who provides man with metaphors that will help him understand what his still-not-understood senses tell him, that life—heroic life—is still possible.

Taken together all the new poems in *Collected Poems, 1917-1952* are fine efforts, and MacLeish was fittingly awarded his second Pulitzer Prize for the book. The publication of this book, his first collection of poetry since 1933, also provided the critics with an opportunity to assess his work in toto. Almost all of them found weaknesses, but many of them concluded that MacLeish had made in one way or another a significant mark in American literature. Reed Whittemore found occasional displays of wit but objected to MacLeish's tub-thumping; Kimon Friar called MacLeish a poet of

action, who attempted "to unite the inner and outer man." Writing later, Signi Falk thought the new poems showed that MacLeish, despite his political involvement, still had his lyric gift.

MacLeish indeed had not lost his lyric gift, for his next work, *This Music Crept by Me Upon the Waters* (1953), a verse play for radio, is more lyrical than dramatic. Most readers find it too chatty. In it Elizabeth appreciates the loveliness of moonrise, as she, her husband, and the Liams await three other couples for a dinner party she is hosting. During the course of the wait, each person recalls having experienced the simple happiness of living. This feeling has been lost by everyone, they decide, but especially by Peter, one of the guests upon whom they wait. The other couples arrive, and the reader learns that on that very evening Peter, and possibly his wife, Ann, had awakened to the beauties of the natural world. Peter and Elizabeth acknowledge that at the moment of his discovery each had thought of the other, and both realize, in Elizabeth's words, that "Happiness is real—the only/real reality that any of us/ever have glimpses of. The rest—the hurt, the misery—all vanishes—/only the blinding instant left us. . . ." The whole company is brought back to the immediacy of the dinner, and, as the play ends, Elizabeth and Peter are called to "potatoes" (the insensitive, unfeeling, unimaginative side of life). The absurdity, for Elizabeth, is that the world of potatoes always comes between the person and her momentary glimpse of beauty and happiness. She is one of MacLeish's Eve-like characters, content to experience the world as it passes; Peter is an Adam/Cain figure, having striven always for some life in the future and realizing only briefly the simple joy of merely seeing.

Perhaps the loveliest of MacLeish's post-World War II work is the collection of twenty-eight poems called *Songs for Eve* (1954), in which the poems recall the idea behind *Nobodaddy*. In the first poem, "What Eve Sang," Eve is conscious of her self, of knowing. Although "Space-time/Is all there is of space and time," there is more than mere existence in space and time. There is also a song of "rhyme/For all of space and all of time." That rhyme is the song of her awareness of human existence and its passing, the knowledge sought by Adam and Eve. Before their awakening they were unconscious of their existence and so merely living in space and time. For all the sorrows of a life of knowledge, Eve is glad to have left the green tree (the garden) and accepted the dry tree (the wasteland where death is certain but known). In the world of the green tree, "Waking is forbidden,"

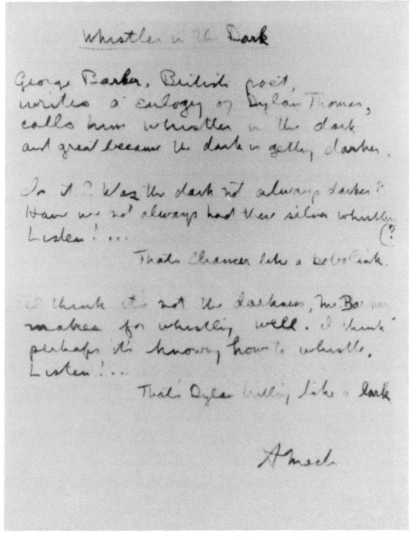

Page from MacLeish's notebook (by permission of the Estate of Archibald MacLeish)

and for this reason Eve says she is thankful for the Fall:

> The Fall! she said—
> From earth to God!
> Give thanks, she said for branch and bole,
> For Eve who found the grace to fall
> From Adam, browsing animal,
> Into the soaring of the soul!

Eve accepts her destiny—the "Dry tree,/Man's tree,/Eternity." It is the tree of her sons, and because of it, man can order and create, make his own world. Ironically, then, his knowledge of his mortality permits him to transcend it through his creations.

Four years after *Songs for Eve* MacLeish pub-

lished *J.B.* (1958), the verse play for which he is best known and for which he was awarded his third Pulitzer Prize. The play generated controversy, especially among those who accused MacLeish of advocating mere sex as a cure for the devastation depicted in the play. Such a reading, MacLeish told a group of college actors at Greenfield, Massachusetts, Community College (15 October 1974), was fatuous. He went on to explain to the young actors that the play was not a conflict between God and man but between justice and love. This theme is twice repeated by Nickles near the opening of the play when he recalls Job's song:

> "If God is God he is not good,
> If God is good he is not God;
> Take the even, take the odd,

I would not sleep here if I could
Except for the little green leaves in the wood
And the Wind on the water."

It is this love for life, expressed in the last two lines of the song, that J.B. loses in the course of the action of the play; it is up to his Eve-like wife, Sarah, to help him regain that love. The function of Sarah is different from the function of Job's wife in the biblical version and constitutes MacLeish's major addition to the story.

The play, MacLeish said, was generated by his haunting recollection of a woman who had been bombed out three times during the London bombings. Where was justice? The play at last took form only when MacLeish conceived of Zuss and Nickles, the two circus workers who play God and Satan, for it was MacLeish's conception of their watching the performance of their "play" that gave him the perspective he needed to complete the work.

The action of the play is distributed over a prologue and eleven scenes. In the prologue, Nickles and Zuss, two has-been and slightly resentful actors who see little justice in their situation, decide to put the story of Job on the stage, Zuss wearing the mask of God (whose eyes are closed, thus reminiscent of the seemingly indifferent or withdrawn God in some of MacLeish's earlier poetry) and Nickles wearing the mask of Satan (cynically aware, his eyes open and "wrinkled with laughter" but his mouth "drawn down in agonized disgust"). The action of the updated Job story then begins. J.B. is a vigorous, prosperous, life-loving New Englander who believes in a just and merciful God who gives freely his gifts to all who will accept them. Sarah, J.B.'s wife, is less certain. Although she holds that God is just (He both rewards and punishes), she thinks that man must earn his rewards and that J.B. is prosperous because he has earned the right to trust to his luck rather than because of God's grace. Sarah's argument for justice is more like Eve's or Cain's; J.B.'s view is more trusting, like Abel's. In any case, J.B. sees Sarah's view as nonsense:

We get the world for nothing, don't we?
It's given to us, gift on gift:
Sun on the floor, airs in the curtain.

During the next ten scenes, J.B. loses sight of the meaning of his words because everything is taken away from him—his wealth, his home, his five children, even his wife. Coming to comfort J.B. are the worldly communist, the psychologist, and the priest. The communist assures him that his only

wrong was being in the "Wrong class" in the "wrong century—/You pay for your luck with your licks, that's all." The psychologist tells him that he is not guilty but is a victim of guilt, or that if he is guilty, the guilt is deep, inevitable, and not yet known. J.B. rejects this argument because it, like the argument of the communist, refuses to recognize human responsibility. J.B. rejects the priest's argument that he is sinful because he is a man; this argument implicates God in man's sin and J.B. refuses to accept God's involvement. Still, J.B. refuses to repent of a sin of which he is unaware and contends with God (the Distant Voice in the play). Job repents of his contentiousness, at last, and accepts God's authority. As Nickles had predicted, God wins, returning to J.B. all that had been taken from him. But MacLeish's point is not that J.B. gets everything back but that he takes it back, accepts it, because even though he cannot understand God's justice he is still able to love life in the world. If justice cannot be seen and so depended upon as a guide for action, love can (as in "Pole Star"), and this then is the meaning of Sarah's words at the curtain:

Blow on the coal of the heart.
The candles in churches are out.
The lights have gone out in the sky.
Blow on the coal of the heart
And we'll see by and by....

J.B. helps her, *"lifting and straightening the chairs,"* as she continues: "We'll see where we are./The wit won't burn and the wet soul smoulders./Blow on the coal of the heart and we'll know .../We'll know...."

John Gassner thought the resolution of the play was undramatic and showed MacLeish to be more poet than playwright. Other negative criticism quarreled with MacLeish's conception of J.B., thinking of him, in John Ciardi's words, as a "shallow, self-righteous fathead." Kenneth Tynan said the play was written in "bumpy alliterative verse" and called it medieval in "narrative technique." But there was positive criticism, too. Joseph Wood Krutch thought the play put the universe rather than sociology at stage center and, succumbing neither to facile optimism nor to nihilism, addressed the tragic aspects of life. Eleanor Sickles argued that *J.B.* reflected MacLeish's lasting interest in the Fall, which began in *Nobodaddy*. She saw J.B. as a tragic hero whose flaw was a "smug arrogant assumption that 'the God of Galaxies' is a special friend and patron of his," and, she explained, J.B. was brought to perceive the "cosmic power and mystery beyond reach of man's thought," and he thus accepted his separation from paradise and "the mystery of the green tree."

Ciardi, for all his criticism of character, thought that MacLeish might be a great dramatist because he forged "a true poetic stage line for our time," the line showing range, poetic identity. MacLeish himself had something to say about the verse. It is, he told the young players at Greenfield, rhythmical, not metrical, based on a four-stress line. There were two ways in which it might be misread—one was to read it as though it were being recited, the other as though it were not verse. As with the verse in *Panic,* the line itself is crucial, the stresses falling where the sense would naturally place them.

After his retirement from Harvard in 1962,

MacLeish became Simpson Lecturer at Amherst (1963-1967), writing *Herakles* (1967) during this time. Like *Nobodaddy* and *J.B.,* as well as *The Trojan Horse, Herakles* updates a myth that speaks to our era. Professor Hoadley has gone to Greece, having just received a prize in Stockholm for his scientific achievements. He and his fellow scientists have made the world safe for man, but in the process they have unwittingly forgotten their own loved ones and the simple joys of their lives. Modern man as scientist, then, is like Herakles, who, having completed the twelve humbling tasks and now ready for the promise of the gods, turns to them and gets no answer. Like the other MacLeish heroes, he seeks his own answers and refuses to accept the gods' refusal to answer him. His wife, like Sarah in

Mark Van Doren and Archibald MacLeish (Warren V. Bush, ed., The Dialogues of Archibald MacLeish and Mark Van Doren, *1964)*

J.B., tries to comfort him for the madness (and the death of his children) that has come to him. But he will not yet accept her efforts and the story ends with Herakles pursuing as he has always pursued. Herakles is like J.B. in that he desires to know, and not for selfish motives, but he is unlike him in that he refuses to accept his limitations. In this respect he is more like Adam or Cain or Peter. The play received as much positive criticism as any of MacLeish's work since *Streets in the Moon*. Richard Eberhart called it "a splendid new creation in American verse drama, splendid, swift, passionate, just." The play has "something to say," said John Wain, "and succeeds in saying it."

The Wild Old Wicked Man and Other Poems (1968) shows MacLeish at his lyric best. The title poem depicts the old man as too old to love yet still loving: "Too old for love and still to love . . ./For what," he asks, answering himself with more questions: "For one more flattering proof/the flesh lives and the beast is strong?" There is for this aging Adam no end to the search. Other poems on this theme are "The Tyrant of Syracuse," "Hotel Breakfast" (a beautiful little love lyric), and "Survivor." For Grover Smith, the collection shows "Adam victorious, fallen upwards into a stasis of art and beauty."

The first twenty-seven poems of *New and Collected Poems: 1917-1976* (1976) continue the themes of *The Wild Old Wicked Man and Other Poems*. This final collection is dedicated to his wife and contains several autobiographical poems—including "The Old Gray Couple (1)" and "The Old Gray Couple (2)" showing in turn how everything that the couple know they know together except for their certain deaths, which each faces separately in the night; the second poem noting that "love, like light, grows dearer toward the dark." Other autobiographical poems in the collection hark back to his years in the army, to the death of his brother Kenneth. "Family Portrait" captures the speaker's feeling of guilt as he thinks about his brother's death. "Pablo Casals" and "A Good Man in a Bad Time" praise excellence, the first in music, the second in politics. "Night Watch in the City of Boston" contrasts Rome, the city of God, with Boston, the city of Man and "Mother of the Great Republic," and expresses the hope that even in the darkness of the present the Republic stands. MacLeish's public voice re-emerges.

The patriotic theme of "Night Watch in the City of Boston" and the public voice in which the poem is couched also are apparent in *The Great*

American Fourth of July Parade (1975), MacLeish's last verse play for radio. In the play Adams and Jefferson are resurrected on the occasion of the nation's bicentennial celebration to counteract the hypocrisy of the political orator who asserts that "THE U.S.A. IS NUMBER ONE!" and the cynicism of the Sweet Young Thing who says "shit" in response to her schoolmarm's patriotic and sentimental response to the memory of Jefferson and Adams. Jefferson recalls his letter turning down the invitation to attend the fiftieth anniversary of the Republic. About the Declaration and the revolution it spawned, he wrote, "May it be to the world . . ./what I believe it will be: to some parts sooner, to others later, but/finally to all. . . ." Jefferson's argument prevails, the voices of the people recalling his words at the end of the play:

Dust jacket for MacLeish's last poetry collection, dedicated to his wife. In "The Old Gray Couple (2)" the poet wrote, "love, like light, grows dearer toward the dark."

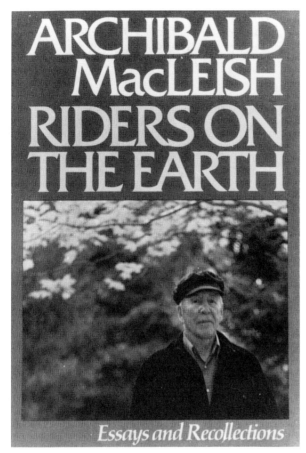

Dust jacket for MacLeish's 1978 collection of prose written in the 1960s and 1970s

The mass of mankind has not been born
saddled and bridled for rulers to ride

but to govern themselves by the grace of God
and they will by the grace of God
                    they will!

MacLeish's life, even during his retirement, was active. Typically, he told Bill Moyers, he would rise early in the morning and write until about noon; he would dine then and work with his hands in the afternoon. Such manual labor, he said, helped him to think, usually unconsciously. The evenings were often capped with conversations with guests or with reading. He was to have been honored by a symposium at Greenfield Community College in Greenfield, Massachusetts, on the occasion of his ninetieth birthday. MacLeish himself had chosen the participants for the symposium. Sadly, the poet-playwright died on 20 April 1982, some three weeks before the symposium on 7 May 1982.

From the very beginning of his career MacLeish was interested in the potential of man to create a society in which he could live justly and happily. To live in this way, he believed, required awareness and love, neither characteristic by itself being quite enough, but love, the way of Jesus, as MacLeish put it to Bill Moyers, was a way that was clearly obtainable even if justice was not.

MacLeish's poetry and verse plays will probably suffer when compared to the work of other poets from his era. Still, his work shows a consistent concern for the craft of lyric and epic poetry as well as verse drama (to which he made important contributions). His effort to develop a wider audience for poetry by adopting a more public voice should also be acknowledged. How, in a world increasingly hostile to the poem, can the poet help shape his society?, MacLeish seemed to ask. His answer was to attach himself to the world in the ways that most men do—through the senses and the emotions. In some of his work MacLeish was unable to realize his intentions. In most, he did. In a few he managed to "capture Heaven and Earth in the cage of form." MacLeish's poetry (in addition to "Ars Poetica" and *J.B.*) deserves to be in the first rank of American literature, and it will undoubtedly receive a critical re-examination in the next decade.

Letters:

Letters of Archibald MacLeish, edited by R. H. Winnick (Boston: Houghton Mifflin, 1983).

Bibliographies:

Arthur Mizener, *Catalogue of the First Editions of Archibald MacLeish* (New Haven: Yale University Press, 1938);

Edward J. Mullaly, *Archibald MacLeish: A Checklist* (Kent, Ohio: Kent State University Press, 1973).

References:

R. P. Blackmur, "Am not Prince Hamlet nor was meant to be," review of *The Hamlet of A. MacLeish, Hound and Horn*, 2 (January-March 1929): 167-169;

Blackmur, "Mr. MacLeish's Predicament," review of *Conquistador*, *American Mercury*, 31 (April 1934): 507-508;

Hayden Carruth, Review of *Actfive and Other Poems*, *Poetry*, 73 (February 1949): 287-289;

John Ciardi, "Birth of a Classic," review of *J.B.*, *Saturday Review*, 41 (8 March 1958): 11-12, 48;

Ciardi, "J.B. Revisited," *Saturday Review*, 43 (30 January 1960): 39, 55;

Ciardi, "The Poetry of Archibald MacLeish," *Atlantic*, 191 (May 1953): 67-68;

Malcolm Cowley, "Muse at the Microphone," *New Republic*, 91 (26 May 1937): 78;

Richard Eberhart, "Archibald MacLeish's Herakles," *Virginia Quarterly Review*, 143 (Summer 1967): 499-503;

Signi Lenea Falk, *Archibald MacLeish* (New York: Twayne, 1965);

Kimon Friar, "The Poet in Action," review of *Collected Poems, 1917-1952*, *New Republic*, 127 (15 December 1952): 19-20;

Michael Gold, "Out of the Fascist Unconscious," *New Republic*, 75 (25 July 1933): 195-196;

Randall Jarrell, "Fall of the City," *Sewanee Review*, 51 (April 1943): 267-280;

Harriet Monroe, "Archibald MacLeish," *Poetry*, 38 (June 1931): 150-155;

Monroe, "The Conqueror," *Poetry*, 40 (July 1932): 216-222;

Monroe, "Tone Poems," review of *The Happy Marriage*, *Poetry*, 28 (April 1926): 44-47;

Theodore Morrison, "Three American Poets," review of *Frescoes for Mr. Rockefeller's City*, *Atlantic*, 153 (January 1934): 6;

Eleanor Sickles, "Archibald MacLeish and American Democracy," *American Literature*, 15 (November 1943): 223-237;

Sickles, "MacLeish and the Fortunate Fall," *American Literature*, 35 (May 1963): 205-217;

Grover Smith, *Archibald MacLeish* (Minneapolis: University of Minnesota Press, 1971);

Kenneth Tynan, "The Theatre," *New Yorker*, 34 (20 December 1958): 70-71;

John Wain, "Mr. MacLeish's New Play," review of *Herakles*, *New Republic*, 157 (22 July 1967): 25-26, 30;

John Brooks Wheelwright, "Toward the Recovery of Speech," *Poetry*, 54 (June 1939): 164-167;

Morton Zabel, "The Poet of Capitol Hill," *Partisan Review*, 8 (January 1941): 2-19; 8 (March 1941): 128-145.

Papers:

MacLeish's papers, memorabilia, tapes, interviews, and manuscripts are collected in the following places: Greenfield Community College, Greenfield, Massachusetts; the Library of Congress; Houghton Library at Harvard; and the Beinecke Library at Yale.

Robert McAlmon
(9 March 1896-2 February 1956)

Stephen Scobie
University of Victoria

See also the McAlmon entry in *DLB 4, American Writers in Paris, 1920-1939.*

BOOKS: *Explorations* (London: Egoist Press, 1921);

A Hasty Bunch (Paris: Contact Editions, 1922; Carbondale & Edwardsville: Southern Illinois University Press, 1977);

A Companion Volume (Paris: Contact Editions, 1923);

Post-Adolescence (Paris: Contact Editions, 1923);

Village:—as it happened through a fifteen year period (Paris: Contact Editions, 1924);

Distinguished Air (Grim Fairy Tales) (Paris: Three Mountains Press, 1925); enlarged as *There Was a Rustle of Black Silk Stockings* (New York: Belmont, 1963);

The Portrait of a Generation (Paris: Contact Editions, 1926);

North America, Continent of Conjecture (Paris: Contact Editions, 1929);

Indefinite Huntress and Other Stories (Paris: Crosby Continental Editions, 1932);

Not Alone Lost (Norfolk, Conn.: New Directions, 1937);

Being Geniuses Together: An Autobiography (London: Secker & Warburg, 1938); revised, with additional material, by Kay Boyle as *Being Geniuses Together 1920-1930* (Garden City:

Robert McAlmon

Doubleday, 1968; London: Joseph, 1970);
McAlmon and the Lost Generation: A Self-Portrait, edited by Robert E. Knoll (Lincoln: University of Nebraska Press, 1962).

Robert McAlmon is one of the major, though neglected, literary figures of the 1920s. He stood at the center of the whole phenomenon known to legend as "the lost generation," that extraordinary company of expatriate writers who for a decade turned Paris into the literary capital of the English-speaking, as well as the French-speaking, world. McAlmon wrote in many forms—fiction, poetry, criticism, autobiography—and, it must be confessed, his poetry is less distinguished than his work in other genres. He also ran the Contact Editions press, which published several seminal works, including Gertrude Stein's *The Making of Americans* (1925) and William Carlos Williams's *Spring and All* (1923). In the end, however, McAlmon's own work degenerated and his reputation has become obscured; too often he appears only as a footnote to more distinguished careers and lives.

Robert McAlmon was born in Kansas on 9 March 1896. His father, John Alexander McAlmon, was an Irishman who had immigrated to Canada; his mother, Bess Urquhart McAlmon, was

born in Chatham, Ontario. His father was a Presbyterian minister who held pastorates around the American Midwest; McAlmon spent most of his youth in South Dakota, until in 1910 the family moved to Minneapolis. McAlmon attended the University of Minnesota for one semester in 1916, and in 1918 he enlisted in the Air Corps, but never got farther than training camp in San Diego. (He later encouraged an apocryphal story that he had joined the Canadian army, and then deserted.) After the death of his father in 1917, his mother moved to Los Angeles. McAlmon sporadically attended the University of Southern California after the war, but in 1920 he left, and headed for Chicago.

Harriet Monroe's *Poetry* magazine had published six of his poems in its March 1919 issue, and he had corresponded with poet Emanuel Carnevali, then working for the magazine. In Chicago he met Carnevali, whom he was to support, years later, when Carnevali was dying of encephalitis in Italy. Later in 1920, McAlmon moved to New York, where he became friendly with the painter Marsden Hartley, and with William Carlos Williams—a friendship which was to be one of the foundations of McAlmon's life for the next thirty years. During this period, McAlmon was living on a garbage scow on the Hudson River, and supporting himself by posing nude for art students at Cooper Union. Together with Williams he founded the little magazine *Contact,* which first appeared in December 1920.

The manifesto which Williams and McAlmon published in this first issue of *Contact* was aimed against the kind of "literariness" which Williams was later to assail in the work of T. S. Eliot. They insisted upon "the essential contact between words and the locality that breeds them, in this case America. . . . We seek only contact with the local conditions which confront us. We believe that in the perfection of that contact is the beginning not only of the conception of art among us but the key to the technique also." These ideas form one starting point for the major line of American poetry which was to lead through Louis Zukofsky's Objectivism to Charles Olson's *Maximus Poems,* its major achievement being Williams's *Paterson.* Indeed, the first line of *Paterson,* "No ideas but in things," is a concise summation of the *Contact* ideology. These ideas also tend to produce long, sprawling, open-ended poems, metonymic rather than metaphoric in structure—and McAlmon's own poetic production is dominated by two ambitious but uneven attempts at the long poem.

In 1921 McAlmon married the English writer

Annie Winifred Ellerman (Bryher), who was visiting America with Hilda Doolittle (H. D.). The circumstances of the marriage have never been fully explained: for Bryher, at least, it was a marriage of convenience, to allow her some measure of freedom from her restrictive family; yet it seems to have left a deep emotional wound on McAlmon. Although Bryher's family was very wealthy, he always denied that he had married for money; he used the Ellerman money to give wide and generous support to many writers. The marriage (which ironically took place on St. Valentine's Day) took McAlmon first to London and then to Paris, which was to become the center for his extensive wandering over the next two decades.

In Paris, McAlmon quickly established himself on the literary scene. He became especially close to James Joyce, who enjoyed his drinking companionship as much as his short stories—stories whose unpolished, rough-and-ready directness appealed to Joyce. It was Joyce who provided McAlmon with the title for his first collection, *A Hasty Bunch* (1922). After the manuscript was indignantly turned down by an English printer, McAlmon had it printed himself, by Darantière of Dijon (the printer of *Ulysses*), as the first of the Contact Editions. McAlmon used Sylvia Beach's bookshop, Shakespeare and Company, as the address for the press.

After a rocky start, McAlmon established a long-standing friendship with Ezra Pound, who always championed McAlmon's writing. It was at Pound's home in Rapallo in February 1923 that he met Ernest Hemingway, whom he initially liked. They went on a trip to Spain (at McAlmon's expense), and Contact Editions published Hemingway's first book, *Three Stories and Ten Poems* (1923); but later the friendship dissolved into rivalry and bitter enmity. An initial friendship with Gertrude Stein also came to grief during a complex dispute over the publication of the first (and for forty years the only) complete edition of *The Making of Americans*—which remains, nevertheless, one of the Contact Press's most impressive achievements.

Some of McAlmon's early poetry had been published, along with prose pieces, in *Explorations* (1921), but in his first years in Paris he concentrated on prose, publishing his finest short stories in *Distinguished Air* (1925), which remains one of the neglected masterpieces of the period. In the second half of the 1920s, however, McAlmon turned more to poetry, publishing *The Portrait of a Generation* in 1926 and *North America, Continent of Conjecture* in 1929. In these books, however, it may be argued

Ernest Hemingway and Robert McAlmon in Spain, 1923

that his poetry is at its best when it sounds most like his prose: that is, when it speaks most directly to his "contact" with the details of local experience.

"We intend no course in literature," *Contact* had claimed. In McAlmon, the wariness of "literature" led to a disdain for "fine" writing: his fiction is always rough, unpolished, fragmentary. Wishing to avoid the impression of highly controlled, intricately revised writing, he shunned "literary" figures of speech, allusions, or metaphors. The results are sometimes unreadable, but at his best there is in McAlmon's writing a remarkable honesty and openness to experience, which enables him to deal directly, movingly, and sympathetically with subjects (such as homosexuality), which Hemingway was unable to treat with similar depth and frankness. The stories are strongest in their use of direct speech or first-person narration, and the same is true of the poetry. The poems eschew traditional "poetic" devices such as imagery or symbolism: they are written in plain, clear American, and present no problems of obscurity. (McAlmon had no liking for surrealism.) They also use mostly free verse but McAlmon was not subtle in his rhythms, and much of the poetry reads rather flat, dull, and prosaic.

The Portrait of a Generation contains some interesting short poems—notably "The Bullfight," which takes the point of view of the bull, and sees the torero's art as merely "butchery," and "Vegetables," which insists that vegetables heaped on market stalls "have an equal amount of fascination" to jewels—but the book's main interest lies in the long poem sequence "The Revolving Mirror." This "Portrait of a Generation" is an attempt to present a contemporary Waste Land, but without Eliot's underpinnings of mythology or literary allusion. It alternates between passages of generalizing commentary in the poet's own voice and portraits of specific individuals caught up in the demoralization of the age. Biographers have speculated on the models for these portraits—that the "Neurotic Correspondence," for instance, refers to Nancy Cunard, "Romance V" to James Joyce, and "Romance VI" to McAlmon's father-in-law, Sir John Ellerman—but they also serve as representative characters. After its exhilarating opening—

> To have as heritage
> SPACE!
> and nothing less

—the poem quickly descends to "that ostracized portion/of degenerate mankind/which lives on the continent/criticizing our home countries." The tone is conversational, and the portraits are often done in monologue:

> Of course Mary had French in her
> and she was gay. She needed it in those days.
> Darnley, you know, was a homosexual.
> Yes. . . . O didn't you know?
> Page boys and all that sort of thing.

The effect is ironic and distancing—so much so that one early review, by Ethel Moorhead, claimed that "in *The Portrait of a Generation* by Robert McAlmon we mostly lose Robert McAlmon." This problem might have been alleviated by organizing the poem around a strong central image, but the "revolving mirror" of the title does not function this way. It keeps on revolving, and there seems no particular reason for it to stop, just as there is no

particular reason for the poem to stop, as it does, at fifty pages, instead of going on for another hundred.

McAlmon himself admitted the open-ended nature of his poetic by subtitling *North America, Continent of Conjecture* "Unfinished Poem." On its last page he writes, "What has happened in America and to her inhabitants,/is a development that is:/incomplete poem." Again the poem works by alternation, this time between discursive sections where McAlmon expatiates prosaically upon the history and nature of North America ("Much may justly be and more has been said/of the warping bigotry of puritanism,/but it can be doubted that this influence/has so affected social and private life as purported") and a series of doggerel "blues," which present the vigorous voices of those outside the official mainstream of society: blacks, Indians, jazz musicians, steelworkers. The contrast is effective, but the general ideas are seldom interesting or original enough to redeem the pedantic tone. The idea of "conjecture," though undeveloped, at least keeps the poem *open*. Although neither of McAlmon's long poems can really be judged a success, they are interesting for what they show about the possibilities of the form. McAlmon was aiming toward that huge, all-inclusive structure which we find in Pound, Williams, Zukofsky, and Olson. Its open-endedness is necessarily metonymic rather than metaphoric: in this way at least, McAlmon was a precursor of postmodernism.

His later work is of diminishing interest. In 1937 New Directions published *Not Alone Lost*, which contained some of his earlier poems as well as some strong political statements on the Spanish civil war. It was not well received critically, and is reputed to be the worst-selling book ever published by New Directions. McAlmon spent the 1930s wandering around America and Europe, until the outbreak of World War II forced him home. His family looked after him: for a while he worked for his brothers as a salesman for medical undergarments in Phoenix, Arizona, and later, suffering from tuberculosis, he lived in Desert Hot Springs, California. Although his literary reputation sank into obscurity, many friends stayed loyal: Pound, Kay Boyle, Katherine Anne Porter. But in his last years his lifelong friendship with Williams collapsed, as a result of what he considered Williams's insensitive treatment of McAlmon's marriage in his autobiography. McAlmon's own autobiography, the caustic and bitterly honest *Being Geniuses Together*, had appeared in 1938; a new edition, with interlaced chapters by Kay Boyle, came out in 1968.

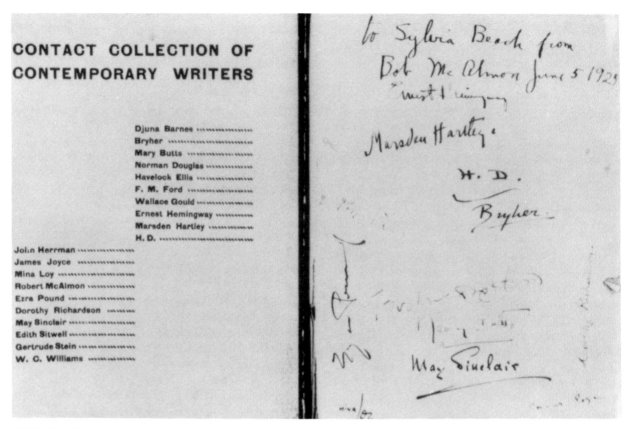

Sylvia Beach's copy of the anthology of avant-garde writing that McAlmon published in 1925 (courtesy of the Sylvia Beach Collection, Princeton University Library)

Robert McAlmon died, of pneumonia, on 2 February (Joyce's birthday, the publication date of *Ulysses*) in 1956, in Desert Hot Springs.

Biography:

Sanford J. Smoller, *Adrift Among Geniuses: Robert McAlmon, Writer and Publisher of the Twenties* (University Park & London: Pennsylvania State University Press, 1975).

References:

Kay Boyle, Afterword to *A Hasty Bunch* (Carbondale & Edwardsville: Southern Illinois University Press, 1977);

Hugh Ford, *Published in Paris: American and British Writers, Printers, and Publishers in Paris, 1920-1939* (New York: Macmillan, 1975);

Robert E. Knoll, *Robert McAlmon: Expatriate Publisher and Writer*, University of Nebraska Studies, new series no. 18 (Lincoln: University of Nebraska, 1957);

Stephen Scobie, *McAlmon's Chinese Opera* (Montreal: Quadrant Editions, 1980).

Papers:

Southern Illinois University, Carbondale, and the Beinecke Library at Yale University have the largest collections of McAlmon's papers.

Claude McKay

(15 September 1889-22 May 1948)

Penni Cagan

See also the McKay entry in *DLB 4, American Writers in Paris, 1920-1939.*

BOOKS: *Songs of Jamaica* (Kingston, Jamaica: Gardner/London: Jamaica Agency, 1912);

Constab Ballads (London: Watts, 1912);

Spring in New Hampshire (London: Richards, 1920);

Harlem Shadows: The Poems of Claude McKay (New York: Harcourt, Brace, 1922);

Home to Harlem (New York & London: Harper, 1928);

Banjo: A Story Without a Plot (New York & London: Harper, 1929);

Gingertown (New York & London: Harper, 1932);

Banana Bottom (New York & London: Harper, 1933);

A Long Way from Home (New York: Furman, 1937);

Harlem: Negro Metropolis (New York: Dutton, 1940);

Selected Poems (New York: Bookman, 1953);

Selected Poems of Claude McKay (New York: Twayne, 1971);

The Passion of Claude McKay: Selected Poetry and Prose, 1912-1948, edited by Wayne F. Cooper (New York: Schocken, 1973).

Claude McKay's poetry and his life display the presence of conflicting forces: his sense of identity as a black man and his desire to write out of a traditional literary heritage. While his poem "If We Must Die" has been heralded as a primary motivator for the Harlem Renaissance movement, McKay made few friends in Harlem during the 1920s, and he resisted characterization as a representative of the Harlem literary community. He was troubled that he was so often identified as a black writer rather than as an individual who was struggling to perfect his poetry, which he wanted to be judged by its merit as verse.

The youngest of eleven children, Festus Claudius McKay was born on 15 September 1889 in south-central Jamaica to Thomas Francis and Ann Elizabeth Edwards McKay, and he spent his earliest years near the hills of Clarendon Parish. When he was six years old he came under the protection of his brother, a schoolteacher and an acknowledged agnostic. This older brother introduced young McKay to literature, science, socialism, and the practice of free thinking. In 1907 McKay was apprenticed to a cabinet maker in order to assist his large and struggling family. He later worked for a wheelwright, and he joined the Jamaican Constabulary in 1909.

While McKay was coming of age, the linguist Edward Jekyll came to the island to study the Jamaican dialect. The two became close friends. Jek-

Claude McKay

yll taught McKay French and introduced him to the literary classics of England, as well as encouraging the young McKay to explore his native dialect and to write poetry. In 1912 McKay published his first poetry: two volumes of dialect verse entitled *Songs of Jamaica* and *Constab Ballads*. *Songs of Jamaica*, in which the poet strongly identifies with earth, nature, and the life of the peasantry, is complemented by *Constab Ballads*, concerned with the problems of urban life in Kingston. These volumes received positive reviews in London, Glasgow, Dublin, and Sydney.

During 1912 McKay won a local prize for his published poetry and used the money to come to the United States and enroll at Tuskegee Institute, but he disliked the structured life he found there and transferred to Kansas State College. He quickly discovered that he had little interest in his chosen field of agronomy and abandoned his plans for a college education.

In 1914 McKay arrived in New York City, where he lived in Harlem but was associated with the left-wing Greenwich Village community, which shared his own traditional educational background. He lost the remainder of his money in an ill-fated restaurant venture and supported himself in a variety of odd jobs, including those of porter, longshoreman, bartender, and waiter. On 30 July 1914 he married Eulalie Imelda Edwards, but the disastrous marriage ended after only six months. In 1917 McKay published his first American poems under the pseudonym Eli Edwards in *Seven Arts* magazine. During the year 1919 McKay became acquainted with Frank Harris, the editor of *Pearson's Magazine*, and Max Eastman, the editor of the *Liberator*.

Also in 1919 McKay's best-known poem, "If We Must Die," was published in the *Liberator*. His most-frequently anthologized poem, it was read by Winston Churchill to the British people during World War II. The poem begins, "If we must die, let it not be like hogs/Hunted and penned in an inglorious spot." It ends with the powerful lines, "Like men we'll face the murderous, cowardly pack/Pressed to the wall, dying, but fighting back!" "If We Must Die," which expresses both love for America and hate for racism, became a rallying cry for justice and freedom during the race riots that broke out in several cities in 1919, and, as racial tensions increased in the South, it had a similar impact.

McKay did not know real racial prejudice until he came to America, and his horror can be found in many of his poems, including "Enslaved," which begins:

> Oh when I think of my long suffering race
> For weary centuries, despised, oppressed
> Enslaved and lynched, denied a human place.

In "Tiger" he wrote: "The white man is a tiger at my throat/Drinking my blood as my life ebbs away."

The duality of McKay's themes is mirrored in the poems themselves: although they are charged with strong emotions, most of them are in the traditional sonnet form, and his poetic inspiration comes from the nineteenth-century romantics. A protest poet with strong traditional ties to England, he did, in fact, have his first volume of verse in standard English, *Spring in New Hampshire* (1920), published in London. The volume is a celebration of nature, and the title poem talks of wasted hours spent indoors "While happy winds go wasting by." McKay was unhappy with most of the reviews because they seemed more concerned with his racial heritage than his skill as a poet. He never again used his native dialect as his poetic language.

In 1920 McKay traveled to London, where he read Karl Marx and supported himself by working for Sylvia Pankhurst's Marxist periodical, *Worker's Dreadnought*. McKay used the opportunity to learn practical journalism. He returned to the United States the following year and became an editor for Max Eastman's *Liberator*. It was during this period that his most widely regarded volume of verse, *Harlem Shadows* (1922), was published, with an introduction by Eastman. He continued to employ the English sonnet form, but his great passion for the plight of black Americans continued to build. This book of poetry heralded the Harlem Renaissance and the literary awakening among black Americans and received glowing reviews from the critics.

McKay traveled to the Soviet Union in 1922 as the spokesman for the American Worker's party and was embraced by the Russian people and Soviet leaders. This journey was the beginning of his wanderings through Europe, a period during which he described himself as an "internationalist." He found himself in Paris during 1923 and supported himself as a nude model until he became ill from pneumonia. He was uncomfortable with the white expatriate world of literary Paris and avoided opportunities to meet Stein, Joyce, and Hemingway. To recuperate from his illness, he went to the Mediterranean coast near Marseilles, where, until 1934, he spent most of his time writing. He completed and destroyed his first novel in 1925, but during these years in the south of France he wrote the novels *Home to Harlem* (1928) and *Banjo* (1929).

Home to Harlem is McKay's most highly regarded novel, but he was sharply criticized by W.E.B. Du Bois for showing the low life of the black people in Harlem instead of their more noble traits. Yet the novel shows that individuals may prove to be much nobler than their environments, a theme also apparent in his poem "The Harlem Dancer": "But looking at her falsely-smiling face/I knew herself was not in that strange place."

During this period McKay was still struggling with his love and hate for America. In "America" he wrote:

> Although she feeds me bread of bitterness
> And sinks into my throat her tiger's tooth
> Stealing my breath of life I will confess
> I love this cultured hell that tests my youth.

When McKay returned to the United States

Claude McKay

in 1934, during the Great Depression, the energy of the Black Renaissance Movement had dissipated. In 1938 he met Ellen Tarry, a Roman Catholic worker, and he underwent a conversion to conservative Catholicism. Through his new-found religion he was finally able to deal with racism, writing in "The Pagan Isms":

> And so I go to make my peace
> Where Black nor White can follow to betray
> My pent-up heart to him I will release
> And surely he will show the perfect way
> of life. For he will lead me and no man
> can violate or circumvent His plan.

McKay spent the last five years of his life in Chicago working for the National Catholic Youth Organization. After his death in 1948, he was given a memorial service in Harlem and buried in New York City. Several years later his *Selected Poems* (1953) was published. Although there has been much criticism of McKay's conventional style and his reputation as a poet has never been as strong as his reputation as a novelist, he will always be considered a poet of deep emotion and remarkable poetic skill.

References:

Wayne Cooper, "Claude McKay and the New Negro of the 1920's," *Phylon*, 25 (Fall 1964): 297-306;

Arthur Drayton, "McKay's Human Pity: A Note on His Protest Poetry," *Black Orpheus*, no. 17 (June 1965): 39-48;

Phyllis Martin Lang, "Claude McKay: Evidence of a Magic Pilgrimage," *CLA Journal*, 16 (June 1973);

Ezekiel Mphahlele, *Voices in the Whirlwind* (New York: Hill & Wang, 1972), pp. 138-140;

Robert Smith, "Claude McKay: An Essay in Criticism," *Phylon*, 9 (1948): 270-273;

Michael Stoff, "Claude McKay and the Cult of Primitivism," in *The Harlem Renaissance Remembered*, edited by Arna Bontemps (New York: Dodd, Mead, 1972), pp. 124-146.

Papers:

The largest collection of McKay's manuscripts is in the Beinecke Library at Yale University.

Edna St. Vincent Millay

(22 February 1892-19 October 1950)

Paula L. Hart

University of British Columbia

SELECTED BOOKS: *Renascence and Other Poems* (New York: Kennerley, 1917);

A Few Figs from Thistles (New York: Shay, 1920);

Aria da Capo, Chapbook (London), no. 14 (August 1920); (New York: Kennerley, 1921);

Second April (New York: Kennerley, 1921);

The Lamp and the Bell (New York: Shay, 1921);

Two Slatterns and a King (Cincinnati: Kidd, 1921);

The Ballad of the Harp-Weaver (New York: Shay, 1922);

The Harp-Weaver and Other Poems (New York & London: Harper, 1923; London: Secker, 1924);

Poems (London: Secker, 1923);

Renascence (New York: Anderson Galleries, 1924);

Distressing Dialogues, as Nancy Boyd (New York & London: Harper, 1924);

Three Plays (New York & London: Harper, 1926; London: Cape, 1927);

The King's Henchman [score], libretto by Millay and music by Deems Taylor (New York & Birmingham, U.K.: Fischer, 1926);

The King's Henchman: A Play in Three Acts (New York & London: Harper, 1927; London: Cape, 1927);

Edna St. Vincent Millay, edited by Hughes Mearns (New York: Simon & Schuster, 1927);

Fear (New York: Sacco-Vanzetti National League, 1927);

The Buck in the Snow and Other Poems (New York & London: Harper, 1928);

Edna St. Vincent Millay's Poems Selected for Young People (New York & London: Harper, 1929);

Fatal Interview, Sonnets (New York & London: Harper, 1931; London: Hamilton, 1931);

The Princess Marries the Page: A Play in One Act (New York & London: Harper, 1932; London: Hamilton, 1932);

Wine from These Grapes (New York & London: Harper, 1934; London: Hamilton, 1934);

Vacation Song (Hanover, N.H.: Baker Library Press, 1936);

Conversation at Midnight (New York & London: Harper, 1937; London: Hamilton, 1937);

Huntsman, What Quarry? (New York & London: Harper, 1939; London: Hamilton, 1939);

"There Are No Islands Any More" (New York & London: Harper, 1940);

Make Bright the Arrows: 1940 Notebook (New York & London: Harper, 1940; London: Hamilton, 1941);

Collected Sonnets (New York & London: Harper, 1941);

The Murder of Lidice (New York & London: Harper, 1942);

Collected Lyrics (New York & London: Harper, 1943);

Edna St. Vincent Millay (photograph by Marcia Stein)

Second April and The Buck in the Snow (New York: Harper, 1950);

Mine the Harvest, edited by Norma Millay (New York: Harper, 1954; London: Hamilton, 1954);

Collected Poems, edited by Norma Millay (New York: Harper, 1956; London: Hamilton, 1957).

OTHER: "Renascence," in *The Lyric Year*, edited by Ferdinand Earle (New York: Kennerley, 1912);

Charles Baudelaire, *Flowers of Evil*, translated by Millay and George Dillon, with an introduction and a biography by Millay (New York & London: Harper, 1936; London: Hamilton, 1936).

Despite a publishing career that spanned three decades and a canon that ranges from lyrics to verse plays and political commentary, Edna St. Vincent Millay is probably best known for her early works, particularly "Renascence" (1912), *A Few Figs from Thistles* (1920), and *Second April* (1921). The first, a 214-line poem revealing a mystical view of the universe, God, and death, caused a sensation as the work of a girl just turned twenty. The second, a sassy celebration of feminism and free love, caught the mood of Greenwich Village life in the racy postwar period of the 1920s. *Second April* showed a more honest approach to the already favorite Millay themes of death, love, and nature. Millay's admirers also commend *Aria da Capo* (1920), a verse play on the foolishness of war, and certain of her sonnets, especially "Euclid alone has looked on Beauty bare" (1923) and the sequences, "Epitaph for the Race of Man" (1934) and "Sonnets from an Ungrafted Tree" (1923).

Edna St. Vincent Millay, the first of the three daughters of Cora Buzzelle Millay and Henry Tolman Millay, was born in Rockland, Maine, on 22 February 1892. In 1900 Cora Millay divorced her husband, an educator with a fondness for poker playing, and settled with her girls in Camden, Maine, providing for the family by nursing. It is little wonder that the poet retained a life-long devotion to the woman who encouraged in all her daughters self-reliance and a love for music and books. The musical talent of Vincent (as she was known in the family) was so obvious that a local teacher gave her piano lessons, hoping to prepare her for a musical career. After a few years the plan was abandoned, but music remained a source of pleasure, a subject for poetry, and undoubtedly the basis for her unfailing sense of poetic rhythm.

It was Millay's early interest in literature that became dominant and soon, augmented by her responsiveness to Nature, found expression in original compositions. At the age of fourteen she had a poem, "Forest Trees," published in *St. Nicholas* magazine, a popular children's periodical that printed a number of her juvenile works. At Camden High School she wrote for and eventually became editor of the school magazine. At her graduation in 1909 she recited an original poem, showing a third side of her early interest in the arts: dramatic performance.

In 1912, at her mother's urging, Millay submitted a long poem, which she entitled "Renaissance," in a contest designed to select pieces for an anthology called *The Lyric Year*. Ferdinand Earle, one of the judges, was delighted with the entry from E. Vincent Millay (as she then called herself), persuaded her to change the title to "Renascence," and fully expected the poem to win first prize. Other judges were not in agreement, and the poem ranked only fourth in the final tally. Nevertheless, when *The Lyric Year* was published in November 1912, "Renascence" received immediate critical acclaim. Two of the earliest to write their congratulations, poets Witter Bynner and Arthur Davison Ficke, became close friends.

The poem, in traditional tetrameter couplets, chronicles the poet's spiritual and emotional development. The enclosed childlike perspective of the opening, "All I could see from where I stood/ Was three long mountains and a wood," soon gives way to the persistence of the inquiring mind, "And reaching up my hand to try,/I screamed to feel it touch the sky." Extending this penetration, the young narrator feels the pressures of a sympathetic response to all humanity, driving her to death underground. A youthful will to live and the reviving power of nature in the image of rain, however, recall the transformed individual, who can now cry, "God, I can push the grass apart/And lay my finger on thy heart!" The heightened spiritual awareness gained by the imaginative experience is shown in the final stanza, which is starkly contrasting in perspective to the first: "The soul can split the sky in two,/And let the face of God shine through."

Many critics were impressed by the poem's youthful freshness, by its strong emotional impact, and by what Harriet Monroe called its "sense of infinity." Caroline B. Dow of the National Training School of the YWCA heard Millay read "Renascence" in Camden and helped her secure a scholarship to Vassar.

Millay, already in her twenties when she en-

Edna St. Vincent Millay on 29 August 1912, the day Caroline B. Dow heard her read "Renascence" and subsequently helped her to secure a scholarship to Vassar College (courtesy of Vassar College Library)

tered Vassar in 1914, after a semester's additional preparation at Barnard College, was very much involved in campus life as well as her studies. She published poems and plays in the Vassar *Miscellany;* acted regularly in school dramas, playing the lead in her own *The Princess Marries the Page* (published in 1932); and composed lyrics for a 1915 Founder's Day marching song. Her studies were concentrated on literature, drama, and both classic and modern languages. Critical biographer Norman Brittin notes, "Her education reinforced the influence of the classics upon her and insured that she would be a learned poet, one more like a Milton, Shelley, or Tennyson than a Whitman or Vachel Lindsay." Indeed, though her poetry would always be termed "American" in flavor, her images and allusions were often based on the classics, while her rhythms and sentiments were forever inviting comparison to established poets from John Donne to A. E. Housman.

The Vassar years, with their feminine collegiality, also had an effect on Millay's outlook, either stimulating or solidifying a healthy regard for the friendship of women and the active feminist principles that were evident in her later poetry. A spirited female independence, to be labeled "flippant" in *A Few Figs from Thistles,* displayed itself also, particularly in Millay's bridling at rigid dormitory rules. This is hardly shocking, coming from a woman in her mid-twenties.

In 1917, not long after her graduation, Millay's first volume of poetry, *Renascence and Other Poems,* was published by Mitchell Kennerley. In addition to the title poem, twenty-two others, many published earlier in periodicals, were included. Critics again responded warmly to "Renascence." The other long poem, "Interim," a blank-verse monologue delivered by a young narrator who has just lost his love, fails to convey the emotional honesty of "Renascence." The dramatic framework, whether it was a device suggested by her reading of Robert Browning and other poets or her own background in theater, was used more effectively by Millay in other works. Her fresh-eyed view of nature, always a Millay strength, is captured in the childlike experience of "Afternoon on a Hill," but it is regrettably clichéd in the often-quoted line, "O world, I cannot hold thee close enough!," of the sentimental "God's World." Its "gaunt crag" and "black bluff" epitomize the artificial poetic diction of which her detractors were often to accuse her.

The last six poems in *Renascence and Other Poems* are sonnets. Though they are not remarkable, they do show indications of the uniquely feminine perspective that was to elicit praise for the best. Sonnet five, in the Shakespearean mode, projects the possible reaction of a young woman if she were to learn of her lover's death while she was in a public place. The realistic detail of the closing lines which should give a sharp sense of the mundane trivia preventing a genuine expression of grief, instead made some readers infer indifference:

> I should but watch the station lights rush by
>   With a more careful interest on my face,
> Or raise my eyes and read with greater care
>   Where to store furs and how to treat the hair

The final sonnet, "Bluebeard," is of interest because she quite suitably transposes the image of Bluebeard's room to that of a feminine bastion, a place of privacy which must be abandoned when profaned by male intrusion. It shows also the prominence of fairy tales as a source of her literary inspiration.

The appearance of this first volume made Millay a presence in the literary world, but it brought her no financial rewards. Millay returned to New York City, hoping to make a living through acting. She and her sister Norma moved to Greenwich Village, home of the Provincetown Players.

In the Village spirits were high and free. It was a new kind of intellectual awakening for Millay, quite different from the formalized education of Vassar. Women's rights and free love were an accepted part of the living code, and the determination to experience life to the full was heightened by the reality of World War I, with its daily records of young lives lost. Millay had long ago shown an independence of spirit which suited her admirably to Village life. The fact that she was an attractive, slender redhead was certainly an added advantage, and the young woman who was so recently surrounded by loving female friendships soon had a line of male suitors vying for her attention. Floyd Dell was the first of the lovers Millay was to have in the Village.

In 1918 Millay finally met Arthur Davison

Arthur Davison Ficke and Edna St. Vincent Millay (Wide World Photo)

Ficke, with whom she had corresponded since his first congratulations on the publication of "Renascence." Ficke, an accomplished sonneteer, had obviously influenced Millay's experimentation with the form. Through their correspondence, she had come to think of the married man as her spiritual mentor. While he was in New York on his way to a military posting in France, however, they had an intense three-day affair. The emotional experience found direct expression in love letters and sonnets written to Ficke (such as "Into the golden vessel of great song") and indirectly in much of her other work. Though they were to remain lifelong friends, the ardor cooled.

The romances and all-night parties made a gay life, but the Village years were ones of poverty for Millay. She made no money from her acting and had to work hard to sell a few poems. One of her chief sources of revenue at this time was *Ainslee's*, a magazine with no literary pretensions. Since she was paid by the line, poetry did not bring a very great return, so she began turning out prose, along with some light poetry, under the pseudonym of Nancy Boyd. These pieces were later collected in *Distressing Dialogues* by "Nancy Boyd," with a coy preface by Edna St. Vincent Millay, in 1924.

In 1920 Millay met Edmund Wilson, who was later, unsuccessfully, to propose marriage to the poet. He was an editor at *Vanity Fair*, a magazine appealing to much more sophisticated tastes than *Ainslee's*. With his influence, Millay began to have most of her work published in that periodical. This brought much-needed capital to the young woman, still involved in the exciting, nonpaying world of theater: acting, writing, and directing. The *Vanity Fair* exposure also gave rise to the popularity the poet was to maintain for many years.

Her second volume of poetry, *A Few Figs from Thistles*, was published by Frank Shay in 1920. The arch tone of this collection did not please reviewers. It did, however, clearly reflect the impression the fast life and fleeting loves had made on the young woman always receptive to emotional experiences. The feelings may have been shallow, as seen in these lines from "To the Not Impossible Him"—

> The fabric of my faithful love
>   No power shall dim or ravel
> Whilst I stay here,—but oh, my dear,
>   If I should ever travel!

—but the saucy kick at convention seen in this

poem and others, such as the "First Fig" with its memorable "My candle burns at both ends," appealed to the postwar generation. Here too was the voice of feminism: women as well as men could be casual in their treatment of sexual love, go on with life when it was over, and look forward to the next affair. Writing much later in his *Lives of the Poets* (1961), Louis Untermeyer most clearly identified the reason for popularity of Millay's poetry during this period: "Plain and rhetorical, traditional in form and unorthodox in spirit, it satisfied the reader's dual desire for familiarity and surprise."

Millay finished *Aria da Capo*, a one-act verse play, for the 1919-1920 Provincetown Players season. It proved to be the outstanding success of the year for them. Starkly dramatic in its concept and construction, the play begins with the stock harlequin characters Columbine and Pierrot exchanging inanities and satirizing current trends:

PIERROT.   Don't stand so near me!
  I am become a socialist. I love

Edna St. Vincent Millay during her years with the Provincetown Players (courtesy of Vassar College Library)

Humanity; but I hate people. Columbine,
Put on your mittens, child; your hands are cold.

The light mood abruptly ends when Cothurnus, the masque of Tragedy, chases the Harlequins from the stage and forces the shepherds Thyrsis and Corydon to play their scene. The two friends play a game, building a wall between them with the stage props constructed of colored crepe paper, apparently cutting Corydon off from a stream. They begin to take the game seriously, their jealousy over possession deepening when Corydon finds a bowl of jewels (confetti) on his side. Before long the two have murdered each other with their carefully guarded possessions: Thyrsis poisons Corydon with tainted water from the stream and Corydon strangles Thyrsis with a string of the precious stones. Cothurnus gives a command to cut the scene, hastily putting a table over the bodies of the slain shepherds and kicking the protruding limbs beneath it. When the Harlequins protest that they cannot continue their scene with bodies under the table, Cothurnus advises them just to pull down the table cover so that the shepherds are out of sight. They do so and resume their chatter. This harsh climax delivers a powerful statement about the folly of war and the callous disregard for human life.

The year of especially hard work brought the additional reward of a $100 prize from *Poetry* magazine for "The Bean-Stalk," which was to appear in her next published collection, *Second April* (1921). Overwork and an active life also brought illness and nervous exhaustion. At the beginning of 1921, however, she was able to sail for Europe, thanks to *Vanity Fair* editor Frank Crowninshield, who paid her a regular wage for pieces she would send from there. In the two years she spent abroad Nancy Boyd articles comprised her chief bread-and-butter writing.

Second April, which came out in 1921, includes much of the same kind of poetry seen in earlier collections. There is the juvenile piece "Journey" with its youthful celebration of nature: "The world is mine: blue hill, still silver lake." The clear, childlike spirit that was such a true voice for Millay is also joyfully exercised in the prizewinning "The Bean-Stalk":

Ho, Giant! This is I!
I have built me a bean-stalk into your sky!
La,—but it's lovely, up so high!

In the same collection, the striking if simplistic

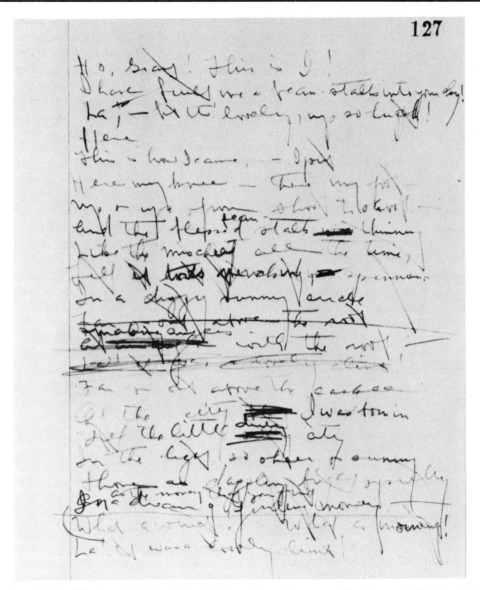

Page from the first draft for "The Bean-Stalk," published in Second April *(courtesy of the Manuscript Division, Library of Congress)*

image of "The Blue-Flag in the Bog" gives voice again to Millay's love of nature and elevates it as the only thing that makes heaven bearable to a child destroyed by a holocaust.

Even in the familiar themes, there is a pervading sense of disenchantment in the volume. "Spring" asks, "To what purpose, April, do you return again?/Beauty is not enough." "Lament" gives a poignant sense of a family's loss of the dead father through skillful use of concrete objects:

> There'll be in his pockets
> Things he used to put there,
> Keys and pennies

Covered with tobacco.

Many readers were reminded of Housman's *A Shropshire Lad*. A more personal record of loss, the moving sequence "Memorial to D.C.," for Vassar friend Dorothy Coleman, culminates in a precise image: "Once the ivory box is broken,/Beats the golden bird no more."

Norman Brittin suggests that Millay's disenchantment with New York City is evident in the collection, especially in "Ode to Silence," a technically accomplished poem on the search for peace, containing the classical allusions and poetic diction which some readers praised and others deplored.

Padraic Colum called it "nothing more than a literary exercise." Undoubtedly it reflected the mental state of the poet just before leaving for Europe.

Perhaps the most highly praised qualities of the collection are the maturing outlook of the poet who cries out for continued life through his work in "The Poet and His Book" and the deft musicality of such lines as "Suns that shine by night,/Mountains made from valleys" from this poem and "There will be rose and rhododendron/When you are dead and under ground" from "Elegy Before Death."

Early in 1921, at the beginning of her stay in Europe, Millay finished the five-act verse play *The Lamp and the Bell*, commissioned for the fiftieth anniversary of Vassar's Alumnae Association. It was published by Shay in the same year. The germ of its story is the Grimm brothers' tale "Snow White and Rose Red," but the play is fleshed out as an Elizabethan drama. At a medieval Italian court the two main characters, Bianca (Snow White) and the robust Beatrice (Rose Red), become sisters when their parents marry. Like the fairy-tale characters, the sisters are devoted to each other and remain so after Bianca's ambitious mother Octavia contrives to have Bianca's warm vulnerability draw King Mario away from Beatrice, with whom he is falling in love. The noble Beatrice never reveals her feelings for Mario to Bianca, and when her father, King Lorenzo, dies, she ably manages his kingdom. After a period of five years, in which Bianca has given birth to two children, Beatrice is attacked by brigands while out hunting. Mario, also hunting in the area, rushes to help but is killed by Beatrice, who mistakes him for one of her attackers. Injured herself, she is taken to her castle to recuperate and is soon visited by Bianca, who wonders why she has not come to comfort her. Beatrice confesses she accidentally killed Mario, and Bianca leaves, now doubly stricken.

In a dramatically charged, if contrived, final act, Bianca is dying and Beatrice has been imprisoned by the arch villain Guido, who has been responsible for much of the duplicity. He agrees to let her go to Bianca, who has sent for her, only after she agrees to surrender herself to him. The sisters are reunited just seconds before Bianca dies. Continuity of their attachment is assured when Beatrice takes Bianca's two daughters (echoes of themselves as children). In the final scene Beatrice's wise fool Fidelio seeks out the mourning queen to tell her that Guido has been murdered by Francesca, the woman he had scorned.

This summary gives no suggestion of the mul-

titude of characters—ladies and lords of the court, servants, pantomime players—that provided a suitable number of parts for the alumnae extravaganza. Probably only for such an occasion could the poet feel free enough to play with the themes of female platonic love as well as feminism so freely. Though the poet herself did not take the work seriously, the drama shows how she could take an essential human truth (the firm friendship of young girls) and make it her own. Unlike the Grimms' heroines, whose adventures in the story are symbolic introductions to sexual love, after which they take their destined places as wives, Millay's protagonists insist that platonic devotion is a genuine feminine trait that does not end when one reaches marriageable age.

Though more-recent commentators, such as Brittin, have deplored the stereotypes and contrivances and though Millay herself thought the play would surely suffer in obvious comparison to Elizabethan works, Mark Van Doren, writing in 1921, found the drama delightful, predicting it would be "best remembered as a delicate riot of gay asides and impeccable metaphors, Elizabethan to the bottom yet not in the least derivative; it bubbles pure poetry."

In contrast to *The Lamp and the Bell*, the other verse play that was published in the same year, *Two Slatterns and a King*, is an easily dismissed farce in regular four-foot couplets that Millay had both written and produced at Vassar. Borrowing again from fairy tales, she used the theme of the king seeking a suitable bride. He desires the tidiest woman in the kingdom, but because of an odd series of accidents that will occur in daily life, he mistakenly chooses Slut instead of Tidy.

Millay's European travels took her to France, England, Albania, Italy, Austria, and Hungary. These were years of adventure and discovery, undoubtedly, but they were also lonely ones for the poet. Both of her younger sisters married, and Arthur Davison Ficke, whose marriage was breaking up, had already formed a close relationship with Gladys Brown. It is not surprising that Millay accepted a long-distance marriage proposal from poet Witter Bynner, Ficke's closest friend. There is some question about the seriousness of the initial proposal. In any case, after a short period of time, both agreed that the match would not work. By the spring of 1922, Millay was able to bring her mother to Europe, boosting the spirits of both women.

Despite her ill health and concentration on the Nancy Boyd pieces in 1922, Millay did publish some poetry in that year, including a pamphlet of her poem *The Ballad of the Harp-Weaver*. Her efforts were crowned with a Pulitzer Prize for poetry in 1923.

Back in New York at a party in the spring of 1923, Millay was paired with Eugen Boissevain, a man she had met at previous Village gatherings, as lovers in a game of charades. Boissevain was a forty-three-year-old businessman and widower. Though the two had shown no interest in each other before, a strong attraction developed on that single night, and the two were married on 18 July 1923. If her public was surprised that the free spirit had succumbed to marriage, it could have no quarrel with the whirlwind way she went about it. Immediately after the wedding, Boissevain took his wife to the hospital for intestinal surgery. This fatherly solicitude was to be a trademark of their marriage, as Boissevain relieved Millay from the burden of everyday details. He was also an ardent feminist and had a high regard for the significance of Millay's writing.

The Harp-Weaver and Other Poems was prepared during her convalescence and was published in 1923 by Harper and Brothers, with whom Millay

Eugen Boissevain shortly before his marriage to Edna St. Vincent Millay

was to form a lasting business association. If readers were looking for a marked maturity or some fresh insights as a result of her European travel, they must have been disappointed, for most of the poems in the collection explored themes already closely associated with the writer. John Gould Fletcher summarily dismissed the title poem as "the unforgettable rhythm of Mother Goose, the verbal utterance of a primer—all used to deal out an idea which is wishy-washy to the point of intellectual feebleness. . . ." The poem is the sentimental story of a little boy's mother, who dies one Christmas Eve, but not before weaving on "the harp with a woman's head" an appropriate legacy:

> And piled up beside her
>   And toppling to the skies,
> Were the clothes of a king's son
>   Just my size.

The poem has been seen as an allegory of the rich cultural gifts Cora Millay had given her children, even when necessities were difficult to obtain. That may be the case, but the poem can also be seen as one of the more successful of the instances in which Millay used the child's voice. The simple quatrains, reminiscent of nursery rhymes, convey the child's sense of wonder, alerting the reader to the imminence of magic, and delivering the essential emotional truths possible only through the folk medium. In the third of the thirty stanzas, Millay introduces the unusual harp, and any child who knows "Jack and the Beanstalk" is aware that special magic is going to be worked. Likewise, while the conclusion may seem maudlin, it has the charm of the concluding image of Hans Christian Andersen's "The Little Match Girl."

The volume also shows the poet's continuing willingness to experiment with form while pursuing favorite themes, as in "Never May the Fruit Be Plucked," a statement about the inevitable staleness of love, delivered in free verse, with a characteristic image in its conclusion: "The winter of love is a cellar of empty bins,/In an orchard soft with rot." Those who found a mature, more-informed tone to the poems on the loss of love and the unwillingness to accept death were surprised to find poems such as "The Betrothal," in which a woman coldly agrees to marry a man she does not love: "I might as well be easing you/As lie alone in bed." This tone is more appropriate to *A Few Figs from Thistles*.

Also in this collection are some of Millay's best-known sonnets. The seventeen-part series, "Sonnets from an Ungrafted Tree," gives a revealing picture of a woman returning to her estranged husband only to ease his death. Not only are the woman's memories and actions sharply focused, but the poems are filled with detailed pictures of homely New England farm life.

By far Millay's best-known sonnet is that which begins "Euclid alone has looked on Beauty bare." Millay had already received praise for her search for beauty in nature and in human beings, but here she transcends the simply personal, elevating beauty through the mathematical conceit. Mere mortals must forego the sight of beauty and hope at most for the sound of the feminized ideal: "Fortunate they/Who, though once only and then but far away,/Have heard her massive sandal set on stone." The Petrarchan octave gains auditory power from enjambment, as in "let geese/Gabble and hiss. . . ." The sestet with its startling representation of Euclid's vision as "light anatomized" is executed with a *cddccd* rhyme pattern, with the final "stone" throwing emphasis back on "Euclid alone" at the end of the eleventh line. Oscar Cargill testified to its continuing power when he wrote in 1941 that this was a poem one could return to and find something fresh.

The years that followed were busy ones, even though no major new work was published. Millay did a midwestern reading tour in 1924, finding to her disappointment that audiences knew only the poems from *A Few Figs from Thistles*. In the same year, showing an increasing public involvement in social issues, she read her poem "The Pioneer" at a National Women's Party celebration in Washington, D.C., to mark the anniversary of the Seneca Falls Equal Rights meeting. Shortly after, Millay and her husband set out on a lengthy tour which took them to the Orient, India, and France. Upon returning, they purchased a rambling old farm, which they named Steepletop, in Austerlitz, New York. It was a retreat from the city and home for the rest of their lives. Yet another peak in this eventful period was the first academic recognition of her poetry when Tufts University granted her an honorary Litt.D. degree in 1925.

In 1926 Millay was able to combine her three major talents and chief interests—poetry, drama, and music—in the libretto for *The King's Henchman*, an opera by Deems Taylor. The story recounts the tragic undoing of a tenth-century liegeman who betrays his lord's trust by marrying the woman he was sent to bring to the king, were she found acceptable. The libretto presented Millay with the kind of challenges she liked best: creating an authentic archaic flavor in the language while charg-

ing it with a genuine music and the freshness of wit, and conveying the heroic ideal of male friendship while delivering a sharp portrayal of a spirited female chafing at the confines of a male-dominated society. She succeeded, and the opera, performed by the Metropolitan Opera, was well received.

Ever sensitive to the problems of the human condition, Millay's demand for justice and equality increasingly took the form of social protest. She wrote to withdraw her name from the League of American Penwomen in 1927 because they had expelled poet Elinor Wylie, who had broken the rules of convention by living with a married man. She marched with protestors in Boston in defense of Sacco and Vanzetti and was arrested. She had an interview on their behalf with the governor of Massachusetts, but it was to no avail.

"Justice Denied in Massachusetts," the poem Millay wrote to raise public feeling against the execution of Sacco and Vanzetti, was included in her 1928 collection, *The Buck in the Snow and Other Poems*. It and the title poem employ nature images to cry against death, and both contain a bitter, poignant note in their suggestion that mankind itself is an accomplice to this waste, the first by suggesting we are willing to sit and wait for death, allowing the good earth to go to waste around us, and the second by the unstated presence of the hunter who has brought the buck to the ground. Some reviewers, such as Babette Deutsch and Louis Untermeyer, saw the collection as more of the same railing against death, but others, including Max Eastman, found more resonance in the lyrics. Though deploring the somber tone, Untermeyer was pleased by the experimentation with line, as can be seen in the final stanza of "The Anguish":

> The anguish of the world is on my tongue;
> My bowl is filled to the brim with it; there is more
>   than I can eat.
> Happy are the toothless old and the toothless young,
> That cannot rend this meat.

The poet insists that death, especially senseless death, must be fought against, and comfort and sense must be found in life. She found them, characteristically, in nature, the bobolink "Chuckling under the rain," and in the sublime order of music, as in the admirable Shakespearean sonnet "On Hearing a Symphony of Beethoven." In addition to her customary deft handling of form, the poet charged the poem with the intensity of the enraptured listener—"Sweet sounds, oh, beautiful music, do not cease!"—and was able to convey as well the

Deems Taylor and Edna St. Vincent Millay at the time of their collaboration on The King's Henchman *(United Press International Photo)*

dramatic moment of the concert itself, as other transfixed listeners for the moment bear no trace of their everyday pettiness.

Edd Winfield Parks, writing in the January-March 1930 issue of *Sewanee Review*, noted the emerging of a philosophy and considered the work a benchmark, predicting that she could not keep up the lyric intensity with the passing years.

Millay's next collection, published in 1931, was a bold undertaking. *Fatal Interview*, taking its title from a Donne line, is a sequence of fifty-two sonnets telling the story of a love affair. Recent evidence has indicated that an affair Millay had at this time with George Dillon, the much younger man with whom she was to translate Baudelaire's *Flowers of Evil*, was the inspiration for this tale of love won and lost. The first sonnet contains an allusion to Selene and Endymion, though they are not named until the final one. Love is elevated by these classical references, but the poet blends them with the voice of the modern woman, who offers love openly and with the freshness of a child. Love runs its inevitable course, echoed by the cyclical pattern of nature.

The sustained theme and its blending of classicism and sensibility gave a more reflective and universal quality to the work than in other Millay love poems, but this quality did not please all contemporary readers. Many missed the strong, purely personal note; others believed, with Allen Tate, that she had failed to probe the symbols she used as frame. But whether they saw the collection as a rejuvenation of the sonnet form or as a clever exercise in its manipulation, reviewers praised her technical performance. Sharp images and musical language abound, and both can be found in the single opening line of sonnet eleven: "Not in a silver casket cool with pearls." The same poem, an artfully constructed single sentence, displays also the poet's dramatic sureness of voice, as the guileless narrator offers love: "I bring you, calling out as children do:/'Look what I have!—And these are all for you.'"

The final sonnet of *Fatal Interview*, which Tate in his review judged her best poem to that time, is richly evocative, bringing together the picture of endlessly sleeping Endymion and a love-distracted Selene, devastatingly portrayed through fragmented images of the moon seen through clouds and reflected on the sea.

By the time *Wine from These Grapes* appeared in 1934, Millay had suffered the death of her mother and was experiencing increasing anxiety over the fate of mankind itself as global tensions escalated. These two events—one personal and one universal—dominated the contents of the volume. In light of their coincidence, it is not surprising to find a more objective viewpoint in her treatment of death. Not only was the poet mature in years, but she had traveled extensively and had obviously responded to the life she had viewed. The prevailing tone seems to be one of anger rather than the bitterness some contemporary readers sensed. In the controlled, predominantly Petrarchan sonnet sequence "Epitaph for the Race of Man," she achieved a sharp picture of the history of living things, the best in man's nature, and the inexplainable certainty of his self-destruction. The style is rhetorical and contains some highly elaborated conceits, such as her comparison of man to a split diamond "set in brass on the swart thumb of Doom." Sonnet two, dealing with the dinosaur, is an equally astonishing but more effective picture that conveys the idea of the transiency of dominant life forms:

His consort held aside her heavy tail,
And took the seed; and heard the seed confined
Roar in her womb; and made a nest to hold
A hatched-out conqueror . . . but to no avail:
The veined and fertile eggs are long since cold.

Reviewers such as Percy Hutchison and Harold Lewis Cook praised the sequence, many considering it one of her best. Association with "Epitaph for the Race of Man" enriches the collection's more personal poems alluding to the death of her mother. In "Childhood Is the Kingdom Where Nobody Dies" Millay, always attuned to the child's perspective, successfully captures the child's voice in free verse. The use of cataloguing and extended line conveys the impatience of children who have to deal with adults who pay no attention to the important things: "To be grown up is to sit at the table with people who have died,/who neither listen nor speak." In the 1930s the whole world was filled with adults who would not listen but relentlessly prepared for war.

Millay spent 1935 working, both in New York with George Dillon and in Paris, on the translation of Baudelaire's *Flowers of Evil*, which was published in 1936. The chief feature of the translation was the retaining of Baudelaire's hexameter line. While the exercise must have appealed to the technician in Millay, the translation seemed to Allen Tate and Mary Colum a flabby English rendering that did not do credit to Baudelaire.

A more interesting project was underway in 1936, however: the controversial *Conversation at Midnight* (1937), the most experimental of Millay's works. The first copy of the work was destroyed in a hotel fire while the poet was vacationing in Florida, so it had to be completely redone. More than a hundred pages long, the work is the script of the after-dinner conversation of several acquaintances at the New York home of the independently wealthy Ricardo. The host is a liberal agnostic, and his guests include a stockbroker, a painter, a writer of short stories, a poet who is also a communist, a Roman Catholic priest, and a young advertiser. The opinions of these guests vary as much as their ages and professions. Although talk begins innocuously enough with hunting, it wanders inevitably to women and eventually to contemporary social issues, eliciting verbal attacks which very nearly lead to blows after the priest has left. At the end Ricardo pours them all a final drink, and they leave.

Though written in play form, the work has no dramatic structure and remains an exchange of diverging ideas, albeit one in which there is increasing tension. Millay used a variety of poetic forms in the delivery. At times the characters speak in sonnets, and in the humorous discussion of women their accents are those of Ogden Nash.

Peter Monro Jack and Basil Davenport applauded this distinctive break from her usual style, hailing the work as a faithful portrayal of the troubled period. Yet John Gilland Brunini, William Plomer, and John Peale Bishop were dismayed by the odd mix of line and rhythms and disappointed by the inconclusiveness of the argument.

In 1936 Millay suffered a back injury in an automobile accident. Added to her already frail health, it was to hamper her work for years. Her next collection of poetry, *Huntsman, What Quarry?*, did not appear until 1939. Its poems, composed over several years, included the same range of themes and styles that characterized the earlier volumes. There are pieces about lost love with the old sass, such as "Pretty Love, I Must Outlive You," and those with a more tolerant understanding of brief love, as "Song for Young Lovers in a City." There are also death poems, notably the sequence "To Elinor Wylie," who had died in 1928, and, of course, nature poems. The title poem, about a dramatic encounter between a young maid and the thee in archaic style—/Words obsolete, words obsolescent" approximate anything like poetry when she read it at Carnegie Hall in 1941. The intense personal voice had been a most successful idiom for Millay in the past, but lovers of poetry had to agree with Babette Deutsch, whose review claimed, "when she turns to political themes, the gay impudence of her girlhood, the sensitive curiosity of her more mature work, are lost in the shriek of a helplessly angry woman."

The Murder of Lidice, a propaganda piece written for the Writers' War Board in 1942, is an overly sentimental ballad recounting the German destruction of the Czech village through the story of two village lovers planning to marry on that very day.

The strain of these years resulted in a nervous breakdown in 1944, and recovery was slow. Several friends died in the 1940s, most notably Arthur Davison Ficke in 1945. Eugen Boissevain, her mainstay, died in August 1949. Though Millay never recovered emotionally or physically, she continued to write, planning another collection. Still at work, she died of a heart attack at Steepletop on 19 October 1950.

Mine the Harvest, published in 1954, seems a suitable concluding volume. The poet's voice often has the refreshing colloquial style that makes her letters so delightful to read, as in the untitled, "I woke in the night and heard the wind, and it blow-

Edna St. Vincent Millay, circa 1939 (courtesy of Vassar College Library)

huntsman she attempts to dissuade from the chase with the offer of a warm bed, has philosophical implications in contrasting the feminine and the masculine approaches to life.

Robert Francis, recommending the collection as representative of the essential Millay, pointed to the dramatic quality of the poems—"the poet appearing in one part after another, effective in each"—as the key to success with readers. He missed, however, a consistent poetic vision. His comments surely were relevant for this volume and, indeed, provide a useful lens for viewing the entire body of Millay's work.

In the 1940s Millay could not maintain her former pacifism. The atrocities of Hitler's Germany forced her to take a different position, and she literally threw her talent into the war effort. She rightly subtitled *Make Bright the Arrows* "1940 Notebook," but this subtitle did not excuse the prostitution of her talent or make the contents any more palatable. It must have taken every bit of Millay's considerable reading skill to make, "If I address

Edna St. Vincent Millay at Steepletop, correcting proofs for The Murder of Lidice *(courtesy of Vassar College Library)*

ing half a gale./'Blizzard, by gum!' I said to myself out loud, 'What an/elegant/Hissing and howling, what a roar!' "

There is much close observation of nature in this volume, and, if there are hints of the wonder seen already in "God's World," the observer is seasoned by experience of many years, surprised that the now-dead snake had shared her garden all summer, and wondering if the seed of love can thrive in her stony heart as the acorn has grown into a mighty oak in "Here in a Rocky Cup."

This reflective cast, of the individual looking for an affirmation of life and the strength to endure one's declining years, is evident in such diverse poems in the collection as the untitled one beginning "The courage that my mother had" and "Tristan," with the dying lover propped against the thriving oak.

Millay's old spirit does break into the collection. "How innocent we lie among/The righteous! . . ." shows her feisty approval of taking love where it can be found. Her poetic philosophy is delightfully put forth in the sonnet "I will put Chaos into fourteen lines."

Contemporary reviewers thought *Mine the Harvest* too intellectualized for the woman who had been their poet of sensibility, but it seems a most fitting conclusion to the work of a sensitive individual who had always used her pen to let people know just where she stood with life.

By the 1950s Millay's voice was no longer reflective of the spirit of the times, and John Ciardi, in an article written shortly after her death, suggested, "It was not as a craftsman nor as an influence, but as the creator of her own legend that she was most alive for us. Her success was as a figure of passionate living." Yet in the same article he admits to being awakened in his youth to a "sudden sense of life" in her saucy lyrics, and concludes by wondering if her place in literature will be as the reflector of youthful discoveries to be outgrown with maturity.

Ciardi was probably right in identifying youth

as the audience with which Millay would always have the greatest impact. The ecstasy of first love and initial sexual experience, accompanied by the bravado necessary to survive its ending, and the stubborn insistence on life seem vital to every new generation, and her poetry continues to attract young readers able to find their feelings matched in her words.

Millay, however, should also be recognized for breaking through the boundaries of conventional subject matter for women writers, while showing the range and the depth of the feminine character. She achieved success in dramatic, operatic, and lyric composition, and her best sonnets demonstrate a masterful handling of form.

Brittin, in his revised *Edna St. Vincent Millay*, blames modernist editors of anthologies for much of the neglect of the poet in the 1950s and 1960s. Nierman's 1977 bibliography of criticism and Brittin's 1982 revision, along with other recent works, give testimony to an increased interest in Millay's work, which may lead to the much-needed consideration of her mature work.

Bibliographies:

Judith Nierman, *Edna St. Vincent Millay: A Reference Guide* (Boston: G. K. Hall, 1977);
Karl Yost, *A Bibliography of the Works of Edna St. Vincent Millay* (New York: Harper, 1937).

Biographies:

Norman A. Brittin, *Edna St. Vincent Millay* (New York: Twayne, 1967; revised, 1982);
Anne Cheney, *Millay in Greenwich Village* (University: University of Alabama Press, 1975).

Papers:

The Library of Congress, the Berg Collection at the New York Public Library, and the Beinecke Library at Yale University have the largest collections of Millay's papers.

Marianne Moore

Elizabeth Phillips
Wake Forest University

BIRTH: Kirkwood, Missouri, 15 November 1887, to John Milton and Mary Warner Moore.

EDUCATION: A.B., Bryn Mawr College, 1909; diploma, Carlisle Commercial College, 1910.

AWARDS AND HONORS: *Dial* award, 1924; Levinson Prize (*Poetry* magazine), 1933; Earnest Hartsook Memorial Prize, 1935; Shelley Memorial Award, 1941; Contemporary Poetry Patrons' Prize, 1944; Harriet Monroe Poetry Award, 1944; Guggenheim Fellowship, 1945; American Academy of Arts and Letters and National Institute of Arts and Letters Award in Literature, 1946; elected to the National Institute of Arts and Letters, 1947; Litt.D., Wilson College, 1949; Litt.D., Mount Holyoke College, 1950; L.H.D., Smith College, 1950;

Marianne Moore

Litt.D. University of Rochester, 1951; Litt. D., Dickinson College, 1952; Pulitzer Prize for *Collected Poems*, 1952; National Book Award for *Collected Poems*, 1952; Youth Oscar (Brooklyn's Youth United for a Better Tomorrow), 1952; Bollingen Prize in Poetry, 1953; M. Carey Thomas Award (Bryn Mawr College), 1953; Gold Medal (National Institute of Arts and Letters), 1953; "One of Six Most Successful Women of Year" (*Woman's Home Companion*), 1953; elected to the American Academy of Arts and Letters, 1955; Litt.D., Rutgers University, 1955; L.H.D., Pratt Institute, 1958; Boston Arts Festival Poetry Award, 1958; Gold Medal (Poetry Society of America's Gold Medal), 1960; Brandeis University Creative Arts medal, 1963; Academy of American Poets Fellowship, 1965; MacDowell Medal, 1967; Gold Medal for Distinguished Achievement (Poetry Society of America), 1967; Litt.D., New York University, 1967; *Croix de Chevalier des Arts et Lettres*, 1968; National Medal for Literature, 1968; Litt.D., St. John's University, 1968; Litt.D., Princeton University, 1968; "Senior Citizen of the Year" (New York Governor's Conference on the Aging), 1969; Litt.D., Harvard University, 1969.

DEATH: New York, New York, 5 February 1972.

BOOKS: *Poems* (London: Egoist Press, 1921);
Marriage, Manikin, no. 3 (New York: Monroe Wheeler, 1923);
Observations (New York: Dial Press, 1924; revised printing, 1925);
Selected Poems (New York: Macmillan, 1935; London: Faber & Faber, 1935);
The Pangolin and Other Verse (London: Brendin, 1936);
What Are Years (New York: Macmillan, 1941);
Nevertheless (New York: Macmillan, 1944);
A Face (Cummington, Mass.: Cummington Press for The New Colophon, 1949);
Collected Poems (London: Faber & Faber, 1951; New York: Macmillan, 1951);
Predilections (New York: Viking, 1955; London: Faber & Faber, 1955);

Like a Bulwark (New York: Viking, 1956; London: Faber & Faber, 1957);

Idiosyncrasy & Technique (Berkeley & Los Angeles: University of California Press, 1958);

O To Be a Dragon (New York: Viking, 1959);

A Marianne Moore Reader (New York: Viking, 1961);

The Absentee, dramatic adaptation by Moore of Maria Edgeworth's novel (New York: House of Books, 1962);

Eight Poems (New York: Museum of Modern Art, 1963);

Occasionem Cognosce (Cambridge, Mass.: Lowell House, 1963);

Puss in Boots, The Sleeping Beauty & Cinderella: A Retelling of Three Classic Fairy Tales, Based on the French of Charles Perrault (New York: Macmillan/London: Collier-Macmillan, 1963);

The Arctic Ox (London: Faber & Faber, 1964);

Poetry and Criticism (Cambridge, Mass.: Adams House & Lowell House Printers, 1965);

Dress and Kindred Subjects (New York: Ibex Press, 1965);

A Talisman (Cambridge, Mass.: Adams House & Lowell House Press, 1965);

Silence (Cambridge, Mass.: Laurence H. Scott, 1965);

Tell Me, Tell Me: Granite, Steele, and Other Topics (New York: Viking, 1966);

Tipoo's Tiger (New York: Phoenix Book Shop, 1967);

The Complete Poems of Marianne Moore (New York: Macmillan/Viking, 1967; London: Faber & Faber, 1968);

Selected Poems (London: Faber & Faber, 1969);

The Accented Syllable (New York: Albondocani Press, 1969);

Prevalent at One Time (Philadelphia: Cypher Press, 1970);

The Complete Poems of Marianne Moore, edited by Clive E. Driver (New York: Macmillan/Viking, 1981).

OTHER: Adalbert Stifter, *Rock Crystal, A Christmas Tale,* translated by Moore and Elizabeth Mayer (New York: Pantheon, 1945; revised, 1965);

The Fables of La Fontaine, translated by Moore (New York: Viking, 1954); republished as *Selected Fables of La Fontaine* (London: Faber & Faber, 1955).

Marianne Moore made a new kind of verse, yet she denied that she was a poet. She worked with words: they were her trade. What she wrote was called poetry, she said, because there was no other category in which to put it. There are, in fact, no commonly accepted terms for describing the whole of her work and few accurate tags for designating the most radical forms she perfected. The verse received attention from the avant-garde poets and critics who were her contemporaries and from the generation of poets that followed them. She also became well-known, in the later years of her life, as an American eccentric who made "good copy," but her accomplished work baffled many readers. She continues, over a decade after her death, to be more highly regarded than widely read.

Moore's vision, a word that she would have thought too grand for the singular modes of perception embodied in her work, is simultaneously aesthetic and religious. For her, as she wrote in her poem "When I Buy Pictures" (1921), art "must be 'lit with piercing glances into the life of things' [a phrase she excised from A. R. Gordon's *The Poets of the Old Testament,* 1912]; it must acknowledge the spiritual forces which have made it." For example, Glenway Wescott recently recalled, "she voyaged to Italy, and what did she notice in the Cathedral of Saint Pantaloon, one of the physician saints, in Ravillo? That all six of the lions guarding the pulpit were equally bowlegged but that each had a different face, and that their sexes were evenly matched, three and three." The pleasure of seeing the modest work of an anonymous sculptor with whom she felt an affinity is characteristic of Moore. The artist's comic particulars or imperfections, his respect for the individuality of the beasts even though they were conventional symbols, his democratic pairing of the sexes, and the sense of harmony within which the enlivened variations are delineated—all serve the function that art, in Moore's view, ideally served: the presentation of a moment of perception that renewed one's consciousness of the communal sacrament.

There is, as yet, no biography of Moore. Early conversation notebooks, reading diaries, poetry workbooks, drawings, and a voluminous correspondence are collected but unpublished. There are on public record, however, interviews she gave, brief autobiographical essays, reminiscences of friends, and articles written about her life. While they do not provide an intimate view of a long and resilient career, gleanings from them indicate the dedication, the exuberance, and the equanimity with which she went her own way in order to write as she pleased. She might be prudent or she might take risks, but she had sufficient confidence to claim the need to be fallible; and the dynamic equilibrium she sought to create in the activities of the imagination corresponds to a strong belief in life's faulty excellence.

As a child, Marianne Moore learned much about "flawed existence" and contingencies. Her family experienced frequent changes of fortune and loss. Her mother, Mary Warner, had married John Milton Moore, an engineer and inventor, in 1885. Suffering a nervous breakdown in 1887 after the failure of a business he had set up in Newton, Massachusetts, to manufacture a smokeless furnace that he had designed, he returned with his wife and son to his family in Portsmouth, Ohio, where they had settled after the American Revolution. William Moore, his father, having been a river pilot and ship owner before the Civil War, had invested money in the Confederacy, but had survived the loss he sustained and was a well-to-do iron founder. John Milton Moore, however, was committed to an institution for the mentally ill and never recovered from the collapse of his career. Mary Warner Moore and their young son went to live with her father, the Rev. Dr. John Riddle Warner, pastor of the First Presbyterian Church in Kirkwood, Missouri. He had moved to the town outside St. Louis in 1867 from Gettysburg, Pennsylvania, where he had served churches during the Civil War. His wife, Jennie Craig Warner, had died three months after the Battle of Gettysburg. Mary Moore, having named her son John Warner, named her daughter in memory of her mother. Marianne Craig Moore, who was born in the house of her maternal grandfather after her parents were separated, never knew her father. After this grandfather died in 1894 when she was seven, her mother took the children to live in Carlisle, Pennsylvania, because she had a good friend there. Living on a small inheritance, the family was often in strained circumstances, and Mary Moore took a job as a teacher of English at Metzger Institute for Girls at which the daughter had begun preparatory work in 1896. Mary Moore had a Presbyterian faith in providence and the goodness of God. Though the poet thought that she herself was too young for the vicissitudes in her life to have been very upsetting, she never married, and, except for the four years that she was a student at Bryn Mawr College, she lived with her mother until her death in 1947. "She advantaged me," the daughter said of her, "when she remarked under crushing disappointment, *Sursum corda:* I will rejoice evermore."

Her family also influenced Moore's literary disposition. Her paternal grandfather, William Moore, was a "bookish man" who owned a large library and during the last years of life read the *Encyclopaedia Britannica* from A through Z. He was also the brother of "Captain Bixby," the steamboat pilot under whom Samuel Clemens was an apprentice on the Mississippi River. The Reverend Dr. Warner had a regard for "serious books," played the flageolet for his daughter to dance to when she was a child, and was remembered by his granddaughter as "a most affectionate person." Believing in the education of women and tolerance for sectarian differences, he had sent Mary Warner to study at the Mary Institute, which was endowed by T. S. Eliot's Unitarian grandfather, Dr. William Eliot, in memory of his daughter. "My mother," Marianne Moore said, "first instructed us—my brother and me—in French and music (the piano) when we were very small" and had "a passion for books." From her, the poet learned verbal decorum, impatience with imprecision, and dislike, if not avoidance, of "the wish for the deed." Describing Mary Moore's sentences as "Johnsonian in weight and balance," Elizabeth Bishop thought she could detect echoes of the poet's own style—"the lighter and wittier ironies"—in the mother's enviable, extreme precision which provided "a sort of ground base for them." Of her education as a poet, Moore wrote that the most important influence on her style was ethical, and she linked the statement with the advice of her brother, Warner, who "once said of a florid piece of description, 'Starve it down and make it run.' "

Moore, who majored in biology and histology at Bryn Mawr College, where she received an A.B. degree in 1909, told Donald Hall in a 1961 interview that she was sure laboratory studies affected her poetry: "Precision, economy of statement, logic employed to ends that are disinterested, drawing and identifying, liberate—at least have some bearing on—the imagination." She thought seriously of studying medicine.

She was interested in the Bryn Mawr literary magazine and, to her "surprise," wrote "one or two little things for it." Two, appearing in 1907, were entitled "To Come After a Sonnet" and "Under a Patched Sail." There was also, among five others printed in the next two years, a simple, old-fashioned quatrain originally titled "Progress" when it was published in 1909. "They tell me, at college," Moore told Grace Schulman fifty years later, "it was the first thing I wrote," but she did not republish it till 1959, when it appeared in *O To Be a Dragon* as "I May, I Must, I Might." Moore defended it as a poem in which she deliberately broke up a cadence that was also continuous:

Marianne Moore at Bryn Mawr College, May Day 1906 (by permission of the Estate of Marianne C. Moore, courtesy of the Rosenbach Museum and Library)

If you tell me why the fen
appears impassible, I then
will tell you why I think that I
can get across it if I try.

"There," she said, "everything comes in straight order, just as if I had not thought it before, and were talking to you. Unrestrained and natural." She added, "Well, that's an extreme example, too. I don't do that well. I'd *like* to."

The verse is hardly notable, but the comments Moore made about it suggest that she discovered for herself the effect of the run-on line and a colloquial manner. As a college student, she had been, she once remarked, "too immature" for English. She liked to tell that she could elect nothing but courses in biology: "the professors in that department were very humane and also exacting, detailed and pertinacious"; they "made biology and its toil, a pleasure and like poetry 'a quest.'" Moore did

"fairly well" in Latin but twice failed the Italian course she had taken so that she could read Dante in the original; she chose a class in torts with a visiting law professor because "he was compassion itself," and praised another professor who created "an appetite for philosophy and dialectic." The work she remembered appreciating in English was "imitative writing" based on prose texts by Bishop Lancelot Andrewes, Francis Bacon, Jeremy Taylor, John Milton, and others. "People say, 'How terrible.' It wasn't at all, the very thing for me," Moore insisted. "I was really fond of those sermons and the antique sentence structure." Equally significant, perhaps, was the fact that the course was taught by Georgiana Goddard King, a lecturer in comparative literature and the history of art, an acquaintance of Gertrude Stein's since the 1890s, and, as Laurence Stapleton observes, "one of the first art historians in America to recognize the importance of Picasso and other modern French painters" as well as the original work being done by Alfred Stieglitz, the New York photographer. Alerted to the controversially "new" developments in literature and art, the young Marianne Moore was as receptive to them as she was to the "antique" structures and sermonics she imitated in the "terrible" writing course. She once said during those years that she would like to be a painter: "I believe I was more interested in painting than poetry." Because she could visualize scenes and enjoyed stories, she also liked fiction: "And—this sounds rather pathetic and bizarre—I think my verse is perhaps the next best thing to it." All of these predilections were seminal in Moore's finding her own voice and topics for a kind of poem of which no one had seen the like before. "I May, I Must, I Might" (or "Progress") certainly does not foretell it.

"Moore's work," as Bonnie Costello has pointed out, "does not conform to a strict chronological development." Each book she brought out not only published or republished earlier poems, sometimes reworked, sometimes resurrected in a revised form from her very early output (as with "I May, I Must, I Might"), but also included a variety of poems in very different styles and on very different themes. In her books she assembled her verse in groups that represent a variety of modes from different periods regardless of chronology of composition. "The past," she states in the title of a poem published in 1917, "is the present," and, for her, poetry, like science, was "never finished." She was not averse to changing her mind.

The Complete Poems of Marianne Moore, published in 1981, sixty years after her first book,

Poems, in 1921, is appropriately both definitive and incomplete. The volume includes 125 poems that Moore chose from eleven books and uncollected work, translations of four of the *Fables of La Fontaine,* snippets she appended as notes from her heterogeneous learning, and authorized corrections of the first *Complete Poems* (1967). Containing all the verse she "wished to preserve" and conforming "as closely as possible to the author's final intentions," the posthumously published text does not satisfy the scholar's need for a variorum edition. Since Moore continued throughout her life to amend, to cull out, to pare down, and to "perfect" the work according to rules or whims of her own, however, the revised edition is representative of her habits and, in that sense, canonical.

The poet's development is a matter of current debate. Is the work a record of an advancement that was relatively steady over a period of more than fifty years, or was there a high mark with the publication of *Observations* in 1924 or *Selected Poems* in 1935 and a decline during the later decades of writing? On the basis of the publication history of individual poems—many of which are excluded from her canon—it is possible to say that the earliest verse has the look of makeshift, not because of indifference but because of an urgent need to use one's frugal resources. Moore was like a girl learning to sew; if the garment was rather plain and not altogether comparable to the work of a modiste, it was lovingly made at home and would suffice for lack of anything better. At least, she made it herself, and that was a pleasure. With diligence she would become more expert. Moore's "authority with language," as Jean Garrigue said, was "gained by an insistent kind of self-schooling." When a few early poems began to look less and less homemade, she attempted more intricate and complex work which she almost never botched. The successes also extend beyond the early *Observations* or the great middle period; and while there are fewer major poems after the *Collected Poems* of 1951, a small number of the last ones are as fine as anything she ever wrote. She once said that her progress was jerky.

Upon graduating from Bryn Mawr, Moore took a business course at Carlisle Commercial College in 1909-1910, went with her mother for the first time to England and Paris in the summer of 1911, and thereafter taught typing, stenography, bookkeeping, commercial law, and commercial English, fixed the typewriters, and coached the boys in field sports at the United States Industrial Indian School in Carlisle. Continuing to write, she contributed ten poems to the Bryn Mawr alumnae magazine during the years 1910-1915. Then she burst onto the literary scene.

Two poems, "To the Soul of Military Progress" (later titled "To Military Progress") and "To a Man Working His Way Through a Crowd," appeared in the April 1915 issue of the *Egoist,* the London magazine which was then serializing James Joyce's *A Portrait of the Artist as a Young Man* (1916). During the same year, the *Egoist* published five additional poems; *Others,* edited in New York by Alfred Kreymborg, included five of Moore's poems in its December issue (in which there was also work by Man Ray and Carl Sandburg); and *Poetry,* in Chicago, printed four poems. The next year saw the publication of fifteen additional pieces. Twelve of these thirty-one poems survived Moore's sifting of her work over the years. As she wrote awkwardly in "To a Man Working His Way Through a Crowd," a poem in praise of the lynx eye of Gordon Craig, critic and revolutionary theorist of theatrical design, "The most propulsive thing you say,/Is that one need not know the way,/To be arriving."

The 1915-1916 poems are a disparate lot, but they set Moore's directions. Some of the titles suggest a determined originality: "In This Age of Hard Trying, Nonchalance is Good and," "That Harp You Played So Well," "Holes Bored by Scissors in a Work Bag," "In 'Designing a Cloak to Cloak His Designs,' You Wrested from Oblivion, a Coat of Immortality for Your Own Use," or "To Be Liked by You Would Be a Calamity." Several of the poems are addressed to writers: William Blake, Robert Browning, George Bernard Shaw, George Moore, Benjamin Disraeli, and William Butler Yeats (on Tagore)—with whom she had imaginary conversations as if her opinion mattered. "Counseil to a Bachelor [*sic*]" is Moore's first *verse trouvé,* an Elizabethan trencher motto (with her own title and a slight change), anticipating her use of lines from either unlikely or familiar sources in verbal collages to follow. "'He wrote the History Book'" is an amusing play on the word *the* in a child's remark about the importance of his professorial father. Among the poems are also the earliest of what Helen Vendler calls portraits of "self-incriminating fools": "a moribund politician" in "To Statecraft Embalmed"; the obtuse and destructive critic in "To a Steam Roller"; and the wooden obstructionist to learning in "The Pedantic Literalist." Vendler says the "deadly anatomies, so impossible in well-bred life, are unsparingly uttered in print," and Moore's "annihilating metaphors" remind her of "the aggression of the silent, well-brought-up girl who thinks up mute rejoinders during every parlor conversation." Although Moore is stringent on the subject of poetry vis-à-vis conscious and unconscious fastidiousness, determination, ambition, and understanding in "Critics and Connoisseurs," the observations are becoming more tempered and speculative. An easy confluence of images and commentary, fine distinctions, and subtle discriminations moves the poem beyond the acerbic tones of the other satirical sketches into a new freedom and openness.

Two additional early poems serve as examples of Moore's later willingness to return to old work she was not satisfied with and to salvage it when she found what seemed right for it. The humorous title "You Are Like the Realistic Product of an Idealistic Search for Gold at the End of the Rainbow" (1916) was sacrificed for the simple "To a Chameleon" when the poem appeared in *Observations* (1924); "Sun" (1916) was changed to "Fear Is Hope" in *Observations*, but that title became the epigraph when the poem was revised and republished as "Sun" in *A Marianne Moore Reader* (1961). "To a Chameleon" is appropriately printed as a calligram in *O To Be a Dragon;* and though it was written early, "Sun" is the concluding poem for *Tell Me, Tell Me* (1966). These two poems are not only examples of the fact that neither text nor chronology was immutable to her but also are significant in tracing Moore's orientations. "To a Chameleon" is her first description of a living animal observed in its own right. The visual sensation, the light and color of this resilient creature, twined "round the pruned and polished stem" of a grapevine, may have symbolic import, but it is the literal and factual that receive primary attention. "Sun" is a magnificent poem celebrating "the multiplied flames" of the resurrected Christ, and the splendid image of light-on-light partakes more irreducibly of the realities of Christian faith than of the phenomenal world. Whatever changes, returns, or advances one can chronicle in Moore's writing, she remained alert to both the natural and spiritual realms of being throughout her life.

The first appearance of Moore's work in little magazines coincided with other important events in her career. Warner Moore had completed studies at Yale Divinity School, had been ordained as a Presbyterian minister, and was appointed the pastor of Ogden Memorial Church in Chatham, New Jersey, where his sister and mother—"two chameleons"—joined him as housekeepers in 1916. The next year, after his training as a reserve officer, he joined the navy and went immediately on a convoy duty. He also became engaged to be married. Marianne Moore, who had gone on a five-day visit to New York in the winter of 1915 and made other visits to the city during the stay in Chatham, moved with her mother in 1918 to a basement apartment at St. Luke's Place in Greenwich Village, where they lived until 1929. And, "trapped by fortuities" (as she phrased it), she was where she wanted to be.

She had tried earlier without success to get work on Philadelphia and Boston newspapers (though she may have been joking when she mentioned that one of them was the *Boston Evening Transcript*—whose readers the young T. S. Eliot, in a 1915 poem, had ridiculed by comparing them to "some" people "with appetites for life"). But "New York/the savage's romance," Moore would say in a 1921 poem, provided (and she borrowed a phrase from Henry James) "accessibility to experience." No matter that it was "the center of the wholesale fur trade" and "a far cry from the scholastic philosophy of the wilderness." At first she worked as a secretary and private tutor in a girl's school.

Having come of age during the period of modernism when writers, following the example of European artists, were incorrigibly experimental, Moore, as she wrote later of Elizabeth Bishop, was "archaically new." She made friends with other young writers, artists, and fledgling critics who gathered at the bohemian parties she attended; she visited museums, galleries, and exhibitions; she read the *New York Times* every day, and the Bible almost every day. As different as she was from the fashionably au courant, she was encouraged by her friends' romantic but common insistence on the right to be oneself, while at the same time she was given to distrusting the self.

There were fewer poems by Marianne Moore published in the years 1917-1918, but among those she collected are four that display the energy of a young moralist whose outrage stimulated the satirical voice she had already learned to use. "My Apish Cousins" (the title had been changed to "The Monkeys" by 1935 when it appeared in *Selected Poems*), caricatures the social scene as a zoo and ends with a contrast between patronizing snobs, who pretend to understand "difficult" art, and a cat, who genuinely appreciates that it is "strict with tension, malignant in its power over us." "Those Various Scalpels" is a scathing condemnation of a woman, dazzlingly bejeweled, "Whetted to brilliance/by the hard majesty of that sophistication which is superior to opportunity," and dressed to kill with a bundle of lances: words. An equally spectacular description, "To the Peacock of France," on the other hand, glories in the color and display, the jewelry of sense—not license—in the art of Molière, who "hated sham" and "ranted up/and down through the conventions of excess." Criticizing British condescension toward Ireland, Moore's "Sojourn in the Whale" is the wittiest of the early poems. Ireland tries to open locked doors with a sword, threads the points of needles, plants shade trees upside down, has lived with every kind of shortage, and has been compelled by hags to spin gold thread from straw. "There is a feminine temperament," "Circumscribed by a/heritage of blindness and incompetence" that "makes her do these things," but "she will become wise," "give in," and "turn back." At least, that is what "she" (Ireland) has heard "men say." Moore writes as if she knew from experience what those men were talking about. "Sometimes," Warner Moore had told his sister, "you have to have paws and teeth and know when to use them." The early poems confirm that she took the advice. Writing, for her, was an act of intellectual self-preservation. She understood combat and rebellion. Otherwise, she would never have become a person to reckon with in modern poetry.

Of the four poems published in 1918, the only one Moore chose to include in the definitive text is "The Fish." It seems to signal a turning point in the poet's development as, in Elizabeth Bishop's words, "the world's greatest living observer" of natural phenomena. While it is like "To a Chameleon" in the nuances of its images, it is not typographically mimetic. "The Fish," however, uses line breaks and stanzaic arrangements to prevent one from darting through the description, while the visual and aural modulations in the poem emphasize the sentience of the poet's response to the seascape, in which there is continual change, and quicken the reader's awareness. The ocean is both beautiful and treacherous, a source of life as well as a place of conflict, danger, and destruction: the final image of the poem is of "a defiant edifice," a wrecked ship but presumably also a fish, which "can live/on what can not revive/its youth. The sea grows old in it." The curious paradox of dying life within the sea, and of the sea dying within what thrives on it, is emphasized in the third and fourth lines of the poem, where a mussel "keeps/adjusting the ash-heaps"— a startling image which tells the reader that this is a world of detritus as well as of edifice. The sense of life dying (and growing) within the sea and of the sea aging (and perhaps renewing) hovers over the poem in much the same way that a theme hovers over a Picasso painting without being obviously articulated, and the poem stimulates a meditation

on time that the dissolving images express. It is perhaps significant that the poem is arranged by syllable count (a device Moore often uses, though—contrary to the views of some of her critics—she was by no means tied to it) in a period of "free" or "cadenced" verse: she eschews the vaguely intuitive, and adopts the mathematical. She is very much a formalist and is unafraid of the arbitrary. Moore was never to write a better poem. There would be others as good, but they would be different.

During the next two years, 1919-1920, she published only six poems, but four of them appear in the final volume: "In the Days of Prismatic Color," "Poetry," "England," and "Picking and Choosing." The best known of them, and perhaps of all Moore's works, is "Poetry" (first published in 1919); by 1967 she had reduced it from thirty strict syllabic lines to a truncation of the first three, thus disconcerting readers familiar with the original. The notorious opening statement, "I, too, dislike it," had been followed in the original by the comment, "there are things that are important beyond all this fiddle," and the poem had set up and then explored a dialectic in which, "Reading it [poetry] . . . with a perfect contempt for it, one discovers in / it, after all, a place for the genuine." Readers used to the earlier version lamented the loss of her memorable phrase, often cited as a figure for poetry: "imaginary gardens with real toads in them" (which she herself placed in quotation marks, although the source has not been found), and of the quotation from W. B. Yeats identifying poets as "literalists of the imagination," with which phrase the dialectical contraries in the poem found resolution. The complete earlier version is reprinted in the "Notes" to the *Complete Poems*, but Moore nevertheless came to repudiate, in the 1960s, the syllabic verse that became, after the first publication of "Poetry," the form she used most often for years. If, when she cut "Poetry" and changed verse techniques, she wished to provoke impatience among admirers, she succeeded. She became known, probably to her delight, as a virtuoso who fiddled.

Moore's humor is irrepressible and occurs at surprising moments in some of the most serious of her poems. The opening of "In the Days of Prismatic Color," for instance, talks nostalgically of pure, original clarity, "when there was no smoke and color was /fine," and (ironically, since the poem is by a woman) locates those days when "obliqueness was a variation/of the perpendicular and plain to see" (itself a humorous rather than a whimsical conceit) in the time before Eve, "when Adam was alone." The poem comically (and to some readers cryptically) says that sophistication is "principally throat," and, in attacking complexity which refuses to recognize itself as "the pestilence that it is" and which is instead "murky," the poem affirms with disciplined passion that "the initial great truths" will "be there when the wave has gone by." It is a highly serious poem, but at moments the reader laughs out loud. In "Picking and Choosing" the patient and discursive tone is at odds with the rueful and comic assertions, and underlying the poem's humor is the poet's anger and *im*patience at a habit of reading (and of literary critical discourse) which *is* perhaps "daft about meaning." It is the "familiarity with wrong meanings" that puzzles one: "*Summa diligentia* . . . Caesar crossed the Alps on top of a '*diligence*'!" "England" praises England and several other countries, but actually is about America and "plain American which dogs and cats can read!" She knew, too, that in America real toads did not turn into Prince Charmings but Mark Twains.

Moore's first book, *Poems* (1921), was published in England. Twenty-four of her early poems had been collected and arranged without Moore's knowledge by Hilda Doolittle (H. D.), Winifred Ellerman McAlmon (Bryher), and Robert McAlmon for the Egoist Press. Among the reviews was one by Edith Sitwell, who thought the verse "strange and interesting, 'thick and uncouth,' a product of life rather than art." An unsigned review in the *London Times* said that Moore wrote "clumsy prose," had not much to say, and disguised "lack of inspiration by means of superficial unconventionality." Mark Van Doren, in the *Nation*, said she had "wedded wit" but forsaken beauty and sense.

The title and the fifty-three poems assembled for Moore's 1924 book, *Observations*, were her own choice, and the impressive variety of her work is evident. In addition to the early verse, there are three long poems that affirm her maturity: *Marriage*, "An Octopus," and "Sea Unicorns and Land Unicorns."

Marriage, which had been published as a single work in 1923 by Monroe Wheeler, is the longest of all of Moore's experimental compositions: collagelike assemblage in free verse of divergent fragments, quotations without regard to either narrative order or contextual relations as principles of design, it exemplifies the art of quotation at its wittiest. It is a precarious contrivance. The play between the opposing voices and divers texts Moore brings to bear on the subject of marriage is appropriate to the tensions, disharmonies, and imperiled happiness of the marital state. Because the

Marianne Moore, circa 1921 (by permission of the Estate of Marianne C. Moore, courtesy of the Rosenbach Museum and Library)

conflicting elements of the poem tend to carry on a sort of guerrilla warfare with one another, the arrangement incurs the risk of seeming impenetrably chaotic or of being arbitrary rather than unified; but the discordant words of Adam, Eve, and their descendants are reconciled by a comment on "the statesmanship/of an archaic Daniel Webster" that "persists to their simplicity of temper/as the essence of the matter: 'Liberty and union/now and forever.' " Moore leaves unstated the fact that these words, later inscribed on the statue of Webster in Central Park, only temporarily resolved the conflict between the states, whose refusal to act on a fundamental issue of human rights resulted in a Civil War that destroyed a union but emancipated a people in bondage. Comparable as an experiment to T. S. Eliot's collagelike *The Waste Land* (1922), *Marriage* is more high-spirited. It is independently indebted to Picasso and the originators of synthetic cubism in 1912-1914 for both the contiguities of the angles within the form and the general action without a center of gravity. Amused that she was "diagnosed as 'a case of arrested emotional development,' " Moore well knew that the *plaisanterie* dared misreading also in relation to the fact that she never married. Having ridiculed an experience that she later said was "the proper thing for everybody but *me*," she later volunteered the quixotic comment that "you don't marry for practical reasons but for *im*practical reasons." These attitudes underlie the bantering tones and good humor, the high and low comedy, the wit and satire of *Marriage*. It is one of Moore's triumphs.

Writing "An Octopus" was for Moore a vital matter. Its subject is the landscape of the spectacular lofty volcano, Mount Rainier, which she identifies by the Indian name, Tacoma. The work has its antecedents in the romantic ode and the traditions of the sublime: the landscape of the soul. She begins the poem with a description of the "deceptively reserved" octopus of ice lying " 'in grandeur and in mass'/beneath a sea of shifting snow-dunes." She is spurred by this sight to move to insight, and returns in the end to renewed understanding of the awesome "unegoistic action of the glaciers" of

Tacoma. Moore and her brother climbed on the mountain when she visited Bremerton, Washington, in 1922 and again in 1923, and a map showing the octopus pattern of its glaciers is in the collection of her papers at the Rosenbach museum. The description of Mount Rainier as an "Icy Octopus" is borrowed from Robert Sterling Yard, author of *The National Parks Portfolio* (1916) and *The Book of National Parks* (1919). Moore's poem is most certainly not set in an "imaginary garden." The accuracy with which the poet describes what she saw on Mount Rainier makes it possible for a reader who checks guide books to identify the trails she took and even the heights to which she ascended: her observation is scrupulous. She creates an extraordinary visual sense of the flora and fauna, the delicate beauty, and the ecology of the park; but she is not the romantic poet looking into nature to find her own image everywhere. She is the self-effacing and invisible observer. At one point, as if by legerdemain, she quickly directs attention from an image of a marmot, "the victim on some slight observatory,/of 'a struggle between curiosity and caution,'/inquiring what has scared it" to a cavalcade of calico ponies instructed "to climb the mountain" by "business men who require for recreation/three hundred and sixty-five holidays in the year."

On Mount Rainier, 1922: Marianne Moore is third from right with her brother, John Warner Moore, standing behind her (by permission of the Estate of Marianne C. Moore, courtesy of the Rosenbach Museum and Library)

The spotted ponies and the businessmen are the first "tame" creatures in the poem. After their appearance, she parodies the platitudes about the "advantage of invigorating pleasures," the "essentially humane" influence, and the stimulation of "moral vigor" for which the American wilderness is praised. But, she says, the laxity and excesses of the children of Adam threaten the "preserve" and its maintenance; one hears "the main peak of Mount Tacoma/ . . . damned for its sacrosanct remoteness"; "it is the love of doing hard things" that has rebuffed and worn the public out.

Then fact takes over. The ode concludes in explosive cadences depicting an avalanche that cuts the claws of the glacier.Humanity is at the mercy of a fatal, sovereign power. The vital affirmation, through the whole poem, is that nature's sovereign power is indeed fatal, must never be forgotten or ignored, and must be *imaginatively* regarded and respected. Couched almost in the language and form of the discursive essay as well as of the romantic ode, the collagelike technique of the poem poses the absurdities and inadequacies of the language of everyday speech, of journalism, of the guide book, and of the bureaucrat, against the sheer grandeur and delicate exactitude of a place the beauty of which "the visitor dare never fully speak at home/for fear of being stoned as an impostor." Those words are from the Department of the Interior Rules and Regulations, *The National Parks Portfolio* (1922) by the "aesthetic conservationist" Robert Sterling Yard, and the sheer variety in his language (comic in its hyperbole and in its context, a context which makes its extravagances sympathetic and insightful while at the same time accurate as a descriptive register of the park) reinforces the reader's sense of the indifferent arrogance of the state and of commerce, confronting nature, seeking to use or control it, seeking to appropriate it to its recreational or commercial ends. Affirming the essential vitality of the world of matter, "An Octopus" is one of the great twentieth-century poems of the planet earth.

Moore draws two word maps—terrestrial and celestial—in "Sea Unicorns and Land Unicorns." The natural world, real as it was for her, was not the totality of existence and the view that rapid but pervasive changes in Western civilization deprive many people of "the sense of the wholeness of life" illuminate the poem. Within a geographic-mythographic context she deliberately chooses for developing the subject of spiritual poise, the poet brings together the emblematic unicorn (which she says amusingly she has not seen) and the lady, the exemplar of mysterious, irresistible grace, "curiously wild and gentle," by which one is qualified for the vocation of blessing the haughtiest, most elusive of beings: the unicorn is "impossible to take alive," but it can be "tamed by a lady inoffensive like itself"—the Virgin Mary. The "unicorn 'with pavon high' "—signifying poise—is willingly submissive to a power that is the equal of its own but paradoxically superior; and the peaceful surrender of the proudhearted animal quietly dramatizes a reverence for mystery beyond human reason. The "matter" is again vital.

Had Moore written no more verse after these three major poems in *Observations*, she would have established the range and versatility of which she was capable. If she rejected the old formalities in the poems, they are hardly prosaic but rather integrate characteristics of different types of writing in a revolutionary way. In 1924 the Dial Press awarded her $2,000 in recognition of "distinguished service to American letters," and Moore, who had become an assistant at the Hudson Park branch of the New York Public Library, benefited from the controversy that the award provoked among readers of new verse. The press brought out a revised printing of the book in 1925.

It contains one additional poem, "The Monkey Puzzler," which had become "The Monkey Puzzle" by the time it appeared in *Selected Poems* (1935). Moore's knowledge of biology and her interest in curios contribute the images in the verse, but it is particularly informed by the historical moment to which it belongs: the time of the Scopes trial (1925) when Americans were engaged in ugly debates over the challenges from the Darwinian theory of evolution and the origin of the species to the biblical account of the creation of man. Like the intertwined monkey-puzzle tree (of rare value to the evolutionary biologist because it is one of a family of conifers that provides a nearly unbroken record of the past), the poem is intricately articulated but has, nonetheless, "a certain proportion in the skeleton." The proportion is evident in the lighthearted attitude toward the many hindrances in the path of human efforts to apprehend the relationships between the past and the present, an appreciative acceptance of the discoveries attributable to that endeavor, and the acknowledgment of the magnitude of human unknowing. The poem's reconciliation of the conflict between scientific fact and Christian faith is ultimately simple and poignant: "but we prove, we do not explain our birth."

The ambitious modesty of these poems, beginning with "The Fish" and culminating with "The

Monkey Puzzle," may be lost, as John Ashbery has pointed out, "in the welter of minutiae" that "people" some of them. Ashbery also notes an "unassuming but also rather unglamorous wisdom that flashes out between descriptions of bizarre fauna and rare artifacts" that is also evident in the work that would follow. The small detail and the monumental are held together conditionally and depend on each other; integrity does not deny the desire for either facts or the elusive truth which, as she put it in "An Octopus," lies "back/of what could not be clearly seen," but finds language itself to serve the need of coping with the problematics. Among the first critics to recognize Moore's objectives in 1925 was Yvor Winters, who wrote that their basis is "the transference of the metaphysical into physical terms." "I am," he said, "sure of her genius."

The year 1925 was pivotal for Moore, who moved from the job of charging out books at the library to that of editor of the *Dial* magazine, where she worked until it ceased publication in July 1929. She remembered later that "those were days when . . . things were opening out, not closing in." The *Dial*, which had a reputation for esotericism in "the other 'école de Paris,'" concentrated on the arts and sought to connect high culture with all aspects of national life. Critical essays by I. A. Richards, T. S. Eliot, Paul Valéry, Conrad Aiken, Kenneth Burke, and Winters aimed to define literary value, the nature of poetry, and their relation to science and civilization. Other contributors included W. B. Yeats, D. H. Lawrence, Hart Crane, Ezra Pound, George Saintsbury, Ortega y Gasset, Thomas Mann, Hugo von Hofmannsthal, Maxim Gorki, Paul Morand, Padraic Colum, William Carlos Williams, E. E. Cummings, Melville Crane, Paul Rosenfeld, Malcolm Cowley, and Archibald MacLeish. The artists whose work was represented were equally significant: John Marin, Charles Sheeler, Georgia O'Keefe, Max Weber, Kuniyoshi, Stuart Davis, Wyndham Lewis, *le douanier* Rousseau, Brancusi, Gaston Lachaise, Picasso, Cocteau, Seurat, Chirico, and American Indians. Moore not only scrupulously edited manuscripts, and wrote editorial comments and more than a hundred "Briefer Mention" reviews, but also assisted Dr. James Sibley Watson and Hildegaard Watson in the selection of the art to be included. The work was, Moore said, "a revel," even though she had to contend with the grudges and griefs of contributors. To her discredit, she rejected a section of James Joyce's *Work in Progress* (*Finnegan's Wake*, 1939) but she was generally clear-sighted and prescient. The editing

helped her to win her first international recognition, and, after the magazine was discontinued, she was able to support herself and her mother by writing verse and independent reviews or occasional essays.

She and her mother moved in 1929 to Brooklyn, where Warner Moore, who was stationed at the Brooklyn Naval Yard, lived with his family. Remaining there until she felt that the neighborhood was no longer safe for her, Moore returned to Manhattan in 1966; and except for a brief period of teaching at the Cummington School in Massachusetts (1942) and at Bryn Mawr (1953), she continued to work as a free-lance writer until she became a semi-invalid in 1970.

In 1935, urged by friends, especially by T. S. Eliot, she brought out *Selected Poems*, for which Eliot wrote an introduction. The book is dedicated to her mother. By 1942 only 864 copies of the American edition had been sold, and in 1940 nearly 500 remaindered copies were sold to Gotham Book Mart for thirty cents apiece. Yet Moore was philosophical about the book's fate. "To have had the book printed," Moore wrote at the time she learned accidentally of the sale to the Gotham Book Mart, "is the main thing, and all will be well if I can manage to produce some first rate stuff." She would say in 1958 that "Discouragement is a form of temptation."

Selected Poems includes forty-two poems from *Observations* and nine poems that had been published in the years 1932-1934. She later retained all of the new verse in her canon and placed the group at the beginning of *Collected Poems* (1951) and *The Complete Poems* (1967), in the same order she established in the 1935 volume: "The Steeple-Jack," "The Hero," "The Jerboa," "Camellia Sabina," "No Swan So Fine," "The Plumet Basilisk," "The Frigate Pelican," "The Buffalo," and "Nine Nectarines" (the original title was "Nine Nectarines and Other Porcelain"). All of them are superbly realized.

"The Steeple-Jack," which has the precision of a Dürer etching and the ambience of an old-fashioned genre painting, describes "the tame excitement," the confusion brought on by a storm, and the peace after its passing on a summer day in a New England coastal town. This setting, Jean Garrigue observed, has "the gusto of a very idiomatic, very home-grown paradise, . . . the one that's found, when it is found, on earth, when 'there is nothing ambition can buy or take away.'" "The Hero," without self-importance, transcends personal likes and dislikes, fears and exigencies, that

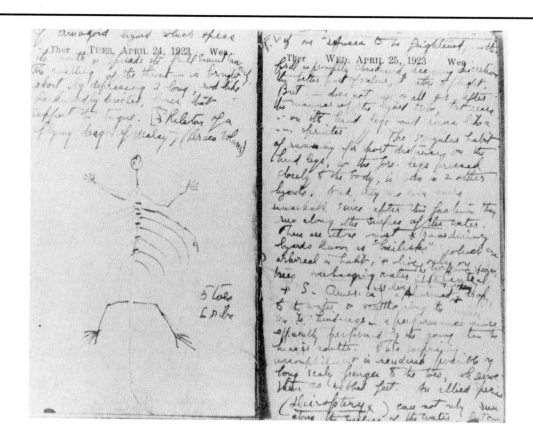

Moore's notes on lizards with a drawing of a Malay dragon, circa 1924-1930, and her 1932 drawing of a plumet basilisk. Both lizards appear in "The Plumet Basilisk," completed in late 1932 (by permission of the Estate of Marianne C. Moore, courtesy of the Rosenbach Museum and Library).

limit action: "He's not out/seeing a sight but the rock/crystal thing to see—the startling El Greco/ brimming with inner light—that/covets nothing it has let go." The understated themes of these two poems are the virtues of hope and courage.

"The Jerboa" has antecedents in the economic crisis of the 1930s and in the Roman Empire, as it is portrayed in Gibbon's *Decline and Fall of the Roman Empire* (1776-1788). The poem is divided into two unequal parts: "Too Much" and "Abundance." The first and necessarily longer part delineates the conspicuous consumption of the Pompeys, popes, pharaohs, princes, queens, and royal households. Describing their good and bad taste, it also points out the servitude of labor and of artists necessary to create the luxuries that such privilege commanded. "Abundance" ironically celebrates the free and vulnerable jerboa. But the complexities of the poem are not resolved by an obvious satirical contrast between "all those things" in "Too Much" and a minimal existence in "Abundance." The jerboa is a resourceful creature living in harmony with its surroundings. "It/honors the sand by assuming its color"; it is self-sufficient, amazingly fast, yet delicate: "it stops its gleaning/ . . . and makes fernseed/footprints with kangaroo speed" (that "fernseed" and the rhyme it then provides for "speed" are both characteristic and astonishing). But still, "Course//the jerboa, or/plunder its food store,/and you will be cursed." The tone is hardly one of sanguine acceptance of threats to the life of the adaptable little animal. And when, at the end of the poem, with characteristically startling humor, Moore says, "Its leaps should be set/to the flageolet" she is not simply affirming that the jerboa should be the subject of art and the source of music, albeit a desert music, haunting, delicate and clear; she is also reaffirming what has been implicit in her description of the animal all along, that it embodies, in itself, those qualities associated (in the first section, "Too Much") with art and music; it is painterly in assuming the color of the sand; in leaping "By fifths and sevenths" it is a musician.

The strains of hunger are also clear in "Camellia Sabina," with its evocative images of food, vintage wines, exotic flowers, circus entertainment, and holiday, all real enough in juxtaposition to the surreality of hallucination and mirage or farfetched allusions to horticulture, French cuisine, the Spanish Order of the Golden Fleece, the children's story of Tom Thumb, and Jean François Millet's well-known painting *The Gleaners*—in which peasants are stooped over to pick up the leavings of grain after the reapers. "I have been finishing a new poem about the camellia and the prune," Moore wrote on 6 February 1933. "Sounds like Will Rogers but it is serious." Rogers, who repeatedly said all he knew was just what he read in the papers, commented during the worst time of the Great Depression that the Senate had "passed a bill appropriating $15 million for food, but the House of Representatives has not approved it. They must think it would encourage hunger."

A mélange of sources and modes serves many purposes in Moore's work. Expressing both religious and aesthetic concepts, her poetry is not without political implications and social criticism. Its moral fervor, furthermore, is inseparable from her close attention to language. "To speak of 'Christ, the beggar,' is inexact," she wrote summarily of Vachel Lindsay's carelessness with words, "since it has never been said of Christ that he begged; he did without." Moore's strategy in the sonnet "No Swan So Fine" points up the difference between an imprecise and a precise use of the word *dead*. Quoting Percy Phillip who had written in the *New York Times Magazine* (10 May 1931) that there was "No water so still as the/dead fountains of Versailles," the poet then contrasts a live swan to a fine china swan perched among "cockscomb-/tinted buttons, dahlias,/sea-urchins, and everlastings" in a rococo candelabrum, and boldly concludes with the statement "The king is dead." In counterpoint to the still water in fountains that are not dead but deathless is the dead king who commissioned their construction. The witty use of the word *fine* to describe a static art object rather than the living but mortal bird also underscores the poet's interest in the accurate use of the right word. And her use of a strict, traditional form—the sonnet—to show without telling the reader that language deserves disciplined regard and care epitomizes the adroitness with which Moore worked.

"The Buffalo" is an original and expressive poem involving the reader in a mental exercise much like that demanded by seeing a face emerge from the overlapping and contrary planes in which it is embedded in Picasso's cubist portraits of Reine Isabeau (1909), Daniel-Henry Kahnweiler (1910), or Ambroise Vollard (1910). After thirty-four lines—"little grids of visual symmetry," as Hugh Kenner called them—the water buffalo comes into focus. The poem's coherence resides in its unstated theme, for which the pre-text is Gerard Manley Hopkins's "Pied Beauty" (1910), with its praise of God for "All things counter, original, spare, strange."

Moore's penchant for employing animals as a

Marianne Moore, circa 1935 (by permission of the Estate of Marianne C. Moore, courtesy of the Rosenbach Museum and Library)

subject for art is pronounced in the decade of the 1930s. *The Pangolin and Other Verse* (1936) continues the interest. Two of the five poems in that volume, "The Pangolin" and "Bird-Witted," show how rarely she repeated herself. The pangolin is initially in the foreground of the poem that bears its name and is described for its own sake: a "model of exactness, on four legs; and hind feet plantigrade,/ with certain postures of a man." Yet pangolins "are not aggressive animals," and, since man "in all his vileness"—his aggressiveness?—has never been long absent from the scene, he inevitably assumes the foreground. (The structure of the poem, rather than narrative, makes this fact apparent. William Carlos Williams said the only help Moore ever gave him in understanding her poems was to tell him she despised connectives.) Whatever similarities or differences between pangolin and man, the two

creatures are not yoked together by oversimplified contrasts. They are seen through and contained in Moore's comic vision, which has room for grace in its devotion to incongruities and absurdities. The poem, indeed, is a meditation on grace: the pangolin ("mechanicked") has "the frictionless creep of a thing/made graceful by adversities, con-//versities." The natural ease of its movements, however, is only one kind of grace, rather a cautious kind. "To explain grace requires/a curious hand," the poet comments. And Moore is nothing if not curious. Who else would choose a pangolin as the embodiment of grace in a bestiary? She considers with seeming ease the manifestations of grace in social behavior, business dealings, "the cure for sins," architecture, and sculpture, but also in the act of writing—the cogent moment: "Bedizened or stark/naked, man, the self, the being we call human, writing-/master to this world, griffons [scrawls, scribbles] a dark/'Like does not like like that is obnoxious'; and writes error with four/r's. Among animals, *one* has a sense of humor." The poet who was so fierce when she was young has, like the pangolin, been tempered by adversities and conversities; she has learned tact; she has grace; she has humor. Not surprisingly, she concludes in "The Pangolin" that yahoo man has "power to grow." If the verse turns on whether one can think well of such an aggressive animal, Moore prefers to give him the benefit of the doubt.

Although "The Pangolin" is one of the most relaxed and discursive of Moore's poems, "Bird-Witted" is fraught with tension and is narratively straightforward. The poet as bird-watcher writes a discordant song of innocence and experience in the face of danger from an "intellectual cautious-/ly creeping cat." The scene is a pussy willow tree where three wide-eyed, open-mouthed young mockingbirds as large as their mother wait for her to bring something that "will partially feed them." Ignoramuses that they are, the fledglings make room on their twig of the tree for the cat, and their tired mother "with bayonet beak and cruel wings" must save them. No poem that Moore ever wrote is as relentlessly clear. For all her good will and politesse, she had her nerve and she knew what it was to be imperiled.

What Are Years, dedicated to John Warner Moore, came out in 1941. The book includes four of the five poems in *The Pangolin*, of which only 120 copies had been printed, as well as ten new poems. The first of them, "What Are Years?," is a wisdom psalm in which the poet meditates on the subjects of fallibility and strength, imprisonment, resolute doubt and mighty singing, mortality and eternity. The syllabic verse has the formality, order, and perfection of ritual; the strophic structure with its questions ("What is our innocence,/what is our guilt? All are/naked, none is safe") and affirmations ("satisfaction is a lowly/thing, how pure a thing is joy") is faithful in form to the antiphonal reading of scriptures at religious services, but the disciplined and subtle rhythms are the poet's own. The poem, she said, was partly written in 1931 and finished in 1939. "The depressing attendant on moral fallibility is mitigated for me," she wrote, "by admitting that the most willed and resolute vigilance may lapse . . . ; but that failure, disgrace, and even death have now and again been redeemed into inviolateness by a sufficiently transfigured courage."

Among the other memorable poems in *What Are Years*, "He 'Digesteth Harde Yron' " continues the moral and aesthetic preoccupations, draws on and amplifies the moral and aesthetic energies, the lines of force that began with Moore's regard for natural history. She writes about extinct birds—the roc known only from its remains and legend, the flightless moa, the great auk—and the flightless ostrich, exploited, threatened, and nearly extinct. The ostrich—a "camel-sparrow"—"was and is/a symbol of justice." The poem, like that on the emblematic jerboa, fuses observation with interpretations. Citing records ("Six hundred ostrich-brains served/at one banquet," the use of the birds' eggshells as goblets and the plumes for decorative purposes, or eight pairs of the birds harnessed to draw carts), she says the facts "dramatize a meaning/always missed by the externalist." The poem continues:

> The power of the visible
>   is the invisible; as even where
> no tree of freedom grows,
>   so-called brute courage knows.
>   Heroism is exhausting. . . .

The revulsion apparent in her account of an endangered species joined with themes that are essentially religious and political is hardly an accident. Among the agonies the poet experienced as she witnessed the menace of totalitarianism to human freedom was the effort to exterminate the Jews of Europe. In an essay on "Feeling and Precision" (1944), Moore wrote that Jacques Maritain, the French moral philosopher, "when lecturing on scholasticism and immortality, spoke of those suffering in concentration camps, 'unseen by any star, unheard by any ear,' and the almost terrifying so-

Marianne Moore (by permission of the Estate of Marianne C. Moore, courtesy of the Rosenbach Museum and Library)

licitude with which he spoke made one know that belief is stronger even than the struggle to survive. And what he said so unconsciously was poetry." Moore did not write directly about the atrocities of the holocaust, but "He 'Digesteth Harde Yron' " commends heroism for contradicting

>   a greed that did not wisely spare
> the harmless solitaire
>
>   or great auk in its grandeur;
>   unsolicitude having swallowed up
> all giant birds but an alert gargantuan
>   little-winged, magnificently speedy running-bird.
>
> This one remaining rebel
> is the sparrow-camel.

The parallels between birds and a people, whose concepts of justice and faith in the power of the invisible are basic in Moore's education, are unspoken in the poem, but the awareness of human suffering because of injustice, intolerance, hatred, greed, and unsolicitude is integral with the work. She had written, in a letter of 1939, of "the wrongful tyranny" of the Germans "in persecuting and being subject to Hitler." She was a student of both natural and human history.

"Rigorists," another of the poems in *What Are Years,* is a tribute to a quiet man, Seldon Jackson, General Agent for the U.S. Education Bureau in Alaska, remembered for actions that prevented "the extinction/of the Eskimo." In "The Labors of Hercules," first published in the *Dial* in 1921 during a postwar period of hysteria and "know nothingism" in the United States, she had protested "age-old toadyism,/kissing the feet of the man above,/kicking the face of the man below," and impatiently asserted

> that one keeps on knowing
> "that the Negro is not brutal,
> that the Jew is not greedy,
> that the Oriental is not immoral,
> that the German is not a Hun."

In that poem, she also stated a principle that motivated the judgments which are pervasive in her writing: "one detects creative power by its capacity to conquer one's detachment," and "while it may have more elasticity than logic,/it flies along in a straight line like electricity." "Light Is Speech," also in *What Are Years,* is for the French people at the time of the Nazi occupation, of the acceptance of fascism by the French radical right, and of the resistance to collaboration with the enemy. The poet's play with words—"free," "frank," "enfranchisement," "France"; "liberty," "fraternity," "generosity," "sincerity,"—*lux et veritas* which animate the poem—prove her sympathy for a people to whom she paid the compliment of light speech, that is, speech which is illumination, light, but not trivial.

"Virginia Britannia" is the poem for Americans in *What Are Years.* The theme, again unspoken, as Marie Borroff has said succinctly, is "E pluribus unum." Moore, says Borroff, "made her country's aspiring motto come true imaginatively in her vision of genuineness: the perceived authenticity of aspect or action that can 'unite' the deer-fur crown of the Indian chief with the coat of arms of the English colonist, and the singing of the hedge-sparrow with the affirmation of human rights in the Preamble to the Declaration of Independence." Moore did not overlook the Irish either. Having written in "The Labors of Hercules" "that we are sick of the earth,/sick of the pigsty, wild geese and wild men," Moore returned in "Spenser's Ireland,"

also in *What Are Years,* to "the greenest place I've never seen." It is tempting but mistaken to read the poem as autobiographical:

> a match not a marriage was made
>   when my great great grandmother'd said
> with native genius for
> disunion, "Although your suitor be
>   perfection, one objection
> is enough; he is not
> Irish."

The Irish, who can "play the harp backward at need," "say your trouble is their/trouble and your/joy their joy? I wish/I could believe it;/I am troubled, I'm dissatisfied, I'm Irish." No poet since Whitman has attempted to give Americans as large an overview of themselves and their relations to humankind as Moore.

Royalty slips record the sale of 1,251 copies of *What Are Years* between 1941 and 1948. The author was beginning to receive serious and praiseworthy attention in academic journals, but she was also damned (by Elizabeth Drew and John L. Sweeney) for "aristocratic quietism," for not speaking "directly to 'general humanity' "; (in the *Christian Century*) for being "a poet's poet" and "sometimes unintelligible"; or (in Clement Greenberg's words) "deficient in energy" and lacking "cultural capital." She was even said (by Randall Jarrell) to represent "a morality divorced from both religion and economics." Ruth Lechlitner, however, remarked on Moore's "comparatively restricted audience" and observed that her gifts "make her a major poet of our time."

Nevertheless (1944) attracted a slightly larger number of readers and went through three printings—a total of 4,000 copies, a figure that probably includes all impressions of the first edition. The war poem "In Distrust of Merits" became one of Moore's most popular poems (indeed Oscar Williams called it "one of the finest poems" of World War II) and the subject of critical debate. Asked about the work in 1961, she said she thought it sincere and truthful, "a testimony—to the fact that war is intolerable, and unjust." But the poem was "haphazard." "As to form," she continued, "What has it? It is just a protest, disjointed, exclamatory. Emotion overpowered me." Yet, honestly critical as she was, she allowed the evidence against her to remain in the canon.

She also retained all of the other poems that make up *Nevertheless.* Among them, "Elephants" is a dream of peace; "A Carriage from Sweden" suggests a travel poster but is a work of deft ironies directed at that country's neutrality during World War II and its belated decision in March of 1944 to receive Jewish refugees who had found sanctuary in Denmark. Toward the end of the poem Moore asks, "Sweden,/what makes . . ./. . . those who see you wish to stay?" The images throughout the poem suggest the answer: "sun-right gable-/ends due east and west, the table/spread as for a banquet," a "Dalén/light-house, self-lit," "moated white castles," or a "bed/of white flowers densely grown in an S/meaning Sweden and stalwartness"—all signify safety and relief.

The two finest pieces in *Nevertheless* are the title poem and "The Mind Is an Enchanting Thing." In "Nevertheless," Moore looks at a strawberry "that's had a struggle" as if she were an analytical cubist. All the poem's fragmented images from hedgehog and starfish to apple seeds and "counter-curved twin/hazel nuts" (split open), from rubber plant and prickly pear leaf to grape tendril and carrots which form mandrakes or ram's horn-roots define qualities of the strawberry. Having taken it apart and looked at it from the varied angles that constitute what is known about the fruit, the plant, and its hardiness, the cubist poet evokes the world's garden and a moral universe: "What is there//like fortitude! What sap/went through that little thread/to make the cherry red!" With the red cherry, the perception not simply of unity but of an identity which runs through seemingly disparate images is complete, and the composition is whole. The poem itself begins by focusing on seeds contained within the fruit, and proceeds—via the leaves—to the roots: the tendril of the prickly pear leaf rooting itself through two feet of air to the ground beneath is echoed in the grape tendril which ties itself in a knot made out of knots (and points the alert reader, perhaps, toward thoughts of those strawberry tendrils called runners, which take root in the ground). The delicacy of the poet's tender attention threads through the complexities of the poem as the sap delicately threads from root to branch to fruit to make the cherry, with its fragile hold upon the tree, so red. The quiet persistence which, the poem tells the reader, enables "the weak" to overcome "its menace" is one manifestation of the force which makes "the strong" overcome "itself"—and which enables the poet to write the poem, and the reader to read it. There is always in Moore's best poems this coherence which is at one with the form: the language itself acts out the theme.

In "The Mind Is an Enchanting Thing," there

is a change of a single syllable between title and first line, as the verse begins:

> is an enchanted thing
>   like the glaze on a
> katydid-wing
>   subdivided by sun
>   till the nettings are legion.

"The speculative, self-correcting attempt to 'define' the mind, advanced through an imagery of light refracted from a smoothly shining yet living, active surface," M. L. Rosenthal has noted, "is true Marianne Moore in both its quiet abstractness and its detailed excitement." The poem becomes, he says, "even more characteristically Moore as it advances through a series of similes ('like Gieseking playing Scarlatti,' 'like the apteryx-awl,' like 'the kiwi's rain-shawl,' 'like the gyroscope's fall') for the mind in action," and nears completion of the figurative network of qualities "through a series of metaphors that gather the intensities of its dominant conception into one last concentrated statement"—"it's/not a Herod's oath that cannot change." The poem itself might be taken as the central piece in all Moore's work: its nettings are legion, its surfaces are often brilliant, its utterances quick and to the point, and its openness to change almost as quick. In the obvious matter of how the poems look on the page, no two are exactly the same. Poetry was, to her, the art of singular forms.

There was a significant change in Moore's life and work after *Nevertheless*. The final illness and death of her eighty-five-year-old mother in 1947 was an ordeal, perhaps the greatest of many in her life, for the poet. Her grief was intense: "The thing must be admitted, I don't care for books that weren't worked on by her." When *Collected Poems* came out in 1951, the dedication was simply: "To/ MARY WARNER MOORE/1862-1947." Among the nine new poems, there is a brief elegy, "By Disposition of Angels." It is one of the two sonnets in *The Complete Poems* (1981) and is the most lyrical verse Moore ever wrote. In a solitary meditation on death and loss and darkness, a high cold star shines steadfastly and inviolate. The star's divine fire is a ministering spirit beyond human reason or mortal grief.

Another short verse, "At Rest in the Blast," was first published in 1948 and became "Like a Bulwark," the title poem for a small volume of new poems published in 1956. Addressed to an unidentified "you," it alludes to two well-known Protestant hymns, "O God, Our Help in Ages Past" (1719) by

The Mind is an Enchanting Thing;

is an enchanted thing
like the glaze on the katydid-wing
    subdivided by sun
    till the nettings are legion.
Like Gieseking playing Scarlatti,

..... How quickly beauty enters it.

Early draft for a poem collected in Nevertheless *(1944). Moore later said its "moral" was "that there is something more important than outward rightness" (by permission of the Estate of Marianne C. Moore, courtesy of the Rosenbach Museum and Library).*

Isaac Watts and "A Mighty Fortress is Our God" (1529) by Martin Luther. It is a poem to God, while it is the validation of a person: "Affirmed. . . . Pent. Hard pressed,/you take the blame and are inviolate." This individual is not abased but "firmed by the thrust of the blast/till compact, like a bulwark against fate;/lead saluted,/saluted by lead?/As though flying Old Glory full mast." Full military honors—a twenty-one-gun salute, as Donald Hall put it—for a heroic person. This fusion of language from religious, military, and secular life is so vigorous that it is difficult to remember the original title was "At Rest in the Blast." Like "By Disposition of Angels," the poem has no explicit dedication; but the first title, the imagery, the new title, the life and character of Mary Warner Moore all suggest that it also expresses the poet's devotion to her. Another impressive poem in *Like a Bulwark* is "Apparition of Splendor," set in a dark wood, where the poet finds a resister, "the double-embattled thistle of jet," the porcupine. The poem might have been entitled "How To Look at a Porcupine or Anything Else": it displays Moore's capacity for enchantment, imaginative appreciation, informed intelligence, sensitivity, and keen eyes.

During the years between the publication of *Nevertheless* and the appearance of *Like a Bulwark*, Moore devoted much of her energy to translation. She and Elizabeth Mayer brought out a version of Adalbert Stifter's *Rock Crystal* ("A Christmas Tale") in 1945. *The Fables of La Fontaine* (on which Moore, doing "the whole thing over four times," spent nine years) came out in 1954. The "glacial style" of the prose for the German story was said to read like the original, but Moore's verse translation of the *Fables* was a subject of dispute among admirers of La Fontaine. Some readers, in comparing it to the original French, thought her verse had lost La Fontaine's music; others commended her success in finding an equivalent to the French in "common American speech" without having betrayed the humor, spontaneity, and intelligence of the original. The French awarded her the *Croix de Chevalier des Arts et Lettres* for the work. The only additional translating she undertook was a "retelling" of Charles Perrault's *Puss in Boots, The Sleeping Beauty & Cinderella* which appeared in 1963. The translation was well-received.

In 1955 she brought out *Predilections*, twenty-two essays and reviews selected from nearly 400 pieces that she had written over a period of four decades, beginning in 1916. The prose is critical, intelligent, penetrating; never hostile, it avoids pedantry and is never assertive. It reveals much of what she valued in life. The book begins with two essays on language ("Feeling and Precision" and "Humility, Concentration, and Gusto") and includes what Moore called "observations" on Henry James, Sir Francis Bacon, George Saintsbury, Wallace Stevens, T. S. Eliot, Ezra Pound, W. H. Auden, Louis Bogan, D. H. Lawrence, Jean Cocteau, E. E. Cummings, Anna Pavlova, and other contemporaries. Like Moore's poems, the essays—to use her own borrowing from Cicero's *Orator* and St. Augustine's analysis of Christian persuasion in *De Doctrina Christiana*—"teach, stir the mind, afford enjoyment."

Moore's zest for learning, her resoluteness, her continuing lively responses to what pleased or troubled her became a matter of public interest. She knew how to grow old without ceasing to grow. During the years of 1955 and 1956, when she was approaching seventy, for instance, she attended poetry workshops given by W. H. Auden and Louise Bogan at the New York YMHA. Having won the triple crown of the National Book Award, the Pulitzer Prize, and Bollingen Prize in Poetry for the *Collected Poems* that appeared in 1951, Moore could well have conducted the classes herself. Instead, the doyenne of American poets, as Elizabeth Bishop recounts, "took notes constantly, asked many questions, and entered into the discussions with enthusiasm." The other students were timid and nonplussed in the presence of Moore, who said she "was learning a great deal, things she had never known before."

Because she liked the tango, she had a decade earlier taken lessons at a Brooklyn dance school. "The young dancers, male and female, may have been a little surprised," Bishop writes, "but soon they were competing with each other to dance with her"; all of them, Moore insisted, had enjoyed the experience thoroughly, and she was taught "a modified version of the tango" as well as several new steps. At seventy she learned to drive a car, although she never owned one; she thought the "policeman," who gave her the test for the license, "a little overlenient." Or, famous for liking baseball—"a game of precision" and grace under pressure—she was asked to throw out the first ball for the opening day at Yankee Stadium in 1968 and showed up in midseason of 1967 to practice. She threw "a sinking slider." Among the things she said she would have liked to have invented were "that eight-shaped stitch with which the outer leather is drawn tight on a baseball," epoxy glue, the zipper fastener, and the collapsible dustpan. She enjoyed being a writer, but, asked when she was seventy-

Marianne Moore on opening day at Yankee Stadium, 1968
(United Press International Photo)

ply bad; "Rescue with Yul Brynner" (1961) is better but prosaic in its commendation of the actor's work with the United Nations Commission for Refugees ("There were thirty million; there are thirteen still—/healthy to begin with, kept waiting till they're ill"). "Combat Cultural" (1959) is an appreciation of the performance, at the time of the cold war, of the Moiseyev Dance Company during its first successful American season—the troupe came to the United States after "the door had been shut" to artists from the U.S.S.R. for forty years. The poem is a jeu d'esprit on seeing and seeming; it is "great fun."

Tipoo's Tiger (1967), which Moore calls a ballad, is the trenchant antiwar poem she had never quite succeeded in writing earlier. Sultan Tipoo's tiger is no paper tiger but a monstrous "toy," a cruel man-eating machine, and the poem is an expression of the poet's genuine need to find effective words—symbols—for the self-defeating arrogance of the will to power, the exercise of brutal force, and the blood-dimmed tide that is loosed upon the world. It is one of her great but not one of her popular poems.

Moore's fury and indignation—that her humor, sense of decorum, and humility helped her to moderate—sometimes are reasserted in the late poems. "Tell Me, Tell Me" (1960) is a plea for refuge from the egocentric people who impose on the weary writer, and it is with some difficulty that she restrains her rancor. She is glad to give her approval to "W. S. Landor" (1964), "who could/throw/ a man through a window,/yet 'tender toward plants,' say 'Good God, the violets!' (below)." In "Charity Overcoming Envy" (1963), the allegorical figures enact the age-old problem of the relation between justice and *caritas*. "An Expedient—Leonardo da Vinci's—and a Query" (1964) is Moore's troubled sketch of the historical personage she most admired, the artist-scientist who inaugurated a radical new style that marked the beginning of the modern imagination. Although "great wrongs were powerless to vex him," Leonardo's dejection and his inability to say "proof refutes me" when he was in error or to take consolation from what he had accomplished perplex the poet. All of these poems, revealing the restlessness of Moore's inquisitive mind, are as good as the best of the early work and are often as significant as any of her spiritual exercises.

Several of the late poems were written for occasions or upon request. "Hometown Piece for Messrs. Alston and Reese," a poem for the Brooklyn Dodgers, appeared on the front page of the

two at what point poetry "had become world-shaking to her," she replied, "Never!"

Critics tend toward the view that as recognition of Moore's achievement increased, the quality of her verse diminished. During the years 1956-1970 she contributed forty-five poems to various magazines, principally to the *New Yorker*, but also to publications as different as *Shenandoah, Sequoia, Sports Illustrated*, the *Ladies' Home Journal, Harper's Bazaar*, the *Philadelphia Inquirer, It's Pencil Week, Art News*, the *Nation*, and the *Paris Review*. Many of the poems seem the work of a writer enjoying success and interested in reaching a wider audience. If they are not all equally impressive, they confirm the amplitude of her imagination and are not to be written off entirely. She chose thirty-five of them for the canonical text.

Some of the poems are for holidays: "Saint Nicholas" (1958), "For February 14th" (1959), and "Saint Valentine" (1960). Among those that speak to a cause, "Carnegie Hall: Rescued" (1960) is sim-

Kenneth Koch, Allen Dugan, Robert Lowell, Stanley Kunitz, and Marianne Moore at the New School for Social Research (courtesy of the New York Times)

New York Herald Tribune during the World Series of 1956. "Enough: Jamestown, 1607-1957" was commissioned for the tercentenary of the first permanent English settlement in America. "In the Public Garden" was written for the 1958 Boston Arts Festival, where she read the poem to a crowd of 5,000 people. "To a Giraffe" was written for *Poetry in Crystal,* published by Steuben Glass in 1963. "Occasionem Cognosce" ("I've Been Thinking") was read in 1963 at Lowell House, Harvard, and first published "in honor of Elliott and Mary Perkins," who were long associated with the house. "In Lieu of the Lyre" was a response to a 1965 request for a poem from the president of the *Harvard Advocate.* "The Camperdown Elm" (1967) commemorates the need for saving the massive old tree in Prospect Park, Brooklyn.

Many of these poems tease if they do not profoundly engage the imagination, and they often experiment with rhythms or rhyme. "I don't see how anyone," Donald Hall said of "Hometown Piece for Messrs. Alston and Reese," "can fail to be delighted by this funny, happy poem. It is meant to be sung, one gathers, but I wouldn't try it." "In the Public Garden" is graver in tone and theme, but the variations on a single rhyme, which recurs forty times, beginning with "festival" and ending with "personal," suggest a prolonged pealing of

bells in gratitude for artistic, intellectual, religious, and political freedom. The final version of "Occasionem Cognosce" is titled "Avec Ardeur" and inscribed to "Dear Ezra [Pound] who knows what cadence is." Moore frolics with language about language in short-lined rhymed couplets: "I'm annoyed?/yes; am—I avoid/'adore'/and 'bore';/am, I/ say, by/the word/*bore,* bored;/I refuse/to use/'divine'/to mean/something/pleasing." The verse concludes: "Without pauses—/the phrases/lack lyric/ force, sound capric— /Attic/Alcaic,/ or freak/ calico-Greek./(This is not verse/of course)./I'm sure of this;/Nothing mundane is divine;/Nothing divine is mundane." This seriocomic tirade against the banal secularizing of the sacred is as close as Moore ever came to showing off. The poet, willing to act as counterpoet, finally succumbs to a facile pedagogic pronouncement by which she gains an equilibrium she really had not lost. It is a pleasure to see that she reveled in whimsy and allowed herself to improvise with words. She could do anything she wanted with them.

She even dared write "To Victor Hugo of My Crow Pluto" (1961) in what she called esperanto *madinusa* ("pidgin Italian") and "My Crow, Pluto— a Fantasy" (in plain American prose), which are parodies of the best-known—and most-notorious—of Poe's poems, "The Raven," and his com-

Ezra Pound, Olga Rudge (behind Pound), and Marianne Moore during Pound's 1969 visit to the United States

panion essay, "The Philosophy of Composition." She was, like their author, crazy about words. "Dream" (1965) is a jubilant satire on "academic appointments for artists": "Bach and his family 'to Northwestern' " and "Haydn, when he had heard of Bach's billowing sail,/begged Prince Esterházy to lend him to Yale." Bach "would not leave home" without his five harpsichords, but all is arranged and in the poet's dream, "BACH PLAYS BACH!" The last verse in *The Complete Poems* (1981) is a finger exercise, "Prevalent at One Time": "I've always wanted a gig/semi-circular like a fig/for a very fast horse with long tail,/for one person, of course. . . . " The pre-text is Emily Dickinson's "Because I could not stop for Death—/He kindly stopped for me—/The Carriage held but just Ourselves—/And Immortality."

James Dickey has written that, if he had to choose a poet to construct heaven "out of the things we already have," he would choose Moore. Her heaven, he said, would be "Much, most probably, like the earth as it is, but refined by responsiveness and intellect into a state very far from the present one; a state of utter consequentiality." He ex-

plained that she "spent her life in remaking—or making—our world from particulars that we have never adequately understood on our own," but that the creative person open to experience can "endow . . . with joyous conjunctions" and reach "conclusions unforeseeable until they were made."

Moore did not, however, presume to an extraordinary vision. Hers is a postlapsarian world that is, nevertheless, rich and manifold; her love of being in the world is realized in an art attentive to one's obligations toward the commonweal and mindful that "After all/consolations of the metaphysical/can be profound. In Homer, existence/is flawed; transcendence, conditional; 'the journey from sin to redemption, perpetual.' "

Despite "the obvious grandeur of Moore's chief competitors," including William Carlos Williams and Wallace Stevens, John Ashbery has said, "I am tempted to call her our greatest modern poet."

Letters:

Letters From and To The Ford Motor Company, by

Moore and David Wallace (New York: Pierpont Morgan Library, 1958).

Interviews:

Donald Hall, "The Art of Poetry IV: Marianne Moore," *Paris Review,* 7 (Summer/Fall 1961): 41-66;

Hall, "An Interview with Marianne Moore," *McCall's,* 93 (December 1965): 74, 182-190;

Grace Schulman, "Conversation with Marianne Moore," *Quarterly Review of Literature,* 16 (1969): 1-2, 155-162.

Bibliographies:

Eugene P. Sheehy and Kenneth A. Lohf, *The Achievement of Marianne Moore: A Bibliography 1907-1957* (New York: New York Public Library, 1958);

Craig S. Abbott, *Marianne Moore: A Descriptive Bibliography* (Pittsburgh: University of Pittsburgh Press, 1977).

References:

Craig S. Abbott, *Marianne Moore: A Reference Guide* (Boston: G. K. Hall, 1978);

John Ashbery, "Straight Lines Over Rough Terrain," review of *The Complete Poems, New York Times Book Review,* 26 November 1967, pp. 1, 42;

Elizabeth Bishop, "Efforts of Affection," *Vanity Fair,* 4 (June 1983): 44-61;

Marie Borroff, *Language and the Poet: Verbal Artistry in Frost, Stevens, and Moore* (Chicago & London: University of Chicago Press, 1979);

Bonnie Costello, *Marianne Moore: Imaginary Possessions* (Cambridge & London: Harvard University Press, 1981);

Melville Crane, "Ladies of the *Dial,*" *American Scholar,* 40 (Spring 1971): 316-321;

Guy Davenport, "Marianne Moore," in his *The Geography of the Imagination* (San Francisco: North Point Press, 1981), pp. 114-122;

James Dickey, *Babel to Byzantium* (New York: Farrar, Straus & Giroux, 1968), pp. 156-164;

Bernard Engel, *Marianne Moore* (New York: Twayne, 1964);

Jean Garrigue, *Marianne Moore* (Minneapolis: University of Minnesota Press, 1965);

Donald Hall, *Marianne Moore: The Cage and the Animal* (New York: Pegasus, 1970);

Germaine La Feuille, Introduction to *Marianne Moore: Poèmes* (Paris: Seghers, 1964);

Gary Lane, *A Concordance to the Poems of Marianne Moore* (New York: Haskell House, 1972);

Ruth Lechlitner, "Fastidious Poetic Craftsman," review of *What Are the Years, New York Herald Tribune Books,* 23 November 1941, p. 6;

Sister Mary Therese, *Marianne Moore: A Critical Essay* (Grand Rapids, Mich.: Eerdmans, 1969);

George W. Nitchie, *Marianne Moore: An Introduction to the Poetry* (New York & London: Columbia University Press, 1969);

Elizabeth Phillips, *Marianne Moore* (New York: Ungar, 1982);

M. L. Rosenthal, *The Modern Poets: A Critical Introduction* (New York: Oxford University Press, 1960), pp. 140-145;

Winthrop Sargeant, "Humility, Concentration, and Gusto," *New Yorker,* 32 (16 February 1957): 38-77;

Laurence Stapleton, *Marianne Moore, The Poet's Advance* (Princeton: Princeton University Press, 1978);

Thurairajah Tambimuttu, ed., *Festschrift for Marianne Moore's Birthday* (New York: Tambimuttu & Mass, 1964);

Charles Tomlinson, ed., *Marianne Moore: A Collection of Critical Essays* (Englewood Cliffs, N.J.: Prentice-Hall, 1969);

Twentieth Century Literature, Marianne Moore issue, edited by Andrew J. Kappel, 30 (Summer/Fall 1984);

Helen Vendler, "On Marianne Moore," *New Yorker,* 54 (16 October 1978): 168-193;

William Wasserstrom, "Marianne Moore, *The Dial,* and Kenneth Burke," *Western Humanities Review,* 17 (Summer 1963): 249-262;

A. Kingsley Weatherhead, *The Edge of the Image: Marianne Moore, William Carlos Williams, and Some Other Poets* (Seattle & London: University of Washington Press, 1967);

Glenway Wescott, "Remembering Marianne Moore," *Partisan Review,* 50, no. 3 (1983): 392-406;

Pamela Hadas White, *Marianne Moore: Poet of Affection* (Syracuse: Syracuse University Press, 1977);

William Carlos Williams, *Selected Essays of William Carlos Williams* (New York: Random House, 1954), pp. 121-131;

Yvor Winters, " 'Holiday and Day of Wrath,' " review of *Observations, Poetry,* 26 (April 1925): 39-44.

Papers:

Moore's notebooks, the bulk of her correspondence, her manuscripts, and her library are at the Museum of the Philip H. and A. S. W. Rosenbach

Foundation in Philadelphia, where her Manhattan living room is also recreated.

Dorothy Parker

(22 August 1893-7 June 1967)

Lynn Z. Bloom
Virginia Commonwealth University

See also the Parker entry in *DLB 11, American Humorists, 1800-1950.*

BOOKS: *Men I'm Not Married To,* bound with *Women I'm Not Married To,* by F. P. Adams (Garden City: Doubleday, Page, 1922);

Enough Rope (New York: Boni & Liveright, 1926);

Sunset Gun (New York: Boni & Liveright, 1928);

Close Harmony, or The Lady Next Door: A Play in Three Acts, by Parker and Elmer Rice (New York: French /London: French Ltd., 1929);

Laments for the Living (New York: Viking, 1930; London: Longmans, Green, 1930);

Death and Taxes (New York: Viking, 1931);

After Such Pleasures (New York: Viking, 1933; London: Longmans, Green, 1934);

Not So Deep as a Well (New York: Viking, 1936; London: Hamilton, 1937); republished as *The Collected Poetry of Dorothy Parker* (New York: Modern Library, 1944);

Soldiers of the Republic (New York: Alexander Woollcott, 1938);

Here Lies (New York: Viking, 1939; London: Longmans, Green, 1939); republished as *The Collected Stories of Dorothy Parker* (New York: Modern Library, 1942);

The Viking Portable Library Dorothy Parker (New York: Viking, 1944); republished as *The Indispensable Dorothy Parker* (New York: Book Society, 1944); republished as *Selected Short Stories* (New York: Editions for the Armed Services, 1944); revised and enlarged as *The Portable Dorothy Parker, Revised and Enlarged Edition* (New York: Viking, 1973); republished as *The Collected Dorothy Parker* (London: Duckworth, 1973);

Dorothy Parker, mid-1920s

The Ladies of the Corridor: A Play, by Parker and Arnaud d'Usseau (New York: Viking, 1954);

Constant Reader (New York: Viking, 1970); republished as *A Month of Saturdays* (London & Basingstoke: Macmillan, 1971).

PLAY PRODUCTIONS: *Chauve-Souris* (revue), by

Parker and others, New York, 49th Street Theatre, 1 February 1922;

Round the Town (revue), New York, Century Root Theatre, 21 May 1924;

Close Harmony, or The Lady Next Door, by Parker and Elmer Rice, New York, Gaiety Theatre, 1 December 1924;

Shoot the Works (revue), New York, George M. Cohan Theatre, 21 July 1931;

The Coast of Illyria, by Parker and Ross Evans, Dallas, Margo Jones Theatre, April 1949;

The Ladies of the Corridor, by Parker and Arnaud d'Usseau, New York, Longacre Theatre, 21 October 1953.

SCREENPLAYS:*Here is My Heart,* Paramount, 1934;

One Hour Late, Paramount, 1935;

Mary Burns, Fugitive, Paramount, 1935;

Hands Across the Table, Paramount, 1935;

Paris in Spring, Paramount, 1935;

Big Broadcast of 1936, Paramount, 1935;

Three Married Men, screenplay by Parker and Alan Campbell, Paramount, 1936;

Lady, Be Careful, screenplay by Parker, Campbell, and Harry Ruskin, Paramount, 1936;

The Moon's Our Home, additional dialogue by Parker and Campbell, Paramount, 1936;

Suzy, screenplay by Parker, Campbell, Horace Jackson, and Lenore Coffee, M-G-M, 1936;

A Star Is Born, screenplay by Parker, Campbell, and Robert Carson, Selznick-United Artists, 1937;

Sweethearts, screenplay by Parker and Campbell, M-G-M, 1938;

Trade Winds, screenplay by Parker, Campbell, and Frank R. Adams, United Artists, 1938;

Weekend for Three, screenplay by Parker and Campbell, RKO, 1941;

Saboteur, screenplay by Parker, Peter Viertel, and Joan Harrison, Universal, 1942;

Smash Up: The Story of a Woman, screen story by Parker and Frank Cavett, Universal, 1947;

The Fan, screenplay by Parker, Walter Reisch, and Ross Evans, 20th Century-Fox, 1949.

Dorothy Parker is known today for her three volumes of verse, *Enough Rope* (1926), *Sunset Gun* (1928), and *Death and Taxes* (1931)—not serious "poetry," she claimed—and two collections of well-wrought short stories, *Laments for the Living* (1930) and *After Such Pleasures* (1933). These stories, characterized by Alexander Woollcott as "a potent distillation of nectar and wormwood," focus on the superficial, empty, directionless lives of well-to-do

women of the flapper and early Depression times. Like the supersophisticated but world-weary personae of many of Parker's poems, these women are devoid of intellectual or emotional resources of their own and are dependent on men for their economic and emotional well-being. There is generally an imbalance of feeling in the relationships depicted in the stories and the verse: the men are either indifferent or inconstant and so wound the faithful, lovelorn women, or vice versa.

Parker was born Dorothy Rothschild, the daughter of a prosperous Jewish clothier, J. Henry Rothschild, and Eliza Marston Rothschild, a Scottish Protestant, who died shortly after her daughter's two-months premature birth. Her childhood was lonely, exacerbated by her ambivalent feelings about her mixed religious ancestry. Her "rather lunatic" stepmother, as Parker's biographer John Keats calls her, sent Parker for some years to the nearby Blessed Sacrament Convent School in New York City and regularly asked, "Did you love Jesus today?" Parker, who characterized her childhood self as "a plain, disagreeable little child," later said she wanted to write her autobiography, if only to call it "Mongrel," which epitomized her detested self-image as "a mongrel that wanted to be a thoroughbred."

She attended the fashionable Miss Dana's School in Morristown, New Jersey, for a year, graduating in 1911, and developed gradually as a writer. After her first job, for *Vogue* in 1913-1916, she became a staff writer for *Vanity Fair* (1916-1920), writing fashion blurbs and drama criticism. She replaced P. G. Wodehouse as chief drama critic in 1920, but her caustic reviews of productions by three of *Vanity Fair's* backers, David Belasco, Charles Dillingham, and Florenz Ziegfeld, led to her being fired. She sharpened her rapier wit in more drama reviews for *Ainslee's* (1920-1933) and the *New Yorker* (1931), writing lines such as *"The House Beautiful* is, for me, the play lousy." Her terse, tart, book reviews for the *New Yorker* (collected in 1970 as *Constant Reader*) and for *Esquire* (1959-1962) have been described as "a combination of acumen and nonsense." Her praise for even mediocre works by Hemingway was inordinate. She had an extreme dislike of perennially popular A. A. Milne. Parker's reaction to Milne's *The House at Pooh Corner*—"Tonstant Weader Fwowed up"—typifies what John Farrar has called Parker's use of "delicate claws of . . . superb viciousness" to make scratches "subtle in phrasing but by no means subtle in [their] sentiments."

In June 1917 she married a handsome Wall

Painting by Will Cotton of the Algonquin group's poker club. Parker is standing, far left; at table (counterclockwise from Parker):
Franklin P. Adams, Henry Wise Miller, Gerald Brooks, Raoul Fleishmann, George S. Kaufman, Paul Hyde Bonner, Harpo Marx
(with George Backer looking over his shoulder), Alexander Woollcott (with Alice Duer Miller looking over his shoulder), Heywood
Broun; standing: Robert Benchley, Irving Berlin, Harold Ross, Beatrice Kaufman, Herbert Bayard Swope,
Joyce Barbour, Crosby Gaige.

Street broker, well-connected and heavy-drinking Edwin Pond Parker II. While he was absent for two years' military service, Parker's social life flourished with the bons vivants of the Round Table at the Algonquin Hotel, including George S. Kaufman, Robert Benchley, Alexander Woollcott, Franklin Pierce Adams (F. P. A.), and Harold Ross, who later established the *New Yorker*. During daily lunches and afternoon drinking bouts they practiced the verbal repartee (some would say smart-alecky style) that typified their writing. Parker's reputation as a punster led others' witticisms to be attributed to her as well, though her quintessential response to F. P. A.'s request that she use the word *horticulture* in a sentence is genuine: "You can lead a horticulture but you can't make her think." After his return from the war, Edward Parker remained an outsider to this self-consciously clever group. Dorothy Parker had an abortion and attempted suicide in 1923; both partners drank more and more heavily, and they divorced in 1928.

During her marriage Parker published two of her three slender volumes of verse, their funereal titles indicative of both her mordant sense of humor and her unstable, intermittently unsatisfying personal life: *Enough Rope* (1926) and *Sunset Gun* (1928). The titles she gave her third book of poetry, *Death and Taxes* (1931), and her collected poetry, *Not So Deep as a Well* (1936), are equally revealing. The years 1926-1936 were Parker's most productive decade; her current reputation largely rests on the poetry and short stories she wrote before 1938.

Even that reputation is slight and depends more on her best stories than on the poetry; "Big Blonde," winner of the O. Henry Award for the best short story of 1929, is the supreme example. John Keats, Parker's biographer, and Arthur Kinney, her only substantial critic, agree that the shallowness of Parker's admirers led them to exaggerate her early talent and seduced Parker into believing too fervently in the importance of not being earnest. As a consequence, Parker settled too quickly for less-demanding writing—satiric repartee, sardonic punch lines, wry shifts of tone—

rather than dealing more thoughtfully with serious issues in ways that would have fulfilled her potential for being a major writer of enduring distinction. To call her, as Kinney does, "the most accomplished classical epigrammatist of her time," is an accolade of ambiguous distinction, given the meager competition.

Parker's poems are highly restricted in scope and in depth. Although they become more technically versatile and controlled, Parker's subjects, personae, points-of-view, and major techniques remain constant throughout her work.

Parker's poetry, like her short stories, treats love, loneliness, and death. Loneliness and death, however, are usually variations on the motif of romantic love—exploited or exploitive, feigned, unreciprocated, betrayed, denied, abandoned. The relations between men and women in both her poetry and fiction are fleeting, false, and inevitably painful: "Scratch a lover and find a foe." In Parker's restricted milieu, women, as epitomized by her narrative personae, are doomed to unhealthy emotional dependence on men whose indifferent fickleness drives these females to the despair implied in the macabre titles of Parker's books. Love relationships are bound to be superficial and ephemeral, based as they are on "dust-bound trivia" ("The Searched Soul"), appearance (eyes "slant and slow," hair "sweet to touch"—"Prophetic Soul"), and youth. If lovers swear their devotion is "infinite, undying," one or both is bound to be lying ("Unfortunate Coincidence"). The woman is more likely to be the victim of her passion, however, for "Woman lives but in her lord;/Count to ten, and man is bored" ("General Review of the Sex Situation"). Lovers are numerous, faceless, interchangeable: "I always get them all mixed up" ("Pictures in the Smoke").

Most of Parker's poems are presented from the point of view of a female persona who plays one of two typical roles. In one guise she is an abandoned lover, "brief and frail and blue" ("Sweet Violets"), smarting from the sense of unworthiness and the pain of rejection, trying to cope with her dismay and despair. Sometimes, in playing this role, she is weighted down by her "heavy freedom" ("Prisoner") and eager to give away her heart, "the wretched thing," "now to that lad, now to this" ("A Portrait"). At other times she despairs over her lost love, "screaming to die with the dead year's dead" ("Willow"), or she imagines herself dead, lying "cool and quiet," finding death a tranquil relief for the heart "that pain has made incapable of pain" ("Testament"). But the grave is not necessarily a quiet place, for she threatens to return as a ghost to haunt her former lover ("I Shall Come Back").

This persona is not convincing, partly because of the conventional language and stale images in which Parker presents the subject, partly because of its divergence from her own view of life as expressed in other contexts. Parker in the 1920s seemed as inconstant as the men whose fickleness her poetry condemns. In 1925 she had an affair with playwright Charles MacArthur, followed by affairs in 1926 with tobacco heir Seward Collins and in 1927 with businessman John Garrett. In 1928 she began a liaison with bisexual actor Alan Campbell which was to last the rest of her life; they were married from 1933 to 1947 and remarried in 1950. Always a hard drinker, she attended, what Kinney calls innumerable "lavish and frenetic" parties, where her boisterous and abrasive manner made her a less-than-welcome guest. On hearing one hostess described as "outspoken," Parker rasped, "Outspoken by whom?"

Parker's public persona, however, gives credence to the other narrative personality in her poetry, a wise-cracking, savvy, jaded female who

Alan Campbell and Dorothy Parker at the time of their remarriage in 1950 (Wide World Photo)

knows "it's always just my luck to get/One perfect rose" instead of "one perfect limousine" ("One Perfect Rose"). Worldly wise, she can also recognize the earmarks of a predatory male ("who murmurs that his wife/is the lodestar of his life"—"Social Note"), her own inconstancy ("I loved them until they loved me"—"Ballade at Thirty-Five"), and the inevitable denouement ("Scratch a lover, and find a foe"—"Ballade of a Great Weariness"). She mocks virginity ("Parable for a Certain Virgin"), scorns sedate society ("Inseparable my nose and thumb"— "Neither Bloody nor Bowed"), and will eagerly engage "in fun and such" until 3 A.M.—for "I shall stay the way I am/Because I do not give a damn" ("Observation"). The hallmarks of this persona are "laughter and hope and a sock in the eye" ("Inventory").

Like the men Parker's melancholy persona laments, this worldly wise persona is bound to be "spectacularly bored" with a constant lover ("On Being a Woman"). If she ever succumbs to sentiment, such as preferring one who is "sudden and swift and strong" to a wealthy wooer, she undermines it with a cynical punch line—"Somebody ought to examine my head!" ("The Choice"). She relishes the calculated insult ("I turn to little words—so you, my dear/Can spell them out"— "Little Words") as much as the imagined deaths of her adversaries, shot with a "shiny gun" ("Frustration")—and sometimes, even the longed-for deaths of her lovers ("I wish somebody'd shoot him"— "Love Song").

The two personae are intermingled in Parker's books of poetry, but the cynic prevails, partly because of Parker's stylistic techniques. Once conditioned, readers expect a witty riposte or a slangy word ("Here's my strength and my weakness, gents"—"Ballade at Thirty-Five") to shift the poem from seriousness to satire, as indeed it often does. Though anticipated, the slang startles, as in "Coda" ("For art is a form of catharsis/And love is a permanent flop"), and provokes laughter in what might otherwise have been serious contexts. Even if Parker meant some of her poems to be taken seriously, as individually they might be ("How shall I be mating . . . Living for a hating—Dying of a love?"—"The Dark Girl's Rhyme"), the flippant, cynical persona and her satiric or ironic language establish the prevailing comic tone of Parker's collected verse. Moreover, the language of the poetry that purports to be serious is predictable, anachronistic ("what shallow boons suffice my heart"), and banal: seas are "stormy," rain "drops softly," "withering flowers" denote an absent or lost lover;

the rejected maiden is "a-crying," or "sleeping chastely," or mourning "whenever one drifted petal leaves the tree." Thus Parker's poetic techniques—far more distinctive and striking in comic than in serious poetry—reinforce the impression that the verse is more an exercise in verbal wit than the interpretation of an authentic emotion or experience.

Parker's lyrics, all short, are written primarily in simple iambic quatrains or couplets ("Men seldom make passes/At girls who wear glasses"— "News Item"). Although she occasionally experimented with ballads, sonnets, and other forms, her poetry on the whole lacks the formal complexity, structural finesse and variations, and metaphorical ingenuity that add interest and stature to memorable love poetry by John Donne, William Shakespeare, John Keats, Emily Dickinson, and Parker's contemporaries, Elinor Wylie and Edna St. Vincent Millay. Kinney has favorably compared Parker's use of meter and line to Horace, Martial, Catullus, and Heinrich Heine, among others; he embeds Parker's work in a classical tradition. Although she may have read these authors, the more immediate influence on her verse appears to have come from the Algonquin Round Table. The verses of Parker and Franklin P. Adams (author of such whimsies as "Give me the balmy breezes! . . . /Wind on my cheek and hair!/And, while we're on the topic,/Give me the air.") exhibit control, compression, precise diction, and an irreverent fondness for puns, which perhaps are all one can expect of light verse. Contemporary reviewers recognized Parker's poetry for what it was, with Louis Kronenberger predicting, "she will survive not only as the author of some first-rate light verse but also as a valuable footnote to the Twenties, out of whose slant on existence that light verse sprang." Yet the public enjoyed her poems, and her books were best-sellers.

In the 1920s Parker collaborated with the Algonquin wits on an ill-fated Broadway revue, *Chauve-Souris* (1922), and in 1924 she and Elmer Rice wrote *Close Harmony*, a predictable comedy of adultery, also short-lived. In the 1930s and 1940s Parker also collaborated, sometimes with Alan Campbell, on several film scripts, including *A Star is Born* (1937), *Smash Up* (1947), and *The Fan* (1949), based on *Lady Windemere's Fan* (1892), by Oscar Wilde. With her film collaborator Ross Evans she wrote a play, *The Coast of Illyria* (1949), about the tortured lives of Charles and Mary Lamb—a failure in its only production, a three-week run in Dallas. Another play, with collaborator Arnaud d'Usseau, was *The Ladies of the Corridor* (1953), three case studies of life-in-death among elderly women. Although George Jean Nathan named it the best play of 1953, other critics disliked it, and it closed after a six-week Broadway run.

Parker's intermittent alcoholism and progressive writing anxiety (she procrastinated on assignments for months at a time) made her later work sporadic and unreliable; only rarely did the glimmer of her former wit illuminate its somberness. She will nevertheless remain known as a writer of comic verse, to which applies the judgment she herself made of the performance of a famous actress, who "ran the gamut of emotions from A to B." Her best verse succeeds within this restricted compass.

Interview:

Marion Capron, "Dorothy Parker," in *Writers at Work*, edited by Malcolm Cowley (New York: Viking, 1957), pp. 71-82.

Biography:

John Keats, *You Might As Well Live: The Life and Times of Dorothy Parker* (New York: Viking, 1944).

References:

James R. Gaines, *Wit's End: Days and Nights of the Algonquin Round Table* (New York: Harcourt Brace Jovanovich, 1977);

Brendan Gill, Introduction to *The Portable Dorothy Parker* (New York: Viking, 1973);

Lillian Hellman, "Dorothy Parker," in her *An Unfinished Woman* (Boston: Little, Brown, 1969), pp. 212-228;

Arthur F. Kinney, *Dorothy Parker* (Boston: Twayne, 1978);

Alexander Woollcott, "Our Mrs. Parker," in his *While Rome Burns* (New York: Viking, 1934), pp. 142-152.

Papers:

The National Association for the Advancement of Colored People owns the bulk of Parker's papers.

Ezra Pound

Wendy Stallard Flory
University of Pennsylvania

BIRTH: Hailey, Idaho, 30 October 1885, to Homer Loomis and Isabel Weston Pound.

EDUCATION: University of Pennsylvania, 1901-1903; Ph.B., Hamilton College, 1905; M.A., University of Pennsylvania, 1906; further study, 1907-1908.

MARRIAGE: 20 April 1914 to Dorothy Shakespear; children: Omar Shakespear, Mary (by Olga Rudge).

AWARDS AND HONORS: *Poetry* prize, 1914; *Dial* award, 1928; Honorary doctorate, Hamilton College, 1939; Bollingen Prize in Poetry for *The Pisan Cantos*, 1949; Harriet Monroe Award, 1962; Academy of American Poets Fellowship, 1963.

DEATH: Venice, Italy, 1 November 1972.

BOOKS: *A Lume Spento* (Venice: Printed for the author by A. Antonini, 1908);

A Quinzaine for this Yule (London: Pollock, 1908);

Personae (London: Elkin Mathews, 1909);

Exultations (London: Elkin Mathews, 1909);

The Spirit of Romance (London: Dent, 1910; London: Dent/New York: Dutton, 1910);

Provença (Boston: Small, Maynard, 1910);

Canzoni (London: Elkin Mathews, 1911);

Ripostes (London: Swift, 1912; Boston: Small, Maynard, 1913);

Gaudier-Brzeska: A Memoir Including the Published Writings of the Sculptor and a Selection from his Letters (London: John Lane, Bodley Head/New York: John Lane, 1916);

Lustra (London: Elkin Mathews, 1916; enlarged edition, New York: Knopf, 1917);

Pavannes and Divisions (New York: Knopf, 1918);

The Fourth Canto (London: Ovid Press, 1919);

Quia Pauper Amavi (London: Egoist Press, 1919);

Instigations of Ezra Pound, Together with an Essay on

Ezra Pound (courtesy of Omar Pound)

the Chinese Written Character by Ernest Fenollosa
(New York: Boni & Liveright, 1920);

Hugh Selwyn Mauberley (London: Ovid Press, 1920);

Umbra (London: Elkin Mathews, 1920);

Poems 1918-21 (New York: Boni & Liveright, 1921);

Indiscretions (Paris: Three Mountains Press, 1923);

Antheil and the Treatise on Harmony (Paris: Three Mountains Press, 1924; Chicago: Covici, 1927);

A Draft of XVI. Cantos (Paris: Three Mountains Press, 1925);

Personae: The Collected Poems (New York: Boni & Liveright, 1926; London: Faber & Faber, 1952);

A Draft of the Cantos 17-27 (London: John Rodker, 1928);

Selected Poems, edited by T. S. Eliot (London: Faber & Gwyer, 1928);

Imaginary Letters (Paris: Black Sun Press, 1928);

A Draft of XXX Cantos (Paris: Hours Press, 1930; New York: Farrar & Rinehart, 1933; London: Faber & Faber, 1933);

Imaginary Letters (Paris: Black Sun Press, 1930);

How To Read (London: Harmsworth, 1931);

ABC of Economics (London: Faber & Faber, 1933; Norfolk, Conn.: New Directions, 1940);

ABC of Reading (London: Routledge, 1934; New Haven: Yale University Press, 1934);

Make It New (London: Faber & Faber, 1934; New Haven: Yale University Press, 1935);

Eleven New Cantos: XXXI-XLI (New York: Farrar & Rinehart, 1934; London: Faber & Faber, 1935);

Homage to Sextus Propertius (London: Faber & Faber, 1934);

Alfred Venison's Poems: Social Credit Themes, as The Poet of Titchfield Street (London: Nott, 1935);

Social Credit: An Impact (London: Nott, 1935);

Jefferson And/Or Mussolini (London: Nott, 1935; New York: Liveright/Nott, 1936); rewritten in Italian and republished as *Jefferson e Mussolini* (Venice: Edizioni Popolari, 1944);

Polite Essays (London: Faber & Faber, 1937; Norfolk, Conn.: New Directions, 1940);

The Fifth Decad of Cantos (London: Faber & Faber, 1937; New York & Toronto: Farrar & Rinehart, 1937);

Confucius: Digest of the Analects (Milan: Giovanni Scheiwiller, 1937);

Guide to Kulchur (London: Faber & Faber, 1938; Norfolk, Conn.: New Directions, 1938);

What Is Money For (London: Greater Britain Publications, 1939);

Cantos LII-LXXI (London: Faber & Faber, 1940; Norfolk, Conn.: New Directions, 1940);

A Selection of Poems (London: Faber & Faber, 1940);

Carta da Visita (Rome: Edizioni di Lettere d'Oggi, 1942); republished as *A Visiting Card*, translated by John Drummond (London: Russell, 1952);

L'America, Roosevelt e le Cause della Guerra Presente (Venice: Edizioni Popolari, 1944); republished as *America, Roosevelt and the Causes of the Present War*, translated by Drummond (London: Russell, 1951);

Oro e Lavoro (Rapallo: Tip. Moderna [Canessa], 1944); republished as *Gold and Work*, translated by Drummond (London: Russell, 1952);

Introduzione alla Natura Economica degli S.U.A. (Venice: Edizioni Popolari, 1944); republished as *An Introduction to the Economic Nature of the United States*, translated by Carmine Amore (London: Russell, 1950);

Orientamenti (Venezia: Edizioni Popolari, 1944);

"If This Be Treason . . . " (Siena: Printed for Olga Rudge by Tlp. Nuova, 1948);

The Pisan Cantos (New York: New Directions, 1948; London: Faber & Faber, 1949);

The Cantos (New York: New Directions, 1948; London: Faber & Faber, 1950);

Selected Poems (New York: New Directions, 1949);

Patria Mia (Chicago: Seymour, 1950);

Literary Essays, edited, with an introduction, by T. S. Eliot (London: Faber & Faber, 1954; Norfolk, Conn.: New Directions, 1954);

Lavoro ed Usura (Milan: All 'Insegna del Pesce d'Oro, 1954);

Section: Rock-Drill 85-95 de los cantares (Milan: All 'Insegna del Pesce d'Oro, 1955; New York: New Directions, 1956; London: Faber & Faber, 1957);

Gaudier-Brzeska (Milan: All'Insegna del Pesce d'Oro, 1957);

Pavannes and Divagations (Norfolk, Conn.: New Directions, 1958; London: Owen, 1960);

Versi Prosaici (Rome: Biblioteca Minima, 1959);

Thrones 96-109 de los cantares (Milan: All'Insegna del Pesce d'Oro, 1959; New York: New Directions, 1959; London: Faber & Faber, 1960);

Impact: Essays on Ignorance and the Decline of American Civilization (Chicago: Regnery, 1960);

Patria Mia and The Treatise on Harmony (London: Owen, 1962);

Nuova Economia Editoriale (Milan: Vanni Scheiwiller, 1962);

A Lume Spento and Other Early Poems (New York: New Directions, 1965; London: Faber & Faber, 1966);

Être Citoyen Romain, edited by Pierre Aelberts (Liège: Editions Dynamo, 1965);

Canto CX (Cambridge, Mass.: Sextant Press, 1965);

Selected Cantos (London: Faber & Faber, 1967; enlarged edition, New York: New Directions, 1970);

Redondillas (New York: New Directions, 1968);

Drafts and Fragments of Cantos CX-CXVII (New York: New Directions, 1969; London: Faber & Faber, 1970);

Selected Prose 1909-1965, edited by William Cookson (London: Faber & Faber, 1973; New York: New Directions, 1973);

Selected Poems 1908-1959 (London: Faber & Faber, 1975);

Collected Early Poems, edited by Michael John King (New York: New Directions, 1976; London: Faber & Faber, 1977);

Ezra Pound and Music: The Complete Criticism, edited by R. Murray Schafer (New York: New Directions, 1977; London: Faber & Faber, 1978);

"Ezra Pound Speaking": Radio Speeches of World War II, edited by Leonard W. Doob (Westport, Conn. & London: Greenwood Press, 1978);

Ezra Pound and the Visual Arts, edited by Harriet Zinnes (New York: New Directions, 1980);

From Syria: The Worksheets, Proofs, and Text, edited by Robin Skelton (Port Townsend, Wash.: Copper Canyon Press, 1981).

OTHER: *Des Imagistes: An Anthology*, edited, with contributions, by Pound (New York: A. & C. Boni, 1914; London: Poetry Bookshop/New York: A. & C. Boni, 1914);

Catholic Anthology 1914-1915, edited, with contributions, by Pound (London: Elkin Mathews, 1915);

'Noh' or Accomplishment, by Pound and Ernest Fenollosa (London: Macmillan, 1916; New York: Knopf, 1917)—edited, with introduction and translations, by Pound;

Guido Cavalcanti, *Rime*, Italian text, edited, with notes and some translations, by Pound (Genoa: Marsano, 1932);

Active Anthology, edited, with contributions, by Pound (London: Faber & Faber, 1933);

Confucius to Cummings: An Anthology of Poetry, edited by Pound and Marcella Spann (New York: New Directions, 1964).

TRANSLATIONS: *The Sonnets and Ballate of Guido Cavalcanti* (Boston: Small, Maynard, 1912; London: Swift, 1912);

Cathay: Translations by Ezra Pound for the Most Part from the Chinese of Rihaku, From the Notes of the Late Ernest Fenollosa, and the Decipherings of the Professors Mori and Ariga (London: Elkin Mathews, 1915);

Rémy de Gourmont, *The Natural Philosophy of Love*, translated, with a postscript, by Pound (New York: Boni & Liveright, 1922; London: Casanova Society, 1926);

Odon Por, *Italy's Policy of Social Economics, 1930-1940* (Bergamo, Milan & Rome: Istituto Italiano D'Arti Grafiche, 1941);

Confucius: The Unwobbling Pivot & the Great Digest, translated, with commentary, by Pound, *Pharos*, no. 4 (Winter 1947);

The Translations of Ezra Pound, edited by Hugh Kenner (London: Faber & Faber, 1953; New York: New Directions, 1953);

The Classic Anthology Defined by Confucius (Cambridge: Harvard University Press, 1954; London: Faber & Faber, 1955);

Sophocles, *Women of Trachis* (London: Spearman, 1956; New York: New Directions, 1957);

Love Poems of Ancient Egypt, translated by Pound and Noel Stock (Norfolk, Conn.: New Directions, 1962).

Ezra Pound's influence on the development of poetry in the twentieth century has unquestionably been greater than that of any other poet. No other writer has written as much poetry and criticism or devoted as much energy to the advancement of the arts in general. Nor has any writer been the focus of so much or such heated controversy. More widely recognized than any other writer by his poet-contemporaries for his influence on their work, he has at the same time been the most widely and bitterly condemned by critics. Opinions about Pound run the gamut from uncritical adulation to vituperative hatred.

Pound's energy was prodigious, and he applied it to his self-appointed mission of revitalizing poetry and the arts in general with an almost obsessive single-mindedness. As the artist and novelist Wyndham Lewis said of him in *Blasting and Bombardiering* (1937), "there was nothing social for him that did not have a bearing upon the business of writing. . . . He breathed Letters, ate Letters, dreamt Letters." T. S. Eliot, Ernest Hemingway, and many others have written on Pound's unselfish dedication to his making new of the arts, to the way in which, if he thought artists had promise, he would go to any lengths to help them, with complete disregard for his own convenience and with no suggestion that they were in his debt as a result. In his introduction to Pound's *Literary Essays* (1954) Eliot explained that, for Pound, "to discover a new writer of genius is as satisfying an experience as it is for a lesser man to believe that he has written a great work of genius himself. He has cared deeply that his contemporaries and juniors should write well; he has cared less for his personal achievement than for the life of letters and art." Pound had an almost infallible sense for talent and genius and a remarkable facility for making contact with major artists, often identifying them before anyone else. He was both friend and literary adviser for many of the greatest writers in English of his time: T. S. Eliot, William Carlos Williams, James Joyce, William Butler Yeats, Marianne Moore, Hilda Doolittle (H. D.), Robert Frost, and Ernest Hemingway. In addition, he helped many other writers by getting their work published, by reviewing it enthusiastically, by introducing them to one another, and even by lending or giving them money.

Knowing that Pound spent much of his life in Europe, insisted that serious American poets should be thoroughly familiar with the great works of the European literary tradition, and denounced the actions of the American government during World War II, many people have thought him "un-American"—an adoptive European. But Pound always considered himself completely American, and, when he was in Europe, he exaggerated his American accent. He wanted American writers to know the heights of European literary achievement, not to be overawed by these, but to surpass them, reasoning that "when an American in any art or *métier* has learned what is best, he will never after be content with the second-rate."

Pound saw in himself the combination of two strong and contrasting American traditions. On his mother's side was the colonial family with its "respect for tradition," in particular his grandmother Mary Parker Wadsworth Weston who, through her mother, was a member of the same Wadsworth family that had produced Joseph Wadsworth (who saved the Connecticut Charter by hiding it in the "Charter Oak") and Henry Wadsworth Longfellow. On his father's side was the pioneer family with "the most rugged kind of idealism," in particular his grandfather Thaddeus Coleman Pound.

Thaddeus Pound's colorful career held a considerable fascination for Pound who, as a child, heard a good deal about how his grandfather had built three railroad lines, owned the second store ever opened in Chippewa Falls, Wisconsin, owned a lumber company and a bottled spring water company, was one of the founders of a bank, was Lieutenant Governor and then Acting Governor of Wisconsin in 1870 and 1871, a United States Congressman from 1876 to 1882, and a strong contender for the post of Secretary of the Interior under Garfield in 1880. After 1928 Pound viewed Thaddeus Pound as the type of the selfless public servant and as an idealist upon whom he could model himself.

In the true pioneer tradition, Pound himself was born on the frontier, in Hailey, Idaho, on 30 October 1885. His father, Homer Pound, ran the land office there, but the rough and ready atmosphere of the town seems to have been uncongenial to Pound's rather self-consciously genteel mother, Isabel Weston Pound. She claimed that she could not stand the high altitude any longer, and the family moved to New York in the late spring of 1887 during the Great Blizzard, behind the first rotary snowplow. The family stayed first in New York, with "Aunt Frank" (Frances A. Weston) at 24 East 47th Street, and then, when Pound was three, at Thaddeus Pound's farm in Wisconsin. In

June 1889 the family moved to Philadelphia, where Homer Pound was to spend the rest of his working life as assistant assayer at the United States Mint. They lived first at 208 South 43rd Street, West Philadelphia, then at 417 Walnut Street, Jenkintown. In 1891, they moved to 166 Fernbrook Avenue, Wyncote. In addition to local schools, Pound at seven attended the Chelten Hills School, run by the Heacock family and founded by Annie Heacock, a suffragette, and at twelve the Cheltenham Military Academy, going from there to the Cheltenham Township High School.

In September 1901, shortly before his sixteenth birthday, he entered the University of Pennsylvania, where his major professor in English was Felix Schelling. At about this time he met William Brooke Smith, a painter and the first of a series of artists in whom Pound would take a keen interest. Smith died of tuberculosis in 1908, and that same year Pound dedicated his first published book of poetry, *A Lume Spento,* to the memory of this "first

Ezra Pound, circa 1903 (courtesy of the Beinecke Rare Book and Manuscript Library, Yale University)

friend": "mihi caritate primus William Brooke Smith. Painter, Dreamer of dreams," as one who loved "this same/beauty that I love, somewhat/after mine own fashion."

In the summer of 1898 Pound had traveled in Europe for three months with Aunt Frank, visiting England, France, Belgium, Germany, Switzerland, Italy, and Morocco. In the summer of 1902 he made a second trip to Europe, this time with his parents. Back at the university he met William Carlos Williams, beginning a firm friendship which was destined to continue, despite a variety of stand-offs, largely on Williams's part, until Williams's death in 1963.

Pound transferred to Hamilton College in 1903 and completed his degree there, receiving a Ph.B. in 1905. His study of Anglo-Saxon under the Reverend Joseph Ibbotson and the instruction he received from William Shepard in French, Spanish, Italian—and by special arrangement in Provençal—helped to turn his literary enthusiasms in a direction that would have a decisive influence on his poetry, criticism, and translations. He claimed that the idea of writing the long poem that would eventually be *The Cantos* came to him in the course of a talk with Ibbotson, and, when he finally decided how to begin this poem, he chose to present the subject of Odysseus's descent into the underworld in a verse form that would imitate Anglo-Saxon prosody.

During this period, Pound was still very much under the influence of his religious upbringing. His parents were very actively involved in the affairs of the Calvary Presbyterian Church of Wyncote, and Pound was to recall many years later, for one of the psychiatrists who interviewed him at St. Elizabeths Hospital, that he "read the Bible regularly up to the age of sixteen years" and was, between the ages of twelve and sixteen, an "earnest Christian." In 1909 he dedicated *Exultations* to the minister of Calvary Church—the Reverend Carlos Tracy Chester—and from the letters that Pound wrote to his parents from Hamilton College it is apparent that he paid close attention to the sermons delivered by the president, Dr. Stryker, and other faculty members. In 1903 Homer and Isabel Pound began missionary work among Italian immigrants in the Philadelphia slums, and by 1905 Homer Pound was superintendent of the First Italian Presbyterian Church of Philadelphia. Pound appreciated the value of his parents' "practical Christianity" and helped them with the children's activities.

Having graduated from Hamilton in 1905, he

returned to the University of Pennsylvania to take a master's degree in Romance languages. He studied English again under Felix Schelling and Latin under Walton McDaniel, working on Catullus, Ovid ,and, on his own initiative, investigating the works of the Italian renaissance Latinists (who appear prominently at the end of Canto 5). Yet when he applied for a fellowship to do research abroad it was to work on Spanish literature—in particular the plays of Lope de Vega—which he had been studying with Hugo Rennert and which he intended to make the subject of his doctoral thesis.

During his fellowship year, 1906-1907, he did research in the British Museum and the National Library in Madrid. He was particularly impressed by Velázquez's paintings in the Prado, and he visited Burgos, where he allowed his imagination to take him back (as in Canto 3) to the days of El Cid. He also spent some time in Paris, where he discovered Joséphin Péladan's writings, which develop the theory that the troubadours were the guardians of a "mystic extra-church philosophy or religion" which dated back to the Eleusinian mysteries.

In 1907, after one more year of graduate study, he took a teaching post in Romance languages at Wabash College in Crawfordsville, Indiana. That summer he had become romantically involved with Mary S. Moore, and wrote to her from Crawfordsville that "you are going abroad with me next summer . . . we need spend no futile time in disputing the matter"; it came as quite a shock to discover that she did not share his assumption that they would marry. By then he had lost his position at Wabash—partly because of the scandal resulting from his having allowed a stranded traveling actress to spend the night in his rooms—and had .definitely decided to go to Europe.

Shortly after this time he began his serious courting of Hilda Doolittle, whom he had first met in 1901. Beginning in 1905, when she entered Bryn Mawr, they had spent a good deal of time together, and, after Mary Moore made it clear that she did not intend to marry him, he became engaged to H. D. Although in *End To Torment*, her memoir of Pound, H. D. claims that he was responsible for the breaking off of the engagement, in *Hermione*, a lightly veiled autobiographical account of this period in her life, it is quite clear that her overwrought state of mind and her strong attraction to a female friend, Frances Gregg, were the real causes of the increasing distance between her and Pound. He had made and handbound for her a small book of twenty-four poems, written between 1905 and

1907, which he entitled *Hilda's Book*, and after their engagement was broken she gave it to Frances Gregg to keep for her. Although the Hilda poems are mannered and archaicized—in the worst he descended to a strained "Miltonism" and describes the perfume of a "flower mortescent" as "Marescent, fading on the dolorous brink/That border is to that marasmic sea"—he was also capable in others of a lyric gracefulness and interesting variations of cadence. He later included four of these poems in *A Lume Spento*, and of these "The Tree" has earned a place among the best known of Pound's short poems—its allusion to the myth of Baucis and Philemon looking forward to the opening of Canto 90, the central canto of the Rock-Drill sequence of *The Cantos*.

Pound left Wabash College in January 1908, and on 8 February sailed from New York to Gibraltar (several of his experiences there are recorded in Canto 22). He then spent three months in Venice. Though he was very short of money, the city was a source of romantic inspiration for his poetry, and he collected forty-four of his poems and published them in Venice under the title *A Lume Spento* in June 1908. A strong undercurrent of studied medievalism of allusion and diction runs through the poems, which—when they are not ballads—are often in the manner of Robert Browning, Algernon Swinburne, François Villon, and William Butler Yeats. Several of them, such as "Plotinus," describe poetic rapture and show his fascination with a Neoplatonic state of visionary transcendence. "Scriptor Ignotus" is dedicated to K. R. H. (Katherine Ruth Heyman), a concert pianist whom Pound had met in 1904. She was on tour in Venice, and at this point was the muse who inspired Pound—in the persona of an eighteenth-century "Dante scholar and mystic"—to conceive a "great forty-year epic." Pound took *A Lume Spento* to London in September. It was favorably reviewed in the *Evening Standard*, and in America by Ella Wheeler Wilcox.

In early December Pollock and Company published a twenty-eight page pamphlet of Pound's poems, *A Quinzaine for this Yule*. In little more than a week the hundred copies of that printing sold out, and Elkin Mathews brought out a second printing of one hundred. Between 21 January and 25 February 1909 he gave a series of six lectures at the Regent Street Polytechnic on "The Development of Literature in Southern Europe," paying particular attention to the troubadours and the renaissance Latinists. At the salon of the wife of Albert Fowler (who is the "Hamish" of Canto 18)

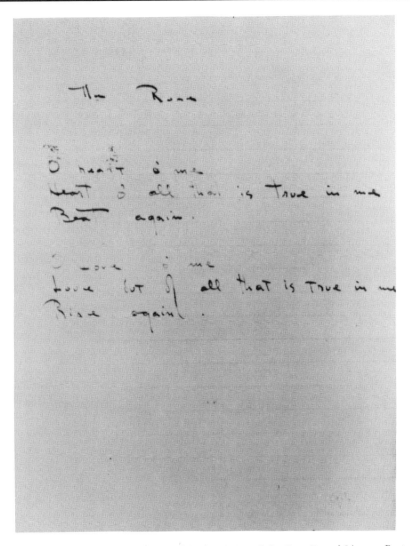

Page from Pound's 1908 notebook (used by permission of the Ezra Pound Literary Property Trust)

Pound met Olivia Shakespear—a novelist, a first cousin of the poet Lionel Johnson, and an intimate friend of Yeats. He was invited to tea at the Shakespear home in Brunswick Gardens, Kensington, where he met Olivia Shakespear's daughter Dorothy, whom he would later marry. He was rapidly coming to know many of the literary personages of Olivia Shakespear's generation. In the spring of 1909 he met Laurence Binyon, Maurice Hewlett, Selwyn Image, Ernest Rhys, May Sinclair, Sturge Moore, George Bernard Shaw, and Hilaire Belloc. In April 1909 Elkin Mathews published Pound's third book of poems, *Personae*, with a dedication to "Mary Moore of Trenton, if she wants it."

While his association with these writers gave him the sense of having made contact with a part of the literary establishment, the contacts that would prove to have a direct and significant influence on his own writing were those he made with the younger group of poets which had gathered around the philosopher-poet T. E. Hulme—F. S. Flint, Edward Storer, Florence Farr, Joseph Campbell, Francis Tancred, and, on occasion Padraic Colum and Ernest Rhys. Hulme, who would be killed in World War I at the age of thirty-four, was the first to expound the aesthetic principles behind imagism and to put them into practice in his poetry. Hulme's ideas about the remaking of poetry in English were much influenced by his reading of French poetry and the philosophical writings of Henri Bergson, and Pound was impressed by the lectures on Bergson's aesthetics which Hulme gave in December 1911 and February 1912. As a consequence of his relationship with Wyndham Lewis,

Pound later misrepresented the nature and extent of his debt to Hulme. Lewis felt a strong sense of rivalry with Hulme, begrudged him his "discovery" of the French neoclassicists, and suspected him of championing sculptor Jacob Epstein over Lewis himself. As Pound came increasingly to admire the vitality and revolutionary nature of Lewis's painting and writing, he started to side with him against Hulme. In "This Hulme Business" (*Townsman*, January 1939) he echoed Lewis's low opinion of Bergson, contending "the critical LIGHT during the years immediately pre-war in London shone not from Hulme but from Ford (Madox etc.) in so far as it fell on writing at all."

Although this is not a fair appraisal in any objective sense of the relative aesthetic influence of Hulme and Ford, it does convey Pound's consciousness of what the development of his writing owed to these two men. His association with Ford Madox Hueffer (later Ford Madox Ford) was an introduction into a literary circle of real distinction. Hueffer's the *English Review* published the work of Thomas Hardy, Henry James, William Butler Yeats, Walter de la Mare, John Galsworthy, W. H. Hudson, Norman Douglas, H. G. Wells, Joseph Conrad, Hilaire Belloc, and Wyndham Lewis, and, in June 1909 it ran Pound's "Sestina: Altaforte" and in October "Ballad of the Goodly Fere." In May 1909 he finally met Yeats, becoming a regular guest at the elder poet's "Monday evenings," and spending his Sundays with Victor Plarr discussing the "old days" of Ernest Dowson, Lionel Johnson, and the Rhymers' Club. The "Siena Mi Fe' " section of *Hugh Selwyn Mauberley* (1920), in which Plarr appears as "M. Verog," gives the reader a good idea of Plarr's topics of conversation.

By July 1909 Pound had made arrangements to give a second series of twenty-one lectures on medieval literature at the Polytechnic. (This material was published in 1910 as *The Spirit of Romance*.) The lectures began on 11 October, and both Olivia and Dorothy Shakespear had signed up for them. On 25 October *Exultations* was published. The volume contains fourteen new poems along with thirteen from his earlier books, and it received largely favorable reviews although the praise was not as unqualified as it had been for *Personae*. Altogether, the speed with which Pound had attracted the attention of the London literary establishment was quite remarkable, and he was even noticed by *Punch*, which gave notice that "Mr. Welkin Mark [Elkin Matthews] begs to announce that he has secured for the English market the palpitating works of the new Montana (U.S.A.) Poet, Mr. Ezekiel

Ton, who is the most remarkable thing in poetry since Robert Browning."

In early March 1910 William Carlos Williams was in London for a week and, before he left for Paris, Pound took pains to make his stay as interesting as possible. On 23 March Pound himself left for Paris, where he stayed for two days with the pianist Walter Morse Rummel before going on to Italy. From Verona he traveled to Sirmione on Lake Garda, where—as apparent in such poems as "Blandula, Tenulla, Vagula," and the first of the "Three Cantos" (which appeared in *Poetry* in June 1917)—he felt strongly attracted to the "genius of the place." He felt himself inspired both by the beauty of the landscape and by his strong sense of the past: he found himself thinking not only of the Sirmio of Catullus's day but sensing also those energies which the ancients had pictured to themselves as "Etruscan gods" and as "Panisks/And oak-girls and the Maenads." Pound, like Emerson, had "transcendental" intimations and found the Neoplatonic way of conceptualizing "the radiant world . . . of moving energies" to be helpful in conveying something of the quality of transcendent experience, which he presents graphically and dramatically by describing the apparitions of pagan divinities. "A god is an eternal state of mind," he said, who becomes manifest "when the states of mind take form."

Pound values the Provençal and Tuscan poets highly, partly because of what he believed to be their Neoplatonic sensibilities: they were the exponents of an "unofficial mysticism"—an "ecstatic religion" that could be traced back to the Eleusinian mysteries and was reserved for an élite of highly developed intellect and sensibility. Where Christianity called for the suppression of the senses as the road to spiritual enlightenment, Pound felt that in the Eleusinian tradition, approach to the divine was *through* the senses—by refining the emotions. In the Tuscan poets and particularly in Cavalcanti Pound found a similar sensibility accompanied by a rigorous intellectualism—a sophisticated "conception of the body as perfect instrument of the increasing intelligence." Although his admiration for Dante remained unwavering, he was fascinated by the "intellectual hunger" of the less orthodox Cavalcanti and his ideal of a strenuous intellectual progress toward "The Truth." At Sirmione he set himself the goal of translating all of Cavalcanti's poetry.

In April he escorted Olivia and Dorothy Shakespear from Sirmione to Venice and then returned, setting out again in the middle of May for

Verona, Vicenza, and Venice, where he stayed for a week before returning, via Paris, to London. On 10 June 1910 he sailed for America and spent the summer and fall in Swarthmore, where his parents were staying, devoting most of his energies to his translations of Cavalcanti. By November he had written the introduction for *The Sonnets and Ballate of Guido Cavalcanti* (1912). In the late fall and winter he stayed in New York and spent time with Yeats's father, artist John Butler Yeats, and with the lawyer John Quinn, who would later be a valuable patron for Lewis, Gaudier-Brzeska, Eliot, and Pound.

On 22 November *Provença*, the first American edition of his poetry, was published and on 22 February 1911 he sailed, via England, for Paris, where he spent a good deal of time with Walter Morse

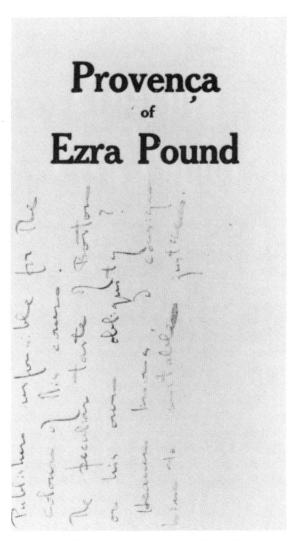

Front cover for Dorothy Pound's copy of the first volume of Pound's poetry published in the United States. Pound's note expresses his distaste for its color—tan (used by permission of the Ezra Pound Literary Property Trust).

Rummel, discussing the music of the troubadours and Debussy. By June he was back at Sirmione and wrote in July of his plans for a study of philosophy from Richard of St. Victor to Pico della Mirandola. He made a brief architectural tour of Northern Italy with Williams's brother, Edward, and then returned to London, stopping at Milan and Freiburg-im-Breisgau to research troubadour poetry, and at Giessen to give Hueffer a copy of *Canzoni* (published on 11 July.) Hueffer literally rolled on the floor at some of the stilted language, a response which, Pound later said, "saved me at least two years, perhaps more. It sent me back toward using the living tongue."

Pound reached London in August and the next month met G. R. S. Mead, a man of many talents and wide education. Musical and a brilliant mathematician, Mead was a lover of Greek literature and a student of Eastern religions. As head of the Quest Society—a group devoted to the study of gnosticism and theosophy—he invited Pound to give a lecture on the connection between medieval gnosticism and the troubadours. In 1901 Mead had published a study of the life of the neo-Pythagorean Apollonius of Tyana, and Pound would later devote Canto 94 to this "philosopher-hero."

In October 1911 Pound was seeing a good deal of Walter Morse Rummel and of Hilda Doolittle, who were both now in London, and he had his first meeting with A. R. Orage, editor of the *New Age*, who was to have a decisive influence on the course of his career. On the practical level Orage made it possible for Pound to continue writing poetry by regularly publishing his articles—and paying for them. Pound called him, in his 1934 obituary notice, "the man whose weekly guinea fed me when no one else was ready to do so, and that for at least two years running." Yet, most important, through his association with Orage, Pound was introduced into a circle of intellectual and artistic discussion which was more rigorous and pragmatic and hardheadedly practical than any he had been exposed to before.

Orage was originally a Guild Socialist, and the *New Age* lived up to its claim of being "An Independent Socialist Review of Politics, Literature and Art." A. J. Penty called it "a centre of free intellectual discussion which in our time has led to nothing less than a revolution in thought on social questions," and its contributors over the next several years were George Bernard Shaw, G. K. Chesterton, H. G. Wells, Arnold Bennett, Hilda Doolittle, Katherine Mansfield, G. D. H. Cole, T. E. Hulme, Wyndham Lewis, T. S. Eliot, and, of course, Pound. With his remarkable breadth of knowledge and vision, and his judicious turn of mind, Orage provided a center of gravity for this wide range of intellectual activity. His own deep interests in social reform and religious mysticism, tempered by common pragmatic sense, by what Edwin Muir called his "incorruptible adherence to reason," had a profound effect on Pound.

The vista of new talents and interests that opened up for Pound as he became acquainted with the writers of the *New Age* circle was exciting and energizing. Pound had an extraordinary affinity for people of artistic talent or genius, and his almost unerring sense of genius in others was balanced by his lack of competitiveness. No talent, however formidable, seemed to overawe him; he felt no jealousy toward other writers whom he considered talented or any need to advance his work at the expense of theirs. He had an instinctive and unselfconscious conviction of his own poetic genius and never felt threatened by the genius of others. Pound's own creativity was quickened when he was in close proximity to other sources of creative energy, and he consistently took pains to be wherever this energy was most intense.

But for his later fascination for economics, Pound's wide range of interests was already established while he was still in America; yet in England and Europe he managed to find increasingly talented exponents of the arts that he admired. In the fine arts he had begun by admiring the paintings of his friends Frank Whiteside of Philadelphia and Fred Vance of Crawfordsville, Indiana, but in Europe he turned to the futurists and vorticists, to the paintings of Wyndham Lewis and Picabia and the sculpture of Henri Gaudier-Brzeska, Epstein, and Brancusi. After his friendship with Katherine Heyman, he became acquainted with Rummel, Olga Rudge, George Antheil, Tibor Serly, and Gerhardt Münch. From his early reading of the Neoplatonists, he graduated to the esoteric investigations of Yeats, Mead, and Allen Upward, another *New Age* writer whose work *The Divine Mystery* (1913) impressed Pound deeply.

Pound's first series for Orage was "I Gather the Limbs of Osiris" (30 November 1911-22 February 1912) and, interestingly, the first of its twelve parts was a translation of the Anglo-Saxon poem "The Seafarer," which his biographer Noel Stock calls "the first clear sign of major ability." The "Osiris" articles and "Credo" (December 1911) set out Pound's new poetic program. In "Credo" he wrote of his belief in an "absolute rhythm" in poetry which "corresponds exactly to the . . . shade of emotion to be expressed"; that "the proper and perfect symbol is the natural object"; that "technique is the test of a man's sincerity," which means "the trampling down of every convention that impedes or obscures . . . the precise rendering of the impulse." He predicted a new poetry that would be "harder and saner . . . 'nearer the bone'. . . . austere, direct, free from emotional slither." These formulations show Pound becoming increasingly clear about the possibilities, suggested by Hulme's aesthetic theories, for innovation in his own poetry. In fact, it was in his note to accompany Hulme's *Complete Poetical Works* (published at the end of *Ripostes*, 1912) that Pound first used the label *Les Imagistes*, whom he identified as "the descendants of the forgotten school of 1909." Before he wrote this note, in about April 1912, Pound, Doolittle, and Richard Aldington had agreed upon three "imagist" principles: direct treatment of the subject, no superfluous words, and poetic rhythm based on the musical phrase and not on "strictness of the metronome." After a walking tour of "troubadour country," Pound was in London in August refining his ideas about poetry in light of Flint's long "Contemporary French Poetry" in that month's *Poetry Review*. Harriet Monroe's invitation to Pound to work on her projected Chicago magazine, *Poetry*, no doubt spurred Pound on. In the following months he sent her poems by Doolittle (which he signed "H. D. Imagiste," thus giving her her pen name) and by Yeats, and prose publicizing the *Imagistes*: a long letter ("Status rerum," published in the January 1913 issue), a self-interview attributed to F. S. Flint and his celebrated "A Few Don'ts by an Imagiste" (both in the March issue). At this time, he met Robert Frost (through Flint) and reviewed Frost's first book, *A Boy's Will*, enthusiastically in *Poetry* (May 1913). He also got verse by Williams published in the *Poetry Review* (October 1912), *Poetry* (June 1913), the *Egoist* (March, August, and December 1914), and elsewhere.

Meanwhile, *Ripostes* had been published in October 1912 by Swift and Company, but the firm failed the next month, and Elkin Mathews took over the bound copies and sheets of the book, bringing out *Canzoni & Ripostes of Ezra Pound* in May 1913 and *Ripostes* alone in April 1915. Hueffer's "roll on the floor" had impressed upon Pound the need to wean himself from his mannered style, and he worked hard in the years between 1911 and 1920 until he had found his own, distinctive voice. The main weakness of the earlier verse had been its inclination to looseness and lack of inevitability. Its presentation tended to the expository and the movement of the verse to a simple forward flow. For presentation he would come to the view that "the natural object is always the *adequate* symbol" (*Poetry*, March 1913), and in the matter of verse flow he would learn how to energize his poems through the use of tension. The act of translating "The Seafarer" from Anglo-Saxon helped by requiring him to work both with the very rigid prosody of the original (with its pattern of three strongly stressed alliterating words in each line and breaks both in the middle and at the end of each line), and also with the tension between the original Anglo-Saxon vocabulary and his own modern (although archaized) English, which sometimes echoed the words of the original and sometimes could not. His close analysis, also in 1911, of Arnaut Daniel's Provençal verse with its short lines, complex rhyme schemes and its frequently brisk, staccato and sometimes even clashing sound patterns provided additional training in tightening up his own verbal looseness. Also, by becoming aware of the extent and persistence of the evocative power of the broken form of Greek poems that have survived only on parchment scraps and fragments, he learned that "less could be more," that he could write a more powerful poem by suggesting rather than stating, by leaving gaps and requiring his readers to exercise their imaginations in making connections and visualizing for themselves.

Already in *Ripostes*, "The Return" shows the effectiveness of combining openness and incompletedness of form and of presentation with various kinds of tension between opposites—in this instance between how the subjects of the poem were and how they are, between the different kinds of meter associated with these two states and between our expectations of forward movement in the verse and the counterforce of hesitation and partial reversal. His efforts in this volume to pare away his esoteric and archaic vocabulary and simplify his verse to greater concision and directness, seeking the "luminous detail," find their first full achievement in "Contemporania" (*Poetry*, April 1913), a group of poems including the much-anthologized "In a Station of the Metro." Attributing this technical breakthrough to the extreme brevity of the Japanese haiku (in an essay significantly titled "How I Began"), Pound pointed to a new area of interest and technical resource: Chinese and Japanese writing. His interest in current French writing was unabated, however; witness his decision in April 1913 to meet in person the group of writers surrounding Charles Vildrac and Jules Romains. He later wrote a seven-part series on this group for

the *New Age* ("The Approach to Paris," 4 September-16 October 1913) and reviewed *Odes et Prières*, by Romains, for *Poetry* (August 1913). He learned from them a sense of indebtedness to Rémy de Gourmont. He also met John Gould Fletcher and Skipwith Cannell in Paris before he left for Sirmione and Venice, where he spent some time with Doolittle, her parents, and Aldington. From here he returned to London via Munich.

Back in London, Pound's association with Frost came to an abrupt end when Pound sent out "The Death of the Hired Man" to the *Smart Set* without bothering to consult Frost first. Characteristically, Frost's annoyance in no way lessened Pound's resolve to promote the older poet's work, and he wrote a favorable review of *A Boy's Will* for the *New Freewoman* (later the *Egoist*), for which he became literary editor in August. The *New Freewoman* published "The Serious Artist" (15 October-15 November 1913), an important statement of Pound's growing economic and political concerns. Concurrently, despite his distaste for D. H. Lawrence personally and for what seemed to him an excessively confessional impulse in *Love Poems and Others* (1913), Pound publicized Lawrence's work by reviewing it in *Poetry* (July) and sending poems by Lawrence to both *Poetry* and the *Smart Set*. He told Harriet Weaver that "If I were an editor I should probably accept his work without reading it. As a prose writer I grant him first place among the younger men."

Pound even persuaded Yeats to consider his call for greater directness and simplicity in poetry, and Yeats was prepared to rethink his own poetic practice to some extent in the light of Pound's ideas. On 3 January 1913 he had written to Lady Gregory that Pound "helps me to get back to the definite and concrete away from modern abstractions. To talk over a poem with him is like getting you to put a sentence into dialect. All becomes clear and natural"; and, Yeats added, he was "writing with new confidence having got Milton off my back." In November of that year, Yeats invited Pound to stay with him for three months at Stone Cottage, Coleman's Hatch, in Sussex, where, in addition to working on their own poetry, they spent a good deal of time following up Yeats's interest in a comparison of Irish folklore and mythology with those of other countries. It was here that Pound first heard of James Joyce, and when Yeats found him a copy of Joyce's poem "I Hear An Army Charging" Pound immediately got permission from Joyce to include it in his anthology *Des Imagistes* which appeared in February 1914 as a number of the *Glebe* and was published as a book in March in the United States and in April in London. It was Pound who persuaded Harriet Weaver to run Joyce's *Portrait of the Artist* serially in the *Egoist*.

At Stone Cottage, Pound was also busy making his own rendering of the Japanese Nō play *Nishikigi* from a verbatim translation made by Ernest Fenollosa, an American who had taught rhetoric in Japan and was finally made Imperial Commissioner of Art in Tokyo. He had died in 1908, and, after his widow came to know Pound in 1913, she chose him as her husband's literary executor and entrusted to him sixteen notebooks of research on and translations of Chinese and Japanese works, as well as an essay, "The Chinese Written Character as a Medium for Poetry." Pound's version of *Nishikigi* appeared in *Poetry* for May 1914.

Pound had, meanwhile, been courting Dorothy Shakespear since 1911; it was not until 23 March 1914 that, overcoming her parents' objections, they announced their engagement. They

were married on 20 April. On 18 January 1914 Pound, together with Yeats, Sturge Moore, Fred Manning, Plarr, Flint, and Aldington, had gone as a delegation to honor Wilfred Scawen Blunt for his services to poetry and as a champion of individual freedom. They had given Blunt a marble "reliquary" carved by the young sculptor, Henri Gaudier-Brzeska. Pound had met Gaudier in 1913 at an art show at the Albert Hall, and the friendship which developed between them would profoundly influence Pound's thinking about the arts and his attitude toward social issues. Gaudier was, as Pound saw, a sculptor of great promise; the body of work that he left—both sculpture and drawings—is an impressive achievement indeed. His death in action in 1915 at the age of twenty-three was a severe blow to Pound, not simply as a personal loss but as a symbolic instance of how those forces in a culture that lead to war simultaneously work to destroy the arts and culture itself. After Gaudier's death Pound dedicated himself with relentless determination to do whatever was in his power as a man of letters

Victor Plarr, T. Sturge Moore, William Butler Yeats, Wilfrid Scawen Blunt, Ezra Pound, Richard Aldington, and F. S. Flint at Newbuildings, 18 January 1914 (courtesy of the Fitzwilliam Museum)

to prevent another world war. That he was bound to fail is only too clear now, but it was a defeat that he refused to concede until long after the cause was lost.

He particularly admired the fact that Gaudier's sculpture required the greatest precision and expertise because he cut directly in stone. When Yeats suggested that Harriet Monroe award £40 of Yeats's £50 *Poetry* award to Pound, this prize money went to buy two small Gaudier statues, as well as a new typewriter. When Pound sat for his bust—the "hieratic head"—he considered this one of the most memorable moments of his life: "Some of my best days, the happiest and the most interesting, were spent in his uncomfortable mud-floored studio. . . . I knew that if I lived in the Quattrocento I should have had no finer moment, and no better craftsman to fill it. And it is not a common thing to know that one is drinking the cream of the ages."

Pound was to write many articles on art, the first of which was "The New Sculpture," a piece on Gaudier and Epstein, published in the *Egoist* for 16 February 1914. His continuing association with the *New Age* made him increasingly familiar with and informed about the works and views of the artists whose paintings were reproduced in its pages—Edward Wadsworth, David Bomberg, William Roberts, C. R. W. Nevinson, Walter Sickert, and most important, Wyndham Lewis. Lewis, a confirmed misanthrope, had made Pound an unusual concession in taking seriously his aesthetic judgments and in sharing his own views on art with Pound. Lewis, after a falling out with Roger Fry, had left Fry's Omega Workshops and set up his own Rebel Art Center, paying Pound the signal honor of allowing him alone to see his latest paintings, which were kept locked in a back room. Pound's admiration for Lewis's creative energy and expertise is clear from a letter that he wrote in March 1916 to John Quinn: "Lewis has just sent in the first dozen drawings . . . and the thing is stupendous. The vitality, the fulness of the man. . . . Nobody has *any* conception of the volume and energy and the variety. . . . It is not merely knowledge of technique, or skill, it is intelligence and knowledge of life . . . every kind of whirlwind of force and emotion. Vortex. That is the right word, if I did find it myself."

Vorticism, this new movement that Pound had named and Lewis had galvanized and focused, seemed to Pound an important step forward from imagism, which was likely to generate poems of fairly limited scope. Vorticism, rooted essentially in painting and sculpture, was concerned with a wider field of composition, with "lines of force," "planes

in relation," and currents of energies which would be moving, yet in a patterned and efficient way, gravitating toward a point of maximum concentration of energy—a vortex. This new theory did not represent any departure from Pound's faith in the poetic power of the image itself, but now, when he tried to identify this power, he found that the idea of the vortex provided a useful analogy. The image was "a radiant node or cluster . . . a VORTEX, from which, through which, and into which, ideas are constantly rushing."

No important poetry came out of his vorticist period, but Pound credited his association with these painters and sculptors with providing him with an entirely new sense of form. It is clear that his thinking at this time had a decisive influence in expanding his conception of the scope of his future poetry. The vorticists' emphasis on energetic and strenuous action and their attacks on whatever seemed stultifying in the society around them en-

THE LEWIS-BRZESKA-POUND TROUPE.
Blasting their own trumpets before the walls of Jericho.

Cartoon by Horace Brodzky, published in the Egoist *on 15 July 1914, a few days after the appearance of* Blast, *number one. The magazine had proclaimed, "BLAST years 1837 to 1900," and had included Pound's "Salutation the Third," which announced "Let us deride the smugness of 'The Times.'"*

couraged Pound to abandon the pose of the indolent aesthete which he had affected and to show his moral earnestness much more openly. The major vorticist assault on establishment complacency was Pound and Lewis's magazine, *Blast: A Review of the Great English Vortex*, with its eye-catching pink cover, "declamatory" typefaces, and its ridicule of whatever it judged to be inane and inert. It was very much in the vorticist spirit of cultivated outrageousness that Pound responded to Lascelles Abercrombie's call for poets to "return to Wordsworth" by challenging him to a duel. Abercrombie responded to the challenge in the spirit in which it was intended and, since it was his privilege to choose the weapons, averted the duel by deciding that they should pelt each other with unsold copies of their own books.

In the meantime, Amy Lowell was busy maneuvering herself into the position of "leader of the Imagists." Having read about imagism in *Poetry*, she had come to London in 1913 with a letter of introduction from Harriet Monroe to Pound. He found her "pleasingly intelligent," introduced her to Yeats and asked for permission to include "In a Garden" in the *New Freewoman* and later in *Des Imagistes*. Their friendship cooled considerably when Pound became impatient because she declined to put up a large sum of money to finance a magazine which he could run for her. In July 1914 she was back in London with a plan of action. Two days after attending a vorticists' dinner given 15 July at the Dieudonné restaurant in celebration of the publication of *Blast*, she gave her own imagist dinner at the same restaurant. Her plan was for a second and much larger "imagist" anthology for which contributors would choose their own poems. Pound, seeing that the result would not be imagist in any precise or authentic way, had no wish to have his work included and suggested that it would be more appropriate to call the book vers libre. She proceeded with her plan, and in 1915 Houghton Mifflin published the first of three anthologies titled *Some Imagist Poets*, with poems by Aldington, H. D., Flint, John Gould Fletcher, Lawrence, and Lowell. Pound dismissed this new pseudomovement as "Amygisme," and his annoyance at Lowell's attempt to pass herself off as the mother of his "brainchild" seems understandable enough: her publisher was billing her as "The foremost member of the 'Imagists'—a group of poets that includes William Butler Yeats, Ezra Pound, Ford Madox Hueffer."

In September 1914 Pound met Eliot, and, as soon as he saw "The Love Song of J. Alfred Pruf-

rock," he reported excitedly to Harriet Monroe that he had been sent "the best poem I have yet had or seen from an American" and that Eliot had "trained himself *and* modernized himself *on his own*." He sent her "The Love Song of J. Alfred Prufrock" in October but was disgusted when she objected to it. It was not until the following June that, by a process of alternating anger and patient justification, he could persuade her, reluctantly, to include it in *Poetry*.

By that time he was working enthusiastically on the Fenollosa notebooks and in October 1914 published his translations of the Nō plays *Kinuta* and *Hagoromo* in the *Quarterly Review*. His poetic resources were challenged even more demandingly by the task of turning Fenollosa's rough translations of Chinese poems into polished verse, a task which he accomplished with impressive skill in the poems of *Cathay*, published on 6 April 1915.

As an imagist, Pound had discovered how to use for his own poetic ends the power of the carefully chosen image to attract to itself and focus and radiate from itself a complex of associations which would provoke a deeply felt and specific emotional response in the reader. As he worked with these Chinese poems, he saw how they also had been constructed around images in a way that showed their authors to have been fully aware of this principle of composition which imagism had identified and, in effect, rediscovered. Pound realized that the imagists had "sought the force of Chinese ideographs *without knowing it*." Often in the poems of *Cathay*, the focal point is an image of leaves, grasses, plants, or flowers described in a way that identifies a season of the year and in turn, at one further remove, highlights the mood of the poem's speaker. In "Song of the Bowmen of Shu" the passage of time and the falling away of hope are focused by the change from "soft fern shoots" to "old fern-stalks." In "The River Song" the coming of spring is made graphic by "the willow-tips . . . half-blue and bluer" whose "cords tangle in mist, against the brocade-like palace," and in "The River-Merchant's Wife" the speaker's sorrow at the five-month absence of her husband radiates out from the lines "By the gate now, the moss is grown, the different mosses,/Too deep to clear them away!"

At Coleman's Hatch with Yeats again in the winter of 1914-1915—this time accompanied by his wife—Pound pressed forward with his researches into Chinese culture. He began to study Confucius in earnest, and in the three-part series "The Renaissance" (*Poetry*, February, March, and May 1915), as well as in the seven-part "Affirmations" (*New Age*,

An imaginative reconstruction of the Vorticists' dinner, painted by William Roberts in 1961-1962: Cuthbert Hamilton (on stool);
Ezra Pound, Roberts, Wyndham Lewis, Frederick Etchells, and Edward Wadsworth (at table); Jessica Dismorr and Helen Saunders
(in doorway) (courtesy of the Tate Gallery, London)

7 January-25 February 1915) suggested that artists bent on a revival of contemporary culture could learn a good deal from the study of Chinese writings.

At the same time Pound was trying to give Joyce all the help he could. He arranged for Joyce to receive a grant of £75 from the Royal Literary Fund in September 1915, and in February 1916 he published a long article praising Joyce's play *Exiles* in the Chicago magazine *Drama*. He took every opportunity to insist on the greatness of *A Portrait of the Artist as a Young Man,* calling Joyce "by far the most significant writer of our decade." In June 1916 he got two more grants for Joyce, one of £26 and another of £100 from the Civil List.

Pound had been increasingly outraged by the spectacle of the war as he came to know more about it from the firsthand accounts of Gaudier. One of

the effects of Gaudier's death in June 1915 was a hardening of Pound's attitude into a new grimness and urgency. He volunteered for service himself, and even after he was rejected by the British authorities, he later tried, again unsuccessfully, to use John Quinn's influence to arrange for him to serve with the American forces in France. A more important result of this sense of urgency was the new resolve with which he turned to the idea which he had held for several years of writing "a cryselephantine poem of immeasurable length which will occupy me for the next four decades." The following month he was working his way through William Roscoe's *The Life and Pontificate of Leo X,* which would provide much of the material for Canto 5, which he was already working on in mid-December, having written early drafts of Cantos 1 through 3.

Finally, after a great deal of effort, he was

able to find publishers for Joyce's *A Portrait of the Artist as a Young Man*. Harriet Weaver agreed to publish the English edition and Pound persuaded John Marshall to bring out the American edition in place of a collection of Pound's own prose articles which Marshall had already accepted.

On 14 April 1916 John Lane published *Gaudier-Brzeska: A Memoir*. Pound's original Cantos 1-3 appeared in the June, July, and August numbers of *Poetry* under the general title "Three Cantos," but Pound continued to revise them, realizing that he had not yet arrived at the degree of formal precision that would be necessary if they were to provide a strong opening for his projected "cryselephantine" poem. When they appeared in the enlarged private and trade editions of *Lustra*, published in America shortly afterward, these cantos had already been revised and pared down. In March with the financial backing of John Quinn Pound was made a London editor of the *Little Review*, an important outlet both for his writing and for that of Eliot and Wyndham Lewis (now with the army in France). Pound and Eliot worked quite closely together between 1917 and 1921: Pound made the financial arrangements for the printing of *Prufrock and Other Observations* under Harriet Weaver's *Egoist* imprint, and their shared interests in Théophile Gautier and in Jules Laforgue led both to turn for a while to writing in more metrically regular forms. *Hugh Selwyn Mauberley* (1920) and Eliot's Sweeney poems were partly conceived as a "countercurrent" to "the dilutation of *vers libre*, Amygism, Lee Mastersism [and] general floppiness."

Pound was actively following up on his interest in music and, as William Atheling, was writing music reviews for the *New Age* (as well as art criticism under the pseudonym B. H. Dias). He was particularly concerned with reviewing troubadour music and with exploring the art of harmonizing lyric poetry with musical settings—an art which he felt had virtually died out since the time of Henry Lawes, Thomas Campion, and Edmund Waller. In Raymonde Collignon, he felt that he had found a singer who could do justice to the kind of marriage of poetry and music which he was working toward, and, when she gave a concert of Rummel-Pound troubadour songs, "William Atheling" covered this event for the *New Age* in May 1918. Collignon appears to be the woman "that sang me once that song of Lawes" to whom the "Envoi" of part one of *Hugh Selwyn Mauberley* is addressed.

Starting in December 1917 Pound began to receive chapters of Joyce's *Ulysses*, which he was arranging to have serialized in the *Little Review*. The first installment appeared in March 1918. On 29 June 1918 Knopf published *Pavannes and Divisions*, a collection of Pound's prose. In August Pound edited a "Henry James Number" of the *Little Review*, and between August 1918 and April 1919 the *Egoist* ran several of his articles on translators of Homer and of Aeschylus, one of which included his "Seafarer" rendering of Andreas Divus' *Odyssey* (which would later become the body of Canto 1). Harriet Weaver planned to publish these collected articles as a booklet, but Pound suggested that a more valuable project would be a first book of poems by Marianne Moore that had been brought to London without Moore's knowledge by H. D., Robert McAlmon, and Bryher (Winifred Ellerman), and it was duly published by The Egoist Ltd. in 1921.

After the February 1919 issue of *Poetry*, Pound was no longer its foreign correspondent; the most immediate reason for his removal after more than six years in the position was the correspondence over "Homage to Sextus Propertius," part of which appeared in the March 1919 issue of *Poetry*. Although his references in the poem to Wordsworth and to "a frigidaire patent" should be conclusive indications that Pound intended no verbatim translation or even fidelity to the original, he was attacked in *Poetry* (April) and the *Chicago Tribune* as being "incredibly ignorant of Latin." When Pound wrote to protest this criticism, in a letter to Harriet Monroe beginning "Cat-piss and porcupines" and then stopped writing to her, she took this action as a tacit resignation from his position with the magazine, and in November wrote to him to formalize it. Pound had several reasons for his highly idiosyncratic rendering of this Latin poet. His statement that he intended to "bring a dead man to life, to present a living figure" suggests a tribute, both to this particular poet and to the power of successful poetry which allows it to be revived many centuries after it was written. To some extent Pound was also using Propertius as a persona by means of which he could present his own feelings in the present—"certain emotions as vital to me in 1917, faced with the infinite and ineffable imbecility of the British Empire, as they were to Propertius some centuries earlier, when faced with the infinite and ineffable imbecility of the Roman Empire." Of course, Propertius is not Pound. Propertius's contentment with writing poetry in a minor key does not at all correspond to Pound's ambitious notion of the poetry that he himself was planning to write. Pound was much less concerned with Propertius's point of view than he was with capturing his shrewd and easygoing tone of voice.

In writing the poem, Pound radically transformed his sense of history: where earlier he tended to adopt the stance of the poet drawn back to the past, even yearning toward its pastness, now he began to draw the past into the present. Instead of explicitly displaying his own emotions, he began to keep himself and his feelings well "behind the scenes," choosing to impress the reader with his discrimination through his artistry and with his self-confidence through his proprietorial attitude toward the great art of the past. Wordsworth and the frigidaire in "Homage to Sextus Propertius" serve as rather extreme instances of this attitude, showing Pound flaunting the advantage which he automatically had by being alive and writing at a time when Propertius was dead. Pound was discovering how to draw on his love of the past for poetic capital without being nostalgic or sentimental and without fleeing from the present. "Homage to Sextus Propertius" is a major step forward in the process of establishing the assured poetic voice that was a prerequisite for a rethinking of *The Cantos.*

In May 1919 Pound and his wife traveled to Paris and then spent most of the summer in the "troubadour country" of the south of France, staying in Toulouse and visiting Nîmes, Arles, Avignon, and the ruins of Montségur in the Pyrenees, the site of the massacre of the Albigensians, where now there was "wind space and rain space/no more an altar to Mithras." (Pound recalled this summer's touring in Cantos 48 and 76.) In September, when they returned to London, the *Little Review* began its serialization of Fenollosa's "The Chinese Written Character as a Medium for Poetry," and in October John Rodker's Ovid Press published *The Fourth Canto* in a limited edition of forty copies. That same month the Egoist press published *Quia Pauper Amavi,* which included both the early Cantos 1-3 and "Homage to Sextus Propertius." Although Eliot and Ford reviewed this book favorably, bad reviews in the *Observer* of 11 January and the *Spectator* of 7 February 1920 annoyed Pound.

Pound was writing drama and ballet reviews for the *Athenaeum.* Also, in March 1920, his review of Major C. H. Douglas's *Economic Democracy* appeared in the *Little Review.* He had met Douglas in 1918 and had come increasingly to share Orage's conviction of the extreme importance of Douglas's Social Credit theories. Also in March he was made correspondent for the American *Dial,* and in April

Boni and Liveright in New York published his *Instigations,* a collection of critical essays and the complete text of "The Chinese Written Character." By 3 May Pound and his wife were in Venice, where he began *Indiscretions,* an account of his childhood and family history which, although it renamed the people involved and affected to deal with their exploits in an "off-hand" or arch manner, was both factually reliable and revealing about the genuine interest he felt in his ancestors. Starting in May 1920, the *New Age* published *Indiscretions* in twelve installments (it was published as a book in 1923). Before *Indiscretions* began to appear in the *New Age,* Dorothy Pound's health dictated a move to Sirmione, and Pound prevailed upon Joyce to visit him there (accompanied by his son) on 8-9 June, during which time Pound persuaded him to make Paris his base, rather than Trieste.

In June Elkin Mathews published *Umbra,* a selection of Pound's early poems, and John Rodker published 200 copies of *Hugh Selwyn Mauberley.* The writing of the Mauberley sequence was a decisive stage in the evolution of Pound's thinking about his role as a poet. The sequence makes clear how the shock of World War I (and of Gaudier's death in particular) and the increasing insight into larger social issues, which he owed to his association with Orage and Douglas, had made his earlier exclusive preoccupation with purely aesthetic concerns seem now to be irresponsible. In the first poem of the sequence he writes of this earlier "aesthete-self," whom he calls E. P., and then disowns him, "killing him off" by calling this poem a funerary ode. In the remaining twelve poems of the sequence, he deplores the "tawdry cheapness" of standards of public taste in the arts; the way in which a writer such as Arnold Bennett, who caters to these standards, is successful while such a committed stylist as Ford is neglected; the hardships of the poets of "the Nineties"; and the death of any Dionysiac vitality or reverence for the mysteries. In particular he deplores the tragedy of the war and the disillusion that followed it, when those who did survive came "home to many deceits,/home to old lies and new infamy;/usury age-old and age-thick/and liars in public places." Poem five leaves no doubt about the relative importance in his eyes of the lives of young men and the cultural monuments of the past:

There died a myriad,
And of the best, among them,
For an old bitch gone in the teeth,
For a botched civilization,

Charm, smiling at the good mouth,
Quick eyes gone under earth's lid,
For two gross of broken statues,
For a few thousand battered books.

In part two of the sequence he presents and decisively disowns Mauberley, the ineffectual, self-absorbed hedonist whom Pound intends to be the exaggerated projection of the kind of writer E. P. might have become had he kept to his purely aesthetic concerns. By creating this caricature, Pound was justifying his belief that a failure to make his poetry more socially conscious would be poetically self-destructive. Mauberley's energies ebb away until he is capable of "Nothing, in brief, but maudlin confession,/Irresponse to human aggression."

Pound's feeling of disgust with the disillusioned mood of postwar London and its hidebound literary establishment had already made him consider living elsewhere, and Paris seemed the most likely alternative. He was back in Paris from Italy in June 1920 and in July helped the Joyce family to settle there, but he still thought of London as his base and moved back there that autumn. One of the reasons for his return was the money he could make as drama critic for the *Athenaeum* and so, when he was fired from this position shortly after arriving from Paris, he was angry at not having been told earlier. His *Dial* letters were increasingly full of praise for the artistic vitality of Paris; he was enthusiastic about his discovery of the poetry of Jean Cocteau, and in January 1921 he left England for France. Until April he stayed at St. Raphael on the Cote d'Azur and then settled in Paris at 70 *bis*, rue Notre Dame des Champs.

Pound's three years in Paris were transitional ones for his career—a time for reorienting his thinking about his future role as a socially committed writer and also for making some important decisions about *The Cantos*. After the stuffiness of London, Paris seemed to be a more energetic place, where it was easier to put ideas into action. In the United States the Society for the Prevention of Vice had managed to bring a halt to the serialization of *Ulysses* in the *Little Review,* and Huebsch as well as Boni and Liveright had decided not to publish it as a book, but in Paris, Sylvia Beach of the Shakespeare and Company bookstore undertook to publish it herself, and Pound took it upon himself to collect subscriptions. It was in Paris at this time that, with considerable help from Pound, Eliot's *The Waste Land* (1922) found its final form. *The Waste Land* manuscripts, published in 1971, show exactly

the extent of Pound's contribution, why Eliot would tell Gilbert Seldes of the *Dial* that Pound is "the most important living poet in the English Language" and why Eliot dedicated the poem "For Ezra Pound/*il miglior fabbro.*" When Eliot was presented with the 1922 *Dial* award of $2,000, he wrote to John Quinn that his only regret was that the award had come to him before having been given to Pound.

In his Paris years Pound established his own assured poetic stance, developing the voice and control that would give unity and integrity to his individual opening Cantos and build up the momentum that would give an inevitability to the ordering of their sequence. We can see how radical a development was involved when we compare Cantos 1-3 as they appeared in *Poetry* to Cantos 1 and 3 of the poem as it now stands. In the early version, the poet's preoccupation with the difficulty of finding an appropriate voice is to a large extent the subject of the poetry. The original Cantos 1 and 2 in particular tend to be rambling, verbose, and, when he discusses his anxiety, prosaic, while his recurring indecisiveness deprives them of any forward impetus. The revised version uses the self-contained second half of the original Canto 3 for revised Canto 1 and cuts most of the original Cantos 1 and 2. The revised Canto 3 contains some greatly abbreviated sections from the original Canto 1 and preserves the passage on El Cid from the original Canto 2; the rest is very heavily cut indeed. (The sources of these, and of all cantos, are recorded in Carroll F. Terrell's *A Companion to the Cantos of Ezra Pound,* 1980, 1984.)

Barbara Eastman has traced the complex history of the text; it is sufficient to note here that Cantos 4-7 first appeared in *Poems 1918-21* (December 1921) and the "Malatesta Cantos" (now numbered 8-11) in Eliot's the *Criterion* (July 1923). They were later revised. These cantos focus on other kinds of difficulty: the dual nature of passion as inspiration and destruction (Canto 4), the apparent incompatibility of any vision of intellectual perfection with actual reality (Canto 5). Pound clearly identifies with the dilemmas of people who struggle to get things done against great odds, perhaps with the hope of only limited success. In a climate of post-world-war disillusion, the achievements of Sigismundo Malatesta, a renaissance patron of the arts whose life is the subject of Cantos 8-11, are a salutary example of what one man can do "outside the then system, and pretty much against the power that was, and in any case without great material resources."

Ford Madox Ford, James Joyce, Ezra Pound, and John Quinn at 70 bis, *rue Notre Dame des Champs, 1923*

Though Pound was living in Paris at this time, he was regularly visiting Italy, and in these cantos he is drawing on his Italian research. These years in Paris are more a source of Pound's musical than of his poetic inspiration: his friendship with the young American violinist Olga Rudge spurred his musical ambitions, and he turned to her (as well as to Agnes Bedford, concert pianist and lifelong friend of Wyndham Lewis) for help in composing an opera using the poetry of Villon as libretto. Unable to play the piano, Pound bought a bassoon, whereupon Lewis, suspecting Bedford's complicity in this purchase, asked her: "do you think it is an act justified by the facts of existence, as you understand them?" Pound also got help from George Antheil, whom he met in June 1923 and whose musical theories became the subject of Pound's *Antheil and the Treatise on Harmony* (1924). Once Pound finished his opera, he turned to composing music for the violin. An abbreviated concert version of *Le Testament* was performed in Paris on 29 June

1926; the whole work was broadcast by the BBC on 26 October 1931.

Pound's "On Criticism in General" was published in Eliot's *Criterion* in January 1923 and in 1929, revised as *How to Read*, was serialized in the *New York Herald Tribune Books* (it was published as a book in 1931). Here he distinguished three "kinds of Poetry"—*melopoeia*, "wherein the words are charged, over and above their plain meaning, with some musical property which directs the bearing or trend of that meaning"; *phanopoeia*, "a casting of images upon the visual imagination"; *logopoeia*, " 'the dance of the intellect among words.' "

There was much about the ambience of the expatriate life-style in Paris that Pound was bound to find uncongenial. The anomie, the directionlessness, and the hard drinking of the "Lost Generation" were antithetical to Pound's energy, earnestness, and optimism—he had no enthusiasm for or even interest in "decadence." He was, however, a strong advocate of sensuousness, and his

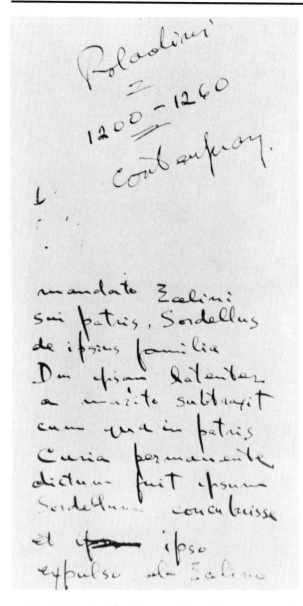

Notes for Canto 6 (used by permission of the Ezra Pound Literary Property Trust)

Cantos" celebrated Sigismundo Malatesta as patron and as survivor in a hostile time, Canto 12 provides twentieth-century contrasts and comparisons with a tribute to John Quinn which in tone foreshadows the "Hell Cantos" (14-15). Canto 13's serene introduction of Confucius sharply contrasts with the "Hell Cantos," in which Pound invents his own counterpart to a circle of Dante's *Inferno*, describing in repulsive detail the fates of corrupt politicians, war profiteers, financiers, agents provocateurs, slumowners, usurers, vice crusaders, newspaper owners, imperialists, and monopolists, as well as "betrayers of language," the pusillanimous, bigots, liars, the envious, the pompous, the litigious, bores, and—sounding like a holdover from *Blast*—"lady golfers." The serious offenders belong in either or both of the major categories—"obstructors of knowledge,/obstructors of distribution." With Plotinus taking the place of Dante's Virgil as his guide, the poet comes up out of this hell into the sunlight, and in Canto 16 finds himself at "Hell-Mouth."

Schooled by the social credit theory of Major Douglas, Pound had become increasingly certain that, were it not for the machinations of the "obstructors of knowledge" and "obstructors of distribution," the common sense of an informed public would have been alert to prevent a tragedy like World War I. Having expressed his outrage so stridently and graphically in the Hell Cantos, Pound settles in Canto 16 for a calm rehearsal of fact. Even the death of Gaudier, which had distressed him so much, is reduced to the matter-of-fact comment "And Henri Gaudier went to it,/and they killed him,/And killed a good deal of sculpture," and to the elegiac vignette of "an arm upward, clutching a fragment of marble," being sucked down into "the lake of bodies."

As the opening canto of a new section of the poem, Canto 17 (set in Venice) is almost a poetic counterpart to the new beginning which Pound has made by choosing Italy as his new permanent home. Although he has made Rapallo his home base, Venice would always be the most important "magnetic center" for him in Italy, personally as well as culturally. From the 1930s on, he spent his summers there with Olga Rudge; he would finally settle there after his return to Italy following World War II and his incarceration in St. Elizabeths and would eventually be buried there. Pound's relationship with Venice was not simple: although its inimitable architecture, painting, and sculpture were a great source of inspiration so that he found "in Venice more affirmations/of individual men/ . . . than any elsewhere," the very excellence of its art

translation of Rémy de Gourmont's *Physique de l'Amour; essai sur l'instinct sexual,* with an earnest and rather embarrassingly silly postscript, suggests that he felt the need to establish his willingness to enter into the Parisian spirit, and to demonstrate that he was, although no decadent, certainly no "Puritan."

In October 1924 the Pounds left Paris for Rapallo, where, after a while, they settled into a top-floor apartment at Via Marsala 12, on the seafront. In mid-December they went to Sicily for several months, and in late January 1925 in Paris William Bird's Three Mountains Press published *A Draft of XVI. Cantos* in a limited edition with capitals designed by Henry Strater. Where the "Malatesta

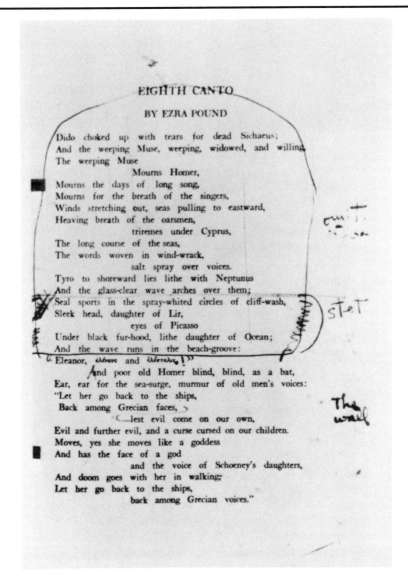

EIGHTH CANTO

BY EZRA POUND

Dido choked up with tears for dead Sichaeus;
And the weeping Muse, weeping, widowed, and willing,
The weeping Muse
                          Mourns Homer,
Mourns the days of long song,
Mourns for the breath of the singers,
Winds stretching out, seas pulling to eastward,
Heaving breath of the oarsmen,
                          triremes under Cyprus,
The long course of the seas,
The words woven in wind-wrack,
                          salt spray over voices.
Tyro to shoreward lies lithe with Neptunus
And the glass-clear wave arches over them;
Seal sports in the spray-whited circles of cliff-wash,
Sleek head, daughter of Lir,
                          eyes of Picasso
Under black fur-hood, lithe daughter of Ocean;
And the wave runs in the beach-groove:
"Eleanor, ἑλέναυς and ἑλέπτολις | "
                          And poor old Homer blind, blind, as a bat,
Ear, ear for the sea-surge, murmur of old men's voices:
"Let her go back to the ships,
  Back among Grecian faces,
                          lest evil come on our own,
Evil and further evil, and a curse cursed on our children.
Moves, yes she moves like a goddess
And has the face of a god
                          and the voice of Schoeney's daughters,
And doom goes with her in walking,
Let her go back to the ships,
                          back among Grecian voices."

Page from the proofs of the original Canto 8 as it appeared in the May 1922 issue of the Dial, *revised by Pound as part of Canto 2 in* A Draft of XVI. Cantos *(1925) (used by permission of the Ezra Pound Literary Property Trust)*

challenged him in a somewhat forbidding way; for the very "completedness" of Venice seemed to exclude him and to send him off to another, less overwhelming setting in which he could create his own art. Two levels of reality alternate in Canto 17: the city itself is never seen in full daylight and so seems strangely artificial and insubstantial. The sunlit landscapes are settings for the apparition of the gods—of Diana, Dionysus, Hermes, and Persephone. For example, in Canto 21, while the city of the present is seen only in the half-light of sunset, the goddesses appear in a moonlight which blurs clear distinctions and the gods themselves have become "discontinuous."

The main event of Canto 26 is the arrival in Venice in 1438 of the Byzantine Emperor and the Patriarch of Constantinople who are on their way to the Council of Ferrara-Florence to ask the Pope for military aid to defend Constantinople against the Turks. Politically a failure, their mission was culturally important for leading to the meeting of Gemisthus Plethon and Cosimo de'Medici and to the founding of the Platonic Academy in Florence. The canto is a focal point for this section of the poem (17-27), since in it appear many of Pound's important renaissance characters who happen to be in Venice on this occasion.

Canto 20—Pound's warning to himself to resist the siren song of an escapist aestheticism—is an organizing center for the autobiographical material and Niccolò d'Este, who made Ferrara a center for arts and letters during the fifteenth century, is important in both, tying these focal points together. Cantos 18, 19, 22, and 27 deal with the problematical present, with 18 and 19 concentrating on crooked financial deals, monopolies, racketeering, and war profiteering. Canto 22 identifies financial success with crooked practice, and castigates economist John Maynard Keynes ("Mr. Bukos") who, at a time when two million men were out of work, said that the reason for the high cost of living was "Lack of Labour," and Canto 27 suggests that Europe, with no responsible political leadership, is drifting out of civilization.

Cantos 17-19 were published in the Autumn/Winter 1925/1926 issue of the Paris little magazine *This Quarter*. On 9 July 1925 Mary, Pound's daughter by Olga Rudge, was born in Bressanone in the Italian Tyrol, and for the rest of this year and the next Pound did very little writing, concentrating mainly on music—on concerts by Rudge and Antheil and on the performance of *Le Testament*. On 10 September 1926 Dorothy Pound had a son, Omar, born in the American Hospital in Paris. On 22 December 1926, Boni and Liveright published *Personae*, Pound's choice of the poems that he wished to remain in print. In spring 1927 he started his own magazine, the *Exile*, which lasted for four issues until fall 1928. At this time, encouraged by Ford, he was considering a lecture tour of the United States—although nothing was to come of this plan—and corresponding with H. L. Mencken, refusing to acknowledge the fact that Mencken's unregenerate cynicism was the antithesis to his own earnest optimism.

In the fall of 1927 he turned, as he so often did, to Cavalcanti and to Confucius for reassurance that harmony and order were still possible despite all evidence to the contrary. He was working on a translation of Cavalcanti's *canzone* "Donna mi prega" and, on 17 October 1927, he finished a translation of Confucius's *Ta Hio*. He had begun reading Confucius seriously in 1915, in connection with his work on Fenollosa, and he came increasingly to rely on the wisdom of the *Four Books* as a source of order and a stabilizing influence in a life that was to become progressively frenetic and chaotic. Originally he was particularly interested in the *Ta Hio* (*The Great Learning*) and the *Analects*. Confucius had studied the histories of China to learn about the operation of moral laws in the state, and Pound came to see the Confucian concern with civic

order as far preferable to "the maritime adventure morals of Odysseus" and to the values of "the Homeric world . . . of irresponsible gods, a very high society without recognizable morals, the individual responsible to himself."

In February 1928 Yeats and his wife took an apartment in Rapallo. Pound, busy preparing an Italian edition of Cavalcanti's complete works, excerpted a part of his commentary for publication in the March 1928 *Dial* as "Medievalism and Medievalism (Guido Cavalcanti)" and sent a translation of "Donna Mi Prega" for the July number. *A Draft of the Cantos 17-27* was published by John Rodker in September. The final issue of Pound's the *Exile* carried forty pages of Williams's writing and the November *Dial* included Pound's article "Dr. Williams' Position." Williams wrote to thank him for his "great interest and discriminating defence of my position" and insisted "nothing will ever be said of better understanding regarding my work than your article in *The Dial*."

In early 1929 Pound was studying the works of the German anthropologist Leo Frobenius, who in Pound's view had revolutionized anthropological study by "reading" surviving artifacts to discern the general state of the culture that produced them. Pound was attracted to his notion that the "reader" could become sensitized to the "Paideuma" of a period, which Pound defined as "the complex of ideas which is in a given time germinal, reaching into the next epoch, but conditioning actively all the thought and action of its own time." It was this "active element" that Pound was particularly concerned to identify and do all he could to strengthen, and his increasing conviction that postwar Europe was drifting toward another war made him turn to Mussolini as the only Western leader who, in his eyes, showed any sign of taking any active and constructive measures against it.

From 1930 on, Pound lived during the summers in Olga Rudge's house in Venice while Dorothy Pound spent time in England. He now began to devote much energy to an ongoing letter-writing campaign to impress upon any American politician or public figure who would listen to him the need for economic reform. In August 1930 Nancy Cunard's Hours Press published *A Draft of XXX Cantos* (with initials designed by Dorothy Pound), and when Cantos 31-33 appeared in *Pagany* for July 1931 his change of emphasis was clear. He had chosen to make the personal take second place to the issues of civic responsibility and the need for economic reform. *Eleven New Cantos: XXXI-XLI* (1934) moves from the good sense of Jefferson and

Homer and Ezra Pound on Lake Garda, Sirmione, Italy

Adams, to Jackson and Van Buren's fight against the Second United States Bank, and ends with a celebration of Mussolini's efforts to curtail the power of the "usurers."

In Cantos 31-33 Pound turned again to the technique he had used in the Malatesta Cantos, building cantos out of extracts from the writings of the characters he is presenting. Now he used *The Writings of Thomas Jefferson*, which Eliot had given him ten years earlier, and *The Works of John Adams*. Pound saw the letters between the two men from 1813 to 1826 as "a Shrine and a Monument," and used these and other documents to comment on human irrationality and the rarity of leaders with good sense. Quoting Adams on the "arbitrary, bloody and . . . diabolical" nature of absolute power, these Cantos remind the reader that the evils of the problematical present, attacked in *The Cantos*, had been diagnosed long ago by the greatest

of America's founders, and point to Senator Brookhart of Iowa's attack on the Federal Reserve Board's practices as a contemporary instance of political integrity.

Canto 34, constructed from excerpts from *The Diary of John Quincy Adams*, and Canto 37, on Van Buren's role in preventing the recharter of the privately owned Bank of the United States, appeared in *Poetry* for April 1933 and March 1934 respectively. In January 1932 Edizioni Marsano of Genoa published *Rime*, Pound's long-projected edition of Cavalcanti. This project had engaged Pound's attention since 1928. Originally planned as a bilingual edition (which was abandoned when the Aquila Press failed), it finally appeared as a critical edition of the Italian texts (with a few translations by Pound). He sent a copy of this work to the University of Pennsylvania but it was not, as he hoped, accepted in lieu of a doctoral dissertation. In the summer of 1932 he drafted a second opera, *Cavalcanti*, which was not performed until 1983.

In 1932 Pound had also been busy writing articles and newspaper items; between 1932 and 1940 he contributed more than 60 to the Rapallo newspaper *Il Mare* and more than 180 to the *New English Weekly*, which Orage began to publish in 1932 after his return to London—and to "full-time Social Credit"—from his stay in America. In the summer of 1932 Pound met the futurist Fillippo Marinetti in Rome and was impressed with his energy and enthusiasm. At this time Ford visited Pound in Rapallo, and Olga Rudge made a transcription of their conversation. She translated it into Italian, publishing it, in an interview format, in the 20 August issue of *Il Mare* (her English retranslation appeared in the August 1947 issue of *Western Review*). Ford arranged for Farrar and Rinehart's publication of *The Cantos of Ezra Pound* (1933), a pamphlet of tributes to Pound by fifteen of his fellow writers, including, in addition to Ford, Hemingway, Eliot, Joyce, Hugh Walpole, and Archibald MacLeish. This pamphlet was to be advance publicity for the Farrar and Rinehart edition of *A Draft of XXX Cantos*, which appeared on 15 March 1933. Louis Zukofsky, who at Pound's suggestion had edited the "objectivist" number of *Poetry* (February 1931), traveled to Rapallo for a visit in 1933.

In 1932 Pound worked with F. Ferruccio Cerio on a film scenario about the history of Italian Fascism which was printed but not published that December (the film was never made), and on 30 January 1933, Pound was granted an official audience with Mussolini. The Duce, looking over a copy of *A Draft of XXX Cantos*, pronounced it "*divertente*," which Pound chose to see as an incisive perception that his purpose in the poem was to "delight" as well as to instruct. Pound was similarly impressed when in response to Pound's comment that he wanted to put his ideas in order, Mussolini asked "Why?" Yet at least as important as showing Mussolini his poem was the opportunity this interview gave Pound to present the Duce with a list of suggested fiscal and economic reforms. Pound's interest in the Fascist régime extended only to its social and economic policies. Early in his régime Mussolini had made significant social and economic innovations, which understandably led Pound to see the Duce as the humane and responsible ruler that he had been searching for; yet he was clearly not justified in closing his mind, as he did, to the mounting evidence during the late 1930s of Mussolini's mental and moral deterioration.

Many of Mussolini's reforms of the 1920s

Ezra and Dorothy Pound (courtesy of Omar Pound)

were in accord with Pound's theories. Under the Fascists a country that was in many ways essentially feudal was modernized and industrialized according to a coherent, long-range program that had been largely worked out as early as 1921 and 1922. A deficit of 400 million lire was replaced, by 1925, with a balanced budget, and by 1929 Italy's industrial output had doubled so that its rate of industrial productivity was higher than that of France, Germany, or England. After 1926 Mussolini created an "insulated economy" to protect domestic prosperity against foreign exploitation and he centralized and increased state control of banking. His social welfare legislation was thoroughgoing and highly successful, and he also involved the government in support of culture and the arts. Pound saw the histrionic face of Fascism—the parades, military drills, and rousing speeches—as unimportant window dressing, reflecting an Italian love of public display and having nothing to do with the commitment to social and fiscal reform which, to him, was Fascism proper. He was annoyed that the British and American press dwelt only on the histrionic and easily mocked.

Right after his interview with the Duce, Pound began *Jefferson and/or Mussolini* (1935), the purpose of which was to assure his reader that Mussolini, like Jefferson, was the "OPPORTUNIST who is RIGHT," that, because he faced such impediments to effective political action, he had to act unilaterally to accomplish any substantial reform, and that his good faith guaranteed that he would not abuse his power. Pound was completely sincere in these statements, but he did acknowledge that "any thorough judgement of MUSSOLINI will be in a measure an act of faith, it will depend on what you *believe* the man means, what you believe that he wants to accomplish." Although the book was written by February 1933, it was not published until April 1935, after having been rejected, Pound claimed, by forty publishers.

On 16 April 1933 Faber and Faber published Pound's short book *ABC of Economics*, the most lucid and helpful digest of his economic views. In 1934 he was busy working on *The Cantos* and writing more than one hundred articles on economic and political reform. On 8 October *Eleven New Cantos: XXXI-XLI* was published in New York. Canto 41, the last of this sequence, begins with a tribute to Mussolini for having provided grain, a safe water supply, and decent housing for large numbers of Italians, and for his stand against usury, graft, and corruption. Although increasingly Pound's impulse was to put economic reform before purely literary matters, 1934 also saw the publication of *ABC of Reading* in May, and of *Make It New*—a selection of his earlier writings on literature—in September. Also in 1934 James Laughlin came to stay in Rapallo as a student-disciple of Pound's. He took on the editorship of the literary section of *New Democracy*, the magazine of the American Social Credit party, and called it "New Directions," the title he would later use when, also at Pound's suggestion, he began his own publishing company.

In 1935 Pound maintained his steady flow of articles on economics and wrote letters to anyone, particularly in America, who would give his fiscal theories a hearing. He had made contact with Henry A. Wallace, Secretary of Agriculture; with the historian and member of Roosevelt's "Brain Trust" W. E. Woodward, and with the Republican Congressman George Tinckham, whom he thought would make a good president. But 1935 was to prove a crisis year for Pound. Mussolini's invasion of Abyssinia on 3 October revealed a new side of the Duce which would alienate the considerable sympathy for his regime that had existed up to that time in Britain and America. The invasion confronted Pound with a dilemma. It had been an article of faith with him that Mussolini was interested only in domestic reforms and was strongly opposed to war. The Abyssinian invasion showed that this belief was unfounded, but Pound had staked so much on his original notion of Mussolini that he could not bear to abandon it. From this point on he began to lie to himself about Mussolini's good faith, trapping himself in a mindset which would require him to rationalize or to try to explain away increasingly blatant evidence that he had been mistaken. This was the beginning of an inexorable process of self-delusion that would lead Pound farther and farther away from contact with the reality of the political situation in Italy. The propaganda of the regime told him what he wanted to hear about the benevolent and peace-loving Duce, and he accepted it at face value. After Abyssinia he carried photographs of alleged Abyssinian "atrocities," which he eagerly presented to people as explanation of Mussolini's change of policy.

Hemingway had already made his dislike of Mussolini clear to Pound back in 1933, but the *New Democracy* for 15 October 1935 carried a very favorable review of *Jefferson and/or Mussolini* by Williams, who was himself strongly committed to Social Credit. The main voice of warning about the Duce and the one that stood the best chance of getting Pound's attention was that of Orage, but to Pound's great shock, Orage died suddenly on 6 November 1935, shortly after having made a BBC broadcast on Social Credit, which Pound had been able to pick up on his radio in Rapallo. It seems as though, at the time when Pound most needed the counsel of common sense and restraint, the voice that could offer him this counsel most persuasively and with most chance of being heard was suddenly silenced. For Pound, Orage was irreplaceable.

Since the summer of 1933, Pound had been actively involved in organizing concerts in Rapallo with Olga Rudge and the pianist Gerhart Münch as "musicians in residence" joined by visiting musicians whenever possible. Pound and Olga Rudge were responsible for a revival of interest in the works of Vivaldi. In addition to presenting these works in concert, Olga Rudge traveled to Turin to catalogue the Vivaldi material in the National Library, and both she and Pound lectured and wrote articles on the composer.

In February 1936 Pound's best-known canto,

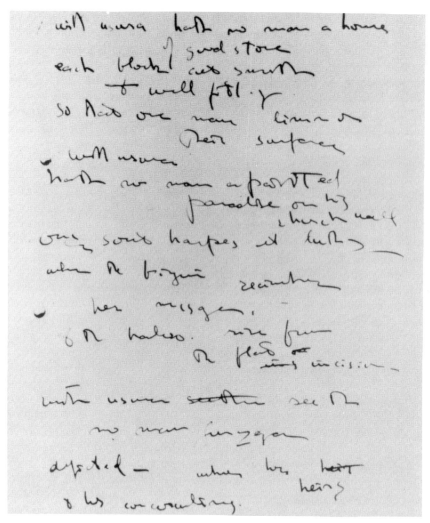

Draft for the "Usura Canto" (used by permission of the Ezra Pound Literary Property Trust)

the "Usura Canto" (45), was included with Canto 46 in the London magazine *Prosperity*, and on 3 June 1937, the complete *Fifth Decad of Cantos* (Cantos 42-51) was published.

Canto 50 follows the history of Tuscany from the time of the Medici until the defeat of Napoleon, which, Pound claimed, had harmful consequences for all Europe by strengthening England and Austria, who gave the usurers free reign. Drawing up his case against the usurers in Canto 46, Pound adopted a new, grimmer mindset and the undertone of the whole sequence is elegiac: the celebration of sexuality in Canto 47 and of precise definition and the value of expertise in Canto 48 are muted by a sense of the transitoriness of human life and human achievements. In the meditative "Seven Lakes Canto" (49) the poet enters the "dimension of stillness," but through a rather claustrophobic isolation, and in his "Lament Against Usura" in Canto 45—the most intense and heartfelt of this sequence—there is not rage against the usurers, as in the "Hell Cantos," but a concern for those who suffer from Usura's stranglehold over all the forces of vitality.

But Pound was not given to despair or inertia, and 31 July 1938 saw the publication of *Guide to Kulchur*. The book is not so much a reliable guide in any objective way to the cultural phenomena Pound considers as it is a revelation of Pound's state of mind: both of the way he thought and of what he thought. It shows clearly the split between the two very different states of mind into which he fell, depending on whether he was dealing with the arts or with economics and politics. This split persisted and widened over the following years: what he said in one state of mind gives at best a partial indication of how he thought in the other. What he said of the arts is generally reasonable, well-considered, and consistent with his earlier views, and this is also generally true of his views about economic theory, but when he tried to account for the current economic and political situation, instead of reasoning carefully he rationalized and relied increasingly on a conspiracy theory about the causes of war and poverty: "We know that there is one enemy, ever-busy obscuring our terms; ever muddling and muddying terminologies, ever trotting out minor issues to obscure the main and the basic, ever prattling of short range causation for the sake of, or with the result of, obscuring the vital truth." More and more, Pound would come to see a deliberate and conscious conspiracy. Altogether, *Guide to Kulchur* provides a highly reliable insight into Pound's state of mind and his most pressing interests in the late 1930s. The similarity of his economic views to those of Odon Por, whose book *Italy's Policy of Social Economics, 1930-1940* Pound would translate in 1941, encouraged Pound to feel that there was a good chance for Social Credit policies to be implemented by Mussolini, as did the ease with which he was able to get his articles on economics published in the Italian press.

In October 1938 Olivia Shakespear died, and Pound traveled to London to help settle her estate. He saw many old friends, including Eliot and Lewis, who painted an oil portrait of the poet and sold him some of his drawings. Shortly after his return to Italy, Pound decided to travel to America the following year, and in April 1939 he sailed from Genoa to New York, where he spent time with Cummings and with Gorham Munson of the American Social Credit Movement, whose *Aladdin's Lamp* (1945) is still the best book on Social Credit. In late April he went to Washington and met the senators and congressmen with whom he had been in correspondence. Williams, who met Pound in Washington by chance, wrote to Allen Tate that he found Pound "very mild, depressed and fearful." Since Pound's purpose in coming to America was to convey his insights into economics and the "real" nature of the political situation in Italy to politicians willing and able to act on them, he was clearly despondent at his lack of success. Back in New York in early May, he saw Ford, Katherine Heyman, Zukofsky, Marianne Moore, and Mencken. He visited Fordham University and Harvard, where he stayed with Theodore Spencer and was recorded reading some of his own poetry. In Cambridge he also met Archibald MacLeish, and he traveled to New Haven and to Rutherford, New Jersey, where he spent

a night with Williams. At Hamilton College, on 12 June, he received an honorary degree, as did the journalist H. V. Kaltenborn, and Pound disrupted Kaltenborn's luncheon speech to protest what he saw as a misrepresentation of Mussolini. On 29 June 1939 Ford died in France at Deauville and Pound wrote an obituary article, "Ford Madox (Hueffer) Ford; Obit," which was published in the August issue of *Nineteenth Century and After*.

Although the burden of all Pound's Social Credit theorizing was that under the present economic system periodic wars were inevitable, the prospect of war in Europe was one that Pound found unbearable. This belief may explain his refusal to "take sides" on the Spanish civil war, as Nancy Cunard's June 1937 questionnaire asked him to. By calling it a "sham conflict" he was trying to pretend to himself that it was not a "real war" and therefore that the cause of preventing war in Europe was not yet lost. By September 1939 this pretense was no longer possible. As soon as war started he wrote to anyone in America whom he thought could be instrumental in keeping the country out of the war, but he found little grounds for hope. In September both Tinckham and Mencken wrote to Pound that Roosevelt was determined to involve America. So desperate was Pound that he considered returning to the United States early in 1940 despite his failure to influence policy on his previous visit.

The Vivaldi "revival" continued, and Olga Rudge arranged a Vivaldi week (16-21 December 1939), sponsored by the Accademia Musicale Chigiana of Venice, in Siena. Some of the works performed were from scores in the Library of Congress and in the Sächsische Landesbibliothek in Dresden—the Dresden library destined to be destroyed in the firebombing—scores which Pound had arranged to have microfilmed. Olga Rudge also compiled a Vivaldi catalogue.

By September 1939 Pound had sent off *Cantos LII-LXXI* to Faber, who published them on 28 January 1940. We can see from the beginning of Canto 52, and from his publisher's cancellation of some of Pound's anti-usury lines, that his decision to concentrate in this sequence on Chinese history and on John Adams was, at least in part, a way of counteracting his growing tendency to fall into rantings against the usurers. This decision enabled him to consider present problems from the vantage point of the past and to adopt a more contemplative perspective on the discouraging prospect of the impediments to social justice. Although the straightforward chronological survey that the "Chinese

History Cantos" supply makes them the most accessible sequence in the poem, they are only of a secondary level of intensity. In writing this sequence Pound, following Confucius's advice, surveyed the whole of Chinese history up to 1780. Inevitably, his commentary is rather cursory; by the middle of Canto 54, the prosaic style and the increasing use of slang and abbreviation suggest that he was moving hurriedly, superficially, and mechanically through material of no compelling interest. But the section on Confucius is of particular interest.

Instead of eulogizing Confucius, Pound presents the events of his life in an understated way which is consonant with the fact that in his lifetime, there was great corruption and suffering, and that he was denied the opportunity to put his ideas into action. Although he was able during his life to make so little impact upon social conditions, after his death his ideas went into action with enormous force, and Pound observes that "every durable dynasty since his time has risen on a Confucian design."

Distressed by the lack of impact that his own ideas were having, Pound felt an affinity with Confucius and, in the next sequence, with John Adams, who continued to reaffirm his disinterested principles throughout his political career even after it was clear, from bitter experience, how rarely political ideals could be enacted without being adulterated by considerations of greed, personal ambition, and "the spirit of party." Earlier, Pound had praised Jefferson as the man of action, the "OPPORTUNIST who is RIGHT . . . who has certain convictions . . . and batters and forms circumstance with them," but now that "circumstance" seemed increasingly intractable, Pound was more inclined to value the deliberateness, steadiness, and tenacity of Adams, whom he calls in Canto 62 "the clearest head in the congress/1774 and thereafter" and "the man who at certain points/ . . . /saved us by fairness, honesty and straight moving."

In these Cantos Pound kept to the order of the pieces in *The Works of John Adams*. Cantos 62-65 show Adams in action; Cantos 66 and 67, taken from his political essays, show how he used his mastery of the law to demonstrate the legality of his countrymen's demands for guarantees of their basic rights and freedoms. Cantos 68 and 69 cover his diplomatic missions to France, Britain, and the Netherlands, and Cantos 70 and 71, taken from his letters, show him reflecting on the destructive effects of factionalism and on religion and human nature in general. Later, Pound would describe the

Ezra Pound (courtesy of Omar Pound)

"Brothers Adam" as "our norm of spirit" and as an "unwobbling pivot"—a particularly apt metaphor for the role of the "Adams Cantos" as a central fixed point for the whole poem. They look backward to Cantos 31-34 and Canto 37, and forward not only to the Thomas Hart Benton and Andrew Jackson Cantos (88 and 89) but to all the many passages in the later cantos that deal with the theme of law.

After Cantos 52-71 were finished, Pound had planned to change the emphasis of the poem from economics to matters of belief and philosophy—to write a "paradiso." He hoped that the American philosopher George Santayana, who was then living in Rome, would be able to answer some of his questions about philosophy, and he did meet Santayana in January and again in December of 1939. Pound invited Santayana to collaborate with him and Eliot in writing a book on "The Ideal University, or The Proper Curriculum," but the philosopher declined, saying that while they were "reformers, full of prophetic zeal and faith in the Advent of the Lord," he was not and so such an undertaking would be "impossible morally" for him.

Mussolini declared war on Britain and France on 10 June 1940, and in late 1940 Pound began to broadcast speeches over Rome Radio. He was still insisting that Mussolini was "for peace" which, by now, required him to rationalize away such overwhelming evidence to the contrary that his view of the international political situation seemed clearly psychotic. He had convinced himself that because Mussolini's main goal was economic justice, he must be antiwar also. For Pound, to oppose Mussolini was to oppose economic justice and peace, so Roosevelt and Churchill were usurers' puppets and warmongers, who had forced their countries into a war they knew they could not win. Mussolini's choice of Hitler as ally "proved" to Pound that the Führer was not a warmonger, so Pound convinced himself that the real villains were a conspiracy of international—predominantly Jewish—bankers. As his paranoia increased, what had been denunciations of bankers became anti-Semitic allegations about a Jewish plot to undermine gentile culture.

By this time he was so obviously speaking out of a personal, psychological compulsion that his views should not be called Fascist propaganda. If Allied listeners had been able to recognize the premises that lay behind Pound's cryptic, staccato commentary, they would have automatically dismissed his allegations as insane, but the abrupt turns of thought and changes of subject made it almost impossible to get any sense of a coherent argument at all. A friend of H. D.'s, who monitored these broadcasts for the British government, said they were "baffling, confused, confusing," and their "message, whatever it was" was not "doing any harm or any good to anybody." His intentions do not seem to have been treasonous, and there is no evidence that the speeches had any effect on the Allied war effort. Pound wrote to the U.S. Attorney General: "I have not spoken to the troops, and have not suggested that the troops mutiny or revolt," and he was sincere in believing that the views he broadcast were not "incompatible with his duties as a citizen of the United States of America."

In 1939 and 1940 Pound had explored the possibility of getting back to America, and in the fall of 1940 he made preparations to leave Italy. In October he tried to get on a clipper ship at Genoa, since the only alternative route was through occupied France to Spain and Lisbon, but no Amer-

ican ships were sailing from Mediterranean ports, and after Pearl Harbor one impediment to his return was the fact that he would have to leave behind his parents, both in their eighties, his father with a broken hip that would not mend. When Italy's surrender to the Allies was announced on 8 September 1943, Pound, who had previously heard on the BBC of his indictment in July for treason, was already on his way by foot from Rome to Gais, in the Italian Tyrol, where his daughter was living with the peasant family by which she had been raised. It was a journey of 450 miles and, although he was able to take a train from Bologna to Verona, he made much of the journey on foot, sleeping wherever he could and arriving with feet swollen and blistered from the ill-fitting walking shoes he had borrowed from the Degli Ubertis. They had also lent him a large scale map, and it was only when he got to Verona that he realized that it was a military map and that, had he been caught with it, he might have been taken for a spy. His main reason for making the journey was finally to tell Mary what had been kept from her until that time—the fact that her mother was not his wife.

He stayed at Gais for several weeks and then traveled to Rapallo via Milan. He seems to have stopped on the way at Salò, where Mussolini had set up his "New Republic" that September, and during the next sixteen months he contributed thirty-five articles to *Il Popolo d'Alessandria*, one of the papers of the Salò Republic. In November at a big Fascist Congress in Verona, Mussolini had presented a new economic program. Its emphases were exactly in keeping with Pound's own views, and it seemed further evidence to him that the Duce was the economic reformer he had taken him for.

Back in Rapallo he clung to the forlorn hope that the cause of economic reform under Italy's leadership was still not lost. Writing in Italian, he issued several manifestos, had posters printed bearing Confucian maxims and Social Credit slogans, and published six books and pamphlets with the Venetian publishing house, Edizioni Popolari. Of these, *Orientamenti* (1944), a collection of his economic and political articles; *Jefferson e Mussolini* (1944), a rewriting of *Jefferson And/Or Mussolini;* and a translation into Italian of Confucius's *The Unwobbling Pivot* were burned after the liberation, the title of this last—*Ciung Iung. L'Asse* ["Pivot/Axis"] *che non vacilla* (1945)—making it almost inevitable that it be misidentified as Fascist propaganda.

By the end of 1944 he had written, also in Italian, Cantos 72 and 73, in which the poet is vis-

Ezra Pound at the dispensary typewriter in the Disciplinary Training Center near Pisa (courtesy of Stephan Chodorov, Signal Corps photograph)

ited by a series of ghosts. First the ghost of Marinetti admits that he wanted war while Pound wanted peace but that they were both blind, Marinetti lacking in self-knowledge and Pound blind to the times. Then the ghost of Manlio Dazzi appears. Dazzi links the two cantos together, having translated Mussato's *Ecerinis* (a place about Ezzelino de Romano, whose ghost speaks later in this canto) and having helped Pound to edit his Italian edition of the *Rime* of Cavalcanti, whose ghost is the main voice in Canto 73. Ezzelino, included among the tyrants in the *Inferno,* here rises up in rage to denounce the betrayers of Mussolini's Italy, while in Canto 73 Cavalcanti celebrates the courage of a peasant girl from Rimini, who, having been raped by a Canadian soldier, deliberately led a party of his fellow soldiers across a minefield, killing twenty of them as well as herself.

In the spring of 1944 the Pounds had had to leave their seafront apartment as it was requisi-

tioned by the Germans, and they had no choice but to move in with Olga Rudge in Sant' Ambrogio on the hill above the bay. Here Pound was working on a translation of Mencius when, on 2 May 1945, two armed partisans ordered him to follow them to their Headquarters at Chiavari. No one was interested in him there, but he was determined to turn himself over to the American authorities and asked to be driven to Lavagna. From there he was taken by MP's to Genoa, where he was interrogated by the FBI. On 24 May he was taken to the Disciplinary Training Center, north of Pisa, an internment camp for some 4,000 American soldiers, and confined in an additionally reinforced "segregation cell" with cement floor and heavy-gauge wire-mesh sides. The heat and dust during the day and the bright light trained specifically on his cell during the night, together with his anxiety about his eventual fate were an increasing mental and physical strain. At his most depressed it seemed as though the sharp spikes of the cut ends of the steel mesh were a tacit invitation to suicide. He was, after a while, allowed a cot and a pup tent, but he was overcome by claustrophobia, panic, and fear, and on 18 June was moved to a tent in the part of the medical compound reserved for those prisoners who were officers. He was allowed writing materials and given use of the dispensary typewriter once the dispensary was closed for the night, on the theory that "letting him write would be good therapy and good preventative medicine." The result was some of his finest poetry.

He had few books—The Bible, The Confucian *Four Books,* a Roman Catholic chaplain's field book, and M. E. Speare's *Pocket Book of Verse,* found in the latrine. He found other material in the details of his surroundings—men entering and leaving through the main gate nearby, soldiers on sick call, identifiable by their names stencilled in white on their green fatigues; the orchards, fields, and mountains surrounding the camp; the moon and stars, the sun and clouds, the morning mists, the birds on the stockade fencing, the grasses, wasps, and crickets. But most of all he could call on what remained "in the mind indestructible"—his memories of the past. The dominant mood of this sequence is meditative, nostalgic, and reverential. Prevented from acting, he was now freed from his irresistible compulsion to carry on his war against *Usura*—freed to rediscover his compassion, humility, and contrition and belatedly to begin the painful process of introspection and self-analysis. The climactic moment of the sequence is the poet's vision, in Canto 81, of the eyes of the women he has loved which, with their reassurance of forgiveness—"nor any pair showed anger"—lead him to his great affirmation: "What thou lovest well remains/the rest is dross/What thou lov'st well shall not be reft from thee/What thou lov'st well is thy true heritage."

At the same time his response to Confucius's writings became more personal and more profound. He became attentive to Confucius's insistence on the need for self-examination and self-criticism and to his advice on attaining self-sufficiency and serenity in adversity. He became interested in the *Chung Yung* (*The Unwobbling Pivot*), the most metaphysical of the *Four Books,* and he translated it into English in a way that "neoplatonized" it, making his description of the "process"—the "perfect way" of the *tao*—echo the radiation of the light of the Neoplatonic One.

It was more than four months before Pound's family was able to see him again. Dorothy Pound

was allowed to visit him on 3 October and 3 November, and Olga and Mary Rudge came on 17 October. On the night of 16 November 1945, Pound was taken by jeep to Rome to be flown to Washington. Omar Pound, serving with the American army, arrived at the camp the next day to find Pound gone, and carried the news to Rapallo. Pound was indicted a second time on 26 November on nineteen counts of treason, a motion for bail was denied, and on 13 February 1946, a jury found him mentally incompetent to stand trial. He was placed in St. Elizabeths Hospital for the insane. In July, Dorothy Pound came to Washington and moved into a basement apartment in a rundown neighborhood near to St. Elizabeths. She stayed there, attending to his correspondence in the mornings and visiting him every afternoon, for the rest of the nearly twelve years that he was there. On 11 February Pound's lawyer Julian Cornell filed a petition for a writ of habeas corpus for Pound to be released into the care of his wife. Although the District Court refused, Cornell was optimistic that an appeal to the Supreme Court would succeed, but on 13 March Dorothy Pound asked him to withdraw the appeal.

On 20 February 1949 the Fellows of American Letters of the Library of Congress awarded the annual Bollingen Prize to *The Pisan Cantos,* which had been published as a book on 30 July 1948. Before this time, reviews of the volume had been generally favorable, with no mention of anti-Semitism. In fact, the only anti-Semitic lines in the sequence, written before Pound had any knowledge of the concentration camps, are a reiteration of the ancient stereotype of the financially naive gentile outsmarted by the sharp practice of the Jew: "the yidd is a stimulant, and the goyim are cattle/in gt/proportion and go to saleable slaughter/with the maximum of docility" (Canto 74). After he was given the Bollingen Prize, however, the *Saturday Review of Literature* mounted an anti-Pound and anti-T. S. Eliot campaign, which soon turned into a broad-based and acrimonious controversy. Robert Hillyer's *Saturday Review* articles drew strong protest, and John Berryman circulated a petition protesting them. Eighty-four critics and writers signed this petition, and after the *Saturday Review* refused to publish it, it appeared in the *Nation* for 17 December.

In the meantime, Pound seemed reconciled to his imprisonment, and quietly complied with the hospital routine. For thirteen months he had been in Howard Hall, the maximum security building for the criminally insane. His mental condition de-

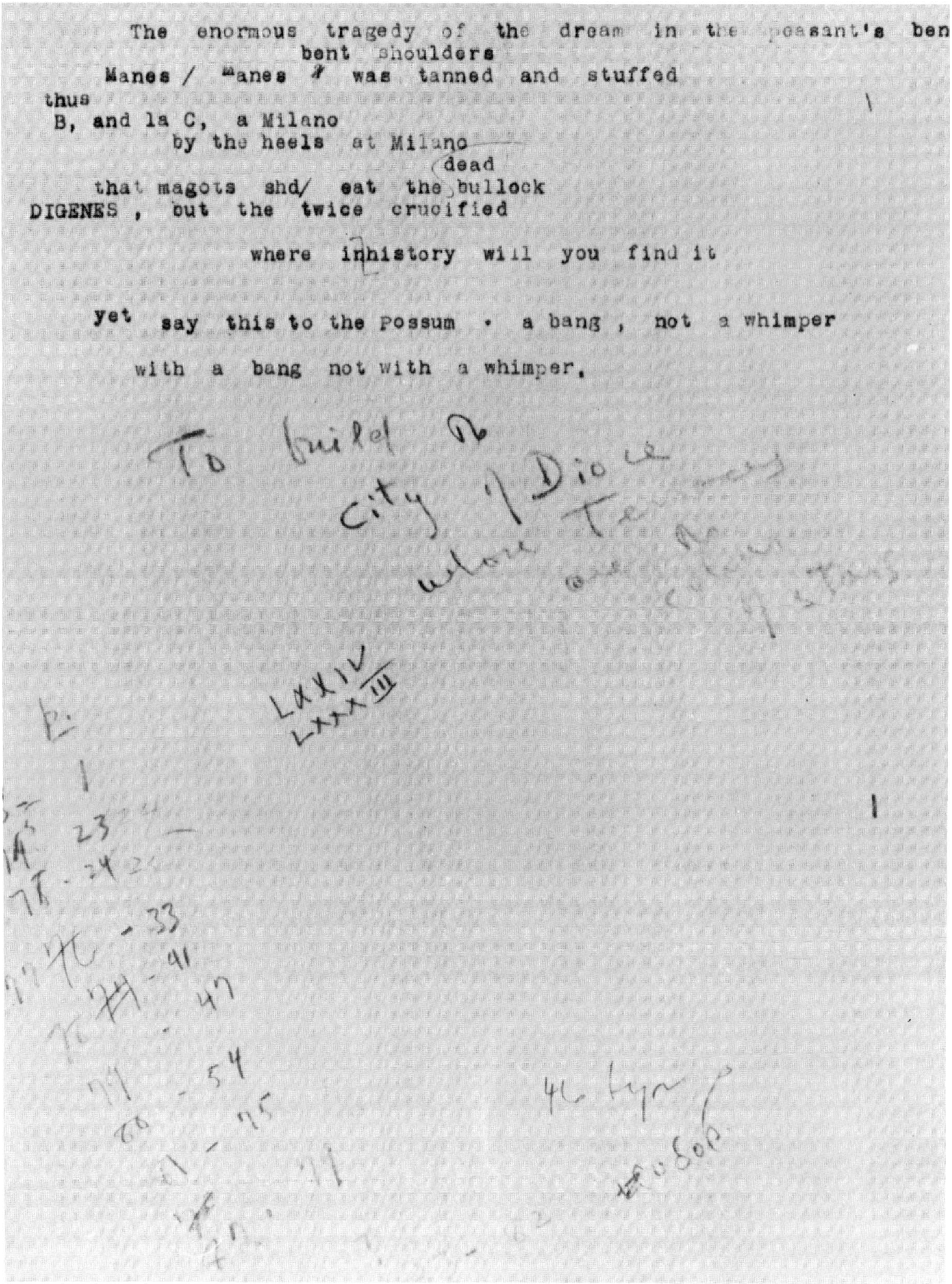

The enormous tragedy of the dream in the peasant's ben
                    bent shoulders
        Manes / Manes # was tanned and stuffed
thus
B, and la C, a Milano
            by the heels at Milano
                              (dead
      that magots shd/ eat the bullock
DIGENES , but the twice crucified

            where inhistory will you find it

    yet say this to the Possum . a bang , not a whimper

      with a bang not with a whimper,

To build a
city y Dioce
whore Terraces
are the color
y stars

LXXIV
LXXXIII

Draft for the beginning of the first Pisan Canto, thought to have been typed in the dispensary at the Disciplinary Training Center
(used by permission of the Ezra Pound Literary Property Trust; courtesy of the Beinecke Rare Book and Manuscript Library,
Yale University)

teriorated under the strain of life in the "hell-hole," and he became claustrophobic and afraid of a complete mental collapse. A second application for bail was denied, but, as a compromise, he was moved on 4 February 1947 to Chestnut Ward, where the inmates were not dangerously insane. Now Dorothy Pound, who had previously been allowed to see him for only fifteen minutes a day, could spend the afternoons with him. Many admirers visited him over the years, mainly writers and critics, including Eliot, Williams, Cummings, Marianne Moore, Tate, Charles Olson, Robert Lowell, Elizabeth Bishop, Conrad Aiken, Langston Hughes, Mencken, MacLeish, Zukofsky, and Juan Ramón Jiménez. Not all who wanted to visit were allowed to come. Requests to visit had to be made in writing and cleared with Pound, and he absolutely forbade any interviews and was able to exercise a good deal of control over the topics of conversation.

During his years in St. Elizabeths, Pound was psychologically in limbo. His wartime views and state of mind remained virtually unchanged. Neither psychiatrists nor friends could diagnose his problem accurately enough to be able to help him to understand and overcome it, and, in the absence of any completely reliable source of psychological support, he was careful to avoid introspection and self-analysis as far as possible. While it might seem logical to assume that the circumstances of his confinement were a painful ordeal which threatened his mental stability, in one sense the fact of his imprisonment offered him considerable protection against the mental anguish that would have accompanied self-confrontation. Certain in his own mind that it had never been his intention to betray America, and, realizing that he was only in prison now because he had been accused of treason, he could see his present condition as punishment for a crime he had not committed. Since his imprisonment must have seemed punitive rather than therapeutic, self accusation must have seemed redundant, perhaps dangerously masochistic.

Depending on the subject at issue, he chose evasiveness, self-protection, or affirmation, and these responses determine the three main levels of intensity of the Cantos in *Rock-Drill* (1955) and *Thrones* (1959). The weakest passages are those born of evasion. Because he had not yet confronted his "usurers' conspiracy" theory of war, he automatically retreated to it under the pressure of anxiety or frustration or—as happened in St. Elizabeths—when someone like the self-avowed white racist John Kasper encouraged him, passing himself off as a serious economic reformer. By

1972 he would come to see that the main cause of economic injustice was human weakness: "re USURY: I was out of focus, taking a symptom for a cause. The cause is AVARICE." But he did not see this fact while he was incarcerated and, because he was still involved in rationalizing his conspiracy theory, he often settled in the Cantos he was writing for commentary which is cryptic and fragmentary, reiterating in a rather pro-forma fashion points he has made frequently before.

The passages written more from a self-protective than from an evasive impulse are more successful, for they follow closely written sources whose own integrity disciplines and tightens the writing, and in those he affirms those values which are the root of civic morality—benevolence, mutuality, filiality, and prudence. But the most successful passages—as fine as anything in *The Pisan Cantos*—are the more personal, reflective, and lyric sections, which affirm without question his faith in a divine force that is the source of all creative power and of all natural order. Borrowing from Neoplatonism, Christianity, and other religions, he visualized this force as a feminine principle, calling it "Lux in diafana./Creatrix," but he could only apprehend it fleetingly, trapped as he was for so much of the time at "the dulled edge beyond pain" (Canto 90). In these passages the poet's struggle to raise himself above despondency long enough to capture a visionary moment of revelation is followed by the inevitable falling back to the drabness of life in the hospital, "under the rubble heap." The paradisal state of mind is authentic but "jagged,/For a flash,/for an hour./Then agony,/then an hour,/then agony" (Canto 92).

Pound called this force, as it operates in human affairs, Amor, choosing as an epigraph for Canto 90 a quotation from Richard of St. Victor, which translates: "The human soul is not love, but love flows from it, and therefore it does not delight in itself, but in the love which comes from it."

In these Cantos the power of Amor emanates from the eyes of a beloved woman, inspiring the intellect to philosophical insight, the moral sense to virtuous action and the imagination to artistic creation such as Beatrice inspired in Dante, Giovanna in Cavalcanti, and Eleanor of Aquitaine in Bernart de Ventadour. Reproaching himself for having shown insufficient compassion in the past, Pound now described himself, in the words of Confucius, as "counting his manhood and the love of his relatives the true treasure." In both *Rock-Drill* and *Thrones* he celebrated the power of benevolence and also the inspirational influence of two young visitors to St. Elizabeths—Sherri Martinelli ("Flora Castalia") and Marcella Spann, in whose presence the hospital grounds become metamorphosed into a temple precinct and the trees into marble columns.

The dominant mood at the conclusion of *Thrones* is one of calm resignation at the realization that there is no triumphant conclusion either to the poet's quest for the earthly paradise or to the poem itself. To keep alive the intellectual light is to be committed to an unremitting struggle against obscurantism. "Oak boughs alone over Selloi" from the *Trachiniae* recalls the revelation of the dying Hercules—"what/SPLENDOUR,/IT ALL COHERES," but this moment of resolution is followed by three references to new journeys to be made. John Bunyan's Christian, beginning his journey to the Celestial City, is directed by Evangelist to make for the light shining "over wicket gate." Odysseus, helped after his shipwreck by Leucothea, must resume his voyage home and Dante, calling back to the reader "in the dinghy . . . astern there," is about to embark upon the writing of his *Paradiso*.

In addition to his cantos Pound also worked in St. Elizabeths on his translations. His *Great Digest and the Unwobbling Pivot* was published in 1951 and a collection of his translations in 1953. Of the three thousand classic Chinese odes, Confucius had selected the three hundred which he considered indispensable, and Pound undertook to translate them all, filling thirty spiral notebooks between 1946 and 1950 with notes and characters, and publishing his translations as *The Classic Anthology Defined by Confucius* (1954). That same year, both his *Great Digest and the Unwobbling Pivot* and his *Literary Essays* were published. In addition, his translation of Sophocles' *Women of Trachis* was broadcast on the BBC (25 November 1954) before appearing in book form in November 1956. In 1952 Olga Rudge visited him, and the following year his now married daughter spent three months in Washington.

By January 1957 Archibald MacLeish was working actively to obtain Pound's release and to this end had drafted a letter to the Attorney General, signed by Eliot, Hemingway, and Frost. On 18 April 1958, the indictment was dismissed and Pound was free to leave St. Elizabeths. Because of passport problems, he remained in the country for two months, during which time he made visits to Wyncote and to Williams in Rutherford. He sailed for Genoa on 30 June 1958, with his wife and Marcella Spann en route to Brunnenburg, his daughter's castle in the Tirol where, for the first time, he met his grandchildren, Walter and Patrizia de

Rachewiltz. At first he was in excellent spirits, working on the manuscripts for *Thrones* and sorting papers and letters, but before long his unresolved anxieties became increasingly oppressive. In January 1959 he went to stay in Rapallo with his wife and Marcella Spann, and, after touring through Italy in the spring, they settled in an apartment in Rapallo for the summer. By October Spann had returned to America, and Pound had written to Mary that he wanted to return to Brunnenburg "to die." His sense that his life's work was a failure was only temporarily alleviated by a birthday telegram from Eliot assuring him that his position as a great poet was secure. The self-punishing effects of his remorse took a heavy toll mentally and physically. He resisted eating and was afflicted with slowness of speech and movement, sometimes remaining completely still for hours at a time. He subjected himself to relentless self-accusation and was obsessed with unfounded anxieties about his health. His physical condition deteriorated because of his resistance to eating, and by the summer of 1960 he had to be treated at a clinic at Martinsbrun, returning there in June 1961 after spending some time at a clinic in Rome the previous month for treatment of a urinary infection. In 1962 and 1963 he underwent prostrate surgery.

By 1962 he was speaking less and less, but his delay and slowness in responding were at the level of communication rather than at the level of thought. This fact is clear from his replies to Donald Hall's questions in the long interview published in the *Paris Review* (Summer/Fall 1962). Neither his memory nor his sense of orientation were impaired, and when he did talk his comments were precise and correct. His holding back from speech seemed of a piece with the problem he had from 1965 on in initiating physical movements and in carrying one through once it was begun. From 11 March to 16 April 1966 he was at the Clinic for Nervous and Mental Illnesses of the University of Genoa, where his condition was carefully studied. His psychiatrist's findings were very much of a piece with those of Dr. Overholser at St. Elizabeths—that, while he was rational and in touch with reality at almost all points, in one area—the assigning of blame—his thinking appeared psychotic. Where in St. Elizabeths he had believed in the culpability of an international conspiracy of usurers, now he castigated himself. He was not suffering merely from "senile depression," and his psychiatrist noted that he was not depressive except in the one area of self-accusation. He also noted that during trips Pound was sometimes capable of essen-

Ezra Pound arriving in Italy, 9 July 1958 (Wide World Photo)

tially normal activity, and this continued to be the case up until the time of his death. On 4 February 1965 he had attended the T. S. Eliot memorial service in Westminster Abbey and then had traveled to Dublin to see Yeats's widow. In the summer of 1965 he attended the Spoleto Festival, and in October, after his eightieth birthday, he visited Greece. In July 1966 he traveled to Paris and in June 1969 spent two weeks in America as the guest of James Laughlin, visiting Hamilton College on the occasion of the presentation of an honorary doctorate to Laughlin and spending time with Valerie Eliot, Hemingway, Lowell, and Marianne Moore.

In 1969 he published *Drafts and Fragments of Cantos CX-CXVII*. On those rare occasions when he could be persuaded to talk, he sometimes dismissed his *Cantos* as a complete failure, saying that they were "a botch" and that his writing was "stupidity and ignorance all the way through," yet *Drafts and Fragments of Cantos CX-CXVII* contains a more balanced assessment. Having chosen all his life to

dwell more on how things might ideally become than on how they were, he had finally to acknowledge that he could neither see a solution to the social problems he deplored nor bring his poem to the "paradisal" conclusion he had projected—that it "nor began nor ends anything" (Canto 114). He confronted this realization steadily, and the prevailing undertone of these cantos is a calm resignation which at times slips into the poignantly elegiac and at other times rises to affirmation. He celebrated the healing power of music and of all forms of beauty and in particular his realization that "the truth is in kindness" (Canto 114)—that "Justification is from kindness of heart/and from her hands floweth mercy" (Canto 113).

He persisted in his self-accusation and now saw clearly "That I lost my center/fighting the world" (Canto 117) but, rather than escaping into rationalization, fatalism, or self-pity, he chose the painful course of contrition without self-exculpation, "the mind as Ixion, unstill, ever turning" (Canto 113). Although he was oppressed by the fact

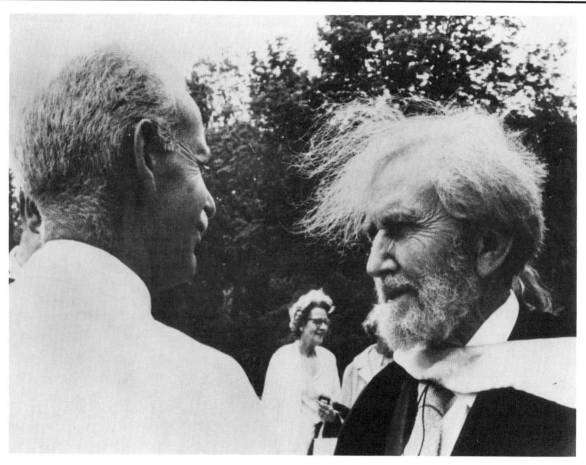

Ezra Pound (right) at Hamilton College, June 1969 (photograph by Robert T. Chaffee, Hamilton College)

that "my errors and wrecks lie about me./And I am not a demigod,/I cannot make it cohere," he had not lost the faith that "it coheres all right/even if my notes do not cohere (Canto 116). Feeling that he was "A blown husk that is finished," he was still aware that "the light sings eternal/a pale flare over marshes" (Canto 115) and that, even if the light is glimpsed only fitfully, even "A little light, like a rushlight [can] lead back to splendour." Here, in this most poignant and moving sequence of the *Cantos,* he managed "To confess wrong without losing rightness" (Canto 116).

Stoic in his silence, he remained active until the end. He could make the long walk from Olga Rudge's house via the Accademia Bridge to the Piazza San Marco, and he was photographed shortly before his death, very thin, but standing dignified and erect, looking at the roses in the garden of friends in Venice. He died in his sleep on 1 November 1972, and his funeral service was performed on 3 November in the Benedictine Abbey on the Island San Giorgio Maggiore. He was buried on the Venetian cemetery island of San Michele.

A summary of Pound's poetic achievement invites the frequent use of superlatives. He saw earliest and most clearly and formulated most thoroughly and emphatically the new principles by which twentieth century poetry would operate. He realized and illustrated in his own work the importance of precision of diction and of vividness and specificity of presentation. He was most bold in experimenting with different kinds of openness of form. He may well have had the most perfect ear of all the poets of his age and, while urging poets to respect the natural cadences of the speaking voice and to resist nineteenth century distortions of word order, he produced the most beautiful and musical verse cadences. In *The Cantos* he wrote the most difficult poem of the period with the most numerous and far-ranging allusions, but also the most moving lyrical passages—a poem that is probably the most unread and so offers the most to be discovered.

Ezra Pound (photograph by Bernhard Durries)

Letters:

The Letters of Ezra Pound 1907-1941, edited by D. D. Paige (New York: Harcourt, Brace, 1950; London: Faber & Faber, 1951);

Pound/Joyce: The Letters of Ezra Pound to James Joyce, edited by Forrest Read (New York: New Directions, 1967; London: Faber & Faber, 1969);

Letters to Ibbotson, 1935-1952, edited by Vittoria I. Mondolfo and Margaret Hurley (Orono, Maine: National Poetry Foundation, University of Maine, 1979);

Letters to John Theobald, edited by Donald Pearce and Herbert Schneidau (Redding Ridge, Conn.: Black Swan, 1981);

Pound/Ford: The Story of a Literary Friendship, edited by Brita Lindberg-Seyersted (New York: New Directions, 1982);

Ezra Pound and Dorothy Shakespear: Their Letters 1909-1914, edited by Omar Pound and A. Walton Litz (New York: New Directions, 1984);

The Letters of Ezra Pound and Wyndham Lewis, edited by Timothy Materer (New York: New Directions, 1985).

Bibliography:

Donald Gallup, *Ezra Pound: A Bibliography* (Charlottesville: University Press of Virginia, 1983).

Biographies:

Charles Norman, *Ezra Pound,* revised edition (New York: Minerva, 1969);

Noel Stock, *The Life of Ezra Pound* (New York: Pantheon, 1970);

Mary de Rachewiltz, *Discretions* (Boston: Little, Brown, 1971);

C. David Heyman, *Ezra Pound: The Last Rower* (New York: Viking, 1976);

James H. Wilhelm, *The American Roots of Ezra Pound* (New York: Garland, 1985).

References:

Michael Alexander, *The Poetic Achievement of Ezra*

Pound (Berkeley: University of California Press, 1979);

David Anderson, *Pound's Cavalcanti: An Edition of the Translations, Notes and Essays* (Princeton: Princeton University Press, 1982);

Massimo Bacigalupo, *The Forméd Trace: The Later Poetry of Ezra Pound* (New York: Columbia University Press, 1980);

Walter Baumann, *The Rose in the Steel Dust: An Examination of the Cantos of Ezra Pound* (Coral Gables: University of Miami Press, 1967);

Ian F. A. Bell, *Critic as Scientist: The Modernist Poetics of Ezra Pound* (London & New York: Methuen, 1981);

Michael André Bernstein, *The Tale of the Tribe: Ezra Pound and the Modern Verse Epic* (Princeton: Princeton University Press, 1980);

Jo B. Berryman, *Circe's Craft: Ezra Pound's "Hugh Selwyn Mauberley"* (Ann Arbor: UMI Research Press, 1983);

Christine Brooke-Rose, *A ZBC of Ezra Pound* (Berkeley: University of California Press, 1971);

Peter Brooker, *A Student's Guide to the Selected Poems of Ezra Pound* (London & Boston: Faber & Faber, 1979);

Ronald Bush, *The Genesis of Ezra Pound's Cantos* (Princeton: Princeton University Press, 1976);

William M. Chace, *The Political Identities of Ezra Pound and T. S. Eliot* (Stanford: Stanford University Press, 1973);

Donald Davie, *Ezra Pound* (New York: Viking, 1976);

Davie, *Ezra Pound: Poet as Sculptor* (New York: Oxford University Press, 1964);

Earle Davis, *Vision Fugitive: Ezra Pound's Economics* (Lawrence: University of Kansas Press, 1968);

George Dekker, *The Cantos of Ezra Pound: A Critical Study* (New York: Barnes & Noble, 1963); republished as *Sailing After Knowledge* (London: Routledge & Kegan Paul, 1963);

L. S. Dembo, *The Confucian Odes of Ezra Pound* (Berkeley: University of California Press, 1963);

Peter D'Epiro, *A Touch of Rhetoric: Ezra Pound's Malatesta Cantos* (Ann Arbor: UMI Research Press, 1983);

Robert J. Dilligan and others, *A Concordance to Ezra Pound's Cantos* (New York: Garland, 1981);

Barbara Eastman, *Ezra Pound's Cantos: The Story of the Text* (Orono: National Poetry Foundation, University of Maine, 1979);

John H. Edwards and William Vasse, *Annotated Index to The Cantos of Ezra Pound* (Berkeley: University of California Press, 1957);

T. S. Eliot, *Ezra Pound: His Metric and Poetry* (New York: Knopf, 1917);

Clark Emery, *Ideas Into Action: A Study of Pound's Cantos* (Coral Gables: University of Miami Press, 1958);

J. J. Espey, *Ezra Pound's Mauberley: A Study in Composition* (Berkeley: University of California Press, 1955);

Wendy S. Flory, *Ezra Pound and The Cantos: A Record of Struggle* (New Haven: Yale University Press, 1980);

G. S. Frazer, *Ezra Pound* (New York: Grove, 1961);

Christine Froula, *A Guide to Ezra Pound's Selected Poems* (New York: New Directions, 1983);

K. L. Goodwin, *The Influence of Ezra Pound* (London & New York: Oxford University Press, 1966);

Eva Hesse, ed., *New Approaches to Ezra Pound* (Berkeley: University of California Press, 1969);

Daniel Hoffman, ed., *Ezra Pound and William Carlos Williams: The University of Pennsylvania Conference Papers* (Philadelphia: University of Pennsylvania Press, 1983);

Eric Homberger, *Ezra Pound: The Critical Heritage* (London & Boston: Routledge & Kegan Paul, 1972);

Thomas H. Jackson, *The Early Poetry of Ezra Pound* (Cambridge: Harvard University Press, 1969);

George Kearns, *Guide to Ezra Pound's Selected Cantos* (New Brunswick: Rutgers University Press, 1980);

Hugh Kenner, *The Poetry of Ezra Pound* (New York: New Directions, 1951);

Kenner, *The Pound Era* (Berkeley: University of California Press, 1971);

Gary Lane, *A Concordance to the Poems of Ezra Pound* (Brooklyn, N.Y.: Haskell, 1972);

Lewis Leary, ed., *Motive and Metaphor in the Cantos of Ezra Pound* (New York: Columbia University Press, 1954);

Peter Makin, *Provence and Pound* (Berkeley: University of California Press, 1979);

Timothy Materer, *Vortex: Pound, Eliot and Lewis* (Ithaca: Cornell University Press, 1979);

Stuart Y. McDougal, *Ezra Pound and the Troubadour Tradition* (Princeton: Princeton University Press, 1973);

Daniel Pearlman, *The Barb of Time: On the Unity of Ezra Pound's Cantos* (New York: Oxford University Press, 1969);

Sister Bernetta Quinn, *Ezra Pound: An Introduction*

to the Poetry (New York: Columbia University Press, 1973);

M. L. Rosenthal, *A Primer of Ezra Pound* (New York: Macmillan, 1960);

Rosenthal, *Sailing into the Unknown: Yeats, Pound and Eliot* (New York: Oxford University Press, 1978);

Peter Russell, *An Examination of Ezra Pound* (New York: New Directions, 1950);

K. K. Ruthven, *A Guide to Ezra Pound's Personae* (Berkeley: University of California Press, 1969);

R. Murray Schafer, *Ezra Pound and Music* (New York: New Directions, 1977);

Herbert Schneidau, *Ezra Pound: The Image and the Real* (Baton Rouge: Louisiana State University Press, 1969);

Grace Schulman, ed., *Ezra Pound: A Collection of Criticism* (New York: McGraw-Hill, 1974);

Richard Sieburth, *Instigations: Ezra Pound and Rémy de Gourmont* (Cambridge: Harvard University Press, 1978);

J. P. Sullivan, *Ezra Pound and Sextus Propertius: A Study in Creative Translation* (Austin: University of Texas Press, 1964);

Leon Surette, *A Light From Eleusis: A Study of Ezra Pound's Cantos* (Oxford: Clarendon Press, 1980);

Carroll F. Terrell, *A Companion to the Cantos of Ezra Pound*, 2 volumes (Berkeley, Los Angeles & London: University of California Press, 1980, 1984);

James J. Wilhelm, *Dante and Pound: The Epic of Judgment* (Orono: University of Maine Press, 1974);

Wilhelm, *The Later Cantos of Ezra Pound* (New York: Walker, 1977);

Hugh Witemeyer, *The Poetry of Ezra Pound: Forms and Renewal 1908-1920* (Berkeley: University of California Press, 1969);

Anthony Woodward, *Ezra Pound and the Pisan Cantos* (London & Boston: Routledge & Kegan Paul, 1980);

Wai-lim Yip, *Ezra Pound's Cathay* (Princeton: Princeton University Press, 1969).

Papers:

The majority of the Pound papers are in the Ezra Pound Archive of the Beinecke Library, Yale University. Other papers are in the Berg Collection of the New York Public Library, the Houghton Library of Harvard University, the Newberry Library in Chicago, and the libraries of Hamilton College, Cornell University, and the University of Pennsylvania. The Lilly Library of Indiana University has about 12,000 letters to Ezra and Dorothy Pound, dating from 1945-1953.

John Crowe Ransom

(30 April 1888-3 July 1974)

Thomas Daniel Young
Vanderbilt University

BOOKS: *Poems About God* (New York: Holt, 1919);
Chills and Fever (New York: Knopf, 1924);
Grace After Meat (London: Leonard & Virginia Woolf at the Hogarth Press, 1924);
Two Gentlemen in Bonds (New York: Knopf, 1927);
God Without Thunder: An Unorthodox Defense of Orthodoxy (New York: Harcourt, Brace, 1930; London: Howe, 1931);
The World's Body (New York & London: Scribners, 1938);
The New Criticism (Norfolk, Conn.: New Directions, 1941);
Poetics (Norfolk, Conn.: New Directions, 1942);
A College Primer of Writing (New York: Holt, 1943);
Selected Poems (New York: Knopf, 1945; London: Eyre & Spottiswoode, 1947; revised and enlarged edition, New York: Knopf, 1963; revised and enlarged again, New York: Knopf, 1969; London: Eyre & Spottiswoode, 1970);
Poems and Essays (New York: Vintage, 1955);
Beating the Bushes: Selected Essays 1941-1970 (Norfolk, Conn.: New Directions, 1972).

OTHER: "Statement of Principles" and "Reconstructed but Unregenerated," in *I'll Take My Stand: The South and the Agrarian Tradition*, by Twelve Southerners (New York: Harper, 1930), pp. ix-xxi, 1-27.

John Crowe Ransom was one of the most versatile and significant men of letters of his generation. As poet, Isabel Gambel MacCafrey has written, "he provided a small but accurate mirror of the modern sensibility. In ... [his poems] are reflected the miraculous virtues of contemporary verse at its best. Its combination of delicacy with strength, of fervor with restraint, of elegance with earthiness.... He has been celebrated rightly, as the poet of perilous equilibrium, of dichotomies and ironies, of tension and paradox." Some critics, nevertheless, think his contributions as critic, editor, and teacher were of even greater importance to modern American letters than his poetry. He was, many believe, the most original theoretical literary critic produced in America in the twentieth century. He not only elaborated exciting and perceptive theories of the nature and function of poetry, but he also provided invaluable demonstrations of how poetry is to be read if it is to function as a legitimate means of cognition, if it is to furnish "the kind of knowledge by which we must know what we have arranged we cannot know otherwise." Others point to the fact that Ransom was a teacher of great dedication and skill. To list the important poets and critics who studied with him is to name some of the best-known authors of the twentieth century: Allen Tate, Robert Penn Warren, Donald Davidson, Andrew Lytle, Cleanth Brooks, Randall Jarrell, Peter Taylor, Robert Lowell, George Lanning, Robie Macauley, Ted Bor-

John Crowe Ransom

gardus, Anthony Hecht, James Wright, Eric Bentley. For more than two decades he was editor of the *Kenyon Review,* one of the most influential and distinguished literary journals of the country.

For his poetry he won many awards, including a Guggenheim Fellowship (1931), the Bollingen Prize in Poetry (1951), the Russell Loines Award in Literature of the National Academy of Arts of Letters (1951), Academy of American Poets Fellowship (1962), and a National Book Award for *Selected Poems* (1964).

Born in Pulaski, Tennessee, the son of John J. Ransom, an erudite Methodist minister, and Ella Crowe Ransom, a former music and French teacher, John Crowe Ransom grew up in the several villages and small towns in Middle Tennessee, where his father preached. Between Ransom's third and eleventh years, his father served four churches: Spring Hill, Franklin, Springfield, and North High Street in Nashville. Because the Methodist Conference came in October of each year, the education of the minister's children was often difficult. Each year when school opened in September, Ransom recalled many years later, the elder Ransom would say, "John, there's no need to enter school because we might move." Ransom, his brother, and two sisters, therefore, were taught at home by their parents. When the Reverend Dr. Ransom was moved to Nashville, however, he enrolled the children in public school. Although John had never been to school before and was only ten years old, after much shifting from grade to grade, he was finally placed in the eighth grade. At the end of the year the principal and several of the teachers convinced Dr. Ransom that his precocious young son should be enrolled in one of the several good preparatory schools in the area, institutions which were preparing their students for the demanding classically oriented curriculum of Vanderbilt University. Young John enrolled in the Bowen School, at 15th Avenue and Broadway, only six blocks from the university. On Thursday, Friday, and Saturday, 14-16 May 1903, only a week before he was to be graduated, he took the demanding entrance examination for Vanderbilt, and made the highest score on all five of the examinations he took: English, American history, mathematics, Latin, and Greek. On the basis of his performance on the examinations, he was admitted, although he was a full year below the official minimum age for admission.

After two years at the university, he had to withdraw for financial reasons and taught in secondary schools, one year in Mississippi and one in Tennessee, before returning in 1907 to graduate Phi Beta Kappa and number one in the class of 1909. He returned to teaching in a private academy for a year before enrolling in Christ Church College, Oxford, as a Rhodes Scholar. In 1913 he earned a B.A. in Litterae Humaniores ("The Greats")—Greek and Latin history, literature, and philosophy, all read in the original languages. From Oxford he went to teach Latin and Greek at the Hotchkiss School in Lakeville, Connecticut, but after one year he returned to teach at Vanderbilt. He took the job because his parents, who lived in Nashville, strongly encouraged their son, whom they had seen only twice in four years, to accept the instructorship offered him by Edwin Mims, head of the English department.

The year following his return to Nashville he joined a group of students, faculty members, and members of the community who were meeting at the apartment of Sidney Mttron Hirsch—a Jewish mystic and etymologist, who lived only two blocks from the campus—to discuss religion and philosophy. At that time the group also included Donald Davidson, Alec B. Stevenson, Walter Clyde Curry, and Stanley Johnson. About a year later Donald Davidson was surprised when Ransom announced that he had written a poem and wanted to read it to him. The poem, entitled "Sunset," was written in free verse, the only poem Ransom would ever publish in that form. (Later, in *The World's Body,* [1938], his first book of criticism, he would explain the reasons for his preference for meter: "When a poet confronts an object, he is tempted to react immediately, but art restrains the natural man. It puts the object out of his reach; or more accurately, removes him where he cannot hurt the object, nor disrespect it by taking his practical attitude towards it." Ransom argued that all aspects of literary form, especially the meter, restrain the poet and prevent him from assaulting the "precious object," the subject of the poem, directly and trying to use it.) Ransom continued to write verse, and when he had completed five or six poems, he sent them to Christopher Morley, with whom he had been at Oxford, and asked if he could place them in an Eastern journal. Upon Morley's recommendation poems were taken by the *Independent, Contemporary Verse,* and the *Liberator.* Morley also published some of the poems Ransom had sent him in his column in the Philadelphia *Evening Public Ledger.*

Ransom also showed these and several other poems to Davidson in the summer of 1917 while they were both serving as cadets at the First Officers Training Camp at Fort Oglethorpe, Georgia. Ransom gave Davidson carbon copies of the poems, and Davidson carried them with him when he went overseas. "When I read those poems in France, by candlelight in some peasant's home in the Côte d'Or or Yvonne, or some ruined village near the Western Front," Davidson wrote in *Southern Writers in the Modern World* (1958), "they still blurred my exploring, eager eyes, even though at that distance I could more gratefully recognize in them the Tennessee country I had left."

Ransom had completed enough poems for a book before he went overseas in August 1917, but, while he was on active duty in France, he carefully revised them before sending them to Morley with the request that he try to place them with a New York publisher. After several abortive attempts, Morley was able to get Henry Holt to agree to publish them. The volume appeared as *Poems About God* (1919), by Lieutenant John C. Ransom, while its author was still in Europe. For a first book of poems by an unknown poet who does not mention the war, except in his preface, the book was widely and generally favorably reviewed, although most of the reviewers missed the general thrust of the book— a young man expressing his amazement, his wonder and awe, and his concern, for the ways in which God makes himself manifest in the world. Several reviewers even found the poet's use of God sacrilegious. The reviewer for *Poetry* found the poems "brittle," but liked the deliberate childlike method of presentation. The reviewer for the *Nation* doubted the poet's "sincerity," saying it seemed "more strained than real." Charles W. Stork compared Ransom favorably with Conrad Aiken and Witter Bynner, writing that Ransom was a "voracious realist," had an "antisocial bent," and found the "religion of uneducated folk . . . ridiculous."

Both Stork and the reviewer for the *Nation* correctly found influences of Hardy and Frost, but none, it would seem, was quite as wide the mark as Louis Untermeyer, who wrote in his review for the *Dial*, "The lines run from the surprisingly powerful to the incredibly banal." He ended his short notice by placing Ransom among the young poets reacting against "purely decorative literature by establishing some previously neglected attitudes toward a free but earth planted naturalism." The members of this school, Untermeyer added, "insist upon a return . . . to brutality." This review, Ransom wrote Robert Graves, who was beginning the correspondence that would result in Graves's bringing out a British edition of Ransom's poetry, gave him most concern because it was so far from what he was attempting to do and "Untermeyer

has established in some circles a reputation as the foremost critic of modern literature."

The reader of Ransom's mature verse may well understand the poet's reason for wishing to suppress *Poems About God*. As Ransom declares in the preface: "Most of these poems about God were complete a year ago, that is at about the time when the great upheaval going on in God's world engulfed our country too. Since then I have added a little only, and my experience has led me so wide that I can actually look back upon these antebellum accomplishments with the eye of the impartial spectator. . . . In this reviewing act I find myself thinking sometimes that the case about God may not be quite so desperate as the young poet chooses to believe. But it is not for that reason that I shall ever think of suppressing a single one of his poems." Ransom's disaffection with this early verse was not because of the subjects treated or the attitudes expressed, but because of the manner in which these subjects and attitudes are presented. The poems put too much emphasis on what Ransom would later call their "structure," their logical argument and paraphrasable content, and not enough upon their "rich but irrelevant local texture"—figurative language, the metaphor, allusiveness, connotation. Wit and irony, the play of literary and archaic language against modern idiom and colloquial usage is not obvious enough in the tone of the poems. Too many answers are given, and too few problems are left unsolved, so the poems are almost completely devoid of ambiguity, dichotomy, and paradox.

The early poems, like their successors, however, are fables, anecdotes, or simple narratives concerned with the inevitable decay of youthful vigor and energy, with man's dual nature and the disparity between what he should reasonably receive from life and what he usually will get. Their obsessive theme is that of the mature poetry: mutability, decay, and death. If the world is not controlled by a malignant sovereign, at least it is under the unseeing, and apparently uncaring eye, of an indifferent one. The poems are obviously set in the Middle Tennessee in which Ransom grew up, and the speaker is Ransom himself. Never again would Ransom write poetry with such an unmistakable autobiographical bias. But even more vexing to the poet than this obvious lack of aesthetic distance— he would later remedy this defect through the use of a fictive persona and the development of the texture of the poem—are the many instances of amateur craftmanship: the flat and conventional diction, the sentimental tone, the awkward and ineffective use of meter, the obvious and heavy-handed irony.

Like many of the characters in Ransom's verse, however, many of these earlier characters are overcome with grief because they cannot accept the nature of the world in which they have to live. In "The Cloak Model" a stranger calls the young protagonist aside to observe a store-window mannequin and to contemplate the following proposition:

> "I wish the moralist would thresh
> (Indeed the thing is very droll)
> God's oldest joke, forever fresh:
> The fact that in the finest flesh
> There isn't any soul."

In "Grace" the young protagonist is deeply puzzled by the manner in which God has allowed the hired man to die—ignobly in his own vomit:

> But this was a thing that I had said,
> I was so forward and untamed:
> "I will not worship wickedness
> Though it be God's—I am ashamed!
> For all his mercies God be thanked
> But for his tyrannies be blamed!
> He shall not have any love alone,
> With loathing too his name is named."

The conflict between body and soul is clearly pointed up in "Morning":

> Three hours each day we souls,
> Who might be angels but are fastened down
> With bodies, most infuriating freight,
> Sit fattening these frames and skeletons
> With filthy food, which they must cast away,
> Before they feed again.

The theme of the passing of youthful energy and beauty, a theme which Ransom found almost excessively attractive throughout his career, is presented, too explicitly he would later think, in "Under the Locusts":

> Dick's a sturdy little lad
> Yonder throwing stones;
> Agues and rheumatic pains
> Will fiddle on his bones
>
> . . . .
>
> Jenny and Will go arm and arm.
> He's a lucky fellow;
> Jenny's cheeks are pink as rose,
> Her mother's cheeks are yellow.

The protagonist of "The School" is surely Ransom the country boy from Tennessee who has studied at Vanderbilt and Oxford:

> Equipped with Grecian thoughts, how could I live
> Among my father's folk? My father's house
> Was narrow and his fields were nauseous.
> I kicked his clods for being common dirt,
> Worthy a world which never could be Greek;
> Cursed the paternity that planted me
> One green leaf in a wilderness of autumn;
> And wept, as fitting a fruitful spirit
> Sealed in a yellow tomb.

While Ransom was serving in the army in France, he seriously considered moving to New York and attempting to make his way in publishing and free-lance journalism—in a manner similar to that in which Malcolm Cowley, among others, earned his living while he was learning his trade—and he even asked Morley to help him find a place with a publishing company. When he arrived in New York, however, he found such positions were scarce and paid little. He left for Nashville, planning to visit briefly with his parents, whom he had not seen for two years, before returning to New York and continuing his search for a satisfactory position. His parents, who had aged noticeably during Ransom's absence, were obviously disappointed that their son intended to leave again so soon. When Edwin Mims offered to promote him to assistant professor and raise his salary to $1,700 a year, Ransom decided to stay at Vanderbilt for one year before returning to New York. He remained not for one year but for almost twenty before leaving not for New York but for Kenyon College.

Early in January 1920 Elizabeth Kirkland, daughter of the chancellor at Vanderbilt, invited three of her friends from Wellesley College to visit her for ten days in Nashville, and Mrs. Kirkland notified four young bachelors on campus that they were to entertain the girls during their visit. One of the visitors was Robb Reavill of Colorado and one of the bachelors was Ransom. These two married after a very brief acquaintance and had three children: Helen Ransom Forman, Reavill, and John Joseph (Jack). The union was broken only by Ransom's death more than fifty years later.

During the years after Ransom's return to Vanderbilt, he had resumed attending the meetings of the Fugitives in the home of James M. Frank, Sidney Hirsch's brother-in-law. The nature of the meetings soon changed. After his first book of poetry was published, although he was already dissatisfied with some of this early verse, he was definitely committed to poetry. He quickly assumed leadership of the group, and the discussions shifted from philology, philosophy, and religion to the details of the form and structures of poetry.

At each meeting one or more poets brought poems they had written and read them aloud, as the other members followed the reading closely on a copy provided each of them by the poet. After the reading a discussion began, and, as Donald Davidson wrote, "it was likely to be ruthless in its exposure of any technical weakness as to rhyme, meter, imagery, metaphor, and was often minute in analysis of detail."

In March 1922, after a little more than a year of the kind of meetings described above, Hirsch suggested that the group had written enough poetry of high quality to publish a magazine. Thus the *Fugitive*, a journal of verse and brief critical commentary, was born, and between June 1922 and December 1925 nineteen issues were published. This little magazine brought the "high modernism" of T. S. Eliot, and Ezra Pound to Southern poetry and, as William Pratt has written, its contributors "have shown greater perseverance" in directing the course of modern poetry than any other group in America."

The split between society and the past is again presented in "Ego," the first poem in the first volume of the *Fugitive:*

You have heard something muttered in my scorn:
"A little learning addeleth this man's wit,
He crieth on our dogmas Counterfeit!
And no man's bubble 'scapeth his sharp thorn;

"Nor he respecteth duly our tall steeple,
But in his pride turning from book to book
Heareth our voice and hardly offereth look,
Nor liveth neighborly with these the people."

With reason, friends, I am complained upon,
Who am a headstrong man, sentenced from birth
To love unusual gods beyond all earth
And the easy gospels bruited hither and yon.

So the poet calls upon his "seven of friends" (Davidson, Curry, Frank, Hirsch, Johnson, Stevenson, and Allen Tate) to "acquit" him of "that stain of pride" and to answer "whether/I am so proud a Fool, and godless beside." When one recalls that a basic critical principle of Ransom's was that a poem should remain "almost anonymous," he can understand why these poems were not reprinted for nearly fifty years. Davidson was surprised that Ransom wanted to suppress the poems that he had pored over in France. A new member of the group, however, Allen Tate was pleased that Ransom was dissatisfied with his early verse. He was delighted with the kind of poems Ransom was then bringing to the meetings. He expressed his reactions to his first Fugitive meetings in *Memoirs and Opinions* (1975): "John Ransom always appeared at the Fugitive meetings with a poem (some of us didn't), and when his turn came he read it in a dry tone of understatement. I can only describe his manner in those days as irony which was both brisk and bland. Before we began to think of a magazine (*The Fugitive* was not begun until April 1922), John had written a poem which foreshadowed the style for which he became famous. . . . I marvelled at it because it seemed to me that overnight he had left behind him the style of his first book and, without confusion, had mastered a new style."

The poet had found his distinctive voice, and no longer was there the confusion of the earlier poems. The poems to which Tate referred is "Necrological," in which, for the first time, Ransom employed the vocabulary, syntax, imagery, rhythm, and persona that would be characteristic of all his future verse. The poem, Ransom said many years later, was suggested by the career of Charles the Bold of Burgundy, who was slain in battle and his body left on the battlefield to be devoured by the wolves. The morning following the battle a young friar says "his paternosters," scourges "his limbs" and goes out upon the battlefield, and what he sees and experiences there brings him face to face for the first time with some of the mysteries of human existence:

Day lightened the place where the battle had been won.
The people were dead—it is easy he thought to die—
These dead remained, but the living were all gone,
Gone with the wailing trumpet of victory.

As the friar wanders among the pillage, he ponders a troublesome question, "With much riddling his head became unruly." Can one understand, justify, reconcile the suffering and death that have occurred on this field with the concept of a personal, loving God? Is there logical cause for human strife and suffering, for sacrifice and love, for devotion to a cause, however sacred, if the winner of this day's engagement goes only to meet death in another the next day or the day after?

The lords of chivalry lay prone and shattered

Newspaper feature on the Fugitives

The gentle and the bodyguard of yeoman
Bartholomew's stroke went home—but little it mat-
tered,
Bartholomew went to be stricken of other foemen.

The young friar, devout and learned in theology,
finds that keeping his faith in the face of this, his
first encounter with the real world, very difficult
indeed.

As he walks through the battlefield, he notes
"the dead wore no raiment against the air/Bartho-
lomew's men had spoiled them where they fell."
Some of the bodies "were whitely bare," "some gory
and fabulous" where they had been pierced by the
sword and then eaten by the "grey wolf." It is easy
to die, the friar concludes. (Note the play of wit on
the word *easy*.) Then, as the friar wanders under
"the blue ogive of the firmament," he notes three

particularized scenes, three tableaux, that seem to
bring together his scattered reflections: one is a
dead warrior whose "leman, who with her flame
had warmed his tent,/For him enduring all men's
pleasantries," had died clutching his knees. The
second is a white stallion who had thrown its rider
and "spilled there his little brain" and the "groin
of the knight was spilled by a stone." The third is
a knife with a "crooked blade," an instrument made
especially for slaughter. The friar pulls it from the
"belly of a lugubrious wight"; he feels its sharp edge
and notes it was "cunningly made." At this point
the poet interposes a comment: "But strange apparatus was it for a Carmelite." Then in a concluding stanza Ransom attempts to demonstrate his
theory that a poem can reveal a quality of knowledge that one can get nowhere else. He endeavors
to reconstitute the friar's experience so that the

reader may share it with him and may learn what he has learned:

> Then he sat upon a hill and bowed his head
> As under a riddle, and in a deep surmise
> So still that he likened himself unto those dead
> Whom the kites of Heaven solicited with sweet cries.

This poem, like so many of Ransom's other poems, ends inconclusively or at best ambiguously. The reason is that Ransom's poetry often asks the difficult questions, those for which there is no easy answer. The ending of "Necrological" seems vague because the friar cannot assimilate all he has experienced. He has surely learned how little value one human being places on the life of another, how precarious human life is. He has learned, too, of how unpredictable the world is. A stallion dies because he is hit in the head; it is a knight who is felled by a stroke in the groin. Most of all he has learned of human love when he sees the leman who has endured "all men's pleasantries" and even given up her life so that she might be near the one she loves. The friar is so deeply engrossed in thought that he is like the dead bodies of the knights in whom only the vultures seem interested. The friar learns that the human body, to which he has given little consideration before, is more than a mere depository for the soul and that there is a kind of love very different from the adoration he feels for his blessed lord. He knows he has broadened the range of his experience. He is on the verge of understanding that the monistic system of his church cannot explain the inexhaustible ambiguities and paradoxes of the world outside his monastery. He is, as Robert Buffington has pointed out, a monist on the point of becoming a dualist.

During 1923 Ransom published twenty-three poems written in what Allen Tate has called his "mature manner," including some of his very best: "Bells for John Whiteside's Daughter," "Philomela," "Conrad at Twilight," "Blackberry Winter," "Emily Hardcastle, Spinster," "Here Lies a Lady," "Captain Carpenter," "Spectral Lovers," and "Vaunting Oak." As he wrote Robert Graves, who had written him a letter praising *Poems About God* shortly after its appearance, he was devoting every moment he could steal from his academic duties to poetry. Also, he often felt "hampered and tortured" as he searched for a form to carry his themes. He had tried, he wrote, "the modern irregular forms effected over here by some clever people," but he was convinced they would not function for him. He was concerned, too, that his verse

would make him unpopular because, if he were honest to his art, he would create the impression that he was "a rebel and a poor admirer of our beloved world." What Ransom was reporting, of course, was that he was attempting in his poetry to recreate a view of reality that depicted a broad disparity between the real world and the fantasy world of the idealists. He was trying to avoid what he later called Platonic or bogus poetry—that is, poetry in which images are used merely to illustrate ideas. With the greatest accuracy and precision possible, he wanted to point up the inexhaustible ambiguities, the tensions, the paradoxes, and the ironies that make up the world in which man must live.

Ransom informed Graves of his dissatisfaction with *Poems About God*, finding them now, he wrote, "very juvenile in spots." In the same letter he enclosed a number of his more recent poems, including "Philomela," so that Graves could see the "sort of things that interests me now." Graves offered to try to find Ransom a British publisher and asked if he would allow any of the poems to appear in periodicals before the book was published. Ransom responded immediately: "You have my permission to use anything of mine anywhere and at any time. And to retitle anything, or to edit as you please." As soon as Ransom had accumulated a sufficient number of poems for a volume, he sent them to Graves, under the working title of "Philomela." The manuscript which Holt had just refused contained forty-six poems of which about half were revised versions of poems from *Poems About God* and about half had been written since that volume appeared. The poems were arranged, he wrote Graves, in the order in which they were written, and he hoped they would be published in this sequence because he thought it would show a "regular progress in technique." Graves liked the new poems—and Ransom's revisions of the old ones—but the title displeased him. He suggested that the book be called *Grace After Meat*, a title to which Ransom objected because it emphasized "Grace," a poem he now found "too raw" and "an artistic offense." "I would rather pass for an artist," he wrote Graves, "than exhibit my history." If Graves did not like "Philomela," he suggested as possible titles: "Vaunting Oak," "Under the Locusts," or "Mortal Oak."

At about the time Ransom sent this manuscript to Graves, he sent Morley *Chills and Fever*, informing him that Holt had refused "Philomela" and requesting him to see if any other New York publisher would be interested in a volume of "all new poems." Just before Graves, with the help of

Philip Blair Rice, John Crowe Ransom, and Norman Johnson at the fonding of the Kenyon Review, *1939 (courtesy of Kenyon College Library)*

T. S. Eliot, had convinced the Hogarth Press to bring out *Grace After Meat*, Morley wrote Ransom that Alfred A. Knopf was delighted to get *Chills and Fever*. On 4 July 1924 Ransom finished reading proofs for *Chills and Fever* and wrote Graves: "I liked the looks of the book, in fact felt weakly tender over it. . . . Then I thought of what the public would think; or rather, how they wouldn't be able to think anything; it would be for them a hopelessly hard nut to crack. For odd as it may seem to you, I can assure you that my simple strains will not find in Nashville, not even among fond relatives, nor well wishers, more frequent than I deserve, more than two persons who will guess what I am after (I make loyal exception to my Fugitive brethren of course); and in the whole United States I should imagine there are not fifty who *could* read it with sympathy and not even ten who *will*."

Chills and Fever appeared in New York in August 1924 and *Grace After Meat* in London three months later. Both of the books were well received by the critics, most of whom recognized them as important volumes by a gifted poet. The reviews were not brief notices, as those of *Poems About God* had been, but serious assessments of the poet's intentions and accomplishments. The poets to whom Ransom was compared this time were not Frost and Hardy, but T. S. Eliot and Ezra Pound. Writing for the *Yale Review*, Louis Untermeyer called Ransom "an imaginative poet, a technician of brilliance, a storyteller of power, whose flavor is as individual as that of any American writing today." *Chills and Fever*, he concluded, "seems the best volume of American verse which has lately come to this reviewer's table. No book of the year—and not many of the last decade—has revealed a finer craftsman,

351

a more sensitive musician, a richer personality. In short—if I may be allowed the uncommon extravagance of the capital—a Poet." The most perceptive statement, perhaps, came from John McClure, associate editor of the New Orleans *Double-Dealer,* an influential little magazine in which the work of many soon-to-be important young writers first appeared. "Mr. Ransom," he wrote in the *Times-Picayune,* "has developed the intellectually expressive cadence to a point probably not excelled by any American—not even by Eliot, Pound, or Stevens, and certainly not by Frost."

Since *Grace After Meat* was published only a few months after *Chills and Fever* and since all of the poems in *Grace After Meat* had already appeared in one or the other of Ransom's two previously published books, it was not widely reviewed. It did provoke, however, what Ransom regarded as "the most philosophic statement of my position that I have seen, though not the most favorable." This "statement" was included in Edwin Muir's review in the *Saturday Review of Literature.* Muir found *Grace After Meat* the second most important literary event in recent weeks, the most important being the publication of Edith Sitwell's *Troy Park.* Looking among his British contemporaries to find the poet Ransom most resembled, Muir wrote, he thought immediately of Robert Graves: "Their ways of apprehending life and handling experience, their preoccupation at the same time with quite ordinary facts and metaphysical problems, their serious attempts to come to terms with themselves and their surroundings, their assumption of intellectual detachment as a means to this." At the same time Muir was persuaded that Ransom was "bolder both in thought and technique" than Graves, as well as more intellectual. Muir insisted that Ransom had what Graves did not, a "heraldic quality ... the ability to translate experience into something which is half myth, half philosophic fable, and in doing that to chill and clarify it." For Muir, however, the basic weakness of the poetry was its cold intellectualism; it thereby missed greatness because the truly "great poet gains freedom from his sufferings by realizing them completely in a living act of the imagination." Ransom's kind of poetry, Muir concluded, had not been written so well since the seventeenth century, and this fact made him "one of the most interesting poets of our time."

Ransom's last book of original verse, *Two Gentlemen in Bonds,* was published by Knopf in January 1927. This volume, not all of which is of the unmatched brilliance of *Chills and Fever,* contains some of Ransom's most enduring poetry: "Antique Harvesters," "Blue Girls," "Dead Boy," "The Equilibrists," "Janet Waking," "Man Without Sense of Direction," "Survey of Literature," "Piazzi Piece," "Our Two Worthies," and "Vision by Sweetwater." This book was greeted by almost all the better-known critics as a major achievement of one of the most important poets of the era. The review that Ransom said had given him the "most honor and inward examination" that he had ever "secured from any source" was written by Allen Tate and appeared in the *Nation* for 30 March 1927. "The fourth volume of Ransom's poetry," Tate began, "is not the equal in brilliant variety of technical effects or in range of subject matter of *Chills and Fever,* issued in 1924"; nevertheless it was "the qualitative equal of anything else he has ever done," and it "precipitates the particular essence" which is Ransom's:

> Mr. Ransom is the last pure manifestation of the culture of the eighteenth-century South; the moral issues which emerge transfigured in his poetry are the moral issues of his section, class, culture, referred to their simple fundamental properties. . . .
> Two of Mr. Ransom's qualities in especial connect him with the culture which in its prime registered its genius in politics and law; rationalism and the code of *noblesse oblige.* These qualities, informing every poem, dictate the direction of his artistic vision. . . . Rationalism . . . stiffens his poetry with an irony and lucidity, and a subtlety, which elevate it with a unique distinction in the present American scene. . . . Mr. Ransom can render a beautiful commentary upon his tragic personal vision because he accepts the code within which the characters struggle. . . . In every poem he is either the satirist or the ironist; and as a fine minor artist he has always the same thing to say, in new and unpredictable images.

Almost the whole of Ransom's poetic career falls within an eleven-year period, from 1916 to 1927. He published fewer than 160 poems, and his first *Selected Poems* (1945) includes only five poems written after 1927. The enlarged edition of *Selected Poems* (1963) contains some new stanzas and many revised lines but no new poems. The last *Selected Poems* (1969) contains eighty poems, including twelve sonnets from *Two Gentlemen in Bonds* along with a revised version of each. Although Ransom wrote poetry for only a brief period and his output during these years was far from prolific, within the restrictions he placed upon himself both in theme and genre his contributions are considerable. Although he wrote only one entirely new poem after 1939, he was, as he expressed it, always "tinkering" with the old ones. William Pratt has noted fourteen different versions of "Tom, Tom the Piper's Son," written between 1924 and 1969. Fortunately, as Robert Buffington and others have pointed out, Ransom changed his best poems very little.

Although in his prose essays Ransom would never admit that he knew exactly what Eliot meant by the "dissociation of sensibility"—he used what he called his "structure-texture formulation" to identify the unique nature of poetic discourse— several critics have pointed out that Eliot's phrase can be profitably used to denote a persistent theme in Ransom's poetry. In one of the first serious attempts to assess Ransom's poetic achievement, Robert Penn Warren pointed out: "To an astonishing degree, in far more than a majority of the cases, the hero or heroine of the poem is a sufferer from that complaint of 'dissociation of sensibility.' The poem itself is a commentary on the situation, its irony deriving from the fact that these otherwise admirable people 'cannot fathom or perform their nature.'" Many later critics have agreed with and elaborated on Warren's thesis. In *Modern Poetry and the Tradition* (1939), Cleanth Brooks suggested that "a divided sensibility" is one of Ransom's major concerns. Like other modern critics, F. O. Matthiessen attempted to explain the schism by pointing out that the modern sensibility is "torn between reason and imagination, between science and faith."

In "Necrological" the young friar is rendered incapable of action by the impact upon his sensibility of the difference between the adoration he feels for his lord and the physical love shared by the knight and his leman. Another of Ransom's characters who cannot perceive the duality of his nature is the protagonist of "Man Without Sense of Direction." Although it would seem that this man should be living a full and satisfying life, something is not quite right. Despite his "noblest mind and powerful leg," he is far from satisfied, and although he is aware that his life is incomplete, he is not fully aware of what is lacking. As Warren pointed out, he can neither "fathom nor perform his nature." His impotence and ignorance make poignant demands on our sympathy:

> And he writhes like an antique man of bronze
> That is beaten by furies visible,
> Yet he is punished not knowing his sins
> And for his innocence walks in hell.

His incompleteness is expressed in physical terms. He has a "small passion," which he "feigns large," and he is "flushed" with passion as he emerges from his wife's bedroom. Almost immediately, however, his lips are cold, and he is "cold as dead." That this man is incapable of genuine human love is obvious; even more pathetic is the alarming fact that not only is his plight hopeless but that he is not really aware of the sad state he is in:

> But let his cold lips be her omen,
> She shall not kiss that harried one
> To peace, as men are served by women
> Who comfort them in darkness and in sun.

This fragmented and incomplete state of man is the basic thematic concern of some of Ransom's best-known poems. In "Winter Remembered" the man is separated from his loved one for no recorded reason—though it is revealed that he has a wound, presumably a spiritual one—and he is deeply affected by the separation. The inability to experience love, or as Ransom expresses it, the "cry of Absence, Absence in the heart" sends him out of the warm house into the icy weather. Metaphorically, Ransom is demonstrating the man's lack of love, and his miserable state is delineated in one of the most evocative images in Ransom's poetry:

> Dear love, these fingers that had known your touch
> And tied our forces first together
> Were ten poor idiot fingers not worth much,
> Ten frozen parsnips hanging in the weather.

Ransom once suggested, as F. Scott Fitzgerald noted, that modern man must hold in his mind simultaneously two contradictory ideas. He is forever confronted by questions that demand answers but for which he has none. This situation is presented in "The Equilibrists," in which two lovers are caught between two equally strong but opposing forces. As the title suggests, they can be likened to the juggler who has to keep two balls in the air simultaneously or the performer who walks the tight wire high in air and must retain his poise and balance, for to fall off on either side would be disastrous. The lovers are in a "torture of equilibrium" for "They burned with fierce heat to come near,/But honor beat them back and kept them clear. The "two painful stars" cannot defy the natural laws but must keep their orbit lest they explode; the two lovers must follow the basic principle behind their humanity even though doing so ruins

Allen Tate, Richard Chase, William Empson, Cleanth Brooks, John Crowe Ransom, and F. O. Matthiessen at Kenyon College, 1948 (courtesy of Kenyon College Archives)

their opportunity to be lovers. They can neither consummate their passion nor free themselves of the compelling desire. Even the woman's mouth, a "quaint orifice," delivers contradictory messages. From it comes heat when the lovers kiss, but this passion loses its force in the light of the "cold words [that] came down spiral from the head." Passion and reason both come from their basic nature; yet, passion tells them to become lovers, reason to remain innocent and pure. The eyes say: "Never mind the cruel words," but "what they said, the doves came straightway flying/And unsaid: Honor, Honor, they kept crying." Ransom is obviously providing a foundation for his own dualism. How much easier it would be if this were a hedonistic world so that the lovers could enjoy each other's body unmolested; or if it were a pure, idealistic world so that they could live without passion or desire. But it is neither and both. Although the persona sympathizes with the plight of the lovers, with their passion demanding fulfillment, he also understands the necessity of the moral restrictions that prohibit the consummation of their desire. (In his essay "Forms and Citizens" Ransom argued that restraining this natural impulse turns what man may feel for any woman into a more complicated emotion that he has for only one woman. The woman becomes, he says, elsewhere, a "precious object," and lust matures into love.)

Although the conflict between the two lovers demands resolution, it remains unresolved. The lovers remain suspended in the terrible void that develops between them, completely at the mercy of the conflicting forces that destroy a unified approach to life, and the polarities will never be terminated. They will remain in this "torture of equilibrium" throughout eternity.

> For spin your period out, and draw your breath,
> A kinder saeculum begins with Death,
> Would you ascend to Heaven and bodiless dwell?
> Or take your bodies honorless to Hell?
>
> In Heaven you have heard no marriage is,
> No white flesh tinder to your lecheries,
> Your male and female tissue sweetly shaped
> Sublimed away, and furious blood escaped.
>
> Great lovers lie in Hell, the stubborn ones
> Infatuate of the flesh upon the bones;
> Stuprate, they rend each other when they kiss,
> The pieces kiss again, no end to this.

Given the nature of the world in which we live and expectations of the one to come, Ransom underscores the plight of his doomed lovers by composing an epitaph "to memorize their doom":

> *Equilibrists lie here; stranger, tread light;*
> *Close, but untouching in each other's sight;*
> *Mouldered the lips and ashy the tall skull.*
> *Let them lie perilous and beautiful.*

Conversing with Cleanth Brooks and Robert Penn Warren in *Understanding Poetry*, Ransom remarked: "Death is the greatest subject of poetry, the most serious, . . . there's no recourse from death except that we learn to face it, to get on speaking terms with it." One is not surprised to find, therefore, that fully a third of Ransom's mature verse is concerned with mortality: the inevitable decay of feminine beauty, the fleetingness of youthful energy, and the awful certainty of death. Many of that small handful of poems which Randall Jarrell certified as "perfectly realized and occasionally almost perfect" treat this theme, including "Bells for John Whiteside's Daughter," Ransom's most-often anthologized poem:

> There was such speed in her little body,
> And such lightness in her footfall,
> It is no wonder that her brown study
> Astonishes us all.
> . . . .
> But now go the bells, and we are ready,
> In one house we are sternly stopped
> To say we are vexed at her brown study,
> Lying so primly propped.

In its movement from "Astonished" to "vexed" the poem delineates exactly how an adult, perhaps a neighbor, is affected by the death of a young girl. Apparently he does not know her very well; her only direct effect upon him has been that of a slight nuisance as the noise of her childhood games in the orchard below has disturbed his adult contemplation. Her energy and vitality seem endless. She is never still; therefore his first reaction when he sees her "brown study"—a lifelike little body lying so still and apparently so meditative—is astonishment. He is surprised that she is so different from the way he remembers her. The thought of a moment, however—rendered by almost three-fifths of the poem presented without any full stops—causes his reflection to move from this individual girl to what she represents. The quality of the icons, to use a critical term of Ransom's, which contribute the rich texture to the poem, clearly reveal the metaphysical nature of the brief reflection—"orchard trees," "arms against her shadow," "lazy geese . . ./Dripping their snow on the green grass," crying "in goose, Alas,/for the tireless heart." Taken together the elements of this meditation portray the human predicament.

After his first reaction of surprise and astonishment, he has now placed the unexpected death of the little girl in another perspective. His astonishment has turned to "vexation." He is outraged at this apparently useless and senseless destruction of youthful vitality. He can only surmise that this death is merely another example of the inscrutability, of the paradoxical and ambiguous nature, of the world in which he must live. There is no way he can make this experience compatible with the view of a meaningful universe controlled by an omnipotent and meaningful God.

The irony of the poem depends upon the contrast of the stock response to death with that which is expressed. The poet employs the same technique in "Dead Boy," which reports several reactions to the death of the little cousin: the simple objective statement "The little cousin is dead" is undercut by the description of his death as "foul subtraction"; the boy, a member of an ancient Virginia family is mourned by many relatives and by the narrator, who belongs to the "world of outer dark." Neither he nor the relatives, but obviously for different reasons, "like the transaction." The death of the boy can hardly be expressed by the vague and scientific word "abstraction," for, although he was a "sword beneath his mother's heart" and although to no one but the mother perhaps was he ever lovable, "never/Woman bewept her babe as this is weeping." Then there are the ritualistic and ceremonial expressions of the elder statesmen, who "have strode by the box of death" and the official statement of the minister who proclaims: "The first-fruits . . . the Lord has taken." But the final statement comes from the "noble house" which suffers a "deep dynastic wound." Although the boy is "a pig with a pasty face," he has been taken "by foul subtraction," a "green bough from Virginia aged tree," and the narrator sees in him "the forebears' antique lineaments." With the death of the little boy passes the expectations for the continuation of the family. The narrator's grief is less personal than the mother's, but he sees in the little boy's death "a deep dynastic wound," a basic description of the elemental process of life.

"Janet Waking" illustrates what Graham Hough has called Ransom's ability to put "massive . . . facts in small or delicate settings." Through the death of her pet hen, a young girl confronts for the first time the most painful and pervasive fact of human existence. Again, Ransom controls his tone by the use of point of view; the simple facts of the poem are presented from the alternating perspectives of a child and an adult. After Janet has slept "Beautifully" until it is "deeply morning," her first thought on waking is of her "dainty-feathered hen." She wonders "how it had kept." Pausing just long enough to kiss her mother and father, she rushes out to the chicken's house, but "Her Chucky had died." Then the perspective shifts from that of the child to that of the adult, and the differing attitudes expressed in this dual point of view produce a tone that is a masterful blending of pathos and humor. Again the poet avoids the soggy sentimentalism that the subject, the death of a pet, seems to demand:

Yvor Winters, John Crowe Ransom, and Allen Tate at Kenyon College, 1949 (courtesy of Kenyon College Archives)

It was a transmogrifing bee
Came droning down on Chucky's old bald head
And sat and put the poison. It scarcely bled.
But how exceedingly
And purply did the knot
Swell with the venom and communicate
Its rigor! Now the poor comb stood up straight
But Chucky did not.

Janet implores her chicken to rise and walk upon the grass as it always has, but it cannot because it has been "Translated far beyond the daughters of men." (Janet does not understand that her hen has been visited by a "transmogrifying bee"—one that has altered, the hen's metaphysical state.) Janet insists that her father awaken her chicken and will not believe him when he says he cannot because she "will not be instructed in how deep was the forgetful kingdom of death." Janet is too young, too full of life, to understand her most significant human trait—the inevitability of death.

Few modern poets have succeeded, as Ransom has, in making his readers aware of the ravages of time, of the shortness of human life, and of the inevitable decay of feminine beauty and vigor. Two of his best-known poems on the subject of change are "Blue Girls" and "Vision by Sweetwater." The vastly dissimilar ways in which this theme is developed in these poems demonstrate both the poet's technical skills and his ability to place his personal stamp on materials far from original. He takes the traditional carpe diem motif and makes it uniquely his own. In "Blue Girls" a group of young girls, students in a fashionable boarding school, are shown parading their beauty, apparently unaware of how time will affect them. The narrator observes them and muses that they should "practice" their beauty and think no more of the future than blue birds that go "chattering on the air." They must not listen to their teacher because their adult rational understanding of how time affects physical beauty might destroy the girls' unself-conscious enjoyment of the moment. The narrator could but does not explain this basic law of life, for if he shared with the girls what he has learned from experience, he might disturb one of the basic patterns of life. The time to practice beauty instinctively is in youth. If one becomes self-conscious and begins to reflect upon experience, to rationalize all of his expectations, he will exaggerate the conflict between abstract thought and natural action. The persona is aware that the girls are silly and vain and in their innocence unawakened, but given the nature of the world and the fragility of their natural

beauty, he cannot advise them to give up their unreflective approach. To think too much about experience is to preclude the possibility of living a complete and satisfying life. In "Vision by Sweetwater" the horror of youthful beauty and energy being inevitably destroyed by the passing of time brings a scream "From one of the white throats which it hid among."

Some of the poems written between 1924 and 1927, particularly "Old Mansion" and "Antique Harvesters," reveal the growing economic and political concerns that led Ransom into the Agrarian movement. But these poems, like so much of Ransom's other verse, are concerned with mutability. Social and political institutions are subject to change, as are their human creators. In "Old Mansion" the poet urges that ideals be preserved even when the institutions which embody them pass away. Although the culture of the Old South is doomed, as all things fall victims to time and change, one needs to participate in the traditions of that culture; for only in a sensitive awareness of the past can one perceive a sense of stability and permanence in the flux of an ever-changing world. In the description of the old mansion one can see the traditional virtues to which the poet refers:

Stability was the virtue of its rectangle
Whose line was seen in part and guessed in part
Through trees. Decay was the tone of old brick and
    shingle.
Green shutters dragging frightened the watchful
    heart.

To assert: Your mansion, long and richly inhabited,
Its porches and bowers suiting the children of men,
Will not forever be thus, O man, exhibited,
And one had best hurry to enter it if one can.

In his use of wit and irony, in the tension and paradox characteristic of his best verse, Ransom is distinctively a modern poet. His attitudes and the poetic forms he employs, however, reflect his interest in the traditional. "Antique Harvesters" opens in autumn, the time of harvest, and the spokesman calls his friends and neighbors together to bring in the bounties that nature has provided. On the surface it seems a modest production: "A meager hill of kernels, a runnel of juice," a few "spindling ears"; "Declension looks from our land, it is old." The young men in the party are disappointed because the yield is so meager. Although the old endure and "shall be older," the young want no "sable" memories; they see only the "spindling ears." They want material values, a bountiful yield of that which can be used; they do not know that "One spot has special yield," that it is a precious object, because it has worth beyond its utilitarian value; it is particularly fertile because it was drenched in heroes' blood.

In *The World's Body* Ransom argued that religion exists for its ritual rather than for its dogma. Ritual combines the attitudes, customs, habits, and rites through which man restrains the more basic side of his nature. The harvest of which the persona speaks is a ritual and from the "ample chambers" of the old men's hearts comes another echo suggested by an activity that is traditionally ritualistic. This activity is fox hunting:

> Here come the hunters, keepers of a rite;
> The horn, the hounds, the lank mares coursing by
> Straddled with the archetypes of chivalry;
> And the fox, lively ritualist, in flight
> Offering his unearthly ghost to quarry;
> And the fields themselves to harry.

The persona calls upon the young men to resume the harvest and reap the real yield that the section has produced. They should get to know their "famous Lady's image"; it is revealed now, though perhaps not in its full splendor, and soon it will disappear, as everything must into nothingness.

This poem, which Ransom often called his Southern poem, suggests some of the thought that went into *I'll Take My Stand* (1930), written by Ransom and eleven other Southerners: Donald Davidson, Allen Tate, Robert Penn Warren, Frank Owsley, Lyle Lanier, John Gould Fletcher, H. B. Kline, Stark Young, Andrew Nelson Lytle, H. C. Nixon, and John Donald Wade. This book, to which Ransom contributed the introduction ("A Statement of Principles") and the lead essay ("Reconstructed but Unregenerate"), argues that modern man must be aware of the evils inherent in a social order dominated by uncontrolled materialism.

Any final estimate of Ransom's achievement must begin with his poetry. Given the severe limits he placed upon his efforts in this genre, the quality of his contribution is remarkable. In a small handful of poems, all of which can be printed in a hundred pages, he accurately mirrored the modern sensibility. He produced a dozen or so poems that are almost perfect and that reflect the virtues of modern poetry at its best, combining delicacy with strength, elegance with earthiness. Not only

is he, as Allen Tate has proclaimed, one of the "best elegiac poets in the language," few poets of his generation have been able to represent with greater accuracy and precision the inexhaustible ambiguities, the paradoxes and tensions, the dichotomies and ironies that make up the life of modern man.

Letters:

Selected Letters of John Crowe Ransom, edited by Thomas Daniel Young and George Core (Baton Rouge & London: Louisiana State University Press, 1985).

Bibliography:

Thomas Daniel Young, *John Crowe Ransom: An Annotated Bibliography* (New York & London: Garland, 1982).

Biography:

Thomas Daniel Young, *Gentleman in a Dustcoat: A Biography of John Crowe Ransom* (Baton Rouge: Louisiana State University Press, 1976).

References:

Cleanth Brooks, *Modern Poetry and the Tradition* (Chapel Hill: University of North Carolina Press, 1939);

Robert Buffington, *The Equilibrist: A Study of John Crowe Ransom's Poems, 1916-1963* (Nashville: Vanderbilt University Press, 1967);

Karl F. Knight, *The Poetry of John Crowe Ransom: A Study of Diction, Metaphor and Symbol* (The Hague: Mouton, 1965);

Thornton H. Parsons, *John Crowe Ransom* (New York: Twayne, 1969);

Louis D. Rubin, Jr., *The Wary Fugitives: Four Poets and the South* (Baton Rouge: Louisiana State University Press, 1978);

Miller Williams, *The Poetry of John Crowe Ransom* (New Brunswick: Rutgers University Press, 1972);

Thomas Daniel Young, ed., *John Crowe Ransom: Critical Essays and a Bibliography* (Baton Rouge: Louisiana State University Press, 1968).

Papers:

The libraries at Vanderbilt University, Kenyon College, Princeton University, Yale University, Indiana University, Stanford University, and Washington University have collections of Ransom's papers.

Charles Reznikoff

(31 August 1894-22 January 1976)

Milton Hindus
Brandeis University

See also the Reznikoff entry in *DLB 28, Twentieth-Century American-Jewish Fiction Writers.*

BOOKS: *Rhythms* (Brooklyn, N.Y.: Privately printed, 1918);

Rhythms II (Brooklyn, N.Y.: Privately printed, 1919);

Poems (New York: Samuel Roth, 1920);

Uriel Accosta: A Play, and a Fourth Group of Verse (New York: Privately printed, 1921);

Chatterton, The Black Death, and Meriwether Lewis: Three Plays (New York: Sunwise Turn, 1922);

Coral, and Captive Israel: Two Plays (New York: Sunwise Turn, 1923);

Nine Plays (New York: Privately printed, 1927);

Five Groups of Verse (New York: Privately printed, 1927);

By the Waters of Manhattan: An Annual [prose, memoirs, and verse] (New York: Privately printed, 1927);

By the Waters of Manhattan [novel] (New York: C. Boni, 1930);

Testimony [prose] (New York: Objectivist Press, 1934);

Jerusalem the Golden (New York: Objectivist Press, 1934);

In Memoriam: 1933 (New York: Objectivist Press, 1934);

Early History of a Sewing-Machine Operator (New York: Privately printed, 1936);

Separate Way (New York: Objectivist Press, 1936);

Going To and Fro and Walking Up and Down (New York: Privately printed, 1941);

The Lionhearted: A Story about the Jews in Medieval England (Philadelphia: Jewish Publication Society of America, 1944);

The Jews of Charleston: A History of an American Jewish Community, by Reznikoff, with the collaboration of Uriah Z. Engelman (Philadelphia: Jewish Publication Society of America, 1950);

Inscriptions: 1944-1956 (New York: Privately printed, 1959);

By the Waters of Manhattan: Selected Verse (New York

Charles Reznikoff (photograph © 1984 Layle Silbert)

& San Francisco: New Directions/San Francisco Review, 1962);

Family Chronicle (New York: Privately printed, 1963; London: Norton Bailey with the Human Constitution, 1969);

Testimony: The United States, 1885-1890: Recitative (New York: New Directions, 1965);

Testimony: The United States, 1891-1900: Recitative (New York: Privately printed, 1968);

By the Well of Living and Seeing, and The Fifth Book of the Maccabees (New York: Privately printed, 1969;

By the Well of Living & Seeing: New & Selected Poems, 1918-1973, edited by Seamus Cooney (Los Angeles: Black Sparrow Press, 1974);

Holocaust (Los Angeles: Black Sparrow Press, 1975);

Poems, 1918-1936, volume 1 of *The Complete Poems of Charles Reznikoff*, edited by Cooney (Santa Barbara: Black Sparrow Press, 1976);

Poems, 1937-1975, volume 2 of *The Complete Poems of Charles Reznikoff*, edited by Cooney (Santa Barbara: Black Sparrow Press, 1977);

The Manner "Music" (Santa Barbara: Black Sparrow Press, 1977);

Testimony: The United States, 1885-1915: Recitative, 2 volumes (Santa Barbara: Black Sparrow Press, 1978-1979).

OTHER: "Rashi," "From 'My Country, 'Tis of Thee,' " and "The English in Virginia," in *An "Objectivists" Anthology*, edited by Louis Zukofsky (Le Beausset, Var, France: To, Publishers, 1932), pp. 87-97, 169-170;

Emil Cohn, *Stories and Fantasies from the Jewish Past*, translated by Reznikoff (Philadelphia: Jewish Publication Society of America, 1951);

Israel Joseph Benjamin, *Three Years in America, 1859-1862*, translated by Reznikoff (Philadelphia: Jewish Publication Society of America, 1956);

Louis Marshall, Champion of Liberty: Selected Papers and Addresses, 2 volumes, edited by Reznikoff (Philadelphia: Jewish Publication Society of America, 1957).

Emerson remarked that the best writers often have the shortest biographies. The genius "draws up the ladder after him," and the world, which had consigned him to obscurity during his lifetime, "sees the works and asks in vain for a history."

Whatever judgment may ultimately be passed upon him, not much more than his works is ever likely to be known of Charles Reznikoff. He left no fervent disciples. The record he wished to preserve is the one he made himself, but it is quite detailed, and will surely have to do for those readers who, treasuring his memory, might like to know more.

Reznikoff was born on 31 August 1894 in—as he himself called it—the Jewish ghetto of Brownsville, in Brooklyn, New York. His parents, who are depicted in *Family Chronicle* (1963), were Sarah Yetta Wolvovsky Reznikoff and Nathan Reznikoff, both immigrant Jews who had recently come to the United States seeking refuge from the czarist pogroms of the 1880s.

The poet was named Ezekiel to honor his maternal grandfather, Ezekiel Wolvovsky, who had died sometime in the 1870s. As he told Reinhold

Schiffer in 1974, his mother's English was very limited, and her doctor, who attended his birth, was "a Jew, but an anarchist," and had "no use for Jewish affairs, as anarchists wouldn't. . . . At every great fast day, he gave a feast." So when the poet's mother told him she wanted to name him after her father, he said, " 'Well, what's your father's name?' She said 'Yehazqel,' which in English is Ezekiel, the prophet. So he said, 'Well,' he said, 'call him Charlie. He'll be grateful to you.' So all that is on my birth certificate and everywhere is Charles." In *Inscriptions* he comments on the meaning of his names, in English and in Hebrew:

Because, the first born, I was not redeemed,
I belong to my Lord, not to myself or you:
by my name, in English, I am of His house,
one of the carles—a Charles, a churl;
and by my name in Hebrew which is Ezekiel
(whom God strengthened)
my strength, such as it is, is His.

According to family tradition, his grandfather Ezekiel had also been a poet who composed his songs while traveling around the Russian countryside with his wagon in search of a living. At his death, the manuscript of his work came into the hands of his widow, Hannah Wolvovsky, who was fearful that the writing might contain nihilistic and hence subversive sentiments dangerous to her family. She destroyed it. The destruction of his grandfather's lifetime literary output haunted Charles Reznikoff, and he took it as a sign that he himself must see to it that his own work was printed even if there was neither public nor market for it, and that he must be sure not to leave any of it to the care of his family, friends, or executors. It is ironic, therefore, that as much as he published during his long life, he should have left perhaps his most interesting prose work, the novel which he mysteriously called *The Manner "Music"* (1977), neatly typed among his papers at his death, where it was discovered when these papers came into the hands of his last publisher, John Martin, of Black Sparrow Press.

While Reznikoff was still a boy, his paternal grandparents and other relatives, who had remained behind in Russia when his parents immigrated to America, came to live near them in New York. Reznikoff's "Early History of a Writer," in volume two of *The Complete Poems* (1977), emphasizes the frequency of his family's moves around the city of New York, and its encounters with the ugly anti-Semitism in non-Jewish neighborhoods.

These experiences contributed much to his feelings of insecurity and to his self-consciousness as a Jew. From Brownsville the family moved to Harlem, then to the Lower East Side of Manhattan, and, by the time he was twelve years old, back to Brooklyn, but this time more than a mile away from the concentration of Jews in Brownsville. This neighborhood, as he wrote in "Early History of a Writer," was "mainly laborers and clerks," mostly cold-water flats without heat. "Among their children," he wrote, "the hatred for Israel smoldered," and any Jew unlucky enough for whatever reason (including following his business) to "blunder" into the neighborhood would, "likely as not, have a clod of mud or a couple of stones whizzing at his head." The poet's grandparents were, in that neighborhood, "the only Jews for blocks." Here, the young Reznikoff would scurry home from high school so as to miss the other children getting out of grade school. Reading on the stoop or playing in the street, he was nevertheless the target of flung stones or garbage. Long afterward he remembered an undersized, red-faced Irish child of six or seven years passing back and forth in front of the house where Charles was sitting on the stoop,

> and chanting at me with a tireless anger that surprised
>   me
> "Yid! Yid!"
> The child's sister, sixteen or so and home from her
>   job just then
> egged him on,
> hatred in her thin pallid face
> and in the eyes that were too bright,
> as if I were somehow to blame for her unhappiness.

There were more violent and traumatic incidents involving his grandfather and an uncle, and from them Reznikoff created vignettes that have the kind of salience that Wordsworth gave to some of his early experiences in *The Prelude*, which he subtitled *Growth of a Poet's Mind*. In "Early History of a Writer" Reznikoff remembers walking with his grandfather through a public park on the East Side when two hooligans ("two strapping Germans—or were they Russians?") decide to have some fun with the sickly looking undersized Jew "with a short grayish brown beard/ruffled by the cold wind." Despite his grandfather's attempts to avoid the confrontation, these fellows will not let him pass but playfully knock him down (showing off, they are "larking with a girl"); they send him "rolling on the pavement until the iron railing along the path stopped him." His grandson helps him to his feet:

> I asked my grandfather if he was hurt
> and wanted to brush his coat with my palms,
> for it was dirty;
> but my grandfather would not stop,
> and did not say a word
> to those who had hurt him or to me.

Another experience which ended even worse took place at the conclusion of the evening prayers on the Day of Atonement, when his grandfather and his uncle were unexpectedly late in returning from the synagogue in Brownsville to which they had walked. Charles was worried and went out to meet them. He saw his grandfather coming down the street alone, tears streaming down his face, unable to answer "where's uncle?" And his uncle appeared "without his new hat and the blood running down his face." As they were passing a bar a little boy, encouraged by a gang of young ruffians, had brandished a stick at them. The uncle had taken the stick away, and some of the gang jumped the old man and sent him sprawling in the gutter. Charles blamed his uncle for going down that particular street; his father blamed him for taking the stick; and the uncle, trying to warm himself next to the stove, said not a word.

> My grandmother was muttering that this country
> was no better than Russia, after all;
> and my parents and I felt ashamed,
> as if somehow we were to blame,
> and we tried to explain that what had happened was
>   unusual,
> that only the neighborhood we lived in was like that,
> and what a wonderful country this was—
> that all our love for it and our praise
> was not unmerited.

Such was the background which prepared him to write not only his long sequential poem *Testimony: The United States, 1885-1915* (1934-1979), a bare and powerful record of human suffering and injustice, but also—during the last years of his life—his major poem *Holocaust* (1975). There can be no doubt that his direct and indirect observation of violence (and his sense of its perpetual immediacy) as a Jewish child in a hostile urban neighborhood lies behind the lifelong concern in much of his work with the continual possibility, potential, and actuality of violence between human beings. In that and indeed in much else—he embodies his time, and he voices the Jewish experience.

In his early years, Reznikoff was a precocious student. He finished grammar school at the age of eleven, three years ahead of the rest of his class, began writing verse when he was thirteen or fourteen years old, and graduated from Boys High School in Brooklyn in 1909, when he was fifteen. He had looked forward to going to this intellectually demanding school as something of a relief from the society of his hostile neighborhood, but, as he recorded in "Early History of a Writer," he was disappointed in his expectations:

It had seemed to me when I first saw the building
that I should be happy there.
The dislike of Jews, however, that was in certain
streets of Brooklyn,
was in the classroom, too;
and sometimes, when Jewish pupils forgot about it
or mistook some careless geniality for friendliness,
they suddenly found, like people who live over a geo-
logical fault,
how uncertain the ground was.

In 1910, a year after his graduation from high school, Reznikoff left New York for the first extended period in his life, going to the newly established School of Journalism at the University of Missouri. His ambition had already been fixed upon becoming a writer. As he says in "Early History of a Writer," in New York he had two friends—whom he calls Eugene and Gabriel—who had also decided to become writers. They would discuss poetry together,

especially the poetry of the new men—new to us—
Francis Thompson, Arthur Symons, and Ernest Dowson.
This was not in our English course,
and Eugene and I felt superior because we read them,
and were proud of ourselves because we, too, were
writing verse,
and trying our hands at sonnets
and the French confectionery Austin Dobson—for
one—was good at.

On weekends, these three friends would explore the secondhand-book stalls and antiquarian bookshops on Fourth Avenue in Manhattan, seeking fresh discoveries modeled on the literary adventures and history they had read about: "for of course we knew that Rossetti or Swinburne had found the Rubaiyat/in just such a pile." Sometimes, he and his friend Gabriel would attempt to meet certain literary challenges or to solve specific problems (such as writing a sonnet on a given theme in a limited period of time) which had become part of romantic history. "We knew that Keats and

Leigh Hunt used to do that./I had Gabriel choose the theme,/for this was to be a test of my skill in writing verse/as against his." Even in those early days, Reznikoff was slow, thorough, perhaps in the eyes of others overscrupulous, overcareful. By the time he finished his sonnet (long after Gabriel, and long after the time had expired) it was twilight, "but there was still light enough to see what we had written./Gabriel's sonnet was something fantastic,/which I did not care for; but he said that he liked mine/And, indeed, I liked it very much."

The Missouri School of Journalism was not what Reznikoff had expected. Journalists, he discovered, were interested primarily in news and not in writing, while he himself was indifferent to what is generally called news and thought it unimportant compared to what could be made of it in writing. In the language of the man he never met but was soon to choose as his first literary instructor and model, Ezra Pound, Reznikoff's real interest lay in "the news that stays news." He would distinguish between journalism and literature by citing the familiar story of the old-fashioned newspaper editor instructing the fledgling reporter in how to find printable news by telling him that if a dog bites a man it is not news while if a man bites a dog it most emphatically *is*. Journalism is interested above all else in the unusual, the sensational, the improbable, the melodramatic. Literature, while it might include such things, can create something out of nothing through its style, its wit, its intelligence. Selection, unity, patient attention to detail, communication of feeling rather than mere facts were everything in literature. It must be devoid of pointless exaggeration or sentimentality as well. The same man might be both a working journalist and a literary artist, but these were different roles, and there was a world of difference between the results achieved.

Reznikoff returned to New York from the University of Missouri after one year and, after working for a year in his parents' hat-manufacturing business, he entered the Law School of New York University in the fall of 1912. He had considered, for a time, taking a Ph.D. in history and embarking on a life of scholarship and teaching, but, as he told Janet Sternburg and Alan Ziegler in 1973, "one day passing N.Y.U. Law School I remembered that Heine had studied law and Goethe had studied law, so that seemed to be fine. They only had two hours a day of studying and the rest of the day I'd be free. So I applied and was admitted. I was just 18 then." Of course he became immersed in his studies: the two-hours-a-day of "case-book" instruction demanded six hours of preparation, and by the time he entered his third year he wanted to quit and get back to his writing: "But my folks wouldn't hear of it—they said correctly that you've only got another year to finish." In 1915 he received his LL.B. degree, graduating second in his class; for the next year he took a few postgraduate courses in Law at Columbia University (and perhaps did some work in the family business), and in 1916 he was called to the Bar of the State of New York. He was twenty-two years old. He practiced law very briefly indeed: "I thought that a young lawyer would get little business, if any," he told *World Authors 1970-1975*, "and if I did not work for another lawyer and just rented desk room I would have plenty of time for my own writing and, indeed, was soon at work at my verse at a desk." When the United States entered World War I in 1917 he joined the Reserve Officers Training Corps at Columbia University, but the war was over before he got any training. The war may, however, have been the reason why he printed, on the press which he had installed in the basement of his parents' home in Brooklyn, a small selection of his poems, which he called *Rhythms*. This little book appeared in 1918, and among the verses was "On One Whom the Germans Shot," lines inspired by Ezra Pound's memorial to his gifted friend, the sculptor Henri Gaudier-Brzeska, killed in battle in France in 1915:

> How shall we mourn you who are spilled and wasted,
> Gaudier-Brzeska,
> sure that you would not die with your work unended,
> as if the iron scythe in the grass stops for a flower?

When he reprinted the poem in 1920 he dropped the title, and in 1927 he dropped Gaudier-Brzeska's name, but the remaining lines (which Zukofsky praised in the February 1931 "Objectivists' Issue" of *Poetry*) are evidence of the thoughts of death which were haunting so many young men like Reznikoff during the war. His work, too, might be "unended," Reznikoff felt, but he was determined that, unlike his maternal grandfather's verse, it would not be unprinted. The book also contained the brilliant short poem beginning "I step into the fishy pool"—in 1918 titled "The Suicide"; in its pacing and sharp clarity of image, in its use of line breaks, it is characteristic of his most mature work. (In all later printings, that is from 1920 on, he wisely dropped the title, and indeed as a general rule from 1927 on Reznikoff left his poems untitled.) Reznikoff lived long enough to see this book

of twenty-three poems, like others of his early works, bring high prices from rare-book dealers.

The training in law marked a decisive turn in his career. By his own account, he had learned to apply the methods of close reading of case books and judicial decisions he had acquired in law school to his own work and to the work of others. Under the sobering influence of the law, he learned to deflate his own romantic rhetoric and, in general, to become much more critical of both himself and others. In this way he acquired the habit, well worth his investment in his law education, of

> prying sentences open to look at the exact meaning:
> weighing words to choose only those that had meat
>   for my purpose
> and throwing the rest away as empty shells.

He lost what literary self-complacency might have come with Harriet Monroe's acceptance of two of his poems in her prestigious *Poetry: A Magazine of Verse*, published in Chicago, when his work was criticized by a friend "Al" (Al Lewin) who was studying Shakespeare with Kittredge at Harvard: "most, if not all, that had seemed good to me/now had the dead sound of a counterfeit coin/on his marble good sense." In his newfound self-critical frame of mind he revised the poems, but Harriet Monroe rejected his revisions and offered some revisions of her own, which Reznikoff strongly disliked. In the end, he withdrew his poems from *Poetry:* "for the judgment of the editor . . ./I had, by this time,/little respect," and he determined on private publication, the form he would come to like best. What he learned from law and from Al Lewin, he wrote more than fifty years later in "Early History of a Writer," was that

> I, too, could scrutinize every word and phrase
> as if in a document or the opinion of a judge
> and listen, as well, for tones and overtones,
> leaving only the pithy, the necessary, the clear and
>   plain.

The law did more than chasten his style; it also appealed to his imagination as he reflected upon the contrast afforded between his quiet classroom and study and the noisy bustle of the street below, and the worry and noise of his parents' shop; what he found was the abstract depersonalization of the language in law, and he was caught up in the play of reason underlying the anguish, the temper, the fear, anxiety, and pleasure of human endeavor:

all the blood—the heartache and the heartening—
    gone out of the words
and only, as a pattern for thinking,
the cool bones of the judge's reasoning.

Abjuring the deliquescent sentiments and soft, imprecise, impressionistic verbiage characteristic of much of the work of the mauve decade, which had once appealed to him and which he had tried to imitate, he now appreciated

    the plain sunlight of the cases,
    the sharp prose,
    the forthright speech of the judges.

His great pleasure—he calls it "delightful" in "Early History of a Writer"—was in discovering how to puzzle through a judge's reasoning and "drag the meaning out of the shell of words": its great appeal was the appeal of "the clear waters of reason" and of using words for their clarity, not for their connotative value. So central did the bare statement of fact become, indeed, that he felt "no regret for the glittering words I had played with,"

    and only pleasure to be working with ideas—
    of rights and wrongs and their elements
    and of justice between men in their intricate affairs.

His delight in the law, indeed, was a delight in the ideal he found it embodied, of rights for individuals, of redress for suffering, of sympathy and practical help for the oppressed and the wronged, all couched in an objective, impersonal, dispassionate, uncluttered and *clear* language, expressing clear principles. It is intimately (and intricately, perhaps) connected with his poetry. At the same time, his devotion to scholarship (and to the study of law, which he impatiently lost interest in because his impulse to write was so strong) indirectly reconnected him to his Jewish heritage which he, and his brother, had rejected as teenagers. Marie Syrkin, whom he married in 1930, has said that he saw his own position as poet and scholar in the light of "a long Jewish tradition according to which a true scholar might spend his days in pious study," and that he "viewed his poetic avocation as a sacred study." The idealization of the law can be seen in the eloquent conclusion of *Rashi* (first published in 1925 and collected in 1927), his little play about a medieval scholar and commentator on the Bible:

Jacob is like the stars
Which rise to their station,

Which the winds cannot blow away
Nor clouds extinguish.
But we become names upon gravestones and upon
    books,
Our desire for the law an inheritance
Among our grandsons.
It was good to labor, and after labor
It was good to rest.

From 1918 on, he continued to write, and for a period he worked as a salesman for his parents' hat-manufacturing business. By and large, however, his life was quiet and uneventful, for he was determined to dedicate his life to his writing. Living in New York almost without interruption, he worked as a free-lance writer, editor, and translator only enough to meet his modest needs and walked the streets and bridges of New York (in his early years as much as twenty miles a day, in his later years six). In his first novel, *By the Waters of Manhattan* (1930), he called walking "that sober dance which despite all the dances man knows, he dances most"; on his walks he always carried his small notebook to jot down lines that occurred to him, things that he saw.

In 1919 he printed on his press another selection of his poems, *Rhythms II*. It is not clear how much, if any, public attention these poems brought him; certainly neither of them was reviewed. That they caught at least one pair of eyes, however, is indicated by the fact that, in 1920, a volume of his poems appeared under modest but commercial auspices. The publisher was Samuel Roth, a bookseller who owned The Poetry Book Shop in Greenwich Village. In his 1930 memoir, Roth indicated that, despite his own admiration for Reznikoff's poetry, the book's sales were insignificant. Roth's enthusiasm was expressed in hyperbolic terms: "I have for a long time been under the impression that in his way [Reznikoff] was doing the only fruitful literary work in America. . . . Indeed, he forms today, in my vision, a solitary lagoon on the vast empty sea of American literary enterprise. . . ." Reviews were mixed. The *Sunday Call*, looking forward to a more substantial later collection, called the work "promising shavings"; Elias Lieberman, in the *American Hebrew*, called himself "a friendly critic" and the book "sordid, with the emphasis on the *sore*"; nevertheless, he said, "there is a wealth of memorable phrases and images in this volume"; the *Dial* gave it a brief but favorable mention, and all the reviews stressed the fragmentary nature of the book. Malcolm Cowley, in the *New York Evening Post*, attacked Reznikoff as "astigmatic. He is unable to focus, and lines of splendid verse are lost to sight among low heaps of rubbish," but he also asserted that Reznikoff "has seen visions, and . . . this, and not the ability to write perfect iambs, is the essence of a poet." As the 1920s progressed, Reznikoff was increasingly able to publish his work in magazines such as the *Menorah Journal,* and *New Palestine:* in the early 1930s he would also be publishing in *Contempo* and *Poetry.*

The publication of *Uriel Accosta: A Play, and a Fourth Group of Verse* in 1921 was followed in 1922 by a collection of playlets, *Chatterton, The Black Death, and Meriweather Lewis.* The form of these, according to Reznikoff, was inspired by the example of the contemporary German expressionist drama being produced in the Weimar Republic, but especially the work of Georg Kaiser. In 1923 he published *Coral, and Captive Israel: Two Plays,* and in 1927, when he met Marie Syrkin, a struggling writer and editor who taught in a New York high school (she was a traditional poet), he was living on a regular allowance of twenty-five dollars a week for his past labors for the family business, and was writing full-time. That year he published *Nine Plays* which collected the previously published plays and added three others (*Abram in Egypt, Rashi,* and *Genesis*), in an edition of 400 copies. The plays, with such heroes as Chatterton, Uriel Accosta, Meriweather Lewis, and Rashi, fill only 113 pages of verse: one friend described them as "dramas with all the interesting parts left out": all of his subjects are historical, and, as Tom Sharp has observed, explore "the difficulties of being true to oneself, one's God, one's family, one's art, one's country, and one's fellow man."

The year 1927 was fruitful for Reznikoff: in that year he also published *Five Groups of Verse* and *By the Waters of Manhattan: An Annual,* a book which he hoped would be the first of a yearly series. It is almost unclassifiable, for it contains a family memoir in prose which purports to be by his mother, but is in fact by Reznikoff, and a series of verse reworkings of Old Testament sources which he called "Editing and Glosses." The book was seminal for Reznikoff, for in the prose he began a work which, after much revision and transformation, would become *Family Chronicle* (1963), and in the verse, he began an activity—the exploration and reworking of his Jewish and biblical heritage—which would occupy much of his later life (these are the works he called "Glosses"). In the *Boston Evening Transcript* for 3 July 1927 W. R. B. (perhaps William Rose Benét) commented that in *Five Groups of Verse* Reznikoff accurately portrays that "seared

and disillusioned humanity which, rightly or not, we associate with the ghetto" and complained that all too frequently the poems lack development: "Most poets do not know when to leave off; by contrast, Mr. Reznikoff does not know when to go on!" Reviewers ignored *By the Waters of Manhattan: An Annual.*

In 1930 he married Marie Syrkin, who was supporting herself and her three-year-old son by teaching high school, a job she detested. Since her income, as she put it in her memoir of Charles, "just about covered my annual expenses" they agreed "lightheartedly that since he had enough income to meet his share—the $25 a week—we would set up housekeeping." They were helped considerably in their plans to marry by Charles Boni's publication of Reznikoff's novel *By the Waters of Manhattan* (1930), with an introduction by the prominent anthologist and critic Louis Untermeyer. Reznikoff received $1,000 from Boni, but shortly after their marriage, in the Depression following the Wall Street crash, the Reznikoff family business failed, and Charles lost his $25-a-week allowance. Reznikoff was thus obliged, after his fruitful years as a full-time writer, to find a job, and he went to work for the publishing firm that produced *Corpus Juris,* which he described as "an encyclopedia of law for lawyers." His job was to analyze law cases and summarize their essentials in a prescribed form. Although he used his legal training in this job, he seems at first to have found it as dispiriting as being a hat salesman (an experience he incorporated into his novel *The Manner "Music"*), but eventually he found in this literary hackwork the materials he needed for *Testimony.* The challenge of combining his vocation with his avocation (to paraphrase Robert Frost) is described in these lines, which he wrote around that time:

> After I had worked all day at what I earn my living,
> I was tired. Now my work has lost another day
> I thought, but began slowly,
> and slowly my strength came back to me.
> Surely the tide comes in twice a day.

The job took up so much of his energy and time that it was 1934 before he published any more books. It is, then, perhaps fortunate that the job failed, for he was too scrupulous in his work. Marie Syrkin records that one well-disposed supervisor admonished him that "when I hire a carpenter I don't want a cabinet-maker," and after a couple of years he was fired because he would not write up the cases fast enough or in proper legal jargon. By

Charles Reznikoff in New York, 1934

this time, however, his parents had settled their financial difficulties, and Charles could make enough money to meet his own needs in occasional free-lance work.

With the 1930 publication of his novel *By the Waters of Manhattan* he acquired something of a reputation as a writer, but once again, Reznikoff's work failed to make a commercial impact (the great success that year, which made use in more sensational fashion of similar immigrant experience, was Michael Gold's *Jews Without Money*), but it did score something of a succès d'estime. Leonard Ehrlich (the author of *God's Angry Man*, a novel about John Brown) reviewed it favorably in the *Saturday Review of Literature*, and Lionel Trilling wrote in the *Menorah Journal:* "Mr. Reznikoff's work is remarkable and original in American literature," and described his prose style as "of the greatest delicacy and distinction."

By 1928, according to Mary Oppen's *Meaning: A Life* (1978), Reznikoff had met fellow-poets Louis Zukofsky and George Oppen, and by 1931 they had become known, with Carl Rakosi, as the principal members of the Objectivist group of poets. February 1931 saw the appearance of the well-

known "Objectivist Issue" of *Poetry*, guest-edited by Louis Zukofsky at the suggestion of Ezra Pound. Zukofsky not only included poems by Reznikoff (his first appearance in *Poetry*) but made him the principal subject of his lengthy essay on "Sincerity and Objectification," which set forth in somewhat cloudy language what Zukofsky saw as the theory of the new movement, and which singled out Reznikoff's work for special praise. (Reznikoff himself suggested that the most accurate description of the group's aims was the simple "writers publishing their own work.") The so-called Objectivist Issue of *Poetry* (it was never officially or formally so titled) was followed up by Zukofsky's *An "Objectivists" Anthology* (1932), which was published in France by George and Mary Oppen's To, Publishers, a new venture which they hoped would be the vehicle not only for books by members of the group but also of major work by Ezra Pound and William Carlos Williams, both members of the group's "advisory board." The Oppens' venture failed, however (it did publish a book by Williams and a book by Pound, as well as Zukofsky's anthology), and Zukofsky, Oppen, and Reznikoff (principally bankrolled by Williams and with Zukofsky as treasurer and secretary and with the interested but geographically distant help of Carl Rakosi) set up the Objectivist Press, which was to be Reznikoff's principal publisher for a brief but important period. In 1934 the Objectivist Press published three titles by Reznikoff: *Testimony* (a prose work), *Jerusalem the Golden*, and *In Memoriam: 1933*, and in 1936 it published his selection of poems, *Separate Way*. The year 1936 also saw Reznikoff print, on the press which was now in the basement of his sister's house, the prose memoir *Early History of a Sewing-Machine Operator*, on which he collaborated closely with his father, Nathan. His sister's basement, incidentally, became the warehouse for the books published by the Oppens in France.

Testimony is a collection of sparse, brief prose narratives, drawn from law records; in his introduction to the book Kenneth Burke said that "in a direct style that frequently helps us to realize what Stendhal had in mind when expressing his enthusiasm for the Code Napoleon as a way of statement, he can contrive by a few hundred 'factual' words to stir our feelings and memories." But the book got a mixed reception, as did *Jerusalem the Golden*. T. C. Wilson, in *Poetry* (September 1934), compared Reznikoff to Williams and found his poetry to be "essentially insignificant" because "what he sees he presents clearly and concisely. But he does not see enough"; Kenneth Alling, in *Commonweal*, said that

Testimony offers "an inner revealment, . . . something incisive and profound," while *Jerusalem the Golden* has "in addition to . . . clarity, also a mystical, clairvoyant quality." Like other reviewers before them, both Wilson and Alling noted Reznikoff's selectivity, arrangement of details, and extreme understatement, qualities which are characteristic of Reznikoff's work throughout his career and which are particularly evident in his late and major works, based in part on what he learned in writing *Testimony*: the two-volume *Testimony: The United States, 1885-1915: Recitative* and *Holocaust.*

In the years after he left *Corpus Juris* Reznikoff had worked as a free-lance editor, translator, and writer, producing an occasional article in order to get enough money to scrape by. On 12 February 1937 his mother died of cancer at the age of sixty-eight, and Reznikoff memorialized her in one of his most moving sequences, the eleven poems of "Kaddish," dedicated "to the memory of Sarah Yetta Reznikoff" and published in *Going To and Fro and Walking Up and Down* (1941). Some time shortly after her death (the date is not exactly clear) Reznikoff's friend Al Lewin, a producer at Paramount Studios in Hollywood, employed Reznikoff as his personal assistant at a salary of seventy-five dollars a week. Separated from Marie (who stayed behind in New York) he wrote to her frequently, sending her the poems he wrote while away. Some of these are collected in the sequence "Autobiography: Hollywood," published in *Going To and Fro and Walking Up and Down.* This, with his posthumously published novel *The Manner "Music,"* which he seems to have written during the 1950s, gives a vivid and poignant depiction of his West Coast experience. He stayed in Hollywood for a little less than three years (Marie spent two summers with him) and then returned to New York, where he went back to his life of free-lance writing.

Reznikoff would not publish another book of verse until 1959. In 1944 the Jewish Publication Society of America published his historical novel about medieval England's expulsion of its Jewish population, *The Lionhearted.* The 1940s were not a happy period for the Reznikoffs—Marie and Charles slowly growing estranged, but neither wanting a divorce. The domestic dilemma was solved in 1950 when she got a job in the English department at the newly established Brandeis University in Waltham, Massachusetts, and Charles agreed to maintain the $60-a-month flat on Eighteenth Street in Manhattan. They would henceforth spend most weekends and all holidays together in New York. Charles took on a number

of projects that provided him with a living; the results of these activities include *The Jews of Charleston: A History of an American Jewish Community* (1950), on which he collaborated with Uriah Z. Engelman; his translation from the German of I. J. Benjamin's account *Three Years in America, 1859-1862* (1956); and an edition of the public papers of Louis Marshall (1957).

By the time the Louis Marshall papers were published, Marie Syrkin was editor of the *Jewish Frontier,* which she describes as "a Labor Zionist monthly with much ideology and little money." As she put it in her brief memoir of Charles, "fortuitously, the only paid employee, the managing editor who ran the magazine in New York, left for richer pastures. My comrades agreed that . . . Charles could be entrusted with the post just vacated. Fear of nepotism made me slash the original stipend radically, but eventually the $100 a week . . . was restored." Though he hated the work (he despised journalism), he was meticulous in its execution and in addition undertook to write the history of the Jewish community in Cleveland: while continually fretting over the time it took and the distraction it was from his poetry, Reznikoff nevertheless labored over this abortive project, eventually turning out, instead of the sociological and historical prose the project's sponsors expected, disparate bits of more-or-less anecdotal information "in neat strips pasted in horizontal and vertical rows."

In 1959 Reznikoff printed a book of poems called *Inscriptions: 1944-1956,* a collection of fifty-nine poems arranged in seven untitled groups. The poem later titled "Te Deum" is thoroughly characteristic not simply of his mature lyrical work, but even of his earliest work at its best:

> Not because of victories
> I sing,
> having none,
> but for the common sunshine,
> the breeze,
> the largess of the spring.
>
> Not for victory
> but for the day's work done
> as well as I was able;
> not for a seat upon the dais
> but at the common table.

The rhythms of these lines (which flow together naturally with their sense and are not determined mechanically by a metronome, in Pound's phrase), the cunningly devised rhyme scheme (victories/breeze; sing/spring; none/done; able/table), the assonance of *day's* and *dais*, and perhaps above all the rocklike democratic faith (shared with Whitman and Dickinson) that its human center is to be found everywhere and its circumference nowhere—all of these elements combine to make a poem memorable as an affirmation of the essential significance and importance of every single human life. It is this unshakable faith that Whitman called "the antiseptic of the soul," and it is certainly the faith of Reznikoff: it informs and sweetens even his most seemingly bitter works.

In 1962 New Directions and the *San Francisco Review* jointly published a selection of Reznikoff's previously published poetry under the by-then-familiar title *By the Waters of Manhattan*. Reviewing this volume for the *Nation*, Hayden Carruth, "captivated, enthralled, swept away.... Delighted, awed, roused," said that "I cannot exaggerate the degree of my enthusiasm for this book" and commended it for the depth of its knowledge of New York and for the depth of its Jewishness. "When you buy this book," he advised the *Nation*'s readers,

"tear out the three pages of introduction by C. P. Snow." For this book Reznikoff was awarded the Harry and Florence Kovner Memorial Award for poetry in English by the Jewish Book Council of America in 1963. In that year, too, he privately published *Family Chronicle*, which was republished in 1969 in England and in 1971 in New York with an introduction by Harry Golden. *Family Chronicle*, a memoir purportedly by Sarah Reznikoff ("Early History of a Seamstress"), Nathan Reznikoff ("Early History of a Sewing-Machine Operator"), and Reznikoff himself ("Needle Trade," first published in part in *Commentary* in 1951), and heavily revised by Reznikoff after his parents' death, is (in the words of Eric Homberger) "among the most vivid of memoirs from the lower East Side." Along with *The Manner "Music"* and many of his poems, it testifies to the strong autobiographical impulse in Reznikoff and at the same time is an important document in the history of that generation of Jewish immigrants who entered the United States after 1880.

In 1965 New Directions published *Testimony:*

Mary Oppen, George Oppen, and Charles Reznikoff in San Francisco

The United States, 1885-1890: Recitative. Geoffrey Wolff in the *Washington Post* (9 November 1965) was impressed with the "muscularity of verbs" and Reznikoff's "lyric sadness." He called *Testimony* "as inevitable as the tale Cassandra foretold, and as moving, too," but what other reviews there were were generally unfavorable. While calling the poem "unique in the history of American literature," James Schevill judged in the *San Francisco Chronicle* that it is "dramatically too bare. The language becomes more sparse than illuminating." William Dickey accused the book of "a very simplistic kind of moral perspective indeed," and Hayden Carruth said that the "cold, neutral language" makes *Testimony* "uninteresting" and "lifeless." New Directions as a result dropped its options on the sequel volumes and indeed on any of Reznikoff's future works; he was thus driven to publish the second volume of *Testimony: The United States, 1891-1900: Recitative* himself, in 1968. The final installments, covering the period 1901-1915, did not appear until the posthumous publication of the complete edition in 1978-1979. Yet *Testimony* is, with *Holocaust* (1975), Reznikoff's major work. Drawing on legal records of the various sections of the United States between the years 1885 and 1915 (Reznikoff said he had read "thousands" of such cases), the poem dispassionately, in a minimum of words, generally with all names and hence personality and individuality removed, records accident, injustice, disaster: Reznikoff's great concern for man's inhumanity to man, and for sheer ill-fortune, makes *Testimony* both a painful book to read and at the same time a profoundly moving assertion of human worth, dignity, nobility, and promise. With the exception of *Holocaust*, it has no parallel in American writing. As Elaine Feinstein wrote in the English journal *PN Review:* "his training as a lawyer taught him there was a continuity in human suffering, and a terribly arbitrary quality in it. . . . Suffering is not only a question of violence; for Reznikoff it is often most deeply a matter of waste."

In 1966 Marie Syrkin retired from Brandeis as Emeritus Professor, and the couple moved into the luxury of a twenty-fourth-floor apartment in Lincoln Towers in Manhattan: "we had a marvellous view of the Hudson," she recalls, "air-conditioning, and a multitude of doormen." Ironically enough, on an early morning walk along Riverside Drive soon after the move, he was attacked by two youths who blackjacked him unconsciousness: he lost his wallet, containing about a dollar, but his glasses were unbroken. After the stitches were removed and he resumed his habit of walking in the city, a major problem was where he could safely go: such diminution of his lifelong habit was an impoverishment he resented.

In 1969 he printed two collections of poetry which he published in one volume: *By the Well of Living and Seeing, and The Fifth Book of the Maccabees;* and in 1971 Reznikoff received the Morton Dauwen Zabel Award from the National Institute of Arts and Letters. In 1974 the Black Sparrow Press brought out his *By the Well of Living & Seeing: New & Selected Poems, 1918-1973*, and the following year Black Sparrow published *Holocaust*, a book which in some sense he had been preparing for all his career, though it was written at his wife's urging. Adopting the techniques he had used so successfully in *Testimony*, Reznikoff mined the Nuremberg Trials and the Eichmann Trial for a bare and appalling narrative of the Nazi extermination of European Jewry. Though he had previously written frequently and movingly about Jewish history, in this book he would permit himself no subjective outcry: the record must speak for itself. As Daniel Lehman commented in *Poetry* (April 1976), "Reznikoff opens the mouth of suffering, and makes it quiver with the voice of survival, a voice capable of the real and tough affirmation implicit in the struggle not at all to sweeten up the story while making it 'literature.' "

Holocaust was to be Reznikoff's final stand as a moral witness, for, following a heart seizure at the apartment where he had dwelt with Marie for ten years, he died at St. Vincent's hospital shortly before dawn the next morning, 22 January 1976. He was buried in the Old Mount Carmel Cemetery in Brooklyn, and a line from the opening section of "Heart and Clock" (1936) was incised on his tombstone: " . . . and the day's brightness dwindles into stars." The poem from which it is taken is especially apt as a memorial for a poet whose sense of his calling made him always conscious of the passage of time.

> Now the sky begins to turn upon its hub—
> the sun; each leaf revolves upon its stem;
>
> now the plague of watches and of clocks nicks away
> the day—
> ten thousand steps
> tread upon the dawn;
> ten thousand wheels
> cross and criss-cross the day
> and leave their ruts across its brightness
>
> the clocks
> drip

in every room—
our lives are leaking from the places,
and the day's brightness dwindles into stars.

Poems, 1918-1936, volume 1 of *The Complete Poems of Charles Reznikoff*, in the press at the time of his death, was published later that year, and the next year Black Sparrow Press brought out *Poems, 1937-1975*, volume 2 of *The Complete Poems of Charles Reznikoff* and his novel *The Manner "Music."* In 1978 and 1979 the complete version of *Testimony: The United States, 1885-1915* was at last published, and only his plays remain uncollected.

Among Reznikoff's papers at his death was found a 30 March 1948 letter from William Carlos Williams, who wrote: "A confession and an acknowledgement! In all the years that I have owned a book of yours, nineteen years! a book you gave me in 1929, I never so much as opened it—except to look at it cursorily. And now, during an illness, I have read it and I am thrilled with it and in this Flossie, who has read it also, gladly joins me. You know, of course, that it is *By the Waters of Manhattan* of which I am speaking. Why have you not gone on writing? Why do you not start again now? This book has so much in it that marks you as a first rate artist that it is shameful of you not to have persisted. It is not by any means too late. . . . I'm ashamed never to have read your book! It took an illness at that even now to make me do it. Such has been my life and I find that I was the loser for it not you—as too often happens when we are neglectful of others, we are the sufferers, not they. . . ."

Of course, Reznikoff never did stop writing as Williams feared he had. Even when the world seemed completely unmindful of him, he went about the work which he had come to do. After Reznikoff's death in 1976, the poet Robert Creeley could still write sensitively in a tone that is reminiscent of Williams's: "One had not known, sadly, that Charles Reznikoff wrote novels. That a man should have such quiet and singular genius so modestly put aside (by himself) is regrettable. So much does shout at us, belligerently claiming attention for its style or its intelligence or its newness. . . ." These words are from Creeley's introduction to Reznikoff's posthumously published novel *The Manner "Music,"* the tragic and triumphant tale of a composer to whose music, no one—not even his wife or his closest friend—had learned really to listen. It is a parable to end all others about the fate of modern art and modern literature. Oliver St. John Gogarty noted that the typical modern

writer was doomed to go on talking to himself but that it was left for James Joyce to go one step further and to talk to himself in his sleep in *Finnegans Wake*. It is this problematical situation which concerns Reznikoff in his last fiction, written in prose embedded with striking imagist and objectivist poetry.

On the death of Yeats in 1939, Auden wrote that, when he dies, the poet becomes his admirers. That is what has now happened to Reznikoff. He is no longer driven by the compulsion to create. It is not up to him now; it is up to those who are left behind and who think that they may have deciphered something of the meaning which he strove faithfully to create. The magnitude of the response to Reznikoff's death by at least one admiring reader may perhaps be indicated by the coupling of names which occurs in the title of a set of Allen Ginsberg's verses in his *Plutonium Ode*. He calls them "After Whitman and Reznikoff."

Interviews:

L. S. Dembo, "The Objectivist Poet: Four Interviews. Charles Reznikoff," *Contemporary Literature*, 10 (Spring 1969): 193-202;

Janet Sternburg and Alan Ziegler, "A Conversation with Charles Reznikoff," *Montemora*, 2 (Summer 1976): 113-121;

Charles Reznikoff and Reinhold Schiffer, "The Poet in his Milieu," in *Charles Reznikoff: Man and Poet*, edited by Milton Hindus (Orono, Maine: National Poetry Foundation, 1984), pp. 109-126.

References:

Hayden Carruth, "A Failure of Contempt," review of *Testimony: The United States, 1885-1890*, *Poetry*, 107 (March 1966): 396-397;

Carruth, "The Tide Comes In," review of *By the Waters of Manhattan: Selected Verse* and George Oppen's *The Materials*, *Nation*, 195 (10 November 1962): 312-313;

William Dickey, "The Thing Itself," review of *Testimony*, *Hudson Review*, 19 (1966): 146-155;

Robert Franciosi, "Charles Reznikoff's Privately-Printed Way," *Sagetrieb*, 4 (Spring 1985): 139-144;

Milton Hindus, *Charles Reznikoff: A Critical Essay* (Santa Barbara: Black Sparrow Press, 1977);

Hindus, ed., *Charles Reznikoff: Man and Poet* (Orono, Maine: National Poetry Foundation, 1984);

David Lehman, Review of *Holocaust*, *Poetry*, 128 (April 1976): 37-45;

Mary Oppen, *Meaning: A Life: An Autobiography* (Santa Barbara: Black Sparrow Press, 1978);

Harold Schimmel, "Historical Grit & Epic Gestation," *Sagetrieb*, 1 (Fall 1982): 220-224;

Kathryn Shevelow, "History and Objectification in Charles Reznikoff's Documentary Poems, *Testimony* and *Holocaust*," *Sagetrieb*, 1 (Fall 1982): 290-306;

Marie Syrkin, "Charles: A Memoir," in *Charles Reznikoff: Man and Poet*, pp. 37-67;

Louis Zukofsky, "Sincerity and Objectification. With Special Reference to the Work of Charles Reznikoff," *Poetry*, 37 (February 1931): 272-285.

Papers:
Reznikoff's papers are in the Archive for New Poetry, at the library of the University of California, San Diego.

Alan Seeger
(22 June 1888-4 July 1916)

James A. Hart
University of British Columbia

BOOKS: *Poems* (New York: Scribners, 1916; London: Constable, 1917);

Letters and Diary of Alan Seeger (New York: Scribners, 1917; London: Constable, 1917);

Lettres et poèmes écrits durant la guerre, réunis par son père, translated by Odette Raimondi (Paris: Payot et cie, 1918).

In the early years of World War I, Rupert Brooke achieved renown throughout the English-speaking world for his sonnet sequence "1914," in which he sang of his devotion to England in emotion-laden lines that possessed, it seemed to many wartime readers, an immortal beauty and permanent significance; England's handsome singer of romantic verse had been transformed by the crisis into a soldier poet. It was, therefore, a great tribute to Alan Seeger that he was called the American Rupert Brooke.

The title fitted him, albeit somewhat loosely, for unlike the "realistic" or antiwar poets of World War I, such as Siegfried Sassoon and Wilfred Owen, Seeger, like Brooke, adhered to the meters and diction of earlier poets and viewed the conflict in a romantic light: it was a crusade and a way of achieving a noble death. Enlisting in the French Foreign Legion in 1914, he expressed, to an unusual but not unique degree, the fervor of many who enlisted in that first year of World War I. Many of his poems are now, with justice, labeled second

rate, but as a manifestation of the idealism that swept over his generation, they deserve attention. Today, the reader—made skeptical of the ideals for which Seeger died by novels such as Hemingway's *A Farewell to Arms* (1929) and by the European powers' pursuit of national self-interest at Versailles—will find it difficult to sympathize with "I Have a Rendezvous with Death" or with the self-serving but sincere fatalism of "Maktoob." In addition, with poetic taste shaped by modernist critics, the reader today soon becomes aware of Seeger's frequent inability to overcome the tyranny of traditional meters and "poetic" phrases.

Despite Seeger's own welcoming, even seeking, of death on the battlefield, the fact is that Alan Seeger died too soon. There is evidence that he would have matured into a better poet. Even though his life included a multitude of experiences and hardships—the Legion and the trenches were harsh instructors—there was always something of the self-centered youth in his behavior, even when he was declaring his willingness to sacrifice his life for his ideals (for "Love and Arms and Song"). He needed more time to move from a stock and outmoded romanticism to a more distinctive and original style, from a style full of abstractions to one more concrete and personal. Ironically, in the light of his firsthand experience in frequent bloody encounters, as a member of the French Foreign Legion, there is a distancing, even a remoteness, in many of his poems and some of his letters and his diary; the literature of the past and his view of the rightful behavior for an aesthete and poet filtered and colored his recording of experiences.

His father, Charles Louis Seeger, and mother, Elsie Simmons Adams Seeger, were of New England ancestry. Alan Seeger, born in New York City on 22 June 1888, had an older brother, Charles, a noted musicologist and father of folksinger Pete Seeger, and a younger sister, Elizabeth. The three children, close in age, spent a spirited and cultured childhood in their home on Staten Island until 1900, when business took the family to Mexico. The romantic picturesqueness of that country is reflected in Seeger's early verse (such as "An Ode to Antares"). Pursuing the interests of an educated middle-class family with a literary bent, the family produced in Mexico a home magazine, the *Prophet*. In 1902 the boys were sent to the Hackley School in Tarrytown, New York. In their reminiscences, Elizabeth and Charles Seeger looked back fondly to their childhood. (Both thought that Alan Seeger's biographer, Irving Werstein, failed to capture the spirit of that time, though they thought the war years well treated.)

By the time Alan Seeger entered Harvard in 1906, he was already shaping his future: he was determined to pursue Beauty by writing poetry and by being a Poet. The emphasis he placed on the music of poetry may have resulted from the musical talent of the Seegers or from what he chose to appropriate from romantic poets and critics. Echoes of Walter Pater, Edgar Allan Poe, and William Gilmore Simms seem to lie behind some of Seeger's pronouncements. Although of the same Harvard generation as T. S. Eliot, Seeger's poetic tastes were quite different. In a term paper he wrote at Harvard he declared that only Laurence Hope would be remembered as a poet of the decade 1900-1910, and not as a result of his "formal excellence" but for the "passionate sincerity of the one signally romantic personality these years have given us."

For his first two years at Harvard, Seeger devoted much of his time to books, but during his upper-class years he participated more widely in Cambridge social life. His wide literary interests were displayed in his translations of Dante and Ariosto. In his last two years at Harvard he became one of the editors of the *Harvard Monthly* and contributed many poems.

After graduation with an A.B. in 1910, he went—to his father's disgust—to New York for two years in order to follow a poetic quest for beauty. These were his years as an American bohemian. Instead of following a career as his parents expected, he sought the enjoyment of the senses. The mind, he thought, had become too powerful.

Dissatisfied with an America unsympathetic, he thought, to the literary, bohemian life he wanted and helped financially by friends who believed in his poetic talent, he went to Paris. For two years, he enjoyed life among artists of the Latin Quarter and occasionally mixed in a more conventional society. Seeger became a devoted admirer of Paris. It was for him the home of the beautiful, even in its seamier areas. His Parisian experiences are embodied in some of his poems (such as "Paris"), and an actual love affair may have stimulated the writing of "Do You Remember Once . . ." ("And breast drew near to breast, and round its soft desire/My arm uncertain stole and clung there unrepelled") and "The Rendezvous," with its plaintive refrain, "She will not come, the woman that he waits." A serious relationship must have been the reason behind this laconic cablegram to his father, "If leave Paris married would you give position in Mexico [and] Passage. Alan."

Soon after the outbreak of war in August 1914, he enlisted, along with other Americans, in the French Foreign Legion. His enlistment did not spring from a hatred of Germany but from other

Alan Seeger

comes to mean to him simply the test of the most misery that the human organism can support." Nevertheless, there is recognition of war's misery and devastation in his poems, including "The Aisne (1914-15)":

> Winter came down on us. The low clouds, torn
> In the stark branches of the riven pines,
> Blurred the white rockets that from dusk till morn
> Traced the wide curve of the close-grappling
> lines.

Yet it is doubtful that an infantryman of 1914 or 1915 would recognize himself and his comrades in lines such as these, from "The Hosts":

> With bayonets and flags unfurled,
> They scaled the summits of the world
> And fade on the farthest golden height
> In fair horizons full of light.

His knowledge of the age of chivalry and his reading of Sir Philip Sidney, the English aesthetes, A. E. Housman, and Fitzgerald's *Rubaiyat* at times prevented him from presenting modern warfare in modern terms.

Having decided that war was the result of nature's inescapable laws and that destiny decides the outcome of all military engagements, Seeger glorified the battlefield. Even decaying human flesh did not dampen his enthusiasm: "I am very confident and sanguine about the result and expect to march right up to the Aisne, borne on an irresistible élan. I have been waiting for more than a year. It will be the greatest moment of my life," he wrote in his diary on 24 September 1915. He thrived on military life and, treasuring the comradeship, supposed or real, of the legionnaires (Victor Chapman spoke of Seeger's unpopularity because of his aloofness), he called fighting men "the hardy, the flower, the elite" ("The Hosts"). Civilians were to be scorned. "A Message to America" is a lively and bitter indictment of America for not coming to the defense of France.

If death came in battle, Seeger asserted, it was to be welcomed, even though it would rob him of the "delicious offerings" of life. Yet despite his frequent references to death, he gave no clear picture of what he expected in afterlife. In "Resurgam" the spirit returns somewhere beyond the grave to the earthly body, which had been and now would forever be "its loved abode."

Typical qualities of thought and phrasing are to be found in his best-known (but not best) poem,

grounds made clear in his letters: avid for adventure and excitement and possessing a deep-rooted fatalism, he was determined not to miss what others were experiencing. Furthermore, he had developed a deep love of France. Once in uniform, he felt himself in the grip of personified Destiny and History, and in poems such as "The Aisne (1914-15)" he viewed the campaigns from a high cosmic standpoint. But in commenting on the larger issues involved, he was so intent on setting the stage for his own performances that the campaigns sometimes appear to exist for his personal benefit. Some of his fellow legionnaires disliked his eagerness for danger and distrusted his wandering off alone to write poetry. One of them even thought he was a spy because of his solitary activities; others wanted him transferred because of his romantic attitude toward death in battle.

Since he viewed the conflict in heroic and idealized terms, and sought in his poetry to create the Beautiful, one does not often find in his war poems the description of war's ugliness and horror that one occasionally finds in his letters, where he says, for example, "Cramped quarters breed ill temper and dispute. . . . Cold, dirt, discomfort, . . . are ever present conditions, and the soldier's life

"I Have a Rendezvous with Death." The whole poem is concerned with his possible meeting with death; the meeting, indeed, is probable, since it has, it seems, been arranged by Death and the author. Although Death may take the speaker into "his dark land," the reader has no sense of horror or tragedy. Spring appears with its "rustling shade," perhaps in an implied contrast with the destruction of the battlefields (Seeger was sensitive to his natural surroundings). Then there are idyllic and lush references to human love to emphasize what the speaker is leaving behind ("Where Love throbs out in blissful sleep,/Pulse nigh to pulse, and breath to breath . . ."). Seeger's fatalism is felt from the opening line to the close: "And I to my pledged word am true,/I shall not fail that rendezvous." The union of fallen soldier and Death is, unfortunately, not based upon any profound philosophical or religious belief, but upon a vague romantic fusion of nature's beauty, sexual love, and life in some undefined other realm.

Seeger's "Ode in Memory of the American Volunteers Fallen for France" is less self-centered and flamboyant. While he still casts a romantic glow over the trenches, this treatment seems somewhat more acceptable in an ode written for public declamation in Paris and Washington on Decoration Day 1916. Furthermore, there are touches of realism that suggest a change in Seeger's poetic treatment of the war:

> And on the tangled wires
> The last wild rally staggers, crumbles, stops,
> Withered beneath the shrapnel's iron showers.

Nature is indifferent to the fallen, who are only "grim clusters under thorny trellises."

On 4 July 1916 Seeger was severely wounded in an attack on Belloy-en-Santerre. The next day he was found dead in a shell hole. Comrades praised his courage and he was posthumously awarded the Croix de Guerre and the Médaille Militaire.

The manner of his death brought forth many comments and reviews of his *Poems* (which were published in the year of his death). The *New York Times,* the *Boston Transcript,* and the *Nation,* for example, praised his work; the English *Poetry Review,* though qualified in its praise, saw great promise. Other publications such as the *Bookman* emphasized his conventional romanticism. It is worth noting, however, that his poems were very popular with the soldiers in the trenches as well as with public-library patrons at home.

Alan Seeger was a man who combined in an unusual degree a wide and deep love of chivalric and romantic literature with a desire to pursue a poetic quest for beauty in one of the most horrible and inhumane environments created by man: the trenches of the Western front. Much of his work, it is true, is derivative and too idealized for modern readers, but there is evidence to believe that he might have developed into a better poet.

In his second group of sonnets, opening lines remind the reader of Donne, Sidney, or Shakespeare, but they have their own liveliness: "Seeing you have not come with me, nor spent/This day's suggestive beauty as we ought" (sonnet five); "There have been times when I could storm and plead/But you shall never hear me supplicate" (sonnet seven). Sensuous and melodious descriptions are sometimes overdone, but in his poems of young, romantic love they seem more fitting. When he becomes scornful, the verse takes on a livelier tone and a fresher diction. In "A Message to America" he assails American isolationism in the early years of World War I:

> You have the grit and the guts, I know;
> You are ready to answer blow for blow,
> You are virile, combative stubborn, hard,
> But your honor ends with your own backyard.

Even if one denies the poetic promise, there remains the fascination of Seeger's life—the change from ostentatiously garbed would-be poet in Cambridge, Massachusetts, to sturdy, hardened legionnaire. The French recognized and appreciated his devotion to their country. Several French translations and tributes appeared in the years after his death, and even in the 1970s, a street in Biarritz was renamed in his honor. The 25 December 1916 order of the day of the Foreign Legion's Moroccan Division included a fitting epitaph for Seeger, which translates as follows: "He was a young legionnaire, enthusiastic and vigorous, who ardently loved France. He volunteered at the beginning of the war and displayed admirable spirit and courage during the campaign. He fell gloriously in battle on 4 July 1916."

Biography:

Irving Werstein, *Sound No Trumpet: The Life and Death of Alan Seeger* (New York: Crowell, 1967).

References:

Conrad Aiken, *Scepticisms: Notes on Contemporary Po-*

etry (New York: Knopf, 1919), pp. 133-135, 222;

William Archer, Introduction to *Poems* (New York: Scribners, 1916), pp. xi-xlvi;

Victor Emmanuel Chapman, *Victor Chapman's Letters from France*, with a memoir by John Jay Chapman (New York: Macmillan, 1917);

Claude de Heeckeren d'Anthès, *Alan Seeger; ou, Le réalisme divin* (Paris: Éditions de la Revue moderne, 1972);

M. A. de Wolfe Howe, *Memoirs of the Harvard Dead in the War against Germany*, volume I (Cambridge: Harvard University Press, 1920);

T. Sturge Moore, *Some Soldier Poets* (London: Richards, 1919), pp. 107-118;

Walter A. Roberts, "The Alan Seeger I Knew," *Bookman* (New York), 47 (August 1918): 585-590;

Paul Ayres Rockwell, *American Fighters in the Foreign Legion, 1914-1918* (Boston & New York: Houghton Mifflin, 1930).

Papers:
There are collections of Seeger's papers at the Houghton Library, Harvard University; the Library of Congress; and the New York Public Library.

Genevieve Taggard
(28 November 1894-8 November 1948)

Janet McCann
Texas A & M University

BOOKS: *For Eager Lovers* (New York: Selzer, 1922);

Hawaiian Hilltop (San Francisco: Wyckoff & Gelber, 1923);

Words for the Chisel (New York: Knopf, 1926);

Travelling Standing Still: Poems, 1918-1928 (New York: Knopf, 1928);

Monologue for Mothers (Aside) (New York: Random House, 1929);

The Life and Mind of Emily Dickinson (New York & London: Knopf, 1930; London: Allen & Unwin, 1930);

Remembering Vaughan in New England (New York: Arrow Editions, 1933);

Not Mine to Finish: Poems 1928-1934 (New York & London: Harper, 1934);

Calling Western Union (New York & London: Harper, 1936);

Collected Poems, 1918-1938 (New York & London: Harper, 1938);

Long View (New York & London: Harper, 1942);

A Part of Vermont (East Jamica, Vt.: River Press, 1945);

Slow Music (New York & London: Harper, 1946);

Origin: Hawaii, selected by Donald Angus (Honolulu: Angus, 1947).

OTHER: *Continent's End: An Anthology of Contemporary California Poets*, edited by Taggard, George Sterling, and James Rorty (San Francisco: Book Club of California, 1925);

May Days: An Anthology of Masses-Liberator Verse, 1912-1924, edited by Taggard (New York: Boni & Liveright, 1925);

Circumference: Varieties of Metaphysical Verse, 1456-1928, edited by Taggard (New York: Covici Friede, 1929);

Ten Introductions: A Collection of Modern Verse, edited by Taggard and Dudley Fitts (New York: Arrow Editions Co-operative Association, 1934).

PERIODICAL PUBLICATIONS: "These Modern Women: Poet Out of Pioneer," anonymous, *Nation*, 124 (19 January 1927): 63-65;

"Hawaii, Washington, Vermont," *Scribner's Magazine*, 94 (October 1934), 247-251.

Genevieve Taggard

NOTE: *The Complete Works of Genevieve Taggard* (3 reels, 1974) are available from University Microfilms.

Although Genevieve Taggard's poetry was well known in her time to both literary and popular audiences, her work as a poet is now largely forgotten, and she is best known as the author of *The Life and Mind of Emily Dickinson* (1930). A passionate, intuitive, and bold interpretation of the father-daughter relationship and of Dickinson's psychology, it proposed George Gould as Dickinson's mysterious lover and her father as a repressive villain. The book was based on Taggard's acquaintance with people who remembered Dickinson, reinforced with meticulous scholarship. It has since been superseded but was well received at the time. In addition to poetry and scholarly work, Taggard wrote short stories, reviews, essays, and articles on poetic theory. She edited literary journals and anthologies. Yet her first commitment was to the writ-

ing of poetry, and at her best, she produced some fine poems containing imagery still vivid today. Her writer friends included Wallace Stevens, who strongly influenced her work, especially her later poems. Yet Taggard's poems are only occasionally derivative, and her best poetry, on art, woman's experience, and social injustice, has much in common with the work of later poets such as Sylvia Plath and especially Adrienne Rich.

Taggard was born to Alta Gale Arnold Taggard and James Nelson Taggard, both schoolteachers in Waitsburg, Washington; the eldest of three children, she was the granddaughter of two Union soldiers. When she was two years old the family moved to Hawaii, where her parents served as missionaries for the fundamentalist Disciples of Christ. Her father built up a public school at Kalihiwaena, near Honolulu. She spent most of her childhood in Hawaii, where she grew up among her father's Hawaiian, Chinese, Japanese, and Portuguese students, and she developed a hearty dislike for American tourists. The Bible was the only book her parents allowed in the house ("I made Bible stories into fairy-tales," she wrote in 1927), but she read Keats and Ruskin secretly, and at school she learned Hawaiian legends. When the family returned to Waitsburg in 1905 (because her father was thought to have tuberculosis) one playmate told her, "Too bad you gotta be Haole [white]"—and later she wrote, "Off and on, I have thought so too, all my life." The family did not like Waitsburg, and in 1906 they returned to Hawaii, where they stayed until 1910, when James's ill-health once again drove them back to Waitsburg. They remained there, her father working a small pear farm for his brother, until 1912. The contrast between small-town rural America and the rich multiracial cosmopolitanism of Hawaii made a lasting impression on Genevieve: the cruel and brutal insensitivity she found in Waitsburg, where the Taggards lived the life of the rural poor, crystallized into a liberalism she later expressed through leftist poetry and commitment to liberal and proletarian causes. In 1934 she wrote that the Waitsburg years had been "the active source of my convictions. It told us what to work against and what to work for." It is quite possible that the family's financial history also contributed to her political and feminist convictions: after many years of saving, her parents had accumulated $2000, and it was earmarked to pay for Alta's college education, but when James's brother fell on hard times, the money went to him. With it he bought a farm in Waitsburg, became prosperous, but never repaid the loan: "my mother," Taggard later wrote, "went as nearly insane with rage as she could permit herself." Instead, he hired James, when he was forced to leave Hawaii, to work on his pear farm—and it was in those years that, in Genevieve's words, "used as my uncle's hired help and wearing his family's cast off clothing, we integrated ourselves into the single struggle to exist."

In 1906, when she was twelve, she entered the missionary Punahou school and began to write poetry; her first published poem, "Mitchie-Gawa" (about American Indians) appeared in the school magazine, the *Oahuan*, in 1910. In Waitsburg she was the editor of the high school paper, *Crimson and Gray*, and in 1914 (the year she became editor of the *Oahuan*) just three months before graduation, her father fell ill again and she took over his teaching at his school. The family moved back to California in the fall, and—with friends contributing $200 toward expenses, she entered the University of California at Berkeley. Since her father was now an invalid, she and her mother became (according to an account she published in 1927) servants in a boardinghouse for Berkeley students; her studies interrupted by work, she took six years to graduate. In her final year she became the salaried editor of the college literary magazine, the *Occident*. She studied poetry at Berkeley with Witter Bynner, and before her graduation she had become a socialist, familiar with radical-literary circles in San Francisco. "At the end of college," she told *Twentieth-Century Authors* (1942), "I called myself a Socialist in a rather vague way. Since then I have always been to the left of center. In those days Frank Norris and Jack London were still heard of as friends of friends. The great city of San Francisco taught me a good deal that I needed to know."

After she graduated from Berkeley in 1920, Max Eastman (editor of the radical *Liberator*) arranged a job for her on the *Freeman* and she moved to New York. In November 1915 the San Francisco magazine *Overland* had published her poem "Lani," and in December 1919 *Harper's* had published her poem "An Hour on the Hill"; once in New York she began publishing her work in such magazines as *Nation* and *Poetry*, and in such journals as *Liberator*. The job with the *Freeman* did not materialize, and she worked for the avant-garde publisher B. W. Huebsch. On 21 March 1921 she married Robert L. Wolf, a writer, and the following year she bore her only child, Marcia Sarah. Also in 1921, she joined with Maxwell Anderson and Padraic Colum to found and edit the *Measure: A Magazine of Verse*, which rapidly became quite prestigious but

folded in 1926. In 1922 her first book, *For Eager Lovers*, was published. Reviewing it for the *Bookman*, Grace Conkling called Taggard "genuinely original in her musical effects. Her imagination is to be trusted"; and Louis Untermeyer, in the *Literary Review*, praised the book highly: "It is a woman speaking; straightforward, sensitive, intense. Instead of loose philosophizing there is a condensed clarity; instead of rhetoric we have revelation." Mark Van Doren, in the *Nation*, said that this first volume "places her among the considerable poets of contemporary America."

The collection consists mostly of rhymed, personal poems about love and nature. A few, such as "Thirst," come close to the imagism of H. D. (Hilda Doolittle), and others, such as "Twentieth Century Slave Gang," look forward to the theme of social injustice which dominates so many of her later poems. The most ambitious poem in the collection is "Ice Age," a long poem which employs rhymed lines of uneven lengths to describe the end of the world. The poem is at times sharp and focused, and at others vague and sensuous. Although *For Eager Lovers* is not particularly memorable, it is notable for its relative lack of sentimentality, its uniformly high level of craftsmanship, and its occasional clear, sharp images.

In the 1920s she and Wolf both served as contributing editors to *New Masses*, but in a 1927 symposium Taggard expressed her uneasiness with pressures to join the proletarian cause. No doubt her experience, in childhood and youth, of intense sectarianism and of the social pressures inevitably attendant on the embracing of a "cause" led her to back off: hers was an independent cast of mind and personality.

Genevieve Taggard's poems were praised by such well-known writers as Edmund Wilson and Allen Tate, but they were often disparaged by the popular press. Her poems tend to reflect the best and worst of the intellectual currents of their times: the lyricism, focus on art, and concern for the image of the 1920s and the 1930s social conscience and sense of place—but they make strongly individual statements as well. From her first poems published in the 1910s and 1920s to her last work in the 1940s, her writing evolved through a series of roughly defined stages, from rhymed poems of nature and love, through protest poetry, to the often experimental poems she wrote in the 1940s about art and women's experience. However, social protest was her overriding concern and it was her protest poetry which was most likely to draw unfavorable criticism from the popular press. *Time*, for instance, once described it as the work of a "worried, earnest, political nondescript."

Hawaiian Hilltop (1923), a small pamphlet of poems that show Taggard's development of a sense of place, was followed in 1926 by *Words for the Chisel*, her first book to be widely read and reviewed with favorable notices in national and popular literary journals. At the time she was working on *Words for the Chisel* she had made some important changes in her life, and investigated and developed major sources: in 1922 she and her husband had spent a year in San Francisco, where she gave courses in poetry and helped edit an anthology of California poems, *Continent's End*, in which she called for more honest involvement in social issues, and less artistic detachment amongst regional writers. In 1923 they had settled in New Preston, Connecticut, and 1925 saw the publication of her anthology *May Days*, drawn from the pages of *New Masses* and the *Liberator*. Some of the poems in *Words for the Chisel* contain strong images from Taggard's Hawaiian childhood, while others deal with social inequities. The collection includes a number of sparse, eco-

nomical poems about love and art. There is a passional and political restraint in this collection not found in the earlier ones, and the intellectual range is wider, although some of the poems are flawed by that very detachment Taggard criticized in *Continent's End*. Katherine Anne Porter, herself politically sympathetic to Taggard's position, wrote in the *New York Herald Tribune* (18 April 1926) that "this is poetry to be read for its own sake"; Joseph Auslander, in the *New York World*, talked of the "sovereign and dextrous craftsmanship"; and Allen Tate, in the 28 April 1926 issue of the *Nation*, praised the work as "intelligently sustained." He went on: "The artistic aim indicated by the title . . . would be pretentious, if it were not accurately realized. Only with excessive zeal could one discover a single failure in her three volumes of poetry." But he then sounded a note which would recur throughout Taggard's career, and possibly haunt her: "It is unfortunately true . . . that she has not yet produced a single perfect utterance." This is a remark that Leo Kennedy would echo in 1946, reviewing *Slow Music* in *Book Week:* "There is not a bad poem in the book . . . but it is like a shop window full of everything from children's toys to bull fighting equipment to hardware and tourist travel literature. I think that what I am regretting is the absence of a unified sensibility in these fine poems." *Words for the Chisel* shows development and redirection of Taggard's poetic skill, which perhaps did not reach its peak until after she had left New York.

Travelling Standing Still (1928), a selection of previously published poems, brought further critical acclaim (though again with reservations about the focus or unity of her career) from such critics as William Rose Benét and Edmund Wilson. Between the publication of this book and the appearance of her next major collection, *Not Mine to Finish* (1934), Taggard produced two brief pamphlets, *Monologue for Mothers (Aside)* (1929) and *Remembering Vaughan in New England* (1933), each containing a single poem, as well as her widely praised biography of Emily Dickinson, published in 1930. *Travelling Standing Still* was a turning point in her career, because for the first time (though she had had favorable reviews before) she was being taken seriously by the major critics of her time.

Not Mine to Finish: Poems 1928-1934 (1934) was published several years after Taggard had left New York City. In 1929, after a year in Southern France, she moved to New England, where she taught at Mount Holyoke College for the 1929-1930 academic year. A Guggenheim award in 1931

Genevieve Taggard

took her to Capri and Majorca with her daughter and sister; from 1932 to 1935 she was teaching at Bennington College in Vermont, going on to Sarah Lawrence College, where she remained on the faculty until 1946. In 1934 she was divorced from Wolf, and on 10 March 1935 she married Kenneth Durant, who worked for Tass, the Soviet news agency. She bought a farm, Gilfeather, at East Jamaica, Vermont, a few miles south of her grandfather's home town of Londonderry. No farmer, she settled into a life of teaching and observing—and writing. *Not Mine to Finish* comes from an eventful and possibly an optimistic period in her life. The poems in this collection—often discursive, philosophical discussions of the relationship between the mind and the world, art and life—look forward to Wallace Stevens's poems of the late 1940s in technique and diction. "Evening Love-of-Self," a long poem (twenty-five pages of text) about a rural woman who desperately scans nature for signs of some vital connection with the self, is filled with parables, shifts in point of view, repetitions; its tone is flat and declarative and is suggestive of Stevens's later poems "An Ordinary Evening in New Haven" and parts of his "Esthetique du Mal."

> a skeleton
> Sitting like a stiff doll on its haunch against a stone
>   wall.
> All summer the fruit swung ripe before the eye-sockets
> And at last fell in purple rot coloring the bones.

The lesson she receives is told simply:

> And when she found this melodrama of bones,
> She laughed. Told no one. Ran the whole way home.
> And that night had no dreams. Death concise and
>   belittled.

The woman's search for a vital link with nature is balanced by her desire not to be absorbed by it, and she ends her reverie as isolated as she begins. The poem is a concrete and complex analysis of the division between the mind and the world, and of the mind's longing for and fear of union. A far less ambitious but equally satisfying poem in the collection is "American Farm, 1934," which may have been influenced by Stevens's poems about trash and dumps but contains Taggard's own strong ideas and images. The farm is a derelict, the place of

> The hard odd thing surviving precariously, once of
>   some value
> Brought home bright from the store in manila paper,

> Now under the foot of the cow, caught in a crevice.
> . . . .
> Edge of a dress, wrappings of contraceptives, trinkets,
> Fans spread, sick pink, a skillet full of mould.
> . . . .

The long list of particulars prepares for the generalization that "Implacable divine rubbish prevails."

On the whole, the book was favorably received, although it was more highly praised for the more conventional pieces than for the complex, experimental ones. William Rose Benèt, who had admired Taggard's earlier work, wrote in the *Saturday Review of Literature* (10 November 1934) that "Her mind is subtle, but . . . she eliminates too much in expressing her thought." Others praised her "lyricism" but said little about her subjects.

At the time she wrote *Not Mine to Finish*, Taggard was fascinated by New England, which seemed to her to exemplify the best America had to offer. In contrast to New York, Vermont seemed unspoiled and humane. But two years later she had changed her mind. Instead of opportunity for self-realization amid natural beauty, New England came to mean exploitation and injustice. After witnessing the treatment of workers involved in the Vermont quarry workers' strike, she wrote in the introduction to *Calling Western Union*:

> I was wrong about Vermont. At first it looked to me the way it looks to the summer visitor who goes up there to get a rest. And then the facts contradicted my hope. I saw canned wood-chuck in the farmers' cellars. . . . I knew a man who worked in a furniture factory for ten cents an hour! I saw his starved wife and children. Slow starvation gives children starry eyes and delicate faces. . . . When they eat, the quarry workers eat potatoes and turnips. . . .
>   And so I say I was wrong about Vermont. The poems in this book were written after I began to see why.

Calling Western Union represents Taggard's most strongly worded social protest, but the subtlety and searching intellectualism of *Not Mine to Finish* are gone. Judged as poetry rather than argument, many of the poems in *Calling Western Union* suffer from the flaws of much social protest poetry and are not completely successful. They contain too much obvious, direct statement and too little imagery. By far the most vivid and evocative part of the book is its long introductory essay, praised by nearly all reviewers, in which Taggard described her Hawaiian childhood, the disappointment of her return to the United States, and her unfulfilled search for a promising and just America.

Reviews were mixed; even those liberal journals to which Taggard was most committed tended to find something negative to say. Reviewing the book for the *New Republic* (21 October 1936), James Daly wrote, "If one had as little quarrel with its poetic accomplishment as with its convictions, 'Calling Western Union' would be an occasion for praise." Others criticized the disparity between the vividness of the introduction and the flatness of the poems, although *Saturday Review* did comment, "The book is very much alive." The poems are simple and direct, their titles—such as "To an American Worker Dying of Starvation," "Up State—Depression Summer," "Feeding the Children," "Mass Song"—proclaiming the contents like labels on cans. In reviewing this collection, no one praised the poet for "lyricism" or even accused her of it. There are a few personal poems in the group, but most were reprinted from earlier collections. Some of the longer poems are attempts to get into the minds of participants in or observers of New England hardships; these dramatizations tend to ring false. A number of poems have rousing assertions as conclusions: "We must feed the children. Vote the strike!"; "I hope the people win"; "For my class I have come/To walk city miles with many, my will in our work." Others express standard condemnations of middle-class complacency. Indeed, it is sometimes hard to believe that *Not Mine to Finish* and *Calling Western Union* were written by the same person.

After the publication of *Calling Western Union,* Taggard pursued various poetic interests. Despite the success of *The Life and Mind of Emily Dickinson* (1930), she wrote no more biography. She worked with composers at putting poetry to music; in 1939 one of her poems, set to music by William Schuman, was sung at Carnegie Hall. Her *Collected Poems* (1938) received mixed reviews, possibly because she included so many poems from *Calling Western Union* that it appeared to be a collection of political poems. But her last major collection, *Slow Music* (1946), draws together poems that exhibit her many abilities and interests.

Slow Music shows Wallace Stevens's influence most clearly, but it is the earlier Stevens of *Harmonium* (1923) whose traces can most easily be found. According to the reviewer for *Kirkus Reviews,* the poetry is "sometimes fanciful, sometimes

profound, brightly-hued and yet often obscure." Rolfe Humphries, in the *Nation* (8 March 1947)— a usually sympathetic journal to which Taggard had contributed often—commented: "Miss Taggard's specialty is a peculiar kind of lyric, very frail, clear, disembodied; larksong descending from way up high in the pure air, or coming down from above the cloud. This is a difficult genre to sustain, or repeat; aiming at effects of innocence, of being 'natural,' Miss Taggard overdoes it a little."

Yet the poems now appear to have more the effect of deliberate artificiality than of affected "naturalness." With the exception of two poems about her sister Ernestine, who died in 1943, and a few somewhat feminist poems, and perhaps one or two social-protest pieces, Taggard wrote about colors, sounds, and shapes. The few social protest poems in this collection often present their subjects obliquely. There is also not much regionalism, though she would later, in 1947, publish a book of regional poems called *Origin: Hawaii.* For *Slow Music,* Taggard created poems about the colors of life and death and devised a system of color symbolism which persists throughout the collection. On the whole, these poems are impersonal, elegaic in tone. In "The Family," the speaker claims that

> The sadness of the old, the veteran old
> Purges the crude
> Metal. Purges the headlong blood
> Of its one-word reply—
>
> The old
>   say nothing wild,
> But take up children on the lap to sit
> . . . Until the planets hoist them, until they lift
> Big on horizons in the chair of sky.
> ....
> So shine the ancients in the wintering void.

The echoes are not so much of Stevens's sequence "The Rock" (first published in the summer 1950 issue of *Inventario*), but of "Cortege for Rosenbloom" (which was first published in the *Measure* in 1921).

Some of the poems seem to explain a turning away from social purpose. An evocative, obscure poem titled "The Little Girl with Bands on Her Teeth" reaches the conclusion that the speaker can do little to help the girl in the discomfort her teeth give her. Given human limitation, there is little anyone can do for anyone.

> Good Christopher the saint! Bless the past for such
>   pity.

The windows of pity shine, holy and vapid.
We need an essential plinth in the gap of such pity.

These poems are not uniformly successful. Some are too obviously imitations of Stevens, including one which begins, "The sombre man in sombrero. . . ." Others, such as "The Aleatory Wind," are far too prosy and discursive to qualify as poetry. Nevertheless, the collection is challenging and intriguing, and if the critic for the *Christian Science Monitor* who said, "There is light, if not heat, in her lyrics" is correct, his statement need not be taken as condemnation.

After the publication of *Slow Music*, illness confined Taggard pretty much to her home in East Jamaica, Vermont, although she took occasional trips to New York for treatment of hypertension and died in a New York hospital. Some of her last poems appeared posthumously. In 1974 University Microfilms published *The Complete Works of Genevieve Taggard*, three reels of microfilm which include juvenilia, reviews, newspaper articles, as well as her magazine publications and her books.

The Life and Times of Emily Dickinson, though provocative and insightful, has been superseded, and Taggard has not been accorded the recognition she deserves. It is easy to dismiss the dated rhetoric of her protest poems, but it is also easy to let those poems with their faults blind one to the very real virtues of her reflective poems and lyrics, which remain unduly neglected. Her best work shows a merging of self and subject, and it may be that a feminist reading of her work will create a new audience for her poetry. Certainly the access to previously unavailable resources casts considerable doubt on Taggard's speculations about the objects of E. D.'s "secret attachments." In her prose work she was a tireless crusader for more involvement—in liberal causes, in art, in life. As early as *Continent's End* (1925), she deplored "the Longfellow-Whittier School—the Lo! here and Lo! there! school in American poetry—a school that never absorbed its environment, but always held it at arm's length in the gesture of a curio-lecturer." When Taggard succeeded in avoiding this flaw herself, she wrote enduring poems. Certainly her work is better than current critical opinion allows, and there is serious need for reassessment.

Papers:
Taggard's papers are in the Berg Collection at the New York Public Library and in the Taggard Archive at the Dartmouth College Library.

Allen Tate
(19 November 1899-9 February 1979)

James A. Hart
University of British Columbia

See also the Tate entry in *DLB 4, American Writers in Paris, 1920-1939.*

BOOKS: *The Golden Mean and Other Poems*, by Tate and Ridley Wills (Nashville: Privately printed, 1923);

Stonewall Jackson: The Good Soldier, A Narrative (New York: Minton, Balch, 1928; London, Toronto, Melbourne & Sydney: Cassell, 1930);

Mr. Pope and Other Poems (New York: Minton, Balch, 1928);

Jefferson Davis: His Rise and Fall, A Biographical Narrative (New York: Minton, Balch, 1929);

Ode to the Confederate Dead, Being the Revised and Final Version of a Poem Previously Published on Several Occasions; To Which Are Added Message from Abroad and The Cross (New York: Published for the author by Minton, Balch, 1930);

Poems: 1928-1931 (New York & London: Scribners, 1932);

The Mediterranean and Other Poems (New York: Alcestis Press, 1936);

Reactionary Essays on Poetry and Ideas (New York & London: Scribners, 1936);

Selected Poems (New York & London: Scribners, 1937);

The Fathers (New York: Putnam's, 1938; London: Eyre & Spottiswoode, 1939);

Reason in Madness: Critical Essays (New York: Putnam's, 1941);

Sonnets at Christmas (Cummington, Mass.: Cummington Press, 1941);

Invitation to Learning, by Tate, Huntington Cairns, and Mark Van Doren (New York: Random House, 1941);

The Winter Sea: A Book of Poems (Cummington, Mass.: Cummington Press, 1944);

Fragment of a Meditation/MCMXXVIII (Cummington, Mass.: Cummington Press, 1947);

Poems, 1920-1945 (London: Eyre & Spottiswoode, 1947);

On the Limits of Poetry: Selected Essays, 1928-1948 (New York: Swallow/Morrow, 1948);

Poems, 1922-1947 (New York: Scribners, 1948);

The Hovering Fly and Other Essays (Cummington, Mass.: Cummington Press, 1948);

Two Conceits for the Eye to Sing, If Possible (Cummington, Mass.: Cummington Press, 1950);

The Forlorn Demon: Didactic and Critical Essays (Chicago: Regnery, 1953);

The Man of Letters in the Modern World, Selected Essays: 1928-1955 (New York: Meridian/London: Thames & Hudson, 1955; London: Meridian/Thames & Hudson, 1957);

Requiescat in Pace: Paul Wightman Williams, Jr., MCMXX-MCMLVI (N.p., 1956?);

Collected Essays (Denver: Swallow, 1959); revised and enlarged as *Essays of Four Decades* (Chicago: Swallow, 1968; London: Oxford University Press, 1970);

Poems (New York: Scribners, 1960);

Christ and the Unicorn (West Branch, Iowa: Cummington Press, 1966);

Mere Literature and the Lost Traveller (Nashville: George Peabody College for Teachers, 1969);

The Swimmers and Other Selected Poems (London, Melbourne & Cape Town: Oxford University Press, 1970; New York: Scribners, 1971);

The Translation of Poetry (Washington, D.C.: Published for the Library of Congress by the Gertrude Clark Whittall Poetry and Literature Fund, 1972);

Memoirs and Opinions, 1926-1974 (Chicago: Swallow, 1975); republished as *Memoirs & Essays Old and New, 1926-1974* (Manchester: Carcanet, 1976);

Collected Poems, 1919-1976 (New York: Farrar, Straus & Giroux, 1977).

OTHER: Hart Crane, *White Buildings: Poems*, includes a foreword by Tate (New York: Boni & Liveright, 1926);

Fugitives, includes poems by Tate (New York: Harcourt, Brace, 1928);

"Remarks on the Southern Religion," in *I'll Take My Stand: The South and the Agrarian Tradition by Twelve Southerners* (New York & London: Harper, 1930), pp. 155-175;

"Notes on Liberty and Property," in *Who Owns America? A New Declaration of Independence*, edited by Tate and Herbert Agar (Boston & New York: Houghton Mifflin, 1936), pp. 80-93;

Philip Wheelwright and others, *The Language of Poetry*, edited, with a preface, by Tate (Princeton: Princeton University Press, 1942);

Princeton Verse Between Two Wars: An Anthology, edited, with a preface, by Tate (Princeton: Princeton University Press, 1942);

American Harvest: Twenty Years of Creative Writing in the United States, edited by Tate and John Peale Bishop (New York: L. B. Fischer, 1942);

Recent American Poetry and Poetic Criticism: A Selected List of References, compiled by Tate (Washington, D.C.: Library of Congress, 1943);

The Vigil of Venus: Pervigilium Veneris, Latin text with an introduction and translation by Tate (Cummington, Mass.: Cummington Press, 1943);

Sixty American Poets, 1896-1944, checklist selected, with a preface and critical notes, by Tate

Allen Tate (courtesy of the Sylvia Beach Collection, Princeton University Library)

(Washington, D.C.: Library of Congress, 1945);

A Southern Vanguard: The John Peale Bishop Memorial Volume, edited, with a preface, by Tate (New York: Prentice-Hall, 1947);

The Collected Poems of John Peale Bishop, edited, with a preface and a memoir, by Tate (New York & London: Scribners, 1948);

The House of Fiction: An Anthology of the Short Story, with Commentary, edited by Tate and Caroline Gordon (New York: Scribners, 1950; revised, 1960);

Modern Verse in English, edited by Tate and David Cecil (New York: Macmillan, 1958; London: Eyre & Spottiswoode, 1958);

The Arts of Reading, edited by Tate, Ralph Ross, and John Berryman (New York: Crowell, 1960);

Selected Poems by Denis Devlin, edited, with a preface, by Tate and Robert Penn Warren (New York, Chicago & San Francisco: Holt, Rinehart & Winston, 1963);

T. S. Eliot, The Man and His Work: A Critical Evaluation by Twenty-six Distinguished Writers, edited by Tate (New York: Seymour Lawrence/Delacorte, 1966; London: Chatto & Windus, 1967);

Complete Poetry and Selected Criticism of Edgar Allan Poe, edited by Tate (New York: Signet, New American Library/London: Signet, New English Library, 1968).

The phrase "man of letters," so often used in praise of Allen Tate, may suggest by its near-obsolescence that Tate and his work belong to the past, perhaps to the Old South, not to the late-twentieth century. That impression is false. Tate may be difficult for literary historians and critics to label: regionalist, Fugitive, Agrarian, Southern gentleman, medievalist, classicist, New Critic, antipositivist, Roman Catholic apologist, neoromantic—these are a sample of the diverse descriptions of him. Yet, his distinctive literary works, whether poetry, fiction, or critical essays, are relevant today, despite his perhaps too great attachment to the Old South, to New Criticism, or to the modernist manner. His poems are sometimes difficult, at times overcompressed and laconic, but works such as "The Cross," "To the Lacedemonians," and "Aeneas at Washington" bring rich and unique rewards for the attentive reader. Detailed knowledge of nineteenth-century Southern history, the *Aeneid*, and basic Christian dogmas may bring extra resonance to his poetry; familiarity with T. S. Eliot or other modernist poets may help one to appreciate

his poems, but often only basic knowledge is needed. The poem creates its own world. For example, a knowledge of Stonewall Jackson and of the battles at Shiloh, Antietam, Malvern Hill, and Bull Run is undoubtedly needed for a full understanding of "Ode to the Confederate Dead" and a comprehension of the key reference to "muted Zeno and Parmenides" may be crucial; yet the poem has meaning even for readers who lack knowledge of the particular historical facts. Indeed, the specific details of the poem are finally the vehicle for conveying a universal truth. One of Tate's strengths is, indeed, his bringing together of concrete particulars—often from Southern, classical, or Christian history—to elicit in the reader thought and feeling.

The son of John Orly and Eleanor Varnell Tate, John Orly Allen Tate was born in Winchester, Clark County, Kentucky, on 19 November 1899. With a Border background he had to face the question of whether he was a Southerner or an American. Affirming the first, he had to confront the dominant positivist and materialistic Yankee values which were supplanting the older values of the South. Tate came of age at the very time that the South was compelled by World War I to end its isolation from the industrial North. The resulting clash of values forced Southern writers to look critically at their inheritance and its successor. Some surrendered to the charm of romanticized antebellum leisure and civility; others, like Tate, felt the attraction of the way things were before the war but viewed them critically. Their South, they knew, was part myth, part fact, part imagination—a region which possessed the social, philosophical, religious, and literary qualities they valued.

Because of his father's business interests the family moved frequently, and Tate had a rather haphazard education at schools in Nashville; Louisville; Ashland, Kentucky; Evansville, Indiana; Cincinnati; and Washington, D.C. By 1918 Tate had written a few poems, decided that he was sufficiently talented for a career as a violinist, and made the crucial decision to follow his brothers to Vanderbilt. Though good at languages, especially Latin, he had to be tutored for the entrance examination in mathematics.

As an undergraduate, Tate began a lifelong friendship with John Crowe Ransom, who was his instructor for freshman composition and then for a course which included Samuel Butler and William Butler Yeats. Ransom noted his student's dedication to literature and his inclination to bring metaphysics and linguistics into essays about the literary imagination in a way "slightly bewildering" to his instructor. Tate's familiarity with Charles Baudelaire, Stéphane Mallarmé, Rémy de Gourmont's concept of "dissociation of ideas," and T. S. Eliot's *The Sacred Wood* (1920) showed a knowledge of a new literature with which Ransom and some of his colleagues were unfamiliar (see Ransom's "In Amicitia," collected in *Allen Tate and His Work*). When Tate graduated magna cum laude as a member of the class of 1922 (though he finished his course work and received his degree a year late because an illness believed to be tuberculosis had forced him to go to the North Carolina mountains in May 1922), he was already a critic, editor, and poet.

At Vanderbilt in 1921 Tate was invited by another of his teachers, Donald Davidson, to join a Nashville discussion group, the Fugitives, who were interested in philosophy and poetry and who had been meeting from 1915 (with an interruption during the war) to read and discuss their own work. Meetings were spirited but nonprogrammatic. Sidney Mttron Hirsch and James Frank were the hosts, but Ransom was the leading poetic figure. The original group, which also included Walter Clyde Curry and others, was joined in 1922 by Merrill Moore and in 1923 by Robert Penn Warren, who shared a dormitory room with Tate in spring 1923. Laura Riding, whose poetry was published in the *Fugitive*, was also associated with the group. Beginning as a group of amateurs, they became an important literary group—comparable in importance to but less avant-garde and aggressive than the imagists—with their own journal, the *Fugitive* (1922-1925). Tate was an enthusiastic member, though he left Nashville in 1924, living briefly in Lumberport, West Virginia, where he taught high school. On 2 November 1924 he married Caroline Gordon, whom he had met through Warren the previous summer, and they took an apartment in New York City.

During the period 1922-1925, Tate contributed more than twenty poems to the *Fugitive*, nine of which he thought worth including in later collections. M. E. Bradford ("Origins and Beginnings," collected in *Allen Tate and His Work*) discerns an important assumption in the early poems: "that the modern reader can be influenced by dramatic presentation of a mind in motion to participate in attitudes of emotions he would not ordinarily tolerate if they were thrust upon him with direct assertion." "Horatian Epode to the Duchess of Malfi" (October 1922) is evidence of this assumption. Another poem, "Homily" (March 1925), contains the author's characteristic distrust of those who want

to banish dreams or thoughts on death. With sharp irony he advises those denying their mortality to "cut it [the head] off, piece after piece,/And throw the tough cortex away. . . ." Here the words of Matthew 18:19 ("If thine eye offend thee, pluck it out") are extended by analogy to the paradox of removing by decapitation the troublesome rumors of mortality in the "tired unspeaking head"; but death cannot be denied, for "The fifth act of the closing night" is inevitable.

Among the Fugitives, Tate played an active role not only as a poet and a critic of fellow Fugitives' poetry but also as a gadfly, making others take note of modernist works. Appropriately, Tate and the younger Fugitives embraced T. S. Eliot's *The Waste Land* (1922); Ransom disliked it. The influence of Eliot seems to be present, indeed, in much of Tate's work, though there are similarities to Eliot's work even in the poems Tate wrote before he discovered Eliot. Indeed, a remark by Hart Crane that he saw evidence of Eliot's influence in Tate's "Euthanasia" (*Double Dealer*, March 1922) led Tate to read Eliot for the first time, starting with *Poems* (1920). Some of the similarities between the two poets resulted from shared attitudes toward the ever-increasing materialism and secularism or from their being familiar with the same French poets, especially Jules Laforgue.

Although during the years 1925-1930 the Tates resided outside the South, in New York City, Patterson, New York, and France, Tate showed a continued concern with the South. His biography *Stonewall Jackson: The Good Soldier* (1928) was followed in 1929 by *Jefferson Davis: His Rise and Fall*, and in 1930 he helped to edit and contributed an essay to *I'll Take My Stand: The South and the Agrarian Tradition*, a collection of essays by twelve Southerners, some of them former Fugitives, in which they argued the superiority of the agrarian, Southern way of life. The collection caused a great stir. To some readers, it seemed that the essayists wanted to stop—even to deny—progress and instead to turn back the clock of American history. Much as Tate opposed the spread of industrialism in the New South, however, his arguments were primarily philosophical and cultural, not economic. The agrarianism he wanted would create or restore something in "the moral and religious outlook of Western Man." He continued to propound his views in later collections of essays such as *Reactionary Essays on Poetry and Ideas* (1936) and *Who Owns America?* (1936), which he edited with Herbert Agar. More important, Tate's poetry embodies the same purpose, though less directly.

Nuptials

When noon-time comes the whistle blows.
Down the crooked street in jagged rows
The multitudinous laborers shamble
Past Mike's saloon, through swarming flies,
To the vacant lot where they may gamble
With loaded dice, and gorge stale pies.
It is a time when stink and sweat
Subside and let the flesh forget
Contact with brick, mortar, lathes,
The cold necessity to bathe —
And certain things one would forget.
The bones rattle, the nickels jingle,
Nuts and sevens alternate
While a pair of shoes balance fate
And Brady's tongue and fingers tingle:
Yet shots be lost or shots be won,
Tonight will be a night of fun,
Two dollars now prognosticate
An image supine and elate,
For she will keep the date early or late.

Manuscript for one of the poems Tate had published in the December 1922 issue of the Fugitive *(by permission of the Estate of Allen Tate)*

During his first year in the North, Tate worked for a few months as assistant to the editor of *Telling Tales*, a pulp love-story magazine, but he was fired after he corrected the grammar in one of his boss's memos. Soon after the birth of their daughter, Nancy, on 23 September 1925, the Tates rented a farm house in Patterson, New York, taking in their out-of-work friend Hart Crane as a non-paying boarder. During the winter of 1925-1926, Tate worked on his best-known poem, "Ode to the Confederate Dead," while Crane wrote part of *The Bridge* (1930). An early version of Tate's ode was published in *Mr. Pope and Other Poems* (1928), a collection that contained some poems that Tate showed no desire to include in later collections; other poems he did preserve are very unlike his later works. For example, the various parts of "The Progress of Oenia," first published in the *Fugitive* when the author was in his early twenties, suggest, in their fin de siècle air, their world-weary disillusionment, a moderately talented young writer under the influence of Dowson. Yet, as Louis Rubin and R. D. Jacobs have shown, even in these poems the language is sometimes not so old-fashioned or mannered as the thought; rather, in lines such as these from the fifth section of "Epilogue to Oenia" the references, contrasting vocabularies, and complex imagery suggest the maturer Tate:

> For now the languid stertorous
> Pale verses of Propertius
> And the sapphire corpse undressed by Donne
> (Prefiguring Rimbaud's etymon)
> Have shrunk to an apotheosis
> Of cold daylight after the kiss.

Another poem shows how quickly Tate's style matured. "The Death of Little Boys," first published in 1926, is both a good poem and a characteristic one. From this poem onward Tate, in Rubin and Jacobs's words, did "increasingly sharp battle with modern times" and made an "ever deeper inquiry into man's plight in a world of materialism and fragmentation of belief." Echoes of Poe are noticeable, those of Ransom and Eliot less so. The poem contains Tate's own intense violence, paradox, and confrontation with mortality in an unbelieving world that has only sterile conventions. The poem opens with the lines:

> When little boys grown patient at last, weary,
> Surrender their eyes immeasurably to the night,
> The event will rage terrific as the sea;
> Their bodies fill a crumbling room with light.

The next three quatrains show the reactions of a community to the death of a boy. Fearful and thrown off balance, they try to repress their natural grief. They seek solace in cold ritual:

> The bleak sunshine shrieks its chipped music then
> Out to the milkweed amid the fields of wheat.
> There is a calm for you where men and women
> Unroll the chill precision of moving feet.

In September 1928 a significant change in life-style occurred when Tate went to Europe on a Guggenheim Fellowship. Ford Madox Ford had been dismayed by the Tates' living standard when he lived with them in New York in 1927 while Caroline Gordon had acted as his secretary, and he had helped Tate obtain the award. At twenty-nine Tate was suddenly in the world of the American expatriates in Paris. He met old acquaintances, particularly John Peale Bishop, with whom he formed a lasting friendship. He also maintained his admiration for Ford, "the last great European man of letters." Other acquaintances included F. Scott Fitzgerald, Ernest Hemingway, whom he accompanied on Sundays to the bicycle races, and Gertrude Stein, whose literary gatherings he regularly attended. Most of the American expatriates remained thoroughly American, and Tate was not the only one to show little influence of the Paris experiences in his work.

In his Guggenheim application Tate proposed to write a long poem of about one thousand lines, but despite devoting considerable attention to it, he apparently never finished it. Significantly, however, he finished his biography of Jefferson Davis.

Early in 1930 the Tates returned to a United States sinking into the Great Depression, moved into an antebellum house that his brother had bought them near Clarksville, Tennessee, and became embroiled in the Agrarian controversy, which centered on the principles, explicit and implicit, in *I'll Take My Stand* (1930). In the introduction to the book, Tate and eleven other Southerners, several of them contributors to the *Fugitive*, supported the Southern agrarian way of life as opposed to the industrialized American way. They believed that industrialism had demeaned man and that there was a need to return to the humanism of the Old South. These ideas brought opposition and ridicule for their real or supposed romanticization of agrarian life and for their denial of American progress.

Also in 1930 he published a collection of three poems: "Ode to the Confederate Dead," "Message

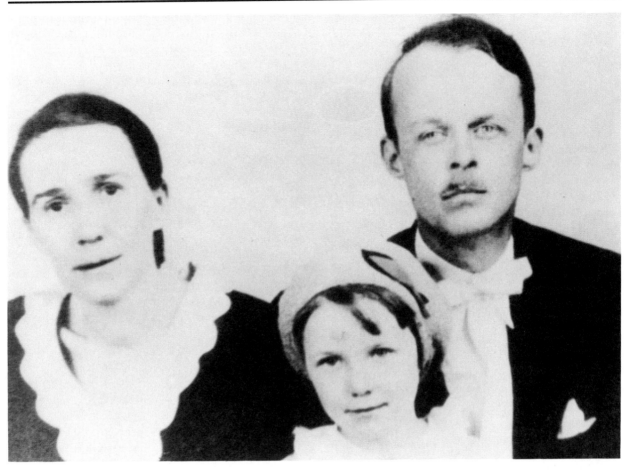

Caroline Gordon, Nancy and Allen Tate, 1928 (courtesy of The Papers of Caroline Gordon, Princeton University Library, gift of Dr. and Mrs. Percy H. Wood, Jr.)

from Abroad," and "The Cross." The first poem (said to be the "revised and final version," though he continued to revise it until 1937), once again shows Tate's use of an idealized, but not romanticized, Southern tradition to convey his view of modern man's plight in a self-centered, industrialized world; the second, dated Paris, November 1929, is mostly the thoughts of a poet in exile, searching for a usable past; exile, the third, one of Tate's most compressed, shows the concern with both religion and history that is so important in Tate's later work. Some readers, including Hart Crane, have found it too condensed and puzzling, but R. K. Meiners has rightly pointed out that only a basic knowledge of Christian dogma and careful reading are required. In his perceptive analysis, Meiners not only elucidates the poem but also shows how the poet is able within its twenty-four lines to convey, without losing control, a large and vital idea: man's "religious predicament and the

consequences of it." Sharpening his usual method, Tate has phrased a problem of religious faith and epistemology in visual terms: "The theme is quite absorbed in its images." By the end of the poem, the spiritually and physically blind protagonist of the opening lines "There is a place that some men know,/I cannot see the whole of it/Nor how I came there. . . ." has to come to know the way to salvation, to accept as truth the existence of hell as well as heaven and in so doing to dismiss paganism or nihilistic narcissism. Some men have known the Christian truth, the cross, but the speaker sees only part. Man, having been given a knowledge of Christianity, can no longer accept the old dispensation, but he has not yet fully accepted the new. A more violent and more original version of Eliot's "The Journey of the Magi," "The Cross" presents modern men as having gained from Christianity a sense of immortality but finding themselves unable to experience the rebirth symbolized by Christian baptism and equally unable to draw spiritual nourishment from this world. They are thus doomed to a type of living death:

> A stag charged both at heel and head:
> Who would come back is turned a fiend
> Instructed by the fiery dead.

This poem and others suggest that Tate was struggling with religious belief. He believed that religion was necessary and wanted to accept it, but he still had doubt. Acceptance of the cross necessitated accepting a God of punishment as well as love. It also required a denial of the supremacy of the intellect and nature.

When Caroline Gordon received a Guggenheim fellowship in 1932, the Tates went for a second time to France, though this time they spent considerable time living outside Paris, particularly at Cap Brun. During their year in France the Tates

Caroline Gordon, Allen Tate, and Sally Wood Kohn at Cap Brun, 1932 (courtesy of The Caroline Gordon Papers, Princeton University Library, gift of Dr. and Mrs. Percy H. Wood, Jr.)

were restless and plagued by financial insecurity. They left in February 1933. Once again living in France seemed to have remarkably little effect on Tate, though he was influenced by European literature and history throughout his life. Tate's first full-length volume of poetry, *Poems: 1928-1931*, published in 1932, was followed in 1936 by *The Mediterranean and Other Poems* and in 1937 by *Selected Poems*, which includes most of the poems from the 1932 collection and all of the 1936 book. He continued his practice of revising his works, and in the preface to the *Selected Poems* he answered those critics who believed his revisions undermined the integrity of spontaneous poetic consciousness. Arguing that his concern was with the readers of his poems not with his own psychology, Tate said that his aim was to achieve *communion* with them, not just communication.

Two of Tate's most important poems, "The Mediterranean" and "Aeneas at Washington," are placed at the beginning of *Selected Poems* and several later collections of his poetry. Both works tie the classical, Graeco-Roman past to the American present, merging the past and the present and abolishing chronological distinction so that the reader sees the contrast between the heroic Aeneas (and his men) and modern men, who are trying to find wisdom by reliving the Trojan's experiences. The poet's profound feeling for classical heritage is fused with his Southern agrarianism to produce a poetic statement about Western man in the 1930s. "The Mediterranean" had its origins in a picnic given by Ford at Cassis in 1932 (an early title was "Picnic at Cassis"), but the occasion is magnificently transcended. The French coast becomes the Roman littoral:

> Where derelict you see through the low twilight
> The green coast that you, thunder-tossed, would win,
> Drop sail, and hastening to drink all night
> Eat dish and bowl to take the sweet land in!

This and later references to feasting and eating the plates are a part of the poet's strategy to have the reader keep in mind various levels of reference: the heroic and meaningful activities of Aeneas, the lesser activities of a modern picnic, and, as the poem moves toward its conclusion, the damaging and unheroic actions of the settlers of North America. In the *Aeneid*, the harpies' curse, that Aeneas would not reach the land he sought until his men were reduced to eating their plates, was fulfilled when the men ate the wheaten cakes that had served as plates. No such curse hangs over a modern picnic, but, on the other hand, the picnic is not part of any heroic quest. Furthermore, when the poet enlarges his view to include early settlers of North America's shores, the reader sees carelessness and waste:

> What country shall we conquer, what fair land
> Unman our conquest and locate our blood?
> We've cracked the hemispheres with careless hand!
> Now, from the Gates of Hercules we flood
>
> Westward, westward till the barbarous brine
> Whelms us to the tired land where tasseling corn,
> Fat beans, grapes sweeter than muscadine
> Rot on the vine: in that land were we born.

"Aeneas at Washington," as the title shows, has a similar fusion of past and present. The poem opens with Aeneas recounting the fall of Troy in words closely following *The Aeneid*. In Aeneas's description of his conduct—"In that extremity I bore me well,/A true gentleman, valorous in arms,/Disinterested and honorable"—Tate presents a view of heroism that is opposed to the conduct of solipsistic modern man. The early European settlers of America brought a prophetic vision, as Aeneas had to the Italian shore, but materialism has corrupted it into "breeding calculation/And fixed triumphs." The poem closes with Aeneas looking back, both as hero of the *Aeneid* and modern man wanting to have an heroic destiny, from "the great Dome" in Washington and "The city [his] blood had built" to Troy, grieving over the corruption of the vision:

> Stuck in the wet mire
> Four thousand leagues from the ninth buried city
> I thought of Troy, what we had built her for.

That the Troy of the epic may be mainly mythical does not matter to Tate; no matter what its factuality, it stands for a usable past and tradition that enable man to exist "objectively" (Tate's term) in the world.

Also in *Selected Poems* is Tate's final version of "Ode to the Confederate Dead," which contains similar ideas, even though the Civil War and Confederate dead have, on the literal level, replaced Aeneas and the matter of Troy. As Ferman Bishop has noted, the numerous revisions made between 1927 and 1937 strengthen the idea that modern man, the onlooker at the gate of the Confederate cemetery, needs to understand his position in the world. The poem itself and Tate's own influential essay on the poem, "Narcissus as Narcissus" (1938), emphasize the plight of modern man imprisoned,

in Tate's words, by his "solipsism, a philosophical doctrine which says that we create the world in the act of perceiving it; or [by his] Narcissism or any other -*ism* that denotes the failure of the human personality to function objectively in nature and society." The poem presents modern man as the isolated individual. Whereas the Pindaric ode implies that the speaker is addressing an audience, speaking on their behalf, Tate's ode is personal. The speaker is alone, speaking only to the dead and struggling to establish communion with the past so that he may find the means for heroic conduct in the modern world.

The man at the cemetery gate, walled off from the Confederate dead and apparently acting in isolation, is shifting his "sea-space blindly/Heaving, turning like the blind crab" (an image that Tate called "an intimation of the nature of the moral conflict upon which the drama of the poem develops: the cut-off-ness of the modern intellectual man from the world"). He can reenact in his mind some of the Civil War events, but he finds in their heroism, based as it was on a firm belief in absolutes, no resolution for him:

> You hear the shout, the crazy hemlocks point
> With troubled fingers to the silence which
> Smothers you, a mummy, in time.

In the last third of the poem, the focus shifts from the viewer at the gate to modern man's search for a heroic code of conduct that will be based on not only moral heroism but also heroism of conduct as defined in the *Iliad* and *Aeneid*. The line "Muted Zeno and Parmenides" refers to Greek philosophers of the Eleatic school who expounded a philosophy which makes such a code possible. As Lillian Feder has persuasively argued, their distinguishing of the objective, unchanging world of being from the subjective world of becoming led to a distrust of "the subjective blindness of mere dependence on the senses for knowledge of the world." Furthermore, in his own act of physical heroism, Zeno "muted" himself, according to tradition, by biting off his tongue rather than giving in to his enemy's demands for information. The man at the gate cannot grasp the heroic vision.

The falling and decaying leaves, which Homer used to show Glaucus's tragic redemption through heroism, in Tate's ode signify mortality and isolation: "We shall say only the leaves/Flying, plunge and expire." The closing dismissal spoken by the man at the gate suggests defeat for the still isolated mortal man:

Leave now
The shut gate and the decomposing wall:
The gentle serpent, green in the mulberry bush,
Riots with his tongue through the hush—
Sentinel of the grave who counts us all!

Yet the poem is not in fact evidence of utter defeat. The reader has been commanded to "Turn your eyes to the immoderate past" and has heard the question "What shall we say who have knowledge/ Carried to the heart?" As Robert S. Dupree argues, Tate answers this question by making use of Oswald Spengler's belief, expressed in *Decline of the West,* that civilizations inevitably grow and decay, only to contradict it. Tate opposes Spengler not only in showing how the present may benefit from the past, but also in believing that memory, as Augustine used it, gives meaning to life and shows a way out of the false dilemma, implied on the surface in the "Ode to the Confederate Dead," that one has either to turn solipsistically inward or to accept a nature dominated by death. Translated in several languages, the "Ode to the Confederate Dead" is deservedly one of Tate's best-known poems.

During the late 1930s and early 1940s Tate continued to publish poems in periodicals and in a brief collection, *Sonnets at Christmas* (1941). According to Squires, Tate was finding it difficult to write poetry at this time. One reason may have been that from 1934, when debt-ridden and doubtful of his ability to survive as a free-lance writer, he accepted a variety of college and university positions that absorbed much of his time. Probably more important, however, was the time he devoted to other literary genres and to his editing.

In 1938 his Civil War novel, *The Fathers,* appeared. The critical reception was mixed, partly because Tate's experimental fictional technique puzzled some readers. Even today, when some critics declare the novel to be Tate's greatest work, the novel is neglected in favor of the poetry and criticism. *The Fathers* is Tate's only novel.

More noticed, admired, and attacked are Tate's critical essays. His first collection, *Reactionary Essays on Poetry and Ideas,* appeared in 1936; his second, *Reason in Madness: Critical Essays,* was published in 1941. *On the Limits of Poetry: Selected Essays, 1928-1948* (1948) and *The Man of Letters in the Modern World* (1955) include essays already published in book form. In his critical essays Tate is a gentlemanly man of letters and also a determined, polemical writer examining and evaluating past and

Allen Tate, 1930s

present writers. As with many poet-critics, his principles support the kind of poetry he writes and the writers he admires, such as Dante, who employ either ideas or forms that he finds useful and valid. A serious, philosophical critic and poet, he opposed the propagandistic writing of the 1930s. He valued form—poetry, he said, is "the art of apprehending and concentrating our experiences in the mysterious limitations of form." Form and meaning are one. By emphasizing the need to pay close attention to the texture of the work rather than to the author's biography, the age, or the paraphrasable content, Tate contributed to the enormous influence of the New Criticism on the reading, teaching, and writing of poetry in the English-speaking world after World War II. In one such essay, "Tension in Poetry," he discusses the uses of denotation and connotation. Yet, while Tate attacked the literary historian's approach to literature, he often examined works in broader contexts. As George Core has noted (see "A Metaphysical Athlete," collected in *Allen Tate and His Work*), certain subjects recur in Tate's essays: the South and its literature, metaphysical and modern poetry, the importance of poetry and criticism in the modern world, and critics past and present.

Tate's writings on Dante and Poe are particularly important. For Tate Dante triumphantly represents the symbolic imagination far greater than what he called Poe's "angelic" imagination. In "The Symbolic Imagination" Tate discusses Dante's use of analogy to create the magnificent movement from the human to the divine, from the natural to the supernatural, from the common to the extraordinary, and from time to eternity. In contrast, Poe's "angelism," which he describes in "The Angelic Imagination," lacks sensuousness; it is like modern man's: "Man as angel becomes a demon who cannot initiate the first notion of love, and we can feel only compassion with his suffering, for it is potentially ours."

In 1938-1939 Tate and Gordon taught English at the Woman's College in Greensboro, North Carolina (later renamed the University of North Carolina at Greensboro). From 1939 to 1942 he was a poet in residence in the Creative Arts Program at Princeton, spending the summers in Monteagle, Tennessee. After leaving Princeton at the end of the spring 1942 term, he spent some time in Monteagle writing poetry, most notably "Seasons of the Soul." In September 1943 the Tates moved to Washington, D.C., where Tate served for one year as the first poetry consultant at the Library of Congress, and in July 1944 they moved again, this time to Sewanee, Tennessee, where Tate edited the *Sewanee Review* until his resignation in early 1946. Under Tate's editorship the journal became an important literary force. One of Tate's reasons for resigning his editorship was his unsettled marital status. He and Caroline Gordon were divorced in January 1946, but in mid-April they remarried and settled in New York City, where Tate went to work as a literary editor for Henry Holt and Company. (Tate was indeed an active editor from his days on the *Fugitive* to his death.)

Two works published during the period 1939-1947, Tate's translation *The Vigil of Venus: Pervigilium Veneris* (1943) and *The Winter Sea: A Book of Poems* (1944), have been grounds for disagreement among critics about the development of Tate's thought. On the one hand, Vivienne Koch (see "The Poetry of Allen Tate," collected in *Allen Tate and His Work*) believes that the translation is "Allen

Tate's valedictory . . . to the South, to the 'classical tradition,' to his masters." She views Tate as a "poet of romantic sensibility who has tried with varying success to compress his talents into a chastely classical form. . . ." To Koch the best poetry comes when Tate the classicist nods, but Lillian Feder declares that Tate's English version of the "Pervigilium Veneris" is more "classical" than the Latin of the original; Tate's language, she says, is "cryptic and economical, as eloquently colloquial as Horace's, and full of incredibly graceful Latinisms" (see "Allen Tate's Use of Classical Literature," collected in *Allen Tate and His Work*). Stanza seven is representative not only of the mixed classical and romantic elements in the original but also of Tate's skill as both translator and poet:

> The blood of Venus enters her blood, Love's kiss
> Has made the drowsy virgin modestly bold;
> Tomorrow the bride is not ashamed to take
> The burning taper from its hidden fold.
>   Tomorrow may loveless, may lover tomorrow
>   make love.

The Winter Sea: A Book of Poems (1944), whose contents include "More Sonnets at Christmas" (a sequel to *Sonnets at Christmas*) and "Seasons of the Soul," leads to a similar split in critical assessment. In this volume, Koch believes, the poet makes an "almost complete break" with his earlier work and displays a "revitalized romanticism." Yet Feder disputes this view, pointing out that in "III: Winter" and "IV: Spring" Tate uses the classical figures Venus and Sisyphus to contrast man's heroic and creative potential with his "tragic fault," the misuse of his strengths. Tate's classicism, Feder declares, "exists not in external, imitative manners (the decoratively neoclassical), but in his way of thought and of feeling in poetry." Thus Tate's nostalgia is related to "Homeric longing for heroism," and in the "Winter" section of "Seasons of the Soul" his distrust and rejection of the contemporary have been deepened through a Virgilian image:

> Goddess sea-born and bright,
> Return into the sea
> Where eddying twilight
> Gathers upon your people—
> Cold goddess, hear our plea!
> Leave the burnt earth, Venus,
> For the drying God above,
> Hanged in his windy steeple,
> No longer bears for us
> The living wound of love.

To George Hemphill, "Seasons of the Soul" is "the real capstone of Tate's career," and R. K. Meiners, emphasizing the links to Dante, devotes a whole chapter to it as an unjustly neglected major poem of our time, concluding that it "sounds the complete death of history and society as a mode of salvation. . . . To the terrible question there is no answer. It is the perfect end to that phase of Tate's work before he carried his critical and poetic themes into the religious conceptions toward which they had been straining for so long."

"Seasons of the South" was reprinted as the opening poem in *Poems, 1920-1945*, published in London in 1947, and followed a year later by *Poems, 1922-1947*, published in New York. Although many of the works in these books had been published before, though not necessarily in quite the same form, the publication of this selection gave critics and literary historians a chance to assess the work of a literary figure who had become increasingly well known through his poetry, criticism, editorial positions, and teaching.

While Tate's poetry had developed and changed over twenty-five years, several critics were struck by the recurrence of certain major ideas and attitudes: Tate's antipathy to man's evasion of responsibility by blaming sociological or naturalistic forces; his rejection of abstractions in favor of concrete presentation; his acceptance of fallen or imperfect man; his sense of the profound effects of isolation or solipsism; his belief in the merging of the living and the dead, of past and present generations; and his intertwining of the religious, ethical, and historical. Since these are indeed some of the important elements of Tate's work, it is not surprising to find Sister Mary Bernetta arguing that Tate recognizes "the struggle of Everyman to win beatitude and to escape eternal reprobation" as the most significant issue in literature (see "Allen Tate's Inferno," collected in *Allen Tate and His Work*). For her, Tate's basic concern is medieval (rather than classical, romantic, or metaphysical in the manner of Donne). It is true that he admired Dante and that signs of his movement toward Roman Catholicism were noticeable in the 1940s. (He converted in 1950.) As early as 1932, in "To the Lacedemonians," a poem written for the occasion of a Confederate soldiers' reunion and revised for *Selected Poems*, the speaker, a veteran addressing such a group, says, "Gentleman, my secret is/Damnation," and the violence of the conclusion seems greater than the occasion requires. The damnational seems more theological than sectional or political:

All are born Yankees of the race of men
And this, too, now the country of the damned:

Poor bodies crowding round us! The white face
Eyeless with eyesight only, the modern power—
Huddled sublimities of time and space,
They are the echoes of a raging tower

That reared its moment upon a gone land,
Pouring a long cold wrath into the mind—
Damned souls, running the way of sand
Into the destination of the wind!

Tate's belief that abstraction is the death of everything has consequences not only for his thought but also for his literary presentation; the violence and sensuousness of his imagery are notable results.

In spring 1948 Tate left Holt to teach at New York University. Soon afterward Tate became embroiled in the controversy over the awarding of the Bollingen Prize to Ezra Pound. Tate voted for and defended the award, even though he thought Pound's ideas crude and anti-Semitic. Pound, furthermore, had scorned Tate's poetry. Tate's defense, which is set forth in "Further Remarks on the Pound Award" (*Partisan Review*, June 1949), is based on Pound's devotion to poetry and to his revivification of the language. In 1951 he accepted a professorship with tenure at the University of Minnesota.

Tate and Caroline Gordon separated once again in 1955 and were divorced for a second time in 1959. Later that year, on 27 August, he married Isabella Gardner. They separated in 1965 and were divorced in March 1966, and on 30 July 1966 Tate married Helen Heinz, one of his students at the University of Minnesota. In fall 1966 Tate served as a visiting professor at the University of North Carolina at Greensboro, and the following spring he held a similar position at Vanderbilt. The Tates became the parents of twin sons, John Allen and Michael Paul, on 30 August 1967.

Following his retirement from the University of Minnesota in 1968, Tate took his family to live in Sewanee, Tennessee, where Michael Tate was killed in an accident. Benjamin Lewis Bogan, the Tates' third son, was born on 18 December 1969.

The Minnesota years saw many public acknowledgments of his literary position. He was a Fulbright lecturer at Oxford (summer 1953) and a Fulbright Professor at the University of Rome for the 1953-1954 academic year. He also lectured in India and various European cities in fall 1956. In addition to accepting numerous honorary degrees,

Allen Tate and T. S. Eliot in Washington, D.C., 1948

he received the Bollingen Prize in Poetry (1956), the Brandeis University Medal (1961), and the Dante Society of Florence Gold Medal (1962). He was elected to the American Academy of Arts and Letters in 1964 and to the American Academy of Arts and Sciences in 1965.

From 1951 until his death in 1979, Tate republished poems and prose in various collections, edited several books, and published numerous prose pieces in periodicals, but he wrote few new poems. Of these, three works have attracted the most attention: "The Maimed Man" (first published in the May-June 1952 issue of the *Partisan Review*), "The Buried Lake" (*Sewanee Review*, Spring 1953), and "The Swimmers" (*Hudson Review*, Winter 1953). Only "The Buried Lake" and "The Swimmers," both considerably revised from their first appearance, were included in *Poems* (1960); all three are included in *The Swimmers and Other Selected Poems* (1970) and again in *Collected Poems, 1919-1976* (1977).

Since all three poems are in terza rima (more as a tribute to than as an imitation of Dante) and

can be related in themes and imagery, they are usually treated as three parts of one poem. In fact, Tate had at one time considered them as sections of a projected nine-part poem. Yet, whether they should be called part of an unfinished longer work is under dispute. Tate also said that each section is complete in itself, but it must also be noted that the three poems gain richness when they are considered together.

The poems are filled with ties and allusions to other poets, in particular to Dante. The influence of Eliot's *Four Quartets*, Milton, Sir Thomas Wyatt, and Augustine is also apparent. The autobiographical element, for Tate reflects on not only his religious beliefs but also his poetic career, also complicates the texture of the poems, especially when it governs the symbolism.

Although the wit and complexity of his earlier work are still to be found, these poems of the 1950s are more religious, Christian poetry. Some readers have seen the effect of Tate's conversion to Roman Catholicism. The poet did not, however, intend his poems to be persuasive tracts; he himself ruled out

Allen Tate (courtesy of Information Services, University of South Carolina)

poetry as a vehicle for religious or moral propaganda.

The opening lines of invocation to "The Maimed Man" display a new didactic style:

> Didactic laurel, loose your reasoning leaf
>   Into my trembling hand; assert your blade
>   Against the Morning Star, enlightening Thief
>
> Of that first Mother who returned the Maid.

Robert S. Dupree is probably right in suggesting that the laurel is to be identified with Phoebus Apollo and the Apollonian understanding of the self, and of Venus, while the Morning Star is associated with Lucifer (Milton's Satan) as well as with sensual Venus; and the blade represents Tate's poetic endeavors. The poet is not going to explore erotic love; he rejects the temptations of the world and instead examines his own past. Thus this poem, like "The Buried Lake" and "The Swimmers," uses incidents from Tate's youth. The horrible figure of the maimed man, who lacks head and feet, dom-

inates much of the poem and represents the ego of both the poet and mankind:

> (By *I* I mean iambics willed and neat;
>   I mean by *I* God's image made uncouth;
>   By eye I mean the busy, lurked, discrete
>
> Mandible world sharp as a broken tooth.)

"The Swimmers" goes back more definitely to a past incident, when the young Tate, enjoying a Kentucky summer day, saw the sheriff take down the body of a lynched Negro and drag it back to town. As he took down the body, the poet says,

> I saw the Negro's body bend
> And straighten, as a fish-line cast transverse
> Yields to the current that it must subtend.
>
> The sheriff's Goddamn was a murmured curse
> Not for the dead but for the blinding dust.

The poem seems to be a straightforward narrative about a lynching obtruding into the simple summer pleasures of a boy in Kentucky; but the various simple elements of the poem, such as the search for water, the laurel and myrtle, and the swim itself, begin to acquire symbolic and mythic overtones. The disposal of the Negro's body, which the sheriff seems to treat so mundanely, is tied to Christ's crucifixion and burial; the town's silent acceptance of the crime leads the reader to consider the question of mankind's guilt for the treatment of Christ and other scapegoat-victims.

The final poem in the sequence as it is now published is "The Buried Lake." The most difficult of the three poems, it is so loaded with mythological, religious, psychological, and personal symbolism that a full explication, such as Robert S. Dupree's in *Allen Tate and the Augustinian Imagination*, risks being considered too ingenious. A reader may ask whether any poet can have so loaded every rift with so much ore. Yet despite the multifarious and complex allusions, one theme is clear: the recognition that man is not omnipotent or complete within himself, and that he needs some transcending power to be fulfilled. Materialism, naturalism, eroticism, and individualism are not sufficient. Dupree is surely correct in seeing the poet move in the closing lines "from recollection to vision to the unified will and sensibility":

> Light choir upon my shoulder, speaking Dove
>   The dream is over and the dark expired.
>   I knew that I had known enduring love.

Allen Tate's final place in the history of modern literature is not known, though the growing numbers of entries in annual checklists of scholarly articles suggest that he is receiving increased critical attention. His position will not depend on his poetry alone, for the title of his 1955 collection of essays describes him most fittingly: The Man of Letters in the Modern World.

Letters:

The Literary Correspondence of Donald Davidson and Allen Tate, edited by John Tyree Fain and Thomas Daniel Young (Athens: University of Georgia Press, 1974).

Bibliographies:

Willard Thorp, "Allen Tate: A Checklist," *Princeton University Library Chronicle*, 3 (April 1942): 85-98; republished in *Critique*, 10 (Summer 1968): 17-34;

"The Works of Allen Tate" and "Works About Allen Tate," in *Allen Tate and His Work: Critical Evaluations*, edited by Radcliffe Squires (Minnesota: University of Minnesota Press, 1972), pp. 309-343.

Biography:

Radcliffe Squires, *Allen Tate: A Literary Biography* (New York: Bobbs-Merrill, 1971).

References:

Ferman Bishop, *Allen Tate* (New York: Twayne, 1967);

John M. Bradbury, *The Fugitives: A Critical Account* (Chapel Hill: University of North Carolina Press, 1958);

Louise Cowan, *The Fugitive Group; A Literary History* (Baton Rouge: Louisiana State University Press, 1959);

Robert S. Dupree, *Allen Tate and the Augustinian Imagination: A Study of the Poetry* (Baton Rouge: Louisiana State University Press, 1983);

George Hemphill, *Allen Tate* (Minneapolis: University of Minnesota Press, 1964);

R. K. Meiners, *The Last Alternatives: A Study of the Works of Allen Tate* (Denver: Alan Swallow, 1963);

William Pratt, ed., *The Fugitive Poets: Modern Southern Poetry in Perspective* (New York: Dutton, 1965);

Louis Rubin and R. D. Jacobs, "Allen Tate: The Arrogant Circumstance," in *South: Modern Southern Literature in Its Cultural Setting*, edited by Rubin and Jacobs (Garden City: Doubleday, 1961);

Radcliffe Squires, ed., *Allen Tate and His Work: Critical Evaluations* (Minnesota: University of Minnesota Press, 1972);

John L. Stewart, *The Burden of Time: The Fugitives and the Agrarians* (Princeton: Princeton University Press, 1965).

Papers:

Significant collections of Tate's manuscripts are held by Princeton and Vanderbilt.

Sara Teasdale

(8 August 1884-29 January 1933)

William Drake

BOOKS: *Sonnets to Duse and Other Poems* (Boston: Poet Lore, 1907);

Helen of Troy and Other Poems (New York & London: Putnam's, 1911);

Rivers to the Sea (New York: Macmillan, 1915);

Love Songs (New York: Macmillan, 1917);

Flame and Shadow (New York: Macmillan, 1920; London: Cape, 1924);

Dark of the Moon (New York: Macmillan, 1926);

Stars To-Night, Verses Old and New for Boys and Girls (New York: Macmillan, 1930);

Strange Victory (New York: Macmillan, 1933);

The Collected Poems of Sara Teasdale (New York: Macmillan, 1937);

Mirror of the Heart, Poems of Sara Teasdale, edited by William Drake (New York: Macmillan, 1984).

OTHER: *The Answering Voice: One Hundred Love Lyrics by Women*, edited by Teasdale (Boston: Houghton Mifflin, 1917; enlarged edition, New York: Macmillan, 1928);

Rainbow Gold; Poems Old and New Selected for Girls and Boys by Sara Teasdale (New York: Macmillan, 1922);

Marguerite Wilkinson, *New Voices*, includes a contribution by Teasdale on writing lyric poetry (New York: Macmillan, 1936), pp. 199-201.

PERIODICAL PUBLICATIONS:

FICTION

"The Sentimentalist," *Smart Set*, 48 (April 1916): 131-134.

NONFICTION

"Two Views of H. G. Wells," as Frances Trevor, *Little Review* (April 1914): 12-15.

Sara Teasdale

Sara Teasdale was one of the most popular poets in America from the years of World War I through the 1920s. Her new work, appearing almost monthly in the major national magazines, was read aloud before large groups (though not by the shy poet herself), quoted and occasionally parodied in the press, and frequently set to music. She was the first recipient, in 1918, of the Columbia Poetry Prize, which later became the Pulitzer Prize for Poetry, and was highly regarded by her literary contemporaries, including Robert Frost, William Butler Yeats, and Edmund Wilson.

Sara Teasdale's success arose from two essential features in her work: her technical mastery of the brief lyric in simple, sometimes ironic language—she called her poems "songs"—and the fact that she typically wrote of love from a woman's point of view. Probably no other figure, except Sappho, whom Teasdale revered, is so closely identified with feminine love poetry. In her later years, however, and in her best work, she extended her range in philosophical depth and self-examination.

After her death in 1933, Teasdale's work gradually disappeared from anthologies, textbooks, and the concern of academic critics. Her popularity with nonacademic readers nevertheless continued, *The Collected Poems* (1937) going through more than twenty printings before being republished in paperback in 1966. With the rise of women's studies and feminist criticism in the 1970s, Teasdale's work emerged in a new light. Although Sara Teasdale thought of her poetry as continuing in a tradition of nineteenth-century women's verse, particularly that of Christina Rossetti and Elizabeth Barrett Browning, she outgrew the conventional Victorian attitudes of her early work to probe in maturity the personal conflicts she experienced as revolutionary changes swept twentieth-century society. Women were thrown to the forefront of those changes, with both greater freedom and the heavier, sometimes confusing, demands placed upon them. Sara Teasdale, however, was not a heroine of the new age as much as its victim, and her later work reflects the cost exacted by disillusion in romantic love, a failed marriage, an abortion, divorce, striving for professional prominence, and eventual loneliness and suicide.

Sara Teasdale was the late-arriving and youngest child of John Warren Teasdale, a prosperous St. Louis wholesaler of dried fruits and nuts, and a pious mother, Mary Elizabeth Willard Teasdale, who strove for perfect middle-class rectitude. Teasdale was sheltered, pampered, educated in private schools, and led to believe that she was frail, chronically ill, and in constant need of protective care. At twenty she joined a group of local young women in an amateur artists' club called the Potters. For several years they published a hand-printed and illustrated magazine, the *Potter's Wheel*, in which Teasdale's earliest work appeared. One of her prose sketches, "The Crystal Cup," caught the eye of William Marion Reedy, publisher of the *Mirror*, who reprinted it in May 1906. Within the following year he began publishing some of her poems as well. One of them, "Guenevere," a dramatic monologue, attracted national attention, and Teasdale was launched on a professional career as a poet whose chief theme was women and love.

In 1907 Teasdale, at the age of twenty-three, put together a collection of twenty-nine poems in a volume she titled *Sonnets to Duse and Other Poems*.

Her parents gave her $290 for a printing of a thousand copies by the Poet Lore Company of Boston. The nine sonnets addressed to the great actress Eleonora Duse—whom Teasdale never saw—are idealized portraits of a classically beautiful woman, blending the image of Duse with Sappho and the Venus de Milo. The additional poems are modeled on the delicate lyrics of the British Victorian poet A. Mary F. Robinson and on Robert Louis Stevenson's *A Child's Garden of Verses* (1885).

Teasdale sent a copy of this first book to Arthur Symons, a friend of Duse, who published a brief notice of it in the *Saturday Review* (London), preferring her childlike lyrics to the attempted heaviness of the sonnets to Duse. Teasdale was eager for criticism, submitting her work to everyone she thought might help her correct and strengthen it. Symons's response was similar to that of others who encouraged her in the direction of simplicity and small-scale forms. This appraisal was realistic, for her background and upbringing as a "lady," and her extended childhood, had deprived her of

Sara Teasdale, 1908 (photograph by Williamina Parrish)

robustness and force in poetry as well as in her life. The lyric with its personal voice was the vehicle most suited to her talents and limitations. Her first book, divided as it was between the celebration of womanhood as beauty and power and an exhibition of actual frailty, expressed the central conflict that would continue throughout her life and run through all her work. In her time other middle-class women, many of whom shared this conflict to a degree, doubtless found their own emotions reflected in her poetry.

Teasdale demonstrated a firm professionalism from the beginning, along with considerable ambition, a keen business sense, and a determination to rise above her crippling problems. In spite of bouts of undefined illness, chronic weakness, nervous exhaustion, trips to quiet retreats around the country in the search of renewed health, and stays at a sanatorium in Cromwell, Connecticut, she labored continually on her poems to achieve vigor and conciseness, freedom from affectation, and stronger emotion. She was stimulated by the example of A. E. Housman, first reading *A Shropshire Lad* (1896) in 1909 and maintaining a lifelong admiration, even making a pilgrimage to visit him while in England in 1932. She tirelessly submitted her work to the magazines that would give her the widest circulation and made a point of never offering a poem to any publication that would not pay.

Teasdale was ready with a second volume of poems in 1910, but circulated the manuscript for nearly a year in both England and America before G. P. Putnam's Sons took it in 1911. This time, however, publication was not subsidized. *Helen of Troy and Other Poems* is a transitional and oddly mixed collection. It begins with half-a-dozen dramatic monologues spoken by famous women in literature who have loved tragically and now look back on their suffering from the wise vantage point of peaceful age, when the storm of love is over. These poems are remnants of her early twenties. Forty-four poems are given the heading "Love Songs." Taken together, they range through demure longing, devotion to imaginary lovers, disappointment, loss, and yearning for death, often employing the Arthurian imagery dear to the Victorians and still in vogue. These were conventional themes the public appreciated, although they were expressed on the whole in engagingly fresh language and rising from Teasdale's own life as a sheltered, inexperienced young woman in a provincial city. Twenty-seven additional poems, headed "Sonnets and Lyrics," offer a miscellany of poems not otherwise classifiable. The volume concludes with a short verse play, "On the Tower," modeled on works by Maurice Maeterlinck or Richard Hovey and interesting because of its heroine, a princess who, fearful of men and marriage, leaps over a battlement to her death. Teasdale dropped this play from subsequent editions of the book.

Helen of Troy and Other Poems is most noteworthy for a single poem, "Union Square." Teasdale had spent several weeks in New York in early spring 1911, attending some of the first meetings of the newly formed Poetry Society of America. Seeing the sights with two St. Louis friends, she composed a series of poems depicting imaginary love relationships in various appropriate locales in the city and added them to the manuscript of her book before it was accepted by Putnam's. In "Union Square" she yearns to express an unspoken love for a man who is unaware of it, and she envies the prostitutes who can take the initiative and ask for love shamelessly. Reviewers pounced on the poem, startled that a decent woman might harbor thoughts of sexual aggressiveness. "Has the woman who speaks in that very unusual poem, 'Union Square,' been always with us but inarticulate?" the anonymous reviewer for the *New York Times* asked.

The woman poet of the nineteenth century had most typically been a stay-at-home, spinning out her work and her unsatisfied longings under the watchful eyes of a male relative or husband. Sara Teasdale's venture into independent professionalism, like those of the new female journalists and scientists, was a departure typical of a new generation. She sensed that the freedom of action she sought also had its corollary in sexual freedom; yet she was too heavily burdened with the inhibitions and submissiveness of her Victorian middle-class upbringing to follow her more rebellious instincts. The result was a troubled ambivalence, a constant wavering between daring and guilt, desire and fear, assertiveness and retreat, that, to paraphrase her own imagery, was an inner wound bleeding ceaselessly.

After 1911 and a taste of New York literary life, Teasdale was never again satisfied to remain in the Midwest. She had made many new friends, including poet and journalist Jessie Rittenhouse, who had advised her that "Union Square" was a strong poem and ought to be published. She returned eagerly to New York the next winter for the Poetry Society meetings, developing a warm friendship with Jean and Louis Untermeyer and arranging to go on a trip to Europe the following summer with Jessie Rittenhouse. But at the age of twenty-six, she was still dependent on her parents, needing their permission for every trip away from home, unprepared to make a living for herself, and writing poem after poem filled with desperate longing for a love relationship which she believed would set her free. She dreaded becoming an "old maid," that point of no return a woman supposedly reached at age thirty.

With the trip to Europe in 1912, a shipboard romance with an attractive but unreliable Englishman, followed by another winter season in New York, a brief friendship with John Reed, and a budding romantic attraction to the poet John Hall Wheelock (later a Scribners editor), Teasdale at last began to distance herself from the oppressiveness of her St. Louis Baptist background and gain a measure of mature self-assurance, even though St. Louis had to remain for a while her home base. The period 1912-1914 was one of a rapid unfolding of her talent and her emotional life, the most voluminously productive period of her life, and probably the only period in which she was ever to feel expansive and free.

This time coincided with a national poetry renaissance, as it has been called. In 1912 Harriet Monroe launched *Poetry* magazine in Chicago; William Stanley Braithwaite started the *Poetry Journal* in Boston; and the Poetry Society of America adopted publicizing poetry as a cause. Critics have since designated this time as the birth date of modernism. But the wave of energy was much broader and deeper, and carried Eliot, Pound, and Stevens into being along with countless poets still writing in traditional modes.

In 1913 Teasdale met Harriet Monroe, who became another close friend and useful critic, publishing her work frequently in *Poetry*. Teasdale spent ten days in Chicago, guided by Eunice Tietjens, Monroe's assistant, into an acquaintance with Floyd Dell and the bohemian crowd. The new sexuality, which she witnessed for the first time, shocked and fascinated her, an experience summarized symbolically in her "queer half-mad ironic" poem (as she called it), "The Star." Later in the summer of 1913 Vachel Lindsay, on Harriet Monroe's suggestion, initiated a correspondence with Teasdale that led to another intimate friendship, one that lasted to his death in 1932.

Teasdale returned to New York in the fall of 1913 with the manuscript of her third volume of poems in preparation, and with the private intention of inducing John Hall Wheelock to marry her. Although her poems still expressed the moods of hopeless longing for freedom in love, of disappoint-

ment, or of self-denial, she had assessed her situation coolly and concluded that marriage was essential to her life, for financial security as well as emotional fulfillment. She was strongly attracted to Wheelock, who, unfortunately unknown to her, was in love with someone else and failed to respond. After nearly a year of futile effort, Teasdale weighed the alternatives: Vachel Lindsay, a penniless small-town eccentric who by now had decided he was in love with her and wanted to keep her for his permanent inspiration; and Ernst Filsinger, a St. Louis businessman introduced to her recently by Eunice Tietjens and also worshipful of her. She had them both come to New York in the summer of 1914, first Lindsay and then Filsinger, in a sort of trial of her affections, and to be introduced to her friends. The competition ended predictably as Teasdale selected Filsinger—a choice of middle-class propriety and security and of a man acceptable to her parents. "I may be all wrong," she wrote Harriet Monroe, "but I can't help it." They were married in a private ceremony at her parents' home on 19 December 1914.

Wheelock had suggested the title for Teas-

Sara Teasdale in her wedding gown, 1914

dale's next book, *Rivers to the Sea* (1915), a phrase from one of his poems. Through Harriet Monroe she had been given a contract by Macmillan, who remained her publisher thereafter. The ninety poems of *Rivers to the Sea* show a marked advance in maturity, self-assurance, and productivity. Teasdale abandoned dramatic verse, except for a last monologue, "Sappho," and French forms such as the triolet, concentrating instead on creating a natural personal voice and an impression of effortless technique in poems that kept close to her actual experiences. The effect was striking to readers whose ears were still attuned to the artificialities of Victorian tradition. Her popularity accompanied that of Frost, Masters, and Robinson in a similar vein. Wheelock, who remained a good friend, wrote her praising the book generously. He noted that it was arranged to lead the reader through cycles of experience, presenting "a world, complete even to its smallest details—the swans, the park, the subway . . . a miniature world grouped and ordered to point the symbol of your own experience." In choosing and arranging the contents of *Rivers to the Sea* Teasdale found the rationale she would thenceforth follow. The final inclusion of a poem was the result of a highly selective process. Probably fewer than half the poems in her notebooks ever saw publication, and many of the poems published in magazines were never gathered into collections. While preparing a book she would write each poem on a separate sheet in a loose-leaf notebook, shuffling and rearranging the pages until she arrived at the order and grouping which represented to her the pattern of her experience.

Rivers to the Sea also marked the point at which she developed her concept of the lyric poem. For her a poem began with emotional irritation and dissatisfaction, personal tension or psychological pain, which needed to be transformed into harmony with the self. A poem was therefore a transmutation of a disturbance or suffering into something beautiful, as she stated concisely in her poem "Alchemy." She viewed her poems as a record of her experience. But, as Wheelock noted, this record was symbolic rather than literal or confessional.

Teasdale's theory that poetry arose from conflict caused her to consider whether marriage might not be adverse to creativity, if it brought the sort of bliss it was supposed to. She had little cause for concern, however, for within six months of a honeymoon she privately termed an emotional "fiasco," she was again chronically ill and depressed. She later admitted that she had forced herself to marry

Ernst Filsinger

a man she did not really love. If she were to marry anyone, however, her friends all agreed that Ernst Filsinger was the best choice. He was hopelessly devoted, willingly allowed her to have her own way in everything, admired her work, much of which he knew by heart, and was intelligently informed about the arts, with progressive opinions. And though they had settled in St. Louis after their marriage, in 1916 he found a position in New York as a foreign-trade specialist, and Teasdale was able to return to her friends and the scene of her literary successes. She made her home there for the remaining seventeen years of her life.

The enormous popularity of *Rivers to the Sea*, the first edition of which had sold out in three months, led Macmillan to pressure her to get another volume ready quickly. She was reluctant to hurry her productivity, fearing a loss of both quality and authentic growth. She compromised by putting together a collection of seventy-one poems, more than half of them from previous volumes, with the title *Love Songs* (1917). At the same time she had begun work on an anthology of love poetry by women, the earliest twentieth-century anthology containing only poetry written by women. This volume, *The Answering Voice* (1917) with one hundred poems by poets ranging from Emily Brontë to Edna St. Vincent Millay, but excluding her own, appeared in the fall of 1917 almost simultaneously with *Love Songs* and another printing of *Rivers to the Sea*.

The prize-winning *Love Songs* remained her most popular volume through the years, with its plaintive moods, its portrayal of youthful longing and disappointment—the voice of an introspective, self-absorbed woman, worshiping beauty and meticulously shaping her stanzas with self-imposed reserve.

In spite of these successes, Teasdale had drifted into morbid depression of the kind that would periodically afflict her with increasing intensity until her suicide in 1933. She did not wish to display such moods in her published work, partly because of reticence and partly because of the public image she preferred to maintain. Yet the first "dark" poems appear in *Love Songs* as a group of seven headed "Interlude: Songs out of Sorrow." World War I was also deeply troubling to her; she felt that the nation had gone mad. She and her husband took a pacifist position during most of the war, influenced in part by his background in the liberal German community of St. Louis. And it was probably in August 1917, judging by indirect evidence, that she underwent an abortion. She confided to Wheelock that her health could not endure a pregnancy and that she could not sustain both a career and motherhood. As with her other major choices, she could see no acceptable alternatives.

At the end of the war, Ernst Filsinger began a series of lengthy business trips abroad. Over the next decade he went to Europe, South America, and the Near East. Teasdale was left alone for many months at a time, gradually becoming more reclusive and self-absorbed. With her fame secure, and her youthful romanticism waning, she became an ironic and truthful observer of her own states of mind and emotion. Her life, she wrote Filsinger during one of his trips, "consists almost wholly of meditation [and] is damned gloomy."

The postwar years were an explosive time for poetry. What began as simply a popular groundswell of interest had broken up into quarrelsome "schools," competing theories, and competing personalities. Temperamentally, Teasdale reacted with distaste to the new modernist productions of Eliot, Stevens, and Joyce. She had formed a personal dislike of Ezra Pound after observing him at a Poetry Society meeting in 1911, remarking that

he had "a miserable coarseness . . . that always crops out when a naturally weak person tries to be 'virile.'" She could never agree with Harriet Monroe's promoting him. For her, poets were free to do what they liked; the only offense was to become doctrinaire and argumentative. She was eager to learn whatever might improve her own work, though she had formed her poetic practice along more traditional lines a decade or so earlier.

While indifferent to, and unchallenged by, modernist experimentation, Teasdale felt a greater impact from poets in the familiar lyric tradition, particularly Frost and Yeats. Frost's tough-mindedness and colloquial realism, much admired by her husband, were influential in the direction her own work took. She felt that Yeats was the greatest poet of the century and counted it as one of the cherished moments of her life to meet him personally in Santa Barbara, California, where she was spending the winter season in 1920. She had come to feel that her earlier, highly successful poetry was weak by the standards she now envisaged.

Two of the major controversies of the war years, free verse and imagism versus the traditional forms, engaged her briefly. Ultimately she felt that both of the new movements were essentially trivial, though she tried her hand at a few free-form pieces, concluding that formal restraints, like social conventions, produced more forceful poems. She already shared with the imagists a taste for the pictorial and for succinct, self-contained imagery. The chief result of her interest in imagism was a stimulating acquaintance with Amy Lowell.

A major shift in her work was under way when she published *Flame and Shadow* (1920), her fifth book in thirteen years. Most of the ninety-two new poems in the book had been written in the troubled time since 1917. Her notebooks from this period show repeated attempts to come to terms with her complex emotional disturbance. She was trying to make the best of a marriage from which she was gradually withdrawing to fight her battle with herself, the conflict between her self-determination as a woman and the grip of the forces of patriarchy. The violence of the imagery in some of her unpublished work is muted into measured tension in *Flame and Shadow*, while despair is softened to nostalgia and grim patience. The title of the book was derived from a poem by Victor Hugo from which she used two lines as an epigraph: "Reçois la flamme ou l'ombre/De tous mes jours." It expressed the bifurcation of her own life and was a conscious attempt for the first time to show the emotional suffering that was the background to the flame of love and beauty, the torch she carried for her public. The poems were arranged with great care to depict a progression of moods from affirmation through a bleak encounter with death to a qualified affirmation at the end. It was a not entirely successful attempt to find beauty and intensity of experience as an adequate exchange for extinction in death and possible meaninglessness. The final section, "Songs for Myself," reveals her retreat into loneliness, her craving for peace, her austere fatalism, and her probing for some sense of design in human life. She had taken up a study of astronomy because the stars had become symbols for her of the vast impersonal forces that inexplicably governed life. For her man was in rebellion against life, but eventually had no choice but to submit.

Technically, *Flame and Shadow* contains Teasdale's best work to that date. Her "music" had become modulated and subtle, her simplicity had lost its immaturity, and her rushes of enthusiasm had been tamed to thoughtful irony. She had begun to master the kind of transparency and effortless ease she had taken as her goal. She now saw the lyric not as a structure, or as requiring a certain content, but primarily as a form of movement, with a rise, a rush, pauses, and a fall, like music or the dance. She studied Yeats endlessly, not only his poems but his remarks on lyric poetry. She had misgivings that revealing her darker side might alienate readers, but *Flame and Shadow* went through four printings within a year.

Always in need of more money than she and Filsinger seemed to earn and always on the lookout for ways to further her professional reputation, she turned again in 1921 to the idea of editing another anthology, this time a collection of poems for children. She selected only poems written for adults, ranging from English ballads to Dickinson, Yeats, and Graves, with an emphasis on nature and the seasons. Her preface stated her belief that poetry is primarily for enjoyment and should not, especially for children, teach a lesson or show condescension. *Rainbow Gold,* published in 1922, was another resounding success, selling more copies than her own work and remaining a kind of classic for many years.

Through the early 1920s Teasdale's productivity began to decline. She fled more and more frequently to country inns in New Jersey or New England for lengthy "rests," and Filsinger was often away on business trips. In 1921 the death of her father, with whom she had always had an adoring attachment, left her feeling depressed and vulnerable for a long time. Becoming fastidious and sensitive to an extreme and more filled than ever with indefinable ailments, she rarely went out and saw few friends. She continued to wear clothing in the styles popular before World War I. She spent insomniac nights working on her poems and rose late. Sometime in the early 1920s she had begun taking Veronal, a sedative, regularly.

In 1923 Teasdale sailed with her husband to England, where she settled down in London for three and a half months while Filsinger dashed about the Continent on business. Here she seemed to come alive again, visiting the Walter de la Mares, Charlotte Mew, and other literary people, and trying to find an English publisher for *Flame and Shadow.* London became *"my* city." This was the first of several trips to a place she would gradually come to think of as a refuge from problems that threatened her. She was proud of her English ancestry, had been reared in the English literary tradition, and pictured herself, with wry self-irony, as a "lady" out of a novel by Henry James.

Longer and longer gaps began to occur between her periods of creativity as she wondered whether she would ever again have enough poems for another volume. By 1926 she was able to gather fifty-nine poems for a new book, almost her slimmest, *Dark of the Moon.* The mood is autumnal, and the themes center on approaching age and death, the incompleteness of life, the inadequacy of wisdom, and the turning to a private inner self for peace. Even as she questioned whether her life and her work were worthwhile, her poems had become increasingly skilled and effective. *Dark of the Moon* contains some of her most satisfactory work.

Her literary taste in these years paralleled the increasing sophistication of her own achievement. She discovered Proust and read with passionate delight, in French, each volume of his great novel as it was published, feeling that only Edmund Wilson among critics had comprehended Proust's importance. Virginia Woolf, in whom she saw aspects of her own personality reflected, became for her the most interesting living writer, and she even contrived to meet Woolf on a trip to England in 1931. Teasdale's critical judgments were pithy and often illuminating, as she observed the antic personalities of her contemporaries—such as Edna St. Vincent Millay and Elinor Wylie—and assessed new work as it appeared. Her letters suggest that she might have produced lively and controversial criticism (her characterization, for example, of Edith Sitwell's style as "sawdust and vinegar") if it not been for her shyness and distaste for public clashes.

In 1926 a young college student named Margaret Conklin wrote Teasdale a charming letter which, contrary to her custom, she answered. On meeting, Teasdale was startled to find someone who, she felt, was herself all over again. At a time in life when she felt herself sinking under a weight of hopelessness, she revived, as if an infusion of youth could restore her to the time before everything began to go wrong. She took Margaret on a ten-weeks' trip to England in 1927, trying to repeat the happy summer she had spent in Europe with Jessie Rittenhouse fifteen years earlier in her own youth. She told friends that Margaret was the daughter she had always wanted to have. From then until Teasdale's death, Margaret Conklin was her closest friend, and afterward became her literary executor.

By 1928 Teasdale had decided to get out of her marriage, which seemed to stand in the way of her finding herself again. The faithful Filsinger reacted wildly to the suggestion of divorce, however, so she consulted a lawyer privately and waited until he went abroad again in the spring of 1929. After giving her friends misleading clues, she secretly boarded a train for Reno in late May. Filsinger was notified of the divorce action while in Johannesburg, South Africa; she persuaded him to go along with it. Suffering much anguish and guilt, she was awarded the divorce in early September 1929. She refused to see him again for over two years.

Instead of finding release and freedom following her divorce, Teasdale lapsed further into loneliness and inactivity, refusing to discuss her problems with her friends and writing almost nothing for two years. She managed to glean a handful of earlier poems from her notebooks, adding a few she had written for Margaret Conklin; and she put them together as a small illustrated volume of verses for children called *Stars To-Night*, which Macmillan published in 1930. Besides a new enlarged edition of her anthology, *The Answering Voice* (1928), she published no other book in the years following *Dark of the Moon*. In 1931 she wrote Genevieve Taggard that she was "almost completely out of the writing game."

But in 1931, when her increasing morbidity began to frighten even herself, she turned to her despair as a subject and began to write again. Over the next two years she produced around fifteen moving and skilled lyrics, recovering her voice as she yielded to the dark side she had not been able to prevail against. Vachel Lindsay's suicide in December 1931, following a mental breakdown, shattered her self-control, partly because she had often entertained the thought of suicide herself.

In search of a project, she had signed a contract with Macmillan in 1931 to edit and prepare an introduction for a collection of love poems by Christina Rossetti. The research seemed endless and took her to England in the summer of 1931 and again in 1932. Her original plan expanded to a larger-scale biographical study entitled "Christina Rossetti: An Intimate Portrait." She completed about 11,000 words before being stricken with pneumonia in both lungs in England in August 1932.

Teasdale then returned to New York, ill and severely depressed; her state of mind was alarming to her friends. She recovered enough physically to spend two weeks in Florida in January 1933 with Jessie Rittenhouse, who urged her to seek psychiatric care. In her apartment at 1 Fifth Avenue in New York, in the early morning hours of Sunday, 29 January 1933, she took an overdose of sleeping pills and lay down in a bathtub filled with warm water. Her body was found the next morning by her nurse.

After Teasdale's death, which was front-page news across the country, Margaret Conklin, following instructions in the poetry notebooks, gathered a last collection of poems, published in 1933 with the title Teasdale had stipulated, *Strange Victory*. The terms of Teasdale's will forbade publication of any other previously unpublished work. Her financial estate was divided between Ernst Filsinger and Margaret Conklin, and on Conklin's death it went to Wellesley College to fund an annual poetry prize. Margaret Conklin, with the assistance of John Hall Wheelock, also edited the *Collected Poems of Sara Teasdale* (1937).

Sara Teasdale's critical reputation declined as the fortunes of modernist poets rose in the 1940s and 1950s. Their "difficult" and "new" poetry, always in rebellion, lost the large popular audience enjoyed by the traditional lyricists and went into the universities. In addition to the tendency to deprecate the older work, there was a decided masculine bias against the women poets who flourished before 1940. Some critics even openly praised Marianne Moore and Emily Dickinson for having minds like men, while deploring feminine emotionalism. But with the passage of time, and the development of feminist points of view, Teasdale's work can be viewed again freshly as a significant contribution in the dominant poetic tradition of 1910-1940. John Hall Wheelock considered her "one of the great lyric poets of the English lan-

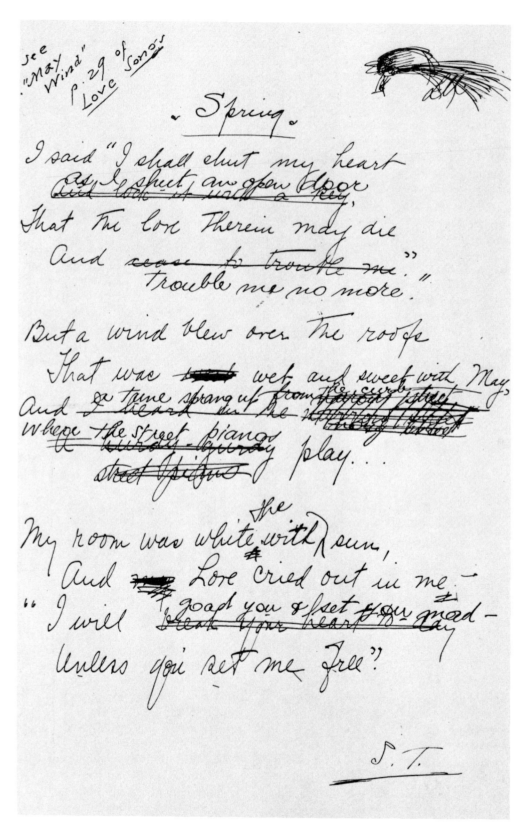

Draft for a poem revised as number four of a group called "Over the Roofs" in Teasdale's Collected Poems *(by permission of the Estate of Sara Teasdale; courtesy of the Lilly Library, Indiana University)*

guage." Her struggle with her identity and conventional role as a woman has emerged as an important concern in the work of recent critics. Teasdale's art is examined in critical detail in Carol Schoen's *Sara Teasdale* in the Twayne Authors series. Cheryl Walker sensitively explores feminist questions in relation to Teasdale in her forthcoming *Masks Outrageous and Austere: American Culture's Legacy to Modern Women Poets*.

While critical estimation of her work is still being formed, there is no doubt that Sara Teasdale's popularity has remained surprisingly constant since she first came to public notice in the early decades of the century. During World War II a Liberty ship was named after her. When *Love Songs* (1917) was republished by Macmillan in 1975, 2,760 copies were sold the first year. And *The Collected Poems* has remained continuously in print since 1937. In 1984, Teasdale's literary executor, Margaret Conklin, gave permission to release previously unpublished works. Fifty-one unpublished poems from the notebooks and twenty previously uncollected poems, together with a selection from *The Collected Poems*, were edited by William Drake and published by Macmillan as *Mirror of the Heart*.

Biographies:
Margaret Haley Carpenter, *Sara Teasdale, A Biography* (New York: Schulte, 1960);

William Drake, *Sara Teasdale: Woman and Poet* (San Francisco: Harper & Row, 1979).

References:
William Drake, Introduction to *Mirror of the Heart* (New York: Macmillan, 1984);
Jessie Rittenhouse, *My House of Life* (Boston & New York: Houghton Mifflin, 1934);
Jean Starr Untermeyer, *Private Collection* (New York: Knopf, 1965), pp. 52-64, 289.

Papers:
The Beinecke Rare Book and Manuscript Library at Yale University has poetry notebooks and Teasdale's travel diary (1905), as well as letters from Vachel Lindsay to Teasdale (1913-1931). The Missouri Historical Society in St. Louis has letters from Teasdale to Ernst Filsinger; "Notes on Sara Teasdale" by Williamina Parrish, a member of The Potters club. The Wellesley College Library has notebooks and the unfinished manuscript on Christina Rossetti. The University of Chicago Library has letters from Teasdale to Harriet Monroe. The Rollins College Library has letters from Teasdale to Jessie Rittenhouse. The State University of New York at Buffalo Library has letters from Teasdale to Jean and Louis Untermeyer.

Jean Toomer

(26 December 1894-30 March 1967)

Motley Deakin
University of Florida

SELECTED BOOKS: *Cane* (New York: Boni & Liveright, 1923);
Essentials (Chicago: Lakeside Press, 1931);
An Interpretation of Friends Worship (Philadelphia: Committee on Religious Education of Friends General Conference, 1947);
The Flavor of Man (Philadelphia: Young Friends Movement of the Philadelphia Yearly Meetings, 1949);
The Wayward and the Seeking: A Collection of Writings by Jean Toomer, edited by Darwin Turner

(Washington, D.C.: Howard University Press, 1980).

OTHER: *Balo: A One Act Sketch of Negro Life*, in *Plays of Negro Life*, edited by Alain Locke and Montgomery Gregory (New York & London: Harper, 1927), pp. 269-286;
"Race Problems and Modern Society," in *Problems of Civilization*, edited by Baker Brownell (New York: Van Nostrand, 1929);
"York Beach," in *The New American Caravan*, edited

by Alfred Kreymborg, Lewis Mumford, and
Paul Rosenfeld (New York: Macaulay, 1929),
pp. 12-83;

"Blue Meridian," in *The New Caravan*, edited by
Kreymborg, Mumford, and Rosenfeld (New
York: Norton, 1936), pp. 633-654;

"Five Vignettes," in *Black American Literature: Poetry*,
edited by Darwin Turner (Columbus: Merrill,
1969).

PERIODICAL PUBLICATIONS: "Banking
Coal," *Crisis*, 24 (June 1922): 65;

"Easter," *Little Review*, 11 (Spring 1925): 3-7;

"Reflections," *Dial*, 86 (1929): 314;

"White Arrow," *Dial*, 86 (July 1929): 596;

"As the Eagle Soars," *Crisis*, 41 (April 1932): 116;

"Brown River, Smile," *Pagany*, 3 (Winter 1932): 29-
33;

"Of a Certain November," *Dubuque Dialogue*, 1 November 1935;

Jean Toomer (photograph by Marjorie Content Toomer)

"See the Heart," *Friend's Intelligencer*, 104 (9 August
1947): 423.

The literary reputation of Jean Toomer is
based primarily on *Cane* (1923), a collection of
poems, impressionistic prose sketches, and stories
on Afro-American topics. He published a few other
poems, stories, and dramas, as well as some essays
and book reviews, in various periodicals, but none
of them equaled his achievement in *Cane*. Though
an influence on black writers of the Harlem Renaissance, he did not identify himself closely with them,
preferring instead to think of himself as a new kind
of man, a blending of races, an American. He was,
as he said, of the human race.

A strong influence on Toomer was his grandfather P. B. S. Pinchback, an important Louisiana
politician of the Reconstruction Era. Toomer spent
much of his childhood in the home of his grandfather, who was living in Washington, D.C., by the
time Toomer was born. Pinchback dominated his
family, including his daughter Nina, Toomer's
mother, who remained most of her life a member
of her parents' household. Pinchback opposed her
marriage to Nathan Toomer, a Georgia planter,
who deserted his wife after about a year. Without
resources, Nina moved with her new-born child
back to her father's home. The child was christened
Eugene Nathan Toomer, but through much of his
childhood was known by the surname Pinchback.
Later in life he changed Eugene to Jean.

In "On Being an American," one of his autobiographical writings, Toomer described his racial heredity as "Scotch, Welsh, German, English,
French, Dutch, Spanish, with some dark blood."
His grandfather's home on Bacon Street was not
in a black neighborhood, and he remembered it as
free of racial prejudice. A leader among the children with whom he played, he remembered their
associations generally with affection. The tensions
he experienced were mainly in the home, primarily
between his grandfather and his mother, and between his grandfather and himself. These tensions,
he thought, were the root in December 1905 of the
one serious illness of his childhood, one which
brought him close to death. When he recovered,
after about eight months, he felt weak and incapable of resuming his old position with his friends.
He reacted by sitting for hours in a kind of haughty
isolation on a post in front of the house. Recalling
this episode in later life, he saw his acting the role
of "candidate-saint" as his typical response to problems too difficult for him to resolve.

When Toomer was eleven, his mother married a second time. This marriage also failed, but it initiated a new phase in Toomer's life, which was marked by frequent changes of residence, a gradual decline in his grandfather's finances, and an increasing racial awareness. The unsettled nature of his life became even more evident when he entered college and tried to decide on a profession. Incapable of sustained effort, he skipped from one interest to another, one institution to the next. In the fall of 1914 he enrolled at the University of Wisconsin planning to study agriculture, but he left after one term. The next fall he entered the Massachusetts College of Agriculture, but again left after a short time. Early in 1916 he was in Chicago enrolled at both the American College of Physical Training and the University of Chicago, where he became interested in evolution and socialism. In the summer of 1917 he registered at City College of New York and stayed on into the fall term but again left without completing the term. He retreated after each failure to his grandfather's home, only to be faced there by increasing irritation and disenchantment. He tried different kinds of work: directing physical education, working in a shipyard, selling cars, working in a store; none of it giving him much satisfaction.

In the midst of this disparate activity he began to write. He also read constantly, seeking authors with whom he felt empathy or in whose work he found useful models. Victor Hugo stirred his sense of social justice, George Bernard Shaw exemplified to him the virtues of candor and independence. Walt Whitman, he thought, had something to teach him about the American experience. Johann Wolfgang von Goethe, in his creation of the character of Wilhelm Meister, gave him a model he could follow. He read Robert Frost, Sherwood Anderson, and the imagist poets as well as books by social reformers, and he heard Clarence Darrow lecture on Charles Darwin. Finally in 1919 in New York, he began to meet authors—Gorham Munson, Kenneth Burke, Hart Crane, Matthew Josephson, Malcolm Cowley, Paul Rosenfeld, Van Wyck Brooks, Robert Littell, Waldo Frank—with whom he could discuss his interests and compare his abilities. The most important of these new acquaintances was Waldo Frank who, during those years in which *Cane* was created, remained his closest literary associate.

In the summer of 1920 Toomer returned to Washington to live with his grandparents. They were old and poor, and his grandfather made demands on him, but he stayed, in part to be with people he loved and who needed him and in part

to have time to write. He wrote, literally, a trunkful of manuscripts: essays, fiction, poetry, drama; but he thought none of it good enough to publish. Yet his confidence in his ability grew, until finally, as he described it in his "Outline of an Autobiography," "I was *inside, I knew literature!* And what was my joy!" But this intense, confining experience also left him exhausted, and his relationship with his grandfather, who by then was almost helpless physically, seemed to Toomer to be a desperate struggle which he feared might end in his own death.

In the fall of 1921, just when he felt most trapped, Toomer was asked by the head of a black school in Sparta, Georgia, who was passing through Washington on his way north to solicit funds for his school, to serve as his replacement during his temporary absence. Toomer jumped at the opportunity. It took him out of a situation that had become unbearable, and it gave him an opportunity to see that part of the South from which the black part of his heritage had come. Though this visit lasted only a few weeks, it became the impetus for *Cane*. What Toomer found was a dying culture, beautiful and sad, and the book he wrote was a swan song. He sent part of the manuscript to Waldo Frank who found a publisher for it. Frank wanted to see the South, so in the fall of 1922 he and Toomer toured the South together. In his foreword to *Cane* Frank praised the book but made more of a point of the author's black heritage than Toomer wanted. For his publicity, Liveright, the publisher, wanted to stress the same racial element, which upset Toomer even more. *Cane* became a critical but not a popular success. The reviewers described it as the beginning of a new era and praised its fidelity and truthfulness. One of the ironies of his life, Toomer thought, was that his readers expected him to write more books like *Cane* when for him that book was a conclusion. That phase of his life was ended.

Cane can be read as one episode in its author's search for self-identity, and the book ends inconclusively. The search led him next to George Gurdjieff, a Russian mystic, whose magnetic personality attracted many disciples in Europe and the United States. Toomer spent the summer of 1924 at the Gurdjieff Institute in Fontainebleu, France, became his disciple, and spent many years explaining and adapting what he learned from him, leading Gurdjieff groups in Harlem (1925) and Chicago (1926-1933).

Toomer sensed in himself a fluctuation between what he characterized as "I-am-I" and "I-am-nothing." Gurdjieff, he believed, offered a means of integrating this duality. Toomer also thought that modern man had insulated himself from nature, and that to achieve wholeness he must attempt to reunite himself with this larger whole, even though the forces of modern society worked against him. He believed that behind the visible world was something even more essential which humanity, in this life, is "out of." Life, then, became an effort at integration and establishing contacts with essentials.

In 1931 Toomer married Margery Latimer, who died giving birth to their child, Margery. In 1934 he married Marjorie Content and lived the remainder of his life with her in Pennsylvania, where he became a Quaker. He wrote little for some years after the publication of *Cane*, but from the late 1920s on he wrote continuously, including several volumes of autobiography, four novels, plays, poetry, short stories, articles and reviews. He tried to find publishers for his work but seldom succeeded. Most of it is still unpublished. In *The Wayward and the Seeking* (1980), Darwin Turner has presented a representative sampling.

In his introduction to the 1923 edition of *Cane*, Waldo Frank characterized Toomer as "a poet in prose," but Darwin Turner, who rediscovered Toomer's work and is probably most responsible for the revival of interest in him, characterized him as "a prose lyricist." Both characterizations suggest that Toomer was not a poet in the conventional sense. He had a good ear for the sounds of words, he could create vivid word images, he was attracted to the gnomic statement, and at times he worked with relatively simple rhyme schemes, but the general effect of his poetry is a loosening of poetic structures, a movement toward prose.

Toomer was not a prolific poet, but the poems he wrote vary greatly in style and purpose. A few poems contain conventional patterns of rhyme and rhythm, but most of them are in free verse. Some present sharp sensory impressions; others use diction that is more general and abstract. Some describe; others argue. Some reflect a contemporary sophistication; others are rooted in old Southern black folkways. At their best, they have a strong sensory and emotional appeal. If they fail, they do so because the intent is not clear, or the experiment does not succeed. Toomer was not a predictable poet; the mercurial quality of his personality is reflected in the variable nature of his poetry.

In *Cane* Toomer integrated some of his poetry into the text as epigraphs, as emotional outbursts, and as refrains. These poetic passages are short and often repeat lines or elements of lines, a char-acteristic which appears to be a carry-over of that African use of repetition which the slaves retained and incorporated into their spirituals and blues. These short passages are the clearest reflection of Toomer's response to the South he experienced in Sparta, Georgia, a South he found "crude in a way, but strangely rich and beautiful." It was there that he heard for the first time blacks singing their spirituals and folksongs, which he found "very rich and sad and joyous and beautiful." Appropriately, almost all of these short poetic passages appear in the sketches set in the South. The few examples of poetry found in the urban sketches seem more prosaic, more negative, less laden with emotion.

The more important body of poetry in *Cane* consists of longer poems set apart from the prose sketches. They range in length from descriptive poems of only a few lines to poems of several stanzas. The topics of these poems vary, but central to them, and to *Cane*, is the theme stated in "Song of the Son":

> An everlasting song, a singing tree,
> Caroling softly souls of slavery,
> What they were, and what they are to me,
> Caroling softly souls of slavery.

This theme of memorializing a dying past recurs in the other poems: portraits, descriptions of nature, poems of work, of longing, of religious trance and erotic ecstasy. Some of these poems relate well to the prose pieces preceding and following them; others seem only tangentially related to the narrative. As with the shorter poetic passages, most of these poems are in the earlier, Southern section of the book. Toomer's impulse to lyric expression did not carry over to his portrayals of urban life in which the characters he portrays seem sterile, more inhibited.

Toomer wrote poetry intermittently in the years after *Cane* appeared, but he failed to get much of it published. Most of these poems he collected in a volume he titled "The Wayward and the Seeking." A few of these poems are published by Turner in his edition of selected works by Toomer, for which he appropriated the title Toomer had given his book of poems. The most important poem Toomer succeeded in publishing is "The Blue Meridian," a long poem different in style and content from his earlier work. On it he spent much time and effort, writing and revising, letting an extract from it, "Brown River, Smile," appear in 1932 before he succeeded in getting the whole poem published in *The New Caravan* (1936). One senses in the poem an urgency lacking in the earlier poetry, a desire to enlighten and persuade quite different from the nostalgia that pervades the poems in *Cane*.

"The Blue Meridian" is both a solution and a vision. All his life Toomer sought a unifying, stabilizing element that would counter what he sensed to be disparities and contradictions within him and around him. His acceptance of Gurdjieff is one evidence of this search. His search for a racial heritage is another; but if Kabnis, the central character in the last section of *Cane,* is a self-portrait by Toomer, that possibility disintegrated before Toomer finished his book. "The Blue Meridian" presents yet another, one which Whitman already had celebrated, but which seems also peculiarly apt for Toomer: America offered the unique possibility that the heterogeneity out of which it was made could be resolved into a unity, a new individual, transcending all his progenitors. America the melting pot becomes an alchemist's crucible refining Emma Lazarus's "Huddled masses yearning to be free" into Toomer's "Free men, whole men, men connected//With one another and with Deity."

As a presentation of a vision "The Blue Meridian" conveys an urgency characteristic of a believer, one who, because of what he has seen, must share it with others. The vision is mystic, having in it images of crosses, lights, vistas, and racial icons. The poem has in it as well the impulse of the mystic to repeat in variant forms a description of that vision which he never feels sure he has described adequately. The poem moves from a negative past to a transcendent future. It exhorts, promises, and strives, seeking to merge the observer with that resplendent light which stirs rapture in his soul. The poem is an amazing statement to come from one contemporary with the members of the Lost Generation, whose "visions" were more characteristically of wastelands, lonely streets, and sterile relationships. That Toomer was so at odds with the dominant sensibility of his times could help explain why he had such difficulty finding a publisher for "The Blue Meridian."

In the 1930s Toomer developed an interest in aphorisms and maxims, some of which he col-lected and had privately printed in *Essentials* (1931). He continued to write more, collecting them in a volume he titled "Remember and Return," which he never succeeded in getting published. His interest in gnomic statement carries over into some of his poetry of the same period. These poems move away from the expansive lyricism of the earlier poetry to a poetic expression closer to that of Wallace Stevens. The few published examples suggest that Toomer was successful in employing yet another variety of poetic talent.

Toomer died with the realization that he failed to accomplish much of what he had dreamed of achieving. He felt isolated and frustrated, sensing within himself some obstacle which prevented him from expressing his thoughts freely. Though the poetry he did publish is not extensive, it displays a variety and richness of expression that makes him a distinctive voice both among the poets of the Harlem Renaissance and among the poets who were developing an American version of symbolism. Poetry, though, is only one aspect of Toomer's literary achievement. It is perhaps best read not by itself, but as part of a unified whole, as but one form in which Toomer chose to describe his quest for identity.

References:

Bryan Joseph Benson and Mabel Mayle Dillard, *Jean Toomer* (Boston: Twayne, 1980);

Alain Locke, *Four Negro Poets* (New York: Simon & Schuster, 1927);

Nellie Y. McKay, *Jean Toomer, Artist* (Chapel Hill & London: University of North Carolina Press, 1984);

Paul Rosenfeld, *Men Seen* (New York: Dial, 1925), pp. 227-245;

Darwin T. Turner, *In a Minor Chord* (Carbondale & Edwardsville: Southern Illinois University Press, 1971), pp. 1-59.

Papers:

Toomer's manuscripts are at the Fisk University Library.

Mark Turbyfill
(29 June 1896-)

Peter Revell
Westfield College, London

SELECTED BOOKS: *The Living Frieze* (Evanston, Ill.: Monroe Wheeler, 1921);

Evaporation: A Symposium, by Turbyfill and Samuel Putnam (Winchester, Mass.: Modern Review, 1923);

A Marriage with Space, Poetry, 28 (May 1926);

A Marriage with Space, and Other Poems (Chicago: Covici, 1927);

The Art of Ruth Page (N.p.: Privately printed, 1931);

The Words Beneath Us, balletic poems by Turbyfill, choreographic tableaux by Charles Bockman, comments by Claudia Cassidy and Ann Barzel, and "The Motion of Poetry" by Samuel Putnam (Chicago: Tower Features Press, 1951).

OTHER: *Five Arts,* by Turbyfill, Waldo Frank, Karleton Hackett, C. J. Bulliet, and W. Roger Greeley (New York: Van Nostrand, 1929).

PERIODICAL PUBLICATIONS: "Thin Day" and "The Rose Jar," *Little Review,* 3 (June-July 1916): 20;

"Windflowers," *Poetry,* 10 (May 1917): 62;

"Reality," *Others,* 4 (June 1917): 28-29;

"Lines Written on a Mountainside at Night," *Youth,* 1 (October 1918): 6-7;

"Journeys and Discoveries," *Poetry,* 15 (October 1919): 14;

"Voluntaries," *Poetry,* 18 (June 1921): 136;

"Outlines," *Poetry,* 24 (June 1924): 124;

"A Note on Cabaret," *This Quarter,* 1 (Spring 1925): 194-195;

"The Poetry of Forces," *Little Review,* 12 (May 1927): supplement, p. 38;

"Absolutely and Sincerely," *Poetry,* 32 (May 1928): 61-74;

"Confessions—Questionaire," *Little Review,* 12 (May 1929): 83-84;

"Dance Poems," *Poetry,* 38 (September 1931): 322;

"The Life of the Bee," *New Review* (Winter 1932): 339-342;

"The Passing of the Author of Life without Death"

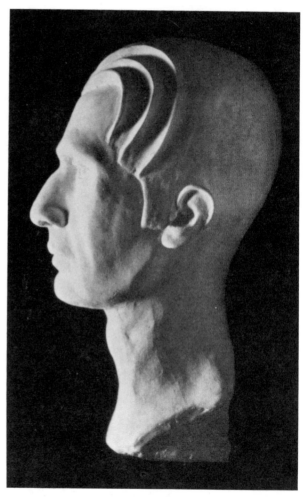

Mark Turbyfill, bust by Tennessee Anderson

and "Youth," *Procession,* 1 (February 1932): 19-20;

"Invitation to the Dance," "Dark Banquet," "Portrait Impression," "The Poet," and "Dance and Transfiguration," *Poetry,* 51 (February 1938): 258;

"Hardy Perennials," *Poetry,* 52 (July 1938): 190;

"Outside a Hothouse; A Lost Dancer," *Poetry,* 61 (January 1943): 546;

"Chicago," *Synthesis,* 9-10 October 1965, p. 4.

There are few American poets of this century who have not combined two vocations (those of teacher and writer are the most frequent). Mark Turbyfill has, over most of his life, combined three: poet, ballet dancer, and painter. His work in all these fields is interrelated, and there is nothing haphazard about his achievements, but such a diffusion of talents must also have carried a price in terms of the more widespread renown he might otherwise have earned.

Mark Turbyfill was born on 29 June 1896 in the small town of Wynnewood, about fifty miles south of Oklahoma City, the administrative capital of what was then known as Indian Territory. His parents were both Southerners, his father from North Carolina and his mother from Texas. His father had begun as a carpenter and then became an architect. He was for a while State Architect for Schools in Oklahoma and later a partner in a thriving architectural practice that built schools, banks, and private homes in Oklahoma City. Presumably a commission of some kind had brought the family to Wynnewood, for soon after the birth of their only child they returned to Oklahoma City, where Turbyfill spent his boyhood. In 1911 a major drought and crop failure in Oklahoma caused a recession in business, and the father—whose partner had earlier returned to Chicago, resumed his architectural practice there, and prospered—took his family to Chicago, where he found a place with Marshall & Fox, a major Chicago architectural firm.

Since then Chicago has been Mark Turbyfill's home and base of operations. He attended Lake View High School and published his first poems in the school magazine, the *Red and White*. It happened that his discovery of his own interest in poetry coincided with the beginning of what subsequently came to be called the Chicago Renaissance, a reawakening of activity in the arts that was in effect the second wave of an earlier literary awakening which began in Chicago during the 1890s. This earlier movement was primarily genteel in impetus (though frequently realist in expression), the product of a desire for native culture and uplift on the part of the newly wealthy commercial class. The only notable poet of the earlier movement was the earnest and romantic William Vaughan Moody.

The new renaissance included less genteel, even antibourgeois elements and was, to begin with, predominantly a poetic revival, as signaled by the appearance of two Chicago-based magazines which so rapidly established national and international reputations that they were for a few years among the chief places of publication for established and emerging poets in America and in Europe. Harriet Monroe's *Poetry*, first appearing in May 1912, and Margaret Anderson's *Little Review* (which also printed prose), following in March 1914, were both aided and abetted for varying periods by Ezra Pound, who, as foreign correspondent, contrived to insinuate into their pages the best writing that he could find in Europe, which was often the work of Americans living abroad, including some of his own. Harriet Monroe was not always easily persuaded of the value of Pound's selections, but she appears to have had no doubts about a group of poems by the then unknown Hilda Doolittle, which Pound had signed on her behalf, "H. D., Imagiste," later drawing from them and other sources the imagist theory of poetic expression.

It was these poems, published in the January 1913 issue of *Poetry*, and also Pound's own work of this period, that particularly excited the young Mark Turbyfill. While still in high school, he began to submit poems in the imagist style to the *Little Review* and to *Poetry* and to have them published, by Anderson in May 1916 and by Monroe in May 1917. Monroe included some of the first group of poems she had accepted in her anthology, *The New Poetry*, which also appeared in 1917 and passed through three enlarged editions to become one of the major collections of new verse. That she championed Turbyfill's work early and late demonstrates her well-known catholicity of taste. His work was far removed in theme and style from the work of the other poets—Vachel Lindsay, Edgar Lee Masters, and Carl Sandburg—who were her best-known "discoveries" and the most celebrated among the poets of the Chicago Renaissance. Turbyfill was twenty or more years younger than any of these poets, and his work exhibited the modernist austerity of language and precision of expression which theirs lacked. Yet, in its preoccupation with aesthetic considerations, with the evanescent beauty discoverable behind the commonplace and the ugly, Turbyfill's poetry connects in some respects with the earlier "genteel" Chicago Renaissance, with the aestheticism of Henry Blake Fuller's novel *The Chevalier of Pensieri-Vani* (1890) rather than the realism of his novel *The Cliff-Dwellers* (1893). It is not surprising that Turbyfill became close friends with Fuller, who was a member of the editorial board of *Poetry* and nearly forty years his senior, while he had almost no contact with Lindsay, Masters, and Sandburg. He was also on terms of friendship with the poet Eunice Tietjens, an associate editor of *Poetry*.

Even before he formed friendships with

Fuller and Tietjens, Turbyfill had made the acquaintance of Amy Lowell, almost meeting her in January 1915, when she had come to Chicago in an unsuccessful attempt to "buy into" the poetry side of the *Little Review*. In the course of her discussions with Margaret Anderson, Lowell had asked "Who is Mark Turbyfill?" and expressed enthusiasm for his poems in the *Little Review*. Learning of her interest, Turbyfill had ventured to write to Lowell at her suite at the Congress Hotel, and soon after she invited him there to meet her. Unfortunately the meeting did not take place because Lowell suddenly had to return home, but she retained her interest in him. Turbyfill recalls a number of later occasions when he was invited to "magnificent parties, they were almost banquets" at Sevenels, the Lowell mansion in Brookline, Massachusetts, where guests included such poets of his own generation as S. Foster Damon, Royall Snow, and Grant Code. They became in the process somewhat typecast as members of Lowell's "group." In the strife that followed her attempt, more or less successful, to take over the imagist movement, this identification was not necessarily fortuitous, since it gave them suspect status in the view of Ezra Pound, whose influence was widespread.

In 1917 Turbyfill also took the first step in what was to be the major artistic activity of his lifetime. While still in high school his imagination had been fired by a performance by the ballet dancer Serge Oukrainsky, and in 1917 he enrolled for a course of private lessons with Oukrainsky. Shortly after completing them the following year he enlisted in the army. He served only six or seven months and never left Illinois, being assigned to duties first at a medical supply depot on Chicago's South Side and later at Camp Grant, near Rockford. For about a year after his demobilization late in 1918 he was in New York, somewhat at loose ends and unsure of a future career, when Oukrainsky offered him a place in the Chicago Grand Opera Company Ballet. His first season in ballet was 1919-1920, and he was retained for 1920-1921. In 1924 he became a principal dancer with Chicago Allied Arts, the first established ballet theater in the United States. This prestigious company was directed by Adolph Bolm, who had previously been associated with the Ballet Russe. In 1928 Turbyfill had a small role in the first performances of Stravinsky's *Apollon Musagète*, to Bolm's choreography at the Library of Congress.

For many years from 1926 onward Turbyfill was associated with the ballerina Ruth Page, who was later ballet mistress of the Chicago Opera Company. He was engaged by her for principal roles and also undertook the promotion of her career as an independent dancer, producing a monograph on her work. During the 1920s Turbyfill was also active as a ballet teacher and as a choreographer. Perhaps his best-known pupil was Katherine Dunham, the great Negro dancer and choreographer. In 1929, while she was still an unknown, they attempted to establish the first Negro ballet company, but the time for such ventures had not yet arrived (she established the first such school in 1931 in Chicago). Turbyfill also served as dance critic for the *Chicagoan* and later as Chicago correspondent for *Dance* magazine; he contributed an essay on "The Dance" to the critical symposium *Five Arts* (1929) which also included essays by Waldo Frank and others. In 1928 he visited Europe for six months, staying in London, Paris, elsewhere in France, and Germany.

During the 1920s writing poetry had become a secondary activity for Turbyfill, but it remained a vital part of his life. His output of verse was never prolific, and it was five years from the appearance of his first poem in the *Little Review* before he had enough to make a slim volume, *The Living Frieze*, published in 1921 by Monroe Wheeler, who at this time was working and publishing in Evanston, Illinois. It is a handsomely produced book, with a touch of Art Nouveau in its design that well suits the hint of aestheticism in its contents, which expressed, in Samuel Putnam's view, "the sculptural note of the exquisite." The title, suggesting a vision of the Parthenon frieze come to life, aptly expresses the mood of the sixty-one short lyrics in the book. These lyrics are fundamentally concerned with the poet's search for the evanescent moment of beauty, the ineffable perception of truth in his day-to-day life. He writes as a young man in love, with an older woman among others, and concerned only to savor the deepest and richest experience that life can offer him, through the senses, the emotions, the passions, the intellect. The threat of romantic hedonism and fin-de-siècle excess which this schema might appear to invite is skillfully avoided by the freshness of the poetic perceptions, which are disarming and spontaneous, yet combined with an elaborate and playful formality of language that suggests a finely tuned sensuousness held in easy control. The implied nearness of surrender to excess is part of that control, perhaps most openly expressed in "The Mind Plays with the Sea Storm," concerned with the delicate apprehension of shades of feeling and emotion discovered in comparing the violence of nature with that of sexual passion:

> And I know your ecstatic response
> Exquisite Monster,
> As I blossom into glittering spray
> Above you!

The perception is, however artful the language, one of natural beauty in unnatural, hostile surroundings. "The Intangible Symphony" is the beauty that is there if we can learn to see it:

>   on trellis, on infinite arch,
> On bridges of fretted iron,
> Frail to thought, acrid to sight,
> Thunderous with traffic of men,
> Red-budding, peach-petalled,
> Beauty flames into view.

The language itself is sometimes of melting beauty, as in the opening lines of "Last Season":

> Oh, once in April late,
> When the slow bee pushed
> Through the thick, sweet air.

Lines such as these recall the enraptured tones of the Cavalier lyricists of seventeenth-century England. As in their work, the tone is prevented from becoming cloying by the occasional use of the humorous conceit. For example, "Bas Relief" compares physical passion for the beloved with the appreciation of a work of sculpted art—"What is low relief/To the heart that seeks the whole/Full-carved from the base!"

In spite of its superficial formal resemblances to the imagist poems of H. D., Turbyfill's work in this volume draws upon a wider range of resources in the poetic tradition. The diction is at times deliberately "antique," with occasional inversions and formalized locutions. If the overall impression is of a playful fantasy built upon a reality which contemporary realists saw differently, the overall direction of the work is not toward escapism but toward some kind of metaphysical statement, an attempt to penetrate beneath surface appearances to discover essences, perhaps best expressed in the poem "Chicago." This poem is not a conscious riposte to Sandburg's well-known 1914 poem with the same title, but an alternative and equally valid account of the city, expressing its nascent promise, its visionary expectation ("in the untrod night/I have looked upon your rapt/Presence./There was a whiteness/as of wings stirring"). The occasional glimpses elsewhere in the collection of a more realistic Chicago, in lines such as "The unmoved city of granite/And noise" in "A Song for Souls under Fire," are the more striking for their rarity and conciseness.

Turbyfill had won *Poetry*'s Young Poets Prize in 1917, 1918, and 1919, and *The Living Frieze* was favorably received in little-magazine circles. Before the book's publication, his uncollected poems had even won guarded praise from Ezra Pound—"Turbyfill has perhaps the cell-nucleus of something about which a book of poems might form itself "— and these words were printed on the dust jacket. Samuel Putnam, a close friend, gave it an enthusiastic and penetrating review in the *Milwaukee Arts Monthly* in 1922. At that time they were collaborating on a small collection of verse and prose, published the following year as *Evaporation: A Symposium*. Turbyfill's contribution was an essay, "The Obstetric of the Idea," and nine poems, including "The Metaphysical Botanists," an aptly titled account of the poet as culler of metaphysical insights into the beauty and joy of the created universe. The "Evaporation" of the title is expounded, with an excess of playful terminology, in the prose essay as a kind of distillation which will remove "the curtains of mist" obscuring "immutable Cause" and "the paradox and potency of Form, the minute shape and delineation of Infinity." For "the truth is, one tiny word symbolizing a patterned proscenium to the absolute, where all rhythm moves and rests, may contain enough voltage of Cause to blow out the fuse of the brewing storm."

This essay presents the playful side of this poet's quest for the absolute, which had progressed beyond the hints and glimpses of *The Living Frieze* toward a more formulated metaphysical statement. *Evaporation* also includes "Prelude," the first section of the long poem Turbyfill had been planning since 1920 and which eventually appeared in its entirety as *A Marriage with Space*, occupying the whole May 1926 issue of *Poetry*, the only occasion on which a single issue of that magazine was devoted to a single poem.

Harriet Monroe's notes, a kind of apologia for the issue, include a transcription of Turbyfill's first plan for the poem. It is to be "The career of an individual consciousness. A poem moving with musical and spiritual flexibility, from narrative to lyric spontaneity. . . . A poem dealing with idealization and manifestation; with creative processes of mind. Capturing the unseen in its transition to the seen. Showing life transcending the limitations of time, space and matter; the enlightened mind

Mark Turbyfill and Samuel Putnam, 1920s (photograph by Jan Fujita, Chicago Evening Post)

accomplishing dematerialization and attaining to an ascension." The enlightened mind is to be "a twentieth-century man, an architect, familiar with contemporary Chicago, individually and aesthetically. . . . He goes to the dunes of Lake Michigan's shores, and in silence, simplicity, compassion, appreciates them and their various life. There he transcends physical sight, having demonstrated his metaphysical understanding . . . and attains to the final beauty—the absolute."

These notes place Turbyfill in the line of twentieth-century American poets who undertook quests for meaning by writing long poems, a line that includes Conrad Aiken, Hart Crane, Ezra Pound, T. S. Eliot, H. D., and Charles Olson. The questing spirit of *A Marriage with Space*, in its final form, is named Emanuel Savoir, perhaps denoting the combination of mystical and scientific knowledge. His troubled musings on the shore recall those of the unnamed seeker in Aiken's *The Charnel Rose* (1918), the first in Aiken's sequence of poems of quest eventually collected as *The Divine Pilgrim* (1949), but there is every difference between the nihilistic angst of Aiken's quester, who sees only a cold and empty shore, and the architectural embodiment of Savoir's final vision of the absolute harmony of the universe as an "edifice of light," a "honeycomb of light,/House of many mansions,/Symmetrical, serene . . . plane through/Shining plane."

After its publication in *Poetry*, where it attracted considerable and controversial attention and won the Helen Haire Levinson prize for 1926, Turbyfill's long poem was collected in *A Marriage with Space, and Other Poems*, published by Pascal Covici in Chicago in 1927. This volume is Turbyfill's most important collection (and also an example of Covici's exceptionally high standard of book production). In addition to the long poem it includes a group of short poems, "Memoria Tecnica," which are mostly different in style from those in Turbyfill's first book. The diction is in general more terse and direct, the subject matter occasionally satiric, as in "Buffet Dinner at an Arts Club," the observation just as acute but less oblique. There is much more reference to Turbyfill's life in the ballet, including a series of tributes to other dancers. "Real-

VOLUME XXVIII   MAY, 1926   NUMBER II

POETRY
A Magazine of Verse
EDITED BY HARRIET MONROE

A Marriage with Space
by Mark Turbyfill
Editorial on the Poem

Subscription $3.00 per year   Single Copies 25¢

Front cover for the only issue of Poetry *ever devoted to
a single poem*

ists" is a slap back at those who had accused his
first book of unreality:

> Hid under a bushel of rubbish
> A poem exists—
> Organized, effulgent.
> They might dig up the vision,
> But they keep throwing on another spadeful:
> "You don't know reality, haven't lived."

All of these changes indicate the directions that
Turbyfill's work as a poet was later to take and also,
unfortunately, the partial waning of his interest in
poetry as the ballet came to absorb more and more
of his life. Yet paradoxically much of his later work
as a poet is more specifically linked to the ballet
than before. The chief change of direction was toward satire, notably in a sequence, entitled "Absolutely and Sincerely," of free-verse satirical
celebrations of the heroes of the age—Valentino,
Lindbergh, Gertrude Ederle, Krishnamurti, and

others. These poems are good-humored but mock-
ingly full of jazz-age zap, advertisers' jingles, and
appropriate hyperbole:

> Earthquakes! Volcanos! Credoes!
> ....
> Everything blown up and out!

The sequence was published in the May 1928 issue
of *Poetry* and, like Turbyfill's shorter poems published after *A Marriage with Space, and Other Poems*,
has never been collected.

During the 1940s Turbyfill appears to have
given up the writing of poetry altogether as his
interest in painting, which had begun as a hobby
in 1931, occupied more of his time. His work in
this medium has had considerable success and is
represented in some of the major galleries. One
phase of his work is in the abstract expressionist
style of Mark Tobey, a close friend for many years,
in which he has adapted the "white writing" techniques of Tobey's white-on-white paintings to include the text of some of his own poems, again
including the "Prelude" to "A Marriage with
Space." The poem is as significant in this context
as in the original one and exemplifies Turbyfill's
search for the moment of absolute perception in
the various media he has tried.

His last published collection, *The Words Beneath Us* (1951), which he considers an amateurish
souvenir of a balletic experiment, is nevertheless
interesting for the light it throws on his notion of
the connection between poetry and ballet. The
poems, about half of which are new and the rest
borrowed from the earlier collections, were recited,
by Turbyfill himself, and without musical accompaniment except in the intervals, as the rhythmic
and aural underpinning of a sequence of short ballet pieces choreographed by Charles Bockman.
The program was presented by the Ballet Guild of
Chicago at the Eighth Street Theater early in 1951.
The "poem-dance" resulting from this collaboration was, to use the words of the prefatory note,
"A fusion of lyric movements and lyric phrases. It
does not interpret nor dramatize poetry. It is poetry. In their sequence here the Poem-Dances tell
their life history little more explicitly than do raindrops fluttering on a cobweb. They form, flash a
color or two, and pass from sight to a world where
there is 'no ground but the words beneath us.'"
The attempt is not to discover through perception
but to create through artifice the moment of vision,
necessarily as evanescent as the performing art itself.

129

ADVANCING TOWARD THE DANCE

Slowly the unknowable couple advances
As a single pear in the orchard
Changing its green to russet
Senses it will ripen and be eaten.

Opal night, still dreaming,
Stirs as if to waken, dazzled by colors
So deeply saturated she can bear no more.

All that breathes is weaving
Into melodic progression,
Apotheosis ringing fortissimo.

Golden chariots rush nearer,
And selves unfold,
Evolving measureless arabesques
To give the day its infinite extension.

Time burns concentrated
As through a reading glass,
And all is clear: stony enigmas crumble,
Plainly to tell no secret.

Undulant forms electric
Illuminate the far-off, shadowy years
Attuning thousands upon thousands
To perpetual, nourishing shock,
As thousands follow thousands
To enter the living dance.

Mark Turbyfill
October 17 - 1971

Typescript for an unpublished poem (by permission of the author)

Turbyfill's most recent published work in verse is the long poem "Chicago" (later retitled "Chicago Alive"), which filled one entire page of a 1965 issue of *Synthesis,* an arts-magazine supplement then included with Chicago Lerner newspapers. In form the poem recalls the brash vigor and jingling rhyming of his satirical poems of the late 1920s. It is Turbyfill's most Sandburgian piece but celebrates Chicago's artistic achievements early and late as much as its commercial and industrial life. More recent still is a group of reflective lyrics, written in 1971 but still unpublished, which retain something of the freshness of his lyrics written in the 1920s. They were suggested by the beauty he found in the urban lakeshore setting to which he had recently moved. A new edition of *A Marriage with Space,* omitting the "Memoria Tecnica" section, was published in 1974.

The key to Turbyfill's multiple effort in the arts is perhaps to be found in the passage from the *Encyclopaedia Britannica* which he quotes in his 1929 essay "The Dance": "the rhythmic principle of motion extends throughout the universe, governing the lapse of waves, the flow of tides, the reverberations of light and sound, and the movements of celestial bodies; and in the human organism it manifests itself in the automatic pulses and flexions of the blood and tissues. Dancing is merely the voluntary application of the rhythmic principle. . . ."

In Turbyfill's vision the natural universe, whether mystically glimpsed or scientifically analyzed, is a unity of motion in harmony, innately joyful, promising an infinitude of beauty if we only know how to find within appearances the organizing principle which lies, like the poem "organized,

effulgent," hidden under the bushel of rubbish. He has continued to live, in reasonable serenity, in his apartment in the Rogers Park District of Chicago, in recent years writing his memoirs, which are as yet unpublished. His work as a poet is long overdue for republication and rediscovery—or perhaps for discovery, since it has never been well known. He is a relatively minor figure, but his association and experimentation with the ballet are unique. His poetry is pleasurable to read in its own right, regardless of poetic fashion, but the best of it has an importance in the history of American poetry of the between-the-wars period.

References:

Ruth Beckford, *Katherine Dunham: A Biography* (New York: Marcel Dekker, 1979), pp. 25-27, 41;

Dale Kramer, *Chicago Renaissance: The Literary Life in the Midwest, 1900-1930* (New York: Appleton-Century, 1966), pp. 260-261;

Pierre Loving, "Dance Rhythms and Crystals," *Youth,* 1 (1921): 32-33;

"Mark Turbyfill [dancer, poet and painter]," *Chicago Review,* 28 (Spring 1977): 33-40;

John Martin, *Ruth Page: An Intimate Biography* (New York: Marcel Dekker, 1977), pp. 71, 83, 87, 152;

Harriet Monroe, "Comment: Mark Turbyfill's Poem," *Poetry,* 28 (May 1926): 92-95;

Ruth Page, *Page By Page* (New York: Dance Horizons, 1978), pp. 108-109, 126-127;

Samuel Putnam, "Curved Attitudes and Elephant Ears," *Milwaukee Arts Monthly* (November-December 1922): 26-28.

Mark Van Doren

(13 June 1894-10 December 1972)

Meredith Yearsley

BOOKS: *Henry David Thoreau: A Critical Study* (Boston & New York: Houghton Mifflin, 1916);

The Poetry of John Dryden (New York: Harcourt, Brace & Howe, 1920; Cambridge, U.K.: Minority Press, 1931); republished as *John Dryden: A Study of His Poetry* (New York: Holt, 1946);

Spring Thunder and Other Poems (New York: Seltzer, 1924);

7 P.M. & Other Poems (New York: A. & C. Boni, 1926);

Edwin Arlington Robinson (New York: Literary Guild, 1927);

Now the Sky & Other Poems (New York: A. & C. Boni, 1928);

Jonathan Gentry (New York: A. & C. Boni, 1931);

Dick and Tom: Tales of Two Ponies (New York: Macmillan, 1931);

Dick and Tom in Town (New York: Macmillan, 1932);

The Transients (New York: Morrow, 1935);

A Winter Diary and Other Poems (New York: Macmillan, 1935);

The Last Look, and Other Poems (New York: Holt, 1937);

Collected Poems, 1922-1938 (New York: Holt, 1939);

Studies in Metaphysical Poetry, by Van Doren and Theodore Spencer (New York: Columbia University Press, 1939);

Shakespeare (New York: Holt, 1939; London: Allen & Unwin, 1941);

The Transparent Tree (New York: Holt, 1940);

Windless Cabins (New York: Holt, 1940);

The Mayfield Deer (New York & San Francisco: Holt, 1941);

Our Lady Peace, and Other War Poems (Norfolk, Conn.: New Directions, 1942);

The Private Reader: Selected Articles and Reviews (New York: Holt, 1942);

Tilda (New York: Holt, 1943);

Liberal Education (New York: Holt, 1943);

The Seven Sleepers, and Other Poems (New York: Holt, 1944);

The Noble Voice: A Study of Ten Great Poems (New York: Holt, 1946); republished as *Mark Van*

Mark Van Doren

Doren on Great Poems of Western Literature (New York: Collier, 1962);

The Country Year (New York: Sloane, 1946);

The Careless Clock: Poems about Children in the Family (New York: Sloane, 1947);

New Poems (New York: Sloane, 1948);

Nathaniel Hawthorne (New York: Sloane, 1949; London: Methuen, 1950);

The Witch of Ramoth and Other Tales (York, Pa.: Maple Press, 1950);

Humanity Unlimited: Twelve Sonnets (Williamsburg: College of William and Mary, 1950);

Short Stories (New York: Abelard, 1950);

In that Far Land (Iowa City: Prairie Press, 1951);

418

Spring Birth, and Other Poems (New York: Holt, 1953);

Mortal Summer (Iowa City: Prairie Press, 1953);

Nobody Say a Word and Other Stories (New York: Holt, 1953);

Selected Poems (New York: Holt, 1954);

An Address Delivered at the Eightieth Commencement, Southern Illinois University, June 12, 1955 (Carbondale: Southern Illinois University Press, 1956);

Joseph and His Brothers: A Comedy in Four Parts (Bryn Mawr: Bryn Mawr College, 1956);

Home with Hazel and Other Stories (New York: Harcourt, Brace, 1957);

Don Quixote's Profession (New York: Columbia University Press, 1958);

The University of Illinois in Retrospect (Urbana, 1958);

Autobiography (New York: Harcourt, Brace, 1958);

Morning Worship, and Other Poems (New York: Harcourt, Brace, 1960);

The Happy Critic, and Other Essays (New York: Hill & Wang, 1961);

Collected Stories (New York: Hill & Wang, 1962);

Collected and New Poems, 1924-1963 (New York: Hill & Wang, 1963);

Narrative Poems (New York: Hill & Wang, 1964);

The Dialogues of Archibald MacLeish and Mark Van Doren (New York: Dutton, 1964);

Insights into Literature, by Van Doren, Arno Jewett, Olga Achlenhagen, and Margaret Early (Boston: Houghton Mifflin, 1965);

Somebody Came (New York: Harlin Quist, 1966);

Three Plays (New York: Hill & Wang, 1966);

That Shining Place: New Poems (New York: Hill & Wang, 1969);

In the Beginning, Love: Dialogues on the Bible, by Van Doren and Maurice Samuels, edited by Edith Samuels (New York: John Day, 1973);

Good Morning: Last Poems (New York: Hill & Wang, 1973);

The Book of Praise: Dialogues on the Psalms, by Van Doren and Maurice Samuels, edited by Edith Samuels (New York: John Day, 1975);

How Praise a World That May Not Last: A Speech Delivered at the 275th Anniversary of St. John's College, Santa Fe, New Mexico, August 8, 1971 (Santa Fe: Lightning Tree, 1977);

The Essays of Mark Van Doren (1924-1972) (Westport & London: Greenwood Press, 1980).

OTHER: *An Anthology of World Poetry*, edited by Van Doren (New York: A. & C. Boni, 1928; London: Cassell, 1929; revised and enlarged edition, New York: Halcyon House, 1939);

The Oxford Book of American Prose, edited, with a preface, by Van Doren (London & New York: Oxford University Press, 1932);

Walt Whitman, edited, with notes, by Van Doren (New York: Viking, 1945);

The Portable Emerson, edited, with an introduction, by Van Doren (New York: Viking, 1946);

William Wordsworth, *Selected Poetry*, edited, with an introduction, by Van Doren (New York: Modern Library, 1950);

Selected Poems of Thomas Merton, introduction by Van Doren (New York: New Directions, 1959);

Carl Sandburg—Harvest Poems, 1910-1960, introduction by Van Doren (New York: Harcourt, Brace, & World, 1960).

As professor of English at Columbia University and literary editor and reviewer for the *Nation*, poet, critic, teacher, and anthologist Mark Van Doren resided through most of his career at the very center of the established literary scene in New York. His older brother Carl Van Doren had been literary editor for the *Nation* before him, and his sister-in-law Irita Van Doren became editor of *New York Herald Tribune Books*. With the publication of major works on Thoreau (1916)—his master's thesis, Dryden (1920)—his Ph.D. thesis, and Robinson (1927), he quickly established his reputation as a scholar. At the *Nation* and Columbia he formed important friendships with such notable figures of his time as Mortimer Adler, John Berryman, Robert Caldwell, Whitaker Chambers, John Erskine, Robert Frost, Joseph Wood Krutch, Thomas Merton, Allen Tate, James Thurber, Lionel Trilling, and Louis Zukofsky.

Mark Van Doren was a prolific writer in almost every genre, and he published more than a dozen volumes of his poetry in his lifetime. In his poetry he consistently eschewed his contemporaries' concerns with image, sound, and language, writing instead in an English tradition of highly formalized verse and recording for the common reader everyday events and the philosophy to be derived from them. "He is not a modern poet," wrote Allen Tate in 1963, "in the sense that most of his contemporaries, poets born in the 1890s, are modern. Has he anything in common with MacLeish, Putnam, Crane, Bishop, or Cummings? Very little, I think. If we are to place him ... we must think of a good deal of Robinson, less of Frost, some of Hardy, a trace of William Browne (the epigrams and 'Britannia's Pastorals,' 1613), traces of Ben Jonson, more than a trace of Robert Herrick—all of them adding up to Mark Van Doren, who is not like anybody else."

John Peale Bishop described him as "a completely integrated person in an age when all we have known disintegrates" and as "almost alone among his contemporaries in this country [in] show[ing] no trace of French influence." Thus, as Richard Howard has pointed out, Van Doren stood out by going against the expectations of modernism, presenting an integrated vision instead of the sharp contrasts of a fragmented voice. "His surface simplicity demands more attention than the obvious complexity of many of the modernists," said Tate, who predicted that Van Doren would "last as a great poet in minor modes."

The son of Charles Lucius and Dora Anne Butz Van Doren, Mark Albert Van Doren was born, fourth in a family of five boys, in Hope, Illinois. Although Charles Van Doren was a doctor, the family owned a farm, and his happy early years there may account for Mark Van Doren's lasting fondness, reflected in much of his poetry, for animals, nature, and rural life.

In 1900 the family moved to Urbana, Illinois, where Van Doren attended public grammar school and high school and then went on to the University of Illinois. He graduated with a liberal-arts degree in 1914 and took his M.A. there in 1915, the same year that his first published poem appeared in H. L. Mencken's *Smart Set.* Then he followed Carl to New York to study at Columbia, where Carl had been, first as a student, then as a teacher, since 1908. His teachers included W. W. Lawrence, G. P. Krapp, John Erskine, and W. P. Trent, who became his thesis supervisor. His fellow students included Joseph Wood Krutch, with whom he formed a lifelong friendship.

When the United States entered World War I, Van Doren interrupted his studies to serve in the infantry from September 1917 to December 1918. He did not serve overseas. After completing his thesis on Dryden—a study which led to the most important literary influence in his own writing—

Carl, Frank, Dora, Mark, Paul, and Guy Van Doren, on the day of Charles Van Doren's funeral, October 1933

he and Krutch were awarded traveling fellowships and went together to England and France. It was during this trip that Van Doren began to think seriously of writing poetry, but in the meantime opportunities opened for him in the academic and public world of letters: before giving him his Ph.D. in 1920, Columbia offered him an instructorship, and almost as soon as he returned from Europe, Carl Van Doren gave him, for the summer, the literary editorship of the *Nation*. On staff at the *Nation* was Dorothy Graffe, who was to write *Strangers* (1926), *Flowering Quince* (1927), *Brother and Brother* (1928), and other novels, and who married Van Doren on 1 September 1922. From 1924 to 1928, Van Doren was literary editor of the *Nation* and contributed reviews (including motion-picture reviews from 1935 to 1938) until 1942 when, as he put it, he became a "private reader" and published

Dorothy Van Doren, 1942

a book of essays under that title. That year, too, after twenty-two years at Columbia, he became a full professor of English.

A prodigious writer and editor, Van Doren during his career edited and wrote introductions for more than thirty collections and anthologies of poetry, as well as other literary works. He also wrote several major critical books, including, in addition to those already mentioned, *Shakespeare* (1939), *The Noble Voice: A Study of Ten Great Poems* (1946), and *Nathaniel Hawthorne* (1949). His *An Anthology of World Poetry* (1928) was so successful that its sales enabled the Van Dorens to buy a house on Bleecker Street in New York city in 1929.

Earlier, in 1923, the Van Dorens had purchased one hundred and fifty acres of land, with a farmhouse and outbuildings, in Falls Village, Cornwall Hollow, in northwest Connecticut—a place described by Van Doren in his *Autobiography* (1958) as "an earthly paradise"—"my *old* home, my first one, long before that other life in Illinois." This farm became their summer and sabbatical retreat and eventually their retirement home. Many of the rural characters, events, and scenes in Van Doren's poetry have their sources in experiences here.

In the summers of 1921 and 1922, Van Doren wrote several long poems but set them aside and brought out instead, in 1924, a book of short poems entitled *Spring Thunder*, which was largely devoted to images of rural life. His next two volumes of poetry, *7 P.M. & Other Poems* (1926) and *Now The Sky & Other Poems* (1928) continue in this vein. Of these books he remarked in his *Autobiography*, "when my poems did not deal with men and the habitations of men (for instance, the houses and barns of Cornwall) they dealt with animals and stars." About animals he said: "To me a work horse in a stable is still the symbol of friendship that cannot talk back. . . . he stands there, benevolent and patient, while you rub his nose and open the most subtle, the most tremendous subjects for him to consider." Parts of *Jonathan Gentry* (1931) and *The Mayfield Deer* (1941), he noted, reflect his concern with this relationship.

In both *Jonathan Gentry* and *The Mayfield Deer* Van Doren achieved at last his ambition to write long poems. The three-part *Jonathan Gentry* is an epic tale of the Gentry family, from its immigration to America ("Ohio River 1800") through the war ("Civil War") to the Depression ("Foreclosure"). As with most of Van Doren's poetry the better sections are those that are not bound by a too-arbitrary form or poetic diction, or bowed down under copious details. In *The Mayfield Deer*, Van Doren tells the story of John Richman, in whom he found "a primitive, a hunter out of old time, a human savage whom civilization could not absorb." To give the story added significance he wove into it parallels from Indian life, and, because he had always been convinced that "no story could be powerful unless it finds room for the supernatural, and makes that natural," he included what he called "bodiless configurations of the truth, which I spoke of as existing somewhere without personality or voice." These "embodiments" proved to be a serious weakness, since, as his friend Scott Buchanan pointed out, these vaguely conceived deities had no integral function in the piece; fifteen years later Van Doren decided Buchanan had been right and he rewrote the poem without them. After these two attempts, Van Doren never returned to the long poem (S. I. Hayakawa called *Jonathan Gentry* "a disaster from beginning to end"), focusing his efforts on lyric poetry instead.

Between the two long poems Van Doren had published three other volumes: *A Winter Diary and Other Poems* (1935), in which the title poem records in heroic couplets "every detail [he] naturally and immediately remembered" of his 1932-1933 sabbatical at Cornwall Hollow; *The Last Look and Other Poems* (1937), which "consisted largely of lyrics with a narrative cast . . . treating actual or imagined persons in crises that revealed their natures" (*Autobiography*); and *Collected Poems 1922-1938* (1939) for which he won a Pulitzer Prize for Poetry in 1940.

In reviewing *Winter Diary* for the *Nation*, Van Doren's friend Allen Tate compared the book to the poetry of Dryden, which included "the whole range of thought and feeling, from emotion at high tension to casual observation." This comparison pleased Van Doren, who said in his *Autobiography*, "I made up my mind to keep on trying to meet that condition; and, fashionably or no, to continue with the record of my thoughts and feelings—always, of course, more interesting to me than any technical performance of which I might be capable."

The Last Look was dedicated to Scott Buchanan, whom Van Doren had met through the *Nation* and who had made him think about poets as philosophers. The poems in this volume begin to reflect a philosophical bent, which in subsequent work touched on education, war, and the spiritual. Concerned about the "poverty of myth" in America, he wrote for the *Collected Poems* (1939) a series called "America's Mythology," which included poems such as "Porch God," "Driveway God," and "Crowd God."

He believed in "the poet as wiser than other men about the very things that all men experience," and that the best thing that poetry could be was "a report of the world as it is without exaggeration or make-believe"—both views which informed *The Noble Voice.* "The whole endeavour of" *Our Lady Peace, and Other War Poems* (1942) he noted, "was to get as close as words would go to the truth as one appalled person felt it day by day, contradictions and inconsistencies notwithstanding."

Through Scott Buchanan and Mortimer Adler he became very concerned with the philosophy of education. He regularly lectured at St. John's College in Annapolis, Maryland, and in his *Liberal Education* (1943) he defended the kind of curriculum offered in the Great Books Program there. A year later in 1944, *The Seven Sleepers* was published. "The Liberal arts lie eastward of this shore," the poem begins, and it goes on to discuss how the arts are like sleepers because they are neglected, but are important as disciplined training.

In 1953 Van Doren partially retired from Columbia (full retirement came in 1959), taking more time to write and travel, including an extensive trip to Europe in 1955. Possibly because of his friendship with Thomas Merton but also from a longstanding interest in the spiritual, his late work—*Mortal Summer* (1953); *Morning Worship* (1960); *That Shining Place: New Poems* (1969); and *Good Morning: Last Poems* (1973)—evinces a greater concern with gods or a God, the significance of death and a reverence for something larger than life. *That Shining Place* includes a series of psalms.

In his later years Van Doren gave considerable time to public lectures and public appearances, including the Hopwood Lecture at the University of Michigan, poetry readings, major addresses on Whitman and Sandburg, lectures at the Johns Hopkins Poetry Festival, and the Bashfield Address at the American Academy of Arts and Letters (where he served as chancellor). When he died on 10 December 1972, he was in every way a distinguished belletrist. He was survived by his wife and two sons, Charles (born in 1926) and John (born in 1928).

Given Mark Van Doren's literary connections, it was difficult for his poetry to get clear-sighted independent criticism. But even the most favorable assessments were little more than lukewarm. Reviewing *Morning Worship* in *Poetry*, Jack Lindeman called him "as thoughtful and meditative as a thoroughly civilized man can be," a poet who can "make honesty and sincerity count" and one who "has a real gift for approximating some of the lyrical high points of the past." The key word is *approximating.*

Mark Van Doren at his Connecticut farm, 1942 (photograph by Helen Taylor)

George Dillon remarked of his *Selected Poems* (1954) that Van Doren wrote "poetry that employs rhyme and metre but keeps mainly within the rhetorical limits of informal prose." Indeed, Van Doren's notions of poetry were prosaic. "Poetry's chief business is the business of story—of mankind in motion," he wrote in "The Possible Importance of Poetry." Such academic concepts, based as they were on years of study and notions about the importance of the classics, likely did much to hamper Van Doren's achievement.

"If he seems to publish too much of what he has done," wrote Allen Tate, reviewing *Collected and New Poems, 1924-1963*, "we must remember once more what kind of poet he is. He is a formalist who is not trying in every poem to write a masterpiece; he is day by day the whole man who submits the whole range of his awareness to the forms that he

has elected to use. . . . If the moment of perception does not get completely into the form, that is too bad for the perception; it will have to try again. The form's the thing." But it was Van Doren's arbitrary use of rigid metrical and rhyme schemes and his overdependence on what Richard Howard called in 1973 a "decorous" and "docile. . . . poetry of a received idiom" that undermined his work. "He has mastered his devices (or they have mastered him) so well that he has fallen into the fatal trap of being able to continue writing extremely plausible verses even after his subject matter has been used up," wrote S. I. Hayakawa, reviewing the *Collected Poems, 1922-1938*. "There are hundreds of unjustifiable personifications . . . as well as other affectations," he continued, noting that "since there is nothing in their contexts to make such locutions inevitable (and if they are not

Mark Van Doren, summer 1972 (photograph by Daniel McPartlin)

inevitable, they cannot help sounding affected), the reader is constantly irritated by them. . . . Mr. Van Doren proceeds, that is to say, in a kind of sentimental automatism of obscure evocations and poetical turns of thought and phrase." It is largely for this reason that Tate's 1963 prediction has proven incorrect; such poetry was out of place in an age that was rapidly coming to understand form and content as indistinguishable.

References:

Mortimer Adler, *Philosopher at Large: An Intellectual Autobiography* (New York: Macmillan, 1977);

John Peale Bishop, "The Poetry of Mark Van Doren," in his *The Collected Essays of John Peale Bishop* (New York & London: Scribners, 1948);

William Claire, Introduction to *The Essays of Mark Van Doren (1924-1972)* (Westport & London: Greenwood Press, 1980);

George Dillon, "Style and the Many-Headed Beast," review of *Selected Poems, Poetry*, 86 (August 1955): 287-295;

William Gilmore, "A Few Ghosts," review of *The Last Look and Other Poems, Poetry*, 51 (December 1937): 164-167;

S. I. Hayakawa, "The Allusive Trap," review of *Collected Poems, 1922-1938, Poetry*, 54 (June 1939): 157-160;

Richard Howard, "To Be, While Still Becoming: A Note on the Lyric Verse (1924-1972) of Mark Van Doren," foreword to *Good Morning: Last Poems* (New York: Hill & Wang, 1973);

Jack Lindeman, Review of *Morning Worship, Poetry*, 97 (November 1960): 109-113;

Thomas Merton, *The Seven Storey Mountain* (New York: Harcourt, Brace, 1948);

Allen Tate, "Center of the Language," review of *A Winter Diary and Other Poems, Nation*, 140 (March 1935): 339-340;

Tate, "Very Much At Ease in Formal Attire," review of *Collected and New Poems, 1924-1963, New York Herald Tribune Book Week*, 29 September 1963, p. 4.

Ernest Walsh

(10 August 1895-16 October 1926)

Melody M. Zajdel
Montana State University

See also the Walsh entry in *DLB 4, American Writers in Paris, 1920-1939.*

BOOK: *Poems and Sonnets* (New York: Harcourt, Brace, 1934).

Ernest Walsh is best remembered as the editor of *This Quarter,* one of the best little magazines in Paris during the mid-1920s. Although he was a poet and experimenter with language himself, it was because of his editorial policy of noninterference, his belief that writers needed to be truly innovative (not merely meeting the demands of the literary establishment), and his publication of work by excellent writers in *This Quarter* that he was best known. Critics then and now have had a mixed response to Walsh's own writing. Although Kay Boyle and Ethel Moorhead, with whom he edited *This Quarter,* perceived Walsh as a doomed genius, others, including Ernest Hemingway and Harriet Monroe, the editor of *Poetry* magazine, found him a poseur rather than a genuine poet. Whatever the merits of his poetry, the quality of his editorship of *This Quarter* earned him a place in literary history.

Born in Detroit, to James and Sara Lampson Walsh, Ernest Walsh spent his childhood in Cuba, where his father was a tea and coffee merchant. Ethel Moorhead's memoir of Walsh presents a romantic picture of this time when his father lived like a "chieftain among the planters," while Walsh himself was "riding bareback in the country, eating on the roadside with Portuguese tramps." After the family's return to Detroit and his father's death, Walsh's life changed drastically, as family finances decreased. A rebel against the rigid Catholicism of his mother and older sister, Walsh ran into trouble with the authorities when he tried to run away with three other young men in a stolen car. At fourteen he left home for good. After three years of working at odd jobs, Walsh became ill. At seventeen he was hospitalized and diagnosed as tubercular. His family, fearing that he would not recover, sent him to a sanatorium in Lake Saranac, where he stayed two

years. Pronounced completely cured, he found work managing first a print shop, then a cafeteria. He also began writing, taking a course at Columbia University from Witter Bynner. Later, he and a friend, Albert Powers, worked their way cross-country from San Francisco to New York. Much of the trip was enlivened and financed by Walsh's talk; frequently his glib and humorous speech, his "briar-pipe talk and dreams," earned them their lodging and food. The experiences of the trip appeared directly in poems such as "To Albert Powers" and indirectly in the images of "America."

When Walsh enlisted in the aviation service as a cadet in 1917, he was sent to training school in Texas. Involved in a near-fatal crash which crushed and pinned him under the plane's engine, he suffered further lung damage, complicated by the tuberculosis from which he had never actually recovered. Experiencing repeated lung hemorrhages, he spent the next four years in and out of military hospitals. In August 1921 while in a hospital at Camp Kearney, California, he wrote to Harriet Monroe, sending her thirteen poems for consideration and explaining, "I have nothing in the world but poetry. Won't you be nice to me, and if you find some of these things *almost* acceptable, tell me what they need." Monroe accepted four poems for inclusion in the January 1922 issue of *Poetry*. Walsh's poems focused on his life in the military hospitals and his illness. In "White Spiders," for example, he described the beds in the hospital wards as spiders on whose backs the patients ride at night, unable to sleep. Similarly, his imagistic poem "The White Death" pictured parts of his body as lifeless and white: his body is desert sand, his brain becomes ice, his soul a ghost.

Monroe was Walsh's first benefactress. In addition to publishing his poems, she furthered Walsh's efforts to leave the hospital by soliciting the assistance of Mrs. Medill McCormack, the Senator's wife, to get Walsh's military and medical records reviewed. As a result, he was awarded a disabled veteran's pension of $3,000 back pay and a lifelong monthly allowance. With these funds Walsh determined to go to Paris and write. After outfitting himself in San Francisco, he traveled eastward, stopping briefly in Chicago. There he visited Monroe, who recalled first seeing him "rushing into the POETRY office like a pillar of fire." His characteristically extravagant, flamboyant, and enthusiastic manner impressed her, and she provided him with letters of introduction to Ezra Pound and other acquaintances in Paris. He lost his money between Chicago and New York and, as would be the case throughout his life, solicited assistance (in this case, from Monroe) to bail him out. Whatever the merits of his writing, Walsh's personality attracted support. Once in Paris, he established himself at Claridge's Hotel, where he suffered another series of hemorrhages. When he could not pay his bills, he was rescued by Ethel Moorhead, a wealthy Scottish suffragette, who continued to care for and finance him until his death.

In Paris Walsh met Pound, who showed him how to edit his poetry. Walsh demonstrated his admiration by dedicating the first issue of *This Quarter* to Pound, "who by his creative work, his editorship of several magazines, his helpful friend-

Ethel Moorhead and Ernest Walsh in Chillon, 1925

ship for young and unknown artists, his many and untiring efforts to win better appreciation of what is first-rate in art comes first to our mind as meriting the gratitude of this generation." Through Pound, he met Constantin Brancusi, whom he greatly admired. With continuing health problems, Walsh wrote little during this period.

By July 1922, with his pension arriving regularly, he began traveling with Moorhead, seeking a healthy, comfortable locale. He visited Germany, Italy, the Riviera, Algiers, and ended, in the summer of 1923, in Edinburgh. The poetry he wrote during this year was predominantly short, lyrical, and depressed. The world he traveled through appeared to him to be "a dying stream/watched by fishermen with anxious eyes," and the silence around him followed him "as silence follows the dead." In Edinburgh, he again met with Harriet Monroe, who had come to give a lecture on modern poetry. She accepted several more of his poems for publication in *Poetry* and described the Walsh she saw as "living carefully, . . . turning out poems now and then."

Finding his health hurt by the dampness of Edinburgh, Walsh returned to the United States, to San Diego, in 1924. According to Harriet Monroe, "a great romance flared up" there, a not uncommon event for Walsh. The poems of this period ("Immortalities" and "A Meeting," for example) are more sensual than earlier works. In them, an unidentified woman intervenes between the poet and the grave, love eclipses death, and a clear carpe diem theme prevails. Also during this visit, Walsh focused his writing on American places and persona. "America" is almost Whitmanesque in its identification with modern American society: "I am the typewriter/All men read me./I am jazz-music/ .../I am the gramophone and cinema/I shall not die." Singling out Carl Sandburg and Ezra Pound as subjects for his poetry continued this identification. In May Walsh returned to Europe.

Fall 1926 found Walsh, with Moorhead, back

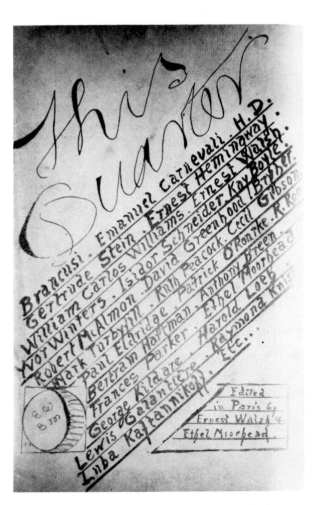

Front cover for the first issue of Walsh and Moorhead's magazine (courtesy of the Thomas Cooper Library, University of South Carolina)

in Paris and preparing the first edition of *This Quarter*. Moorhead funded the journal to provide Walsh with a vehicle for both his poetry and his ideas on modern literature. The editorial policy, established by Walsh, was to encourage new writers by tampering with their writings as little as possible. Indeed, contributions to the magazine were printed unedited. As he explained, "The artist will be edited in these pages in terms of himself . . . we are against literary politics and literary politicians. . . ." Walsh used his reviews and editorial essays to oppose the literary establishment, which was frequently synonymous to him with T. S. Eliot's the *Criterion* and the *Dial*. In his essay "What Is Literature?" (for the third issue of *This Quarter*), he called the *Dial*'s effect on the creativity of young writers "insidious" and accused it, along with the *Criterion*, of representing "a tradition without individuality." The first issue of *This Quarter* published works by Carnevali, H. D. (Hilda Doolittle), Gertrude Stein, Ernest Hemingway, William Carlos Williams, Yvor Winters, Kay Boyle, Robert McAlmon, and Bryher (Winifred Ellerman). The second and third issues published a portion of Joyce's *Work in Progress* (published in 1939 as *Finnegans Wake*), poems by Ezra Pound, Kenneth Fearing, and Eugene Jolas; fiction by Morley Callaghan and Kay Boyle; and, of course, Walsh's own writings. The poems Walsh wrote in 1925 and 1926 were free verse, frequently love lyrics. Many juxtaposed the sensuousness of physical lovemaking with Walsh's sense of his imminent death. In "Irish," for example, even while his lover is "holding my head to her breast," he recognizes "She might have been telling a dead man her love." Other poems of the period catalogue his travels and rail against those circumstances and people who would keep the poet from the women he loves and from experience, which has become his anodyne.

After publishing Boyle's fiction in the first issue of *This Quarter*, Walsh invited her to join him in the south of France. The result was a passionate liaison. Still aided financially by Moorhead, Walsh lived with Boyle throughout 1926. As Walsh's health worsened, Boyle became his nurse as well as his lover. Boyle's recollection of their time together appears in her additions to Robert McAlmon's *Being Geniuses Together* (1968). Fictionalized accounts of their relationship appear in both Walsh's poems and Boyle's novel, *Year Before Last* (1932). The relationship allowed Walsh to finish the editorial work on the second issue of *This Quarter* (Autumn-Winter 1925-1926). After

Walsh's death, Boyle gave birth to his daughter in March 1927.

While in Milan in late 1925 Walsh, in accordance with his pension requirements, was examined by a medical board and informed that he needed absolute rest. From October 1925 to January 1926 he was virtually bedridden. The result of this enforced seclusion was his most experimental poetry, written in an invented language resembling Middle English. Walsh sent one of these poems, "To Begin Withe," to the *Dial*, where editor Marianne Moore rejected the poem, explaining "We are not insensible to its self-evident talent but we cannot give it our unqualified assent." For Walsh, this rejection confirmed his belief that publishers in general were unsympathetic to experimentation. However, several of these poems were later accepted and published by Michael Gold, editor of the *New Masses*. The others appeared in the third issued of *This Quarter*. Many were playfully addressed to a young love, mixing modern commonplace actions and colloquial language with pseudoarchaic spelling. An excellent example was "A Songge for Merrie Companye": "Bacon andde Corne andde potatos andde pees/Brewe inne the barel to drink as ye plese/A saucye yongge thinge to holde andde to squeese/Withe a dimple inne mor than her prety knees."

Walsh's health continued to worsen throughout 1926. Successive hemorrhages weakened him until, nursed by both Moorhead and Boyle, he died in Moorhead's Monte Carlo villa on 16 October 1926. Moorhead published the third issue of *This Quarter*, making it a memorial to Walsh and a forum for his final criticism and poems. She created a literary scandal by retracting the first issue's dedication to Pound and denouncing his poetry because he had refused to write against Walsh's detractors. Walsh's criticism published in this issue illustrated both his perceptivity and his idiosyncrasies: Gertrude Stein is a "profound artist but a poor writer"; Pound, Robert McAlmon, Carl Sandburg, James Joyce, William Carlos Williams, and Emanuel Carnevali are "the six greatest living literary artists"; and T. S. Eliot, at least critically, "has been dead a long time." His opinions were extreme and, as Monroe noted, "a matter of personal loyalties." Still, they were often not unrealistic assessments of the modernist experimenters in poetry.

Walsh's own poetry did not, as Moorhead later noted, "meet with acclaim and praise." Although both she and Boyle continued to view Walsh as a genius, other critics were less kind. In 1932 Harriet Monroe assessed him as "a man of keen creative energies who could not quite make them work efficiently. . . ." Less gentle critics, such as Hemingway, viewed him as a "conman," a man who played the romantic (albeit real) role of the doomed writer, a "man who was marked for death."

In 1934, Moorhead edited Walsh's complete poems, adding to his previously published works what she called "the plums of the poems" written in his final months. Fewer of these last poems were in his invented language and many returned to the stronger lyric voice of his early poems. A few, such as "Eight O'Clock" and "Anger and Silence," are among his best. They confirm that in his deathhouse vision of life, "The only thing that is alive . . ./And lit and warm is my head." They are no less sensual in their details, but they shift the poet's concern from action to reflection. *Poems and Sonnets* received little critical attention and went out of print in two years, having sold only 500 copies.

Like other writers and publishers of the 1920s, Walsh's primary interest was in exploring new forms and encouraging other young experimenters. In *This Quarter*, he and Ethel Moorhead published many of the best new writers and provided them with an uncensored, unedited forum for presentation. Challenging the editorial stances of more established journals, they actively sought writers who opposed the literary tradition. Although Walsh's own writings were not first-rate, his commitment to growth and exploration in poetic form deserves commendation.

References:

Sylvia Beach, *Shakespeare and Company* (New York: Harcourt, Brace & World, 1959), pp. 138-140;

Emanuel Carnevali, *The Autobiography of Emanuel Carnevali*, edited by Kay Boyle (New York: Horizon, 1967), pp. 231-235;

Edward Dahlberg, "The Expatriates: A Memoir," *Texas Quarterly*, 6 (Summer 1963): 50-55;

Ernest Hemingway, *A Moveable Feast* (New York: Scribners, 1964), pp. 123-129;

Frederick J. Hoffman, Charles Allen, and Carolyn F. Ulrich, *The Little Magazine: A History and A Bibliography* (Princeton: Princeton University Press, 1947), pp. 82, 279;

Robert McAlmon, *Being Geniuses Together 1920-1930*, revised, with additional material, by Kay Boyle (Garden City: Doubleday, 1968);

Harriet Monroe, "Ernest Walsh," *Poetry*, 41 (December 1932): 208-214;

Ethel Moorhead, Memoir of Walsh, in *Poems and*

Sonnets (New York: Harcourt, Brace, 1934);
Winfield Townley Scott, "Ernest Walsh: The Poet Against Despair," *Decision*, 11 (August 1941): 36-46;

William Wasserstrom, "Hemingway, *The Dial* and Ernest Walsh," *South Atlantic Quarterly*, 65 (Spring 1966): 171-177.

John Hall Wheelock
(9 September 1886-22 March 1978)

Robert H. O'Connor
North Dakota State University

BOOKS: *Verses by Two Undergraduates*, by Wheelock and Van Wyck Brooks (Cambridge, Mass.: Privately printed, 1905);

The Human Fantasy (Boston: Sherman, French, 1911);

The Belovèd Adventure (Boston: Sherman, French, 1912);

Love and Liberation: The Songs of Adsched to Meru, and Other Poems (Boston: Sherman, French, 1913);

Dust and Light (New York: Scribners, 1919);

A Bibliography of Theodore Roosevelt (New York: Scribners, 1920);

The Black Panther: A Book of Poems (New York: Scribners, 1922);

The Bright Doom: A Book of Poems (New York & London: Scribners, 1927);

Poems, 1911-1936 (New York & London: Scribners, 1936);

Poems Old and New (New York: Scribners, 1956);

The Gardener, and Other Poems (New York: Scribners, 1961);

What Is Poetry? (New York: Scribners, 1963);

Dear Men and Women (New York: Scribners, 1966);

By Daylight and in Dream: New and Collected Poems, 1904-1970 (New York: Scribners, 1970);

In Love and Song: Poems (New York: Scribners, 1971);

This Blessed Earth: New and Selected Poems, 1927-1977 (New York: Scribners, 1978);

Afternoon: Amagansett Beach (New York: Dandelion Press, 1978).

OTHER: *Happily Ever After: Fairy Tales Selected by Alice Dalgliesh*, translated in part by Wheelock (New York & London: Scribners, 1939);

The Face of a Nation: Poetical Passages from the Writ-

John Hall Wheelock (photograph by Danford Barney)

ings of Thomas Wolfe, edited by Wheelock (New York: Scribners, 1939);

Editor to Author: The Letters of Maxwell Perkins, edited by Wheelock (New York: Scribners, 1950);

Poets of Today, volumes 1-8, edited by Wheelock (New York: Scribners, 1954-1961).

Although John Hall Wheelock could admire the less-obscure experiments of his poetic contemporaries, his own poetry was firmly grounded in the poetic past, especially in the romantic tradition of William Wordsworth, Ralph Waldo Emerson, and Walt Whitman. Combining formal regularity with a passionate clarity of expression, Wheelock's poems are most often concerned with the wondrous beauty of life and the sublimity of artistic accomplishment. He imbued many of his early poems with an athletic vigor which suggested the influence of William Ernest Henley to several critics, while his later poetry is more mystical and often darker in tone. More than a dozen volumes of Wheelock's poetry appeared between 1905 and 1978, and, during his unusually long career, Wheelock won many of this nation's most-prestigious poetry awards, including the 1962 Bollingen Prize. His position as assistant and then successor to Maxwell Perkins of Scribners allowed him, too, to advance the careers of other poets, including James Dickey and Louis Simpson. Especially important was his editing of *Poets of Today* (1954-1961), an innovative series which presented new poets in annual, multiauthor volumes rather than the single-author volumes which critics so often ignored.

Wheelock was born on 9 September 1886 in Far Rockaway, New York, to William Efner and Emily Charlotte Hall Wheelock. Money from his father's prosperous medical practice built the family a home in East Hampton, on Long Island's South Fork. Later in life he returned to this beloved area, which he referred to in his poetry by its Indian name, Bonac, as often as his work allowed, walking the beaches for hours at a time, bathing in the ocean surf, and gathering images for his poetry.

Wheelock attended New Jersey's Morristown School and showed a fascination with poetry from very early in his academic career. He wrote his Latin translations in verse and published some of his poetry long before leaving for Harvard in 1904, where he was to be recognized as official poet of the Class of 1908. While at Harvard, he was active in the Stylus (a literary society) and contributed frequently to the *Harvard Advocate*, thereby becoming acquainted with such other aspiring literary men as Van Wyck Brooks and Maxwell Perkins. With Brooks, Wheelock collaborated on his first book of poetry, the privately printed *Verses by Two Undergraduates* (1905). The volume drew no critical attention, selling perhaps a half-dozen copies.

Graduating Phi Beta Kappa, Wheelock was urged by his practical father to travel to Europe to seek a doctoral degree. Working toward a doctorate would allow Wheelock to exploit his obvious talent for scholarship, and the degree itself would provide him entry into the stable, reputable profession of university teaching. Temporarily giving in to his father's argument that poetry could never provide a man with an adequate living, Wheelock left for the Continent, spending much of 1909 at the University of Göttingen and much of 1910 at the University of Berlin. He brought back several fashionable dueling scars, a tourist's knowledge of Germany, France, Italy, and Dalmatia, and many new poems, but no doctorate.

Subsequent to the temporary detour of his European studies, Wheelock was hired at Scribner's Book Store in New York City, thereby beginning an association with Charles Scribner's Sons that would last for half a century. At about this time, too, he published his second volume of poetry, *The Human Fantasy* (1911), a work which brought Wheelock considerable critical acclaim.

In addition to pleasing the critics, most notably Louis Untermeyer, *The Human Fantasy* attracted the attention of Sara Teasdale, who wrote the startled Wheelock an appreciative note and began visiting him at the bookstore. Soon, the two were taking long walks together through the streets of New York, and Teasdale had fallen in love. The smitten Teasdale, certain that the diffident but handsome Wheelock was equally in love with her and would eventually confess his love, remained in quiet pursuit of the remarkably naive young poet for several months before Wheelock realized the depth of her attachment. At the time involved in a hopeless relationship with another woman, Wheelock could offer her no more than his continuing friendship, a friendship which remained intense until Teasdale's tragic death and whose emotional complexity inspired some of her finest lyrics.

The man Teasdale had fallen in love with was, at this stage in his life, extraordinarily shy. In a letter to Harriet Monroe, Teasdale described Wheelock as "the shyest person I ever knew," a man whose dread of meeting new people was "almost . . . a nervous disease." To prove her point, she mentioned the following incident: "We were at a large formal dinner together and had to sit opposite each other. He talked in his company manners way with the woman next to him, who happened to be a stranger to him. When we finally left the table and stood together he said in a low voice absolutely grey and tortured: 'This has been

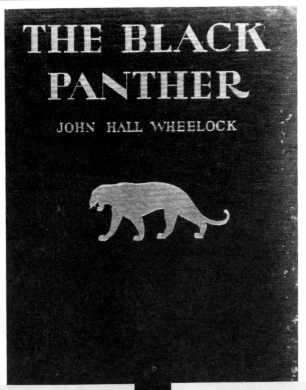

Front cover and inscriptions in copies of Wheelock's 1922 book

terrible.' A little minute afterward I noticed a drop of blood on his hand. 'Where did that come from?' I said. And then I was ready to beat myself for my lack of care for his feelings, for I saw his pain at my question. The foolish creature had pressed his finger nail into his hand out of sheer nervous torture."

Despite the difficulties of his friendship with Sara Teasdale, her interest in *The Human Fantasy* gave a boost to Wheelock's confidence which the young poet sorely needed. She was equally enthusiastic about *The Belovèd Adventure* (1912), as, again, were many of the critics. There was, however, a slight diminution in the fervor of the praise. Louis Untermeyer, for example, heard "Echoes of Whitman, Shelley, and Edwin Arlington Robinson" in *The Human Fantasy* and was impressed with its author's "wide-sweeping love of existence," but in *The Belovèd Adventure*, he detected "a slight dilution of the strain so prominent in the initial volume; there are times when the poems, animated by nothing so much as sheer high-spirits, seem boyish rather than buoyant." In *The Human Fantasy*, Wheelock had anticipated Frost in lines about "the dear, sensual Fact of things" and "the clear reality of life, filled with laughter and eternal strength." It was, according

to Untermeyer, their "sense of casual beneficence" that gave these "earliest rhapsodies so sympathetic a touch" and that made stanzas such as the following, from *The Human Fantasy*'s initial poem, so effective:

> I see you stand before me,—
> Bizarre, absurd, enchanting,—
> (The swinging, silver satchel,
>   The dear, ridiculous dress),
>
> A little, dauntless figure,
> Half lost in the enormous
> Gay picture-hat bowed forward
>   Across the eager face.

The Belovèd Adventure, on the other hand, might have been improved by "a judicious use of the blue pencil," Untermeyer said, especially by "the omission of such adolescent verse as 'Twilight and Dawn,' 'Parting in Spring' and one or two others. . . ." In Untermeyer's opinion, the volume was largely successful despite Wheelock's careless inclusion of weak materials, but this problem became acute in the poet's next book, *Love and Liberation* (1913). In Untermeyer's damning words, *Love and Liberation* "poured repetition on repetition, sugar on treacle, beauty on banalities." This condemnation was echoed by others.

With *Dust and Light* (1919), *The Black Panther* (1922), and *The Bright Doom* (1927), Wheelock recouped some of his critical losses, but there continued to be doubts expressed concerning the ultimate value of his work. Particularly called into question were his characteristic adherence to traditional rhyme and meter and his ever-increasing indulgence in romantic idealism. On the matter of his romanticism, Alfred Kreymborg called Wheelock "a belated Transcendentalist" and complained of his mystical tendency to drift off into the ether: "One does not question Wheelock's integrity. The man is an artist untouched by mundane appeals. One only asks of his idealism, a little more reality, a more down-right humanness, a less self-conscious concern with the universe, a little more humor in dealing with unearthly factors." Kreymborg's opinion was shared by some, but certainly not by all, of those concerned with the state of American poetry. That the nineteenth-century tenor of much of his work was, in fact, welcomed by a significant portion of the literary community is suggested by the largely positive reception of his *Poems, 1911-1936* (1936), which received the New England Poetry Society's Golden Rose Award for 1937.

John Hall Wheelock, 1951 (photograph by Pach Brothers)

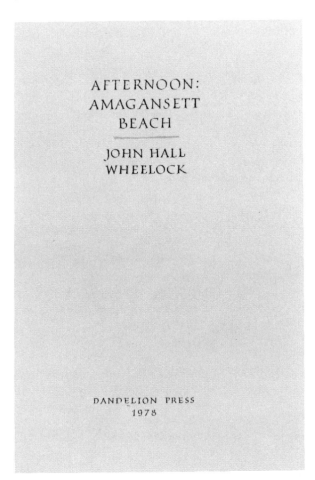

AFTERNOON:
AMAGANSETT
BEACH

JOHN HALL
WHEELOCK

DANDELION PRESS
1978

FOREWORD

Much of my work reflects the countryside of Long
Island's South Fork and, more especially, of the
area comprising Montauk, Springs, Amagansett,
Wainscott, and East Hampton, an area affectionately nicknamed "Bonac" by its native inhabitants.
There, in a house surrounded by woodlands,
within sound of the sea, I have spent some part
of almost every summer for eighty-six years. The
poems in this selection describe that house and
that sea-country, its birds, and insects, its woodlands, dunes, and beaches, and they record the
thoughts and emotions these inspired in the man
who dwelt among them from early childhood
into the fullness of age.
     Though a Long Islander born, I am not entitled
to call myself "a Bonacker." But you will find me
to be such, at heart — Bonac is my heart's country.

John Hall Wheelock
1977

Pages from publisher's brochure for Wheelock's 1978 book

While continuing his poetic career, Wheelock was also rising through the editorial ranks at Scribners under the tutelage of Maxwell Perkins. Wheelock once described editorial work as the "dullest, hardest, most exciting, exasperating and rewarding of perhaps any job in the world," and though it considerably limited his poetic output during the most onerous years of his editorial career, he performed his duties for Charles Scribner's Sons with an effectiveness that led, finally, to his appointment as senior editor, the position held for so many years and with such distinction by Perkins himself. Although no one has chronicled Wheelock's editorial accomplishments in the way A. Scott Berg has done for Perkins, Wheelock's importance to the careers of many of America's finest writers cannot be denied. He was, for example, second only to Perkins in giving editorial assistance to Thomas Wolfe, and his *Poets of Today* series was highly significant.

Despite the long hours he devoted to his duties at Scribners, Wheelock found time for a belated courtship, marrying Phyllis de Kay on 25 August

1940. The comparative lateness of this marriage was paralleled by the lateness of many of his finest editorial and poetic achievements. He was past sixty when he ascended to his senior editorship; he initiated *Poets of Today* when he was nearly seventy; and two years later, he published his ninth volume of verse, *Poems Old and New* (1956). Twenty years had passed since his eighth volume, but despite his advancing age, Wheelock's poetic capacities remained strong, and he published several more volumes of poetry during his seventies, eighties, and nineties. A growing awareness of death gives a bittersweet poignancy to many of these later poems, but even in the bleakest of them, such as "Night" from *By Daylight and in Dream* (1970), that "wide-sweeping love of existence" which had so long ago impressed Louis Untermeyer is still to be found:

In the darkness of the night,
When the high stars stand over the house,
In a house of many empty rooms
(They have all departed into the night),

On an ancient planet, naked to the stars,
Together—oh, together still,
In the darkness of the night,
Your hand in mine.

Even a partial list of Wheelock's honors suggests a man of considerable literary importance. He served as vice-president of the Poetry Society of America from 1944 to 1946 and Honorary Consultant in American Letters to the Library of Congress from 1967 to 1973. He received the Torrence Memorial Award in 1956, the Borestone Mountain Award in 1957, the Harvard University Signet Society Medal in 1965, and the Gold Medal of the Poetry Society of America in 1972. He was a member of the American Academy of Arts and Letters, the National Institute of Arts and Letters, and the Academy of American Poets, which he served as chancellor. Nevertheless, his poetic reputation has failed to remain strong and threatens to fade further. Wheelock himself was aware that the gentleness, clarity, and regularity of the bulk of his poetry made him something of an anachronism in an age of poetic complexity, obscurity, and dissonance, and in one of the more insightful sections of *What Is Poetry?* (1963), he acknowledged the vulnerability of the poet who writes in a style proscribed by the spirit of the age. Not only does the zeitgeist create poetic opportunities but it also establishes poetic taboos, and Wheelock violated a number of those taboos with regularity. His essentially romantic sensibility left him open, during his lifetime, to attacks by antiromantic critics, and his posthumous neglect is largely an extension of the critical doubts expressed about the value of his poetry while he was alive. Perhaps with a shift in poetic fashion, his reputation will revive.

References:

A. Scott Berg, *Max Perkins: Editor of Genius* (New York: Dutton, 1978);

William Drake, *Sara Teasdale, Woman and Poet* (San Francisco: Harper & Row, 1979);

Louis Untermeyer, "John Hall Wheelock," in his *The New Era in American Poetry* (New York: Holt, 1919), pp. 215-230.

Papers:

The Library of Congress has a collection of Wheelock's papers.

John Wheelwright

(9 September 1897-15 September 1940)

Alan M. Wald
University of Michigan

BOOKS: *North Atlantic Passage* (Florence, Italy: Privately printed, 1925);

A History of the New England Poetry Club, 1915-1931 (Boston: Privately printed, 1932);

Rock and Shell: Poems 1923-1933 (Boston: Bruce Humphries, 1933);

Footsteps (Boston: Poems for a Dime, 1934);

Masque with Clowns (Boston: Poems for a Dime, 1936);

Mirrors of Venus: A Novel in Sonnets, 1914-1938 (Boston: Bruce Humphries, 1938);

Political Self-Portrait, 1919-1939 (Boston: Bruce Humphries, 1940);

John Wheelwright: Selected Poems, edited by R. P.

Blackmur (Norfolk, Conn.: New Directions, 1941);

Collected Poems of John Wheelwright, edited by Alvin H. Rosenfeld (New York: New Directions, 1972).

OTHER: S. Foster Damon and Robert Hillyer, eds., *Eight More Harvard Poets*, includes poems by Wheelwright (New York: Brentano's, 1923).

Among the most likely candidates for belated recognition as the best American socialist poet of the 1930s is John Brooks Wheelwright, a rebel Boston Brahmin and heretical Christian who combined

John Wheelwright, 1920s (courtesy of Brown University Library)

his experimental poetry with Marxist political activities. At the time of his premature death—at the age of forty-three he was struck down by a drunken driver—he was both an influential figure among Boston poets and a member of the Trotskyist Socialist Workers party.

Much of Wheelwright's literary sensibility and outlook were shaped by the cultural history of New England, a region to which he was bonded by birth and upbringing. Some of his poems even drew sustenance from the works of rebels from the colonial and pre-Civil War eras. In fact, he was named after one of the leaders of the Antinomian Rebellion (1636-1638), the Reverend John Wheelwright (circa 1592-1679), from whom the poet was tenth in direct descent. His father was Edmund March (Ned) Wheelwright, an architect who designed many of Boston's most imaginative buildings. His mother, Elizabeth Brooks (Bessie) Wheelwright, a

remarkable deaf woman noted for her skill at lip reading and for her aristocratic bearing, was the great-granddaughter of Peter Chardon Brooks, the wealthiest of Boston's colonial "merchant princes." The mystique of the Brooks family was rendered so vivid to young Wheelwright by his mother that, as a teenager, he went to court to have his middle name changed from Tyler to Brooks.

While he was a student at St. George's preparatory school in Newport, Rhode Island, the young poet was profoundly shaken by his father's mental breakdown in 1910 and by his suicide in 1912, after two years of confinement in a sanatorium. Soon afterward young Wheelwright experienced a religious conversion. He repudiated the Unitarianism of his ancestors and became an Anglican, pledging to become a priest.

As a Harvard student (1916-1920), however, Wheelwright found that his natural sympathies clashed with the dogma of that church. He became a central figure in the circle of Harvard Aesthetes, which included poets such as S. Foster Damon, Robert Hillyer, E. E. Cummings, John Dos Passos, and Malcolm Cowley. After his expulsion from Harvard for irregular attendance at classes and examinations, Wheelwright had many close connections with lost-generation writers in New York and Europe. But even though he engaged in the "decadent" life-style of these bohemians while living in Florence and visiting Greenwich Village, his need for a belief in the Christ myth remained ardent.

Politically, Wheelwright was first attracted to the English expatriate and Fabian socialist Harold Laski, with whom he studied government at Harvard. At the time of the Russian Revolution he was sympathetic to the overthrow of Tsarism. In the later 1920s he episodically studied architecture at Massachusetts Institute of Technology, without receiving a degree, and set up a short-lived practice with Zareh Sourian. When the execution of the anarchists Sacco and Vanzetti occurred, he was outraged. However, as much as he railed against the immorality into which he believed New England society to have fallen, Wheelwright initially rejected the uneducated and uncultured proletariat as a force for change. Instead, he believed in the revival of a priestly caste of poets who could provide ethical guidance.

Many of Wheelwright's religio-mythic poems from the volumes *Rock and Shell* (1933) and "Dusk to Dusk" (in preparation at the time of the poet's death and published in 1972 as part of his *Collected Poems*), as well as the entire sonnet sequence *Mirrors of Venus* (1938), have Wheelwright's philosophical and emotional conflicts as their subject. These were especially intense during his late adolescence and student years and persisted through the 1920s when he was torn by the contending claims of his elitist training and his passionate hatred of injustice.

North Atlantic Passage, privately printed in 1925 in Florence where he and his mother vacationed and reprinted in *Rock and Shell,* is usually noted for its surrealist technique, but this long poem is in fact an attack on those poets who adulate surrealism, Dadaism, or other art forms elevated above philosophic substance. Wheelwright states that the basic "enigma" in life is the relationship of the individual to the rest of humankind. In the poem he refutes various solutions others have proposed to resolve this problem—solutions that rise and dissolve like waves. His conclusion is that a belief in "external Authority" (religion) is a necessity but that the achievement of an "internal Authority" (belief in himself) must come first.

Wheelwright tried to achieve this "internal Authority" through two major literary projects. One was a series of poems about Thomas, the "Doubting Apostle" who is supposed to have questioned the resurrection until he was permitted to touch Christ's wounds. The other was the sonnet sequence *Mirrors of Venus.* He referred to both of these efforts as "novels." This was in part a response to the new conceptions of the novel genre engendered by the literary experiments of the 1920s. But calling the works novels was also a way of emphasizing that the two groups of poems concerned character development. And in each of these works the main character was actually Wheelwright himself, represented by various personae.

The published sections of the first "novel" include "Twilight" in *Rock and Shell* and "Morning" in "Dusk to Dusk." These works reflect Wheelwright's study of apocrypha, lost gospels, and other religious materials excluded from the Old and New Testaments. These texts are usually considered to be of questionable authorship and heretical content.

Wheelwright's method is to "correct" the legend of St. Thomas by retelling or paraphrasing it and introducing various changes. In two such changes, Wheelwright presents the argument for sexual chastity as a false and dangerous perversion of Christian thought and contends that upholders of morality must name the true enemies of humanity, such as hypocrisy and social oppression, more specifically as a preparation for action.

The thirty-five poems that compose *Mirrors of Venus: A Novel in Sonnets* also invoke a spiritual journey, disclosing contradictory elements in a central figure. (Once more the main character is a Wheelwright persona, here called "Z.") The background of the sonnet sequence is more explicitly Wheelwright's own—the death of his architect father, World War I, the boarding school and Harvard days, bohemian life experienced during visits to New York City in the 1920s, and his religious ordeals.

The stated theme of the sequence is the transitory nature of human friendship. Wheelwright juxtaposes memories of and fantasies about a friend who dies (and whose friendship thereby becomes immortalized) with a narrative about an unidentified friend who lives (but who becomes estranged from the poet). The list of dedications in the "Argument" to the sequence indicates that the friend who died was Ned Couch, a Harvard student who was close to both Wheelwright and S. Foster Damon. Couch was killed in an accident in a training camp during World War I, and the poem suggests that he may have been a pacifist. Wheelwright links Couch with the memory of his own dead father, also called Ned.

The intense experience described in this poem culminates in a repudiation of Wheelwright's belief in an afterlife—startling for an avowed Christian. The sonnet sequence turns to four elegies aimed at discrediting a blind optimism that Wheelwright associates with the romantic poets. He criticizes Shelley in particular for his belief in the immortality of the individual self—a view that fosters a false perception of human existence.

In "Autumn," the third elegy, Wheelwright rejects the analogical proofs of immortality forwarded by the Greeks and others. In "Winter," the last elegy, he concludes that after death the human body is not immortalized at all but is merely a shell, not much different from an inorganic rock. Thus human existence is only a delicate, transitory phase of human nature. The ending is emotional in tone but stoical in perspective, as he rejects his former idealization of his dead friend and father:

> Our bold-voluted immortality, fallen
> is only rock
> —though proud in ruin, piteous in pride—
> Ned. Ned.
> Snow on a dome, blown by night wind.

Wheelwright's changing outlook was also shown in the way he settled accounts with the suicide and atheistic ideas of Harry Crosby in a poetic obituary that first appeared in *Hound and Horn* in 1931. Crosby and Wheelwright shared important similarities in their moneyed Brahmin backgrounds, their Episcopalian schooling, and their overlapping periods at Harvard. But they represented two contrasting responses of alienated writers in a world where their cultured family traditions had become superfluous. In Wheelwright's view, Crosby carried out the Henry Adams perspective to its logical conclusion: He broke in disgust from the world of commercial corruption (identified with Boston's State Street in Wheelwright's poem) but saw no alternative social class with which to identify. Instead of forging a new social identity for himself as an artist, he immersed himself in artistic activity that became increasingly divorced from the real world. ("Crosby tried to live art rather than ... to live for art ...," Wheelwright later wrote in a note to the poem.) Wheelwright's poem was titled "To Wise Men on the Death of a Fool." He made it clear, however, that even though he deplored Crosby's philosophy, he sympathized with his rebellion:

> State Street, maintain your silence.
> His mad impiety is holier than your sane
> Infidel doubt. . . .

Still, Wheelwright's only alternative for the wise men, to save them both from the corruption of State Street and the madness of Crosby, was the vision of classical culture with which he closes the poem:

> Magnanimous in bronze, straddling a stallion
> Over the Roman capital, diffusing
> A green benediction, rides serene Aurelius.

Such writings as the Thomas poems, *Mirrors of Venus*, and the verse obituary for Crosby show how Wheelwright divested himself of the romantics' Christian belief in an afterlife, as well as of bohemian aestheticism and hedonism. Thus Wheelwright was psychologically and philosophically prepared to assimilate Marxism. He began to do so at the start of the Great Depression, when the working class emerged as a visible agent for effective change. At that time Wheelwright concluded that he had a distinct role as a poet: to assist in the cultural development of the revolutionary movement.

Although he first joined the Socialist party of Massachusetts in 1932, he was not an opponent of Russian Bolshevism. To the contrary, from 1934 on he was openly sympathetic to the ideas of Leon Trotsky. He believed that Trotsky—whom he compares to Prometheus in his poem "Titanic Litany"—sought to continue the age-old struggle to develop humanity to its fullest potential, and that Stalin's triumph over Trotsky represented a retrogression from that goal.

In the Socialist party Wheelwright's main activities centered on education: he was in charge of literature distribution; he gave classes; he was poetry editor of *Arise* (the Socialist party's cultural journal) and a leading member of the Rebel Arts Society (which was affiliated with the party). But he also participated in demonstrations and was arrested on picket lines; he ran for local office in elections on the Socialist party ticket; he worked in defense of political prisoners and in antiwar organizations of the 1930s.

Wheelwright's several poems against the threat of a second world war indicate that his so-

John Wheelwright, 1930s (courtesy of the Clifton Waller Barrett Library, University of Virginia)

cialist views were not based on mere sentimental feelings; they stemmed from an understanding of the class basis of war. "You-U.S.-US" is a satire underscoring "the chief difficulty in proletarian revolution, the subservience of the masses to war hysteria. . . ." "Skulls as Drums" is an answer to the Civil War poetry of Walt Whitman, which Wheelwright felt was naive about the nature of the conflict. His philosophic "Train Ride," dedicated to Horace Gregory, uses as its refrain a slogan attributed to the German socialist Karl Liebknecht: "Always the enemy is the foe at home."

Much of Wheelwright's writing in this period defies conventional perceptions of the literary culture of the 1930s. His poems exhibit not only revolutionary fervor but also profound ties to New England culture, an impulsive temperament, self-parodying mannerisms, and an indissoluble technical affinity with the modernism of Pound and Eliot. "You-U.S.-US," for example, is a paradigm of radical modernism in an extreme form. Replete with the techniques of clashing fragmentation, word surprises, abrupt appearances and disappearances of emotions and imaginings, the poem is also bonded to canonical modernism in its attempt to function as a moral adviser to a misguided society.

In this poem Wheelwright also attempted to transform his poetry into a more public instrument. He departed from his style of the 1920s by writing in a virulent tone and colloquial language. Many of his lines are essentially sarcastic parodies of common expressions, children's songs, and advertising slogans, and he refers frequently to familiar Depression scenes (the urban and rural unemployed, industrial working conditions); or to famous political figures (Wilson and Roosevelt). His political ideas are as aggressive as they are lucid.

None of Wheelwright's books were money-making ventures; indeed, he had great difficulty in locating a publisher for his first collection, *Rock and Shell*, until he worked out an arrangement with Bruce Humphries, a small Boston printer, which obligated Wheelwright to sell a certain number of copies of the book in advance to subscribers. The printing was of only 500 copies. Nevertheless, *Rock and Shell* was reviewed favorably in numerous publications. Reviewing the book for the *New Republic* (16 January 1935), Horace Gregory called Wheelwright "one of the few matured poets in our time," characterizing the book as "an epilogue to the tradition of New England culture." He suggested that "one has only to remember Jonathan Edwards and to read passages from Emerson, Thoreau, Oliver Wendell Holmes, to find the emotional sources of the book."

Several reviewers did complain about the difficulty of the poems; and others failed to recognize the authentic political implications of Wheelwright's idiosyncratic religious stance. However, most reviewers perceived his left-wing sympathies. Morton Dauwen Zabel pronounced Wheelwright one of the three leading revolutionary poets in the *Nation* (8 December 1934), along with Horace Gregory and Norman MacLeod. Muriel Rukeyser wrote in the *New Masses* (12 March 1935) that the book "outlines the development of a poet passing from religious preoccupation to activity in the revolutionary movement"; she urged that his work not be "dismissed as confused or confusing." In his review for the August 1934 issue of *Poetry* R. P. Blackmur cited the balance in which the diverse elements in *Rock and Shell* are held. Noting that Wheelwright wrote "with a kind of constant fitfulness, requiring of the reader an ability to receive a rapid and tightly bound succession of disparate observation," he concluded that the "impact of mass" is given to "what is usually fragmentary, disjunct, and irreconcilable." This resulted in "tough, squirming, gnostic verse, modified and exhilarated by New England wit and New England eccentricity, and the unique heresy of New England Anglo-Catholicism—and the whole qualified by New England political radicalism."

Four years later when *Mirrors of Venus* appeared, it was also much admired but even less understood. In the *Nation* (15 October 1938) Paul Rosenfeld called it a "brainy, realistic, and reserved little book of a true poet who is also a loving friend." Kenneth Patchen wrote in *Books and Writers*, "It is above all the work of a poet whose gifts are major. . . . When recorders begin the work of sorting the chaff from the wheat, the name of John Wheelwright should find its way to a great many lips." In the *New Republic* (8 March 1938) Muriel Rukeyser wrote that "John Wheelwright's sonnet sequence is brilliant and sage, full of diagrammed exercises, inventions and variations on the sonnet, and his valid eccentric note." In the *Boston Transcript* (28 August 1938) Merrill Moore, well-known for his own experiments with sonnets, judged that "Complete originality is the outstanding characteristic of Wheelwright's newest book."

However, for a number of reviewers two aspects of Wheelwright's originality caused perplexity, sometimes provoking hostility. One was his subtitle, "*A Novel in Sonnets*"; the other was his inclusion of diagrams of the structure of each sonnet.

Harry Roskolenko wrote in *Voices* (20 February 1939) that "Mr. Wheelwright really has written separate sonnets, though he insists that the book is a novel . . ."; and in *Commonsense* (June 1939) Louis MacNeice complained that Wheelwright "spoiled his book by attaching to every poem rather pedantic or exhibitionist pieces of commentary."

In 1934 Wheelwright initiated a new project called Vanguard Verse, which sponsored the pamphlet series *Poems for a Dime* and *Poems for Two Bits*, as well as a correspondence course on "The Form and Content of Rebel Poetry." Assisting Wheelwright in this venture were Kenneth Porter, a Christian socialist poet who later became a historian of the American frontier, and Sherry Mangan, a friend from the Harvard Poetry Society.

The fourth number of *Poems for a Dime*, appearing in 1936, was entirely devoted to Wheelwright's *Masque with Clowns*, a verse drama that was included in "Dusk to Dusk," a collection published for the first time in *Collected Poems* (1972). The masque, which describes a national election campaign as though it were a circus, in many ways resembles a play by Bertolt Brecht. For didactic purposes, Wheelwright defamiliarizes his characters and divests them of personal attributes. To underscore the oppression of farmers and workers during the Depression, he clutters the setting (the corner of Milk and Mill Streets) with signs reading "No Help Wanted." He then satirizes existing political parties. The Democrats and Republicans are to be shown as twins, and the Socialist party is mocked as dainty, middle-class, and politically effete.

As Wheelwright continued his study of Marxism, the positions of the Trotskyists became increasingly attractive to him. After the Trotskyists of the Workers party were admitted into the Socialist party in June 1936, Wheelwright joined their caucus. In late 1936 his friend Sherry Mangan also joined the Trotskyist caucus, and the two poets collaborated in cultural activities and in work on behalf of the American Committee for the Defense of Leon Trotsky during the Moscow trials. When the Trotskyists were expelled from the Socialist party in the fall of 1937, both poets became founding members of the Socialist Workers party.

As a member of the Boston chapter, Wheelwright continued his literary and educational activities. He also did public speaking on soapboxes. The rebel Brahmin made a rather startling sight with his bowler hat, full-length raccoon coat, and walking stick. Wheelwright was also active in the League for Cultural Freedom and Socialism, an organization of revolutionary writers in the United States inspired by a manifesto signed by Trotsky, surrealist author André Breton, and painter Diego Rivera.

In the last year of his life Wheelwright produced *Political Self-Portrait* (1940), containing a number of poems that offer insight into his gradual abandonment of Christianity and his ultimate political stance. For example, "The Word is Deed," which was first published in *Partisan Review* in 1938, is clearly an attempt to reconcile his waning faith in Christ with scientific socialism. Wheelwright argues that Friedrich Engels was incorrect in *Anti-Dühring* (1878) when he changed St. John's statement to read that the deed preceded the Word. Nevertheless, Wheelwright says, he agreed with Engels that humanity transforms itself through its deeds, and therefore he can share Engels's strategy for liberation.

In addition, *Political Self-Portrait* shows that Wheelwright felt he had a special obligation to understand and interpret from a revolutionary point of view the culture of New England, his own region. It had now become clear to him that his studies of rebel divines and their theological disputes were to be undertaken for precise political purposes. His intentions were made clear in "Bread-Word Giver," his poem celebrating his radical Puritan ancestor, the Reverend John Wheelwright:

> Keep us alive with your ghostly disputation
> make our renunciation of dominion
> mark not the escape, but the permanent of rebellion.

Wheelwright died under the wheels of a car in the early morning hours of 15 September 1940, at the intersection of Massachusetts Avenue and Beacon Street in Boston. Later, Kenneth Rexroth wrote that "Dead in his prime like so many other American poets, he was not, like most of them, already burned out. No one has ever taken the place of this dynamic, inexhaustible and lovable mind and completely original talent." And it is true that Wheelwright's enchanting personal qualities— a quirky but piercing power of perception, a wit that shuttled between the mirthful and sardonic, a zealous devotion to principle lightly covered by a veil of capriciousness—remained embedded in a literary achievement that continued to be much admired by a small band of poets and scholars of his generation who pledged themselves to keeping his memory alive.

Austin Warren eulogized him in the concluding chapter of *New England Saints* (1956): "Wheelwright was a saint; he was also a poet whose books will one day take their rightful place in American poetry and scripture." Reviewing *Political Self-Portrait* for the *New England Quarterly* (September 1940), Dudley Fitts praised Wheelwright's "consummate craftsmanship" and wrote that "every line of John Wheelwright's verse confirms his position among the few perfectionists writing English poetry today." Comparing Wheelwright with other left-wing poets of the 1930s, Matthew Josephson judged that "it is Wheelwright's political poetry of that epoch that documents the Depression and New Deal for us better than any of his contemporaries' verses."

Proof of the enduring vitality of his poetry came in 1972 when his *Collected Poems* was published in one volume by New Directions. Wheelwright was compared favorably with John Berryman, Robert Lowell, Ezra Pound, Sylvia Plath, and A. R. Ammons in leading literary journals. Reviewing the volume for the *New York Review of Books* (22 February 1973), John Malcolm Brinnin observed that because of the relatively small quantity of Wheelwright's work, "He cannot be accorded major status; yet, had he lived to expand the achievement of this volume, he would very likely share rank and status with his close contemporaries Allen Tate, E. E. Cummings and Hart Crane." As recently as 3 June 1979 John Ashbery named Wheelwright's *Collected Poems* in the *New York Times Book Review* as one of the hundred most important books of Western literature since the end of World War II.

References:

S. Foster Damon and Alvin H. Rosenfeld, "John Wheelwright: New England's Colloquy with the World," *Southern Review*, 7 (April 1972): 311-348;

Horace Gregory and Marya Zaturenska, *A History of American Poetry, 1900-1940* (New York: Harcourt, Brace, 1946), pp. 347-354;

Matthew Josephson, "Improper Bostonian: John Wheelwright and His Poetry," *Southern Review*, 7 (Spring 1971): 509-541;

Winfield Townley Scott, "John Wheelwright and His Poetry," *New Mexico Quarterly*, 24 (Summer 1954): 178-196;

Alan M. Wald, "From Antinomianism to Revolutionary Marxism: John Wheelwright and the New England Rebel Tradition," *Marxist Perspectives*, no. 10 (Summer 1980): 44-67;

Wald, *The Revolutionary Imagination: The Poetry and Politics of John Wheelwright and Sherry Mangan* (Chapel Hill: University of North Carolina Press, 1983);

Austin Warren, *New England Saints* (Ann Arbor: University of Michigan Press, 1956), pp. 165-178.

Papers:

The central depository of Wheelwright's manuscripts and letters is the John Hay Library at Brown University.

Elinor Wylie

(7 September 1885-16 December 1928)

Karen F. Stein
University of Rhode Island

See also the Wylie entry in *DLB 9, American Novelists, 1910-1945*.

BOOKS: *Incidental Numbers*, anonymous (London: Privately printed, 1912);

Nets to Catch the Wind (New York: Harcourt, Brace, 1921; London: Knopf, 1928);

Black Armour (New York: Doran, 1923; London: Secker, 1927);

Jennifer Lorn: A Sedate Extravaganza (New York: Doran, 1923; London: Richards, 1924);

The Venetian Glass Nephew (New York: Doran, 1925; London: Heinemann, 1926);

Elinor Wylie, edited by Laurence Jordan (New York: Simon & Schuster, 1926);

The Orphan Angel (New York: Knopf, 1926); republished as *Mortal Image* (London: Heinemann, 1927);

Mr. Hodge & Mr. Hazard (New York: Knopf, 1928; London: Heinemann, 1928);

Trivial Breath (London & New York: Knopf, 1928);

Angels and Earthly Creatures: A Sequence of Sonnets (Henley on Thames: Borough Press, 1928);

Angels and Earthly Creatures (New York: Knopf, 1929; London: Knopf, 1929);

Birthday Sonnet (New York: Random House, 1929);

Collected Poems of Elinor Wylie (New York: Knopf, 1932);

Collected Prose of Elinor Wylie (New York: Knopf, 1933);

Last Poems of Elinor Wylie (New York: Knopf, 1943).

In her lifetime Elinor Hoyt Wylie won notoriety for her unconventional private life and acclaim for her poems and novels. Carl Van Doren celebrated her as a "poet and queen of poets." Prominent members of the New York literary scene in the 1920s—such as Edmund Wilson, Carl Van Vechten, and her third husband, William Rose Benét—admired her beauty and literary achievements.

The daughter of Henry Martyn and Anne McMichael Hoyt, Wylie was born into a socially and politically prominent family in Somerville, New

Elinor Wylie (courtesy of the Beinecke Rare Book and Manuscript Library, Yale University)

Jersey. (Later, believing Somerville insufficiently romantic, she hoped that people would imagine Paris or Persepolis as her place of birth.) Her family moved to Rosemont, Pennsylvania, a suburb of Philadelphia, in 1887. In 1897 her father became assistant attorney general of the United States, taking the family to Washington, D.C. Although her life outwardly traced a romantic course, her three marriages never brought her the emotional fulfillment she sought, and her poetic success never erased her self-doubts. A perfectionist, shy and uncertain of her talents, Wylie required unqualified approval from others. Hers was a complex and contradictory nature. Her poetry articulates her central conflicts: a desire for love that led to a series of disappointing marriages, a delicate sensitivity which often made her wish to escape a hostile and unlovely world, a yearning for transcendent spiritual vision that she felt was beyond the reach of her limited gifts.

As a young woman growing up in an aristocratic family, Wylie was groomed for the life of a socialite. Yet she had a questing intellect as well. Her sister, Nancy Hoyt, asserts that Elinor was "passionately interested in her school work," with a love of books and an artistic avocation. Her scholarly interest is reflected in the meticulous research underlying her novels. But, despite the urging of her teachers at Miss Baldwin's School in Bryn Mawr, Pennsylvania, and at Mrs. Flint's (later the Holton Arms) school in Washington, her parents did not allow her to continue her education. Instead, she was launched as a debutante. Although the social career her parents deemed appropriate began brilliantly, it could never absorb her interests and energies completely.

In 1905, apparently on the rebound from a short-lived romance, Wylie married Philip Simmons Hichborn and gave birth to his son Philip Hichborn III in September 1907. Hichborn proved to be emotionally unstable. During this difficult marriage, Wylie began to suffer from the high blood pressure and migraine headaches which would plague her throughout her life. Wylie's first two novels, *Jennifer Lorn* (1923) and *The Venetian Glass Nephew* (1925) describe women suffering in disastrous marriages. The husbands in both books compel their wives to become decorative objects. Attempting to meet these needs, the heroines are destroyed. Undoubtedly, Wylie's account is at least partially autobiographical.

She left Hichborn in December 1910, eloping with a married lawyer, Horace Wylie, and leaving behind her son, who was raised by Hichborn's sister Martha Pearsall. Wylie's elopement and abandonment of her child became a highly publicized scandal in conservative Washington. The couple lived in England as Mr. and Mrs. Horace Waring to escape publicity and social ostracism. (As late as 1927, the League of American Pen Women in Washington countermanded an honor-guest breakfast invitation they had extended to Wylie.)

Horace Wylie encouraged Elinor's literary interests. In 1912 she published privately a small book of poems, *Incidental Numbers*, none of which she later found worthy of inclusion in her subsequent volumes. The poems, written between 1902 and 1911, indicate some of the themes she would continue to explore—magic, love, entrapment and isolation—and reveal her indebtedness to the poets of the aesthetic movement. Wylie kept this anonymous collection secret, claiming in a 1919 letter to Harriet Monroe, editor of *Poetry*, "I have never published anything—never tried to, until the last few weeks."

When Britain entered World War I the Wylies returned to the United States, living in Boston, Augusta, Georgia, and Washington, D.C. They were distressed by family coldness, bad financial straits, social disapproval, and Elinor's poor health. Perhaps out of guilt for the loss of her son, Elinor eagerly wished for a child. From 1914 to 1916 she had several miscarriages, one stillbirth, and a premature child who died after a week. She perceived this inability to produce a child as a personal failure. She felt estranged from Wylie and wrote bitterly about her frigidity in poems such as "This Hand" (*Black Armour*, 1923). After Horace Wylie at last succeeded in obtaining a divorce from his wife and Hichborn had committed suicide, they were married on 7 August 1916. But the strains of their position had already damaged the fiber of the relationship. Elinor withdrew emotionally from Horace as she grew increasingly involved in her literary career.

Friends such as John Dos Passos, John Peale Bishop, and Edmund Wilson convinced her to take her writing seriously. In November 1919 she sent some poems to *Poetry*, hesitantly, for she feared her work was not "modern enough" for the magazine. Wylie's reluctance is understandable, for her work looked back toward her literary forerunners, and did not participate in the contemporary experimentation with free verse. Throughout her career, Wylie wrote in rhyming stanzas, often working with ballads and sonnets. But Monroe allayed her concerns, and asked for more poems, publishing four in the May 1920 issue ("Atavism," "Fire and Sleet and Candlelight," "Silver Filigree," and "Velvet Shoes," which would become her most widely anthologized poem). As her work began to gain recognition and acceptance, Wylie devoted herself to her writing.

One of her strongest supporters at this time was her brother Henry's friend William Rose Benét. Benét encouraged Wylie to submit her work and frequently acted as her literary agent, placing her poems and advising her about contracts and projects. On the strength of her growing literary reputation, Wylie separated from her husband and moved to New York in 1921. Here she captivated the literary world with her slender, tawny-haired beauty, personal elegance, acid wit, and technical virtuosity. Her success was almost legendary: Carl Van Vechten organized a torchlight parade to cel-

Elinor Wylie and William Rose Benét

ebrate publication of her first novel, *Jennifer Lorn*, in 1923. In the same year, at perhaps the height of her powers and fame, she divorced Wylie and married Benét. Yet, remarks which Edmund Wilson quoted in his diary before the wedding suggest that the marriage was doomed from the start. According to Wilson, "When I expressed my doubts about their union, she said with her harsh and callous laugh: 'Yes, it would be a pity that a first-rate poet should be turned into a second-rate poet by marrying a third-rate poet.'"

During the period from 1921 to her death in 1928, Wylie's literary output was astonishing. She published four volumes of poetry and four novels, as well as—less significantly—essays and reviews, and served for a time as literary editor of *Vanity Fair*. *Nets to Catch the Wind* (1921) won critical acclaim, receiving the Poetry Society's Julia Ellsworth Ford Prize. The book, a substantial advance over her juvenilia, contains much of her best work. Writers such as Edna St. Vincent Millay, Louis Untermeyer, and Edmund Wilson praised it for its precision, its clarity, and its jewel-like brilliance.

Nets to Catch the Wind articulates Wylie's continuing conflicts over the suffering she endured at the hands of an uncaring world (as in "A Proud Lady"), and her desire to escape (as in "The Eagle and the Mole," "Sanctuary," "Winter Sleep"). Another prominent theme of the volume is her celebration of the world's beauty ("Madman's Song") to which others may be unreceptive ("The Church-

Bell," "A Crowded Trolley Car"). The grandeur of the natural world and the artist's imagination may provide alternate satisfactions ("Sunset on the Spire"), but the poet remains aware that imaginative escape must fail ("The Fairy Goldsmith").

Her technical mastery enabled her to create precise images of great beauty. When the image itself is the poem's subject, as in "Velvet Shoes," "August," and—for the most part—"Wild Peaches," the results could be superbly successful. Yet, because her style was a miniaturist's—elegant, with muted colors, small compass, and minute attention to detail—she often produced, in her novels and some of her verse, a crystalline, polished surface with little sustaining depth. These tendencies may derive from Wylie's aristocratic upbringing and the influence of the aesthetic movement, with its admiration for detail, precision, and design.

Wylie, however, was aware of her limitations. In her poetry and prose she satirized the aesthetic excesses of which she herself was often guilty. Her first two novels, *Jennifer Lorn* and *The Venetian Glass Nephew*, deal with the conflicting claims of Art and Nature, depicting the destruction of heroines who succumb to others' demands that they become art objects. Yet, even as she satirized the inhumanity of an aesthetic sensibility that values decorative objects over humans, she often allowed the sensual richness of her prose to subvert thematic development. Similarly, her essay "Jewelled Bindings," written in 1923 while she was composing *Black Armour*, is both defense and critique of her technique. She contended that she is a minor writer, defining herself in the images of a crafter rather than an artist; hers is a "small clean technique." The article explains her vision, but also admits to its shortcomings: Wylie believed that she might create a "gilded bird," but not the living bird who could sing in the work of an "authentic genius." Such a genius was Wylie's idol, Percy Bysshe Shelley.

To some extent, as Judith Farr contends, *Black Armour* reflects the poet's knowledge of her limits, both personally and poetically. In "Let No Charitable Hope," for example, she begins:

> Now let no charitable hope
> Confuse my mind with images
> Of eagle and of antelope:
> I am in nature none of these.

This modest recognition contrasts with the poet's triumphant earlier identification with the proud, soaring eagle ("The Eagle and the Mole"). Yet Wylie's self-criticism falls short of the mature awareness Farr commends. Most of the personae in this volume are suffering victims, outcasts from society, like the alienated heroes of "Simon Gerty," "Peregrine," "Lucifer Sings in Secret," "Preference." The second stanza of "Let No Charitable Hope" continues:

I was, being human, born alone;
I am, being woman, hard beset;
I live by squeezing from a stone
The little nourishment I get.

Thus, most of the poetry in this volume evokes the adolescent self-pitying aspects of the romantic mode, as in Shelley's anguished cry: "I fall upon the thorns of life. I bleed." Furthermore, the book's governing metaphor of armor continues the theme of escape from a world that wounds the poet's vulnerable sensibilities. In identifying with the outcast heroes of this book, Wylie remains apart from society, glorying in her wounds as badges of a finer sensitivity. Where Shelley almost always transcended personal suffering, Wylie rarely escaped self-consciousness. It is ultimately this narrow personal focus that prevents her from attaining the Shelleyan heights of visionary inspiration for which she wished.

Wylie's interest in romanticism grew from her strong identification with Shelley, dating from her first reading of the poet when she was seven. Her enthusiasm for Shelley may have occasionally verged on obsession: she spent early royalties to purchase some of his letters; she sometimes entertained fantasies of Shelley's return to life; she argued Shelley's merits at dinner parties, and she wondered how he would have responded to her. In a poetic self-caricature, "Portrait in Black Paint," she mocks her "peculiar schism."

The highest tribute she paid Shelley was to write two novels about him, *The Orphan Angel* (1926) and *Mr. Hodge & Mr. Hazard* (1928). The first of these is an elaborate fantasy of Shelley's returning to life and traveling through the American West in the company of David Butternut, a Yankee sailor, searching for a mysterious and beautiful woman whom he hopes to rescue. Critics were polarized in their responses to this novel. Its chief difficulty is that it fails to achieve Wylie's purpose, that of kindling admiration for the heroic poet. Instead, the novel becomes a picaresque exploration with minimal plot interest. The second of these novels recounts the decline of romanticism in the tale of "the last Romantic poet" (a composite of Shelley and Wylie) vanquished by the bourgeois

1927 caricature of Wylie by Katherine Anne Porter (by permission of Paul Porter; courtesy of the Beinecke Rare Book and Manuscript Library, Yale University)

world of the Victorians, a world that cannot accept his values and his poetry. Critics agree that this book is her best novel.

Wylie dedicated her third volume of poetry, *Trivial Breath* (1928), to Shelley. In the second of four sonnets celebrating her idol, "A Red Carpet for Shelley," she expresses most poignantly her wish for greater poetic powers:

If I possessed the pure and fiery pulse
By true divinity informed and driven,
I would unroll the rounded moon and sun
And knit them up for you to walk upon.

The book explores Wylie's continuing interests, but happily, leaves behind the theme of suffering so prominent in *Black Armour*. The only poem alluding to suffering suggests a more mature view. "Desolation Is a Delicate Thing" speaks of a heavy sorrow which leaves her: "It was not my heart; it was this poor sorrow alone which broke." Her mingled love and suspicion of the aesthetic passion for beautiful objects is reflected in "Miranda's Supper,"

444

"Minotaur," and "True Vine." "Miranda's Supper," a long poem in iambic-tetrameter rhyming couplets, tells the story of a "gentlewoman" who survives the Civil War and the Union invasion of her Virginia home. The poem's climax is the supper Miranda eats on the precious china she has unearthed from its hiding place. Her meal is ironically contrasted with Christ's Last Supper, satirizing the confusion of spiritual and material values.

Also new in this volume is the cynical treatment of love in such poems as "The Puritan's Ballad." In another, "Speed the Parting," reminiscent of Dorothy Parker, Wylie writes:

> Therefore die when you please;
> It's not very wise to worry;
> I shall not shiver and freeze;
> I shall not even be sorry.

Biographical evidence suggests that the cynicism was a mask to conceal the pain of yet another failure of love.

Like "This Hand" (which spoke of her guilt for the collapse of her marriage to Horace Wylie), poems in *Trivial Breath* indicate the poet's continuing self-blame for her failures in love ("Confession of Faith"). In the chilling "Where, O, Where?" the poet describes her retreat from her lover,

> I need not die to go
> So far you cannot know
> ....
> You shall see me no more
> Though each night I hide
> In your bed, at your side.

Her marriage to Benét had lost its charm for Wylie. Although she would not divorce him, she had begun to live apart, spending her time in and near London. In May 1927 she wrote to Horace Wylie, affirming a continuing love for him, in spite of her remarriage, but the following year, she experienced a new love which she felt to be the supreme one of her life. The object of this affection was Henry de Clifford Woodhouse, whose home Wylie had visited, and whose wife she had befriended. Wylie and Woodhouse took walks together and discussed philosophy.

While arranging the poems for her 1929 collection *Angels and Earthly Creatures*, Wylie returned to New York for a Christmas visit to Benét. On the evening of 16 December 1928 she set down the completed typescript of her poems, picked up a volume of John Donne's sermons, and called to Benét for a glass of water. When he brought it to

her, she walked toward him, murmured "Is that all it is?," and fell to the floor, dead of a stroke.

Out of her love for Woodhouse, Wylie had written a series of nineteen sonnets first printed privately in 1928 under the title *Angels and Earthly Creatures*, then included as the first section of a larger volume with the same title. These sonnets, which many critics consider her best work, describe love, separation, and resignation. The first begins "Now shall the long homesickness have an end," a powerful statement of contentment and the achievement of a long-desired objective. The sixth relates that she had previously lacked passion, and now recognizes it. The ninth sonnet announces that she is now liberated from her former reliance on Shelley, for she no longer has the wounds which he alone was able to heal. Yet, the poems express her willingness to "uphold your house," that is, to subdue her passion for the sake of Woodhouse's marriage. In the sixteenth sonnet she returns to the house image, stating "I am not the hearthstone nor the cornerstone."

Wylie's life and work point to a contradiction between her continuing belief in the ideal of love and a dissatisfaction with her actual experiences. From childhood she had won accolades for her beauty and social accomplishments, while her intellectual achievements were not encouraged. An attentive and charming father and grandfather were the strong figures in her family. She was used to being petted and made much of by devoted men. Growing up in a society with clearly defined expectations for women, Wylie may have felt compelled to act out a feminine submissiveness and emotionality that was at odds with her strength of will, ambition and emotional control. She was looking for men to rescue her from entrapment and "provide her with the intellectual and emotional satisfaction she could not seek independently." But she chose as her romantic heroes men who could not sustain the roles she cast them in. Both Horace Wylie and Benét were her literary mentors (and even Hichborn had minor literary pretensions), but Elinor Wylie's talents far surpassed her husbands'. It is suggestive that in an unconsummated love Wylie found the passion and fulfillment denied her in her three marriages. Her adulation of Shelley raised the ideal of love to empyrean heights; Woodhouse, alive but unattainable, was a foil for Wylie's passion. Frustrated in her marriages, Wylie came to prefer the fantasy of love to the potential disillusionment of marriage. Like her other cynical love poems and marriage novels, the bitter "From the Wall" of *Last Poems* (1943) points to a distrust of

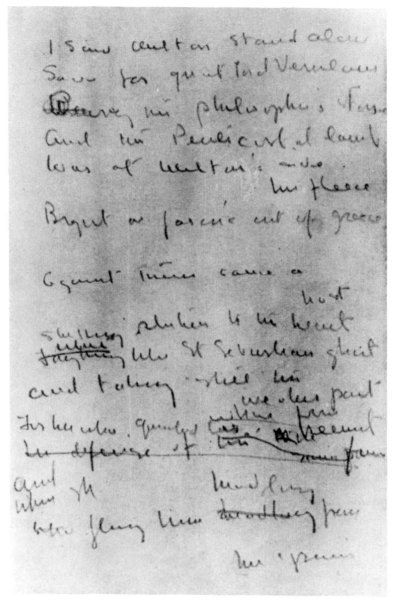

Manuscript for a poem published in Wylie's Last Poems *(1943)*

love, and to a fear that love destroys women:

> Woman, be steel against loving, enfold and defend
> you,
> Turn from the innocent look and the arrogant
> tongue;
> You shall be coppery dross to the purses that spend
> you.

If a human lover might undervalue and demean her, then a fantasy lover could affirm her femininity to herself and to the world without trapping her in a disappointing marriage.

It is certainly the nexus of her personal and poetic lives that proves most perplexing to the student of Wylie. Biographer Stanley Olson argues that it was her inability to love that prompted her to pursue a poetic career. Olson alleges that "she turned herself into a writer when she discarded the idea, and hope, of being simply a woman." Surely Carl Van Doren is closer to the mark in his assessment: "She was a woman who had beauty and genius. Doubly driven, she was doubly sensitive. Two careers side by side in one woman. No wonder she often seemed ruthless, often hysterical, habitually bewildering." Van Doren's observations, along with

Wylie's identification with Shelley, invite the reader to ask (as Virginia Woolf did of Shakespeare): what would have happened had Shelley been born a woman? Woolf's Judith Shakespeare, maddened by her inevitable frustration, killed herself; Wylie, who aspired to incarnate Shelley's genius, was wounded, but survived.

Wylie's talent is notable, but problematic. Tensions between opposing impulses—romanticism and aestheticism, poet and woman—often led her to miss her mark, but when the tensions were confronted and examined, her work achieved its full potential in powerful poems of heightened irony. In her best poetry, Wylie was able to deal more pointedly than in her novels with the conflicts that drove her: the problem of the feeling self smoldering beneath its decorative surface, her struggle to define herself both as woman and as poet. Statements of this theme appear in "Sleeping Beauty," "Sanctuary," "Where, O, Where?" and "Full Moon," where the speaker, dressed elegantly in "silk and miniver," cries: "There I walked, and there I raged;/The spiritual savage caged." Images of falsehood—masks, disguises, and costumes—convey the tension between beautiful exterior and turbulent interior, between felt passion and enforced restraint. Similarly, in "Sanctuary" the poet's attempt to escape from her struggles behind walls is doomed, for enclosure means death. Similar images of disguise and entrapment are frequent in the work of Emily Dickinson, Marianne Moore and other American women poets. These image patterns indicate Wylie's participation in a woman writer's tradition of struggle to escape from the bonds of expectation and convention.

Perhaps in part because they were under her spell, Wylie's contemporaries praised her work effusively. Louise Bogan's 1951 evaluation places Wylie in a literary context: "Wylie . . . brought to the feminine lyric a mature emotional richness, as well as an added brilliance of craftsmanship. . . . Her work as a whole was far more complex than that of any feminine predecessor." Subsequent criticism has been scanty and less favorable. Until recently, Nancy Hoyt's chatty biography and Thomas A. Gray's unsympathetic study were the only full-length works in print. However, new works on Wylie indicate a reawakening of appreciation. Stanley Olson's 1979 biography, despite its questionable central hypothesis (that Wylie became a poet to compensate for her failure as a woman), is well-written and brings together materials useful for study of the poet and her milieu. Judith Farr's study sets biographical material into the context of a careful and thorough reading of Wylie's work. Inclusion of Wylie's poetry in recently published anthologies testifies to a continuing interest, and may hopefully lead to further examination of her poetry and prose.

Biographies:

Nancy Hoyt, *Elinor Wylie: The Portrait of an Unknown Lady* (Indianapolis & New York: Bobbs-Merrill, 1935);

Stanley Olson, *Elinor Wylie: A Life Apart* (New York: Dial/James Wade, 1979);

Judith Farr, *The Life and Art of Elinor Wylie* (Baton Rouge: Louisiana State University Press, 1983).

References:

Louise Bogan, *Achievement in American Poetry, 1900-1950.* (New York: Regnery, 1951), pp. 76-77;

Julia Cluck, "Elinor Wylie's Shelley Obsession," *PMLA*, 56 (September 1941): 841-860;

Mary M. Colum, "In Memory of Elinor Wylie," *New Republic*, 57 (6 February 1929): 317-319;

Thomas A. Gray, *Elinor Wylie* (New York: Twayne, 1969);

H. Ludecke, "Venetian Glass: The Poetry and Prose of Elinor Wylie," *English Studies*, 20 (December 1938): 240-250;

Donald Pizer, " 'Symbolic Romances of the Mind': The Novels of Elinor Wylie," *Centennial Review*, 24 (Summer 1980): 284-301;

Allen Tate, "Elinor Wylie's Poetry," review of *Collected Poems of Elinor Wylie*, *New Republic*, 72 (7 September 1932): 107;

Carl Van Doren, *Three Worlds* (New York & London: Harper, 1936);

Carl Van Vechten, Introduction to *Jennifer Lorn* (New York: Doran, 1923);

Rebecca West, *Ending in Earnest* (Garden City: Doubleday, Doran, 1931), pp. 19-22.

Papers:

The Berg Collection of the New York Public Library contains the papers of Horace Wylie and the Hoyt family's collection of Elinor Wylie's letters. The Elinor Wylie Archive in the Beinecke Rare Book and Manuscript Library at Yale University contains the papers of William Rose Benét and Elinor Wylie.

Books for Further Reading

Aiken, Conrad. *A Reviewer's ABC: Collected Criticism of Conrad Aiken from 1916 to the Present.* New York: Meridian Books, 1958.

Aiken. *Scepticisms: Notes on Contemporary Poetry.* New York: Knopf, 1919.

Aiken. *Ushant: An Essay.* New York: Duell, Sloan & Pearce/Boston: Little, Brown, 1952.

Anderson, Margaret. *My Thirty Years' War; the Autobiography: Beginnings and Battles to 1930.* New York: Covici Friede, 1930.

Beach, Sylvia. *Shakespeare and Company.* New York: Harcourt, Brace, 1959.

Benét, William Rose, ed. *Fifty Poets, An American Auto-Anthology.* New York: Duffield & Green, 1933.

Berg, Andrew Scott. *Max Perkins, Editor of Genius.* New York: Dutton, 1978.

Bogan, Louise. *Achievement in American Poetry, 1900-1950.* Chicago: Regnery, 1951.

Borroff, Marie. *Language and the Poet: Verbal Artistry in Frost, Stevens, and Moore.* Chicago: University of Chicago Press, 1979.

Brooks, Cleanth. *Modern Poetry and the Tradition.* Chapel Hill: University of North Carolina Press, 1939.

Brooks, Gladys. *If Strangers Meet; A Memory.* New York: Harcourt, Brace & World, 1967.

Brooks, Van Wyck. *Scenes and Portraits: Memories of Childhood and Youth.* New York: Dutton, 1954.

Coffman, Stanley K., Jr. *Imagism: A Chapter for the History of Modern Poetry.* Norman: University of Oklahoma Press, 1951.

Cowen, Louise. *The Fugitive Group: A Literary History.* Baton Rouge: Louisiana State University Press, 1959.

Cowley, Malcolm. *The Dream of the Golden Mountains: Remembering the 1930s.* New York: Viking, 1980.

Cowley, ed. *Writers at Work: The Paris Review Interviews,* series 1. New York: Viking, 1958.

Crosby, Caresse. *The Passionate Years.* New York: Dial, 1953.

Cunard, Nancy. *These Were the Hours: Memories of My Hours Press, Réanville and Paris, 1928-1931,* edited by Hugh Ford. Carbondale & Edwardsville: Southern Illinois University Press, 1969.

Davidson, Donald, ed. *Fugitives: An Anthology of Verse.* New York: Harcourt, Brace, 1928.

Dembo, L. S. *Conceptions of Reality in Modern American Poetry.* Berkeley: University of California Press, 1966.

Duffey, Bernard. *The Chicago Renaissance in American Letters; A Critical History.* East Lansing: Michigan State College Press, 1954.

Fitch, Noel Riley. *Sylvia Beach and the Lost Generation: A History of Literary Paris in the Twenties and Thirties.* New York: Norton, 1983.

Ford, Hugh. *Published in Paris: American and British Writers, Printers, and Publishers in Paris, 1920-1939.* New York: Macmillan, 1975.

Ford, ed. *The Left Bank Revisited. Selections from the Paris Tribune, 1917-1934.* University Park & London: Pennsylvania State University Press, 1972.

Fowlie, Wallace. *The Clown's Grail; a Study of Love in its Literary Expression.* London: Dobson, 1948; republished as *Love in Literature: Studies in Symbolic Expression.* Bloomington: Indiana University Press, 1965.

Gaines, James R. *Wit's End: Days and Nights of the Algonquin Round Table.* New York & London: Harcourt Brace Jovanovich, 1977.

Gould, Jean. *American Women Poets: Pioneers of Modern Poetry.* New York: Dodd, Mead, 1980.

Gregory, Horace, and Marza Zaturensha. *A History of American Poetry, 1900-1940.* New York: Harcourt, Brace, 1946.

Guggenheim, Peggy. *Out of this Century: Confessions of an Art Addict.* New York: Universe Books, 1979.

Hall, Donald. *Remembering Poets: Reminiscences and Opinions.* New York, Hagerstown, San Francisco & London: Harper & Row, 1978.

Harriman, Margaret. *The Vicious Circle; the Story of the Algonquin Round Table.* New York: Rinehart, 1951.

Hoffman, Frederic. *The Twenties; American Writing in the Postwar Decade,* revised edition. New York: Collier Books, 1962.

Huggins, Nathan. *Harlem Renaissance.* New York: Oxford University Press, 1971.

Hughes, Glenn. *Imagism & the Imagists; A Study in Modern Poetry.* Stanford: Stanford University Press, 1931.

Jarrell, Randall. *Poetry and the Age.* New York: Knopf, 1953.

Jones, Peter, ed. *Imagist Poetry.* Harmondsworth, U.K.: Penguin, 1972.

Kenner, Hugh. *The Pound Era.* Berkeley: University of California Press, 1971.

Kermode, Frank. *Romantic Image.* New York: Random House, 1957.

Kramer, Dale. *Chicago Renaissance: the Literary Life in the Midwest, 1900-1930.* New York: Appleton-Century, 1966.

Kreymborg, Alfred. *Our Singing Strength: An Outline of American Poetry.* New York: Coward-McCann, 1929.

Kreymborg. *Troubadour: An Autobiography.* New York: Boni & Liveright, 1925.

Locke, Alain. *Four Negro Poets.* New York: Simon & Schuster, 1927.

Lowell, Amy. *Tendencies in Modern American Poetry.* New York: Macmillan, 1917.

Mariani, Paul. *William Carlos Williams: a New World Naked.* New York: McGraw-Hill, 1981.

McMillan, Dougald. *Transition: The History of a Literary Era, 1927-1938.* New York: Braziller, 1975.

Mellow, James R. *Charmed Circle: Gertrude Stein & Company*. New York & Washington, D.C.: Praeger, 1974.

Moore, Marianne. *Predilections*. New York: Viking, 1955.

Paz, Ottavio. *Children of the Mire; Modern Poetry from Romanticism to the Avant-Garde*. Cambridge: Harvard University Press, 1974.

Perkins, David. *A History of Modern Poetry from the 1890's to the High Modernist Mode*. Cambridge: Harvard University Press, 1976.

Plimpton, George, ed. *Writers at Work: The Paris Review Interviews*, series 2, 4, 5. New York: Viking, 1963, 1976, 1981.

Pratt, William, ed. *The Fugitive Poets; Modern Southern Poetry in Perspective*. New York: Dutton, 1965.

Pratt, ed. *The Imagist Poem; Modern Poetry in Miniature*. New York: Dutton, 1963.

Quinn, Sister M. Bernetta. *The Metamorphic Tradition in Modern Poetry; Essays on the Work of Ezra Pound, Wallace Stevens, William Carlos Williams, T. S. Eliot, Hart Crane, Randall Jarrell and William Butler Yeats*. New Brunswick: Rutgers University Press, 1955.

Ransom, John Crowe. *Beating the Bushes; Selected Essays, 1941-1970*. New York: New Directions, 1972.

Ransom. *The New Criticism*. Norfolk, Conn.: New Directions, 1941.

Ransom, Allen Tate, Donald Davidson, and others. *I'll Take My Stand: the South and the Agrarian Tradition, by Twelve Southerners*. New York & London: Harper, 1930.

Rubin, Louis D. *The Wary Fugitives: Four Poets and the South*. Baton Rouge: Louisiana State University Press, 1978.

Schwartz, Delmore. *Selected Essays*, edited by Donald A. Dike and David H. Zucker. Chicago: University of Chicago Press, 1970.

Smoller, Sanford. *Adrift Among Genuises: Robert McAlmon, Writer and Publisher of the Twenties*. University Park & London: Pennsylvania State University Press, 1975.

Stewart, John L. *The Burden of Time: The Fugitives and Agrarians; the Nashville Groups of the 1920's and 1930's, and the Writing of John Crowe Ransom, Allen Tate, and Robert Penn Warren*. Princeton: Princeton University Press, 1965.

Tashjian, Dickran. *Skyscraper Primitives: Dada and the American Avant-Garde, 1910-1925*. Middletown, Conn.: Wesleyan University Press, 1975.

Tate, Allen. *Essays of Four Decades*. Chicago: Swallow, 1968.

Tate. *The Man of Letters in the Modern World, Selected Essays: 1928-1955*. New York: Meridian/London: Thames & Hudson, 1955.

Tate. *Memoirs and Opinions, 1926-1974*. Chicago: Swallow, 1975.

Tate. *Reactionary Essays on Poetry and Ideas*. New York & London: Scribners, 1936.

Tate. *Reason in Madness: Critical Essays.* New York: Putnam's, 1961.

Turner, Darwin. *In a Minor Chord; Three Afro-American Writers and Their Search for Identity.* Carbondale & Edwardsville: Southern Illinois University Press, 1971.

Waggoner, Hyatt. *American Poets, from the Puritans to the Present.* Boston: Houghton Mifflin, 1968.

Wald, Allen. *The Revolutionary Imagination: The Poetry and Politics of John Wheelwright and Sherry Mangan.* Chapel Hill: University of North Carolina Press, 1983.

Weatherhead, A. Kingsley. *The Edge of the Image: Marianne Moore, William Carlos Williams, and Some Other Poets.* Seattle: University of Washington Press, 1967.

Wertheim, Arthur Frank. *The New York Little Renaissance: Iconoclasm, Modernism, and Nationalism in American Culture, 1908-1917.* New York: New York University Press, 1976.

Wickes, George. *Americans in Paris.* Garden City: Doubleday, 1969.

Wilson, Edmund. *Axel's Castle; a Study in the Imaginative Literature of 1870-1930.* New York & London: Scribners, 1931.

Winters, Yvor. *In Defense of Reason.* Denver: University of Denver Press, 1947.

Wolff, Geoffrey. *Black Sun: The Brief Transit and Violent Eclipse of Harry Crosby.* New York: Random House, 1976.

Contributors

Shelley Armitage ....*West Texas State University*
Lynn Z. Bloom .... *Virginia Commonwealth University*
Jewel Spears Brooker...*Eckerd College*
Penni Cagan ....*New York, New York*
Bruce Comens ....*State University of New York at Buffalo*
Stephen Cummings....................................... *University of Western Ontario*
Motley Deakin ....*University of Florida*
Richard S. Donnell...*Miami University*
William Drake ....*San Francisco, California*
Wendy Stallard Flory .... *University of Pennsylvania*
Susan Stanford Friedman .... *University of Wisconsin-Madison*
Harlan Greene ....*South Carolina Historical Society*
John Griffith .... *University of Washington*
James A. Hart ....*University of British Columbia*
Paula L. Hart..*University of British Columbia*
George F. Hayhoe ....*Aiken, South Carolina*
Robert W. Hill... *Kennesaw College*
Milton Hindus...*Brandeis University*
Milne Holton .... *University of Maryland*
Victor H. Jones ....*Indiana State University*
Shirley Lumpkin.. *University of Tennessee*
Janet McCann..*Texas A & M University*
Russell Murphy .... *University of Arkansas at Little Rock*
Robert H. O'Connor .... *North Dakota State University*
Berkley Peabody..*Salem, Massachusetts*
Alice Hall Petry ....*Rhode Island School of Design*
Elizabeth Phillips ....*Wake Forest University*
Peter Revell .... *Westfield College, London*
Stephen Scobie .... *University of Victoria*
Robert Ian Scott ....*University of Saskatchewan*
Carol Shloss... *Drexel University*
Karen F. Stein .... *University of Rhode Island*
Thomas C. Tulloss ....*University of Maryland, European Division*
Alan M. Wald ....*University of Michigan*
Edna Cunningham White ....*Columbia, South Carolina*
W. Ross Winterowd.................................... *University of Southern California*
Meredith Yearsley .... *Vancouver, British Columbia*
Thomas Daniel Young .... *Vanderbilt University*
Melody M. Zajdel ....*Montana State University*

Cumulative Index

Dictionary of Literary Biography, Volumes 1-45
Dictionary of Literary Biography Yearbook, 1980-1984
Dictionary of Literary Biography Documentary Series, Volumes 1-4

Cumulative Index

DLB before number: *Dictionary of Literary Biography*, Volumes 1-45
Y before number: *Dictionary of Literary Biography Yearbook*, 1980-1984
DS before number: *Dictionary of Literary Biography Documentary Series*, Volumes 1-4

A

D

E

G

H

K

M

T

LIBRARY
ST. MICHAEL'S PREP SCHOOL
1042 STAR RT. - ORANGE, CA. 92667

6251